FOUNDERS OF WESTERN PHILOSOPHY

FOUNDERS OF WESTERN PHILOSOPHY

THALES TO HUME

LECTURES BY

LEONARD PEIKOFF

EDITED BY MICHAEL S. BERLINER

AYN RAND INSTITUTE PRESS

Grateful acknowledgment is made for
permission to quote copyrighted material:

Gordon H. Clark, *Thales to Dewey: A History of Philosophy*
(Boston: Houghton Mifflin, 1957), by permission of Elizabeth Clark George.

To the extent that efforts to trace copyright holders have been unsuccessful, the publisher will be pleased to include any necessary credits in all subsequent reprints or editions.

Ayn Rand Institute Press
Santa Ana, California

AYN RAND INSTITUTE PRESS

ISBN: 978-0-9960101-7-7

Design by Simon Federman
Cover design by Jesse Hashagen

aynrand.org

CONTENTS

FOREWORD

In the early 1980s, while I was an undergraduate, I was torn between going to graduate school or to law school. It was at that time that I first listened to Leonard Peikoff's lectures on the history of Western philosophy, from Thales to Hume. It was a *tour de force*, covering the essential ideas of the most significant and influential philosophers, from the dawn of philosophy in ancient Greece up to the eighteenth century, and it influenced my decision the following year to pursue in graduate school the serious study of the history of ideas. This history in the hands of Dr. Peikoff did not consist of discrete and disconnected episodes or units; rather, it was an integrated presentation of the unfolding of the history of philosophy, with the major figures of each period responding to those who came before them and influencing those who came after. Moreover, Dr. Peikoff throughout tied the abstract ideas in this history to the "real world," acting as a "philosophical psychotherapist" (in his apt description) diagnosing Western civilization.

I eventually received my PhD in philosophy, with a specialization in ancient Greek philosophy and especially Aristotle. Over the past three decades, as a historian of philosophy, I have devoted most of my research to individual trees (and, so to speak, to their roots, branches, and leaves); but I have never lost sight of the forest, in large part owing to my introduction to the subject.

"Philosophy is not a bauble of the intellect," as Dr. Peikoff would later begin his magnum opus, *Objectivism: The Philosophy of Ayn Rand*, "but a power from which no man can abstain." Anyone interested in a history of this crucially important subject is fortunate to have available this course in book form and can do no better than to begin here.

—Robert Mayhew
Seton Hall University
March 2023

EDITOR'S PREFACE

> The lectures present the ideas of the philosophers who shaped Western civilization, the meaning and practical consequences of these ideas, their unidentified influence on the minds of modern men—and a critical analysis, which will provide a defense against many of today's prevalent intellectual fallacies. The course concludes with a lecture on the Objectivist answer to selected philosophic problems.

So reads the announcement in the August 14, 1972, issue of *The Ayn Rand Letter* for Leonard Peikoff's course Founders of Western Philosophy: Thales to Hume. The twelve-lecture course, beginning on September 14, 1972, took place at the Hilton Hotel, 6th Ave. and 53rd St., in New York City and was immediately offered worldwide on tape to groups of ten or more on a rental basis.

Because the course was presented orally, a significant amount of editing was required to make the book more amenable to the reading audience. I hasten to add, however, that I did not edit for philosophic or historical content, nor did I rewrite on the premise of "This is what I think Dr. Peikoff meant to say." I did eliminate repetition and a number of colloquial and conversational expressions, and I made some grammatical changes. I also moved some questions and answers so that they follow the lectures that contain those topics, and I retained some answers that repeated material in the lectures, on the premise that Dr. Peikoff thought that material important enough to warrant repetition. I also added the footnotes, including citations for quotations from secondary sources. I did not cite quoted material from the philosophers discussed by Dr. Peikoff: Not only are there multiple translations of the non-British philosophers, but web searches make it easy to find and compare different versions. Bracketed material was added by me, except where noted as asides from Dr. Peikoff during the lectures. All punctuation is mine, because Dr. Peikoff did not see either the original transcription or the edited version, and I had access only to the recordings of the live lectures, not to any of Dr. Peikoff's notes or manuscripts. A word-for-word transcript of the tape recording of the course resides in the

Ayn Rand Archives, and audio recordings of all sessions are available free of charge on the Ayn Rand Institute's website under the course title History of Philosophy.

I would like to thank Donna Montrezza, my longtime colleague, for her diligent and thoughtful proofreading and copyediting and her helpful comments in the difficult task of turning oral material into written. Thanks also to Simon Federman for his skillful production work and to Ziemowit Gowin for creating the highly valuable index.

—Michael S. Berliner
March 2023

FROM LEONARD PEIKOFF

People have often asked for a written version of my oral lecture courses, on the premise—with which I agree—that written lectures are much more accessible to the student. Writing, however, is in this context virtually a different language from speaking; a raw transcript of an extemporaneous speech, however excellent, is almost always filled with defects and confusions of one sort or another—and so is frequently boring as well. To turn a lecture course into an accurate, clear and valuable book, a huge amount of time-consuming editing is required, a task which can be performed only by an individual with the necessary motivation, knowledge of the subject and editorial skills. My own age and priorities make it impossible for me to undertake such a task.

I have therefore decided to authorize several individuals who possess the necessary qualifications to edit and bring out in book form certain of my courses, and to do so entirely without my participation. Although I have confidence in these editors to the extent that I know them, I have had no part in their work at any stage—no guiding discussions, no reading of transcripts, not even a glance at early drafts or final copy. Even a glance might reveal errors, and I could not then evade the need to read more, etc., which is precisely what is out of the question.

In my opinion, the lecture course in this book is of real value to those interested in the subject. But when you read it, please bear two things in mind: Michael Berliner is an excellent, proven editor—and I have no idea of what he has done in this book.

PS: If you happen to spot and wish to point out seeming errors in the text, please email Dr. Berliner at mberliner@aynrand.org. If you like this book, I may add, do not give me too much of the credit. My course provided, let us say, the spirit, but Dr. Berliner gave it the flesh required to live.

LECTURE ONE

The First Problem: Are There Any Absolutes?

I want to begin by asking you to imagine that you've just taken a trip to Mars, where you encounter a race of men who are just like us in all physical and psychological respects, and you observe one peculiar thing about them, namely, that they walk around on their hands only. This is utterly senseless. Their hands are torn and bleeding. Their hearts are pounding. Their faces are flushed. This is a misery-invoking, widespread insanity. Your first question would be "What could explain this kind of behavior?"

Hold that in mind and then look at our world on earth. If you look at the realm of art, you will see that the dominant school represents smears, which art historian Mary Ann Sures divides into two categories: the neat ones and the messy ones. You'll see that modern music represents a progression of unintelligible noises, and that a good deal of modern literature is an unintelligible succession of letters of the alphabet, that the theater alternates between characters and garbage cans and engages in orgies with the audience. In the realm of education, you will see that teachers are militantly against teaching and in favor of social adjustment and/or student power, that they're opposed to facts or the teaching of laws, that they regard thinking as abnormal, and that they tell little Johnny to express his feelings, with the result that he cannot read. If you look at the realm of religion, you will see that there are some three hundred warring sects, all claiming their insight into the appropriate other dimension by means of revelation, and that one of the crucial conflicts in the field is between the Orient, where they worship various types of animals, and the West, where they worship the pope. You'll see that the latest development in avowedly Christian philosophy is atheism, the view that God is dead. And in the age of atomic energy and space travel, we hear excerpts from Genesis broadcast from outer space. If you look to the realm of modern science, one school tells us that cause and effect no longer holds; another tells us that the theory of light has refuted the law of identity. Almost all tell us that science is based on arbitrary presuppositions, just like religion and no more objectively valid. Many tell us that there are no such things as laws, simply statistics. And a few chime in that the latest discovery is that electrons can move from one place to another without traversing the space in between.

This is a brief sample. What are the net results of this rampant irrationality? Well, if you look at it psychologically, you will see that the percentage of neurosis and psychosis in the West has reached epidemic proportions. If you look at it politically, you will see the escalating violence, the threat of nuclear war, the spreading worldwide slavery, the vicious, senseless political murders, and the inexorable march on the part of the West toward some version of fascism or communism.

If you want a philosophic barometer of the state of the culture, there are three questions that will tell it to you: What do people regard as certain? What do they regard as realistic? And what do they regard as human? We are told today that nothing is certain but death and taxes, and the skeptics aren't even sure of that. We are told that the characters of Tennessee Williams, or the ones inhabiting garbage cans, are realistic, but Cyrano de Bergerac is not. We would be told that Eleanor Roosevelt is human, but John Galt is not.

I submit that this is crazier than the example of Mars that I began with, and that the question therefore is: Why? But it's more complex than that, because there are great things, good things, rational things in the world, and particularly in Western civilization. There are the rational elements left in modern science, which is an enormous achievement. There is the legacy of the Industrial Revolution. There is the remnant of America's individualist political heritage and the remnants of nineteenth-century Romantic art, side by side with all the rest.

How are we to understand it all? How are we to understand such an incredible mixture? If you want a symbol that is no more eloquent than ten thousand others that could be used, what I myself think of as a symbol of this mixture is a New York City skyscraper with everything that that implies, with the thirteenth story labeled "fourteen," because thirteen is an unlucky number.

This is a symbol of the mixture of modern technology and ancient numerological mysticism. Why? There have been better periods in the past—why didn't they last? Where will we look for an explanation of it all? The answer is: the history of philosophy. If you want to know why, consider an analogy. Suppose that you were a psychotherapist, and you had a patient, an individual of mixed premises, partly rational, partly irrational, and he was accordingly tortured, stumbling, groping, and you wanted to understand him. The first thing you would have to do is understand the cause of his troubles. You'd have to understand what his bad premises are, why he holds them, and how he came to hold them. And then you would have to guide him in uprooting his bad premises and substitute correct ones in their stead. To do this, the crucial thing you would have to do is probe the patient's past, because his present can be fully understood only as a development and result of his past. Because he is one continuous entity, he builds conclusions on conclusions, and to understand the crucial events in his past life is therefore urgent. You'd have to understand those events, the conclusions he drew from them. You'd have to see how and why, across the course of his development, he was led to form and accept certain errors, and then to build upon them, thereby compounding his original problems, progressively stifling his better premises, making himself more and more twisted, confused, helpless. You would have to reconstruct the main points of the man's intellectual development, from childhood on.

This analogy applies to an entire culture. The stand-in for the neurotic of mixed premises is Western civilization, the world you live in. The stand-in for the psychiatrist is each one of you. You live in this culture; your lives and futures depend in thousands of ways on its future. If you pursue values in this world, you have a responsibility to your own lives and values, to correct the course of the world, to put it on the right track again. To fight for your values in a world such as ours, you must regard yourself as a psychotherapist of an entire culture. And just as in the case of an individual, so and even more so in the case of an entire civilization, which develops across time. Its present state at any given time cannot be understood except as an outgrowth from its past. The errors of today are built on the errors of the last century, and they in turn on the previous, and so on back to the childhood of the Western world, which is ancient Greece. To understand what exactly the root errors of today's world are, why these errors developed, how they clashed with and are progressively submerging its good premises, to understand, therefore, what to do to *cure* the patient, you have to reconstruct the intellectual history of the Western world.

I don't want to take the time now to give you a lot of examples. I'll give you just one, schematically. How would you explain the phenomenon of progressive education except by reference to John Dewey? But Dewey simply applied to education the principles of William James, and James made an obvious deduction from Hegel, and Hegel is a minor variant on Kant, and Kant was trying to answer Hume, who was the last consistent consequence of the trend inaugurated by Descartes and Locke, who were simply reformulating, in a somewhat more secular way, the principles of Augustine, who was reformulating in a somewhat more religious way the principles of Plato, who was trying to answer the dilemma posed by Heraclitus and Parmenides, who took off from four sentences of Thales, with whom we are beginning tonight.

The history of philosophy is like a philosophical psychotherapist's biographical report on a civilization. And it is therefore a precondition to understanding, and therefore to changing, the nature and present course of the civilization. That's the first and primary purpose of any course on the history of philosophy.

And there is a second purpose. The history of philosophy is *not* like the history of science. It is not an historical, antiquarian interest—it is not a dead subject. The only issues that a history of philosophy properly deals with are living, fundamental issues, perennial issues of philosophy. And in the course of a proper history of philosophy, you have presented to you all the main positions on all the main questions that have ever been formulated in Western philosophy. And consequently, it is valuable in its own terms as an introduction to the whole subject of philosophy. In particular, it's helpful because I will present to you not only the conclusions of the various philosophers, but also the arguments that they offer in favor of these conclusions.

Almost all of the philosophic errors that are undermining the world were originally—and still today are—advanced by their supporters with an array of arguments, claiming to prove that the viewpoint in question is true. And in fact, these viewpoints could not have acquired the power that they have over people's minds, if they didn't have this structure of apparently supporting arguments, which gives the errors at least the appearance of plausibility and rationality. So, if you are to fight the errors, you have to know clearly the main arguments advanced for them. You have to hear the Devil's case presented as strongly as that case permits. You have to be sure you know on each issue what really is true, and what is wrong with the arguments advanced for the erroneous view. If you don't know this, then you are not in a position to fight successfully against the errors. And therefore, in each case, I am going to present as strongly as I can the arguments by which the various views are defended by their supporters, particularly those arguments that are still widespread in terms of their public acceptance today. And at the appropriate point, I will present to you the Objectivist criticism. For the opening lectures, I will defer all criticism. My criticisms will essentially come either in the section on Aristotle, who took care of a great many errors, or in the last lecture on the Objectivist answers, where I'll take care of everything that hasn't been covered up to that point. In the end, therefore, I hope you have not only an increased understanding of the causes of today's world, but a philosophic arsenal to help you combat successfully what needs combating and to defend what needs defending.

Because this is a history of philosophy, it will be appropriate to tell you very briefly what philosophy consists of. The word "philosophy" comes from two Greek words, *phile* meaning "to love," and *sophia* meaning "wisdom," so etymologically it means "the love of wisdom." And at the very beginning, it was the subject that you studied if you studied anything; there was no other subject. Anybody who loved wisdom and wanted to acquire knowledge was by that fact a lover of wisdom; he was a philosopher. The ancient philosophers, therefore, all had views on things that we would not now regard as philosophy but as science (such as physics, mathematics, biology, etc.). But progressively, as each of these disciplines acquired a certain stock of information on its own, it split off and set up shop on its own. Mathematics was the first to do so, and subsequently, many hundreds of years later, physics and chemistry and so on.

What is philosophy as we use the term today? Essentially, it consists of five main divisions. One is metaphysics, and that is the branch of philosophy that studies the nature of the universe as a whole. Metaphysics embraces two types of questions: One, what are the main ingredients of the universe? Is there another dimension or only this one? Is there only matter, or is there also mind, or is there only mind, or what? And the second type of question under metaphysics: Are there any laws that are true of *everything* that exists? For instance, some philosophers say the law of cause and effect is true of everything, and therefore, is metaphysical.

The next division is epistemology—the branch of philosophy that defines the nature and means of human knowledge. It is concerned with all questions on the order of "How do you know you know?" What does knowledge begin with? Are the senses valid? Does man have some means of knowledge over and above the senses? For instance, reason. If so, what is reason? How does it operate? If you say "by logic," what does it mean to be logical? If you say "by concepts," what *are* concepts, and how are they related to sense experience? If you say man has some faculty of knowledge over and above reason and the senses, then what faculty? For instance, faith? Revelation? LSD? Women's intuition? Etc. What are the claims of any of those candidates to means of knowledge? Can man acquire knowledge? Is there anything outside man's province of knowledge? All of that is epistemology.

There's an offshoot of metaphysics and epistemology, which it's helpful to know just for purposes of ancient philosophy, and that's something we can call *philosophical psychology*. It's not really a separate branch of philosophy. It really is the application of metaphysics and epistemology to a philosopher's view of the nature of man—the basic philosophical nature of man, not experimental observations, which would be scientific psychology—but philosophical psychology. And that would deal with such questions as: Does man have free will or is he determined? What is the relationship between reason and emotions? Things of that order. In presenting Plato and Aristotle, I will present their views of man under the title of their psychology, although you could call that the application of their metaphysics and epistemology to the theory of the nature of man.

Then there is ethics, or morality (I'll use the two terms as being synonymous)—the branch of philosophy concerned to define a code of values to guide human choices and actions.

And then there is politics—the application of ethics to social questions; the branch of philosophy that defines the proper nature of society and, particularly, the proper function of government.

And finally, there is esthetics, which is the branch of philosophy concerned with art, the nature and purpose of art, and the standards by which it is to be objectively evaluated. We will not discuss esthetics except very peripherally in this course. We'll concentrate on the big four—metaphysics and epistemology being the base of any philosophy, ethics being the application to how an individual should live, politics being the application of ethics to social questions.

Philosophy, therefore, really consists of three basic questions: "What is there?"—that's metaphysics. "How do you know?"—that's epistemology. And "So what?"—that's ethics and politics. If you wanted an overall definition of philosophy, I would simply repeat it all in one sentence as follows: Philosophy is the subject that studies the nature of the universe, man's means of knowing the universe, and, on those bases, a code of values to guide human actions and institutions.

In the early days of philosophy, they did not have complete systems of philosophy with organized views in all of these branches; they had only isolated ideas on separate, individual questions (at least so far as we know from the few fragments that remain). The first overall systematic philosopher, who has views of an organized kind in every branch, is Plato. And thereafter, all major philosophers have systematic philosophies.

Before we plunge in, one point regarding the chronological division of the history of philosophy—so you'll have a perspective of what's coming and won't sit in suspense, wondering who's coming next. The history of philosophy is divided into three broad periods: ancient, medieval, and modern. Ancient is dated from the sixth century BC until about the sixth century AD, a period of about ten or twelve hundred years. It's officially declared to be dead in 529 AD, when all the pagan (i.e., non-Christian) schools were formally closed, and non-Christian philosophy was prohibited in the West. Medieval philosophy is the period when Christian philosophy dominates the scene, and it picks up two or three hundred years after Jesus, around the fourth or fifth century AD and dominates the field entirely until the Renaissance in the fifteenth century AD; so, that's a thousand years. And modern philosophy is the period from the Renaissance—the fifteenth century to the present. By convention, the present century (the one in which you live) is called "contemporary" philosophy (which we won't address in this course, since we stop in the eighteenth century). This gives us a big program; we have about 2400 years to cover from the sixth century BC to the 1800s, and we have twelve lectures, so that averages two hundred years per lecture. We can be thankful for the Dark Ages because we'll cover hundreds of years in one second.

Within ancient philosophy, there are four main divisions. There are a group of people of whom we know very little that came before Socrates and who are, therefore, very logically called the Presocratics. In most of these people, we do not know when they were born or when they died, but simply that they were alive and working in some year, and that is called their *floruit*, which means that they were flourishing in this year, and you assume that they were born thirty or forty or fifty years earlier, and/or died thirty or forty or fifty years later. We don't have any connected works from this period, just little excerpts, fragments. From the father of philosophy, Thales, we have four sentences. From Heraclitus, we have one hundred thirty, and so on. And that is enormously difficult to interpret, but we won't get into the scholarly difficulties. We'll be looking at those philosophers in this and the next lecture. And then we come to two philosophers who are really a unit—Socrates (Plato's teacher, whose years are 469–399 BC) and then Plato (427–347 BC). As I said, we'll be treating those as one unit, and we'll be regarding Socrates as a man who gave Plato some very seminal ideas, which he proceeded to develop. And then Aristotle (384–322 BC), Plato's pupil for twenty years, who then developed a philosophic system diametrically opposed to Plato. And then a group of second-rate philosophers stretching across hundreds of years, as ancient philosophy waned and died. They include the followers of Epicurus, the Stoics, Skeptics, Neoplatonists, and sundry others, and they are collectively called the post-Aristotelians, the winding up phase of ancient philosophy, and we cover all of those in one lecture here.

Medieval philosophy has two main eras: Augustinian and Thomistic. The Augustinian is named for Saint Augustine (354–430 AD), who represents the attempt to develop Christianity on a Platonist basis. And that dominates the scene for hundreds and hundreds of years, until the time of the second main era, the Thomistic, under the influence of Thomas Aquinas (1225–1274), who represents the attempt to combine Christianity with the philosophy of Aristotle, thereby (as we shall see) opening the door to the collapse of Christian influence and to the development of the Renaissance.

The fifteenth and sixteenth centuries have nothing of any interest. They represent the time when the modern world went back to school to study ancient philosophy and find out what had happened that they had lost knowledge of during the medieval period. So, a modern philosophy of any distinctive kind begins in the seventeenth century and divides into two famous schools: the "Rationalists," fathered by René Descartes in the seventeenth century, and the "Empiricists," fathered by John Locke and culminating in David Hume. So, that is a chronological survey of what to expect. And now let us plunge in at the very beginning.

Why do we say that philosophy and science started with the Greeks in the sixth century BC? After all, there had been human beings for a long, long time before that. There had been flourishing civilizations, and, surrounding Greece, there were the Phoenicians, the Egyptians, the Babylonians, and many others, and they had acquired a fair amount of primitive knowledge in fields like astronomy, mathematics, and so on. But none of them, except the Greeks, had anything that you would call "philosophy." They had philosophy implicitly, of course—every human being has some kind of code of values and view of reality and knowledge. But these non-Greek civilizations held these views essentially by implication. Insofar as philosophy was explicit, it was metaphorical, enormously mystical, mythological, filled with parables and dogmas, and so on, nothing that you would call a self-conscious or systematic or critical or rational attempt to raise and answer philosophic questions. In this latter sense, philosophy, as a self-conscious discipline, a rational phenomenon, began in the sixth century BC in Greece.

What prevented all these other civilizations from developing philosophy? Two things: In regard to their view of reality, they believed that true reality was some other dimension, superior to this one. They believed accordingly that nothing in this world was intelligible. This world was a series of events operated by the gods behind the scenes in another dimension and thus there was no way of trying to explain or understand this world. All you could do was bow, pray, and beg, because this world was basically a byproduct of another dimension. They had the same view with regard to ethics: Morality was merely a series of injunctions by the appropriate gods, and you could make no more sense of morality by reason than you could of physical phenomena. And therefore, there was no possibility of understanding the world. In other words, they were supernaturalist cultures, and they meant it.

A consequence of that was a second viewpoint that prevented them from developing philosophy: They held that this life and this earth are not only unintelligible but also evil. If you want to get their perspective (and this varied to some extent depending on the civilization, but it's a pretty fair statement), imagine that you are caught in a jail cell. You will not, in the normal case, have a passion to discover the molecular structure of the bars or the viscosity of the air, and so on—you will want to get out of the jail cell. That will be your overriding concern. And that was the overriding concern of most of the non-Greek cultures. This is perhaps best typified in regard to Egypt. The thing you think of is the pyramids, and they are a monument not to life, but to death, and the important thing in Egypt was not how good a life you could live, but how good a death you could die. In other words, these previous cultures took religion seriously, and the result was complete stultification, the failure to develop philosophic ability.

Greece was, however, an exception. As one commentator (M. T. McClure) puts it, Greece was "an oasis almost completely surrounded by barbarian custom and savage practice."[1] Why? What about the Greeks made the "oasis" possible? Two things: one political, one religious. Politically, what it amounts to is that by the sixth century BC, the Greeks, owing to various factors, had achieved a comparative degree of political freedom. The powerful monarchies of the earlier centuries had given way to the freer city-states, and in that climate, philosophy and science could develop. (I might note parenthetically that wherever government remained strong, philosophy never took root. The classic example of that is Sparta, which never had a philosophic thought so far as you can tell from what they left.)

The other factor in Greek development was religion. They had a very peculiar religion, based on the gods of Mt. Olympus. According to that view, the gods were not creators of the world; they were not rulers or directors of the world. The Greeks believed—*all* Greeks believed—that the universe had always existed, that it was a natural phenomenon, that the gods are one natural evolutionary development, along with everything else. The gods, therefore, could not interfere in any major way with the operation of the universe. The Greeks had a saying (which is dubious, but neverthe-

---

1. M. T. McClure, "The Greek Conception of Nature," *Philosophical Review*, March 1934.

less, they had it), "Nothing in excess." And the idea was that that applied to the gods also: They have their own place, and as long as they keep their place, okay, but if they get out of hand, reality will fix them. So, the gods were, in effect, streamlined men. They were elder brothers to man, in effect; they were not something you groveled before. They were not omnipotent, they were not omniscient, you were not to fear them. As a result, the Greeks held that this world is intelligible, and it was a *good* place in which to live. You know their statues—that is *their* concept of what is realistic. They thought that this was a good world, a friendly, happy place where you could achieve enjoyment and ease during life on earth, and therefore, they wanted to make something of life on earth. Now, they did believe in a shadowy immortality of sorts, but they didn't yearn for it. For instance, in one of Homer's works, the ghost of Achilles says, in a very representative statement, that he would rather live on earth as the slave of a man, even of a poor man—and it was a big disgrace to be the slave of a poor man—rather than be the king and the ruler of the whole other world. And that is a typically Greek attitude, you see, a very pro-this-life attitude. (There were exceptions, as we'll see later, but this was the dominant trend.) For these reasons—because knowledge was possible, because it was worthwhile, the Greeks developed a love of knowledge. They developed a *phile* for *sophia.* They took ideas seriously, and we had for the first time a development of a civilization of thinkers.

What did they think about? The first things that interested them were two different phenomena. I emphasize that they were at a period where we know essentially nothing—there's no philosophy yet, and no systematic science, so the first observations are going to be, by their nature, very elementary. The first two things that interested them were *change* and *multiplicity.* Let's explain what we mean by each of those things because they're going to appear throughout the course. By "change," we mean *anything* that happens, mental or physical—any occurrence, any event, any motion, any activity. Winter and then spring and then summer and then fall, and so on, in a cycle—that's change. A thing is born and grows and reaches its maturity, and then dies and decays and turns to dust—that's change. Life and death, waking and then sleeping, day becomes night, wet things become dry, cold things become hot, and light things become dark, etc. You know about rivers rushing off to where they're going, and landslides—the idea is clear.

What interested them about change? I'll take an example that they obviously did not use, not having paper matches made in Nevada. I'll engage in a process of change before your eyes and light a match. This is a process of change. Observe this match that I have. When I strike it, it undergoes a process of change, in fact, two of them—there was something white and flickering and hot, and now it's vanished, and something black has taken its place, and it's hot. That is a simple example of change, and the question that the Greeks wanted to know is: How do we make sense of this? Where did the flame come from? It wasn't there, and now it is. Where did the smoke come from? It wasn't there, and now it is. Where did the white tip go? The cold, hard, white tip that was there and now isn't? How did we get from one state to the other state? How are the two states related? That was the first question that they asked with regard to the phenomenon of change.

And now with regard to multiplicity—what does that mean, and what was the question? Multiplicity is a word for "many." The Greeks were impressed by the fact that there are a great many things making up the physical world—there are shoes and ships and sealing wax and cabbages and kings; if there were only cabbages, this question wouldn't have come up, but there are all kinds of different things. And the question that they asked is, "What is the relationship between all of these different things?" There must, they thought, be some sort of common denominator uniting or tying together all these different things. Could it be, they asked, in effect (not using these examples), could it possibly be that the only thing to say about bananas is that they're made out of banana stuff, and that's it? And tomatoes are made out of tomato stuff, and that's it? No, they said, that's impossible. There must be some sorts of relationships tying all these many things together, making them part of one universe. After all, some of them change into others—so the two issues are tied together; water becomes ice. So, there has to be something in common to make it possible for one of them to become the other. And how are we going to determine this?

Thales

Against this background, we can introduce the father of philosophy, the man who put forth the first answers to these questions and, as far as we know, was the first one to ask the questions. His name was Thales, and he flourished in 585 BC. As I said, we have only four sentences of his left, so you can become a world authority on Thales. He came from a town in Asia Minor called Miletus, and therefore, the school that he founded is called the Milesians. And he put forth essentially the following hypothesis (now I'm reconstructing, but it seems to be justified)—he put forth the idea that there is one fundamental stuff that makes up the entire universe, everything—bananas, philosophers, and sealing wax and everything else is made of this one ingredient that he called (or which subsequently was called) the "world stuff," the stuff that makes up the world and everything that's in it. This view—that there's only one stuff that makes up the world—came to be called "monism," from the view that there's one such stuff.

Thales's reasoning seemed to be that if there was one stuff, we could explain how everything is related. All the many things will just be many different forms of the one stuff.

And we'll be able to explain change, because change will be one form of that stuff becoming another form of that stuff. And therefore, we'll have a common denominator uniting and tying everything together. Of course, there's no warrant for the view that there's only one such stuff. But the approach that he is attempting here was of incalculable importance. It is the approach that, to this day, is the essence of the scientific approach: the attempt to find unity amid diversity, to find common denominators that enable us to integrate a whole wealth of disparate observations. The whole process of physics, for instance, started with a series of laws, and then Newton comes along and shows that you can reduce them to just a few laws, and Einstein to even fewer laws, and so on, constantly seeking for unity in the face of diversity. The same is true of chemistry, which took the endless stuffs of the world, and tried to find them in ninety or one hundred-odd elements, and then the physicists came in and tried to reduce those elements down to eight or ten building blocks, and so on. That attempt was inaugurated by Thales. And what he was looking for, if we use the Greek terminology, was the *one in the many.* Another way in which it is described is: *the permanent amid the changing, the thing which is always there*, and which all the changing things are simply different forms of.

As to Thales's view as to what *is* the one in the many, what is the world stuff, it is very primitive: He held that it was water. And he is sometimes jocularly described as a "hydromonist," but that is carrying terminology to the point of insanity. He held that view on the basis of observations, which are sensible within his frame of knowledge. Water was the one thing that he could observe that could take on solid, liquid, and gaseous form. Water seemed to be able to turn into air, because when you put out a dish of it, the next day it was gone, and all that was left was air. (And that, of course, is evaporation, a phenomenon he didn't know about.) Earth seemed to turn into water, because if you dig in the earth, you'll find water. (Those were underground springs, which they regarded as earth turning into water.) Water can become solid, as in the form of ice. Water dries up, and sometimes you find little wriggling living creatures, which suggests a central connection between water and life, and so on.

For all of these types of reasons, he said that water is the one in the many. He's wrong, but the importance of Thales is the question and the category of answer, not the specific answer. He was the one who (1) established the idea of a *naturalistic* approach to the world, rather than a supernaturalistic one, (2) dispensed with the supernatural, with gods as explanatory principles, and (3) introduced the idea that there are natural laws in the nature of things governing what takes place—we can account for the entire phenomena that we observe by reference to one logical reality. And he also suggested by implication that the indispensable precondition of it all was sense observation—that that alone would tell us the nature of reality.

All of this is implied from the four sentences that he left us, but it was essentially there. Hence, the "Father of Philosophy."

He had a number of successors in the Milesian school, which we are going to pass over without mention—you can get them from a history book if you want. Some of them weren't as good as he was, and some of them were more advanced, and they speculated that the world stuff wasn't water. One of them thought it was air, one of them thought it was earth, and another one had his own weird view as to what it was. But in any event, that's a detail that we can pass over. Science, philosophy, although very primitive, was nicely started.

Heraclitus

And now we reach the next philosopher in the progression—Heraclitus. He is not a Milesian; he is a Presocratic who started his own school. And from the Objectivist perspective, he is the first villain in the history of Western thought. He is also the first enduringly influential philosopher, in that his particular views are still widespread today: Nobody today is a hydromonist, but there are all sorts of Heracliteans wandering around. Heraclitus flourished about 500 BC. We have about a hundred thirty fragments, and they are so obscure that even in the ancient world he had the nickname "The Dark," because he was wont to deliver aphoristic, cryptic utterances without explanation, sort of oracular.

The essence of Heraclitus's views is an attack on what Aristotle later defined as the basic laws of logic. Now, obviously, he could not have attacked the laws of logic explicitly, because the laws of logic were not even known until the fourth century BC, when Aristotle defined them. But in retrospect, we can say that the essence of what Heraclitus was getting at, and what all of his followers promptly made explicit, is an all-out attack on the law of identity and the law of contradiction. For now, I'll just say them succinctly and explain their nature and importance properly when we get to Aristotle. The law of identity is the simple view that everything that is, is what it is; everything that is possesses a nature, possesses an identity; it is something, and is nothing else. A is A. And the law of contradiction, a corollary of the law of identity, says, well then, if things are what they are, a thing is not what it isn't; nothing can be A and non-A at the same time and in the same respect. If you are six feet tall, then you're six feet tall; you can't also be not six feet tall. You might grow, but at a given time you can be only one height. Aristotle claimed that these laws were the basis of all logical reasoning, the basis of science, the basis of sanity.

Heraclitus's point is that these laws are out (not explicitly, but that's the meaning). Why? Well, he said, everybody is so interested in change, I propose to show that the phenomenon of change is incompatible with these laws of logic. Or, put it another way, the phenomenon of change requires the existence of contradictions, requires things that are and are not at the same time. Well, if so, we'd like to know how. I'll use the same example I gave of the match, and this time derive Heraclitus's conclusion from it. I'm now going to put this match through a process of change, and ask you to observe it closely, and at a certain point we'll see if we can show, from Heraclitus's point of view, why it ends up being contradictory. Now I just pluck this match; this is still the same match that I had a second ago. I didn't take the original match and throw it away and substitute a new match; that would be substitution, but I didn't do that. I still have the same match. I'm now going to make it go through a process of change. Here's a process of change—as I light the match. Obviously, it is still the same match—I didn't substitute another one. But it obviously is *not* the same match, because it has changed—the tip is now hot, and it used to be cold, and it's now black and it used to be white. According to Heraclitus, this match is therefore the same as it was at the beginning, and yet it has changed, it is *not* the same as it was at the beginning. At the same time (namely, after the change), it *is* what it was, but it is *not* what it was—it is and is not—it's the same and not the same—it's A and not-A at the same time, which is a contradiction.

Could we give another example? Oh yes, Heracliteans can give all sorts. For instance, take any one of you. Remember the little baby who was born twenty, forty, whatever years ago—are you the same as that little baby, the same entity? Well, obviously, yes you are. I mean, we didn't take that little baby and bring in somebody new. You are it. We didn't substitute. You are the same. On the other hand, what in the world is the same about you? As the Heracliteans would say, your mental content is certainly completely different (your values, ideas, and so on). According to certain biologists, every cell in your body changes every seven years, so there's nothing physically left the same. So, you're completely different mentally and physically, and yet you're obviously the same. You're the same and you're not the same. You're A and you're non-A.

If you want it applied to Thales, the way Heraclitus himself seemed to argue is like this: Everything is water, Thales says. Well, okay. Then after a change, the water is still water. But since it's changed, it *isn't* water anymore. It is and it isn't. In other words, we can generalize: Wherever there is change, at the end of the change we have the same thing. That is what is involved in it being a change rather than substitution. Whenever there is change, at the end of the change we have a different thing, because that's inherent in its changing. Therefore, at the end of the change, we have the same thing and not the same thing, and therefore, change necessarily involves a contradiction.

Change is the most obvious fact there is. No one could possibly deny it. The only conclusion can be is that the world is riddled with contradictions. The world is filled with things that are and are not. In fact, you can put it even better: The world is filled with things that are and are not, what they were and were not, and what they will and will not become. As B.A.G. Fuller summarizes Heraclitus's view: "[Reality's] essential nature lay in being both the same as itself and different from itself. For in order to change, a thing must become different from itself. If it remains the same as itself, it hasn't changed. But also, after it has changed, it must still be the same thing, otherwise there has been no change, but simply the substitution of one object for another. A changing thing then is an identity of opposites. It both is and is not what it was and what it will be."[2]

You may think that that is a primitive viewpoint, that it has an obvious flaw (even if you might not know right offhand what it is), but that there's something obviously wrong with it, and that surely no one, after the development of modern science and Aristotelian logic and so on, could *ever* have been taken in by that, so I'll read you a quotation. Who said the following? "The law of contradiction is afflicted with falsity. It says nothing can both be and not be. But anything that can change defies it—it can both be and not be with the utmost ease."[3] Now, that is not Heraclitus. That is F.C.S. Schiller, one of the leading American pragmatists, who

---

2. B.A.G. Fuller, *A History of Philosophy*, Volumes 1–2 (New York: Harcourt Brace, 1955), p. 51.
3. F.C.S. Schiller, *Logic for Use* (London: G. Bell & Sons, 1929), p. 381.

taught for many, many years in the twentieth century at the University of Southern California. Or if you want another one: "Life consists precisely and primarily in this—that a being is at each moment itself and yet something else. Life is, therefore, also a contradiction which is present in things and processes themselves, and which constantly originates and resolves itself; and as soon as the contradiction ceases, life, too, comes to an end, and death steps in."[4] Pure Heraclitus applied to life. That's Friedrich Engels, the sidekick of Karl Marx, and what the Marxists made is essentially a three-step waltz out of Heraclitus's viewpoint.

As to what is wrong with this, think about it. I'm going to leave it for Aristotle, who took care of it definitively. So, if you don't figure out an answer by then, you'll be sure to get it then. Let's go on to Heraclitus's next point.

He took change very seriously. Everybody at this time, as you know, was looking for the world stuff, the one in the many. Heraclitus looked, as did everyone else. But, he said, I couldn't find anything that was everywhere. It couldn't be water, because there are things that *aren't* water, and for the same reason, it couldn't be earth, and it couldn't be air, and so on. There is, he said, only one thing that I can find everywhere without any exception, and that is: the process of change itself. Everything is changing, slow or fast, but at least everything is changing. Therefore, he said, if we really want to know the key to reality, if we want the metaphysical phenomenon (of course, he didn't use those words), the essence of reality is change. That is the metaphysical essence. The word that he used is "Becoming," usually spelled with a capital "B," Becoming—everything is becoming, changing, evolving, developing, in process. Since he made this metaphysical, it follows that it applied to everything—not just to sticks and stones, but to sealing wax and kings and the whole works—and therefore, Heraclitus took the view that everything is changing, in every respect, at every instant. Change governs everything. Therefore, nothing remains the same for two consecutive instances in any respect.

His famous sentence illustrating this is "You can't step into the same river twice, for fresh waters are always flowing in." For him that is the paradigm of reality. You try to put your foot in it the next time, it's different—it has changed. And *everything* is like that. There are many obvious examples of change to which he could appeal—landslides, volcanoes, earthquakes, biological growth, the slow changes of erosion and so on—but you might ask, "Well, what would a follower of Heraclitus do with such a thing as this lectern?" This seems to be the most peaceful,

---

4. Friedrich Engels, *Anti-Dühring*, 1877.

quiet, motionless, unchanging thing you could ask for. It just sits there. What's happening? Well, Heraclitus might personally have had a little difficulty with it, but his followers don't bat an eye when you give them an example of that sort, because, they say: "When looked at from your crude human senses, it looks like it is motionless. But if you could see it as modern science reveals it to us, you would see that this table is a holocaust of activity. There are all sorts of subatomic particles busily racing off and on to it, all the boundary interchanges. And there are electric charges coursing through it, and energy pulsations, and cosmic rays," and you can, you know, get any cheap science fiction and put in whatever you want there—the idea being that actually this lectern is a whirl of activity, and it is the crudeness of human senses that makes this activity undetectable to us. But that is the defect of our senses. We can, however, confidently generalize and say that *everything*, even the most apparently stationary things, are constantly changing.

From this point, Heraclitus drew a momentously important consequence: There are no *things* at all. No entities. For example, a table, a person, a mountain, a cigarette, a plant. To the normal person, it seems blatantly obvious that there are all kinds of things, all kinds of entities. But Heraclitus observed that if you accept his principle that everything is changing in every respect at every instant, there are no entities.

How does this follow? Suppose that he asks you to find an entity (in a reality, remember, that is constantly changing). You point to this lectern and say, "There it is." But you no sooner get the "it" out than the lectern is gone completely. It's vanished in the flux, it's completely different from what it was. Nothing stands still for one instant. Therefore, try to find something and say, "There's a thing," and you just get to the "th–," and the "thing" is gone. Therefore, Heraclitus summarized in two famous aphorisms (which are two of his fragments), "Nothing is, everything is becoming." Which is surely a paradoxical utterance. And the other famous one is *panta rhei*, in other words, "Everything flows and nothing abides."[5]

I'm going to read you a fairly lengthy passage from one historian (Gordon H. Clark), who outdid himself in the presentation of this point. He's a modern commentator summarizing Heraclitus's view. I could not

---

5. Note this caveat: "Πάντα ῥεῖ" (panta rhei), i.e., "everything flows," seems either not to have been written by Heraclitus or did not survive as a quotation of his. This famous aphorism used to characterize Heraclitus's thought comes from Simplicius, a Neoplatonist, and from Plato's *Cratylus* where it is translated as "everything moves."

equal his level of clarity on this point.

> All things flow. No man can ever step twice into the same river. How could he? The second time he tried to step, new waters would have flowed down from upstream: The water would not be the same. Neither would the bed and the banks be the same, for the constant erosion would have changed them, too. And if the river is the water, the bed and the banks, the river is not the same river. Strictly speaking, there *is* no river. When common opinion names a river, it supposes that a name applies to something that will remain there for a time at least. But the river remains there no time at all. It has changed while you pronounce its name. There is no river. Worse yet, you cannot step into the same river twice because you are not there twice. You, too, change, and the person who stepped the first time no longer exists to step the second time.
>
> Persons do not exist. When anyone says that something exists, the meaning is that that something does not change. An object that is real must be an object that stands still. Suppose a clever sculptor takes a lump of children's modeling clay and begins to work it rapidly. It shortly takes on the appearance of the child's teddy bear. And if the sculptor should stop, we could call it a teddy bear. But he does not stop. His nimble fingers keep working, and the momentary bear turns into a small statue of Zeus, only quickly to disappear into the form of the Empire State Building. "What is it?" we ask. The answer is not that it's a bear, or a god, or a building. Under these circumstances, all we could say is that it is modeling clay. And we could call it clay because the clay remains the same throughout the changes. But if the clay itself never remained the same—if it changed from clay to wax to papier maché and so on and never stopped changing, we could call it nothing. Nothing; it does not exist, it is unreal.[6]

Nothing is. Everything is becoming. Change is the world stuff.

This type of philosophy is called a *process* philosophy because it holds that process, activity, motion, change, is reality. Do not take this superficially to mean merely that he thinks a lot of things are happening in the world. That a lot of things are happening in the world is not a philosophic viewpoint; that is a *Reader's Digest* homily. The Heraclitean view is that *all* that exists is change—a stream of shifting, restless, transitory, seething, boiling, bubbling, melting, fusing, swirling activity, riddled

6. Gordon H. Clark, *Thales to Dewey: A History of Philosophy* (Boston: Houghton Mifflin, 1957), p. 19.

with contradictions, as though the whole universe were plunged in a kind of cosmic food blender, and just flowed in all directions (and didn't flow, because . . . you know).

Heraclitus himself, apparently in an attempt to get a metaphor to capture this, picked on fire, because fire was the closest he seemed to be able to get to the idea of motion without an entity—the tongues leaping and darting, and yet there's nothing solid there to get a hold of; it seems to be like the visual embodiment of pure motion. And therefore, in that terminology, he said the world stuff is fire. But he did not mean by "fire" any kind of material substance, but rather, sheer process or activity.

I should point out that Heraclitus had a follower in the ancient world named Cratylus, a disciple of Heraclitus and a teacher of Plato, so he's between the two. And Cratylus drew a perfectly obvious conclusion from this principle: He stopped talking. He took the view that no one should ever speak, on the grounds that there is no way to give words meaning, because the only way that you can give words meaning is by giving them a referent, and there's nothing for words to refer to. If you try to say "lectern," by the time you say "lec–," it's gone. And therefore, words are just noise, and a respectable man does not utter noise. According to Aristotle, from whom we learn about this, Cratylus, at a certain point in his conversion, therefore, stopped speaking, and simply wagged his finger when he was hungry, presumably beckoning the non-Heracliteans to bring him food. (We will see Aristotle's answer later.)

So much for Heraclitus's fragments dealing with metaphysics, and now one epistemological issue in connection with Heraclitus. He's the first man in the history of philosophy to regard the senses as invalid. The reason is very simple: By the evidence of our senses, it appears that there are permanent, motionless, unchanging things. And yet, he says, we know that that's not true. We know that everything is changing, and so we must say that our senses are deceptive, they're invalid, they are too gross to detect the degree of change that is actually taking place. Sometimes his followers say that the change taking place is analogous to letting water into a bathtub via one pipe and out via another at the same rate, so that an unwary spectator looking at the surface will say no change is taking place, but, in fact, two opposite changes are taking place and canceling each other out. Their viewpoint is, "We have shown by reason that reality is filled with nothing but change, and therefore we reject the senses."

Therefore, an earthshakingly important distinction is implicit in Heraclitus, the distinction between two realms—reality and appearance. Reality is that which really exists. In Heraclitus's view, it's a mass of change.

His "reality" is very often referred to as "Heraclitean flux," that being a way of describing nothing but change, which is riddled with contradictions besides. So, there's reality and, on the other hand, there is the world as it appears to us, the world that the Greeks called "the world of appearance." Reality is known by reason, reason apart from the senses, reason in contradiction to the senses. And the world of appearances is the world as given to us by the deceptive senses.

This duality between reality and appearance, and its corresponding epistemological duality of reason versus the senses, runs all through Greek philosophy with one or two exceptions. And Heraclitus is the first in which you find it. Anyone who subscribes to this view and who says that reason is what we should follow (reason in this sense of the term, reason as *opposed* to the senses) is called a philosophic *rationalist.* Therefore, Heraclitus can be regarded as the first Greek rationalist. That's obviously not "reason" in any Objectivist or Aristotelian sense of the term, but that's the way the terms are used. You will see that Plato is a rationalist in this sense also.

Now, in order to be fully fair to the historical Heraclitus, I would like to point out that he himself believed (quite inconsistently with the rest of his philosophy) that change was actually orderly, lawful, intelligible. He was, in fact, one of the earliest formulators of the view that the events in the world occur according to law and can be understood by the human mind. He thought that there was a law of change governing all the particular changes. But he was in this respect a good rational Greek. The Greeks, almost without exception and no matter how awful they became, had something good to say. It's only since Christianity took over that you have philosophers who are black from top to bottom. But the Greeks almost always have something good, and that's true even of Heraclitus. Unfortunately, the good element in him was not nearly as influential as his flux side.

I don't think I have to point out to you the prevalence of Heracliteanism today. Anybody who says it's a changing world and uses that in anything other than an utterly innocuous sense, is a Heraclitean. Anybody who says that there are no absolutes, that everything is relative, is a full-fledged orthodox Heraclitean, because "absolute," in such a context, means invariant, unchanging in time or place, something that holds for all times and places. And for Heraclitus, there is no such thing; there are no absolutes. If it's true today, it won't be true tomorrow, and so on. And the same kind of relativism will be generated not only for knowledge in general, but for ethics and value theory in particular. There will be no absolutes in ethics any more than in anything else, a viewpoint at which Heraclitus himself actually hinted (but simply hinted in one of his fragments, that ethical relativism is the conclusion to draw). If you ever have found anybody who equates "old-fashioned" with "false," that is Heracliteanism at work, the idea being (to take an example that I hear frequently), "The American Constitution, for instance, must be wrong." Why? "Well, it was formulated in the eighteenth century." So? "Well, now it's the twentieth century." Period. That argument is pure Heraclitus. If the person attempted to say, "In the intervening years, there have been changes and so on," well, that would be one thing, "specific changes that require a specific change." He'd be wrong, but at least that would be a different argument. But if he says, "Time has passed, and the eighteenth century can't be applicable in the twentieth," why can't it? "Because everything flows and nothing abides." And that is Heraclitus.

Most skeptics base themselves partly on Heraclitus. "How can you say that you know that such and such is really true? Maybe yesterday it was true, but how do you know about tomorrow? Everything changes, everything is becoming." John Dewey says at one point that Aristotle's logic must be no good because it's worked for so long, we must need a new one.

As to what it would be like to live in the Heraclitean world—well, physically you don't and you can't. But you can get a good taste of it (unless you're very fortunate) in your social existence because most people, to some extent, live in a Heraclitean world socially. A great many children live in that kind of world thanks to the wanton irrationality of their parents, whose behavior is characterized by constant contradictions, constant switching, so that nothing ever holds true from one moment to the next. That is the perfect recipe for the Heraclitean world. Most citizens, in relation to the government of a mixed economy, live in exactly that Heraclitean world. And if you want a kind of perfect example, most businessmen in regard to the antitrust laws live in an absolutely clear-cut textbook Heraclitean world. What are their complaints about the antitrust laws? One is: "Everything flows and nothing abides. Interpretations change from moment to moment, and you never know what's coming next." And another is: "Everything in that world is and isn't. Is competition good? Yes, because monopoly is bad. Is competition good? No, because the efficient people will then take away the markets of the inefficient. It is and it isn't." Now, that is Heracliteanism, and you see where it's getting us. If you want a marvelous portrayal of it, I suggest that you reread the scene in *Atlas Shrugged* between Cherryl and Dagny, where Cherryl comes at the climactic part in her relationship with Taggart and is saying that everything is switching, everything is swimming, everything is changing, and she can't enjoy or understand it, and Dagny tells her what she needs to know in essence, and tells her that there have been philosophers working for centuries to bring about just that state. The first and most influential of the philosophers that she refers to in this scene is Heraclitus.

Parmenides

Let us now turn to Parmenides, who flourished about twenty years after Heraclitus, about 480 BC, and who represents a diametrically opposite philosophic viewpoint. Parmenides comes from the town of Elea, and so his philosophy is frequently referred to as Eleaticism, or the Eleatic philosophy. Parmenides is the first (judging by the fragments that we have) to support his conviction with reasoned arguments. We have a whole poem of his, where he does not just announce his conclusions in Heraclitus's oracular fashion but lets us in on the actual reasoning that he adopted. He is profoundly opposed to Heraclitus's view, the view that everything is an identity of opposites, or that nothing *is*, everything is becoming. His entire philosophy derives from one basic principle (which I will give you in my own words): "What is, is, and what is not, is not, and what is not can neither be nor be thought about." That is the essence of Parmenides. If you want to hear Parmenides's own formulations of this, I'll quote you from some of his fragments: "Come now, I will tell thee, and do thou harken to my saying and carry it away—the only two ways of search that can be thought of. The first, namely, that what is, is, and that it is impossible for it not to be, is the way of belief, for truth is its companion. The other, namely, that what is, is not—that, I tell thee, is a path that none can learn of at all, for thou canst not know what is not; that is impossible, nor utter it." As you gather, that is unmitigated repudiation of Heraclitus. Heraclitus says everything is and isn't, and here Parmenides says: Absolutely not. If it is, it is, and if it isn't, it isn't. What is, is, and what isn't, isn't. In regard to the Heracliteans, he has very pointed words. He refers to them in one fragment as "mortals knowing not who wander two-faced. Helplessness guides the wandering thought in their breasts, and they are borne along, stupefied like men deaf and blind, undiscerning crowds who hold that it is and is not, the same and not the same, and that all things travel in opposite directions." In other words, out with the Heracliteans. And one more fragment from him, "For this shall never be proved, that the things that are not, are, and do thou restrain thy thought from this way of inquiring."

What does it mean, his basic principle? It is the earliest formulation in the history of thought of what Ayn Rand in Galt's speech formulates as "Existence exists," and its meaning is the same. And therefore, it includes the following elements: First, there is a reality, which he refers to as "what is, that which exists." Reality exists. And *only* reality exists. What is, is, and *only* what is, is. What is not, is not. And another point implicit: What is not can never be thought about. In other words, all thought must be thought about existence, about what is. It is impossible, according to Parmenides, ever to think about what is not, or to know what is not, or to have any cognitive relation of any kind to what is not.

If you doubt this, perform a mental experiment right now—try for a second to think about nothing. I don't mean the letters n-o-t-h, etc., because that's something, and I don't mean a black wall—that's something. I mean *nothing*, absolutely nothing, what is not. Go ahead and have the thought. You see, you cannot do it, because as soon as you think, you think about *something*, you think about what is. And thus, Parmenides's famous line, "Thou canst not know nor utter what is not." It is empty; there *is* no "what is not," and therefore, you can't think about it. And this is the view that ultimately appears in Galt's speech as the view that consciousness is the faculty of perceiving that which exists. In this sense, the earliest source of these crucial ideas is Parmenides. And he is, therefore, an extremely important, and in this respect, an extremely good, philosopher.

We can put his viewpoint another way in order to prepare ourselves for the consequences that he derived from it. If thought is always about reality, always about what is, then it is untenable and invalid ever to hold a concept of sheer nonexistence, in other words, of what is not. Because that would be a concept of nothing; in other words, it would be no concept. His key point in this respect is (to put it in a sort of funny way, but this is really the essence of it): There is no nothing, only somethings. And the thought about nothing is therefore not a thought about anything; it's not a thought at all. All concepts must be formed within existence and refer to existence. And therefore, according to Parmenides, any theory or philosophic position that at any point requires a concept of sheer nothing, of nonexistence, is invalid and must be dismissed right away.

On this basis, Parmenides drew a number of systematic deductions: Number one, the universe must have been uncreated; it could never have come into existence. Why? If there was a beginning to what is, then what existed before? Well, if it wasn't "what is," it had to be "what is not." But what is not, is not; there is no nothing, and therefore, there could never have been a state of nothing preceding a state of something. In other words, the universe must always have existed; it could not have been created. So much for the religious view. I may say that on the basis of this reasoning, no Greek philosopher ever believed that the universe was created out of nothing. That is a distinctively and exclusively Jewish/Christian doctrine, never accepted by the most mystical Greeks.

Secondly, in the other direction, the universe must be indestructible; it could never go *out* of existence; because if it went out of existence, what would be left? What is not. But what is not, is not, and can never be. Therefore, the universe must be indestructible; it always will exist. If you put these two points together, we can say that, according to Parmenides, the universe is therefore eternal; it has no beginning and has no end.

Third point—focusing now *within* the universe—can there be such a thing as a vacuum, as an empty space? Completely empty now, a real little zero, inside the physical world. To which Parmenides answers, "Absolutely not. What is not, is not. All there is, is what is, and therefore, there's no such thing as a vacuum." This later came to be expressed in Latin, "The universe is a *plenum*," which means that it is solidly packed; the actual word means "full"—it's completely full. There are no little holes, no little spaces, no little nothings; it's one big slab of stuff, a huge ball of tightly packed matter. Now, for other reasons that are irrelevant, he happened to believe that it had the shape of a sphere, apparently because he thought there was no good reason why it should bulge in one direction but not the other. But that's beside the point.

So far, having given several of his deductions, his principle "What is, is," is really the basic law of logic, and in that sense he's sometimes called the "father of logic" (although that's pretty indirect, because he didn't know that it had anything to do with thinking, as a principle of guiding thinking). He certainly launched an all-out attack on Heraclitus, and raised hell with religion, so he's made a good start.

But Parmenides drew another deduction from his basic principle, which, in his opinion, was just as obvious as all the preceding ones, and that's where all the trouble comes in. He drew, as a fourth conclusion, the idea that change is impossible. Change of any kind—motion, alteration, occurrence of any kind. Therefore, according to his viewpoint, there are no such things as talking, moving, writing, swimming, planets orbiting the sun—all of that is a gigantic illusion.

How did Parmenides draw such a conclusion? Take a simple example of change: a seed growing into a flower. At the beginning of the change, the seed represents what is. What about the flower at the beginning? The flower is not. At the end of the change, what happened to the seed? It's gone; it's what is not. What happened to the flower? It's now there, it's what is. And that is true of every change—something goes away, and something comes to be. What does that mean? He concluded that change is a double violation of his principle. Every change is a simultaneous passage from what is to what is not, and, from the other aspect, from what is not to what is. But there *is* no "what is not," and you can't think about what is not, and therefore: out. Change, according to him, is just as irrational as the idea of the universe being created or going out of existence. It involves reference to what is not. And what is not, is not. Therefore, he concluded, there is no change at all. The world is completely motionless in every respect.

Now, you see here that there is a sense in which he is in complete agreement with Heraclitus. Both of them agree with the following crucial viewpoint: Change implies a contradiction; change implies a violation of logic. Heraclitus, from the aspect that at the end of a change a thing is and isn't what it was, and Parmenides from the aspect that at the end of the change, you have what is *not* becoming what is, and vice versa, and that is a contradiction, since what is not, is not.

Given this common premise, they take diametrically opposite views. Heraclitus says, "Change is obvious, therefore, to hell with logic." Parmenides says, "Logic is obvious, therefore, to hell with change." But the common denominator is that you have to make your choice—it's either logic or change, either identity or change.

Just to make it a little worse, the two things I said that the Greeks were primarily concerned with at this early stage were change and multiplicity. Having denied change, Parmenides went on, with apparently equal consistency, to deny multiplicity. There is no multiplicity. There is no variety of things. Why? He, like everybody at this early period, was a monist. Remember that "monist" means somebody who believes there's only *one* stuff that makes up the world. But in addition, he believes that the world is a plenum, solidly packed; there are no spaces. Well, then, he asked, what in the world would make one thing different from anything else? How would you draw the line and say, "Here's one thing and here's another"? The world is one solid, undifferentiated slab, one stuff that has no spaces between it, so there's nothing to separate one thing from another thing. Therefore, we have to say that multiplicity is an illusion. The world is just a hunk of undifferentiated stuff. There's nothing to distinguish one part from the other. Again, there are no entities, or putting it another way, there's just *one* entity—*everything*, which he called "the One," and you can see why. It's no longer the one in the many, because "the many" are gone now; it's just the One. That, believe it or not, is the ancestor of the Christian God. By several transmutations and permutations, Parmenides's One became the God of

Christianity, but it took quite a while for it to happen.

So the world is just a motionless, changeless, undifferentiated ball of tightly packed matter. Needless to say, this is not the way that it appears to our senses. It appears as though there is multiplicity; it appears as though there is change. What is Parmenides's answer? The same as Heraclitus's: The senses are deceptive; they give us only the world of appearances, which is not true reality. True reality is the motionless One, and it is arrived at by logic, not by the senses. And therefore, again, we have rationalism epistemologically from both Parmenides and Heraclitus, but coming to opposite conclusions.

What is wrong with his reasoning? Wait until we get to Aristotle, because one of Aristotle's main assignments in metaphysics was to answer both Heraclitus and Parmenides, and to do so, Aristotle carved out certain concepts that he originated and which we use to this day, and he said those are the only concepts by reference to which we can answer Parmenides.

You see that people are now in a very dreadful philosophic position. We have a catastrophe almost at the very outset of Western philosophy: One philosopher with an array of arguments that seemed persuasive at the time, to prove that everything is change and there are no things; another philosopher with an array of arguments which seemed convincing, to prove that nothing changes and there is only the motionless One. What are we going to do to reconcile these two philosophers, to take their arguments and somehow make sense of it all? That was the task of subsequent philosophy, never properly answered until the time of Aristotle.

Zeno

We haven't finished with Parmenides, though, because he had a famous follower, namely, Zeno (approximately 490–430 BC). Zeno is famous for devising a series of paradoxes that purport to prove two things: Some of them purport to prove that motion is impossible, thus carrying out Parmenides's principle. And some of them purport to prove that multiplicity is impossible. They all involve the same kind of reasoning, sometimes more obvious than others. I'm not going to answer them now, because Aristotle devoted his attention to answering them, and in the process said some very valuable things about the nature of infinity. I'll just present to you two of Zeno's paradoxes, and you can get an idea of what a dreadful position people were in at the time because they couldn't answer Zeno, and they knew that something had to be wrong.

His most simple one about motion is that it's impossible to cross a room. Why is it impossible to cross a room? Consider: To cross a room, you first have to cross half of it. But to cross half of it, you first have to cross half of *that* (a quarter of it, in other words). And to cross that, you have to cross half of it (an eighth). And of course, cross half of that (a sixteenth), and so on. He asks, how many times can a distance be subdivided? And his answer was, there's no end. If you say one-zillionth of the distance, well, there's always one half-zillionth of the distance. You can divide without end. In other words, you can subdivide infinitely. But how can you possibly cross an infinite number of distances, no matter how tiny they are? Because, to cross any distance would take some time, no matter how little, and to cross an infinite number of distances would take an infinite amount of time, but you die in forty or fifty or sixty years. Therefore, you obviously couldn't cross a room, or *any* distance, for that matter. And therefore, motion is an illusion.

This would apply to the motion of his tongue in uttering the argument. To get from the upper palate to the lower, his tongue has to cross half the distance, and so on. But that's his viewpoint.

Here's one of his paradoxes on multiplicity: Multiplicity is the view that the world consists of a number of things. For instance, you and you and you and this. Or you can take it on the level of atoms, or galaxies; it doesn't make any difference to the argument. Zeno is going to argue that this is impossible. The world has to be one indivisible slab, not a whole comprised of parts. Why? Well, he says, I'll show you that the idea that the universe has parts is filled with impossible contradictions. For instance, let's imagine the universe is a whole with many parts, and let us ask what the size of the universe would be? How many parts does the world have, he says, according to the people who believe in such a thing as parts? If we keep on subdividing, how many parts will the world end up having? Obviously, he says, it will end up with an infinite number of parts, because every magnitude is theoretically divisible without limit, so if we break the world up into one-foot-long things, we can break each of those up into two six-inch things, and each of those into four three-inch things, and so on, and there's no theoretical end. So, if we keep going, you have to grant that there's an infinite number of parts. And if there's an infinite number of parts, no matter how small each of them is, we must have an infinitely big universe, because infinity times any amount is infinitely big. Thus, we reach the conclusion that *if* the universe consists of parts, it must be infinitely large. But look at it another way: What will be the size of the ultimate parts, the ultimate constituents when we ultimately reach them? Now, he says, there have to be such ultimate indivisible parts; otherwise, we can't talk meaningfully about the world being a whole consisting of parts. If you're going to claim it's a whole, there have to be parts. And that means that there ultimately has to be something that is no longer divisible. But any magnitude, as we've seen, is divisible. So, what must be the size of the ultimate parts if they're to be indivisible, even in theory? They must be zero in size. The ultimate particles, or constituents, of the world, must have no magnitude. But if a universe has parts that have no size, what will be the size of the whole? Obviously, it won't have any size; an infinite number of zeros is still zero. So, if there is multiplicity, on the one hand, we must have an infinitely big universe with endless parts and, on the other hand, an infinitely small universe with size-less parts. And that's an impossible contradiction. Therefore, the premise must be wrong. There is no multiplicity. Therefore, Parmenides was right after all: There's only the One. The universe is in principle indivisible. That's the end.

This involves the same kinds of issues pertaining to infinity and infinite subdivision that the other paradox did, and you need a certain theory of the nature of infinity to answer it. But, in the meantime, you can assume, pragmatically, that *you* are one part, and your *home* is another, and that motion between the two is possible. But how we validate that philosophically is something we'll discuss later.

Pythagoras

Let us now turn to the last Presocratic school that we are going to consider in this lecture, the Pythagorean school. Pythagoras flourished about 530 BC, so technically, he's actually right after Thales in order and prior to Parmenides and Heraclitus. Because of the absence of documents, we don't know what was held by Pythagoras himself, as distinct from his followers, so it's common to talk about the Pythagoreans as a school, and not attempt to differentiate which one was responsible for which particular idea. And the Pythagoreans endured right to the very end of pagan philosophy and underwent various modifications in their views, so it's common to talk about early, middle, and late Pythagoreans, but we'll hover around middle Pythagoreans.

Pythagoras founded an enormously influential school. It had overwhelming effects on Plato and later, therefore, on Christianity. Neither Plato nor Christianity would have been possible without Pythagoras and his school or some equivalent.

The early Pythagoreans were a basically mystic sect. They lived communistically without private property. They were, in effect, a religious order, or brotherhood. They were far and away the most otherworldly, the most mystic, of all of the Presocratics. They are actually the first religious philosophers that we encounter in this course. Therefore, I have to tell you at the outset something about the religion to which they subscribed. They were not adherents of the religion of the gods of Olympus. They did not take the anthropomorphic view of the gods, the polytheistic view. They represented a somewhat different—or rather, take out the "somewhat"—an *enormously* different trend in Greek religion. They advocated what was called a *mystery* religion, which is much more religious than the Mt. Olympus divinities ever dreamed of. This is really religious. In the early years, it was a rabid, mystic, supernaturalist cult, of a very primitive order. And there were quite a number of them. And the ones that the Pythagoreans subscribed to was called the *Orphic* mystery religion.

So, what did Orphism teach? Orphism is not a philosophy; it's an Oriental mystery cult imported into Greece and advocated by only a minority. The Orphics preached such tenets as: Man has two parts, a high part and a low part. The low part is the body, the high part is the soul. These two are in eternal conflict with each other. The soul is akin to God, to another dimension. Once, it was a God-like creature, inhabiting another, superior, spiritual world. But it sinned. And the result was that it fell from grace and, as a punishment, was included in the body on this earth. The body is therefore the prison, or the tomb, of the soul. And we are destined, each of us, to go through a series of reincarnations. At the end of our earthly span, our soul goes back to the other world, and it gets its appropriate reward or punishment (depending upon its behavior), and then it comes around again—what they called the "wheel of birth." Sometimes it comes up in another human body, sometimes in an animal body. It lives out its cycle and goes back again, round and round the wheel of birth, until (and this was their ultimate hope) one day the soul can escape from the body and this earth permanently, reunite once and for all with God, and thereby achieve true happiness and salvation. In effect, the idea was: Go back home. How do you get to do it? You have to engage in a process they called *purification.* That's essentially a process of decontaminating the soul of any physical influences. You have to live a good life, which means essentially an ascetic life, a pleasure-denying life. I remind you that we are in ancient Greece, and therefore, the Pythagoreans, at their most ascetic, are frenzied hedonists in comparison to the Christians that are yet to come. But nevertheless, they made a start. And you must also engage in the rituals of the Orphic mystery religion. In the early days, these rituals included something on the order of what goes on off-Broadway now—mass orgies, intoxication, frenzied dancing, secret initiation rites (that's why they were called "mystery" religions)—it was highly primitive, to say the least. Here's a description from one commentator (B.A.G. Fuller). Orphism worshiped the god Dionysus, whom Fuller describes in some detail. In an act of heroic commentator self-abnegation, I will steadfastly abstain from commenting or drawing parallels to any subsequent Western religion:

> [The god Dionysus was] elaborated in the Orphic Mysteries. Originally a Thracian deity of vegetation, and particularly of the vine and wine, and of the sense of liberation from human bondage and of access to divinity that intoxication bestows, he was worshiped in the beginning by orgiastic rites of frenzied dancing and drunkenness. Probably in the beginning, his priest, in whom he was supposed to be incarnate, was sacrificed and eaten by his worshipers, who thus partook of the *mana* or strength of their god. But before the cult entered Greece, the sacrifice of the priest had given way to that of a sacred animal, the wild bull, which now became the vehicle for communicating the divine substance of the god to his devotees. Brought down into Greece from the north, his cult became more civilized and developed a complicated theology. First begotten by Zeus from a divine mother, Persephone, he [Dionysus] was slain in the form of a wild bull by the evil Titans and was torn to pieces and devoured by them. But his heart was saved. This Zeus ate, and begot him a second time, from a human mother, Semele. She, demanding to see her divine lover face to face, was consumed by a thunderbolt. Her unborn child was preserved and placed in the thigh of Zeus, from which, in the fullness of time, it was brought forth and made Lord of the world. The Titans, also, Zeus slew with a thunderbolt and formed man from their ashes. Hence man is a dual creature, a mixture of the evil substance of the Titans and of the divine substance of the god they had devoured. His soul, or mind, is a fragment of Dionysus, his body a heritage from the Titans. Salvation consists in freeing the divine within us from the bondage of the body. This can only be accomplished by a long series of reincarnations, at the end of which, if she has sufficiently purified herself, the soul may escape from the wheel of birth and rebirth and be reunited with her divine source. This purification, however, could only be effected by joining the Orphic cult, assisting at its mysteries, and following its rule of life.[7]

---

7. Fuller, *A History of Philosophy*, p. 22.

Historically and philosophically, this is the primary source of the soul-body opposition in Western civilization. No better argument for that opposition has ever been put forth. I read recently that something like fifty percent of the women on the continent of Europe suffer from some type of sexual frigidity, caused partly by the feeling that sex is vulgar and materialistic. You know how many businessmen feel guilty because they are after money and are considered "money-grubbers"—look at how many people attack capitalism because it's just physical. If you asked the ultimate root of that view, it goes back to these tales on Dionysus, back to the Orphic. And prior to that, it has a long, long history.

The Pythagoreans subscribed to Orphism. They believed in two different worlds, the world of god and this world, the soul-body conflict. They yearned for immortality and escape from the body. They believed in reincarnation. Pythagoras is alleged to have seen a dog being beaten one day, and he asked the man to stop, because he recognized from the cries a friend of his from a preceding life. The Orphic religion is obviously enormously primitive. There's a whole series of typical taboos. Here are a few examples: If you are a good Orphic, you have to obey divine commandments to: abstain from beans; not to pick up what has fallen; not to stir the fire with iron; not to walk on highways; not to let swallows share one's roof; when the pot is taken off the fire, not to leave the mark of it in the ashes, but to stir them together; when you rise from the bed clothes, roll them together and smooth out the impress of the body. One commentator (John Burnet) says, "It would be easy to multiply the proofs of the close connection between Pythagoreanism and primitive modes of thought, but what has been said is sufficient for our purpose."[8] And that is certainly sufficient.

This sort of thing, I may say, was looked at askance by most Greeks. It was certainly not in the mainstream of Greek religious views but was regarded as a lunatic fringe. The question is, how did any of these beliefs get into the history of philosophy? Because of the caliber of beliefs that existed for thousands and thousands of years prior to Thales. And the answer is that Pythagoras had a scientific side to him also. He and his school were concerned with the same questions as were all the other Presocratics, namely, what is the nature of the universe, what is the world stuff? And in this connection, they made some valid and enormously important points. The result was that their scientific discoveries and their mystic

---

8. John Burnet, *Early Greek Philosophy*, 3rd edition (London: Adam and Black, 1920), pp. 96–97.

Orphism were propagated together as a kind of package deal, and, in fact, the combination became very influential.

So, now I want to look at their more philosophical side. They asked the question: What is the nature or the essence of the universe? What is the world stuff? Is it water, is it air, is it fire, is it change? No, they said. In order to understand their answer, you have to know something about their special interests and achievements. The Pythagoreans were really the discoverers of mathematics in any serious way. Other civilizations had discovered mathematical knowledge, but the Pythagoreans were the first to discover that mathematics is somehow everywhere. They did a lot of work in mathematical theory. You know about the Pythagorean theorem, still called that to this day. They discovered many interesting things about the connection of mathematics to *musical* phenomena, a thing that was absolutely unheard of prior to their discovery of it. They discovered, for instance, that harmony in music (as distinct from noise) is based on mathematical ratios, the length of the string being plucked. They discovered that musical relations can be expressed numerically. This was a staggering discovery. And to this day, we use mathematical terms to talk about musical relationships—we talk about the interval of a fifth, or a fourth, or an octave, which is an eighth, and so on. They discovered that mathematics is relevant to astronomy. They uncovered the first hints that mathematical law governs the heavens. They discovered that mathematics is somehow relevant to medicine—they had the idea that physical health consists of the mathematical ratio of the various elements of the body, and that if you have just the right amount of each, you're healthy, but if one grows voraciously and destroys the right mathematical balance, today we would say, you have cancer; they would say you're sick, you're out of harmony. Whenever they looked at the subjects known at this time—astronomy, mathematics, music, medicine—they found a fact that had not been known—that somehow or other, the distinctive character and action of things is governed by numerical relationships, by mathematical laws—in a word, by numbers. Numbers popped up everywhere, and who would have expected it? Consequently, they did what Thales did when he thought water was the key, or what Heraclitus did when he thought change was the key: They seized on their particular "thing" with avidity and proceeded to make it metaphysical. By a gigantic leap, they generalized, and they said: "You want to know what the world stuff is? You want to know what all things really are? All things are numbers." That's their famous fragment—"All things are numbers." Numbers are the world stuff.

Commentators have worked for centuries to try to figure out what this could have meant. Because, how can you talk about numbers if there isn't something being numbered? Suppose I point to this glass, and you ask me, "What is it?" and I say, "It's six." You say, "Six what?" How can you have a universe made of quantity, without any *things* being quantified? Heraclitus has a universe of activity without any things performing it, so why shouldn't Pythagoras do likewise? A lot of this is speculative, because there are no surviving data, fragments, or documents that would establish it definitively. But some people suggest that, because of the primitive stage of knowledge, the Pythagoreans represented numbers by physical things, for instance, three little pebbles would be three, and six little pebbles would be six, or sometimes by dots, the way we have on dice. And so "six" for them meant six dots or six pebbles arranged in a certain way. In other words, they confused numbers with the physical entities that represent them or symbolize them. And so sometimes, when they said, "All things are numbers," they meant, "All things are composed of tiny physical particles." So, this was like a primitive version of what later became the atomic theory, but the Pythagoreans never developed it.

In part, the explanation of this is their Orphism, their errant mysticism. They were the real numerological mystics, and they carried that to fantastic lengths. For instance, there was a quarrel among the Pythagoreans as to whether justice was four or nine. The idea is that it would have to be a square number, because it had to return equal for equal, but whether it was two times two or three times three, they hadn't decided. Marriage was five. Love was eight, because love is harmony between people, and the octave is a harmony. Man, if I remember, was 250, plants 360. This is just nonsense and does not require a deep explanation. This is the Western source of those skyscrapers, I mentioned earlier, that have the thirteenth floor blanked out. Except that isn't fair, because the moderns are worse than the Pythagoreans—if the Pythagoreans thought that thirteen was bad luck, they would stop the building on the twelfth floor; they wouldn't bring in subjectivism and call the thirteenth "fourteen."

Besides these other features, there is a crucial point disguised in this primitive, mystic statement. And that crucial point is the vital importance of mathematics in discovering the laws of the world, in making sense of the universe. Today, people take this for granted. Modern physics would have been impossible without the discovery that physical laws have to be formulated in mathematical terms. This discovery actually developed from the Pythagoreans. Although they didn't *discover* any laws, they're the ones who discovered that mathematics was the keystone. For instance, Kepler, in the modern world and the beginning of modern science, the man who discovered the first mathematical laws of planetary motion, couldn't find them for years, but he was a devout Pythagorean, and he went on looking on the grounds that all things are numbers and there must be mathematical laws governing the planets, and sure enough, he found them. In this sense, modern science is, in part, a development of this discovery of the Pythagoreans. However, it did not bear fruit until the Renaissance, when it was combined with other theories.

But for our purposes, what is important is what the *later* Pythagoreans did to make sense out of the theory that all things are numbers, that numbers are literally the ingredients of things—for they realized that's too primitive. So, they took the line that numbers, or numerical relations, somehow governed the behavior of things. Things, they said, are formed, or behave, according to numbers, and they took this in a very literal and still quite primitive sense. If you consider people today saying, for instance, that the law of gravity governs the behavior of bodies—you understand today that that use of the word "govern" is metaphorical, i.e., you don't think that there's a disembodied law of gravity in another dimension, which says to things, so to speak, "You better follow, or else," like a king governs his subjects. But the Pythagoreans apparently did. When they said that numbers governed the things of this world, the later Pythagoreans apparently believed that there were two dimensions: a world of numbers, of numerical relations, and then this world in which we live, which was somehow formed in accordance with the world of numbers. What are the characteristics of the two worlds? The world of numbers can't be grasped by the senses. You can't perceive the world of numbers—you can perceive two people, but not just "two." Two itself is something you have to grasp by reason. And, on the other hand, this world is a world graspable by the senses. Another point of difference: The world of numbers is unchanging. "Two and two makes four" goes on forever, without any alteration. Any two things can come into existence, grow, decay, die and vanish; but two, as such, goes on forever. Two is two, and two plus two is four, and so on. The world of numbers is immutable, whereas the world in which we live is constantly changing. So, we have a metaphysical dualism, two realities, and, of course, the true one is the world of numbers.

They thought that they had thereby solved the problem posed by Heraclitus and Parmenides, because they provided one world for each. Heraclitus said that true reality must be constantly changing. And the Pythagoreans said, "Okay, there is a changing world for you. In this world, you are right—everything is flowing." Parmenides said, but true reality has to be *un*changing. They said, "You're right, too. True reality is the world of numbers." This particular attempt to solve the Parmenidean/Heraclitean dilemma, by apportioning two worlds, one for each, was picked up from the Pythagoreans by Plato (in a somewhat different form, as we'll see the next lecture). In any event, the Pythagoreans had now given a philosophic grounding to their Orphic religion. They now had their heaven and earth tied in with their two philosophic worlds (the world of numbers and this world). They had a philosophic basis for their soul-body opposition. They had, so to speak, synthesized their religion with their science, and they were happy.

A few last points about the Pythagoreans. One legacy in the epistemology of Pythagoreanism is the view that only mathematics qualifies as true knowledge. That is a common view among a certain type today, expressed in the fact that if you do not give him statements with numbers in them, he will not accept them as scientific. If you tell him, for instance, that human beings need self-esteem, that claim is considered "vague, qualitative, unscientific, inexact." But if you say they need 3.9 units of self-esteem, and they need an extra point for every time they commit one-eighth of an act of immorality or something, then that makes it mathematical. That's a legacy of the Pythagorean number fixation.

In regard to ethics, the major legacy left by the Pythagoreans was the mind-body, or soul-body, dichotomy, of which they are the founders in Western philosophy: the idea that the ultimate goal is to escape from the body and have the soul be pure. We will see in Plato the development of that view. You may ask, "Well, why didn't they commit suicide if they were so anxious to escape the body?" And they had an answer to that: God giveth, and God taketh away. In effect, you belong to God, and if you commit suicide (I'm parodying), you're violating God's property rights; it's up to him to decide whether or not to let you come home. Well, what should you do while on earth? You should purify yourself by withdrawing from the physical. And how are you going to do that? Here, the Pythagoreans made a famous observation—they distinguished three types of men who come to the Olympic games. (This was picked up by Plato and became the basis of a whole theory of human psychology.) Three types of men ranging in hierarchy from the lowest to the highest. The lowest is the one most directly involved with the physical: the guy who comes to make money, for instance, to buy himself popcorn. The lover of gain, the man obsessed with the almighty drachma—that's the lowest. But above the lover of gain, there are the athletes, and they are motivated qua athletes (according to the Pythagoreans) not by the desire for money, but for something *somewhat* more spiritual, namely, honor, fame, triumph, glory. They are still materialistic to an extent because they still want their fame and glory in this physical world, but at least they're not wallowing in the crude physical, and so they're one rung higher. And then there is the third type, the type most detached from the physical world, the type that doesn't want money or fame: the people in the stands, the spectators, who just want to look out and see what's happening, the ones who have *phile* for *sophia*, who want to acquire knowledge in a completely disinterested way. Those are the ones, if they're properly disinterested, who are cut off from the physical world (and they surely are). And therefore, the Pythagoreans preached the supreme importance of knowledge, but it had to be "disinterested" knowledge of philosophy and science, divorced entirely from any physical, practical consequences or action regarding life on earth. They preached philosophy, science, knowledge, as a religious rite, as a rite of purification of the soul, so long as it was disinterested, noncommercial, and non-materialistic. This is the earliest severing in Western philosophy of knowledge from life. It's the idea of knowledge as an end in itself. You'll see in Plato what happens to this and to the whole Pythagorean view of three types of human beings, where it develops into a full-blown psychology and ends up with the view that there should be complete communistic dictatorship. That, however, is all we're going to say about the Pythagoreans. They are the first major two-reality school that we've met. In this sense, they are the oldest religious/supernaturalist school in Western philosophy. As we continue, we're going to trace the line from the Pythagoreans to Plato to the whole Christian axis. But all of it, including the mind-body opposition, the yearning for an otherworldly immortality, the scorn for this life on earth, goes back originally to the Orphic Pythagoreans.

Lecture One, Q&A

Q: How could Parmenides think of a shape for the universe? What would be outside that shape? Wouldn't the universe have to be infinite without shape?

A: No, it would not. I agree with Parmenides on that point. (Not necessarily with the idea of it being a sphere; I don't pretend to know what shape the universe has.) But I agree with Parmenides, and so did Aristotle, and so in his own way did Einstein, if you want me to give you a modern, scientific authority, that the universe is finite and has some structure, and some kind of shape. And that does not imply anything outside of the universe. The simple answer to "What is outside of the universe?" is, *there is no outside of the universe.* "Outside of the universe" is a meaningless phrase. It does not designate a locality, which is empty. It designates no locality. There is no such place as "outside the universe." All that exists is the universe. When asking that question, you necessarily have to project yourself as being outside the universe, and you're looking at it from the outside, and you see this big ball, and there's all this space outside. But you can't project yourself outside of the universe; you can project yourself only within the universe. And therefore, from that perspective, there is no difficulty in thinking of the universe as finite, limited, shaped, but you cannot *visualize* its shape, because to do so, you'd have to stand outside. The best I can recommend to you as a mental exercise is to imagine a little dot in your mind, and let it fill up from the inside out until it occupies your entire mental screen, and do not try to peek beyond it, and then you've got the universe.

Q: What does "shape" mean, then? Anything that I can think of that has a shape, I can stand outside and see what the shape is.

A: "Shape" means the relative configuration of the constituents at the boundary. And they have a configuration relative to each other, quite independently of whether you can get outside and look at it.

Q: Did Oriental thought have any influence on the early Greek philosophers?

A: To my knowledge—and I emphasize that I do not know a great deal about Oriental philosophy (to put it mildly)—Oriental philosophy was influential primarily on Pythagoreanism. I do not believe that it had any significant influence on the Milesians, on Heraclitus, on Parmenides, on the Atomists, on the Sophists, on Socrates. It *did* on Plato, through Pythagoras. But that's all that I know of.

Q: If the universe were finite, and you thought about yourself as traveling in a straight line—

A: I get it. If you traveled in a straight line through the universe, wouldn't you have to come to the end at some point, bump your head into the end of the universe, and look out, and wouldn't that imply there's an outside? The contradiction to that would be that there *is* no outside of the universe, and therefore, obviously, you couldn't do it. If you asked me what are the scientific laws that make it impossible for you to go straight through the universe and go out the other side, I would have to refer you to a scientist. Relativistic physics is one possibility, but I wouldn't comment on that. It is very important that you distinguish clearly between philosophy and science. Philosophy can lay down the basic principles of reality (if it can prove them) and the basic principles of a scientific methodology. To that extent, it is capable of exercising a veto power in relation to science. If a scientist comes up with some theory that violates an established philosophic principle, a philosopher is entitled to show that his theory *must* be wrong, and that the scientist better try again. However, it is not within the competence of the philosopher qua philosopher to speculate about the actual structural laws of the physical world. There is no distinctively philosophical means to do that; it has to be done by experiment and observation, and it is therefore outside the competence of philosophy. So, I refuse on principle ever to be drawn into scientific speculations.

Q: Why must the dualist choose one of their realities as the real one, and the other as just a result of our distorted senses?

A: Well, "reality" means "everything that exists," so two of them would be a big problem. Therefore, they have to say that the one of them doesn't really exist. But they can't say it's nothing, and so they carve out the concept of "appearance," to give it a metaphysical half-status: it sort-of is. For a fuller discussion, we'll wait until Plato next time.

Q: Why wouldn't the same argument Zeno used to disprove a whole of *many* parts apply to a whole of *one* part? In other words, why couldn't the one be divided infinitely?

A: If it's divisible, it would be more than one part, and the idea is you can call it one part if you want, but the crucial thing is that it's an *indivisible* part. Since it's only one, it *is* the whole, and, therefore, it's senseless to talk about it being "a part."

Q: Is there any such thing as a vacuum, or is the universe completely filled with matter of some sort?

A: I agree with Parmenides. I believe his argument on this point is unanswerable—that there is no nothing, and consequently, no such thing as a true vacuum, in other words, a true zero inhabiting reality anywhere. This does *not* mean, however, that everything is necessarily solidly packed with matter in the form that we now know it. It's that it must be packed with *something*. What it is that it's filled with, I do not purport to know. There used to be theories in the nineteenth century that the world's so-called empty places were filled with ether, and that the universe was solidly filled, and that the ether was the medium by means of which energy traveled, action at a distance was able to take place, and so on. I believe ultimately that some form of that theory, *some* form, will have to be sustained on philosophic grounds. But again, I refer you to the distinction between philosophy and science. I wouldn't *dream* of speculating what is it that is present in what we regard as vacuum. After all, we do *not* know everything about the physical universe, and the fact that we are able to pump out or discover areas with the absence of most matter that we can now identify, does not per se prove the existence of a vacuum. A long time ago, some of us used to use the term (humorously, I may say) "little stuff," and "little stuff" was the name we gave to that which *is* where nothing isn't. But what it is, we do not purport to know.

Q: Would you say that a major problem for the Presocratics was not really understanding the natures of time and space (for example, the problems of change and multiplicity), and that time and space are poorly understood today?

A: Time and space are poorly understood by some schools of philosophy, but Aristotle gave the essentially correct view of them, so if they're poorly understood today, that per se wouldn't prove anything. As to this point, certainly the issue of time and space is relevant to Zeno's paradoxes because that brings in the question: Is time and space infinitely divisible? But in regard to the rest of their questions, I don't see that this is a contributing factor. I think their major problem was they didn't know very much, and you can hardly blame them for that. They started, and they made some gigantic leaps forward in a very short time.

Q: I'd like to know if any of the early Greek philosophers had any influence on the politics of the time?

A: I do not know of any influence that the early Greek metaphysics had on the politics of that time. I'm not very familiar with the politics of that time. As far as I can tell, it was too abstract prior to the fifth century. When you get to the fifth century BC, the theories had direct influence. As you'll see, the Heracliteans and the Sophists of that period had direct political effects, and Socrates had enormous influence on Plato and had enormous influence going on to the fourth century. But, when you say, "All things are water" or "All things are numbers," you can't do anything with it politically.

Q: Did the politics of the time have an influence on the philosophy?

A: So far as I know, only in that at that period they were freer, as I said, and therefore freer to look at the world and think and come up with answers. But I can't, for the life of me, imagine how you could correlate the kinds of views we were discussing today with specific political systems. In a general way, I oppose the idea that existential conditions determine philosophic viewpoints. I think quite the reverse is true.

Q: Would you elaborate on the definition of philosophy, explaining why the five main branches you included are grouped together, while psychology, mathematics, etc., are omitted?

A: Yes. There are two common denominators to the five main branches. One is the universality of their scope. And the second is their necessity as guides to human action, *any* human action. Philosophy is, above all else, the all-embracing subject. Metaphysics studies the *entire* universe, not just any one species or subdivision, not just matter or mind or life, but *everything*. Epistemology does not ask how you acquire knowledge of physics or chemistry or astronomy or of cooking, but of *everything*. And the same for the other branches—ethics does not ask how should a tailor, a butcher, or a candle maker live, but how should *any* man live, how should *any* government be organized, how should *any* work of art be judged? The essential element of philosophy is that it is *universal*, not specialized. Which is why philosophy deals with the kinds of issues that *anybody* can think about. It does not require specialized information of one particular subcategory of reality. The other common denominator is that all these branches provide indispensable guides to action. Metaphysics does not directly tell you how to live, but it gives you the precondition—the nature of reality. But every other branch tells you how to act. Epistemology says, "Do this if you want to know." Ethics says, "Do this in your choices." Politics says, "Do this in your government." Esthetics says, "Do this in your art." And therefore, the essence of philosophy is telling man how to function, conceptually, existentially, socially, esthetically. Those are the two common denominators. In contrast, all the so-called special sciences—psychology, mathematics, etc.—are either restricted to one subcategory of reality, like human behavior (which psychology used to describe), or mathematics (which is restricted to quantitative relationships)—and they are not normative; they do not tell you how you *should* behave in any field, but just describe the way things are.

Q: Why did Heraclitus not say that the *law* of change was the world stuff, rather than the change itself?

A: First of all, he did not have a very clear idea of what the law of change consisted of; it was pretty much to the effect that there has to be a balance, and change in one direction, in a so-called upward way, has to balance change in another direction, the "downward" way. But I think the main point is that the *law* of change is merely a description of how change operates, and consequently is not something apart from change. Although, I grant you that according to some commentators, the law of change is reified by Heraclitus into an entity distinct from change, and many people think that it is one of the sources of the Christian God, too. So, you can throw that in the pot along with the Parmenidean One if you want.

Q: Since Heraclitus invalidated the senses, by what means did he discover changes?

A: He would say "by reason." But if you then asked him, "Well, but how does reason operate if it doesn't begin with sensory data?" he would have said, "I never thought of that question." However, they did come up with many ways by which, according to them, you *could* arrive at knowledge by reason without the use of the senses. One of Plato's most famous theories is specifically an attempt to answer that question. But we're at the very beginning. If Heraclitus had thought of all the questions that his theory implied, he would have had a full-fledged system of philosophy, and we wouldn't be talking about the importance of Plato anymore, but of Heraclitus.

Q: Do you recommend any history of philosophy text for this course?

A: The best introductory history of philosophy that I know is *The History of Western Philosophy* by W. T. Jones; it comes out in a four-volume paperback edition, published by Harcourt Brace. And it covers the waterfront for complete beginners, and it is perfectly respectable. Another good and much shorter one is by Gordon H. Clark, called *Thales to Dewey*, and it is the one that I quoted from that has that excellent summary of Heraclitus's river and why it doesn't exist. The two unquestionably best histories of philosophies ever written, but they are not for beginners, but they are without question the best, are Émile Bréhier, the famous French historian of philosophy, who wrote an enormously lucid, detailed work, covering everything right until the time of his death (in 1952), and that has been put out by the University of Chicago Press in a whole series of paperbacks; and my own personal favorite, Wilhelm Windelband, *A History of Philosophy* (and not *A History of Ancient Philosophy*—that's a different one, which is good, but it's not the one that I have in mind), which I regard as a truly superlative history of philosophy, and I would say without any doubt that I learned more history of philosophy from Windelband than all the rest put together. But it is difficult reading, not because it's unclear, but because it's enormously compressed, and to follow it, I averaged, the first time around, about forty-five minutes for one side of a page. If you want to do any readings in particular periods, there are many good histories of ancient philosophy that are much more detailed. I think, offhand, of Joseph Owens's *A History of Ancient Western Philosophy*, Appleton Century, very scholarly and detailed. There is the massive, multivolume, thick multivolume work by W.K.C. Guthrie; the last I heard, he had three volumes out on the Presocratics alone, I think; and that will really tell you everything if you have that kind of passionate interest in it. There are all sorts of anthologies which give you little excerpts, fairly generous excerpts, on any philosopher, or all of them. There are many works on the Presocratics, but unless you asked me for them particularly, I wouldn't urge you to read any particular one of them unless you have a special interest. Certainly, if you want to do any reading, read some of Plato's famous dialogues; they're all collected in one volume called *The Collected Dialogues of Plato,* edited by Edith Hamilton and Huntington Cairns, and that's Pantheon Books, and that's a one-volume edition of everything of Plato's. I don't think we need to go on. There's Richard McKeon's edition of the works of Aristotle, or you can get the whole twelve volume Oxford series if you want. And if you want to read the *Confessions* of Saint Augustine, the best translation is by R. S. Pine-Coffin. There's also the pocket Aquinas, if you want, edited by Father Copleston, but that should hold you for a while.

Q: When you say, "That which is not, is not," is that a principle about nothing?

A: No, it's a principle *denying* nothing. It's a principle saying that you cannot have principles about nothing, because there is no nothing. So, it's not *about* nothing; it is indirectly about something; it tells you one thing about something, namely, something is all there is.

Q: Did Zeno derive this mathematical approach from his views on infinity, time, and space?

A: So far as I know, Zeno originated the implications of the paradoxes that he put forth. There was no work done on the nature of infinity, time, or space at this time.

Q: Can you think of nothing if you think of it in relation to something?

A: I would say in one sense, yes, you can, but not in the example you use. I believe Parmenides's argument is valid in regard to vacuums, and, therefore, I wouldn't take that as an example of your point. But there is a sense, I would say (speaking for myself now, not for Parmenides) in which you *can* think of nothing, in a qualified or relative sense, in relation to something. For instance, I can say perfectly meaningfully, "I have nothing in my pocket." I obviously mean, *in relation to some specific type of existents*—I have no money, or no peaches, or no bananas, or whatever it happens to be. And by reference to whatever form of existence is the standard, I can refer to the absence of that form of existence. In that relative, limited sense, you can talk about nothing. But Parmenides was talking about the *absolute* nothing; not the absence of a particular type of something, but the sheer zero. And in that sense, I think he is correct.

Now, I don't want to end on the note of nothing, so we have one minute if I can get a question about something.

Q: You say that one of the difficulties of the ancient Greek philosophers was the failure to differentiate between various kinds of change.

A: What kinds of changes did you have in mind? Like locomotion versus growth, and so on? [Questioner responds: Yes]

You're asking me, would I say that one of the problems of the early philosophers was their failure to differentiate various *kinds* of change? Certainly, they *didn't* differentiate, and certainly it was a major step forward when Plato and Aristotle began to classify and say there's change of place (locomotion), and change of substance (when a thing comes into existence, such as the flower versus the seed), and change of quantity (when a thing gets bigger), and change of quality, and so on. And by the time you get to Aristotle, you have a sophisticated view of all the types of change. You find that many of the problems that they got into disappear because they were confusing one type of change with another. In that sense, yes, that was a problem. But I would never want to say anything that would imply that they should have done differently, or that that is a criticism of them, because after all, this is the kindergarten of mankind, and they are, regardless of their errors, the heroes who made the first steps. So, I mean, surely if they had known what came centuries later, they would have been better, but on the other hand, if they hadn't done what they did, the later centuries couldn't have developed. So, when somebody in the twentieth century says, "Everything flows and nothing abides," I have a completely different attitude than I do toward Heraclitus.

Q: If, according to Heraclitus, all is flux and nothing exists, how can definitive laws of change exist, and why are these not subject to change? Is this not logically contradictory?

A: Yes, it certainly is. He should not have said that, but that was his better Greek side coming out in the midst of his Heracliteanism.

Q: If, according to Heraclitus's "Nothing is, and everything is becoming," how can it be that the quote you read last lecture from a modern commentator on this subject defined "modeling clay" as still being merely modeling clay after going through a series of changes in form?

A: You misunderstood the quote. He said that you could call it "modeling clay" only if it didn't change from being modeling clay. But he went on to say that in the Heraclitean world, even that wouldn't remain the same, so the modeling clay would change into papier-mâché, and that would change into something else, and something else, and therefore, nothing would ever remain constant, and therefore, nothing is. It's simply a misunderstanding of the quotation.

LECTURE TWO

The Triumph of the Metaphysics of Two Worlds

The philosophers we have looked at, although extremely influential on all later philosophy, did not have complete systems of philosophy to offer. They had leads, individual ideas, particular observations and arguments—and these were accepted by many later philosophers—but these early Presocratics had no definitive, systematic, all-embracing approaches to philosophy that they had yet worked out. We're now going to look at the first actually developed, worked out, systematic approaches to philosophy, the first attempts at complete systems or, at least, overall approaches to philosophy. We're going to look at three kinds of philosophy that were formulated in Greece and endure to this day, with legions of supporters right to the present. The three kinds are *materialism*, *skepticism*, and *idealism.* I'll say a word at the outset defining each of these three basic approaches.

Materialism is a technical term in metaphysics. It does not mean "a preoccupation with money or sex." It is the view that reality is basically matter in motion and that all so-called nonmaterial or mental phenomena are to be explained entirely in physical, material terms.

Skepticism is the view that no objective or certain knowledge, of anything, by anyone, is possible. In other words, what we call "knowledge" is really a guess, a hunch, a subjective feeling, a probability, or whatever you wish to call it—but not true knowledge.

Idealism, again, is a technical term in philosophy; it does not mean "devotion to the good." It is the view, again from metaphysics, that reality is basically nonmaterial, and that the material world is not an irreducible primary, but actually a byproduct or expression of something more fundamental, something that is nonmaterial in character.

I note for the record that these three are not the only possible approaches to philosophy. Aristotle is not one of them, and neither is Objectivism. But of that we'll say more later.

All of these three that we're now going to look at are derivatives of various of the early philosophers that we looked at previously. In a way, you can say that materialism is implied by Thales's view that everything is water, since water is a form of matter (although Thales is too early to have grasped or stated the materialist implications of his statement, and it's highly doubtful that he would have accepted materialism if he had realized that it was entailed in his statement). Materialism's major Greek spokesmen are the Atomists.

Skepticism is primarily a derivative of Heraclitus. You remember his disciple Cratylus, who stopped speaking altogether on the grounds that there was nothing to refer to. And its major exponent is the Sophist school, the last pre-Platonic school. I don't call them "Presocratic," because they are contemporary with Socrates in the fifth century BC.

And idealism, in Greece, is a derivative essentially of the Pythagorean viewpoint, with a large boost or assist from Parmenides and Heraclitus. And its major exponent is Plato, helped along by certain suggestions of Socrates.

Of these three movements, I should say at the outset, the idealism of Plato was incomparably more influential in the ancient world, in the medieval world, in the modern world, and in the twentieth century, than either materialism or skepticism alone have ever been. In fact, one of the great attractions that Plato offered his followers, and does to this day, is that his approach to philosophy enabled them to escape the materialist or the skeptic approaches. So, we're going to look briefly first at materialism and skepticism as general background, and then begin on Plato.

The Atomists

Let us turn to the materialists, i.e., the Atomists, as they were called in Greece. We saw the problem raised by the opposition of Heraclitus and Parmenides: "Everything is change and that's all that exists" versus "there is no change, only the motionless One." And we saw the Pythagoreans attempt to solve the problem by postulating two worlds—one that is constant flux, this one (and that should satisfy Heraclitus in their view), and one that is immutable (and that should satisfy Parmenides). So, there was an attempt to reconcile these two views.

The Atomists are the outcome of a very different kind of attempt to reconcile Parmenides and Heraclitus, a very different attempt from the Pythagoreans. The Atomists belonged to a general approach that is called *pluralism.* The pluralists were a group of philosophers who agreed with elements of Parmenides and elements of Heraclitus, as follows: They agreed with Parmenides that the stuff that makes up reality has to be uncreated, indestructible, eternal, unchanging. They agreed that there can be no "what is" becoming "what is not," or vice versa—there is no "what is not." To put it another way, they agreed that nothing really new can ever come into or go out of existence. But they agreed with Heraclitus that there is such a thing as change, process, action, motion, becoming, and they regarded this as too obvious a fact to deny. The question was: How can we reconcile these two views?

And they got this idea: "What we if we abandoned monism?" Monism, if you recall, is the view that there is only *one* world stuff (that everything, for instance, is water or air or whatever it happens to be). Suppose we abandon that view and say instead that there are *many* different stuffs that make up the world. (The name "pluralism" comes from the idea of many stuffs.) Let us endow each of these stuffs by itself with all the Parmenidean characteristics, so that in itself, each of them is unchanging, eternal, indestructible, like a little miniature Parmenidean universe. But, they said, the one thing that we'll allow these stuffs to do is to move around in space; that's all—we'll allow them to change their position; we'll allow *loco*motion as the only type of change permitted. We will not, therefore, allow any internal alteration in the stuffs—no change in their individual qualities. And, they argued, locomotion doesn't violate Parmenides's principle, because it doesn't require anything new to come into existence or to go out of existence. Locomotion involves just a rearrangement of the stuffs that always exist in new combinations, a constant mixing and un-mixing (as they put it) of the stuffs in different arrangements. So, we will never have a case of "what is" becoming "what is not," or vice versa. We are going to explain every other kind of change exclusively as being, in reality, a process of changing position and, therefore, changing rearrangements of these unchanging stuffs. If you want to think of it this way, we'll take Parmenides's One and smash it into a bunch of separate little stuffs, and we will explain all change, growth, becoming, development, as merely a process in which these eternal stuffs constantly shift around and rearrange themselves. So, we won't need any reference to nonexistence as the beginning or the end of the process of change. And the key point will be: Nothing new ever comes into existence.

The question was: What are these many stuffs? The early pluralists are primarily of historical interest. The first advocate of this approach was Empedocles (490–435 BC). He was not very original in his concept of what the stuffs were; he just picked up the various stuffs of his predecessors and combined them into one view. He said that there were four basic kinds of stuff, four "roots," as he called it—earth, air, fire, and water—and everything else is merely combinations and rearrangements of these four.

Empedocles had a successor, Anaxagoras (born around 500 BC), who disagreed with him. Although also a pluralist, he argued, in effect, as follows: "You say there is supposed to be nothing new coming into existence. You say that on your philosophy, you never have what is *not* becoming what *is*. But I don't see it. As far as I can tell, on your viewpoint, you are violating Parmenides's basic principle all the time. Consider, for instance, tomatoes, or bananas, or tobacco, or chalk, or flesh, or hair, and so on. You say that these things are formed when earth, air, and so on, get into different combinations. But even so, all these things I mentioned are *different* from earth, air, fire, and water. They have different qualities—different tastes and different colors and different sounds and different odors, so something new is actually coming into existence when various changes take place. Banana-taste comes into existence, and then when the banana disintegrates, it goes out of existence, and so on." We have to be consistent here. If there are truly to be no new qualities in reality (and that's the basic Parmenidean principle), there have to be way more than four stuffs. There must be an indefinite *number* of stuffs. There must be as many different stuffs as there are different types of things. There has to be tomato stuff, with *its* distinctive qualities, and banana stuff, flesh stuff, hair stuff, tobacco stuff, etc. And each of these will have to be regarded as irreducible, inexplicable in terms of anything else, a basic ingredient of reality. Now, he said, "if we take this view, and we say that little tiny bits of all of these stuffs are actually in everything . . . —'little seeds,'" as he put it— "are actually in everything," you might say, "But I don't see banana stuff and tomato stuff when I look at somebody's hair," and the answer would be, "Only little seeds are there, and your senses are too gross to detect them; your senses deceive you; you see only the dominant stuff." But suppose that little bits, little seeds, of everything were in everything. "Then," he says, "change would really be only a rearrangement, and nothing new would ever come into existence. If we burned wood, for instance, and converted it to ash, well, it wouldn't be new qualities coming into existence, because the ash-stuff was always in the wood to begin with, and all that happened is that a certain rearrangement made us able to perceive the ash-stuff and temporarily obscured the wood-stuff, which is still there." And so on for all changes. "This," he said, "is the only thing to do, if we're to obey Parmenides's principle."

On the other hand, this was a total dead end from the task undertaken by Thales. It was a total collapse, because Thales wanted to find unity in the midst of diversity—he wanted to find the one in the many—and here we end up with diversity, with the many as absolutely irreducible and inexplicable. It's a hopeless theory, one that would be the end of science. All you can say about tomatoes is they're made of tomato-stuff, and so on for everything else. And yet it seemed to follow from Empedocles if you're going to be consistent with Parmenides.

At this point, the Atomists entered the scene. The two famous Atomists are Leucippus (who lived sometime in the sixth century BC), and almost nothing is known of him; the much more famous one is Democritus (who, as far as we can tell, lived a whole century, from 460 to 360 BC). These two were also pluralists. They agreed that the world was composed of many elements, each of them by itself too tiny to see, and all change was merely the mixing and un-mixing, the rearranging, of these elements.

But, they said, Anaxagoras's theory is hopeless; what can we do to get out of it? And they came up with a theory that was destined to be fantastically influential. They said we have to distinguish two kinds of characteristics that physical things possess, two basically different kinds of characteristics—the *qualities* and the *quantities*—the qualitative characteristics versus the quantitative (mathematical or numerical) characteristics. Among the qualities were things like colors (red, orange, yellow, etc.), sounds (loud, soft), odors, tastes, temperatures (warm, cold), textures (rough, smooth, etc.). Those are the qualities. In the quantities are the attributes, which are mathematically measurable (and here you see an obvious influence of the Pythagoreans). And they include (1) size (the exact amount of extension of a given particle); (2) shape (is it triangular, or rectangular, or what?); (3) motion or rest, and at what rate (is it standing still or is it moving, and if so, at what rate?); and (4) number (is a thing one particle or is it ten particles making up a peach). Those are the big four of the quantities—size, shape, state of motion, and number.

On the basis of this distinction, they said, there is only one way out of Anaxagoras's dilemma, and that is to strip qualities from the things in the world altogether, to say that the things in the physical world actually have only quantitative characteristics—only size, shape, motion, and number. Because, if you say that qualities like colors, odors, tastes, temperatures are real, then you've got two choices, and it's disaster either direction: Either you have to say that *some* of them are real, but not all (and that's in principle the position of Empedocles—some qualities are real, and not the rest; but then the others emerge, come into existence, and go out of existence, and that's forbidden by Parmenides); or else you have to say that *all* qualities are real, all are equally basic and eternal (and that's Anaxagoras's position, which is hopeless). Well, our only alternative, if we're to escape the disasters implicit in saying some qualities are real or all qualities are real, is to say no qualities are real. We'll say that reality in itself is exclusively quantitative. The various stuffs that make up reality have only size, shape, motion, number. What we call "qualities" are just the way that what's really out there affects us; they are merely the subjective effects on human beings, merely the way things appear to us. And if we take that view, they said, we will be able to explain change without violating Parmenides. When wood becomes ash, no new qualities are taking place in reality, because in reality, there aren't any qualities at all. The *appearance* of new qualities is taking place *in our minds*, as a result of different rearrangements of purely quantitative particles out there in the world. Therefore, reality consists of a huge—actually infinite—number of tiny stuffs, or particles, possessing only these quantitative features.

What will we call these particles? Each of them is absolutely Parmenidean; it's a little tiny Parmenidean One; it's solidly packed within any given particle; it's a plenum, completely full—there are no little holes in it. So, if you tried to get the point of a knife, or even a needle, into one of these particles, you couldn't do it, because it's solidly packed. It's completely un-cuttable. And since the Greek for "un-cuttable" is *a-tome*, it came out that these little particles are *atoms*. Therefore, they took the view that all change is nothing but spatial change of atomic position. And thus the name "Atomism," which now supersedes pluralism because the old pluralists fell into disrepute. This became the sophisticated form of pluralism.

The question becomes: How do you differentiate one atom from another? Since they have no qualities at all, what makes one atom one atom and separates it from another? And the answer was that there must be empty space between them, because if there was no empty space—if it was all one solidly packed mash of atoms—then it would be the same as one big atom. In other words, we'd be back to Parmenides's One. Therefore, over and above atoms, there have to be the empty spaces between them. And therefore, they said, there are *two* constituents that make up reality—atoms and the *void*, the void being the empty spaces that separate the atoms. The void is a crude violation of Parmenides's principle; it's a blatant "what is not" sitting out there as a constituent of reality. They tried to get around it by saying, "Oh no, it isn't a violation of Parmenides; it's just that there's two kinds of reality, full reality and empty reality," but that's a pretty crummy way out. In any event, the universe is atoms and the void, and that's all.

How do these atoms operate? What determines how they behave? And their answer was: They operate exclusively as a result of physical pressure and impact from other atoms. They smash each other and collide strictly according to what we now call "the laws of mechanics." And this is sometimes referred to as "billiard ball metaphysics." If you imagine that a person has struck the balls, broken them up, and they are now just caroming back and forth, smashing each other, and moving back and forth strictly by mechanistic law—according to the Atomists, *everything* operates that way; everything that happens, happens exclusively according to the laws of mechanics.

Which means, first of all, that nothing ever happens by chance. They were opposed altogether to the idea that something causeless could happen; everything is determined by the atomic configurations and the various pressures and reactions, by mechanical law. It also means, they said, that nothing ever happens for a purpose, or an end, or a goal, because atoms (or billiard balls, if you want to think of that analogy) do not move around in order to get into the side pocket; they move around simply as a *result* of the forces operating upon them. In other words, the laws of mechanics have no purposes, no goals.

You may be tempted to think, "Well, billiard balls move that way, but the man who wields the cue was motivated by a different principle of behavior—he had a purpose (whether it's to enjoy himself, or show off his skill, or make money, or pass the time, or whatever it happens to be)." But you see, if you are an Atomist and you subscribe to this philosophy, you say that the man wielding the cue operates on exactly the principle that the billiard balls do—once he's hit, he also is a quivering system of atoms, certain atoms struck him in the appropriate places, and that caused parts of his body to start quivering, and that caused him to pick up the cue, and that caused so on and so on, and at a certain point, the motion is communicated to the balls, which start to jostle back and forth, and then they hit the table, and others jostle, and so on and so on and so on, and that's it.

A metaphysics such as this is called, technically, "mechanistic materialism." Each of those words has a meaning. "Materialism" I've already defined as the view that matter is the fundamental reality, and that anything nonmaterial is a derivative or a byproduct to be explained entirely in physical terms. "Mechanism" is the view that everything happens according to the laws of mechanics. In other words, it is contrasted with the view known as *teleology*. Teleology is the view that purpose is operative somewhere in the universe. Teleologists do not agree among themselves where. A religious teleologist will say that the universe as a whole has a purpose, and everything has a purpose. A more naturalistic type of teleologist will say no, only certain parts of the universe have a purpose—for instance, only living creatures or only conscious creatures or, conceivably, only human beings. But in any event, the mechanists deny purpose on any level anywhere; there simply is no such thing. Purposeful behavior is a myth. That is the essence of the meaning of the metaphysics of mechanistic materialism. And these are the first mechanistic materialists in history.

Since this is put forth as a metaphysics, it encompasses everything, including man. It follows that man is governed by strict, rigid determinism. Determinism is implied by materialism, because there's no mind to make any choices; and it's implied by mechanism, since everything happens according to the laws of mechanics. So, they're double determinists. They are the first orthodox, systematic, principled, self-conscious determinists in philosophic history.

If you asked them, "But don't you believe in any such thing as a mind, or a soul?," they would say, "Oh yes, we believe in the soul, but the soul is made of soul atoms, and it's the presence of those particular atoms that give rises to life and consciousness." I might mention that they also believed in gods, apparently because people dreamed of gods, and at this primitive time, they thought that if something appears to you in a dream, it must have some counterpart in reality. But the gods, they insisted, were also made of atoms, which eventually perished the same way human beings did. They had no divine characteristics, they were indifferent to men, and at a certain point, their various atoms split up and went off in new combinations, and that was the end of the gods. So, for practical purposes, Atomists are atheists, although you will find that they believed in gods of an utterly unreligious and insignificant kind.

The soul atoms, I stress, are completely physical. On this philosophy, you could have a good handful of soul. Soul atoms are fine, round, smooth, polished, mobile, they said. They are diffused throughout the world. When a cluster of them enters a combination of grosser atoms and starts quivering, then you have a living—or even a conscious—entity, if it's appropriately organized. Consciousness is nothing but a quivering of the soul atoms. Periodically you have a slight deficiency of them—a few of them exodused; that's called going to sleep. Sometimes there's a sudden exodus during the day—that's fainting. And at a certain point, all of them leave permanently—that's dying. There's no such thing as immortality on this philosophy. Death is disintegration, after which there is no "you" left at all. Your various atomic constituents wander off according to the laws of mechanics, to take part in new combinations, and you are obliterated, and that's the end, since *you* are just the combination. So much for the metaphysics of the Atomists.

What about their epistemology? I'll mention only one point here, namely, their attitude toward the senses. You remember that Heraclitus thought the senses were invalid, and he distinguished between reality and appearance; and so, on his own grounds, did Parmenides, and the Pythagoreans. The senses deceive us. The Atomists hold the identical view. They hold that you cannot rely on the senses. Why? Judging by the senses, it appears that things have colors. Nothing seems clearer to me than that this tablecloth is green. And yet, in reality, we know (if this theory is correct) that there are no colors; the green is a subjective effect on me. Nothing seems clearer than that this feels cool, and yet we know that there are no temperatures in reality. Nothing seems clearer than that I'm hearing a sound now (namely, my own voice), but there are no sounds, and there are no tastes, and there are no textures. All that exists is size, shape, and so on. Therefore, the senses are deceptive.

Democritus uses the term "convention" (he copies that from the Sophist school) to stand for anything that is a product of man's subjective constitution, as against the actual facts of reality. The Greeks frequently contrasted what came from convention and what came from nature, or reality. And using that terminology, Democritus says in a famous quotation, "By convention, sweet is sweet. By convention, bitter is bitter. By convention, hot is hot. By convention, cold is cold. By convention, color is color. But in reality, there are atoms and the void. That is, the objects of sense are supposed to be real, and it is customary to regard them as such, but in truth they are not. Only the atoms and the void are real." The Atomists subscribe to the same dichotomy between reality, known by reason, and appearance, known by the senses. They carry out what we've seen in many other cases, and therefore, philosophically, they too are rationalists.

Those of you who know any modern philosophy will know that this distinction between what the Atomists called "quantities" and "qualities," although it never went anywhere in the ancient and medieval world, was picked up at the time of the Renaissance by almost all the influential scientists and philosophers. It was accepted by Galileo, Descartes, Spinoza, Leibniz, Locke. And Locke gave it its modern name: Instead of calling it "qualities versus quantities," he called it "the primary versus the secondary qualities" (the primary being the quantities, the secondary being the subjective effects on us). These philosophers made it the basis for invalidating the senses. So, we're going to encounter it again. Its source is the Greek Atomists, and it's enormously influential when we get to modern philosophy. I'm going to leave it for now. It's a complex issue to untangle what is wrong with it; there are several different factors involved, and I'm going to present the

Objectivist view on this question in lecture twelve, at a time when you will be especially eager to know the answer, because you will see the catastrophes that derive in the modern world from this distinction.

I do want to make one final comment before we leave Atomistic metaphysics. Do not be misled by the primitive idea of atoms, because in more sophisticated form, this theory is enormously common today, particularly among psychologists, who are desperate to be regarded as scientific, and who regard that as requiring that they be materialists. Perhaps the arch example is B. F. Skinner, but there are many, many others. Today they don't talk about soul atoms, but what they agree with, in relation to the Atomists, is the view that we can explain all human behavior without reference to mind or consciousness, Of course, they disagree among themselves whether the relevant parts of matter are genes or electric charges or SR (stimulus-response connections) or reflexes or super reflexes. But that is all irrelevant philosophically. It's merely subtler forms of the Democritean theory. Philosophically, however, it is identical to Democritus. Scientifically, it's more sophisticated, but philosophically, it's identical.

As for what is wrong with mechanistic materialism as a philosophy, I'm going to refer you to some readings, first, to Miss Rand's article on Skinner in *The Ayn Rand Letter*.[9] You can look at W. T. Jones's *History of Western Philosophy*, volume one, which has a chapter on Atomism, where he presents many of the criticisms that are applicable to it. I can recommend Brand Blanshard's *The Nature of Thought*, which has a very good chapter attacking and dissecting behaviorism ("behaviorism" being the name of mechanistic materialism as applied to modern psychology). And I might also recommend J. B. Pratt's *Matter and Spirit*, which has many, many things wrong with it, but also has many, many good points attacking materialism.

As a theory of *physics* (not metaphysics, but physics), mechanistic materialism was a brilliant idea. And in fact, modern science began when somebody got the idea of combining Democritus with Pythagoras—that is, of looking for mechanistic laws that were mathematically formulatable. (But they didn't get that until the Renaissance, as we'll see when we get there.) But as a metaphysics, it is completely invalid, because it denies the existence of mind. And as such, it's immediately self-refuting, as its opponents have pointed out from antiquity to the present day. If there's no such thing as a mind capable of observing evidence and reasoning according to

9. Ayn Rand's critique of Skinner's *Beyond Freedom and Dignity* was later reprinted in her *Philosophy: Who Needs It*.

the laws of logic, then every man's conclusions express nothing but blind mechanistic reactions. Each man is then a machine—he's a physical puppet guided by the laws of motion. His conclusions are dictated by factors such as the density of his tongue, the viscosity of his saliva, the charges coursing through his nervous system, etc. He's a little billiard ball system, rattling and quivering by mechanistic necessity. No one on this philosophy, therefore, could ever claim to be guided by logic, by reason, by evidence, because there's no mind that can grasp, think, or relate the evidence. How, then, is anyone to decide which of all the conflicting positions on all the different subjects is true? The situation is this: You rattle the way *you* have to rattle, and I quiver the way *I* have to quiver, and that's it. No one can say his position is knowledge, simply that that's the way he has to quiver. In other words, materialism entails skepticism, and in that respect is self-refuting. You couldn't even know that *materialism* was true if you didn't have a mind to acquire knowledge.

The Sophists

Let's leave the Atomists, and go on to the Sophists, who were not so much a school as a professional class in the fifth century BC. *Sophia* means "wisdom," so a Sophist, if you go by the etymology, is a wise man, a knower. However, what they knew and what they taught, if we put it briefly, was how to win friends and flatter the multitude and thereby gain political power. They appealed, above all, to unscrupulous office seekers, and they taught them all the debating tricks, all the fallacies, all the confusing gimmicks that they could think of, so that the aspiring politician could bamboozle his opponent. They were like debased Dale Carnegies on the political level. The result was that they acquired a bad name, and the word "sophist" has come to have its present negative connotations. (The negative connotations are, I must say, partly undeserved, because they were held in opprobrium for accepting money for teaching philosophy, which was regarded as a breach of moral principle—and apparently still is, by many universities.)

The main Sophists were Protagoras (the father of Sophism, 480 to 410 BC) and Gorgias (483–375 BC). You may have heard of others, such as Thrasymachus and Callicles, but the main ones are Protagoras and Gorgias.

Philosophically, the Sophists are the first avowed skeptics in history (if we ignore Cratylus, who never would *say* anything). And I've given you the definition of "skepticism": No objective or certain knowledge is possible to anyone, about anything; nothing can be known. How, you ask, do they know this? What arguments do they put forth? Primarily they base their skepticism on an all-out attack on the senses. When I say "all-out," I mean *all*-out. They claimed to prove that every sense perception, by *any* creature, is necessarily invalid. This is a much more sweeping argument than the *Reader's Digest* type—I mean by that the obviously popular type. For instance, there is the argument from illusion—you know, you put a stick in water, and it appears bent, and it's really straight—and there's a certain mentality that concludes that, therefore, the senses are unreliable. Or there's the argument from hallucinations—you see a dagger before you, or pink rats, after having a drink, and they aren't really there—and there's a certain mentality that concludes that the senses are unreliable. Those arguments are very poor arguments. They wouldn't stop anybody seriously for five minutes. The Sophists were not above using those arguments, but that was not the essence of their case. Their case was a much more important argument. It was an all-out attempt to show that *every* sense perception is wrong. Not just that we can be taken in by an occasional illusion or hallucination, but that you can *never* trust *anything* from the senses. Why? Here's the famous argument.

Whenever we perceive, what we perceive depends upon two factors. One, it depends upon the object being perceived. That much is obvious. If I look at a person, that's one object, and I'm going to have a different experience than if I look at a pitcher of water, and so on. If I listen to Rachmaninoff, I'm going to have a different experience than if I listen to Beethoven; I'm hearing a different object. That much is obvious. But the crucial point is point two: What you perceive, they say, depends not only on the object, but also on the nature of your sensory apparatus, the nature and condition of your sensory apparatus.

For example, the color-blind man and the man with normal vision look at the same rug, and one says it's red, and the other says it's gray. They're looking at the same object, but their experience is influenced by the type of sensory apparatus they have. You taste a piece of cherry pie and it tastes sweet. You then develop a cold, or smoke four packs of cigarettes and coat your tongue appropriately and taste the pie, and it tastes bitter—same object. You look at the sun from the earth and it seems to be about the size of a fifty-cent piece; you travel closer and closer to it, and it gets huger and huger. The size that you experience varies with the condition, in this case, the distance to the object. Or you take three beakers of water—a freezing cold one, a medium warm one, and a boiling hot one—and you have one person plunge his hand in the ice cold one and then in the lukewarm one, and he says, "Oh, how warm"; and you have another person plunge his hand in the boiling water, and then into the *same* medium warm one, and he says, "Oh, how cold"—same object, different experience, the Sophists say, because the sensory apparatus is different. You can do this with anyone, with any sensory quality. If you want an example, put your finger gently on your eyelid and press in, and you will see two of me.

The Sophists hold that we can't go by majority rule on this question. What if there were a race of Martians, with their fingers tied into their eyes at birth, so they saw two of everything? Would you say the way to tell whether there's really one or really two is to take a population count, and if there are more Martians than us, there's two, and if there are more of us than the Martians, there's one? Obviously, that would be senseless. You can't go by majority rule in epistemology.

What conclusion, then, do we come to? Who is right? They said there's only one fair conclusion to come to: *Nobody* is right, because nobody can ever perceive reality, except as processed by his particular sensory apparatus. Nobody ever perceives reality directly. You can't just take your consciousness and wrap it around something. Impulses have to be given off, which go through your particular apparatus, and the kind of apparatus you have affects what you at the other end finally experience.

Therefore, all we ever can know is the way reality appears to us because of our senses. And if our senses differ, the appearances differ. Therefore, we can never say—*no one* can ever say—what the case *is* objectively, in reality. All you can ever know about is *what appears to you*, and *now*, because tomorrow your senses may change. To put it another way, you never can say "It is"—you always must begin your sentences with "It seems to me," "It appears to me." There is no way of knowing how things really are. All we know are our own subjective experiences, the private effects on each of us of the world out there. And since these effects vary from individual to individual, from species to species, from time to time, each of us lives in his own private, subjective world, and we have to dispense with all talk about "reality."

Some of them went so far as to say, "We may as well get rid of the whole idea of reality—how do you know there even *is* such a thing, since you never perceive it?" Others weren't quite so radical, and they held that there is one, but what's the difference since it's unknowable anyway?

This is the most influential argument ever advanced against the validity of the senses; in fact, it's the *only* influential argument ever advanced against the validity of the senses. Although rejected by Aristotle, it was accepted in full by Plato and then by the whole Christian era, by almost all modern philosophers without exception, and in a blown-up cosmic, gigantic form, it's the basis of Kant's whole philosophy. Therefore, it is urgently important that you know what is wrong with this argument.

Please observe that two things are true and can't be contested: It is true that perception is impossible without sensory organs, and it is true that the type of organs you have, in some way, affect the type of experience you have. That much is true. From those premises, Protagoras draws the conclusion, "You can never perceive reality." So, what is wrong with his reasoning? Think about it, and we'll deal with it in lecture twelve.

Where do the Sophists go from here, having annihilated (in their view, at least) the senses? You might say, what about reason? Couldn't reason give us knowledge of reality, even if the senses deceive us? The earlier rationalists would have taken exactly that position, and Plato subsequently will take that position. But the Sophists do not. They hold the view that reason depends upon the evidence of the senses (which is quite correct). But if the senses give each of us only our own private, subjective world, then our so-called rational conclusions are each of them true only for that private individual, only for his private world—are true only *for him*. The arch mark of a Sophist in today's world is anybody who puts the word "for" after the word "true." There are two kinds of people—the people who say, "This is true," and the people who say, "This is true—for me, for you, for him, for her, for it, for us, for . . .," etc. As soon as anybody puts "for" on, that is the tip-off that he is a subjectivist, that he does not believe you can make a statement about reality, that everybody has his own private little world, and in your little world, there might be a God, and therefore, it's true for you, but in my little world there isn't, and therefore, it's not true for me, and so on. That goes back to the Sophist viewpoint. Most people today can't even defend that viewpoint; the Sophists at least derived it from an overall epistemology.

Nor was the deficiency of the senses the only thing they held against reason. They also put forth *the argument from disagreement*. This argument is very simple: Everybody disagrees about what is rational; who is to say what's really true? Thales says everything is water; Heraclitus says no, it's fire and change; Parmenides says, oh, there is no change at all; and Pythagoras says that it's a world of numbers, and the Atomists say, oh no, it's little particles. And the Sophists at this point come in and say that this is hopeless. If human beings had a way of arriving at the truth, they would agree, and if they don't agree, it must just go to show that reason is incapable of arriving at the truth. That argument, by the way, is *enormously* widespread, almost as widespread as it is fallacious.

The Sophists had still a third objection to reason: Being followers of Heraclitus, they held that everything is constantly changing. Nothing, therefore, is an absolute. So even if, by some miracle of good luck, you hit on the truth, it wouldn't *stay* true for two seconds anyway. Nothing is true for two consecutive instances, so you can't even say, "It seems"; you have to say, "It seems to me *now*."

Two famous statements express this view. One is Protagoras's famous statement, the manifesto of subjectivism: "Man is the measure of all things, of things that are, that they are, and of things that are not, that they are not." By "man" there, he means each individual man subjectively. In other words, if you believe, if you feel, that something is so, it *is* so . . . for you now, and if you don't, it *isn't* for you now, and so on. That is the famous "Man is the measure of all things." And it's complete subjectivism and complete relativism. There are no absolutes, no objective truth. And the even more succinct formulation comes from Gorgias, who was the perfect example of a twentieth-century skeptic transplanted into ancient Greece. He wrote a book (they were all writing books on nature, on reality, on the nature of reality), so his book, in the true Sophist tradition, was titled *On Nature*, subtitled, *or the Nonexistent*. And it maintained three basic propositions: One, nothing exists; two, if anything existed, you couldn't know it; three, if you could know it, you couldn't communicate it. That is what you call *skepticism*! It is useless to ask him if he exists. Does he know the things that he claims? Has he communicated it? There's no use asking him that, because he'll say "No." He'll say it's highly probable that nothing exists. And if you ask him how he knows that, he'll say, "It's highly probable that it's highly probable that nothing exists," and so on. That's what they used to call in the ancient world *reduction to babbling*—the skeptic would finally stand in the corner and say, "It's highly probable that it's highly probable that it's highly probable" and so on.

As is true of all skeptics, the Sophists prided themselves on being enlightened, on having escaped the superstition and the dogmas of the past—they said, "We *proudly* know that you can't know anything, and we don't pretend to have any knowledge."

This is a historical cycle, and we are at the end of an era. As you will see, the whole history of philosophy is in cycles like this—a constructive era collapsing into total skepticism, and then into a still deeper skepticism, in comparison to which even Gorgias seems to be a champion of cognition. This has been repeated over and over again. There's a fascinating parallel to the history of countries with mixed economies, that is, there will be a constructive period, a boom, and then a bust, a depression, and then another constructive period (frequently with inflated speculation), following which there is a more severe depression. And that has been the entire pattern of the history of philosophy. Whenever you reach complete skepticism, you've finished cycle one, and since people can't live by it, that is the time when a new philosopher of great importance appears, because he is the one who tells mankind what to do. I'll say that in the twentieth century, skepticism reached the most intense level ever, which augurs well for the future of a new constructive period.

Let us turn in conclusion to the ethics of the Sophists, because they had very definite views on this matter. Can ethics come from reason? Obviously not; reason is deficient. Can it come from God? Obviously not. Remember, the Sophists, as good skeptics, are not atheists, because atheists claim to know something for certain, namely, that there's no God; the skeptics are agnostics, the Sophists are agnostics—they don't know one way or another whether there's a God. But in any event, they don't know that he *does* exist, so he's no use for ethics. The question is, where does ethics come from then? It can't come from reality, it can't come from God, and their answer is very simple: It *doesn't*—it comes from nowhere—there is no objective ethics. There is no basis for it, no source of it, and man has no cognitive faculty to grasp it. Therefore, they are, as you would expect, complete ethical subjectivists, and complete ethical relativists.

Man is the measure of all things, including of all things that are good. You say to them, but don't you recognize certain virtues that man should follow? Answer: Virtue is an arbitrary social convention. Their position is that if you *feel* that something is good—and by "something," I mean *anything*, whether it's having an ice cream cone or massacring a continent—if you feel that it's good or right, it *is* good, for you, now. All desires are ethically equal, because there's nothing to go by, *except* arbitrary desires and passions. If they were starting out their ethics systematically, the first proposition would be "I want it, whatever it happens to be." And if you ask them, well, what about facts or reality? the answer would be "Who knows anything about facts or reality?" If you say, shouldn't your desires be rational? the answer would be "What's rational for you isn't rational for me. Man is the measure." And so we have an ethics (putting it in Objectivist terminology) of avowed whim-worship. According to the later Sophists, the more intense your whims, the better. The ideal life, they said, is one in which you should burn with passionate, arbitrary desire, of *any* kind at all, and then go out and satisfy it by any means at all. All desires and all means of satisfying them are equally valid. Live by your desires. That's the natural element in you, that's what's given you by nature, by reality. All the talk and argument and reasoning and philosophy—that is artificial, conventional, just society's arbitrary dictates. And so the Sophists are profoundly anti-intellectual (as they would have to be, considering the intellect to be completely impotent), and they believe that the way to achieve morality, as they construe it, is simply to express your passions (a view which has been adopted intact by many schools of contemporary psychotherapy, exactly this same view, except instead of saying, "This is the way to be moral," they say, "This is the way to be uninhibited and healthy").

The later Sophists contributed another point because the question came up: What happens if your desires conflict with somebody else's desires, and you have to deal with other human beings—what do you do then? And the answer was, smash him with a club before he smashes you. In other words, there is only one method of dealing with other men, and that is brute physical force. It's useless to try to argue with men or convince them by reason. Because reason is helpless, the only "argument" is a club. Thrasymachus in particular is famous for this view. It's the first time we've had in philosophy the view that might makes right.

According to the Sophists, there's only one trouble with what people call "immorality"—like lying, cheating, robbing, raping, murdering, etc.—the only trouble is that you get caught. But suppose, they said, you could put on a veneer of virtue—you could join some appropriate charitable organizations, so that it looked like you were a good law-abiding citizen, and you make appropriate sacrifices at religious temples, and therefore, you bribe the gods. Suppose you could put on this outer covering of virtue, and at the same time live a subterranean life of roaring vice. Well, they said, that would be terrific. You would then have the best of both worlds—the rewards of virtue (the social approval) and the pleasures of vice. Or if you can't do that, what about trying to become a dictator—get the police and military on your side, and then you don't have to worry about any retaliation. And, they went on, this is not simply our theory; *all* men are like this. This is human nature. Why, then, do most men say you shouldn't live this way? Why does society say you shouldn't cheat and rob and kill and rape? And their answer was: Society is hypocritical and cowardly. The people who make up society secretly lust after just this kind of life, but they're afraid. They figure if they do this, and they start the rule "Slaughter other people to get what you want," somebody's going to do it to them and beat them to the punch. And therefore, they get together, and they say, "Let's compromise—I'll give up what would be the ideal life of killing you if you give up what would be the ideal life of killing me, and so we'll follow these rules." But, they said, society does this strictly out of fear, cowardice, and hypocrisy, not out of conviction. Every man would run riot, like a whim-worshiping Sophist, if he thought he could get away with it.

The famous story illustrating this is told by Plato, who profoundly opposed the Sophists, and it's the story of the Ring of Gyges, a mythical character, but it's used as a parable to illustrate a point. Gyges was a shepherd who had discovered a ring, and this ring had the magical power that when you turned the stone to the ground you became invisible (so it was like an anticipation of H. G. Wells's invisible man). And the Sophists said that if you had the magic ring of Gyges, life would be magnificent. You could then run riot. You could do anything you wanted, satisfy all desires, and you would be in a perfect state. And, they held, everyone is like that, and the only question is, do you have the courage to approximate this condition, or are you going to be a coward?

Let me read to you from Plato's presentation of this view. His dialogues represent different views that he tries to answer, and this is a famous description by Thrasymachus speaking in Plato's dialogue *The Republic*, book 2.

> Suppose there were two such magic rings, and one were given to the just man, the other to the unjust. No one, it is commonly believed, would have such iron strength of mind as to stand fast in doing right, or keep his hands off other men's goods, when he could go the marketplace and fearlessly help himself to anything he wanted, enter houses and sleep with any woman he chose, set prisoners free and kill men at his pleasure, and in a word, go about among men with the powers of a god. The so-called just man would behave no better than the other; both would take the same course. Surely this is strong proof that men do right only under compulsion. No individual thinks of it as good for him personally, since he does wrong whenever he thinks he has the power. Granted full license to do as he liked, people would think a man a miserable fool if he refused to wrong his neighbors or to touch their belongings, though in public they keep up a pretense of praising his conduct for fear of being wronged themselves.

You have to become a real skilled expert in injustice, however, so that you can get away with it.

This viewpoint is given a philosophic name, and it is called *egoism*. It is called "egoism" because the Sophists certainly do not preach that you should sacrifice for God or for others, and they say you should achieve your own advantage, and that should be your only goal. You see, it *is* egoism—I mean, you'd have to classify it as that, as against altruism or sacrifice for God or some other type of theory—but it is egoism that is thoroughly relativist, skeptical, and subjectivist. And one of the worst errors, one of the worst tragedies of Western philosophy, is that egoism at its inception was tied to these other views. The result is that ever since, egoism has been associated with two cardinal points: One, with whim-worshiping, with the idea that the egoist is the man who arbitrarily follows his subjective passions wherever they lead him. And two, brutality—the idea that an egoist is someone who tramples over others. And, you see, arbitrary whim-worship and brutality are all that's left when you abandon reason. And since the Sophists were egoists who abandoned reason, they were the first to give egoism the image and the concept that it has to this day in many people's minds. There were exceptions, however. Aristotle was an egoist of a radically different kind—but it was to the interest of the centuries of Christianity to ignore the existence of Aristotle and to present Sophism as the only concept of egoism. And so, in the mass media today, if someone is referred to as "selfish," that is taken as a synonym that he is a brute whim-worshiper.

This is the sort of position that Plato is going to try to answer. Above all, he was concerned to answer the Sophists.

Socrates

Let me now begin with Socrates and Plato, the two philosophers who set out to answer the Sophists and to ground objective knowledge and objective morality. Between them, they founded the first complete philosophy, the first complete system, including an integrated presentation in metaphysics, epistemology, ethics, politics, esthetics. So, we finally have passed the era of fragments and of background and reached the beginning of the new constructive era.

First, a few words about Socrates (470–400 BC). It is very difficult to separate him from Plato because Socrates left no writings; he is known primarily through Plato's dialogues. It's impossible to say exactly how much of those dialogues are historically accurate, and how much are words that Plato put into Socrates's mouth after Socrates died. You can find commentators and interpreters who range from one extreme to the other. Some of them say that there was no such person as Socrates, that he was a myth invented by Plato and Xenophon. Other people say that there was no such thinker as Plato, that he was just a secretary who took down what Socrates had to say. But I think in this particular case, moderation is the best policy, and I agree with the standard viewpoint, which is that the early dialogues of Plato, written when he was young, represent the historical Socrates on the whole, and the so-called middle and later dialogues of Plato represent Plato. But it doesn't really make any difference, because if you want to get around this problem, call it the "Socratic-Platonic" philosophy, and don't bother to apportion credit or blame.

If we interpret Socrates in this way, his interest was basically in ethics, rather than in metaphysics. He was the first major moralist of the Western world, a champion of absolute objective ethics, an arch opponent of the Sophists. He himself did not have a complete system of ethics, but he had a number of characteristic ethical ideas and approaches that were picked up and developed subsequently by Plato and by Aristotle in different ways. In the next lecture, we'll look at some of these typical Socratic ethical tenets in connection with our discussion of Plato's ethics.

But I want to say a few words about Socrates's method of philosophizing in order to acquaint you with a discovery of his, a very fundamental one, of an epistemological kind, which is indispensable background for Plato.

Obviously, Socrates employed the Socratic method, the conversational method, the question-and-answer method. In essence, he would collar an unsuspecting Athenian (usually of a pompous and ignorant kind, but who thought he knew a lot)—he'd collar him at his home or in the marketplace, engage the man in a philosophic conversation, and ask what seemed to be perfectly innocuous questions. He would get un-thought-out, apparently obvious answers, and then he would begin to reason, and say, "If you said this, wouldn't this follow?," and the man would say yes; "And then wouldn't this follow?," yes; "And what about this?"—and the man begins to feel quite uneasy because he doesn't want to say that, but he doesn't see how he can get out of it, given what he's said—and in not too long a time, the man has stopped completely; and the tradition was that he was rendered entirely speechless and couldn't utter a word.

Socrates's motive, apparently, was that he had a divine mission, and his mission was to be a philosophical gadfly, to rouse people from their unthinking, complacent slumbers. He was *not* a skeptic, but he was concerned to make people really think and question their hasty assumptions and their un-thought-out ideas and their conventional bromides and their sloppy formulations. His famous line in this connection is "The unexamined life is not worth living."

The unfortunate result of his method of procedure was that he was highly unpopular in Athens. He made many powerful enemies, particularly because a band of young men followed him around eating up the spectacle of him demolishing the prominent citizens. One member of that band was Plato. You probably know the consequences of it all: Socrates was arrested, charged with corrupting the youth and worshiping false gods. He was brought to trial, a famous trial. He was asked to defend himself, and he refused to concede that he had done anything wrong at all. The custom of the time was that the prosecutor and the defendant were each to propose a penalty, and then the court voted on which penalty should be given. The prosecutor demanded death. Socrates was asked, "What penalty do you propose?" and he said he thinks that the only appropriate result of his action is that he should be kept in luxury until the end of his days by the state for the service he has rendered them. Needless to say, the court voted for death by hemlock, and that was subsequently administered. So, he is the first philosophic martyr. If you want to read his story, it's contained in three dialogues of Plato: *The Apology*, which is Socrates's trial; the *Crito*, which is the episode in which a friend of Socrates tries to get him to escape from the jail, but Socrates refuses on the moral grounds that this was the will of the people, and although he disagrees with them, he believes that he is morally obligated to obey the law of the people; and then the third dialogue, the *Phaedo*, in which the last hours of Socrates are recounted, and it ends with him drinking the hemlock and becoming paralyzed.

The question is: What did he find in his philosophic method that was so crucial? What did Socrates discover? He found in the course of his discussions with people that the reason that people were so confused, so unclear, so chronically in disagreement and collapsing into subjectivism and skepticism, was that their concepts were unclear, that their concepts were undefined. For instance, they would argue whether a certain man was just, but they would argue back and forth vigorously without any definition of "justice." And Socrates asks: How could you possibly resolve this dispute objectively without a definition? The Sophists would say, well, it's a matter of opinion; for me he's just, for you he isn't. Socrates would say that you can't ask the question until you have a definition of "justice." You have to know what is common to just men, just actions, just governments, that makes them just. Once you have this definition, then there's no difficulty in applying it in a particular case. Once we know the definitions of our concepts, we can resolve all disputes in particular cases. And this is true not only of justice, but of *all* such cases. Is a given country a democracy?

Well, there's no use arguing until you know what *is* a democracy, and once you know, it's very easy to answer. Are you in love? No way to answer unless you know what is love—what is common to all instances of love? Once you know, it's easy enough to answer. And the same for what is religion, what is courage, etc.

In discovering the importance of the need for definitions, to that extent, Socrates is the father of definition. He did not use the term and didn't give the rules; he simply discovered the urgent need of them. So, let us pursue this.

What do you want when you ask for a definition? You want a statement of the characteristics that are common to some class. You want those characteristics possessed by *every* member of the class, in virtue of which they're members of *that* class, and not some other. When you define, you don't concentrate on one particular example; you don't try just to describe it. What you do is concentrate on what's common to a whole group of particulars. So, for instance, if you're trying to define "triangularity," you don't make an exhaustive study of one triangle on the blackboard and say, "Well, it's white, and it's got a three-inch hypotenuse, and it has a right angle, and so on." You survey all triangles in your mind, and you think, "Now, what is it that's common to them all, on the basis of which we classify them as triangles?"

To introduce terminology that didn't come into existence until later but is appropriate here, you concentrate, when you want a definition, not on particulars, but on *universals*. By "universal," we mean here something very specific: that set of properties which is common to every member of a class, and which is the basis of a classification. We do not mean universal *truths*, like the law of gravity; we mean universals in the sense of universal properties running through a class. Let me give you some examples.

I point to one book, and another book, and another book—those are three particulars—what is the universal? That set of properties common to all books on the basis of which we call them "books." If you want a single word for the universal—in English you usually have to put a suffix on it—you have to say something like "bookness," or "bookhood" (which is pretty bad). If you wanted to use it the way the Greeks talked about it, you would talk about "the idea of books," or "the essence of books," or "the universal book." And the same applies to people, and it applies to *every* time you have a classification. For instance, I move my hand, and that is one particular in the realm of motion; you move your head, and that's another particular; the earth moves around the sun, and that's another particular. What is the common, what is the universal? Motion. Or I point to this shade of green, and that's a particular, and that shade of green is a particular, and that shade of green is a particular, a particular quality. And what's common to them all? Greenness would be the universal. And it applies to relationships—this cup is on top of the desk, my body is on top of the stage, this floor is on top of the preceding one. And what is the universal? If you wanted to coin a grotesque word, you'd say it's "on-top-of-hood," the relation of one thing being above another.

What Socrates established was that the crucial problem of human knowledge was the knowledge of universals. Wherever we have a word, we have a universal, except for proper nouns ("John Smith" is not a universal but rather a particular, unless you're using "smith" to mean someone engaged in a certain occupation, with a small "s," and then it's a universal). Socrates believed, and Plato believed, and Aristotle believed that the thing that made man distinctive from the animals, everything that was distinctive about him, derived from his ability to grasp universals. They said that's what it means to say man is a rational being—he can abstract, he can grasp common denominators, he can conceptualize, he can classify—and therefore, he can generalize, he can grasp laws, he can apply to all the other particulars he's never encountered the information he gets from merely some particulars. He can predict the future, he can satisfy his desires and control his environment. But if you take away that one crucial capacity, the ability to grasp universals, you're left with animals, who merely are able to perceive particulars and react to them, but can't abstract universals and, therefore, can't draw conclusions, can't formulate principles, and are comparatively helpless. A dog, for instance, likes a bone; he likes a number of bones. Now, the question is: Why doesn't it occur to him to start a bone store, or to start a science of bones (boneology) and find out where bones come from and how you get them? And the trouble is that the poor dog can't get the idea of bone-ness; he gets this bone, and then the next one, he forgets the first one, and then the next one, and so on. And so, his problem is that he's enmeshed in particulars, and he can't rise to universals.

To put it in more modern terminology, Socrates was the one who really discovered for the first time in the West the importance of *conceptual*, as distinct from *perceptual*, knowledge. And conceptual knowledge was knowledge of common denominators, knowledge of universals. If we can validate knowledge of universals, said Socrates, then we'd have no difficulty answering the Sophists. Because the Sophists go around arguing, "What should this man do, what should he not do?" They never solved the problem; they say it's all subjective. What's wrong? They don't ask: What is *man*, man as such now—what kind of a being is he, what characteristics are common to all men and peculiar to them, in virtue of which they *are* men? The Sophists say that men vary, circumstances vary, and it's *true* that men vary, but *man* remains the same. And, if we didn't restrict ourselves to perception of particulars—if we focused on the universal, or the essence (which is essentially a synonym for the universal here), then we would have means to answer questions about individual men. In other words, human beings have to rise to the conceptual stage. Once we grasp universals conceptually and see particulars as simply instances or examples of them, we will have universal standards, universal definitions, and that will be the end of all our disagreements and our subjectivism. So, to talk about validating human knowledge is to talk about acquiring knowledge of universals. That is essentially the legacy left by Socrates in epistemology, although he did not use any of that terminology. ("Universal," "particular," "definition," etc., are all later terms.)

Plato

Now let's take up Plato (427–347 BC). One of Socrates's disciples, Plato wrote a great deal, a lot of which is lost. What we have is primarily (aside from some letters) a series of dialogues, twenty-odd dialogues, and he wrote in that form in order to reproduce and perpetuate the conversational method of his master. You know that Plato founded the first university of the Western world, the Academy, and therefore in the ancient world, his followers were frequently called "the Academics." His motto was supposedly emblazoned over the doors: "Let no one ignorant of geometry enter here," which can suggest to you the influence of Pythagoras on Plato. His major work, in terms of popularity and known by just about everybody, is *The Republic*.

To do him credit, Plato is undoubtedly one of the two most influential philosophers of all time (the other being Aristotle). He is the first great philosophic genius in human history, and I say that deliberately and advisedly, not from the perspective of the truth of his ideas, or even the rationality of them (because Objectivism disagrees *entirely* with Platonism, with its conclusions and its approach), but he is nevertheless one the greatest geniuses philosophically, in three ways: (1) in his abstract ability, which was superlatively greater than everyone else in the history of thought but for Aristotle; (2) in his originality—he was the man who essentially created philosophy from the tentative bits and suggestions that I've given you so far; and (3) in his power of systematic integration—he was the first to put it all together into a comprehensive view of man, of reality, of knowledge, of life, of ethics, of politics, of art. And this is an achievement not to be underestimated.

Plato was in complete agreement with Socrates's view that the crucial knowledge needed for man was the knowledge of universals. He himself, however, drew metaphysical conclusions from this that Socrates, as far as we can tell, did not. I want to follow Plato here step by step, because this is the most crucial part of his philosophy. It's the basis of his distinctive, world-famous, staggeringly influential metaphysics.

We start with premise, then, then that universals must be knowable; otherwise, we're going to be back in the position of the animals and the Sophists. If universals must be knowable, we can conclude one thing right away: They must actually exist; they must be real, because Parmenides made it perfectly clear that *thou canst not know what is not.* And therefore, if universals are knowable, they must exist. Which raises the question: Where do they exist? How do they exist? For Plato, this is a grave problem. It was later called (for perfectly obvious reasons) *the problem of universals.*

You might say in advance that you don't see any problem. And since, in order for you to understand Plato, I have to get you to see a problem, let me tell you what is probably on your mind. You're probably thinking: You say universals exist in particulars. "Manness," you would say, for instance, is merely a name for all the similar characteristics possessed by individual men, not something over and above individual men, as though you have Tom, Dick, and Harry, etc., and then another one called "manness." And so, you say, where's the problem? When you're thinking about universals, you are really thinking about particulars from a certain point of view.

Plato says no, this is wrong. He is proposing to argue that universals and particulars have radically different characteristics and, therefore, must in logic be radically different kinds of things. Universals cannot be names for aspects of particulars; that's what he's going to argue for.

His method here is: How do you know that Smith and Jones are two different people? Suppose somebody said, "Smith is just a name for parts of Jones." You'd say, "Well look, I know that Smith and Jones are two different people because Smith is a plumber, Jones is a philosopher, Smith is rich, Jones is poor, etc." You make a list of all the different characteristics, and you say that they have to be two completely different entities because they have completely opposite characteristics.

Plato proposes to do exactly that with universals and particulars. He's going to find a whole list of differences, complete opposites, on every count, and he's going to show how universals couldn't possibly be a name for groups of particulars when they're completely opposite. The conclusion we're going to come to is that there must then be two worlds: a world that has the characteristics of particulars, and another one that has the characteristics of universals.

How do universals and particulars differ? Plato makes four points. Remember that the Greeks were fascinated with multiplicity, so let's look at the question from the point of view of multiplicity, of the one and the many. How many particulars are there in a given class? How many men, for instance? Obviously, millions. If we don't bother to quantify, we'll just call them "many." How many universals are there in that class? How many mannesses? Obviously, one. How many triangles, particular triangles? Endless number. How many triangularities? Obviously, only one, says Plato. Suppose you proved a theorem about triangularity, about all triangles, in other words, and somebody said to you, "Well, that's true of this triangularity, but it's not true of that one"—you would look at him, baffled, and say, "What do you mean? there aren't two triangularities, there's only one." The universal *is* what's common to all the different particulars. It is the unifying common denominator. It is, if we hark back to the early phrase, "the one in the many." So, on your list, you can put down "one per category" under universals and under particulars, "many."

Now we go on to the second point. The Greeks were not only fascinated with multiplicity, but with change. What about the contrast between universals and particulars from the point of view of change? Plato says that particulars are obviously changing. They come into existence, they hang around for a while, they decay, they grow old, they rot, and they pass out of existence. In fact, he believes with Heraclitus that particulars are changing all the time in every respect in every instant, that this world is a stream of Heraclitean flux, unchanging, eternal, indestructible, immutable. How does he defend that? Think of the idea of "manness" or the idea of "triangularity"—we are able to formulate unvarying laws. By his very nature, man requires self-esteem, and this is an immutable law. How would that be possible unless manness, the thing the law is about, were immutable, unless it were unchanging? Or we can say, "Triangles must have an angle sum of 180 degrees"—how is that possible as an immutable law, unless there is some thing such as immutable triangularity? Therefore, when we think of a universal, says Plato, we're not thinking of particulars, because particulars change in every aspect, but universals go on unchanging.

And now point three—think of it from the point of view of the constitution of the two—particulars are primarily material or physical; animals can see them, hear them, taste them. But what about universals? Are they accessible to animals? Can you see manness or boneness? Obviously not. The dog can see bones, but it can't see boneness. So, boneness is somehow abstract, it's nonphysical, and that's proved by the fact that we can't grasp it by the senses. So, we have another contrast—something nonphysical (that's universals) and something physical (that's particulars).

And fourthly, as a consequence of that, how do we *know* the two different things: We know particulars by means of our senses, and we know universals not by means of the senses but by the mind, reason, intelligence, the thinking capacity, the intellect. Well, says Plato, the conclusion to draw is inescapable. How can we deny that there are two different worlds—on the one hand, a world in which there is one universal per category, unchanging, nonmaterial, knowable only by the mind; and the other, a world of multiple, changing, physical, sensory particulars? They're not the same. One can't be explained as just a name for the other. And yet we know that universals must exist, must be real. Conclusion: There must be two worlds, two realms: the world of universals and the world of particulars. Q.E.D. That's argument one.

There are many arguments for this metaphysics in Plato. If you want to give them names (names that I, not Plato, have given them), you can call this first one the *argument from the differences between universals and particulars.* I'll give you three more arguments, all leading to the same conclusion from different aspects.

You can call the second one (my order, not Plato's), the *argument from perfection.* And this one begins: Where do we get our concepts and standards of perfection? In any category, Plato uses mainly mathematical and ethical examples, like the perfect triangle or the perfectly just man, but it applies to any category—the perfect straight line, a perfect government, a perfect banana, a perfect innerspring mattress, you name it. Where do we get our concepts of perfection? You might say, by seeing individual perfect instances and then abstracting. Plato says no, you could not have gotten your concept of "perfection" by this means, because *nothing* in this world is perfect—a fundamental principle of Plato's philosophy. There is no such thing as perfection in this world. Why not? He says that that's proved by the fact that things in this world change—if a thing changes, it couldn't be perfect, because if it were perfect, it would stand still; it would lack nothing. Take, for instance, a man—suppose a man were perfect, he lacked nothing, completely perfect. Then he wouldn't have to eat, he doesn't lack food; he wouldn't have to go to school, he doesn't lack knowledge; he wouldn't have to breathe, he doesn't lack air. He'd be the way the Christian–Jewish God is supposed to be—he'd just sit there motionless because he's already perfect. On the other hand, if things change, that means they *lack* something—they're imperfect, they have to grow and develop, etc., they're not perfect.

Even in mathematics, the Platonists say, you'll never find perfection. You know the standard example: Have you ever seen a perfect straight line? And the Platonist will say no; if you look at the most beautiful straight line through a microscope, you'll see little wiggles, so it's not perfectly straight. And even aside from that, the Platonist will say, you've never actually seen a perfect triangle. In fact, they'll go further: You've never even seen a triangle of *any* kind. If I draw a triangle on a blackboard, you'd say, "Isn't that a triangle?" And the Platonist would say that it is not—a triangle is defined as a plane figure bounded by three straight lines. What I have on the board is not a line; a line is simply extension in one dimension; it's a three-dimensional phenomenon—it comes out from the board a certain distance, and it has a certain thickness; so if it was to be just a line (which is how a triangle is defined), we would have to erase the chalk from the board to get rid of the thickness, and we'd have to erase the width of it, and of course, we'd have nothing left. In other words, we don't have a perfect triangle; we don't even *have* a triangle. What we have is a crude approximation of a triangle, which is not a sensory phenomenon according to Plato. If we can't get a perfect triangle in mathematics, we can't get it anywhere. But what do we then conclude? We must have gotten our concepts of perfection from *somewhere* because we *have* those concepts. We criticize things as imperfect, and the fact that we say something is imperfect presupposes that we know in some way what perfection would consist of. So, we have a knowledge of what perfection consists of, and yet we couldn't have gotten it from this world. From where then? Plato says we must have gotten it from contemplating another world, a world that contains the perfect embodiment of everything in this world, a world of perfect archetypes, or universals.

Notice that whenever we think of a universal, we typically have a perfect, unblemished representative in mind. If I say, "Think of man," well, to most of you at least, John Galt and not some welfare recipient, will come to mind. If you say "university," with all due allowances for deterioration, you probably think of Harvard and not of a teachers college in Tennessee. If you say "the human body," you think of an Olympic athlete, and not some broken down hulk, etc. So, the association between the universal and the perfect is very firm, very strong, and Plato cashes in on it to conclude that the world of perfection that we need is precisely the world of universals. And he concludes that there must *be* a world of perfect universals, which we have contemplated at some time prior to this life, thereby gaining our standards and knowledge of perfection, and thereby, by contrast, being able to say that the things in this world are imperfect.

Notice, therefore, that we've not only established by this particular argument the world of universals, but two other things. We've established *innate ideas*, knowledge possessed in us at birth, because we had to be born with this knowledge of perfection, since we have it, and since (as he claims to have proved) we couldn't have acquired it during this life. So, it had to come from another world, and that means we had to have knowledge at birth. So, we've laid the first groundwork to the theory of innate ideas in epistemology. And, in regard to another point, we've proved that the soul must be independent of the body because the soul must have been in this other world apart from and prior to the formation of the body. Therefore, we've laid the groundwork to establish the immortality of the soul. So, this argument brings in a whole bunch of Platonic themes.

Let's turn to argument three, which I call the *argument from the order of knowledge*. It takes off from the question: Which, in logic, would you have to know first: universals or particulars? You might think that you know particulars first and then you arrive at universals by abstraction from what they have in common. Plato says absolutely wrong. He says it's impossible to know particulars, to classify them, to categorize them, unless you knew universals in advance. And he goes into an elaborate criticism of the theory that you arrive at universals by a process of abstraction. The advocate of the Aristotelean view that you arrive at universals by abstraction from particulars says: If you want to define "justice," for instance, or arrive at a knowledge of justice in general, the way to do it is to collect before your mind all the particular instances of justice, or at least a great many, and then abstract and see what they have in common. To which Plato says, this is an impossible thing to do, because if you *didn't* know what justice was in advance, how would you know what was a particular instance of it? How would you know what things to collect together and form the abstraction from? How would you know what particulars to group together?

Plato says that we have a real tricky question. To define a universal, we have to assemble the instances before us (for instance, in the case of justice), and then grasp what's common. But we're in this position: If we knew in advance what was common, we would never have to inquire, because we know all the definitions in advance. If we *don't* know in advance, then we have no idea *how* to inquire, because we don't know what particular to collect or group together. Suppose I told you to go out and find the definition of "gloop," and you say, "How?" and I say, "Find all the particular gloops and then abstract what they have in common." You'd say, "That's ridiculous, I don't know what to look for." Plato says we're in this paradoxical position. Somehow we have to know universals in advance to be able to organize particulars, and yet we *don't* know them in advance; if we did, we'd be able to whip off the answers, and we obviously can't. We have to know and not know, and how is that possible?

He says there's only one solution: There must, again, be a realm of universals, independent of this world, which we knew before this life. (Of course, here he's relying on the previously mentioned Pythagorean wheel of birth.) It must be the case that we were born with innate knowledge of all these universals, so, in a certain sense, we're born omniscient. We know every category, and all the relationships, which means all the laws; and in that sense, we *do* have all knowledge. But the knowledge is unconscious when we're born. It's deep in our subconscious, to use modern terms. And you have to go through a special process to unearth it. And therefore, in a sense, yes, we *are* born with it, in the sense that we have it, but in a sense no, we're not; we have to unearth it by a deliberate process. In any event, the point is proved—there must be a world of universals, and we must have had knowledge of it in some form prior to this life; otherwise, we would gape like animals at particulars and have no idea how to proceed.

And now the last argument that I'll look at—the *argument from the possibility of knowledge*. Knowledge must be possible, knowledge of reality—that's Plato's basic premise. And the question, therefore, is: What must reality be like if knowledge is to be possible? And here he draws the final conclusions of all his predecessors. Heracliteans held that you can't know a world of flux, but *this* world *is* a world of flux. Plato says true enough. Therefore, if reality is to be knowable, it must be immutable. That means another world. Heraclitus and Parmenides had both said that if a world is changing, then it's contradictory, and you can't know the contradictory, because it both is and it isn't. And Plato says true enough: If a world is to be knowable, it must be made of consistent entities, and that means entities that don't change, and therefore, again, an immutable other world. The Sophists had said knowledge acquired by the senses is invalid, subjective, not of reality. And Plato agrees. Therefore, he says, if we are to have knowledge of reality, it must be knowledge that is acquired by a non-sensory means, and if it's acquired by a non-sensory means, it must be of a nonmaterial object, because material objects could be known (in theory) by the senses; and if this has to be the kind of world that's inaccessible to the senses, it must be nonmaterial. Socrates had said the crucial thing to know is universals, and universals happen to have all the characteristics that the knowable world has to have: They're immutable, self-consistent, motionless, nonmaterial. The conclusion must therefore be: If there's to be knowledge of reality at all, if that's to be possible, it must be of a world of universals, and not of this world. And therefore, Pythagoreanism wins out in Plato: There are two worlds. Knowledge, true knowledge, is knowledge of the other world, but now it's not the world of numbers—numbers are just one small constituent—it's the world of universals, which includes numbers and everything else that has any instances, actual or possible. There is reason to believe that, in his very late life, Plato reverted to pure Pythagoreanism and converted the universals back into numbers, but that is not what he is famous for, so we'll treat him as a Platonist (as that's understood).

Plato thought he had the final answer to all the problems of the skeptics. The Heracliteans had said that this world is a world of flux, and we can't speak or acquire knowledge of it. Plato said true enough, but there is an immutable knowable world, the world of universals. The Heracliteans had said this world is contradictory because it's constantly changing. Plato said true enough, but there is a non-contradictory reality, the motionless world of universals. The Heracliteans and Sophists said we can't rely on the senses, and Plato said true, but there's a non-material world we can know by non-sensory means, a supernatural realm of universals. This is Plato's solution to the problems of earlier philosophy: There are two worlds, the world of universals (also known as the world of essences), the world of Forms (with a capital "F"), the world of Ideas (Platonic Ideas), and the intelligible world, because it's the world that you grasp by intelligence, by mind. And as against that, there's the world of particulars, or the physical world, or the "sensible world" (as it's called), that being the world you grasp by the senses.

Let me now give you an overview of the differences between the two worlds. For Plato, universals are entirely different from the particulars in this world. They're independent of the particulars in this world and independent of our thoughts. If you wiped out all of our thoughts about manness, that would not touch manness; manness is real and immutable. Whether we think of it or not has no effect on it. Indeed, if we wiped out all particular men, that would not touch manness. Manness is immutable, it's eternal, it's indestructible. Therefore, universals are to be thought of not as thoughts and not as particulars, but actual entities, things—real, external objects. They're not physical, but they are nevertheless real. And that's why, although Plato's word for them is a Greek word for "idea," it's very common not to call them the world of Ideas, because "idea," suggests a thought in somebody's mind. And that's why most people translate the actual word "idea" into the word "form," which has the virtue of being entirely meaningless, and therefore doesn't mislead people into thinking that Plato's "Ideas" are ideas in a mind. They are free-floating universals. Up there, there is subway-hood and banana-split-ness, and you name it. There are no banana splits. It's not sensory. It's the *essence* of banana split as such. Whereas down here, there are particular, individual things. How many of them? For every class of particulars, there is a corresponding universal, for every abstract word that we use, and undoubtedly for a great many that we haven't yet discovered. There is one such to every group of many in this world. Universals are unchanging, immutable, eternal; particulars are changing, temporal, and Heraclitean. Universals are perfect, and particulars are imperfect—they simply approximate the perfection of the Forms. Universals are non-material. I should point out that they are also non-mental, because minds are also particulars—your mind, her mind, his mind. What's up there is not a particular mind, but mind-ness, the universal that's common to all minds. Therefore, universals are neither mental nor physical. They're . . . universals. Whereas the things down here, if we leave aside minds, are essentially material. Universals are knowable by thought, particulars only by the senses. But particulars are not really knowable, according to Plato, because down here in this world, all you can have is subjective opinions. On that, he agrees with Heraclitus and the Sophists. True knowledge is always knowledge of the Forms, of the Ideas, never of the particulars in this world.

Of these two worlds, which do you think Plato regarded as really real? Obviously, the world of Forms—that's reality. Why? Well, for a number of reasons. Ask yourself what it means to say that something is real. What are the tests, so to speak, of reality? Plato gives a number of tests, and on every test, the world of Forms comes out with flying colors, and the world in which we live fails miserably. Here are four such tests:

One, to be real, a thing has to exist. For instance, you say Santa Claus isn't real, he doesn't exist. But follow that out: According to Plato, for a thing to exist, it can't be contradictory (which is true). But for a thing to be noncontradictory, it has to be motionless (that's the Heraclitean view, because change involves a contradiction). What can we say about the things in this world then? Are they real? They're contradictory, which means they are and they are not. They are somehow, says Plato, a union of what is and what isn't. They are being and nonbeing. They are therefore not real. They are partly illusory. They have about the status of a dream—it's there, but it isn't; it is and it isn't. For Plato, the real must therefore be the immutable. That's test one.

Or second, we can use the test that a thing is real when it's knowable. Plato held very firmly the view that reality is that which is the object of knowledge. And as we've seen, if knowledge is of reality, and knowledge is only of the world of Forms, then the world of Forms is reality, not this world.

With the third test, Plato equates the real with the perfect, with the ideal. And this is a usage of the word "real" that has survived to this day—you serve somebody a piece of apple pie, and he says, "That's real apple pie"; or you say about him, "He's a real man"; or there used to be a newspaper that said: "The paper for real New Yorkers." They obviously didn't mean, "As opposed to hallucinatory New Yorkers"; by "real" they meant "good." And that usage was firmly accepted by Plato. So, on that count also, the equation of the real with the ideal, the world of Forms comes out as reality.

And finally, we characteristically use the word "real" to stand for the original, as against the imitations. For instance, the other night, somebody said to me when I was praising Potato Buds (a form of instant mashed potatoes), somebody said to me, "Oh, they're not real; that isn't really mashed potatoes." They didn't mean that it was hallucinatory or nonexistent, or even that it didn't taste good; they meant this isn't *real, original, natural,* mashed potatoes, just an imitation. On that test also, the world of Forms is the original, and the world in which we live is just an imitation, derivative, or projection of the world of Forms. So, on that count of originality also, the world of Forms emerges as reality.

What then is the status of this world in which we live? Plato says it is like a byproduct or a derivative or a projection or a reflection of true reality. If you want an analogy, you have to project being in an amusement park and looking into one of those distorted mirrors. In this analogy, *you* represent the world of Forms, and the distorted, twisted, garish reflection of you represents the imperfect image of you projected into the mirror. To make it a proper parallel, we have to assume that the mirror is multifaceted, so that where there's one of you, there's a whole variety of images, and an ignorant person looking at them might confuse it and think there are many different people, but there's actually only one. It's just that the image is splintered. And now we have to imagine someone there with a crank whirling these facets around, so that the images seem to be racing around even though you are standing motionless. That is approximately Plato's view of this world. Up there in Platonic heaven is the single, motionless, perfect, nonmaterial reality. But it projects itself outward and assumes the illusory appearance of a world of imperfect, multiple, moving images. And that world is the world we're living in temporarily.

Plato does not use the example of a mirror. He does say that this world is the world of Forms reflected, or projected, into a medium, but not into a physical mirror. What does he think that the world of Forms projects into? This is a fairly technical point from Plato, but just to satisfy your curiosity, I'll mention that in one of his later dialogues, the *Timaeus*, he reasons as follows: This world, we know from Heraclitus, must be a union of what is and what isn't; it must somehow be a union of reality and unreality. And this world in which we live must therefore be a compound. The Forms, we know, represent the element of reality. But what represents the element of unreality that is an essential part of this world? We need a nothing, a "what is not," which sort of *is*. This world, according to Plato, has to arise from a union of the Forms with a principle of non-being that somehow is. That's a big problem. What could it be, the nothing that is (sort of)? Plato took his cue here from the Atomists—the answer is *empty space*. Space, according to Plato, is nothing, and yet it exists, it *is*. It is, therefore, the stand-in for the mirror in my example; it is the actual medium that enables the Forms to take on physical location (not the Forms themselves, but their images). And space, being extended in three dimensions, being spread out, is suitable to be that element that gives material, physical character to the non-material Forms. And therefore, this world is really the Forms shining out into empty space. That's Plato's final theory of the relation between the two worlds. Therefore, if we took away empty space and wiped out this world, the Forms would go on untouched. But if we did anything to the Forms, this world would vanish in the same way that the image in the mirror would if you went away. But you don't have to worry about that happening, because the Forms are by their nature immutable. Nothing can happen to them.

As to how this world came about, Plato, being a Greek, did not believe it was created *ex nihilo* (out of nothing)—he believed that the stuff of the world always existed, the Forms were always projecting into space, and therefore, matter in a primitive form always existed—but he tells a story which is the forerunner of many religious views, the story of the Demiurge. This is another myth. Whenever Plato tells a myth, it means: Take it seriously but not literally. It means he's trying to say something that he doesn't know how to say, but he means it, but not literally. The myth of the Demiurge is as follows: The Demiurge is a sort of godlike, but very limited, soul that wanders free in the universe. Not a Form, and not matter, but kind of a third category—sort of like a god, but nothing like the Christian God. Well, this Demiurge wandered by one day and saw all this chaotic matter, and being good, he said to himself, "Isn't there some way I could organize things better?" So, with one eye on the perfection of the world of Forms, he shaped and organized the matter, molded it like an architect, to produce as much order, harmony, symmetry, and perfection as he could. And that was the actual source of the lawfulness and the order of the world that we observe. This is the most primitive (and influential) early form of what later became the *argument from design* for the existence of God (that is, the world is so orderly, it must have had an orderer, a designer). In any event, Plato is insistent that the Demiurge is not all-powerful. He did as well as he could, but remember, this world had a very recalcitrant element in its constitution, and that element is: nothing, which you can't do anything with; it is deficient. And consequently, there was a certain imperfection that had to remain in this world that is beyond anyone's power, and that's the reason why the world is imperfect—it's imperfect because it's partly not here.

Now you know the basis and the essence of Plato's metaphysics, but there's more to say, because I haven't yet brought in Plato's god, or to be exact, the ancestor of what later became the God of Christianity. It wasn't the Demiurge; he appears in just one dialogue and never comes back. We have to leave this world and embark on an excursion into the world of Forms in order to discover its content in greater detail and that excursion begins in the next lecture, which we will devote to the consequences that Plato drew from his metaphysics for epistemology, psychology, ethics, and politics.

Lecture Two, Q&A

Q: How could Plato's Forms project into the world if they were unmoving and incapable of any sort of change or action?

A: It's some motionless process. The Christians had exactly the same problem—God created the world, and God, they held on Platonic grounds, was completely motionless. How could he create the world if he didn't do anything? And their answer was, he did it the same way Plato's Forms projected. And to grasp that, you have to go into the higher mysteries beyond the problems of human reason.

Q: In the history of philosophy, there have been both the empiricist and the rationalist sides to the reason-senses dichotomy. Why did the Greeks take the rationalist side, instead of "the senses are valid or good and the reason is not" side?

A: That's an excellent question, and my answer to that would be that these two views as presented here are both false. The view that reason is right and the senses are wrong, or that the senses are right and reason is useless—are both false. But it is significant that the Greeks took the rationalist side, rather than the empiricist side in the way that's being used in this question.

And I would say the answer is: because the Greeks were thinkers. If you're going to be wrong (and I don't mean to say that some errors are less wrong than others), but if you're going to be wrong, it is much better to be a rationalist, *in a certain limited respect.* Because if you take the other side and say the senses are valid but you can't trust the mind, like David Hume did, you are then in the position of an animal or a skeptic. You're in the position of saying that nobody can know anything. And under that viewpoint, knowledge immediately comes to a halt—you can't know anything—because a human being who denies the ability of reason wipes out the possibility of intellectual development. Ideally, mankind would have started with the proper relationship of the two faculties. But if they had to start wrong, it's perfectly understandable that they would start by accepting the validity of thought, and then if they were led to primitive conclusions that seemed to defy the evidence, they clung to their reason as they understood it and wrote off the sensory evidence. That is profoundly wrong, but if you're going to make a mistake and continue to think, you cannot abandon thought. In this sense, the rationalists have *always* been philosophically superior to the skeptics (although Objectivism repudiates both). And they have always been infinitely more influential on mankind. The skeptics set up the next rationalist, that's all. The Sophists allowed time for Plato to come in, and the later skeptics opened the door to Augustine, and the Renaissance skeptics opened the door to Descartes, and David Hume opened the door to Kant, etc. The whole pattern has been that the skeptics wipe out everything, and the next rationalist comes in to institute his own new form of mysticism. But in that respect, of these two errors, it is the rationalists who are the only ones who think and have influenced mankind for good or evil. The skeptics disqualify themselves on the face of it.

Q: If the Sophists believed that one can't know anything, how do they know what a desire is?

A: A perfectly good question, to which I can only say the Sophists were inconsistent. They were not properly skeptical. Their modern followers are much more consistent, and they say that we can't talk about desires because we haven't the faintest idea of what a desire is, nor can you ever know what your desires are—how can you be sure of anything? For instance, Kant says that your real desires are entirely unknowable to you; all you can know are your desires as they appear *to you*, the so-called phenomenal desires, not the "noumenal" desires. And he has modern disciples who go one step further: "How do you even know the way your desires appear to you? How do you know that they don't appear to you differently than the way they *really* appear to you?" Therefore, you can't know anything. From this point of view, Gorgias, as I said, was a half-hearted, fair-weather skeptic compared to the twentieth century.

Q: Did the Atomists hold that all atoms are the same? How do soul atoms differ from regular atoms?

A: No, they're all the same in the sense that they all have only the characteristics of size, shape, motion, and number. But the soul atoms are finer (whatever that means—smaller, I guess), more polished, more mobile—they quiver a lot—things like that.

Q: Please give some additional argument against mechanistic materialism.

A: The first question to ask is: What is the argument *in favor* of materialism? What is to defend that? If you take an unprejudiced view of reality, if you truly are going to go by observation, you observe that there's an external world and an internal world. We have direct awareness of matter on the outside and of consciousness in your own head. The standard materialist will say: "I don't know what you're talking about when you talk about consciousness or mind. I can't taste it, I can't feel it, I can't weigh it, I can't dissect it. I *can* crack open your head and stick my fingers in your brain; that's good, solid and physical, but I can't find any mind, and therefore, it's a myth." That argument, in actual fact, is fantastic. What it consists of doing is setting up the characteristics of matter as the criterion of reality, and then saying since mind doesn't have those characteristics, it isn't real. If that method of reasoning were valid, you could do exactly the same thing in reverse—you could make a list of all the things that matter doesn't have. For instance, you can't psychoanalyze electrons or matter; you can't discuss their motivation; you can't discuss its feelings, its sensations, its premises, etc. Suppose I were to say that since you can't do any of this with matter, obviously matter doesn't exist, only mind. Your immediate answer would be: "How can you take characteristics of consciousness and arbitrarily say that all of reality must fulfill it, when there are obviously two kinds of things?" The same principle applies equally to matter. Then the materialist will come back and say: "Yeah, but you can't define consciousness. All you can do is give synonyms—you can say consciousness is awareness, and so on—or list its properties. But you can't say what it *is*." To which the answer is: In exactly that same way you're in that position with matter. You can give synonyms—you can say it's material, it's physical, it's extended—but you cannot define it in terms of other concepts, any more than you can consciousness. All definitions presuppose some cognitive primaries that are the basic categories in terms of which you define everything else, but which themselves cannot be reduced back further—in effect, the axioms of definition. And there is every reason to hold that consciousness as a phenomenon is descriptively different from matter, and consequently, that you cannot do any more than say, if you want to know what I mean by consciousness, you point ostensively, the same way you do with matter, or with green for that matter—now how would you communicate green to someone who didn't know? You'd have to point to several instances and say, "That's green." That's what's called an "ostensive" definition, a definition by pointing.

And it's the way that all primaries are defined. How would you define "existence"? Same thing. Since everything exists, you can't distinguish existence from anything else. The only way you define "existence" is just wave your arm and say, "It's that," covering everything. And the same principle is applicable to consciousness (not that it covers everything, but that you grasp it by direct introspection).

Let me remind you of a crucial point: We have to distinguish what philosophy can do and what science can do. I, and Objectivism, put forth no theories on the ultimate relationship between matter as we now know it and consciousness. It might be the case—I say it might be, I'm not ruling this out—that consciousness is a phenomenon that results from a certain enormous complexity of organization of matter and, in that sense, is a derivative phenomenon. It might be the case that there is, irreducibly, consciousness and matter as two distinct phenomena, which in some form always exist, and combine in certain ways under appropriate conditions. It might be the case that there is a third, or a tenth, phenomenon that we yet do not know, of which matter is one product and consciousness is another, or one form and another, some world stuff that is yet outside our knowledge, some type of energy. I don't know, nobody knows, and nobody has any business speculating, given the state of our present knowledge. Nor will philosophy have any means of answering this question. That will be a question to be answered by the appropriate scientific discoveries in physics, biology, psychology. I don't prejudge those questions. I say that on philosophic grounds, you cannot get away from the following: One, there is consciousness, which is not reducible to matter as we now understand the phenomenon of matter; it has its own characteristics and its own method of being known; and it is as real a phenomenon as external physical matter. Two, the conclusions of consciousness are efficacious—they have effects on the actual behavior of conscious entities; three, consciousness is, in the human case, volitional. The proof of these latter points is in the Objectivist literature, and I won't get into them. Those are the points on the mind-body question that are philosophically untouchable. I don't know the ultimate physical or metaphysical relations of the two, and it makes no difference *philosophically.*

Materialism comes in two varieties. One is *reductive materialism*, and the other is called *epiphenomenalism*. Reductive materialism is the crudest type. That is the type claiming that thinking is nothing but a quivering of the brain cells; love is a squirting of glandular juices, etc. This is a crude confusion of necessary conditions and identity. Maybe it's true that certain glands have to squirt before you can experience love. That does not mean that love *is* its necessary condition. Obviously, it has to be something different from the thing that gives rise to it or is presupposed by it. As one philosopher put it, you cannot argue with a man who says love *is* a squirting of juices (that's distinct from love is *caused* by, or *presupposes*, but love literally *is*), because, he said, to argue against a position, what you try to do is show that it leads to an absurdity, but if somebody comes in the room and utters an absurdity as his formal position, there is nothing you can say.[10] If somebody comes in and says, "My view is that elephants are peaches, now do something." That's reductive materialism.

The more serious form of materialism is epiphenomenalism, and that is the view that there *is* such a thing as mind that is distinct from matter—but it's a completely helpless byproduct of matter, it is incapable of initiating any action, it's a passive result of physical processes, it's completely determined, completely purposeless—sort of like a useless waste product that nature gives off. The problems with this are all of the problems that we indicated, and even more. If mind is metaphysically helpless and has no efficacy, but then the theory is self-refuting—its advocates are mindless by their own statement, or rather, they have useless minds that have no effects, and therefore, their mind had nothing to do with the motion of their hands or their tongues as they were busy propounding their theory. Insofar as there's no mind, there's no possibility of choice, and therefore, materialism necessarily implies determinism, and that, as you must know from Objectivist literature, is thoroughly self-refuting. The determinist can't know anything, including that he's determined. And, insofar as it implies a denial of purpose, it's *also* self-refuting—that means there's no way in principle of distinguishing between a man whose hand shakes because of palsy and a man whose hand shakes because he wants to express a certain thought, because there's no such thing as *wanting* to express; everything that happens is purposeless, mechanistically caused. If that's the case, no one has a right to expect you to consider the results of his palsy-shaking. Beyond all of these, there is a simple fact, and it's often very helpful to appeal to facts in philosophy—it is not a common practice, but it is a very desirable one.

I put it to you that you cannot look at the actual facts of the world and entertain for a moment the belief that ideas (mental phenomena) have no effects, which is the essence of materialism. You could not account for the facts of human behavior, i.e., the obvious fact that behavior is dictated by ideas, including value judgments; that when men change their values,

10. Source unknown.

they change their actions; that they go to psychotherapists in order to change their mental processes, in order to act differently, and that's the only way that they can do it. But knowledge is a vital necessity, without which a man cannot cross the street or satisfy the most minimal hunger pains. And that knowledge means something mental—the acquisition of awareness, of ideas, of information. You could not begin to make sense of human history, from the Industrial Revolution through the self-flagellation of the worst medieval saint, on mechanistic-materialist grounds, that somehow, in some funny way, the atoms started to quiver, and Saint Francis went out and plunged himself into a snow heap every time he had a sexual desire—I mean, it's just bizarre. I regard mechanistic materialism as senseless. I think Plato's philosophy is *infinitely* more sophisticated, more thoughtful, much better reasoned—it's wrong, but I'd take Plato over a materialist any day.

Q: Don't you need to know about music to have a philosophy of music, and about painting to have a philosophy of painting?

A: First, let me clarify something. I said last time that in philosophy, no special knowledge of any one area of reality was required. I didn't say that as a defining characteristic, but a consequence of the fact that philosophic principles are universal; you can find them anywhere. So, it's not that you don't have to know anything about reality, but wherever you look, for instance, whatever you look at, it is what it is. And so, you can get the law of identity from peaches or art or battleships. It's not that you don't have to look at reality, but you can find philosophic principles anywhere, precisely because they're universal.

As to your specific question, yes, when doing esthetics, you do need knowledge of the arts, but then that is already applied philosophy, that is specialized philosophy. That is a union of abstract philosophy and a particular field. As soon as you start to apply philosophy to a particular area, you obviously have to have specialized knowledge of that area. If you're going to have a philosophy of education, epistemology by itself will not give it to you. It will give you the base, but then you have to think about what kind of curriculum is proper, and what age children should be taught certain content, and with what motive, etc. If you're going to have a philosophy of law, politics will give you the base, but it won't tell you what the Constitution should say, and how many sessions of Congress should there be, and how many houses of Congress should there be, and who owns the oil rights to what kind of land, and so on. So, you have to know a great deal of particular material. And the same is obviously true with the philosophy of music, or the philosophy of science, or whatever it happens to be. I was talking about philosophy abstractly, the basic branches, not the detailed applications of them.

Q: If the world is made up of ultimate particles, there must be something between them if there's to be no vacuum. Is that something between them *itself* made of particles, or is it continuous? If it's made of particles, then is there something between them, and so on?

A: This is a question, which, as far as I know, there's no philosophic method of answering. I would not speculate about that type of question. I am not a physicist, and I despise armchair metaphysicians who become physicists. If you want to become a physicist, then go out and get facts. I don't believe in doing it by deduction. It can't be done that way.

Q: Do you regard Plato's metaphysics as being motivated primarily by his ethical viewpoint, that is, his opposition to the Sophists?

A: That is a question I don't know the answer to, nor know that the answer would make any difference, and so I'm reluctant to speculate about it. There are two entirely different questions: (1) What does a philosopher say (and is it true or false), and (2) what is his motive? Now, it's deuces wild with regard to the motives, unless they have written something that explicitly says that this is their motive. And it doesn't make any difference. Suppose Plato was motivated by a passion for the all-powerful state, or by a passion for truth as he saw it. In either case he put forth the ideas that he did for the reasons that he did, and they had the influence that they did. And so it's a question of your private, personal evaluation of Plato's character, which I don't see as having any philosophic significance. Therefore, I stay away altogether from questions of the motive of philosophers, unless we're specifically in a psychological (not philosophical) context, which is not the context of these lectures. Plato was passionately concerned with value questions. He thought that what had been done to Socrates was vicious and evil—the death by hemlock—and that there was something fundamentally wrong with Athens and that it had to be reorganized politically. He thought the Sophists were depraved. But he was also fascinated by mathematics, by questions about the nature of the universe, and I defy anybody to say that one interest was greater than the other, and this is what gave rise to his views, and as I said, I don't see the relevance.

Q: You said that Socrates was the first philosophic martyr. Could you tell us about some others?

A: Well, that's anecdotal history, not philosophy. Aristotle came close to being one, only he, having a very different philosophy from Socrates, wouldn't let it happen. In fact, he deliberately fled Athens at a time when he knew he was going to be persecuted, and rather than submit to the will of the people, his famous line is: "I'm not going to give the Athenians the chance to sin against philosophy twice." Galileo is very close to being a martyr, having been forced to recant his view, and you know the famous story that after he got up from his recantation officially regarding whether the earth moves around the sun, he whispered, or is alleged to have whispered, "But it *does* move, it *does* turn." But he whispered it, which is perfectly justifiable. I mean, he'd have to have been crazy to yell it aloud at a time when he'd be burned at the stake. Spinoza is a perfect example of a philosophic martyr—the only famous major Jewish philosopher in the history of Western thought, who was formally excommunicated by the Jews of his time (I don't regard Marx as a serious philosopher) on the grounds that he was an atheist. Which in fact, in his special Spinozistic way, he was and wasn't. He is simultaneously an atheist and the most religious man in the history of thought (but we'll get to that when we get to him). But he certainly was made to go through hell for his views. There were many others.

Q: According to Plato, what is the status of mythical concepts, concepts that have no actual embodiments in this world?

A: "Santa Claus" is a proper name, so that's not a concept. But suppose you say "unicorn," or "centaur" or something that could have many instances. An individual can't exist in the other world; only universals can. What is their status? Yes, they are universals that exist in the other world. There is centaur-hood, and unicorn-ness, and all the rest of it. There's even square-circle-hood, according to many Platonists, on the grounds that we can think of those things. If we can think of those things, there must be something; we can't think about what is not. And since they don't exist here, they must exist in Plato's world of Forms. In a late dialogue, the *Parmenides*, Plato raised the question of what kind of universals are there. He has Socrates as his mouthpiece. And he was disturbed by the question because it seemed that there had to be all kinds of universals that he didn't care to have in his perfect world. For instance, there had to be universals of evil—there had to be perfect rotten-ness, because rotten-ness is a universal—and Plato was disturbed at the idea that there had to be all these corrupt things, in their perfect form, in the other world, but by the logic of his argument, there have to be. Also, he didn't very much like the idea that there must be universals of mud, universal dirt, universal toenails, and he has Socrates say at this point in the dialogue that he feels he's being driven into absurdity, and yet he doesn't know what to do with it. And one of the speakers in the dialogue, Parmenides, reassures Socrates and says that he's disturbed by those things only because he's still young, and when he grows older, the implication is that he will accept with equanimity the complete assortment of things in the other world and not be disturbed by it. So, Plato himself was in debate. But his followers made it all-embracing—there are witches up there, and fairies, and everything.

Q: What is Plato's empty space filled with, if not with matter?

A: Well, technically, Plato's empty space is not matter, but an *ingredient* of matter. Matter is the union of empty space with the Forms. However, you could look at it from this point of view: If you ask Plato what is the essence of matter (since he believes that all the secondary qualities, i.e., colors, sounds, tastes, etc., are subjective in the same way that Democritus and the Atomists believed), all that's left for matter to have is the quantitative characteristics (extension and three dimensions). Extension and three dimensions are precisely what space is. And therefore, it's very common for advocates for the Democritean view to hold that matter is only quantitative, to reduce matter to space, and say that, therefore, out there in the real world, there's only space. And you can find that in Plato since he subscribes to that dichotomy. Now, that has the effect of dissolving the physical world altogether into nothing, and it's another reason why that dichotomy between the primary and the secondary qualities is disastrous. But you can find it in Plato.

Q: If Pythagoras's influence is responsible for the premise that only quantitative statements can be scientific, is it not also then Pythagoras's influence that gives rise to the outright philosophical mysticism and irrationalism of thinkers in the abstract sciences?

A: I don't know quite what you call "abstract." Do you mean *mathematical* sciences? It certainly is significantly Pythagoras's influence that mathematicians have such a tendency to otherworldliness and mysticism. That is pronounced among particularly modern mathematicians. They believe their axioms have no relationship to reality, their concepts have no relation to observation, that they start off in their own little world of numbers, except that they don't believe that there's a *real* world of numbers that they're trying to learn, that they make it up as they go along according to their whim. They're kind of the union of Pythagoras and the Sophists—man is the measure of all numbers, numbers are as they are, etc.—that's modern mathematics, and it's kind of subjectivist Pythagoreanism. Would I hold Pythagoras responsible? Ultimately, he's the first, but there's a long, long chain in between, certainly including Plato and the centuries of Christianity and Descartes and Leibniz and Kant and then Hegel, so Pythagoras is comparatively innocent.

Q: Are philosophical psychology and epistemology synonyms?

A: No. Philosophical psychology, in the sense that I used it in this course, is the philosophic theory of the nature of man, his basic nature. And it includes questions such as: Does man have free will, or is he determined? Is he motivated by purpose, or is he simply a mechanistic being? Are emotions basically opposite to reason, or is there some relationship between the two? All of those questions, in a way, are really resolved in metaphysics and epistemology, so "philosophical psychology," as we use the term in this course, is the application to the theory of man of your conclusions in metaphysics and epistemology. It's not really a separate subject, just a convenient pedagogical device. Epistemology is specifically the theory of the nature and means of knowledge. It will have an effect on your view of man but is not exactly the same thing. It will have a *crucial* effect—if you say that reason is impotent, that's a Sophist view of man (or some equivalent). But that doesn't mean that it's exactly the same thing.

Q: How does Plato account for the fact that particular men are not omniscient, if all men are born knowing everything?

A: Partly because the knowledge is born in your unconscious, and therefore, a complex process is required to dig it out. It doesn't surface by itself. That's Plato's epistemology, how you acquire this knowledge and make it real, and that we'll look at next lecture. But the point is that a complex process is required; it doesn't just pop up by itself. And it's a process of such a nature that if you are interested in the physical world and physical pleasure, you won't perform it. You'll turn away from that process and instead concentrate on money and sex and things like that, and so you'll remain ignorant all your life. But if you follow Plato's epistemology and ethics, you will one day hit the jackpot and know everything.

Q: Are there any non-mechanistic materialists, or non-materialistic mechanists?

A: Let's take it one at a time. Are there any non-mechanistic materialists? Yes, the Marxists. The Marxists are *dialectic* materialists, not mechanistic materialists. As materialists, they agree that reality is essentially matter in motion. But as dialectic advocates, they do not believe that the laws controlling the development of matter are the good old-fashioned laws of Galilean mechanics and Newtonian mechanics. They believe that the laws controlling the entire world are Hegel's dialectic triad—something happens, and then the opposite, and then the two blend which gives rise to a new opposite, and so on, and reality waltzes to destiny. That's a very different type of materialism; it's not mechanistic materialism. Are there non-materialistic mechanists? I can't imagine what they would consist of. If mechanism is the view that everything operates according to the laws of mechanics, I don't know what else would obey the laws of mechanics other than material things. And if everything occupies that wave, then presumably everything is material, so I can't imagine it in reverse.

Q: Is mechanism valid in physics?

A: If all you mean by "mechanism" is "the denial of teleology as applied to inanimate nature," then I would say yes. In other words, Objectivism does not subscribe to the idea that the inanimate world is animated by purpose. It holds that purpose is coextensive with consciousness, and is therefore possible, at most, to the animals, and primarily in the form of a conceptually directed goal, to man. In this broad respect, Objectivism would subscribe to mechanism in physics. However, as soon as you become more specific and you mean by "mechanism" Galileo's laws or Newton's laws or Einstein's laws, or whatever a particular scientist tells you about the principles by which matter operates, that is a question for science, not philosophy.

LECTURE THREE

The Results in This World

In the previous lecture, I presented the essence and the base of Plato's metaphysics, but not yet the climax of it, to say nothing of the rest of his philosophy—his epistemology, his psychology, ethics, politics. That is now our assignment.

As to the climax of Plato's metaphysics, I'll begin with an excursion into the world of Forms, to find out something about the characteristics of true reality.

The first thing to know is that the Forms, according to Plato, are not a disconnected grab bag of universals. It's not as though you have a motley collection of banana-ness, subway-hood, justice, etc., without interrelationships. The fact is, the Forms are all connected by various logical relationships. They are bound together into one integrated system. And indeed, says Plato, every scientific law, every mathematical theorem is merely a statement of how certain specific Forms are logically interconnected. If I say, for instance, "The sum of the angles of a triangle is 180 degrees," that is not a statement about any one particular triangle; it is a statement about triangularity, triangularity as such. And it says that triangularity is intrinsically connected with 180-degree-hood, an unavoidable logical tie. Or if I say, "All men are mortal," again, I am talking about man as such, and I am saying that manness by its very nature entails mortality as such. And so for any universal law or principle we can state.

For Plato, the sciences are attempts to discover the structure of the world of Forms, attempts to show the order or organization or connection uniting the various Forms. How do the sciences do it? Each science, says Plato, starts with certain basic premises, certain basic statements of how the Forms in its particular field are related. And it proceeds to deduce a whole host of consequences from these basic premises. Each science, in this sense, is a description of some part of the world of Forms. This is obvious in the case of mathematics—it starts with certain premises, and then deduces its consequences. It's true of ethics—you must start somewhere, with some basic premises, and then deduce your whole system. It's true of physics—whatever theory of physics you have, it begins somewhere with your physical axioms, and then deduces the consequences.

Every individual science assumes certain relationships among certain Forms, and then deduces the consequences.

This poses a problem, says Plato: Unless we can validate the basic premises in each science, all of our knowledge remains hypothetical. All of our science is reduced to the level of assumption. It's on the order "*If* the premises are true, *then* everything we deduce from it is true," but how do we know the premises are true? In each field, we need *true* axioms. Which means, says Plato, we need some foundation point from which we can deduce the axioms of the various individual sciences.

Just imagine that you could find one fundamental Form, one that was self-intelligible, or self-luminous—in other words, you need no explanation of it, you need no proof of it—once you grasp it, once you mentally come in contact with it, by that act you understand what it is and why it must exist. And now suppose, says Plato, that having grasped this one Form, we could see that absolutely everything else followed from it. We could deduce from it all of the axioms of all of the individual sciences. Well, says Plato, if we could do that, we would have put every science on absolutely firm ground. And in addition, we would have achieved a marvelous result of intellectual unity. Instead of having psychologists talk their language, and moralists talk theirs, and physicists talk theirs, all in a splintered, unconnected, disintegrated, and often contradictory form, we would have tied all the areas of human knowledge together into one whole by deducing the basis of each separate science from one fundamental principle. After all, says Plato, we live in one integrated universe. There must, therefore, be one ultimate principle from which everything else follows.

It's crucial to find this, so we are embarked again on a quest for the one in the many. But now the whole quest is transferred to the world of Forms—we are looking for the one supreme Form uniting the many Forms. Plato believed there was one such Form, the ultimate axiom from which everything else follows—indeed, if you grasp it, you are truly omniscient, because you grasp all the other Forms, and, since this world is just the reflection in space of the other world of Forms, you would therefore (insofar as this world is intelligible at all) have understood everything there is to know about it. You would have explained the total of existence on every level if you grasped this Form.

Plato's reality can therefore be analogically compared to a pyramid, but what we are looking for now is the apex, the climax, the jackpot: the ultimate key to reality. Of course, Plato gives no argument to prove that the supreme Form must be single in nature, that there must be only one.

On this point, he is simply reflecting the monism that was characteristic of most of Greek philosophy. It's another reflection of the Greek desire to reduce the many to the one, otherworldly Form.

What could be the nature of this fundamental Form? We know it is to explain the entire universe. It's to be the explanation of everything. That raises the question: What do you take as an explanation? And Plato has a firm answer to that question. Plato is a thorough teleologist. Remember that I defined "teleology" as the view that purpose is operative somewhere in the universe, and perhaps in the universe as a whole (there are various forms of teleology, and it is contrasted with mechanism, the view that everything happens by mechanical law, devoid of purpose, à la the Atomist viewpoint). Plato is a universal teleologist. He believes that *every* event in the universe has to be explained in terms of the purpose it serves, in terms of something the events of the world are striving to accomplish, in terms of goals, of ends, of a good of some kind that everything is aiming at. Plato regards the Atomists as completely wrong in their concept of what constitutes an explanation. The Atomists, he says, at best tell us *how* things happen. They tell us that under these circumstances, this is the way the particles of matter jostle—these are the *descriptive* laws that characterize the actual behavior of the physical world. The Atomists merely describe, says Plato. And that's true of any mechanist, he says. If we want to know *why*, and not just *how*—if we want *explanation*, and not just description—it must be in terms of purpose, and "purpose" means some good that everything is aiming at.

On the human level, this is obvious. If Bobby Fischer makes a move in chess, no amount of mechanistic explanation will explain it. You can talk about the quivering of his cortex until you're blue in the face, but you will not capture the *reason* he made that move, as apart from his motive, the goal he was aiming at (namely, to defeat Boris Spassky). Plato adopts this pattern of explanation for the entire universe. That is an unjustified overgeneralization, but he does it, nevertheless. As he sees it, the alternative is atomistic mechanism across the board versus teleology across the board, and he takes the latter. Consequently, he called the ultimate Form "the Form of the Good," since the good is that which everything is aiming at. Another word for it is "goodness," and therefore the expression "Goodness gracious" is pure Platonism.

What are the functions of the Form of the Good? It has two fundamental functions in Plato, one metaphysical, one epistemological. Metaphysically, it is the purpose of all existence, the purpose of the universe. Epistemologically, it is *the* single axiom of all knowledge. Metaphysically, to restate, it is the source of existence; it's what makes all of reality possible. On a teleological model of the universe, if you removed the purpose, you would remove everything that exists to serve the purpose. If Fischer did not have any purpose, he would not play the chess game; it couldn't exist. Similarly, if you hold that the entire universe exists to serve a purpose, if you remove the purpose, the whole universe would vanish. In that sense of the term, the Form of the Good for Plato is the source of all existence. And epistemologically, as a result, it is the source of all intelligibility. It's what makes anything understandable because it's the thing that leads to the axioms of the sciences and all the way down. Short of reaching the Form of the Good intellectually, reality remains a mystery to us—we wouldn't understand why.

In this respect, the Form of the Good performs for Plato a function enormously similar to the function that God performed for later Christian philosophy. God, for Christianity, is the source of reality, and the ultimate source of intelligibility. Until you grasp him and, in Christian terms, "his plan," you cannot make any sense of the universe. In this respect, Christianity took over Plato's view.

But Plato's Form of the Good is not yet itself a god. It is, remember, a universal—impersonal, unconscious—it is abstract universal goodness. It has no plan, no will, no awareness; it just exists in the world of Forms, and everything strives for it. To get God out of Plato's Form of the Good, you have to do two things—drop an "o," and add a personality (which was very shortly done).

Plato himself compares the Form of the Good (in an analogy only) to the sun because, he says, the sun, in a certain sense, enables everything to exist on earth. At least it enables living things to exist by providing the heat and the life sustenance that is required; otherwise, the earth would turn cold and die, and in that loose analogical sense, it enables the earth to exist; and, epistemologically, the sun makes everything visible (this is in the age prior to Thomas Edison), and without it, the whole world would be black, and no one could have any awareness of it. In that same sense, the Form of the Good now has these two functions applied to the entire universe.

The most urgent philosophic question will be "What is the Good?" We have to know it to understand anything, to make the universe intelligible. What is Plato's answer? What is the nature of the Good? What is the ultimate purpose of everything? Unfortunately, I can't tell you. I can't tell you because Plato held the view that his deepest thoughts should not be put in writing. He held that the Form of the Good is *ineffable*—"ineffable" is a technical philosophic term meaning "outside the power of human conceptualization, beyond human language, logic, discussion, concepts." To grasp the Form of the Good, you do not do any intellectualizing; you must transcend the intellect and have an intuition, or a vision—a vision that, when you have it, is completely, blindingly self-illuminating, and which, if you don't have it, there is nothing anyone can say to you. To those who understand, no explanation is necessary; to those who do not understand, no explanation is possible. In either case, we don't explain it.

This is mysticism, *technical* mysticism (mysticism being the view that knowledge is attainable by means other than reason or the senses). And in this respect, Plato is the father of mysticism in Western philosophy. As the course proceeds, you will see the extent of his following if you don't already know it. I should say that Plato himself believed that there was a definite course of action that you should take to have this special vision. Although he couldn't tell you what the vision was like, he could tell you the necessary steps to attain it, and he outlines them in detail. It amounts to a rigorous period of essentially mathematical training, stretching across decades and becoming progressively more abstract. Plato felt that mathematics was very valuable because the more you engage in higher mathematics, the more tenuous your tie to the physical world becomes, and at a certain point you cut your ties altogether, and at that point you are free to go on to the Form of the Good. You can see the mathematical influence of the Pythagorean mathematical mysticism on Plato.

To sum up Plato's metaphysics: There is a world of Forms presided over by the Form of the Good, all of it reflected into space, thereby generating this half-real reflection that we call the physical world, and if we're not Platonists, we mistakenly call it reality.

Now let us turn more systematically to Plato's epistemology. I said previously that one main purpose of Plato's philosophy was to answer the Sophists, to show that objective knowledge is possible. But here we immediately have a question—how can we ever come to know the Forms? After all, they constitute a completely different world—a nonmaterial world, and as such, not in space, not in time—and yet here are we on earth, limited by our bodies and our senses. How are we ever to come in contact with them? Plato's answer: by thought. But the question is: How does thought down here ever come in contact with the Forms up there? Keep in mind that "up" and "down" are here just metaphors because the Forms aren't anywhere; they're not spatial. We have already touched on the answer to this. We proved, at least in Plato's opinion, that we must have been in contact with the world of Forms prior to this life. We must have lived in the world of Forms in a preceding life. And Plato believes that he's proved that, and therefore adopts intact the whole Orphic/Pythagorean view, with the wheel of birth and successive reincarnations—the ultimate goal being escape. But in any event, our souls knew all the Forms, and therefore all the laws, and therefore our soul was actually omniscient prior to its birth in this world. When, however, it was immersed in the body and thrust into the Heraclitean flux, it had what modern psychologists would call "a birth trauma." And the effect is that the soul forgot all the things that it knew. Put in modern terms, all that knowledge descended into the unconscious. But it is still there, still in us, still real. What we call "acquiring knowledge," says Plato, is really not acquiring *new* knowledge at all; it is a process of digging out from your subconscious or unconscious what is already there.

This is Plato's famous theory of knowledge as reminiscence (*anamnesis* in Greek). Therefore, for Plato, there is definitely innate knowledge, knowledge born in us. The senses, the physical senses, are not means of getting new knowledge of reality. What then is their function? Does Plato believe that if you took a young baby and mutilated his senses, he would then be able to go along merrily and still remember the Forms? No. Plato says that we definitely need the senses in the early stages of knowledge. Not to teach us something new but to serve as a stimulus—to jog our memories. The best analogy you can think of (the one I was taught when I was first taught Plato) is this: Imagine that twenty or thirty or forty years after you have left college, you come across an old, faded yearbook with pictures of your classmates, and your grandson is busily jostling back and forth, so you get only a fleeting glimpse of a faded photograph. If you didn't know the man in the photograph from twenty, thirty, forty years back, you'd never get anything from that little stimulus. But given that you knew the man well, even if you have forgotten him completely, that corrupt, imperfect, flickering stimulus is enough to remind you; you say, "Oh, yes, Jones, I remember him, I haven't thought of him for years." For Plato, in essence, that's true of all knowledge. You see a few horses and you say, "Ah, yes, horse-ness, now it comes back to me." But after an initial period of thus stimulating your memories, knowledge thereafter is a matter of looking *inward,* not of looking outward. It is a matter of turning away from the world, of *introspection.* Because, we have in us all the basic truths and laws and concepts, and what we do is look in, find them, and proceed to deduce their consequences logically, quite apart from any further sensory observation.

This view of knowledge is called *rationalism.* And with Plato we have a fully worked out answer to the question that has been asked several times: *How* does reason operate if it doesn't base itself on sensory data? Heraclitus and Parmenides and those early figures were rationalists, but if you had asked them that question, they had no answer. Plato has an answer. His answer is that reason is capable of acquiring knowledge apart from the senses because we are born with innate ideas.

From the time of Plato on, "rationalism" acquires a fuller definition. It becomes the epistemological theory that knowledge is acquirable solely by reasoning from innate concepts, and that sense perception is, in principle, dispensable (except as a stimulus). It's called "rationalism" because Plato called the faculty that studied universals "reason." It's the idea that reason alone can give you knowledge, apart from the senses. I should say for accuracy that this definition of "rationalism" holds true descriptively of philosophers in this camp up to the eighteenth century, at which time Kant introduced a quite different version of rationalism, a variation on Plato, but nevertheless a significantly different one. From the eighteenth century to the present, rationalism is quite different and does not accept innate ideas.

What proof does Plato offer for innate ideas? In general, there is only one argument in favor of innate ideas, and then it's a matter of all of the various forms of it. The general argument for innate ideas raised by Platonists, from Greece to the present, is: "We have a certain type of knowledge that we *could not* have acquired by sensory observation. But we have it. Therefore, it must have been acquired from somewhere else. We must have got it from some means apart from the senses. We must be born with it. It must be innate." And then the various sub-arguments under this are specifications of the *types* of knowledge which various philosophers feel could not have been acquired by experience. For instance, Plato himself mentions the knowledge of perfection. He mentions the argument from the *order* of knowledge, from man's ability to define and classify, which, in his opinion, presupposes that we knew universals prior to this life, and we couldn't have acquired them from sensory particulars. And he gives us several other equivalent arguments. One famous, although very weak, argument is given in the *Meno*, where Socrates says to a man who owns a slave: "Bring me your slave boy"—this boy is completely uneducated—"and I will show you that he possesses knowledge of complex geometric theorems that no one has ever taught him. I will elicit them from him by judicious questioning. Watch and see that I am not going to tell him anything, I'm merely going to question him." And sure enough, Socrates, by a series of questions (with nothing in the declarative form, everything interrogative), the boy at the end comes out with a complex geometric theorem. And Socrates draws the moral: "You see, he had it in him all the time; he just needed to be reminded of it." Needless to say, critics for centuries have said Socrates was feeding him information right and left and doing it in the form of questions. It's not as crude as the following, but what it amounts to is, "Don't you *see* that the angle sum of a triangle is 180 degrees?" and the slave boy says, "Yes, yes I do." So that is not very convincing, but it's famous, nevertheless.

In the *Phaedo*, Plato gives four proofs for the immortality of the soul. I mentioned one of them previously, i.e., that the soul must have existed prior to the body, and that is proof of the immortality of the soul (if it were valid), because if it could exist prior, it could just as well exist *after* the body, because the essential point in an immortality argument is to prove the *independence* of the soul from the body, and Plato would have done that. He gives three others in the *Phaedo*, but they are very poor arguments, so I will not take your time discussing them, except in the question period if you're interested.

In any case, he is convinced to his satisfaction that he has established the existence of innate ideas, and this becomes a challenge to Aristotle to explain how all knowledge is possible without innate ideas. And Aristotle accepts that challenge and proceeds to define for every category of knowledge that Plato said we *couldn't* get from experience, *how* you get it from experience, as we'll see when we get to Aristotle.

Let us continue with Plato's epistemology by giving you some detail on the steps you have to go through to recollect and reawaken all of your knowledge. You must, says Plato, pass through four stages on the road from ignorance to complete mastery of the entire universe. (I must amend that there is no real ignorance, but "ignorance" in quotes, the ignorance of a baby who doesn't remember anything.) He illustrates this by a famous divided line that has four segments, and you travel up the line through the four stages.

The first stage he calls the *state of imagining*. This is the stage in which you are wholly ignorant, confused, and unenlightened. As far as cognition is concerned, you take all superficial appearances at face value. For Plato, you are, in effect, a baby, for this is the stage where babies begin: You do not distinguish between dreams and physical things. If you dream that somebody hit you, you wake up mad at them, because you take the dream and the physical thing as interchangeable. You look in a mirror and you see an image or reflection or shadow of yourself, and you think it's another person; you can't even tell the distinction between images and physical things. In other words, you are being bombarded with an unidentified stream of sensations. The moral counterpart of this first level of imagining is where you accept anything that you want, any desire, utterly unthinking. This would represent the moral mentality of an animal (one that desires and goes out and gets what it wants, without any questions of right or wrong), or of a Sophist (who does the same thing as a matter of philosophic principle). This is the lowest mentality that there is.

The second stage is the *stage of belief*, or the *stage of opinion*. By this time, you've grown some years and have learned to distinguish some facts in regard to the physical world. You can now tell the difference between fact and fancy, between physical objects, on the one hand, and dreams or images, on the other hand. And you've even risen to the level where you've made a variety of scattered, empirical observations, and some crude, approximate, rough generalizations, on the order of empirical rules of thumb. At this stage, you do not know *why* any of these facts or generalizations hold true, and therefore, you have no capacity to be certain that they will continue to hold true. For instance, you've observed that if you follow any given man around long enough, he drops dead, but you have no idea *why* all men are mortal—that just happens to be a brute observation. Or if you went in for specializing in triangles, you kept measuring them and their angle sum kept coming out to be 180, but as far as you know, the next one might be 179 or 250? So, you have a certain degree of probability here, but not true knowledge. And that is why Plato calls this the "stage of belief"—you *believe* certain things, but you don't yet know them. And there are other reasons why you don't have knowledge yet at this stage: You're using your senses to study physical objects, and, of course, they're not real, they're contradictory, they're in flux, they can't be known, and the senses are invalid. So, for all those reasons, we have only *belief* at this particular state. The moral counterpart on this particular level would be the average man, who has absorbed a certain set of rules—you shouldn't kill, you shouldn't cheat, you shouldn't tell lies—but he couldn't for the life of him say why, or prove that they're universal, or in what context they're universal. They're just rough and ready common-sense rules of thumb. Notice that your opinion, or your belief (Plato uses the two synonymously), might be right, and it might be wrong. But even if it's right, it's still just an opinion, a belief; it isn't yet knowledge.

Stage three, going up the line, is the stage he calls *thinking*. That's the point, the stage, where science begins. Which means, having gone through the stimuli of the preceding stages, we now are able to turn away from the physical world, the sensible world, altogether, and focus our attention on the Forms—individual, separate Forms at first, in this particular stage. And the crucial thing we find is that every time we grasp any one Form, it illuminates and makes intelligible everything that we had observed on the preceding levels. As soon as we grasp a Form, that explains *why* the rules that we have empirically observed are true.

This is true of every level—every stage explains the preceding stage. We can illustrate this by imagining for a moment that for some fantastic reason, you wanted to study the shadows of a particular physical horse. And you never had seen the horse; you were watching its reflections in a pond, and you decided to study them. You could learn something by studying the shadows; they might follow a certain progression in a certain order, and you might be able to tell that this is obviously not a banana that's involved here, and so on. But you couldn't learn very much. And whatever you learned would be just a series of brute observations—the shadows move this way and this way, but *why* they do, you don't know. What makes it possible for you even to study the shadows? The fact that there is a real physical horse. Suppose that you turn around and see the real horse after years spent studying the shadows, you would say, "Aha, this makes sense of it all; now I see what all these shadows were doing, and why they were doing what they were doing." The higher level illuminates and explains the lower. That is exactly true of the third level in relation to the second, but on the third level, you discover horse-ness, and when you get to it and you grasp the abstract nature of horses as such, then everything you observed about particular physical horses now falls into place and you see how it follows from the very nature of horse-hood.

If you want an example of the three stages, a baby would be the example of stage one—he doesn't know anything about horses; he can't tell a physical horse from a merry-go-round horse. The second stage would be a racing fan, who has discovered that certain horses are good mudders and others aren't and so on, but he couldn't explain why, and therefore it's just probability. And the third stage would be the theoretical biologist (or, if you wanted a science of horses, the hippologist), and he would deduce from the very *nature* of horse all the preceding rules. Or, with regard to mechanical phenomena, the first stage would be the layman who is completely ignorant of mechanical things; the second would be a garage mechanic, who knows by rule-of-thumb experience that if you smack this particular thing the car will start, and if you pour oil in here it won't, but he doesn't know why; and the third stage would be the theoretical physicist, who could tell him the laws from which his particular empirical observations are deducible. On the moral level, the three stages would be:

the lowest stage, the Sophist; the second stage, the average man (who may have correct, but unexplained, beliefs); and the third stage, the moral philosopher, who explains the reasons behind those correct beliefs. The general principle is: The abstract, the universal, the general—always explains the particular, giving you the *reason* for the particular.

At this stage of thinking, or science, we are almost at the stage of certainty, but not yet. It's not yet true knowledge, for the reason that I mentioned at the outset, namely, we go only to a certain point and then we come against the blank wall of the axioms of the various sciences themselves at this stage, and they are not yet validated; they are just assumptions, so our whole structure is precarious and is not true knowledge. And thus we reach true knowledge, stage four, *true* knowledge, where we grasp the pinnacle, the Form of the Good, and at that point we are able to reason down the whole chain and show that everything we had discovered *ascending* follows deductively from the Form of the Good. At this point, we have true understanding of the universe. We've hit the epistemological jackpot. So, there are four stages and to each corresponds its appropriate type of object: (1) the stage of imagining, which has as its counterpart images—the man is lost in a world of images of a baby; (2) the stage of belief, which studies physical objects; (3) the stage of thinking, which studies the lower Forms; and (4) the stage of knowledge, which grasps the Good. Each stage makes the existence of the lower one possible. It gives you knowledge of why and thus illuminates the lower stage.

These four stages were illustrated by Plato in a famous parable, or allegory, which he invented. It's a marvelous story because it captures not just his epistemology and metaphysics, but the essence of the whole Platonic philosophy. And I don't believe that any course is ever given anywhere on Plato in which this story is not told, and so I want to take five minutes to tell it to you. It is called the Myth (or Allegory) of the Cave, and it is presented in *The Republic.*

Imagine, for instance, that you are all in a dark, dank, gloomy, underground cave, and imagine that you have been prisoners in this cave from the time of your birth. You cannot get up and move around, you're chained at the neck and the ankles, you can look only straight ahead at the wall in front of you. Behind you, unknown to you, there is a group of people that you've never seen, and they are carrying various objects, and behind them is a fire which casts the reflection of those objects onto the wall in front of you, so that you see only the moving shadows of those objects on the wall and are completely ignorant of the actual objects in the fire behind you. Now you, the prisoners of the cave, would necessarily take the shadows to be reality, because you've never seen or conceived of anything else. And consequently, you would attach great importance to proficiency in shadow detection. You would (I'm here elaborating slightly to make it more modern, but the idea is Plato's) give out your Ph.D.s to the man who was best able to detect the shadows, and you would make him the president of the country and heap honors upon the shadow experts because, after all, they are the ones who are the exponents of the ability to deal with reality as you see it.

Now, says Plato, let us release one of these prisoners. He's very stiff—he's been sitting there for years in chains and, therefore, it's painful. When we take him to the back, he has to shade his eyes at first because it's awfully bright back there with this big fire. However, at a certain point, his eyes become accustomed to it, and he says: "So this is what's really going on. I was just looking at shadows; all of us were deluded," and he is amazed, and we say to him, "You haven't seen anything yet."

We take him up the long sojourn to the surface of the earth, and he emerges from the underground tunnel, and he sees this fantastic new realm that he never even dreamed of. He is completely overwhelmed by the variety, the beauty, and so on, compared with the dingy, dark cave. This, he sees, is what's really real, and the cave world is just a meaningless appendage. Of course, he can't see very well at first. Because it's really blindingly bright, he has to keep his eyes down, but after a while he grows accustomed to the light and begins to wonder where all of this light is coming from And finally he looks up and sees the brilliant sun, the ultimate source of energy and life, which illumines everything, and he's reached the end of his journey. He wants nothing but to live up there in the world of beauty and sunlight, but he feels that it's his duty to return to the cave in order to enlighten his fellow prisoners and free them from their delusions. So, he starts back down. But he stumbles because he can't see very well now in the dark. But he makes his way back to the cave, and he finds the prisoners arguing excitedly about some shadow or other. And he rushes in and says: "Forget this nonsense. This is all shadows. I have seen *true* reality." And so, the prisoners say to him, "Well, what's it like?" And he says: "I can't tell you. It's incommunicable. You couldn't imagine it. You'd have to see it for yourself." Well, the prisoners are skeptical, and, if we update the myth, they give him a sanity test because they think he's crazy. And, since they define "sanity" as the ability to deal with reality (and thus with shadows), they measure his ability to deal with shadows, and since his eyes are not accustomed to the dark anymore, he does poorly and he fails and they put him to death (which is an obvious allusion to what the masses did to Socrates). In other words, they are hopelessly out of touch with reality.

That's the famous Myth of the Cave. And you see the meaning of it—the four stages, the shadows and the physical objects at the back correspond to the first two stages, imagining and belief, and the ascent to the surface of the earth corresponds to the ascent to the ascent to the world of Forms, and the sun is the stand-in for the Form of the Good. The people caught in the cave, who are doomed to believe that that is reality, are the masses of mankind. The few who can escape from the cave and see the true reality are the philosophers (needless to say, the *Platonic* philosophers, not the Sophistic ones).

What does it illustrate? On Plato's view, knowledge requires you to leave this world, to turn your intellect away from the physical, to reorient your whole soul, disposition and interests, to leave the half-real shadow kingdom—if you want knowledge, it is not of this world. Another point it illustrates: The crucial and final knowledge required is to reach the Form of the Good. Until you know that, you cannot organize your knowledge into an understandable vision of reality, and therefore, you have no way of knowing how to live a proper life, because you don't know what is the good, what is it all for, what is the purpose of it. You can't make sense of anything without that knowledge of the good, and therefore, your actions are hit and miss, chance, self-defeating and self-destructive. Notice also that it is a painful process. It's difficult, because of the constant physical pain in adjusting to the light. It's difficult because to grasp that, you have to turn away from everything familiar—from the senses, from the physical—and achieve a vision, which takes years and years of more and more abstract preparation. The result is that most men never reach it; they never learn about even the world of Forms, let alone the Form of the Good. They spend their lives in the shadows.

Now, exercise your ingenuity and predict the political implications of this viewpoint. Just ask yourself if the crucial knowledge needed to live is painful, difficult, incommunicable—if you require a mystical insight that only a very few will ever be able to achieve—then who is going to be qualified to tell men how to live their lives and govern their political affairs? Only those few. This is the epistemological base of Plato's politics. And it is the first instance of an invariant law of philosophy: Mysticism leads to dictatorship.

If an opponent of Plato were to say to him: "I don't believe in your world of Forms. I believe in physical objects that I can see and hear and taste and so on, and that's what I take as real," a true Platonist would say that that answer gives away everything; that answer is the proof that you are one of the ignorant masses caught in the cave, and that it is therefore hopeless to try to reason with you. But you don't have to worry, because the sojourner from the cave promises to come back down and give you all the guidance you need. That is the essence of Plato's metaphysics and epistemology.

Before we turn to his ethics, you can see from the Myth of the Cave the general direction that Plato's ethics will take. What will be the goal of the moral man? Obviously, to escape from the cave, to reach the higher world of beauty, truth, and sunlight. His attitude to the cave (i.e., to this world) will be disdain, dislike, a yearning to get out. How, in actual life, does a man escape from this world? His body is doomed to remain in this world—it's physical, it's part of the sensible world. Only his soul can go to the to the world of Forms. And this it does, *when the man dies*. And consequently, the ultimate goal of such an ethics is *death*, in other words, escape from this world, the freeing of the soul from the body, the shadows, and the imperfections.

You may think that I am reading something into Plato, implicitly criticizing him from the framework of the Objectivist ethics, so I quote you a passage from the *Phaedo* (this is Socrates speaking, representing Plato's view):

> Ordinary people seem not to realize that those who really apply themselves in the right way to philosophy are directly and of their own accord preparing themselves for dying and death. If this is true, and they have actually been looking forward to death all their lives, it would of course be absurd to be troubled when the thing comes for which they have so long been preparing and looking forward. If a man has trained himself throughout his life to live in a state as close as possible to death, would it not be ridiculous for him to be distressed when death comes to him? It is a fact that true philosophers make dying their profession.

You may ask, why not commit suicide? And Plato's answer is the same as the Orphics before him and the Christians after him: They create this world, this other world, which they regard as magnificent, but after all, if you exhort your followers to suicide, it is very difficult to have a mass movement. So, suicide is prohibited. God giveth, God taketh away is the idea.

Nevertheless, what you *can* do during life is free the soul as much as possible from domination by the body. In other words, live an *ascetic* life. Here's another brief excerpt from the *Phaedo*, a conversation between Socrates and another philosopher:

> "Do you think that it is right for a philosopher to concern himself with the so-called pleasures of food and drink?"
>
> "Certainly not, Socrates."
>
> "What about sexual pleasures?"
>
> "No, not at all."
>
> "And what about the other attentions that we pay to our bodies? Do you think that a philosopher attaches any importance to them? I mean things like providing himself with smart clothes and shoes and other bodily ornaments. Do you think that he values them or despises them, insofar as there is no real necessity for him to go into that sort of thing?"
>
> "I think the true philosopher despises them."
>
> "Then it is your opinion in general that a man of this kind is not concerned with the body, but keeps his attention directed as much as he can away from it and towards the soul?"
>
> "Yes, it is."
>
> "So, it is clear in the case of physical pleasures that the philosopher frees his soul from association with the body, so far as it's possible, to a greater extent than other men."

Plato has a legion of followers on this point, stretching all the way from the early Christians to the hippies: In their anti-materialism right down to their attitudes to their own bodies and to the clothes they wear, their basic attitude is Platonic. (They do not, however, apply it to sex in the way that Plato recommended.) And I should say on Plato's behalf that he was much neater. And I should also point out that the hippies do it on the same metaphysical-epistemological base as Plato, from whom they got it (although they actually got it directly from the comic strips, but ultimately from Plato)—namely, the idea that there is another reality that transcends this one, and that you grasp it by mystic vision. However, they represent a new modern version of mysticism, in which the key to the mystic vision is not forty years of higher mathematics but one dose of LSD. That, however, is simply the transformation of mathematics into chemistry as the supreme key. That does not alter the philosophy involved.

You see here an exact parallel that Plato explicitly draws in his epistemology and his ethics. In epistemology, the bodily senses deceive us; true knowledge comes from pure reason itself, severed from the physical. Just as the bodily senses deceive us in epistemology, so the bodily desires corrupt us in ethics. And true virtue lies in being anti-physical. So, both knowledge and virtue require leaving the cave (in other words, leaving this world). And you see here the Pythagorean–Orphic influence on Plato. I remind you that Plato is a Greek, and he is not fully consistent; certain of his dialogues are much more this-worldly, insofar as he writes qua Greek. Greece was too healthy a civilization to produce anything such as the aberrations that came when Christianity took over.

Let's now look more systematically at Plato's ethics, having laid the overall foundations. But first I want to backtrack in time for a moment and say a few words about Socrates's views on ethics. Socrates was Plato's teacher, and he developed certain ethical views of his own (rather generalized, but still very important), and they were subsequently taken up and developed by Plato and, in a different way, also by Aristotle. I will not give you a full presentation of Socrates's views but will concentrate on those that are essentially valid, mentioning an occasional error but not focusing on it.

Socrates was a champion of an absolute, objective, universal code of ethical principles. An arch opponent of the Sophists, he believed that ethics was a science, not a matter of feelings and impulses. Although he never worked out a full system of ethics, he had leads to it. Perhaps his most important lead was the parallel that he was fond of drawing between the soul and the body. Consider for a moment the body—it obviously has a definite nature, and there are, therefore, definite conditions that have to be fulfilled to keep it healthy. And there are definite sciences, whose function is to determine those conditions. There are, in the Greek world, gymnastics (the method of taking care of and exercising the body and keeping it healthy) and medicine (the method of curing its various ailments). There are certain options—you can do sit-ups or pushups, for instance, or eat one kind of food with so and so many vitamins, or another kind which has the same number—there are options, but the *principles* of bodily care are mandatory and not optional. If you disobey them, you have a diseased, sick body. Certain things may give you temporary pleasure—for instance, dope—but there is, nevertheless, an objective basis for declaring that these things are wrong, because they subvert the life of the individual by destroying his body. And the result is that after a few flickers of pleasure, we have the ravaged dope addict, the alcoholic with DTs, and so on. The general rule is: Definite physical conditions have to be met to achieve physical health and, therefore, true bodily welfare, and this requires that you tend to your body scientifically—to exercise reason and self-control, as against acting on any whim or urge you get.

For Socrates (and he was the first to emphasize this), the same is true of the soul, and by the soul, we mean the psychological, or spiritual, element in man. The soul has a definite nature, and there are definite conditions required for *it* to be healthy, universal conditions deriving from the nature of the soul. In modern terms we don't talk about an unhealthy soul, but we recognize the phenomenon he was referring to—we talk about a tortured neurotic, a man who is anxious, guilty, depressed, self-doubtful, torn by conflict, etc. That's what Socrates would call a "sick soul." And you must live a certain way if you are to have a healthy soul, as proved by the fact that there are such things as sick souls. You have to live *virtuously*, so you must understand what the Greeks meant by "virtue": They meant "excellent performance of function," whatever the function happens to be. If the function of a knife is to cut, then a sharp knife is a virtuous knife, a knife with the power to perform its function. A virtuous man, therefore, is a man who performs *his* function correctly, and looks after his soul accordingly. You mustn't associate virtue, as used by any of the Greeks, with the meaning it came to have under Christianity. "Virtue," the actual word that we use, is the same root as "virility," and *vir* is Latin for "man." As someone once pointed out, it's a fascinating commentary on the development of civilization that the word "virtue" passed from meaning the manliness in a man, to chastity in a woman. That is the legacy of Christianity.

Ethics, for Socrates, is the science of achieving health in the soul. It is on the level of the soul what gymnastics and medicine are on the level of the body. And therefore, there are objective, absolute principles in ethics, just as there are in the case of the body. If you follow them, you will achieve happiness. But Socrates insists—and Plato and Aristotle agree with him—that there are definite conditions imposed on human nature for the achievement of happiness. It is not, they all insist, a matter of acting on any desire you happen to have. Happiness has objective, universal conditions. Today it's a bromide that people can achieve happiness anyway they choose, that it's arbitrary and subjective, but the Greeks are right (not the Sophist Greeks, but the main line, from Socrates on). It is not true that the way to achieve happiness is to have any arbitrary desire and then satisfy it. The proof of that is endless. Without the right psychological conditions, you can have a passion for money and acquire it and end up a miserable Park Avenue neurotic, or a passion for fame and acquire it, and end up a movie star on a Beverly Hills couch in psychotherapy forever, or a passion for love and acquire it, and end up one of those self-doubting neurotics who feels that he's a fraud and worthless and the love makes him feel worse. Socrates is right: Misery is the consequence of a diseased, or unvirtuous, or unjust soul. Along with the Greeks, in general, he demands proof when you say about a man, "He's happy." They take that as an achievement because it means he is a completely moral man. They do not sling the term "happiness" the way the moderns do. And therefore, if somebody tells three jokes at a party and gets roaring drunk, they do not say he is happy; they say he is having a temporary titillation. And they clearly distinguish—there are two different Greek words, one meaning "pleasure," one meaning "happiness"—"pleasure" is *hedone*, from which we get "hedonism," and "happiness" is *eudaimonia*, which is the much broader term, encompassing the whole condition of the soul.

It follows from Socrates's view that no man can really be harmed by anybody else, and he says this because, in the basic sense, the crucial determinant of his soul and of his state is up to him, how he conducts himself; nobody can make you unhappy in this fundamental sense. Here we must distinguish, as he did, between what we can call "inner" and "outer happiness"—the external conditions (how people treat you) and your inner state. As Plato depicts him, Socrates is a man of inner tranquility, peace of mind, serenity—he has a healthy soul. If true, other people can defame him, rob him, even kill him, but in this deep sense they cannot get to him, they can't destroy his inner serenity. And conversely, others cannot *give* you happiness in any basic sense; they can give you money, fame, love, etc., but not the inner harmony or health that makes them enjoyable. I should say that "ideally," for the Greeks, it's nice to have both, the inner and the outer, but the crucial thing is the inner, because that's what determines your whole direction. The crucial thing is to have a healthy soul. Not just life, but the good life. Never to commit injustice no matter what, never to commit evil, because evil is like poison, in a literal sense—it brings only suffering and self-destruction in its wake. That's the substance of the Socratic contribution to ethics.

There's one more crucial Socratic point, and that is that virtue requires *knowledge*, in the same way that medicine or architecture or any practical art requires knowledge. It is a very common device for Socrates to draw a parallel between the various practical arts and ethics, the art of living. It requires knowledge, knowledge of the proper end and of the means to it. And thus, Socrates's famous principle, "Virtue is knowledge." What exactly did he mean by that? As far as we can judge, he meant two quite different things, one of them I would say is correct, the other false, both package-dealt together in this famous statement. The first is that knowledge is a *necessary* condition of virtue—knowledge of what is required for the health of the soul. This is obviously correct, and there's an exact parallel, for instance, to architecture—if you don't have any knowledge, you will not be able to build sensibly; it would be a matter of chance, and your building nine chances out of ten will collapse (if you even get it up). For Socrates, the same thing is true of the art of living—if you do not know the principles by which to live, you are going to have a life that collapses. That's point one under "Virtue is knowledge." Apparently, however, Socrates *also* believed a second point under this formula, namely, that knowledge is a *sufficient* condition of virtue. In other words, that if you know what is right, you will automatically and necessarily do it. You have no choice about it. There is no such thing as *deliberate* evil, just ignorance. How did he claim to prove that knowledge is *all* that's required, and itself guarantees virtue? His argument is like this: He says that everyone necessarily pursues that which he thinks is going to lead to his own welfare, to his self-interest, to his own good, to his happiness. I should say here that Socrates, along with most of the Greeks, assumed without question that all men are egoists and want to achieve their own happiness. This is wrong, but it is evidence of the comparative health of Greek culture. If you combine that premise with Socrates's definition of virtue ("that which is indispensable to a man's welfare"), the conclusion follows unavoidably that everyone who knows what virtue is and sees that it leads to his welfare will necessarily pursue it and live the good life, because the only alternative would be that he's deliberately and willfully pursuing his own destruction. And according to the Greeks, that is impossible. Therefore, said Socrates, everyone who doesn't live the good life does not know the nature and the rewards of virtue. Sin is simply ignorance. Once you know the good, you cannot betray it. All wrongdoing is involuntary. And thus, you see the urgent importance for Socrates of studying philosophy: It gives you the knowledge that *makes* you good, and therefore *makes* you healthy, and therefore *makes* you happy. The study of philosophy is therefore the key, the *only* key, to a successful life.

I must briefly demur that knowledge is sufficient to guarantee virtue, because the effect has been to wipe out the distinction between errors of knowledge and breaches of morality. On this view, there is no such thing as volitionally immoral behavior just involuntary ignorance. And today there are all sorts of people excusing all sorts of crimes on the grounds that "He couldn't help it, he wasn't educated, he didn't know any better, if he had had the right knowledge he would have been okay." Of all the possible criticisms you could make of this view, I'll confine myself to two very briefly. It assumes, first of all that all men are rational egoists, acting always for what they believe will be their own welfare, something that is demonstrably false. Anyone who knew the history of Christianity (which Socrates didn't have the chance to know) would see that. And I don't mean to pick on just Christianity; atheists are no better. You could just look around at the state of the world and read any newspaper as far as this point is concerned. To become a rational egoist is an *achievement*, not an innate endowment. And Socrates's view is a version of determinism. Human beings are not determined to be rational or irrational, egoistic or non-egoistic. There are men who are actually indifferent to their own personal lives and happiness. There are men who are positively eager to destroy themselves, to sacrifice themselves. Socrates's error is to project onto human nature the general pro-reason healthy egoism of the Greek civilization. It is a noble error, but it is an error.

And another criticism: The fact that you know something does not mean that you will automatically apply that knowledge. You can know that something is good for you, and yet refuse to allow that knowledge to come into focus. The point I make to my students is a perfect example: You know there's going to be an exam tomorrow, but you have the capacity to push that unpleasant fact out of your mind by an act of evasion. Socrates implies that your knowledge must always be operative. But if you understand the Objectivist theory of free will, it's an essential aspect that you not only have to know, you have to *summon* your knowledge and concentrate on it in any given situation by consistent acts of focusing. This is what Socrates leaves out. So, he is right that when you know that something is the right thing, and when you volitionally focus on that thing, keep it real to yourself, then, and in that moment, you have no choice but to act on what you know. But it doesn't follow that whenever you commit a wrong action, you didn't have the knowledge; it could very well have been the case that you had the knowledge but chose to evade it. That's inherent in free will. You can never become an automatically good person just by stuffing yourself full of enough lectures on ethics.

So much for Socrates's views. You see that, apart from certain errors, his general view is sound, if undeveloped and generalized. It's true that man has a nature, and, using his terms, the soul has a nature. It's true that happiness depends on having a happy soul, on living in accordance with your nature, that Sophistic whim-worshiping is the means to guaranteed misery. And it's true that a knowledge of man's nature and requirements is indispensable to virtue and happiness.

But we don't yet have anything very specific. We have to know what the specific nature of man or the soul is. What *are* its requirements? What *are* the laws of happiness? What *is* the knowledge we need? And thus, we have to turn to Plato to fill in Socrates's generalized scheme and deduce a concrete set of virtues from it.

What then is Plato's view of the nature of man, the nature of the soul? What is Plato's "psychology"? (I don't mean the workings of his mind but rather his theory of the nature of the soul, the nature of man.) *Psyche* is the Greek for "soul," and therefore, "psychology" is literally "theory of the soul." You can think of it as the theory of the personality, theory of the spiritual-psychological component of man.

To understand Plato's psychology, you need to remember his metaphysics. There's a sharp dualism between the world of perfect Forms and the world of Heraclitean particulars. According to Plato, man is a creature with ties to both worlds. He is a composite creature, of two parts, soul and body. His soul (his reason) belongs to another world and came from there. Its nonmaterial essential function is to study the Forms. But in this life, the soul is encased in the body, and as a result, man has drives, urges, and desires that a disembodied soul would never have; he has loves and lusts for physical things. Basically, there is a part of man urging him to the world of Forms, to study, to think, to philosophize, and there is a part that pulls him down to this world, the part influenced by the body. And therefore, there must be two parts to man's personality reflecting the two different worlds. Man, for Plato, is a dualistic creature, with a higher nature and a lower nature. His higher nature is his reason, or call it his "mind," the thinking part, the part that studies the Forms and acquires knowledge. His lower nature is the irrational element in him, and that is the emotions, the feelings. Those, says Plato, are always feelings and emotions for things in this world, for the sensible world. You do not feel passions for abstract Forms. Emotions and desires are inherently this-worldly; they're directed to particulars. You may feel a craving lust for bananas, but nobody feels a lust for banana-hood. So, on this point, he's right—emotions are directed toward particulars.

These two elements, according to Plato, are present in *every* man. They are fundamentally independent and, in fact, *opposed* components making up the essence of man's soul. Notice that they are opposed by nature. What is the proof of that? It's what you can call the *argument from conflict*, which Plato puts forth in *The Republic*, and which has been going like a house on fire ever since. It's perhaps best illustrated by the story of Philip and Mildred in Somerset Maugham's *Of Human Bondage*, supposedly illustrating the eternal conflict between man's reason and his passions. That story, very briefly: Philip is an artist and he meets Mildred, a green-tinted slut from the gutter, who, intellectually speaking, he finds repulsive, and yet he is caught in helpless emotional bondage to her. On the other hand, he meets Norah, a nice girl whom he intellectually approves of, and he's completely indifferent to her sexually, emotionally. And he runs through the book, wailing about the eternal plight of man: His emotions pull him one way and his reason the other. There are ten thousand such examples that the followers of Plato have written. Plato's argument is that if a man like this is urged in two opposite directions at the same time, there must be two different opposite parts at work, two independent, autonomous, motivating sources, one pushing one way and one the other.

You see here the influence of Plato's metaphysics: If you held a one-reality metaphysics, you would never come to such a conclusion. You could easily account for conflicts without taking emotions as irrational elements, severed from reason and functioning independently. You would do it by reference to a person's contradictory ideas, contradictory premises. And you would say that the person holds a contradiction and is in intellectual conflict, and one half is usually not within his conscious awareness, but in principle if he introspects properly and engages in self-analysis, perhaps goes to psychotherapy, he will be able to bring it all to the surface, get rid of the contradiction, restore harmony to his emotional life, and proceed about his business. *But*, if you come to man in advance with a metaphysics of dualism and conflict, you will find that conflict in man also. And for Plato, therefore, in every man's soul, there is a basic conflict of reason versus emotion.

And in fact, it's a little bit more complicated because Plato proceeds to subdivide the lower emotional element itself into two parts, ending up with three. The lowest element of the lower part he calls the *appetites*, those desires that are grossly, crudely tied to the physical world—the desires for physical things like food, shelter, wealth, money, sex. Then there is the higher part of the lower part, and it's more or less intermediate. He calls it the *spirited* (note "spiritual") element. And it is the passionate, more violent part of your emotional life, the part that is higher than the appetites. It's not directly tied to physical things, but it's still oriented to this world, so it's nothing like the high parts. It's responsible for intense anger, indignation, ambition, hatred, the desire for power, honor, glory. If you ask why Plato made this latter subdivision between the appetites and the spirited, it is the same argument from conflict. He observed that a man's sexual desire can point in one direction, and the man can feel violent anger at his own sexual desire, in which case his indignation, his spirited element, is aligning itself with his reason, and both of them are against his appetite. On the other hand, the spirited can jump in the other direction. It, so to speak, holds the balance of power in the soul. And if the voice of reason says, "You shouldn't have that particular desire," and the spirited element chimes in with hatred for reason and lends its weight to the appetites on top of it, then the man is pretty much cooked, you see. So, the spirited is like an intermediary part that can go either way.

You can see here the obvious influence of Pythagoras—remember the three men at the Olympic games, the lover of gain, the lover of glory and fame, and the spectator—that has now been blown up into a full-fledged theory of human psychology. Plato's own analogy is that inside the skin of every man, there are three creatures—a little man (representing the reason), a raging lion (representing the spirited), and a many-headed, slobbering, drooling beast (representing the appetites).

Those of you familiar with Freud will see that there is a close correlation between Plato's trichotomy here and Freud's—at least the id of Freud is Plato's appetites put into Latin. And Plato himself held that the appetites contain, among their other parts, desires so evil that we can't face them in real life, and that they come out only in dreams. I hasten to add in defense of Plato that Freud is a nineteenth-century irrationalist, and that by comparison, Plato's trichotomy is a paragon of virtue in relation to the Freudian corruption.

The upshot, in any event, is that for Plato, there is a tripartite soul, three parts, three autonomous, separate, distinctive, independent sources of behavior, three springs of action in man, so that man is in conflict metaphysically, by his very nature. His parts are inherently at war with one another; that's human nature, that is not neurosis. It is this psychological theory that sets the problem of ethics, and the problem is how to achieve peace and harmony among these parts. Health of the soul, for Plato, would equal peaceful coexistence among the man, the lion, and the many-headed beast. Ethics is the science that's going to tell us how to do it. How?

How should you live? How will you achieve harmony of the soul, and therefore happiness? Plato says the answer lies in the fact that each of these three parts of the soul has a specific function, a specific job to do, a specific purpose to serve in the organism as a whole. If we grasp the function of each, that will guide us as to how to use each properly. The function of reason is to acquire knowledge of the world of Forms, and, on the basis of this knowledge, to rule the other parts of the personality and, therefore, to guide man's life. The spirited and the appetited elements are blind; they roar and drool, respectively. It is only reason that can see the consequences of an action, the conditions of a goal, that can plan long range, so it must be reason that rules. When a man has acquired the knowledge, and reason is ruling his life, the man as a whole, says Plato, has the virtue of *wisdom.*

I might mention here as background that the Greeks conventionally recognized four cardinal virtues, the stand-ins for the Christian virtues of faith, hope, and charity. Plato is going to show how he can accommodate these standard four according to his particular scheme.

What is the function of the spirited element? It is the executive part of the personality, the part that incites you to action. Plato holds that disembodied reason itself would merely contemplate motionlessly; it would never do anything. He says that no man would ever act out of his theoretical intellectual conclusions. And therefore, in his view, the spirited (or passionate) element is required to get a man moving, doing something, on the basis of his rational conclusions. It's the thing that gives you the drive, the energy, the enthusiasm, to go out into the world and fight for your values, rather than merely sit back and contemplate them. Its proper function is to let itself be guided by reason. So, it will act only for values sanctioned by reason, and it will fight in battles only approved by reason. In other words, it has to align itself on the side of reason. And if so, says Plato, a man will have the virtue of *courage*. He calls it "courage" because he thinks of the spirited element as functioning most obviously in military campaigns. When a soldier is guided by reason, he will know exactly how much to endure, what to fear, and what not to fear. He won't either act blindly, taking foolish risks, not knowing what he's doing, or on the other hand, turn tail and run when he should have stood his ground. In such a case, he'd be neither foolhardy nor cowardly; he'd be courageous. And thus, Plato gets the second virtue, courage.

As to the appetitive element, it performs the life-promoting functions. Essentially, it's the concern for food, sex, material sustenance, physical goods. This is the most dangerous element because there is a chronic tendency on the part of the beast to spring. There is a chronic temptation to start enjoying these pursuits as pleasures in themselves, rather than merely as a means to promoting life. And therefore, the appetites come to dominate most men. Here again, says Plato, we must be guided by their function. We must never indulge in them as ends in themselves, but we must willingly submit to the rule of reason. We must, to use Freudian terms, keep the lid on the id. And if you do this, you have virtue number three, *temperance*. "Temperance," as used in ancient Greece, does not mean complete abstinence; it doesn't have the same meaning as the Women's Christian Temperance Union. But it's a little closer to that in Plato, in particular, because he's a Platonist.

Assume that these three parts are acting properly, as I've described—each is doing its job. We have, in effect, a psychological division of labor—each is doing what *it* is suited for, and not interfering with the others. And the result is that we have an integrated, harmonious personality. And then, says Plato, the man as a whole has the virtue of *justice*. He called it "justice" because the Greeks tended to think of justice not as one virtue among others, but as a synonym for virtue or good behavior in general. On the other hand, injustice or evil would be a lower part of the personality gaining control, seizing the reins and growing cancerously out of all proportion. So, for instance, Plato would say that Hitler represents a cancer of the spirited element (a power-luster); or Don Juan represents the cancer of the appetitive element. And I might say, Plato would equally say that an industrialist, like Henry Ford, represents a cancer of the appetitive element. Virtue is cancer of some part of the soul—spiritual, improper growth. And therefore, Plato's final answer to the Sophists is that you shouldn't live this way, the way the Sophists advocate, because you are killing yourself spiritually, you are undermining your soul, you are instituting a civil war that will lead to your destruction. And here, you see, he has given a fuller account of Socrates's view of the health of the soul. He's now developed that view into a whole theory of what the soul is, and what parts it has, and therefore how it should live, and he's done it by tying it to a whole overall metaphysical-epistemological base. And if you now ask Plato the question with which he began *The Republic*, "If you give a man the Ring of Gyges, how should he live, when he can get away with murder if he wants?," Plato would say don't do it. Even if you could get away with it, it isn't worth it, because you are obviously destroying yourself in the process.

And notice, therefore, that Plato's answer to the Sophists amounts to this: We have to turn away from the concerns of life on earth; we have to repress our passions and our appetites and concentrate on another super-reality. The choice these two schools offer you is whim-worshiping subjectivism or otherworldly asceticism. Plato does not say that emotions are consequences of your premises, and that if your premises are rational, your emotions will be rational and your personality stable and healthy. He says emotions are absurd, irrational elements waiting to spring up and seize control, and health consists in sitting on them and not letting them get too violent.

The effects on subsequent Western civilization of Plato's view of human nature, and particularly of the nature and source of emotions, are overwhelming. Here are some of the more blatant effects that are Platonic in origin. First is a certain type of determinism because you have no control over the content of your emotions, your likes, your dislikes, your feelings, your passions. They're independent of your thinking; they're thrust on you by your body. Consequently, you're helpless to change your character. If you happen to be born with strongly developed appetites, you're stuck with that kind of soul and there's nothing that you can do. For Plato, this becomes the basis for the division of men into three types with innately different characters. I should mention that, at certain points, Plato hints that in the other world, you had a choice about which soul you were going to be born with; you picked your soul, so to speak, at the last moment before you came back around the next time; but that doesn't do you much good in this world.

A second consequence: Because the passions in general are bad, and since all men necessarily feel them to some extent, there is an Achilles heel in human nature, a fundamental weakness: Man has emotions. Therefore, the ground is prepared for the theory of Original Sin, the theory that there is an inherent weakness, deficiency, evil built into man at birth. Now, in Plato, the metaphysical basis of this is the idea that *anything* in this world, man or banana or triangle, is imperfect and semi-real and contradictory, and man, therefore, is imperfect, too. Later, in the theological period, it was tricked up to be explained via Adam's Original Sin, but that just is a mythological version of Platonism.

Third, if you advocated the view that you should live entirely by reason, did you ever hear anybody respond: "How would that be possible? What about the emotional side of human nature?" If you ever heard that, that is Platonist. The idea being that emotions exist, are basically antithetical to reason, demand some expression, and therefore, a completely rational man would have to be a man without emotions, which is impossible. I remember years ago having a conversation with a Platonist, and I was taking the view that you should always act by reason, and he said to me: "This is obviously impossible. Suppose that you had a girl in the car, and you were driving to the top of a mountain to look at the moon. If you go by reason, what would you do, discuss astronomy with her?" This is automatic Platonism on his part. He just routinely assumed that to be rational means to have no feelings, always to be impersonal. Reason is the *anti*-feeling, the *anti*-emotional, not just the scrupulous observance of facts without using emotions as evidence, but the actual *antithesis* of emotion. Therefore, reason requires the destruction of the emotions, which, since it can't be done, people can't live completely rationally. That Platonic view is everywhere.

A fourth consequence: Ranking of careers is dependent upon the part of the soul that is most involved. For instance, businessmen, industrialists, producers come out as very low types of people on this view, as against philosophers or *pure* scientists ("pure" as against the applied type), or "pure" mathematicians (you'll notice the word "pure" is a Platonic legacy—they are uncorrupted, you see, by the crude physical concerns; they are off, according to this dichotomy, in their own super-dimension). One of these is materialistic, appetitive, and therefore irrational. That view is everywhere and influences *every* variety of intellectual. To take just a tiny example, the theory that the great American self-made capitalists are robber barons. There's no such evidence or documentation for such charges, but the historians who uttered them and the people who accept them expect such tales to be true on philosophic grounds because they know they are dealing, by definition, with a low, depraved, irrational type of man. And they know that from Plato. Therefore, you don't have to scrutinize the evidence very carefully; you just get the Ford Foundation to finance a grant, and come out with a few smears, and that's it. I should mention that Plato himself did not include artists on the good side of this particular career dichotomy. He had several reasons, which I won't take the time to go into, but later Platonists included artists on the spiritual, as against the material, side, and they also were elevated into this higher category (of course, only so long as they're not popular, because if they're popular and their works sell, they're commercial, and that plunges them back down again).

Fifth—what about the attitude toward money and wealth? What about the idea that the love of money is the root of all evil? Here is Plato's description in *The Republic* of how the true philosopher lives his life:

> None of [the true philosophers] must possess any private property beyond the barest necessaries [Peikoff: private property being materialistic]. Next, no one is to have any dwelling or storehouse that is not open for all to enter at will. Their food they will get in the quantities required by men of temperance and courage, and their wages fixed so that there will be just enough for the year with nothing left over. And they will have meals in common and all live together like soldiers in a camp. Gold and silver, we shall tell them, they will not need, having the divine counterparts of these metals always in their souls as a God-given possession, whose purity it is not lawful to sully by the acquisition of that mortal dross current among mankind which has been the occasion of so many unholy deeds. They alone of all the citizens are forbidden to touch and handle silver or gold, or to come under the same roof with them, or wear them as ornaments, or drink from vessels made of them. This manner of life will be their salvation.

That, I think, speaks for itself. What is Plato's view of sex? I've alluded to it before, but I'll read you one brief passage, also in *The Republic*:

> "Is excessive pleasure compatible with temperance?"
>
> "How can it be, when it unsettles the mind no less than pain?"
>
> "Is it compatible with virtue in general?"
>
> "Certainly not.
>
> "It has more to do with insolence and profligacy?
>
> "Yes."
>
> "And is there any pleasure you can name that is greater and keener than sexual pleasure?"
>
> "No, nor any that is more like frenzy."
>
> "Whereas love rightfully is such a passion as beauty combined with a noble and harmonious character may inspire in a temperate and cultivated mind, it must therefore be kept from all contact with licentiousness and frenzy, and where a passion of this rightful sort exists, the lover and his beloved must have nothing to do with the pleasure in question?"
>
> "Certainly not, Socrates."
>
> "It appears, then, that in this commonwealth we are founding, you will have a law to the effect that a lover may seek the company of his beloved [Peikoff: I should interrupt to say that this is written in a discussion on homosexual love, but the principles are more broadly applicable], a lover may seek the company of his beloved, and with consent kiss and embrace him like a son with honorable intent, but must never be suspected of any further familiarity on pain of being thought ill-bred and without any delicacy of feeling."
>
> "I quite agree."

Now that we're on the subject of love, let me say something about *Platonic* love. You might think from the passage I just read that, according to Plato, the essential element is to love your beloved's soul or character, even if not his or her body. But that isn't true. And Plato is very explicit on this. Even the soul is too tied to this world. In his dialogue the *Symposium*, Plato gives you instruction on how true love should operate. And the idea is that you start with loving the body—that's the lowest kind of love—then you proceed to love his or her soul—and then you go to the next step, and you come to recognize that, after all, what you love in the body or the soul is its beauty, and that the same beauty is common to a great many other things: the beauty of works of art, the beauty of scientific discoveries and so on—and so ultimately you see that the thing that you love is *beauty as such*, the *Form* of beauty, not its particular embodiments. Therefore, Platonic love is, technically, the love of the Form of Beauty, and since the Form of Beauty is for all practical purposes the same as the Form of the Good, it's the same as love of the Form of the Good. It is a completely otherworldly love, and, as popularly understood, the phrase "Platonic love" is much too earthly for Plato (the idea that you should love only the soul). We have another ladder, an amatory ladder (all of Plato's philosophy is a series of ladders). In metaphysics we have the ladder of being: from images to the half-real physical things to the lower Forms of the Good. In epistemology we have a ladder of cognition: from imagining to belief to thinking to true knowledge. And now we have a ladder of love: from a particular body to a particular soul to a whole bunch of concrete instances of beauty wherever they may be found, to the Form of Beauty itself. And just as the senses awaken in us the remembrance of the Forms that we had in a previous life, similarly the perception of physical beauty, which excites sexual desire, also revives in the soul the memory of the perfect beauty that is contemplated in a former existence. And once you recollect this beauty, that inspires in you a yearning for the higher life associated with the world of Forms. And therefore, sexual love and the yearning for the Form of Beauty really derive from one basic impulse. But the trouble is, says Plato, that most men settle for the lowest, crudest, most vulgar form of its satisfaction, namely sex, or, at most, personal love of other individual human beings, whereas properly their love should be for the ineffable pinnacle of the world of Forms (which later became the view that the supreme virtue is love of God).

I think that I've said enough to give you an idea of Plato's ethics. So, let us turn in conclusion to the famous politics that he bases on his ethics. The first thing to note is that the three parts of the soul are not present in equal amounts in each person. Each man, says Plato, has a certain amount of each, but they're not equally developed in all men, the reason being that every person is simply an image or a reflection of the Form of Man, and there are variations among the images as there are among any reflections. Some reflect better than others. Some are more distorted by this-worldly influences, more mixed with nonbeing. And therefore, in those people, the lower elements will be stronger. In general we will expect, with maybe some intermediate cases, to find three general classes, or types, of men: the men in whom reason is the dominant element, and that type is the philosophers; the men in whom the spirited is the dominant element, and that type is the soldiers, the warriors, the military class; and then men in whom the appetites are most developed, and those are the masses in their economic capacity, business and labor, producers and workers.

Plato says that these distinctions among men are innate, and he tells another myth, the famous *Myth of the Metals*, to illustrate. For instance, he says, imagine that some men are born with gold in their souls—those are the philosophers. And some men are born with silver in their souls—that's the military. And some men are born with iron and brass in their souls—and those are the economic people, the majority. These three types of men are innately determined by the kind of spiritual metal that makes them up. Notice that this is not necessarily hereditary. You might be a gold soul, and your children might be iron and brass. Or the other way around, too—you could be brass and have come from a gold or a silver parent. Plato does not hold that it's hereditary, but it is innate.

The question of politics for Plato is: Who should rule? To which group should we give control? Should we give it to the men in the cave, to the men who are dominated by their appetites or by the spirited element? Obviously not; we would have chaos. The group that has to receive ruling power in the state is the philosophers, because they are the only men of reason, the only ones who know the Form of the Good, the only ones who know what's right and how to act, the only truly just men, the only ones whose souls are healthy. All the other men are, in varying degrees, inherently irrational, unjust, blind, bestial. There is, therefore, an exact parallel for Plato between the individual soul and the state as a whole. When the lower parts dominate the individual soul, we have a rampaging Sophist on a spree of self-destruction. When the lower parts dominate the state, the same thing happens. And therefore, Plato is an avowed opponent of democracy, of majority rule of any kind or for any purpose. His view is that just as reason has to rule in the soul, so the men of reason (the philosophers) have to rule in the state. And just as reason must have *unlimited* power in the soul, it must be the *absolute* ruler, so the philosophers must have unlimited power in the state; they must be the absolute rulers. Philosophers must be kings, absolute kings. And this is Plato's famous theory of the *Philosopher King*. We will have harmony in our lives on earth, says Plato, only when philosophers assume total power, or else when some king who already has absolute power is converted to Platonism. That's the only choice, the only way to have sanity on earth. And Plato actually tried to convert one such king to Platonism, with conspicuous lack of results.

After all, says Plato, why should we allow the masses any voice in ruling the country? Ruling is a specialized art. Think of it—the government is to have complete control over the fine arts, sciences, industries, foreign policies, you name it. How can we open this up to untrained, uneducated, ignorant masses? Imagine what would happen if we arrived at the design of buildings in architecture by majority vote. Well, says Plato, exactly the same thing would happen if we ran the state by majority vote. Virtue is knowledge, but the masses don't have the virtue, don't have the knowledge, and therefore can't conduct themselves virtuously. And the other half of "Virtue is knowledge" answers the question, "But is it safe to trust philosophers with such absolute power?" Oh yes, because they have absolute knowledge, and therefore they *cannot* misuse their power. They must act correctly since knowledge guarantees virtue. So, it's all set.

When you get to politics, the moral to draw is that you cannot argue with any philosopher. If you have accepted his conclusions in metaphysics and epistemology, by the time you get to politics, he just takes you by the hand and leads you wherever he's going. It is hopeless to argue politics with someone unless you first argue metaphysics and epistemology, and *once* you argue metaphysics and epistemology, you would be amazed that political disagreements fall into place within minutes.

You might object to Plato and ask why have rulers at all in the sense he means. He plunges in and says *who* should rule. You might say, "Well, why not let each man rule his *own* life by his *own* reason, and have the function of the state solely to protect the individual rights of each citizen from violation by force and fraud?" In part, the answer is that the very concept of "inalienable individual rights" inhering in man qua man had not yet been discovered (it is post-Aristotelian). But there is a much more important answer. Even if it had been discovered, Plato would have rejected it, because in his view, it is *impossible* for most men to live their own lives rationally. They are in the cave dominated by their appetites; they are savage barbarians at heart. Therefore, *any* kind of stability is possible *only* if there is a strong government ruled by the elite in whom reason is the most powerful element. You see the progression: (1) this world is unreal, true knowledge is otherworldly; (2) most men are this-worldly and incapable of a mystic vision; (3) conclusion, most men are incurably irrational, helpless to live by themselves. Therefore, we need rule by an authoritarian few who have specialized knowledge. The lesson: Mysticism leads to dictatorship; irrationalism leads to statism.

In Plato, we have a three-class society, exactly parallel to the individual soul. The philosophers, whom Plato calls the "guardians" (because they are the guardians of the state) perform all the legislative and judicial functions, and when they are properly in charge, the state as a whole has the virtue of wisdom. The military performs the executive functions.

Plato calls them the "auxiliaries," the assistants or helpers to the guardians, and when they have properly performed their functions, the state as a whole has virtue number two, courage. And the masses are the third class, the economic productive class, and their primary virtue is temperance, which in this context means obedience. And when the three classes are appropriately following their proper functions, the state as a whole will have the right division of labor and the right harmony, and that will therefore be the virtue of justice. I say again, out of fairness to Plato, this is not a caste society. In other words, you're not necessarily in the same class as your father. He may have been a philosopher, and you're going to have to be a worker, or vice versa, up and down the scale. And Plato has a whole series of tests worked out, and a whole educational program, to pick out at the appropriate age who is really in which class and shunt him up and down the social scale appropriately.

If you're worried about the philosophers abusing their absolute power, Plato's answer is in part what I alluded to—"Virtue is knowledge"—since these philosophers know the Good, they have lost interest in everything that could possibly tempt them to abuse their power. They don't want money, fame, anything of that sort; they want only wisdom. But, says Plato, just to make doubly sure that the guardians don't misuse their power, we're going to deprive them of all private property, and thus they can't be motivated by money. They're not allowed to have any money, and so all temptation is removed from their path.

Suppose that we had constructed such a Platonic state. We have a huge human being, like a single giant organism. We have a whole entity unto itself, with all the parts of an individual human being, but blown now into huge proportions. Each of the three classes corresponds to the three parts, functioning as one entity. This view is known as the *organic theory of the state*, the view that the state collectively is a separate and distinct organism, and that the individual has the same relation to the state that a cell on the body has to the body. Originated by Plato, it is a particularly virulent form of collectivism.

How does it relate to his metaphysics? According to Plato, individuality is not real. Only universals are real, and as far as men are concerned, individual men, insofar as they are individual, are unreal. What is real about them is only the thing they have in common, and that is manness. The appearance of a whole bunch of different men, remember, is in the images. They are not real metaphysically. They are not separate, autonomous individuals. We are all of us just varying reflections of one entity. And we are therefore all, ultimately, metaphysically identical. At bottom, the unit of reality and the unit of importance is the group, the state, not the individual. In metaphysics, universals are real, particulars are illusory, which means in politics, the collective is real, the individual is illusory. This is the philosophic basis of collectivism in politics, full collectivism being the view that the group is the unit of reality and of value. And this, by the way, is one reason among dozens why the most crucial question in philosophy is the problem of universals.

As a citizen, what is your obligation? To recognize your identity with all other men and act accordingly. And what is the arch vice you could embody? To treat yourself as an autonomous, self-sufficient entity living for your own happiness. You must live for the welfare of the state as a whole.

Again, I point out that, as a Greek, Plato is not a total altruist. He did say that you could legitimately be concerned with your own happiness also, on the side. And he did say that in his state, that would not only produce the collective happiness, but also your *individual* happiness. But those are concessions to the prevailing Greek viewpoint and are not characteristic of Plato. Qua Platonist, as against qua Greek, Plato is an active, ardent state-worshiper, an advocate of the view that individuals should live to serve the state and should systematically sacrifice themselves and their personal happiness. "Excessive love of self is the greatest of all evils." What is the ideal? I'm quoting now from his very last dialogue, *The Laws*. The ideal is "that the private and individual be altogether banished from life, and the things which are by nature private, such as eyes and ears and hands, become common." What is Plato's attitude toward private property, private concerns, the kind of person who would say, "This is mine, that is thine (yours)," the kind of person who is concerned to establish ownership, "Who owns this, whose is it?"? Quoting from *The Republic*:

> Disunion comes about when the words "mine" and "not mine" and "another's" and "not another's" are not applied to the same things throughout the community. The best-ordered state will be the one in which the largest number of persons use these terms in the same sense, and which accordingly most nearly resembles a single person. When one of us hurts his finger, the whole extent of those bodily connections which are gathered up in the soul and unified is made aware, and it all shares as a whole in the pain of the suffering part. And hence we say not only the finger, but the *man*, has a pain. The same thing is true of the pain or the pleasure felt when any other part of the person suffers or is relieved.
>
> Yes [says the other speaker in this dialogue], I agree that the best

organized community comes nearest to that condition.

> In our community then, above all others, when things go well or ill with any individual, everyone will use that word "mine" in the same sense and say that all is going well or ill with him or his. People will not rend the community asunder by each applying that word "mine" to different things and dragging off whatever he can get for himself into a private home where he will have his separate family forming a center of exclusive joys and sorrows. Rather, people will all, so far as may be, feel together and aim at the same ends.

That is a formal and explicit advocacy of the exact view of man and of society that Ayn Rand dramatizes in *Anthem*, and that is, therefore, hardly an extreme projection. It is a dramatization of Plato's political ideal (and not only of Plato's but of all collectivists thereafter). The ideal is for men to form one unit with all goods in common. And in this respect, Plato is the father of communism. And it is instructive to observe that he is the father of Western religion *and* of Western communism, and that both of those are beautifully integrated in his philosophy to form one coherent whole (a very helpful thought when you observe that the two branches of descendants today pose as warring antagonists). I should mention that Plato, however, regarded communism as the ideal but as impractical when applied to the masses, because the appetites are so strong that they wouldn't stand for it. They have to have their own little families and private property and so on, and Plato said we may as well appease them because it's useless to try to get them to live the ideal life. Nevertheless, the true philosophers live that way, according to Plato. As we've seen, they have all property in common, and Plato insists they must also have all wives and children in common, But that won't bother them, because, as true philosophers, they're not interested in sex anyway, and, says Plato, it will also help to remove any conceivable temptation from their paths, because there's no longer the possibility that they'll be ambitious for their children, who will be taken away at birth, brought up, supervised and educated by the state. Plato adds that there will be yearly mating festivals among the philosophers, and that although the lower philosophers will be told that this is taking place by lot—that the partner you get is your good or bad luck—the actual truth is that the oldest, most senior philosophers will have studied the eugenic construction of the philosophers, and will mate the ones who are eugenically best to produce the highest breed, and the others will just have bad luck at the lots.

You might ask, won't the guardians, the philosophers, be unhappy living in this life, living this manner of life? And Plato says in answer to that: "Our aim in founding the commonwealth was not to make any one class especially happy, but to secure the greatest possible happiness for the community as a whole. We are not trying to secure the well-being of a select few. It is as if we are coloring a statue, and someone came up and blamed us for not putting the most beautiful colors on the noblest parts of the figures. The eyes, for instance, should be painted crimson, but we have made them black. We should think it a fair answer to say, 'Really, you must not expect us to paint eyes so handsome as not to look like eyes at all. This applies to all the parts. The question is whether by giving each its proper color, we make the whole beautiful.' So, too, in the present case. You must not press us to endow our guardians with a happiness that will make them anything other than guardians."

You see the complete collectivism of the Platonic mentality: Individuals are unimportant; what counts is the group. And the group is something over and above the individuals—*it* can be happy, even if all the constituents are miserable. Manness is getting whatever it deserves, even if men are miserable. So, we have a giant organism with the men of reason living communistically, ruling over the lowest class, the lower classes assisted by the spirited auxiliaries, everybody as much as possible being systematically inculcated by the desire to serve the state and obey the rulers.

Which brings us to the question: What are the functions of the guardians; what areas of man's life are they to control? Everything. Plato's theory is total, and if you make an adjective out of that, you get "totalitarian." He modeled himself on Sparta, which was completely statist and heavily admired by Plato. Education, says Plato, must be thoroughly controlled by the state. We must have a thoroughgoing censorship of literature, music, philosophy, science. We will allow people to hear only those ideas that are good for them, as judged by the authorities, the philosophers. We will tell people lies, so-called *noble lies*, that is to say, lies that are for the good of the people, as and when it turns out to be necessary. In other words, we're going to engage in out-and-out brainwashing. And there's no objection to this, because the masses' reason is so weak that they won't respond to arguments, and so we have to condition people emotionally to blind obedience. As one unsympathetic but accurate commentator, W. T. Jones, says, describing this point: "It is pointless, for instance, to try to explain to the masses the organic nature of the state and the corresponding need of each individual to subordinate his immediate interest to the whole, for they cannot grasp such abstract concepts. But loyalty and patriotism are attitudes of mind easily inculcated, and they serve the same purpose of producing social cohesion, self-sacrifice, obedience to command, etc. Flag waving, patriotic music, and tales about heroic forefathers must therefore occupy a large part of the school curriculum. It is quite beside the point if the tales told the children are untrue, provided they are thus inspired to conduct which is best for the state."[11] (I can't resist pointing out the blatant parallel between this and Nazism, among dozens of other movements.) And Jones continues: "If, on the one hand, we see to it that certain things are taught, we must be careful to see that other things are *not* taught. Since the whole basis of this education is an appeal to emotion, rather than intellect, it is of vital importance that the wrong sorts of emotion or desire—fear, for instance, or greed—are not stirred, that good emotions are not associated with the wrong sorts of objects (loyalty to one's family or class, for instance, instead of loyalty to the rulers as the symbol of the state as a whole). Thus, in Plato's state, the ministry of propaganda and public enlightenment, and its complement the ministry of censorship, are of the first importance." And so they are.

Needless to say, all careers are to be completely controlled. Vocational tests will be given, and the board of philosophers assigned to vocational guidance will determine your ability and assign you to the job where you best fit the state, *regardless* of your desires. And if you say, "I object. What about my own happiness? I don't want to do this particular work," they will say, "Look, you are a cell of the body of society. Suppose a man had to walk through mud to reach his goal, and his foot could speak and said to him, 'I don't want to get dirty,' you would say, 'You're a foot, and if necessary you'll get dirty or get cut off.' And the same applies to an individual in relation to the state." There will, of course, be economic controls. Extremes of wealth have to be controlled, said Plato—we can't have poverty and we can't have extreme wealth.

It's complete totalitarianism. In *The Laws*, Plato sets forth the details of totalitarianism, with specific laws covering everything from the banishment of atheists to the rules of trading various types of commodities. He has the whole pattern worked out in exhaustive detail. It is, by the way, not a popular dialogue among Platonists, because it is blatantly totalitarian. They prefer *The Republic*, which is earlier and somewhat woozier.

Plato's philosophy has been the blueprint for dictatorial totalitarian schemes of every variety. He is the rock underlying and appealed to by

---

11. W. T. Jones, *A History of Philosophy* (New York: Harcourt, Brace & World, 1969), p. 178.

medieval theocrats, defenders of absolute monarchies in the early modern world, and communists, fascists, and Nazis. And therefore, I suggest that you read *The Republic*, where it's clearly outlined and very easy to follow.

It's common on the part of people who don't like totalitarianism, but who accept entirely the basic ethics and metaphysics of Plato—in other words, they accept the altruist-collectivist viewpoint, but don't like complete totalitarianism—it's common for them to say: "It won't work. We shouldn't have this kind of society. It would be good, but it won't work." And of course, it's true that it won't work. But the reason it won't work is the anti-life ethics and the underlying otherworldly metaphysics on which the ethics is based. Life on earth *is* impossible under such a system, and no such system will work. But you can't combat it by saying it wouldn't work, not if you accept the foundations from which it comes. And I'll go you one better—you might be surprised to know that Plato was the first one who *said* it won't work, and he even gave an explanation of why it wouldn't work. It wouldn't work, he said, because after all, my whole political philosophy is *theory*, and what's good in theory doesn't necessarily work in practice. He originated that one, too. And it follows directly from his metaphysics, because when we theorize, what are we focusing on? The world of Forms. When we practice, when we act, what world are we in? This physical, imperfect, transitory, appetitive, sensory world. So, we couldn't expect that all our theories are going to work perfectly down here in this world. In fact, we *have to* expect they *wouldn't* work very well, because of all the nonbeing and contradictions and imperfection in this world. And therefore, there *has* to be a dichotomy between theory and practice. And therefore, the people who say it's good in theory but won't work in practice are thoroughgoing Platonists even if they have never heard of universals. That dichotomy between theory and practice has had its own devastating effect. It's led to two kinds of men: (1) the self-declared practical men (who despise theory and the intellect) and (2) the self-declared theoretical men (who despise practice and the physical world and float free in their own dream dimensions of constructs). Both types sever the intellect from life. And that is a fundamental Platonic contribution. Even though my theory won't work perfectly, says Plato, it's better than any alternative we have. I should say that he grew progressively pessimistic about it as he got older, but he never abandoned it. The truth is that it would not work in practice, because the *theory* on which it is based is defective, opposed to reality. But for that you need a different metaphysics and epistemology.

In conclusion, I want to point out to you a fundamental similarity between two schools that seem to be the exact opposite: Plato and the Sophists, who have fought each other from Greece to today. Observe the similarities: The subjectivist-skeptic side says we have no standard to resolve disputes among men. The only thing we can resort to in human relations is force—we must become tyrants in politics. The Platonic mystic says truth is accessible only to a privileged few, the mass of men is irrational and needs to be dictated to, we have to resort to force in dealing with them—we must have a politics of tyranny. The Sophists say to hell with theory, we scorn it, let us feel and kill. Plato says the intellect will take you only so far, and then let's have a vision and kill. The friends of Plato say this is unfair. After all, they say, the Sophists are tyrants in the name of selfishness, whereas the Platonic philosophers dictate in the name of the unselfish welfare of the masses. One kills, if he does, for personal selfish pleasure, whereas the other kills altruistically, for the happiness of society. Now, I don't propose to bargain about this question. You are dead either way.

Which brings us to an important question: What about the possibility of a philosophy that would provide the foundation for a *third* alternative, a philosophy that would say there is one objective reality, *this one*, that all men can know it by the use of their senses and their reason, that neither subjectivist skepticism nor otherworldly mysticism is true, a philosophy that would lay the groundwork for an ethics of man's rational happiness on earth, and a politics of individualism and freedom? Was there such a philosophy? Yes. And we will come to that in the next lecture when we turn to Aristotle.

Lecture Three, Q&A

Q: How, if at all, did Plato reconcile his opposition to democracy with Socrates's acceptance of the majority's will?

A: Good question. I do not know of any way by which these were reconciled by Plato, because one is the elitist authoritarian view, and the other is the view that the will of the majority is the standard. Hegel, however, found a way, and Hegel's way of reconciling the two was to say that the elite that has absolute power *is* the masses and isn't. But to "grasp" that, you have to understand that Hegel repudiated Aristotelian logic.

Q: Didn't Plato consider what would happen to his ideal state if two philosopher-kings disagreed?

A: He would say that there could be no such thing. Two philosopher kings, properly trained (since they're all being guided by the world of Forms), will have to end up, when they have the ultimate vision, with the same vision, since there's only one Form of the Good, and therefore there's no possibility of disagreement.

Q: You distinguished between what philosophy can and cannot discover concerning consciousness and its relation to matter. Is it within the province of philosophy to determine the *status* of consciousness, that is, whether it is a separate substance or entity, or a state, or attribute, or action of certain living entities? If this is a philosophic question, what is the answer?

A: The only respect in which this is a philosophic question is: Consciousness must *in some respect* have at least one attribute of an entity, that is, it must be capable of initiating action. It must be capable of that if we are to preserve the philosophic principle of the *efficacy* of consciousness and its ability to direct human behavior or animal behavior. And in that one respect, it must be *akin* to an entity, but what its exact status is and its exact relation on anything further than that, philosophy has nothing to say.

Q: How are we supposed to have grasped the universals prior to birth? By what means? It seems to be the idea that we saw the perfect man, but how do you see freedom?

A: A perfectly good question, but you make a certain concession here: You think, "Well, it's easy enough to see the perfect man," but remember, the perfect man is *manness*, and that's not physical. It doesn't have a head, just head-ness, and so on. So, it's a perfectly good question, but there's no answer to it. All that Plato's epistemology does is move the question of how you acquire knowledge of concepts back one step. You can't get them in *this* life, but get them in another. But then the question is, how did you get them in the other? And Plato says you got them *somehow*, which is always true of reversions to supernaturalism. The exact same principle applies to the question "Where did the world come from?" And people think, "Well, we've got an answer if we say it came from God." But then the question is, where did God come from? And you're back where you started. Supernaturalism explains nothing. And therefore, Plato has commonly been criticized on the grounds that his theory does not answer the question it's designed to answer.

Q: Wasn't Plato's theory of reminiscences directly opposite to empirical evidence?

A: That depends on how you interpret "empirical evidence." If you take empirical evidence as being the obvious need of sense perception before you can rise to a knowledge of concepts, Plato would say he has accommodated that fact by virtue of the fact that we need the senses as a stimulus. If you take your "empirical evidence" much more rigorously and define in detail what goes on, then Plato's theory is incompatible with the actual facts, as Aristotle points out, as we'll see in the next lecture.

Q: Please explain in more detail the parallels between the Platonic and the Freudian theories of personality, and the nature of the Objectivist objections to the Freudian constructions.

A: I could give a whole lecture on that. They're both wrong, but there's a big difference in the nature of the errors, and the difference is: For Plato, the supreme element of the three is reason, granted that he ultimately defines "reason" in mystical terms. Nevertheless, it's the mind, the thinking faculty, the part that judges, comes to conclusions, and, to some extent uses logic (at least on the lower stages). For Freud, reason is demoted to the *middle* level of the trinity. It is essentially the ego—it has exclusively a mediating function. Between two alternatives, so far from being the *ruler* of the personality as in Plato, it is just a little helpless puppet shunted back and forth between the two. So, that is a profoundly more anti-rational view. And, in addition, what is the nature of the third element in Freud? Plato, at least, has two emotional elements, both of which represent you, your emotions, and one rational element; so, to that extent, there's a certain individualism about it—it's all parts of *you*. Freud, however, has the id (which is your innate depraved passions), the ego (which is essentially your thinking, reasoning faculty), and the superego, which is the *mores of society* that you have interjected and made a part of you. In other words, for Freud, your basic conflict does not even *involve* reason, not even *mystically* conceived. The conflict is not, as in Plato, between passion and reason, but between arbitrary passion and arbitrary society, between feeling and people, with reality dropped out of the picture altogether. Freud's is an infinitely more corrupt trichotomy, and it could not have been formulated until after Kant in the nineteenth century, i.e., it would have been impossible philosophically, before reality was pushed out of the picture altogether by Kant.

As to the nature of the Objectivist objections to Freudian constructions, the first thing to mention is that Freud's theory is all constructions—in other words, arbitrary, baseless, senseless, ungrounded, irrational dogma, made up as he went along, with the actual observational evidence twisted to support the most bizarre theories (Oedipus complex and the death instinct, etc.). It is, of course, completely deterministic, and Objectivism objects on that ground. Insofar as it advocates instinct (which is essential to it), it is Platonist, representing the theory of innate ideas. Since, in fact, all drives to action presuppose knowledge or awareness, any such theory as *innate* motivation, or *innate* drives, means innate ideas. And therefore, those are just a couple of obvious things on the face of it. But what I would say if someone said to me, "What is your objection to Santa Claus?" And my answer to that would be: "What is your reason in *favor* of it?" The onus of proof is on the man who asserts that something exists. And until such evidence comes up, it's a philosophic mistake to dignify it by treating it sufficiently seriously to try to refute it.

Q: Isn't Plato contradictory by allowing the masses private property and simultaneously saying that once you've seen the sun you have to go back down to the cave?

A: No, you've misunderstood. First of all, only philosophers see the sun, and secondly, they have to go back down and control the way the men in the cave live. But the men in the cave can't be expected to live the right way. All that the philosophers can do is keep some kind of control over them and see that they don't run hog wild. So, you have "private property" for the masses in exactly the sense you do in a fascist state—that is, private property in name, subject to complete government control. And in that respect, Plato is the simultaneous father of fascism and communism—the guardians representing the communist element, the masses representing the fascist element.

Q: In the world of Forms, are the Forms that are closely related to the Form of the Good more real?

A: Yes, there are gradations of reality in the world of Forms. The higher you get, the closer you get to the world of Forms, the more real it is. There is a continuum of reality from the lowest image on through physical things through the lower Forms until you hit the jackpot. And that, translated into religious language, the big Form became God, the lesser Forms became the angels, and you had a whole hierarchy. And you had a whole science of the hierarchy of angels (which ones were better and which were lower), and that was angelology.

Q: Did Plato originate the idea of teleological explanation in philosophy?

A: No. So far as I know, that idea was originated by Anaxagoras, the Presocratic upon whom I touched in a few sentences—the man who said that everything was little seeds, and everything had little seeds of everything. He also had the idea that there was some kind of cosmic mind, defused throughout the world, motivated by a purpose of its own, and that that was the ultimate explanation. And in that respect, Anaxagoras is really the father of teleology, but that's too historical to have covered in this course.

Q: How does Plato know that the ultimate Form is the Good, not the Bad?

A: That's a good question, to which there's no answer. The only thing you can say is this: If you are going to be a universal teleologist at all (and I tried to indicate the reasons for it), it is infinitely healthier to be a Platonic type than the opposite type. There is the opposite type, but again, it couldn't have developed until the nineteenth century, and that was Schopenhauer. Schopenhauer holds that everything happens for a *wicked* purpose. He is what is called a *metaphysical pessimist.* He believes that the goal of everything is to make life as miserable as possible, so the thing to do is to sacrifice everything and hopefully extirpate the entire universe. A typically nineteenth-century thought. Compared to that, Plato is a benevolent life-lover.

Q: Did Plato have any checks against the *spirited* element (the military) misusing its power (as he did for the philosopher-kings)?

A: The check was in the nature of the system: A man is allowed into the spirited class, into the military class, only after: (a) exhaustive education—drumming into him the necessity of absolute obedience to the philosophers—and (b), only after passing tests of character to prove that he is a silver man.

Q: Did Plato have any check against the spirited element manifesting itself in the guardians?

A: Only the ones I mentioned—thorough education, complete absence of property, complete absence of private family, mystic insight. But he granted that the guardians are imperfect along with everybody else. And that was why Plato wasn't so sure it would work. But, he said, what can you do when you deal with people?

Q: Do you agree with Plato's distinction between belief, or opinion, and knowledge? Do you have to know why in order to have knowledge or be certain? If so, wouldn't that mean that the Greeks couldn't be certain that the sun would rise, or that man was mortal (presumably, you see, because they didn't know the full scientific explanation)?

A: I'll answer it briefly. Yes, I agree with Plato's distinction between belief and knowledge, although not the Platonic interpretation of that as reflecting two different dimensions. I agree that you have to know *why* in order to call something knowledge, i.e., you have to be able to prove that it must be so on the basis of fact. It does not, however, follow that the Greeks couldn't be certain that the sun would rise or that man is mortal. Because the question is, what do you take as a proof? What do you take as an answer to the question why? And here, the crucial Objectivist point is, *knowledge is contextual.* You can be certain within the context of a certain amount of knowledge and proceed to expand your knowledge accordingly when more evidence comes in. You do not have to know the latest discoveries from biology to know that man is mortal, and you do not have to know the Newtonian theory of the heavens in order to know that the sun will rise tomorrow. If you have further questions on the conditions of certainty and of the nature of an explanation, I will cover them in part when I present Aristotle's view of explanation.

Q: How would the industrial-military complex rank in Plato's world?

A: To begin with, that is an invalid concept; it does not designate anything in reality. It is a leftist slogan attempting to imply that there is some kind of conspiratorial link between business and the military to take over the country and to seize control from the people ("the people" in this connection being those left over, those who don't work and aren't concerned with the defense of the country). And therefore, it is interesting that it's President Eisenhower who introduced that. It's always the Republicans who do the worst things (almost always), and therefore I simply repudiate it. But, trying for the moment as a kind of hypothetical and utterly detached thought experiment to see what Plato would say, he would say it's a big mistake. The military should be absolutely under the thumb of the philosophers and so should the industrial class, but the two should have no links to each other. And therefore, I guess you could say that Plato is the father of that idea, although he didn't discuss the possibility of such a conspiracy; that took the detachment from reality of twentieth-century intellectuals (the post-WWII intellectuals even; with each decade, it gets worse).

Q: If a man's reasoning part is fully dominant, and he has an inactive spirited and appetitive part, would this be called a cancer?

A: Oh no, that would not be called a cancer, because a cancer is not just bigness, but improper bigness, and reason *can't* be too big.

Q: Does Plato hold that there are no degrees of truth, only no knowledge or omniscience?

A: Ultimately, he does hold that—either you know everything, or you know nothing—if you use "knowledge" in its strict sense. You either know the Form of the Good or you don't. If you don't, then you have probability, you have hypotheses, you might have whole worked-out systems but they're hanging in the air; and in that sense, you don't have true knowledge. But he makes a distinction between a baby and a scientist, who wouldn't know the Form of the Good and yet have a lot of accumulated data about the unreal world and a lot of hypotheses about the Forms. So, in that sense, he makes a cognitive distinction.

Q: If you have a basically appetitive soul, is it possible for you to succeed in converting yourself to a moral life, or are you doomed to immorality by the nature of your soul?

A: That's a good question, and Plato, I think, would be inclined to answer it both yes and no. Yes, from the point of view that he does not feature the deterministic element implicit in his philosophy. He wants to suggest that men are really free, and that they're responsible for what they are. But no, in the sense that he does believe you have an innate character, and apart from the state molding you, there's nothing you can do about it. So, like the whole of Western religion that grew out of him, he has one foot in the free-will camp and one foot in the determinist camp. And you'll see that pattern repeatedly throughout religion. On the one hand, for instance, Adam had to have free will, because otherwise it makes a mockery of God's punishing him for his Original Sin. On the other hand, God is all-powerful, according to Christianity, and actually determines everything that happens, and therefore he himself is the *cause* of Adam's sin, and therefore Adam had no choice. And Christianity juggles those two desperately, with every possible device to try to make sense of it, and of course it can't.

Q: When you dealt with Plato's epistemology, you discussed how there is a corresponding level of morality for every level of epistemology. Would that be your own point, or is that Plato's point?

A: The examples might have been mine, but the idea that there is a cognitive and moral state on each level is his.

Q: How does a philosopher know he's seen the ultimate Form when he actually does?

A: You can't miss it. The answer of the whole Platonic tradition is that the experience you have when you get it is so overwhelming, so revolutionary, so soul-penetrating, that no one could possibly be mistaken. You know, for instance, the Hollywood movies about when you're in love, bells go off? Well, that is nothing compared to what goes off when you hit the Form of the Good.

Q: Duty seems very important in Plato, because the guardians are supposed to leave their beautiful world of sunlight in order to come down to the cave. Where did the concept of "duty" originate?

A: It did not originate with Plato. It is implicit in Plato because it is implicit in any ethics that advocates self-sacrifice. But to have a formal ethics declaring that right and wrong is explicitly a matter of duty means to have a formal ethics declaring that happiness is irrelevant to ethics—of any kind, your happiness or anybody's happiness—and you must blindly obey certain rules because they have been laid down, period. But Plato is not that corrupt. It is implicit, but it's contradicted by his pro-happiness Greek side. The earliest formulations in the West of something approaching a duty-morality are in (a) the post–Aristotelian Stoics, who came close to a duty-morality and in (b) the more religious Christians, who said that duty was a matter of allegiance to God's commandments, no matter what. But even those schools are not really duty-schools in the full sense, because the Stoics said you would achieve happiness if you did your duty, and the Christians said you would achieve otherworldly happiness in Heaven if you did your duty. And therefore, it is not until Kant that "duty" became the central ruling concept in philosophy. Kant launched an all-out polemic against happiness, as such, which he considered a despicably low state in relation to morality. And it's only from that time that duty has become the central concept. Kant took what was beneath the surface in Plato, the Stoics, and Christianity, and what had sometimes emerged into the surface, and blew it up into a gigantic, full-fledged, explicit system of morality.

LECTURE FOUR

A Revolution: The Birth of Reason (Part I)

Aristotle

Up to now, you have been offered the spectacle of two basic alternatives in the history of philosophy: the Heraclitean–Sophist approach and the Pythagorean–Platonist approach. And in each major branch of philosophy, these two have their characteristic positions. In metaphysics, one side says there is no objective reality, nothing exists, everything is becoming. The other side says that's wrong; there are two realities: a true reality, which is nonmaterial and superior to this one, and this imperfect semi-real reflection in which we live. In epistemology, one side says that knowledge is impossible, it's all a matter of opinion, man is the measure of all things, he can only say what seems to be now. That's the skeptic viewpoint. The other side says that this is wrong, there *is* objective knowledge, and it is gained by coming into contact with the superior dimension, not with the facts of this world. And as Plato interpreted that, it meant that you recollect your innate ideas (the ones that you acquired from the previous life), and you achieve this ultimately by a mystic insight into an ineffable principle. In ethics, we have whim-worshiping subjectivism, accompanied by might makes right, versus the claim that ethics is objective but consists of turning away from life on earth, and if you remember the quote from the *Phaedo*, "practicing the profession of dying," and if you remember *The Republic* and *The Laws*, also of ruling men by force. So, we have no reality and two realities: skepticism, mysticism and whim-worshiping subjectivism or ascetic supernaturalism.

What about the possibility of a philosophy that would advocate one reality—this one—that would hold that objective knowledge is possible—knowledge of this world, gained by logic operating on the evidence of the senses—that would say that there is such a thing as an objective ethics, and that its standard is man's happiness on earth as an end in itself to be achieved by being rational here on earth? Is there such a third alternative? Yes. There is one philosopher who lays down for the first time the fundamental basis for a rational philosophy, one that is neither skeptic nor mystic. That philosopher is Aristotle.

When I began the lecture on Plato, I said that he was a great philosophic genius, and on at least three counts: in his originality, in the depth and the grandeur of his power of abstraction, and in his capacity for systematic integration. I now wish to say the same things about Aristotle. He was as original as Plato, in a way even more so, inasmuch as there were no significant precursors of Aristotle's approach to philosophy, whereas Plato had the Pythagoreans to set his overall direction, and many of the other Presocratics contributed to Plato's view. Before Aristotle there was only Platonic mysticism, Sophistic subjectivism, and millennia of barbarism and ignorance. Aristotle had as profound a capacity for philosophic abstraction as Plato, and if you judge by the scope of his works that have survived, he had an even greater power for all-encompassing, systematic integration. But there is still another factor here, one crucial difference between Plato and Aristotle—besides their common originality, profundity, and brilliant capacity for integration—and that is that Aristotle's philosophy, in its essentials, is true. And that makes Aristotle a phenomenon without precedent in the history of thought. Dante, many centuries later, called Aristotle "the master of them that know," and this was a simple statement of the exact truth. During the medieval period, after Aristotle's thought was rediscovered, he was characteristically referred to as "The Philosopher," and this also was an exact statement. Because if truth—I mean truth on essential, fundamental issues—is a vital part of philosophy, then Aristotle's is the only philosophy (in other words, the only true philosophy speaking of an essential, fundamental approach). Aristotelianism in this sense *is* philosophy. It is philosophy as a rational science, as opposed to viewing philosophy as a rationalization for subjective whims or mystic trances. Aristotle is *the* philosopher. Whatever his errors (and he made many, as we'll see), his system has been the base and the foundation on which every major human achievement ever since has been built, and without which none would have been possible—whether you take the development of modern science, or the Industrial Revolution, or the creation of the United States of America. As Ayn Rand has observed, the history of the West has been in a certain way a duel between Plato and Aristotle across all the centuries. Whenever and to whatever extent Platonism was dominant, the results on earth were mysticism, regression, brutality, suffering. Whenever and to the extent that Aristotelianism was dominant, the results were reason, progress, freedom, human happiness.

Aristotle was born in 384 BC in Stagira in Thrace, a colony in northern Greece, and he is often called "the Stagirite," after his birthplace. At the age of eighteen, he came to Athens and entered Plato's Academy (the first university in the Western world). He studied under Plato for about twenty years, until Plato's death. And during most of those years, Aristotle (judging by the available evidence) was a whole-hearted Platonist. He believed in the world of Forms, in the immortality of the soul, in the wheel of birth, and he believed that death was a release from the body, where the soul was enabled to go back to the perfect unchanging world. He believed that knowledge was reminiscence. And he wrote a number of Platonic-type dialogues in this period, expounding these typical Platonist themes. But Aristotle was not only a student of Plato—he was also Aristotle. And he came gradually to question, one issue at a time, to question and to reject Plato's views, developing finally his own philosophy in fundamental opposition to Plato's. In 335 BC, he opened his own university, the Lyceum, in Athens in direct competition with Plato's. And since he characteristically instructed the students by strolling back and forth with them in a covered walk called a *parapatos*, he is frequently called the "the Peripatetic philosopher."

During his years at the school, he wrote an incredible number of treatises for his students on all subjects then known, and on many that had not been known and that he started. He was one of the very few universal geniuses in human history. His works encompass physics, metaphysics, logic, epistemology, ethics, psychology, biology, rhetoric, theology, politics, esthetics and more. Today, unfortunately, much of his writing has been lost. Only a small fraction of his work remains, and yet what we have fills twelve volumes.

A word on his writings should you want to read them: Almost all of his works written for the general public have been lost, and what we have today are largely notes that we conjecture he made for himself and his pupils and had not intended for publication. Indeed, some people take the view (and there is a certain plausibility to it) that the works we have are written by Aristotle's students, and that they represent class notes that were later compiled and ascribed to Aristotle. In any event, the works are terse, telegrammatic, highly technical, difficult to read. Moreover, after centuries of confusion, various people have added various bits to them, pasting them usually in the midst of a completely different subject and treatise. The order got all mixed up, and so, for instance, elements of Aristotle's early Platonism periodically pop up in a mature work and make a hash out of the total volume. Generally, therefore, do not blame yourself if you find Aristotle difficult to untangle or read. It is not your fault, and it is not his fault. It does have the effect that Aristotle is particularly difficult to interpret in several instances because of the fragmentary, elusive nature of what we have. And in those cases, insofar as they're relevant to this course, although my presentation will be generally the standard presentation, I will indicate where other possibilities of interpretation exist.

Let us begin with Aristotle's epistemology, but as a preface, I must acquaint you with the essentials of his metaphysics as a base to understand his epistemology. The fundamental principle of Aristotle's metaphysics I've already given you—there is *one* reality, *this* reality, the world we live in. That is contrasted with the Sophistic view. Aristotle believed that reality is objective, it's absolute, it is what it is independent of consciousness, independent of the thoughts, the hopes, the wishes of anybody or everybody. And, in contrast to Plato, it is anti-supernaturalistic. It's sometimes called "naturalism," a dubious word, so you need to understand its meaning, i.e., that there is this reality and no supernatural world—no world of Forms or of universals. In due course, we'll see the arguments that Aristotle offers against the Sophists. As for Plato's world of Forms, Aristotle's works contain a repeated polemic against them. I'll give you just a sample, some of his many, many arguments attacking Plato's world of Forms. These arguments will help you to get the flavor of Aristotle's approach to philosophy.

To begin with, he says, the Forms are a useless theory, because they do not explain this world. This world in which we live is a world of particular things, which move and change and develop. How are we going to explain the events of this world by reference to another world that is defined as static, motionless universals? And yet *this* is the world that we want to understand, and this is the world we need to understand, not some other world. Therefore, he argues, Plato's supernatural world is a useless duplication. Down here we have shoes, ships, and cabbages, and Plato's idea of making sense of it is to say, "And besides that, there's another world of shoe-ness, ship-ness, and cabbage-hood." That is senseless, says Aristotle. And again, if Plato tries to reply to that by saying, "Well, yes, the Forms *do* help us to understand this world, because after all, this world somehow reflects the Forms," Aristotle says: "Your answer is unintelligible. *How* does this world reflect the Forms? All you use, Plato, are empty metaphors. You say that the Forms project out into space, or somehow this world imitates or shares in or participates in the Forms, but it's completely unclear what the actual relationship between the two worlds is. In actual fact, you have two sundered worlds without any real connection between them."

Aristotle also uses the famous *third man objection.* That argument goes as follows: Plato says that whenever you have two or more things that are similar to each other, then the common denominator exists separately, and the things are similar because they all share in or reflect the same common denominator, the same one Form, so that Socrates, Plato, Plotinus, for instance, are all similar (taking them as examples of men), and they must be similar because there is a manness that they all reflect. Well, says Aristotle, do Socrates and the Form of Man have something in common? Are they similar to each other? If not, why do we call them both by the same name and say the Form of Man, and Socrates is a man? Obviously, there must be something similar. But if there *is* something common to Socrates and the Form of Man, then by Plato's own principle there must be still *another* Form that *they* both reflect, and in virtue of which they are both similar. So, if Socrates is man one, and the Form of Man is the second, then there must be a *third* man (and thus the third man argument). And of course, it goes on to infinity. In other words, Aristotle claims, the theory of Forms leads to an infinite regress. There must be a Form for what particulars have in common, and a Form for what particulars and the first Form have in common, and so on. And this is hopeless. I should say in fairness that Plato himself was the first to raise this objection in his late dialogue the *Parmenides*, and he admittedly had no answer to it. Aristotle adds, "You have no answer because your theory is hopeless."

Aristotle's major objection to Plato's world of Forms is that it's self-contradictory. What Plato does is make the universals into concrete, individual, particular things. And this, he says, obliterates the whole distinction between the universal and the particular. What is that distinction? By a particular, we mean a self-contained, self-enclosed thing: *this*, *this*, *that*, i.e., a thing which exists in itself. However, a universal, by definition, is what is *common to* a number of particulars. It's the set of characteristics possessed by *many* different instances. Therefore, it can't exist in itself, but only in other things, only in particulars. To say, as Plato does, that the universal is a separate thing existing as an entity in itself is to make it a particular thing, which is to make the universal a non-universal, which is directly self-contradictory. What, then, was Plato's error? Aristotle says that Plato confuses abstraction with entities, with things. We can separate the common characteristics running through a group of particulars from the differences among them. We can do that as a mental process, as a process of thought. We can form an idea of what is in common among the group of particulars, ignoring the differences. But this does not mean, says Aristotle, that this common denominator can exist in reality apart from its particular accompaniments. It is simply an abstraction, a result of selective awareness on our part. For instance, we can look at a whole bunch of colored surfaces of all different shapes that are, let us say, all of the shade of red. We can focus on the red and ignore the varying shapes, and we can make a mental abstraction and arrive at the idea of "red" *regardless* of shape. But that doesn't mean that there can be a dimension in which color floats free without *any* shape whatever. And the same is true of all abstraction.

Plato thinks that because we can separate two different elements in thought, therefore, they can exist separately in reality, one in one reality and one in another. This is, says Aristotle, the *fallacy of reification*, which means literally "thing-making," i.e., making a *thing* out of what is an abstraction. Therefore, as to Plato's argument in favor of the world of Forms, Aristotle says you're committing the fallacy of reification. It's true, for instance, that the universal is one and the particulars are many, but that is because we are focusing on the one identity running through the class that *is* the same for each example. But that doesn't mean we're thinking of a single super-entity, merely of the identical element in all the otherwise different particulars. And the same for the point that universals are unchanging and particulars are changing. True, says Aristotle, but that merely means we are abstracting mentally away from all the changes in the particulars and are focusing our attention mentally on the permanent, enduring element that gives them a certain character. We are ignoring in our thought all of the changing accompaniments (so that, for instance, particular men change, but we can concentrate in thought on the element of them that doesn't change, the element they have in common, by a process of abstraction). And therefore, it's true that we can think about one unchanging element, ignoring the many differences. That does not mean it exists by itself in another dimension. The conclusion is that only particular, individual, concrete things exist in reality, and they are the units of reality.

What, then, is Aristotle's own position on universals? He holds that universals *are*, in a way, distinguishable from particulars. To that extent, Plato is right. And universals are *real*—they are the basis of conceptual thought, and they are the *objects* of conceptual thought. To *that* extent, Plato was right. But, only particulars exist. That's Aristotle's essential principle. How, then, will we interpret universals? Aristotle's famous answer is that universals do exist, they are real, but they exist only in particulars. There are, he says, two elements in each thing that exists. Each thing that exists is a metaphysical compound comprised of two elements. On the one hand, everything is an individual, particular, concrete, what Aristotle calls a "this," and it has something unique about it. But, it also has a certain nature, and there are certain characteristics that it shares with other things on the basis of which we can classify it as not only a "this" but as a "such," a certain *kind* of thing. So, everything is a "this-such," a particular of a certain kind, an individual that belongs to a certain class. For example, if I point to the gentleman in the front row, you are in one respect an absolutely unique, unrepeatable individual. Even if by a fantastic science-fiction method, we would create another individual who was identical to you in all physical and psychological characteristics so there was no way qualitatively of distinguishing you, you would still be you and not him, and he would still be him and not you. Individuality is an irreducible element; there is something unique about you. (In the next lecture, I'll present the full answer about what that unique thing is.) But in any event, there is something unique about you. On the other hand, obviously you have many characteristics in common with other entities on the basis of which we call you "human," "living," etc. So, there are two elements, what are sometimes called the "universalizing element" and the "particularizing (or individuating) element."

Aristotle has his own terminology for these two elements. For the universal element, he uses the word "form" (borrowing from Plato). For the particular, individuating element, he uses the term "matter," which means the this-ness, the uniqueness, of any particular. This is a very specialized Aristotelian usage of the word "matter," and it does not mean "matter" as we use the term today. For now, I just want to introduce the term. In this preliminary stage, you can think of "matter" as standing for those aspects of a thing that make it unique and "form" as standing for those aspects of a thing it shares with other things.

In these terms we can, says Aristotle, formulate a philosophic law: You can never have matter without form, or form without matter. Plato and Heraclitus, each with his own perspective, violated this law. Plato's perspective has form without matter all over the place in his World of Universals without particulars—manness apart from individual men, etc. Heraclitus made the opposite mistake—he's got matter, but without form. There's *some* kind of stuff in Heraclitus's world, but it has no nature, no identity, it isn't anything—it is and it isn't and it's constantly changing. Aristotle's position is: no matter without form, no form without matter. If something exists, it's *something* (in other words, it has form), and if it exists, it exists as a real, particular *this*, a concrete here and now matter. So much for Aristotle's attack on Plato's world of Forms. Aristotle's own position on universals is given the technical name *Aristotelian realism*, indicating that universals are real but exist only in particulars. Plato's view is called *Platonic realism* in the theory of universals, for obvious reasons.

I have a further preliminary metaphysical point to make: What does Aristotle have to say to the earlier Presocratics, who held that this world exists, but that it is only actions, process, change, not entities (ala Heraclitus)? Or, turning to the Pythagoreans, that reality exists, but it really is numbers or quantities? In a famous work called the *Categories*, Aristotle classifies the basic types of existents, kind of an inventory of the most fundamental categories of reality. In that work, he takes the view that the fundamental constituent of reality is the *entity*, the thing, the individual thing. Actions, he insists, are actions of entities, actions of things. You can't have a room filled with running, unless there's something running, nor can you have a room filled with digesting unless there's something doing the digesting, etc. "Change," "action," "motion" are names for what entities do. Wipe out the entities, you wipe out the action. And the same principle applies to quantities—you can't have a room filled with six or twenty thousand, because the question is six or twenty thousand *what*? Quantities, in other words, are quantities of entities. The fundamental constituents of the world are entities, which Aristotle calls "primary beings," or "primary substances." That means "entity," if you encounter that phrase in Aristotle. There are, he says, many derivative types of existents that are not entities, such as actions or quantities or qualities (for instance, red, loud, beautiful), or relationships (e.g., above or below or similar to or uncle of), and he mentions several other such categories. But his main point is that these are all *derivative* forms of existents. None of these categories can exist apart from entities. If there are no entities, there are no actions, because what could be performing them? No qualities, because what would be possessing them? No quantities, same question. No relations, because between or among what would those relations in here? So, to summarize this point, the world consists of primary substances, individual entities, each a particular with a certain nature, engaged in various actions, possessing various qualities, bearing certain relationships to each other. In other words, reality is the world of common sense. It is the everyday world we live in. It is not a reflection, or a flux, or a contradiction, or a dream, or a nothing, or a string of essences, polluted by empty space. Reality is this world as it appears to human senses. This is the world we want to know and understand.

Given this preliminary metaphysical sketch, and before we proceed to look at Aristotle's epistemology, let's identify one cardinal metaphysical principle implicit in what I've said so far (although not explicitly identified by Aristotle himself). Aristotle is the true author of the principle of the Primacy of Existence as against the Primacy of Consciousness. For those of you unfamiliar with this distinction, I will explain it here briefly, because otherwise you cannot appreciate the significance of Aristotle's philosophy.

The Primacy of Existence is the view that reality, to put it colloquially, comes first. It is the metaphysical primary. Reality is what it is independent of the content or actions of any consciousness. It is the irreducible primary that sets the terms for consciousness, and consciousness is just a man's or an animal's faculty for perceiving, grasping, identifying, coming to know the facts of reality. On the primacy of existence, consciousness has no power to alter the facts of reality. No matter how much it wishes, hopes, fears, believes, opines, etc., it cannot magically change reality. Facts are what they are, independent of consciousness.

The opposite view is the Primacy of Consciousness, and this is the view that consciousness in some form comes first, and *it* is the metaphysical primary, the irreducible entity that sets the terms for reality. Reality is somehow an offshoot, or derivative, or byproduct, of the activities or content of consciousness. On this view, consciousness has magical powers, and it has the power to produce or shape reality. Facts are not what they are, but rather whatever the ruling consciousness chooses them to be. If you want a simple daily example of the primacy of consciousness, any act of evasion implies it. You come into your bedroom after a day of work, and you find your wife in another man's arms, and you find this a shattering experience. You don't want it to be true, so you evade—you blank it out, you push it out of your mind. What is your premise? "This is too horrible to be real. If I don't see it, it won't exist." What is the implication? "My consciousness controls reality. Facts are whatever I want them to be." That is the primacy of consciousness in homey, daily action. The point here is that, in terms of philosophic approach, every fundamental approach opposed to Aristotle's represents the primacy of consciousness, either explicitly and nakedly (as was primarily the case in the modern post-Kantian world), or else implicitly and indirectly (as was true largely in the ancient world). But if you want an explicit example of the primacy of consciousness in the ancient world, the Sophists would be that example: Man's arbitrary feelings and opinions are the measure of all things, according to them. What does that mean? It means that facts are whatever any individual arbitrarily chooses them to be. His feelings and opinions, the content of his consciousness, are omnipotent for him and shape reality, which somehow snaps into line and becomes for him whatever his consciousness dictates. That is the primacy of consciousness on an individual level—each individual consciousness has primacy over existence. And in this respect, all subjectivism, all skepticism, represents the primacy of consciousness.

Or consider Platonism—now here, the primacy of consciousness is indirect, but nevertheless real. If the father of the primacy of existence is

Aristotle, then the most influential father of primacy of consciousness is Plato. What is his world of Forms, to take just one point? What are they? As Aristotle was the first to observe, the Forms are actually abstractions, phenomena pertaining to man's method of organizing and grasping the facts given to him by his senses. But Plato erects them into separate entities that shape and control this world, which means that he makes this world a reflection of phenomena of consciousness. This is the primacy of consciousness by implication. I say "by implication" because Plato himself did not regard the Forms as having any connection to consciousness and thought of them as special non-conscious entities. But in actual fact, abstractions is all that they are, and in this way his philosophy reduces by implication to the primacy of consciousness. Take his myth of the Demiurge—how do we account for order in this world, asks Plato? Why does the physical world have law and order? And his answer is that a soul—a *consciousness*—wandered by and desired order and perfection, and thereby shaped the physical world in accordance with its wishes. That's the primacy of consciousness. Law and order in the physical world are not irreducible natural facts, but rather the resultant of the operations of a supernatural consciousness. Or consider Plato's very approach to philosophy at the deepest level and at the outset. His starting point is the demands of man's methods of acquiring knowledge: Man must know, knowledge must be real, *conceptual* knowledge must be real. Now, he goes on, what must reality be if it is to satisfy, fulfill, live up to man's need of a certain kind of knowledge? As an approach, that is the primacy of consciousness (again by implication) because the starting point is: Consciousness *needs* something, it *wants* something, it has to have something (a certain kind of knowledge in this case); therefore, reality must have such and such a nature. That implies that reality is determined by man's method of knowing it. That is the primacy of consciousness.

Aristotle is the exact opposite of Plato on all these points. Not only does he dispose of Plato's Forms and Demiurges and supernatural consciousnesses of all sorts, he refuses to endorse Plato's approach to the whole subject of philosophy. According to Aristotle, the question you start with is not "What must reality be in order to make it possible for us to acquire knowledge of it?" but "What as a matter of fact *is* reality?" And then, given that it is that way, by what processes are we able to acquire knowledge of it? First comes reality, and then we turn to the question: "What processes of knowledge are suitable for acquiring knowledge of such a reality?"

The title for this lecture is "A Revolution: The Birth of Reason." But the metaphysical meaning of this is actually the birth of reality (and I mean here the *discovery* of reality). Because, in this profound sense, it was Aristotle who first identified the primacy of existence, the primacy of reality. All the others in their various ways engage in disconnected, free-floating theorizing. At some point they come to a contradiction, to some conclusion in conflict with the facts of reality as reported by our senses, and they proceed to say: "This isn't reality, but appearance. True reality is the world that lives up to our theories." Aristotle refuses to endorse any dichotomy between reality and appearance. Reality is what we observe, and any theories that are counter to it are wrong. Aristotle's most characteristic attitude comes across when he deals with the theories of various Presocratics, the kind who say, "There is no permanence" or "There is no change," and Aristotle responds, "That can't be. Zeno gives whole pages of arguments as to why you can't walk across a room." And Aristotle's typical procedure is to present their arguments conscientiously, and then he says, matter-of-factly, "But we *see* these things, *they are obvious, they are facts*, and *facts are facts*." And then, since he's a great philosopher, he proceeds to make mincemeat of the arguments that led to the denial of those facts. In this sense, he is preeminently the *realist* in philosophy. That's why I had to start with the rudiments of his metaphysics, of his own view of reality, and only now can proceed to his epistemology. I should mention that Aristotle is not a fully consistent representative of the primacy of existence. There was always a vestigial contradictory Platonic element in him to the very end of his days, and this you need to know for historical accuracy. I'll point out occasional touches in these lectures, but that is unimportant to him qua Aristotelian, which is our primary concern in these lectures.

Let us now turn systematically to Aristotle's epistemology. And the first question that we ask is: What do we begin with as far as knowledge is concerned? What cognitive legacy do we have at birth? And Aristotle's answer to that question is very simple—nothing. We have no innate ideas. To *know* reality, you have to come in contact with it. There is no life prior to this one. At birth, therefore, we are, he says in a famous simile, like a blank tablet, a *tabula rasa*, which simply means "a blank slate." All knowledge, says Aristotle, must start with sense experience. This viewpoint is often called *empiricism* and contrasted with *rationalism*. Empiricism in this sense is the view that all knowledge is based on and derives from the evidence of the senses, in other words, there is no innate cognitive content. In that sense of the term, it's fair to say that Aristotle is an empiricist (in contrast to a rationalist). However, since the eighteenth century and the time of David Hume, empiricism (for reasons we will see later) became synonymous with subjectivism and skepticism. It became the view that we can acquire knowledge *only* by the senses and there is no such faculty as reason at all. In that sense of the term, Aristotle is not an empiricist any more than he's a rationalist. He's rational (that is to say, Aristotelian). But if you use "empiricism" in its pre-Humean sense, you can call Aristotle an empiricist. And his philosophy is the first influential statement in history of the obvious fact that knowledge begins with the evidence of the senses. Knowledge, for Aristotle, is looking out to discover the facts of the world, not introspecting, not reasoning from constructs. And if you ever reach an allegedly rational conclusion that contradicts the evidence of the senses, you know you've made a mistake somewhere. All theories have to take the facts as their point of departure. You cannot write off the evidence of the senses as a deception, because that's where knowledge begins. The senses are valid. They give us an awareness of reality as it is.

In his defense of the senses, Aristotle was the first influential philosopher to say in regard to illusions that we must make a distinction between (1) what the senses contribute and (2) the interpretations supplied by the mind. If you look at a bent stick in water (a stick that's actually straight but appears bent), all the skeptics across the centuries moan, "Oh, you see, our senses deceive us because it looks bent and it's really straight." Aristotle says the senses do not deceive you. They give you the actual evidence of the facts because the senses *cannot* deceive you. The error comes in the *conclusion* that you make and the *theory* you put forth to interpret the data, and you're saying that the cause of it is that the stick actually bends in the water rather than some other explanation. But don't blame the senses for your confused or erroneous intellectual interpretation. That is an Aristotelian point in defense of the senses.

As to the deeper questions about the senses, i.e., the arguments of the Sophists that the senses are across the board invalid because they distort by their very nature, I will postpone Aristotle's answer, because you need to know more of his fundamental philosophy to understand his answer.

Let's assume for now that the senses are valid. The senses, however, are simply the *beginning* of knowledge. We must go on from there. And to this extent, says Aristotle, Plato is absolutely right: We must come to grasp universals, not merely sense particulars. We have to form concepts, we have to grasp common denominators, in order to be able to classify and systematize our percepts and thereby make sense of the world. Plato, however, was wrong in his view of the process by which this is done. Plato thought that you had to have concepts in advance of coming in contact with particulars in order to be able to group particulars. That is the argument that I presented as argument three, the argument from the order of knowledge. Aristotle says this is all wrong. Concepts, he says, can be grasped by a process of abstraction from particulars without any antecedent knowledge, and therefore, first, you know particulars and only subsequently do you know concepts, nor do you need concepts in order to get them, as Plato claimed.

The process, he says, is simple. Point A, you start with sense experience. In some cases, he says, the living creature doesn't have the capacity to retain sense data, in which case it never gets any farther. It sees one sense datum, and then it's gone, and it sees the next one, and that's all. Salmon are supposed to be like that, but, he says, some living creatures are able to remember past sense experiences, they have memory, they can retain their percepts. In the case of man and man alone, they have not only sense perception and memory, but a third capacity: After a number of similar percepts are repeated, a man has the ability to detect common denominators among them. He has the ability to abstract, to concentrate selectively on the common denominators, ignoring the differences. And that is how we form concepts. We see one example of green, and another, and another, and at a certain point, you get the message that there's something similar in those instances, and even if their shapes and locations and sizes differ, you focus on the similar element and you form the concept "green," and so on for all others.

We don't need to know concepts in advance. At the outset we are, said Aristotle, bombarded by sensory chaos. In the beginning, we don't know, and when the green thing hits us, we haven't a clue what it is. It's just something, but we haven't any idea what. And if we could take this Aristotelian baby and somehow conduct a philosophic discussion with him and ask him what is this, he'd say, "I haven't the faintest clue," whereas, if you took a Platonist baby and asked him, he'd say, "Well, I don't know yet, but I'm shortly going to know that it's green and it comes under 'color,' and so on and so on, because I knew it all once, I just forgot it." So, we don't need all that. All we have to postulate, says Aristotle, is the basic ability to be able to recognize similarities when they hit you in the face, and to grasp them when they confront you, and then abstract and ignore the differences. Every time we do so, we bring order into a certain range of our percepts. We form classifications by detecting identities among differences.

If you ask Aristotle, "But why? How come human beings have this kind of capacity?" Aristotle gives his same answer as to why they have the senses or why they have memory—it is simply a fact. It is not a fact that philosophers should make mystical or try to explain away. His famous line in this respect is "The soul is so constituted as to be capable of this process," and he proceeds about his business. Facts are facts, and they are not to be made into mythology.

Once you have formed a given concept, that permits you to recognize and identify new instances when you encounter them. So, the next time a little green thing comes by, you can now say, "Aha, I know what that is. It's green." And this process continues on progressively more abstract levels, when you abstract from your abstractions—so you get "green" and "red" and so on, and then "color"; or "man" and "animal" and so on, and then "living thing"; or "table" and "chair" and so on, and then "furniture." And you go still wider. From "furniture" and "art," you might abstract "manmade object," and from "rocks" and "tomatoes" and "mountains," you might abstract "natural object"; and by combining "manmade" and "natural," you get the widest, namely, "thing," "primary substance." In the other areas you'd get "action," "quality," "quantity," "relationship," the "categories," as he called them, the widest universals, the climax at the end of the abstracting process, the widest abstractions in any area. In other words, we build up our conceptual apparatus by a process of successive abstraction, which enables us to classify facts that we observe, bring order out of the sensory chaos, identify facts conceptually. So, instead of being bombarded with unintelligible shapes and colors and sounds, we say, "A man just died," "A piece of ice just melted," etc.

I insert here Aristotle's answer to Plato on the question of perfection because it's relevant and can be easily discussed in connection with his view of abstraction. Remember Plato's argument as I gave it to you: We never encounter the perfect in this world, and therefore, we must have gotten our knowledge of it from another world (e.g., all the beds in this world have something wrong with them, for instance, a lump). Well, Aristotle says, leaving aside every other argument you could use, why can't you just abstract away from the lump? Why can't you just find from your observations what a bed is and what its function is, and then grasp, "Okay, it has a lump, I'll ignore that," and say a perfect bed would be a bed just like this but without the lump? Why did you have to meet it in another dimension? And the same thing is true of lines that have a wiggle. Even if it were true that every line has wiggles, human beings have the power of abstracting away from the wiggles. And as to Plato's view that there is no triangle in this world because a triangle is straight lines and lines are only one-dimensional, and only the three-dimensional exists in this world, and therefore, we must have encountered the one-dimensional in another dimension (we must have encountered the one-dimensional in the fourth dimension), Aristotle says that's false: The one-dimensional *does* exist in this world, but it doesn't exist apart from the other two dimensions. But the way to find it is to focus selectively—take any surface and ignore its extension and just focus on the extension in one dimension, and there is the real one-dimensional, exactly as real as color is real, only it doesn't exist floating free. But neither does color. So, why do we need another dimension for that? In other words, if you can abstract, you can abstract.

To continue, let us suppose we have acquired a certain conceptual apparatus and are thus able to discover a host of particular facts. Is this the end of knowledge or science? No, says Aristotle, that's actually just the beginning, because the goal of knowledge is to understand, to explain, to find out *why* things happen as they do—to see their necessity. The goal of science, says Aristotle, is to reach the stage where you would be amazed if anything were *different* than it was. When you start and you're ignorant, everything is a big surprise to you. You're amazed that the sum of the angles of a triangle is 180 degrees, or that all men are mortal, etc. You can't figure out why that is. By the time you acquire enough knowledge of geometry and mathematics, or biology, you would be amazed if anything else took place. And that, says Aristotle, is the goal. In other words, to get to the stage where you know the two crucial things, as he puts it, the "that" and the "why," the facts and the causes that make them what they are, the causes that explain them. But that raises the question: "What would you take as an explanation? What *is* the cause of a thing's having the characteristics and behavior that it does?" So, we have to look at Aristotle's theory of explanation, which in turn depends upon his metaphysics.

Before we can look for causes, we have to know what, in fact, are the causes of the actions of *things*, i.e., what makes things act as they do? For instance, if you believe in an all-powerful God as the source of everything, you will then hold that the explanation must be theological, i.e., "This happened because God willed it." That would be the Christian viewpoint. Or if with Plato you believe that the Form of the Good inspires everything and it's the ultimate cause, then your explanation will have to be in terms of the striving of everything for the Form of the Good. However, since Aristotle denies any supernatural realm, his viewpoint is that things act as they do because of what they *are*, because of their nature, because of the kinds of things they actually are in reality. Why does this particular thing boil when you raise it to a certain temperature? Because it's water, not sand. Why does this one explode? Because it's gunpowder, not paper. Why does this one fly? Because it's a bird, not a teaspoon. In other words, what a thing basically or essentially is determines its characteristics and its behavior. And to explain any particular thing, therefore, we must know to what class it belongs, and what its essential characteristics are. And thus, we reach the question: "How will we discover the essential characteristics, the essence, of each class of things?" How will we find out what makes water water, or what makes a man a man? What methodology will we take to answer these questions and thereby tell us how to find the essence of each class and explain all the other characteristics?

By asking how to find the essence, we have reached another theory of Aristotle's, his *theory of definition*, because Aristotle's definition of "definition" is that a definition is "the statement of the essence of a class." In other words, it is the statement of those fundamental characteristics that make the class what it is and differentiate it from all other types of things in the universe. For Aristotle it is crucial to discover correct definitions of every concept because these definitions tell you the essence of something, which therefore permits you to understand why it behaves at it does.

How, then, do you arrive at correct definitions? Aristotle wrote a great deal on this subject and had many crucial things to say, so I can give you just a sample. For instance, he said that all definitions must have a certain structure, and the structure must consist of two parts. Suppose, for instance, you wanted to define "man." First, you must state the general kind of thing he is. He is an *animal.* That gives you the basic, the fundamental kind of thing he is. What you've done then is place man in a wider, general, class, and that class is known as the *genus* (from which we get our word "general"). What is a triangle? It is a plane figure. What is a church? It is a building. What is capitalism? It is a political system, etc. But obviously, the genus is not enough, because there are other members of the same genus—there are other types of plane figures, other types of buildings, etc.—therefore, we have to add a further element specifying how the thing that we're defining differs from everything else within the genus. Man, for instance, is an animal *with the capacity to reason*, and that's what distinguishes him from the apes and the bumblebees. A triangle is a plane figure, but it's bounded by three straight lines as against circles and squares. The word that represents what's distinctive within the genus is the *differentia* (from which we get our word "differentiate"). If you have these two, and if you have chosen them correctly, says Aristotle, you will have reached the essence of the class. The genus guarantees that you are stating the basic fundamental kind of thing it is, and the differentia guarantees that you've stated something that's true *only* of this class, that you've differentiated it from all others. So, the two together have given you the essence of the class and told you what it is in a fundamental way distinct from all other classes. It is important to choose the *correct* genus and differentia. I could say, "a cigarette is a pig with wings," and thus, I've given a genus and a differentia of sorts, but that is hardly a valid definition, so a whole series of further rules is required. Aristotle goes into complex and very valuable detail on this issue. I will mention just two of his many rules to give you an idea of the nature of his view and achievement.

To begin with, he says, your definition must be *commensurate* with the class you are defining. In other words, it must be true *only* of members of the class and of *all* of those members. So, you can go wrong in two ways on this rule: Your definition might be too wide or too narrow; it might take in too much territory or not enough. For instance, suppose I were to say, "man is a member of reality"—well, as a definition, that obviously takes in everything and therefore doesn't define "man." It is not much better to say, "man is a social animal," and by this same count, what about ants? Or to say, "man is a featherless biped," a two-legged thing with no feathers (which is how some Platonists once defined "man," and according to the legend, a group of Aristotelians walked by and threw a plucked chicken into their midst to indicate that this definition is too wide, that it takes in too much territory, and that it can't be the essence that makes man, man). And on the other side, the too-narrow type is all around us today, too. If I say, "man is an American living in the twentieth century," that's obviously too narrow. Or "man is an Aryan" (the Nazi working definition of "man") or "man is the entity who feels compassionate benevolent self-sacrificial love for the sufferer" (the newspaper editorialist definition of "man"). That is all too narrow, and it does not take in all members of the species. Definitions must be commensurate.

But that's not enough. Going on to one more rule, it is not enough for the definition to be commensurate. The definition must also state the *fundamental* characteristics of the class to be defined. There are such things as commensurate but derivative characteristics, that is, characteristics true of all and only members of a certain class. But they are not basic, but rather the results of something deeper that *is* basic. For instance, suppose I say, "man is the being (assuming he's not damaged) with the capacity to talk" or "the being with a sense of humor." He has those qualities because he has reason, and therefore, they cannot validly be definitional of "man," because they are *effects* of his essence, not his essence. Or if I say, "a triangle is the plane figure whose angle sum equals 180 degrees"—it's true, it's true only of triangles, but it is not the definition of "triangle," because it can be explained by reference to the *structure* of a triangle, combined with the axioms of geometry. Or if I said, "capitalism is a system that is highly productive, prosperous, and brings about the greatest happiness of the greatest number"—this, as you know from Objectivism, is true of capitalism and only of capitalism, but that is not what is the essence of capitalism, merely its consequence. (That last example, needless to say, is not Aristotle's.) Consequently, says Aristotle, we must make a firm distinction between the essence—the *fundamental* commensurate characteristics—and the derivative characteristics. Aristotle called these derivative characteristics by the technical term "properties," and he means by "property" those commensurate characteristics that are not fundamental but are results or effects of the essence of the class. I'm using his "essence/property" terms—what we do when we want to understand a fact is learn the connection between the essence of things and their properties. That's just a reformulation of the point I made before, that the nature of a thing determines its characteristics and behavior. Therefore, in our definitions, says Aristotle, we must keep a firm line between causes and effects, between essences and properties. If we don't—if we start including properties in our definitions and thus lose the distinction between essence and property—then we will never be able to explain properties, and we will become hopelessly confused.

Suppose we know how to formulate correct definitions, know how to state the essence of some class. We want to know that because the essence of a class determines its properties, determines its behavior. Things with the same essence will behave the same way. Same nature, same properties. There are—and I'm introducing a new topic now, but obviously related—there are general laws in reality governing how things behave. And these laws, according to Aristotle, always take one form: A thing of such and such a nature has such and such properties. A thing of such and such an essence behaves in such and such a way. If we could discover these general laws, we could then explain the initial observations that we made at the outset. We observed, for instance, that Socrates is mortal. But if we can grasp the nature of man, and then say, "All things of this essence—all men—are mortal, and Socrates is a man," we would thereby have explained the fact of his mortality. And therefore, the essence of Aristotle's theory of explanation is: *Explanation consists in seeing the particular events that we observe as instances of a general principle that relates the nature of some class to its mode of action.* To understand any particular fact or observation, we must subsume it under general principles.

There is an obvious influence of Plato on Aristotle on this point because it is derived in a certain way from Plato's divided line. Recall that when you get to stage three of Plato's divided line and reach the Forms (the universals), they illuminate and make intelligible the particulars. Aristotle's point is actually the same one that Plato makes, that the general explains the particular, but now stated in a scientific fashion stripped of metaphor and mysticism (but Plato here gets credit for the insight, even if buried in a mystical framework).

The question is: How do we discover these general principles? All men are mortal, or to vary the example, all hot stoves (assuming they're hot enough) burn you (assuming you keep your fingers close enough to them for long enough), and so on. You don't observe general principles, and yet they're indispensable to explain what we do observe. We observe only particulars. There must then, says Aristotle, be a process of acquiring the knowledge of the general principle by observing the particular facts. And this process he calls *induction* (*epagoge* in Greek), and that is defined as "the process of passing in thought from particulars to a general principle." And it is, according to Aristotle, a fundamental procedure of human knowledge, because it is the ultimate source of all of our general principles. General principles are not reached by a recollection of another dimension, but by generalization from particulars that we actually observe. And therefore, there's an exact parallel between concept formation and the arriving at general laws. We go from percepts to concepts, or from individual facts to general laws, in both cases not by recollection, anamnesis, or mysticism, but by being able to abstract. How can we do this? "The soul is so constituted as to be capable of this process."

Aristotle wrote very little about induction. But, leaving aside certain hints from Socrates and Plato, he was the first officially to recognize that it was indispensable to human knowledge. Like all the Greeks, he had a primitive concept of induction. He had what's called induction *by simple enumeration*, which is induction by enumerating instances, e.g., you see man one die, man two, man three, and after a while you say, "I guess all men must be mortal." Aristotle had no knowledge (none of the Greeks did, nor did the medievals) of the experimental methods that are a modern discovery. He did not know about controlled experimentation, whereby on a few instances you could with assurance validate a general law. And consequently, he did not think that by induction alone you could prove the truth of a law, because, after all, he was aware that you might have struck a coincidence. How do you know that the instances you've observed are really representative of a general principle? Or perhaps there was a necessary condition concealed from you that won't always operate and will invalidate your generalization. And therefore, in Aristotle's opinion (lacking the more sophisticated, modern concepts of "induction"), he thought the best you could get by induction was the *suggestion* of a law, which you then had to validate by some other means. In this sense, his epistemology is deficient, and I mention this for the record. His basic view of the indispensability of induction is correct, but it does require supplementing with a theory of the rules of validating induction. I do not wish to suggest that the modern experimental method is a full answer to that question. It is a partial lead. The full answer to that question awaits formulation. It has never yet been presented in writing.[12]

Let's assume that we've arrived at general laws by induction and have validated them. Now we can take our laws and apply them to new particular cases, predicting what will happen in advance because we know the laws, and explaining what we observe. We can now go in the opposite direction: Starting from Socrates, Plato, Plotinus, and a number of other individual men, we *induced* to reach the conclusion that all men are mortal. Now we can turn around, when we encounter Joe Blutz, and say, "All men are mortal, Joe Blutz is a man, therefore, even though he hasn't died, I know Joe Blutz will be mortal, too." And that process of starting with the general principle and applying it to a particular case is, of course, *deduction*. And therefore, knowledge, for Aristotle, is the integrated employment of induction and deduction. Induction gives you the basic general laws; deduction uses these laws to explain and understand particular instances. And you do not stop with your first inductions. You don't stop with "All men are mortal" or "All hot stoves burn," any more than on the level of concept formation would you stop with "green," "red," and "bananas." You go on again to ask *why* this general law is so. And, says Aristotle, again, by a process of broader induction, you find a more general law from which you can *de*duce the law that you first arrived at by induction. So, for instance, we first arrived by induction at the conclusion that all men are mortal, just by observing instances. Now, by taking a wider field of vision, we observe that carrots, bumblebees, pigs, and pussycats are mortal, and we induce "all living things are mortal." Thus, we say to ourselves: "All living things are mortal, and man is a living thing; therefore, man must be mortal." And we have now deduced, and thus explained, a law that we originally arrived at by induction. And the process continues. The process of knowledge, therefore, is a systematic, integrated employment of induction and deduction, going progressively deeper into the laws of reality, finding

12. Peikoff's theory of induction is included in *The Logical Leap* by David Harriman (New York: Penguin, 2010).

more and more basic ones by wider and wider inductions, each new induction permitting you to deduce the preceding level, and so on, more and more of reality being explained at each step so your laws are organized into a systematic chain of deductions.

If Aristotle had little to say about induction, he had a great deal to say about deduction, and I want to look very briefly at his views of deduction, because that is what wins for him the title of the "Father of Logic"(i.e., of deductive logic). For the first time in human history, he asks this question: What do we actually do when we defend a conclusion by stating premises? What is the actual structure of human reasoning when we engage in deduction? Let's take the simple example, "All men are mortal; Socrates is a man"—those are our premises, and on their basis we come to the conclusion: "Therefore, Socrates is mortal." Our conclusion ("Socrates is mortal") relates two terms, "Socrates" is one, "mortal" is another. Our conclusion says that there's a connection between those two, "Socrates is mortal." Somehow our premises justify this conclusion. But how? Observe, says Aristotle, that there is a third term besides "Socrates" and "mortal" that appears in the argument, namely, the term "man." It appears in each premise. In one case, it's linked to the term "Socrates" when we say, "Socrates is a man." In the other premise it's linked to the term "mortal" when we say, "men are mortal." What we do, says Aristotle, in reasoning, is discover such a linking term, what he calls the *middle term*, which relates the two terms that we connect in the conclusion. And reasoning, therefore, is really the discovery of a middle term connecting two others. Therefore, every argument will have three terms: (1) the *subject* of the conclusion (in the example I gave you, the conclusion is "Socrates is mortal," the subject will be "Socrates," and that was called by later logicians the *minor* term); (2) the *predicate* of the conclusion (in this case, "mortal," that's called the *major* term); and (3) the linking or middle term, which occurs once in each premise but not in the conclusion, and that's called the *middle* term, the term that enables us to ground the connection in the conclusion. Aristotle himself discovered this type of reasoning, which he called a *syllogism.* I will give you not his, but a modern (but legitimate) definition of "syllogism": "A syllogism is a deductive argument with two premises. It contains only three terms, two of which are linked in the conclusion as a result of the linking of each of them with the third or middle term in the premises." Reasoning, therefore, and explanation, and ultimately science, according to Aristotle, is always a quest for the right middle term, the term that explains and proves the conclusion. To give an example, suppose you want to show that price controls are wrong—one term is "price controls," one is "wrong." What is the middle term that explains and proves? The answer would be "compulsion." Then you'd say, "Price controls are a form of compulsion; compulsion is wrong; therefore, price controls are wrong." And you would continue. Why is compulsion wrong? What is the middle term between "compulsion" and "wrong"? If you take Objectivist philosophy, you'd say, "Compulsion is anti-mind, and the anti-mind is wrong, therefore, compulsion is wrong," and so on.

The middle term does not always function correctly. For instance, "Pigs are mortal; men are mortal; therefore, men are pigs"—I have a middle term, namely "mortal," but it certainly failed in its function. Or "Communists are atheists; you are an atheist; therefore, you are a communist"—we have three terms, but the conclusion doesn't follow. So, when does it and when doesn't it? Aristotle answered exhaustively for every possible type of syllogism, and there are, if I remember correctly, 256 varieties. That means he had to classify all the types there are. The work in which he did this is the *Prior Analytics*. He had to define all the types of premises, because it makes a big difference whether you say, "All men are mortal" or simply "Some men are geniuses," and if you have an argument with "some," all your reasoning is affected thereby. And it makes a big difference *where* the middle term is placed. Is it the subject of a premise, or the predicate? Therefore, he had to define all sorts of fallacies that could be committed in reasoning syllogistically. This is the first time that any of this was ever dreamed of being done. He formalized and systematized the rules of reasoning. His later followers proceeded to give a name, particularly in the medieval period, to every valid type of syllogism, and they got to be so familiar with them that as soon as somebody uttered an argument, they'd call out the logical name for that particular type of syllogism. For instance, "All men are mortal; Socrates is a man; therefore, Socrates is mortal" is *Barbara*, and whenever they had such an argument, somebody would call out "Barbara," and there's also Derio and Fesio and Braniteria, etc. Aristotle didn't go that far—that was for his Scholastic followers. But the point is that he is the first man ever to think about the thinking process and define its rules. He did not say the last word on this or indeed any other subject (I take that back; on certain subjects he said the last word). There are other types of deductive argument besides syllogisms. But Aristotle is nevertheless correct that the syllogism is the essential deductive argument. He carved out the entire subject of logic for the first time. He identified the most common and crucial type of reasoning. He defined for the first time what it means to *prove* something, to prove it or explain it, *objectively*, on the basis of facts. And that was the sense I meant when I said "the birth of reason"—it means specifically the birth of reason, reason as an explicit, conscious, defined objective method. In that sense, he is the father of reason and logic.

On the topic of proof, I want to make one other point. Aristotle observed that it is not valid to demand a proof of everything. Because, he said, what does proof consist of? Proof is the demonstration of a proposition by inference from premises. Suppose you did that, and somebody says to you: "How do you know your premises are true? You have to know that the premises are true in order to establish the conclusion, so give me some proof of your premises." Suppose you give a proof, and that person says, "Ah, but your proof itself has premises, and what is the proof of those?" And so on. But, says Aristotle, there cannot be an infinite regress. There must be starting points for all human knowledge: basic axioms. The alternative would be that knowledge is impossible. Either we'd have to have an infinite regress, which is impossible, or our starting points would have to be arbitrary, in which case our conclusions would be equally arbitrary. If there were no axioms that we could know to be true without the need of proof, all knowledge would be hypothetical. It would be of the form, "If this, then . . .," but we'd never know whether anything really was true. And that would be a contradiction, and we'd be in the position of saying, "We have reached the knowledge that there is no knowledge."

There must, therefore, be basic self-evident truths, beginnings of knowledge. And Aristotle calls these the *archai*, which is Greek for "beginning," or "first principle" (in the singular, *arche*). These are the foundation of human knowledge. Of these it is improper to ask for proof, because they are the ultimate foundation of everything else. All proof consists of deriving from these *archai* their consequences. Deny them and you wipe out the very concept of "proof." Quoting Aristotle, "To demand a proof of everything argues want of education." By which standard there are many uneducated people today, not excluding many Ph.D.s. But, said Aristotle, we must very, very carefully specify what we are entitled to regard as a self-evident axiom and what we are not. He wrote a great deal on this subject—the types of axioms, how they come to be known, at what point in time different ones come to be known, and so on. One could give a whole lecture on his theory of axioms, but I'll make just a few points.

Aristotle identifies two general types of axioms: (1) those at the base of just *one* science or *one* branch of knowledge (for instance, "If equal is added to equal, the result will be equal," which is a geometrical, or broader, a mathematical axiom); and (2) the universal axioms, the axioms you need in order to know *anything* (for instance, the laws of logic, to which we'll return in a moment). Aristotle's view is that in each science there are special axioms unique to it, basic laws of its particular genus or area of study. The ultimate goal of a science, since its purpose is to understand, is to find these ultimate first principles. You induce and induce and induce deeper and deeper, but there can't be an infinite regress. It's a finite universe. Consequently, says Aristotle, in each science we must ultimately reach its basic laws. When you reach these, you will grasp them to be self-intelligible, and they will not require explanation or proof by reference to anything outside of themselves. Just as in mathematics when you finally reach "A straight line is the shortest distance between two points," that is self-luminous, self-intelligible, and from it in conjunction with others like it, you can deduce all the geometric theorems. He thinks the equivalent will take place in all subjects. And thus, we reach the ultimate axioms at the *end* of our quest, so that the thing that is first in reality is the last to be discovered. And then, once we have reached this first principle, we turn around and travel backwards, deducing from it all of the laws and facts we had earlier reached by observation and induction. You see here the obvious influence of Plato's divided line: You travel up the line, hit the top, and turn around and deduce what you formerly had not arrived at deductively. But there are two crucial differences in Aristotle's version. To begin with, the basic definitions are, for Aristotle, abstracted ultimately from sense experience and must be objectively defined. There is no mystical Goodness that you reach at the end. And secondly, Aristotle insists, there is no one ultimate principle from which every subject is deducible. After all, as the father of logic, he knows something about the structure of reasoning, and he says you cannot have a term in your conclusion that did not appear in your premises, and therefore, if you want a mathematical conclusion, you have to have specifically mathematical premises. If you want a conclusion in the realm of physics, then your premises have to contain terms in the realm of physics, and so for psychology, etc. Therefore, Plato's goal of one all-encompassing insight from which everything flows is a myth. There are distinct sciences, each with its own basic premises, and the goal of each science is to grasp these.

In this theory, Aristotle carved out for the first time the idea of *a* specific science. Prior to his time, there was only *sophia*, wisdom—you want to know *anything*, you come under the lover of *sophia*. Aristotle is, therefore, not only the father of logic, but of science, i.e., of the very idea of a specific science, from the aspect of a specific, delimited subject matter and of an objective scientific methodology

I said that there are universal axioms presupposed by all knowledge no matter what the subject matter, and of these, the most famous are the laws of logic, which, in a way, is Aristotle's supreme achievement. There is the law of contradiction: Nothing can be A and non-A at the same time and in the same respect. The law of excluded middle: Everything is either A or non-A at a given time and in a given respect. (It's called "excluded middle" because the middle is excluded and it's either A or non-A. It can't be sort-of A or partly non-A. Therefore, it either is or it isn't, but there's no middle ground—that's why he called it the law of excluded middle, which is metaphysically the antithesis of "moderation" and the middle of the road.) As to the law of identity, just for the record, although it always goes along with the other two in this regard as an Aristotelian law, and although it's obviously everywhere in Aristotle implicitly, as a formally defined law, the law of identity was not discovered as far as I can tell until the twelfth century AD by Antonius Andreas. But that's just a minor wrinkle—it's always called an Aristotelian law because it's so obviously the same essential point as the law of contradiction and excluded middle, which Aristotle defined and named.

These laws, says Aristotle, are laws of *all* of reality. They are not laws only of reality insofar as it consists of living things, or of reality insofar as it consists of quantitative things. They are laws of everything that exists insofar as it exists. In his famous expression, they are laws of "being qua being," in other words, of everything by virtue of the fact that it is, no matter what it is. Knowledge of these laws is the precondition of any acquisition of knowledge on any level in any field. You can't know anything without knowing them. You couldn't make the most rudimentary reasoning, because, being the laws of logic, they are presupposed in moving from the premises to the conclusion. And the first time you grasp an argument—if I say, "All men are mortal; Socrates is a man; therefore, Socrates is not mortal"—you either can tell that there is something wrong with that or you can't. If you can't, obviously you're in a bad way. If you can, it's because whether by knowing it explicitly or not, you know that you can't say all men are mortal but here's one who isn't, because it's an A and a non-A. And in that implicit form, no one can get off the ground cognitively who doesn't know the laws of logic.

How do we arrive at these laws? Obviously not by reasoning. If we tried to arrive at them by reasoning, that would be impossible—how can we reason if we didn't know the principles of reasoning? And therefore, the only way that we can arrive at them is by direct abstraction from self-evident sensory facts. You observe that this cup is not both red and not-red, and this table is not both green and not-green, and this lady is not both tall and not-tall, etc. And at a certain point, if we're not too dense, we get the message: *Everything* must be consistent, nothing can be A and non-A. That is self-evident.

In the translations of Aristotle, the faculty that grasps the self-evident is given the forbidding and misleading name *intuitive nous*, "nous" being the Greek word for "mind." Aristotle was called "the *nous* of Plato's Academy" (in other words, the "brain" of the school). "Intuitive," as used in translations of Aristotle, has no mystic connotations at all. It means the human mind in its capacity to grasp self-evident principles, as opposed to the deductive or reasoning *nous* that draws conclusions from these principles. I trust that you appreciate the importance and indispensability of the laws of logic, so I won't comment further on them. The titles for the three parts of *Atlas Shrugged* are, of course, Miss Rand's testimonial to her view of the importance of this discovery.

Aristotle also had to deal with skeptics, who said: "It might be self-evident to you but it's not self-evident to me. I don't accept these laws. Maybe that's just the way you were brought up." The standard hot-off-the-griddle modern skepticism that is only two or three thousand years old. And in a famous chapter of his *Metaphysics*, chapter Gamma, or "Book Four," as it's called, Aristotle offers a classic refutation of such opponents of the laws of logic, and I want to give you an indication of it here. He devised a brilliant technique to deal with all these objectors and skeptics with regard to the laws of logic. His reasoning was like this: If the laws of logic are truly the foundation of all human thought, then we should be able to demonstrate that even the objector has to rely on them, that even he can't escape them, that these laws are truly inescapable. And so, he says, I propose to show that even the man who denies the laws of logic must count on the laws of logic even to utter his denial. If you can do that, you have taken care of the objectors. This technique is called the technique of *reaffirmation through denial*, that is, the skeptic is forced to reaffirm the laws in the act of denying them. How does this work? Aristotle is filled with valuable tips on how to argue with skeptics, because he had the Sophists around him (who were good, if not better, than anybody in that department today, because they were honest, straightforward, and you could know what they were talking about). So, tell the skeptic to say something, anything, a word—he doesn't even have to say a whole phrase—but he has to say something meaningful or significant, not gibberish. If it's meaningful, it has to mean what it means, it has to mean something, it has to have one meaning, and in other words, it has to exclude its opposite. In other words, it has to adhere to the law of contradiction. If the skeptic utters "man," then he's got to mean by "man" man and exclude non-man. Why? Because A is A, and it's not non-A. If the law of contradiction weren't true, you couldn't utter an intelligible word or sentence. Every time you opened your mouth, you would not only say "Yes" but also "No." Your words wouldn't mean what they mean; you wouldn't be saying what you're saying. Perhaps the simplest way to illustrate this technique is by the following hypothetical conversation. (I'm paraphrasing Aristotle's presentation.) The skeptic says to Aristotle, "The law of contradiction is false." Aristotle says, "I'm glad to hear that you accept it." The skeptic says, "What do you mean accept it? I just said it's false, it's completely wrong, I don't believe it." Aristotle says, "I'm glad that you are such an avid champion of the law of contradiction." And the skeptic says: "Look, I said my view, I reject it, and I think everything is riddled with contradictions of A and non-A. I can't be any clearer than that. If it's false, it's false. After all, A is A." That is the technique of reaffirmation through denial, and it's completely inescapable. It follows, says Aristotle, that the true opponent of the law of contradiction cannot speak and can maintain nothing. And I quote to you now from book Gamma of the *Metaphysics*: "And at the same time, our discussion with such a man is evidently about nothing at all, for he says nothing, for he says neither yes nor no, but yes *and* no, and again he denies both of these and says *neither* yes nor no, for otherwise there would already be something different. One who is in this condition will not be able either to speak or to say anything intelligible, for he says at the same time both yes and no." And then the thought occurs to him, well, what about somebody like Cratylus, who would just think the contradiction in his own mind but not speak? So, he had this sentence: "And if he makes no judgment, but thinks and does not think indifferently, what difference will there be between him and a vegetable?" He means that literally, not as an insult, i.e., it would be a man who has renounced his conceptual faculty, in fact, has renounced his consciousness, and therefore is back on the level of vegetables, which are living entities devoid of consciousness. Such a man can maintain nothing, can distinguish nothing, because from his point of view, nothing is anything, i.e., there is no identity, and consequently, there's no distinction between anything and anything else. And by the same token, such a man can take no action at all. Here's a longer passage from book Gamma of the *Metaphysics*. It's a marvelous demonstration of Aristotle's interests and concern for life on earth, and the actual practical meaning of abstract theories. He's talking about the people who deny the law of contradiction, and what it would mean in actual practice if they lived by the theories that they preach:

> It is in the highest degree evident that no one of those who maintain this view, nor anyone else, is really in the position he claims. Why does a man walk to Megara and not stay at home when he thinks he

> ought to be walking there? Why does he not walk early some morning into a well, or over a precipice, if one happens to be in his way? Why do we observe him guarding against this? Evidently, because he does not think that falling in is alike good and not-good. Evidently, then, he judges one thing to be better and another worse. And if this is so, he must judge one thing to be a man and another to be not a man, one thing to be sweet and another to be not sweet, for he does not aim at and judge all things alike when, thinking it desirable to drink water or to see a man, he proceeds to aim at these specific things, yet he ought to do the other if the same thing were alike a man and not a man. But as was said, there is no one who does not obviously avoid some things and not others. Therefore, as it seems, all men make unqualified judgments. And if this is not knowledge but opinion [Peikoff: I interject here: He has in mind the Sophists who say, "Yes, we make unqualified judgments, but after all, that's just a practical, pragmatic assumption that doesn't represent knowledge, just opinion on our parts"], the skeptics should be all the more anxious about the truth, as a sick man should be more anxious about his health than one who is healthy, for he who has opinions in comparison with the man who knows is not in a healthy state as far as the truth is concerned.

And therefore, here is the famous summary of his view of the law of contradiction and the laws of logic, which I will read just to summarize Aristotle's position. It is the one quoted [in part] by Miss Rand at the very end of *Atlas*, where Ragnar is reading passages from book Gamma of the *Metaphysics*.

> The most certain principle of all is that regarding which it is impossible to be mistaken, for such a principle must be both the best known and non-hypothetical. For a principle which everyone must have who understands anything that is, is not a hypothesis; and that which everyone must know who knows anything, he must already have when he comes to a special study. Evidently, then, such a principle is the most certain of all; which principle this is, let us proceed to say. It is that the same attribute cannot at the same time belong and not belong to the same subject, and in the same respect.[13]

Well, that was Aristotle on logic, as far as these lectures are concerned.

---

13. Although the passages read by Dr. Peikoff and the passages reprinted in *Atlas Shrugged* are both from the translation by W. D. Ross, the material preceding "For such a principle which everyone . . ." differs.

Let me mention two other epistemological achievements of Aristotle. He was the first to give a formal definition of "truth" that is valid, truth being the goal of reasoning. And his famous definition has subsequently come to be called the *correspondence theory of truth*, the idea that an idea is true if it corresponds to the facts, if it states the way things actually are. His wording, as I recall, is: "To say of that which is, that it is, or of that which is not that it is not, is true. To say of that which is that it is not, or of that which is not that it is, is false." That's all. Truth is the relationship between a statement and reality when the statement corresponds to reality. I know that sounds like just common sense, and no one could appreciate it until they steeped themselves in Kant, Hegel, Dewey and the Pragmatists. Only then would you be able to appreciate it, so I give up any attempt to make you appreciate it now, until and unless you are familiar with the followers of Kant.

And the second brief point that I wanted to make is that Aristotle was the first to organize and define in a systematic way a great many common and widespread fallacies of reasoning. For instance, he formally defined for the first time and named: *begging the question*, *equivocation*, *complex question*, *oversimplified generalization*, *composition*, *division*, *ignorantium elenchi*, and a host of others. You can get them out of any logic text or in the question period. But it has been the basis ever since for the classification of fallacies taught in logic courses.

In general, and given all the omissions, we are still in a position to assess Aristotle's epistemological achievement. In summing up, he was the first man to recognize the sensory basis of all knowledge and the validity of the senses, the first to recognize the nature of scientific explanation, the first to define the principles of definition, the first to grasp the need of induction, the first to grasp the nature and rules of deduction and to create the syllogism from scratch (the theory of it). And he was the first to grasp, both in content and method, the concept of a specific science. He was also the first to grasp the need for and the nature of axioms and the first to enunciate the laws of logic. He did not say the last word on most of these subjects, but he did say virtually the first. He is, therefore, the father of reason and of the scientific method in all of its essentials. This is his great imperishable achievement in the field of epistemology.

But that is only what he did in epistemology. Let's now take a more detailed look at some of his metaphysical ideas. Let's go back to the subject of universals and particulars. You'll recall that I said that for Aristotle everything that exists is a particular, i.e., it's a "this," and it's also a certain kind of thing, a "such." It has common properties that it shares with other things on the basis of which we can classify it. So, there are two elements comprising each thing—a particularizing or individuating element, that which makes it a "this" (which Aristotle called "matter"), and the common or universalizing element (which he called "form")—two aspects that are separable in thought but not in reality.

Aristotle asks, in effect: Can we specify more clearly what we mean by "matter" and "form"? Matter, we know, is what makes a thing a particular, a "this," the principle of individuation. But what is it about a thing that is unique to it? What is it within a given thing that is the element responsible for its particularity? What makes a thing particular? And equally, he says, we say that form is what makes a thing "such," what makes it a kind of thing. But what is the element that is responsible for universality? What is the element in common? So, we want to perform a metaphysical dissection of things into two elements and say exactly what they are.

To understand Aristotle's answer, imagine that I confront you with a large quantity of bricks (this is my own example, but it's his point), and I ask you to build me a number of houses out of these bricks. You take one lot of the bricks, you put them together in a certain way, and you have a house. Notice I said to put them together *in a certain way*, to give the bricks a certain structure—that's what makes it a house. If you took the same bricks and put them together differently, you'd have a bridge or a fence or a table or whatever, but not a house. Suppose you take another lot of bricks, and you make another house, and so on. Let us suppose you build ten houses—what is common to them all? The same structure, the same pattern of organization, the same way of relating the elements (the bricks). And that's why they're all houses, rather than bridges, tables, etc. But now suppose we point to one particular house and say, "Well, what makes this house this one, as distinct from all the others?" The obvious answer would be that it's made of *this* lot of bricks, rather than *that* lot of bricks, and the stuff of this house, the matter of it, is different and unique to it. The structure is common and makes it a house, or the stuff, or material, is unique and makes it *this* house. We can descend a little deeper and do the same thing with the bricks: Take any individual brick—it too is made of some stuff, some material, suppose cement. What makes it this brick rather than that one? It was made of *this* glob of wet cement, rather than *that* glob. What makes it a brick, a certain kind of thing? The structure or organization of the cement, as against making a statue or a vase out of that same cement. In general, says Aristotle, everything is made of some stuff, some material, and that material is organized, structured, formed in some particular way. The form (which is now synonymous with the structure) is what gives the thing its character, its such-ness, its classification. The material, or stuff, is what's unique to it, what makes it this particular instance of its class, as against all others. And therefore, Aristotle identifies the universal-particular distinction with the structure-stuff distinction. Universal comes from structure, particularity from stuff. And so, form and matter come now to mean structure-stuff (a very, very crucial point of his with which Objectivism does *not* agree).

If this is the basis for all universals (as it is for Aristotle), then obviously the concepts of "stuff" and "structure" must mean more than just physical stuff and spatial structure (as in the example that I've given so far of the bricks in the house), because there are universals of things *other* than physical entities like bricks and houses. So, now we have to greatly broaden our notion of what we mean by "matter." "Matter," for Aristotle, is going to mean any content, any stuffing, any filling, so to speak, of any kind, and "form" is going to mean any structure, any organization, any pattern of relationship that is imposed on that filling or stuffing, in virtue of which the thing has some specific nature. Let's take a completely non-physical example: two syllogisms, the Socrates one that I've quoted and one that I'll make up. "All bright students get an A in this course; you are a bright student; therefore, you get an A in this course." What makes each a syllogism? What is the common denominator? The structure of the terms. In each case, we have three terms, one is the middle, one is the minor, one is the major, and the organization is the same, and that's what makes it a syllogism. But what makes the Socrates syllogism *this* one, as against the getting-an-A syllogism *that* one? The "stuffing" is different. In other words, the particular terms. The terms of one are "Socrates," "man," and "mortal," and of the other, "bright students," "get an A," and "you." "Stuff" and "structure" here mean the content of the terms and the organization. And that's why, to this day, Aristotelian logic is called *formal logic*, because Aristotle's discovery was that the validity of your reasoning (the *validity*) depends exclusively upon the form, upon the structure. It doesn't make any difference what the content is; if it's organized a certain way, the conclusion has to follow. That doesn't mean the conclusion is *true* (the premises could be wrong), but on the technical question of whether the conclusion follows, it's dictated by form, not by matter.

Take a different example, a sonnet. A definite form is required to be a sonnet; that's what makes it a sonnet. A certain number of lines, rhyme scheme, etc. But what makes this sonnet *this* one rather than *that*? Its particular content, or subject matter, as we would say. Therefore, for Aristotle, "matter" is used in a much broader sense than physical matter since physical matter is only a type of matter (as Aristotle uses the term). "Matter" means the stuffing, the filling, the ingredients, the raw material, whether it be the physical stuff, or for instance the stuff of a novel (which would be the episodes, the situations, the characters), or the stuff of a word (which would be the syllables or the letters making it up), or the stuff of a person's character (for instance, his passions, his thoughts, his tendencies), or the stuff of a concept—what is the stuff, or the matter, of a concept? A concept is a certain organization imposed on sense data. It is sense data integrated, organized in a certain way. So, a concept is also a structure imposed on a matter (in this case, a mental structure imposed on a sensory matter). In every case, matter of whatever type will always be organized, put together, structured in some way or other, giving us a certain kind of product owing to the kind of structure imposed on the matter (whether the product be a house, a syllogism, a novel, a concept, whatever). So, for Aristotle, the following statements all mean essentially the same thing: Everything is a particular of a certain kind, everything is matter of a certain form, and everything is comprised of stuff, structured or organized or formed in a certain matter.

That is the basic concept of Aristotle's metaphysics, this form-matter, structure-stuff distinction. And a good deal of the rest of Aristotle's metaphysics consists of applying this basic distinction (which has, I should hasten to add, validity in many contexts): It consists of applying this distinction to various crucial philosophic problems, showing how, if you grasp this distinction, we can answer many hitherto unsolved dilemmas. I now want to follow him through just one such dilemma, and I mean the problem of change. You remember the problem as bequeathed by Heraclitus and Parmenides: Heraclitus had said change implies a contradiction because at the end (remember when we lit the match), it's the same thing but it's not the same thing. Aristotle says true enough: It's the same and it's not the same, but in two different respects. There are, after all, two elements making up a thing—the thing making it this, and the thing making it the kind of thing it is, that gives it its qualities. When the match changes, it's the same individual match at the end. Right. That means the matter is the same. But it has new qualities at the end. True enough. And that means that the matter has taken on a new form, that the matter is now different in respect of its organization, and that's why it's now black, hot, and smoky, instead of painted, cool, and non-smoky. So, there is no contradiction in change.

Change, for Aristotle, is simply the process of the same matter taking on new forms. The result *will* be a thing that is the same thing and different. But that's no contradiction if you specify the two respects. Or look at the problem from the perspective of Parmenides. Parmenides asked how there could be change. What is not is becoming what is, and vice versa. When the seed becomes the flower, at the beginning the flower was not, and at the end it is, and vice versa, at the beginning the seed is, and at the end it is what is not. And therefore, change really involves a miraculous appearance out of nothing and a miraculous disappearance into nothing, and that's all. Aristotle says that the basic material has always existed—it merely changed its form. When the seed becomes the flower, nothing comes into existence or goes out of existence. It's merely a different form imposed on the same fundamental material. And Aristotle draws the conclusion that change does not involve a contradiction. A changing world (and this is his main concern) is an intelligible, understandable world. As against Plato, Parmenides, and Heraclitus, he refuses to degrade this world into a semi-reality, mixed with being and nonbeing on the grounds that change is contradictory. He says no, this world is fully real and noncontradictory. As for the idea that change conflicts with the law of identity, he also says—in addition to the points I made—that the truth is the exact opposite: Change, he says, *presupposes* the law of identity. Because what do you mean by "change"? Change is change *from something to something*, from one identity to another. If there were no identity—if nothing is anything, and everything is riddled with contradictions—then you can't have change. Change *of* what? *From* what? *To* what? Obviously, it would be impossible. What is his ultimate conclusion? You are right that it is a changing world, he says to Plato, but change is perfectly logical and rationally understandable.

For Aristotle, it's very important to examine and understand the phenomenon of change thoroughly, because that is the means, he says, of saving this world from the Platonic degradation into a semi-real, unintelligible world. And therefore, he devoted a great deal of time and attention to an analysis of the phenomenon of change, to try to carve out the conceptual categories in terms of which change would be fully intelligible. And I want to follow his analysis of change for a few minutes, and to introduce you to some of the further concepts that he originated to make change fully intelligible.

Change, we said, is the process of matter taking on new forms. Therefore, we can use the term "matter" somewhat differently than I've so far indicated, and we can start to speak of a thing as a whole as being matter *relative to a later stage of development*, relative to a future form it can take on. We can start to speak of a thing as a whole as being matter *for* some future state. For instance, consider the bricks becoming a house. First, the bricks by themselves are matter (namely, cement), organized a certain way into a brick, giving form. But now, regard the bricks not in themselves, but in relation to the house they are going to become. If you look at them from that perspective, you can say, relative to the future house, the bricks themselves are matter. In themselves, they are matter and form. But relative to the house, they are matter, i.e., they are matter of the house that is to come, matter for the house. And the house, relative to the bricks, is form, i.e., it is the new form imposed on that matter. Or take Aristotle's favorite example of an acorn becoming an oak. In itself, abstracting away from any change, the so-called static analysis, an acorn is a combination of form and matter like everything else—its various compounds, which are its stuff, organized a certain way to make an acorn. But acorns and various other chemicals in the soil can be combined, can be reshaped, can acquire a new form and become a tree. And so, relative to the oak tree, the acorn is matter, and it's matter for the oak. And the oak relative to the acorn is form, and it is form, the new form given to the acorn.

There are these two senses, the so-called *static sense*, in which a thing is always matter and form, and the so-called *dynamic sense*, when you think of a thing as matter relative to the next form, as a form relative to the preceding matter. And to avoid confusion, Aristotle carved out a new set of terms, a new set of concepts, to stand for the dynamic changing use of this concept—the terms *potentiality* and *actuality*. We can say that bricks are matter for a house, but it's clearer to say (although it means exactly the same thing), bricks are *potentially* a house. And the house, when it comes, is the *actuality* of the bricks, the actualization of their potentiality, the thing that gives a new form to the bricks, the thing that contains in full reality what had previously existed only potentially. Or the acorn, we can say, is potentially an oak: It is matter for an oak, and the oak is the fulfillment, or actuality, of the acorn's potentiality. You're familiar with this because you all use the terms "potential" and "actual," but this was their actual genesis, in Aristotle's metaphysics. In this sense, therefore, matter is any material that has potentialities for reorganization, any material that can become or do something else. And form is any structure in which these potentialities are actualized. So Aristotle's literal sentence will be something like "A closed eye is matter for seeing." Can you translate that? That means simply a closed eye has the potentiality to see (assuming it's not blind), and when you open the eye, you then have the actuality, the form, whereas previously you had only the matter. The thought here is actually quite simple, but you have to get used to the terminology. It still survives today in an attenuated sense (Aristotle's actual usage of "matter")—if you utter a sentence like "He's got good stuff in him," that's Aristotle's use of the term "stuff": He's got good potentialities. Or if you say, "He's good material for football," that use of "material" is Aristotle's sense. Or "He's great presidential timber," that use of "timber" is actually the literal original Greek sense because the original Greek word *hulé*, which Aristotle uses for "matter," in a time before Aristotle, actually meant "timber." All of those are ways of saying he has potentialities: And sometimes we see when he actualizes his potentialities, "Well, he's really in form today." And you see, that's the Aristotelian "form equals actuality."

So if we use the potentiality-actuality terminology, we can say that change for Aristotle is the passage from potentiality to actuality. And thus, we have another way of putting the answer to Parmenides. Parmenides said that when the seed becomes the flower, we have nothing becoming something (namely, the non-flower becoming a flower). Aristotle says this is wrong, because you don't have nothing becoming something; you have one kind of reality, *potential* reality (namely, the flower at the start) becoming another kind of reality, *actual* reality (the flower at the end). Change is a passage, therefore, from one form of being to another, from potential to actual, all of it taking place within the confines of reality and what is, at no point depending upon what is not.

Observe that everything that is matter, relative to a later stage of development, is formed relative to an earlier stage. Everything—let's be very precise, *almost* everything, and you'll see some exceptions next lecture—everything is the form of some preceding matter (in other words, the actualization of earlier potentialities), and, at the same time, it is matter for a future form. It is potentialities for a yet future actualization. The universe consists of entities constantly realizing their potentialities, passing from matter to form, which is matter for a future form, and so on. And you get a whole chain here, or a whole hierarchy, where each step is successively more formed than the one before. For instance, start with grass. Grass comes from something, some potentiality (e.g., grass seed). So, grass seed would be the matter, the potentiality, of which grass is the actuality. But, in relation to what's coming, grass is *also* potentiality because it can be eaten by a cow and turned into beef. And we say grass is form in relation to the seed, but matter in relation to the cow, part of which it can become. And then, the beef of that cow can be incorporated by us and become human flesh. Or the oak is actuality in relation to the acorn, potentiality in relation to timber, and the timber is actuality in relation to the potentialities of the oak, which could be split, and so on. And in relation to the ships that you'll build out of the timber, the timber is potentiality. Or take a concept—that's the actuality of the potentialities of the sense data, and in turn, once you have concepts, you have the potentiality for a new organization, namely, combining several concepts together into a premise or a proposition, which is the actuality of the potentialities of a concept. And in turn, a proposition is the potentiality of being combined in a new organization with other principles to make a whole argument, which in turn is the potentiality of a whole science.

What is the significance of these chains? It is the actual metaphysical foundation for the view that reality is lawful and orderly because what a thing is matter *for* depends on its nature, on what it is actually. You can make a ship out of timber, but not out of acorns, and man can live on beef, but not on grass seeds. You can make a science out of syllogisms, but not out of sheer unorganized sense data. In other words, within certain limits, the order of these cycles of actualization is necessary. It is not true that anything is possible, "possible" meaning "potential." And as the father of potentiality, Aristotle insists emphatically that it is not true that everything has just any potentiality, and it is not true, therefore, that anything *could* happen ("could" is just a synonym for "potentiality"). It is not true that anything can be followed by anything, because there are laws governing what occurs in the world. The world is an ordered structure, or hierarchy, of things that are related as matter to form. And therefore, if we grasp the rules by the appropriate inductive-deductive method, we can predict, we can explain, the thing's behavior in terms of its nature and know what to expect. It is not a wild, chaotic, lawless universe. What a thing *can* do, its potentialities, depends on and derives from what it *is*, its actualities. Actualities determine potentialities, a fundamental law of Aristotelian metaphysics. And that actually is the real metaphysical basis of the distinction we covered in epistemology between essence and properties because the essence is really the actuality of the thing, and the property is the consequences of that essence. So, this really is the metaphysical basis of Aristotle's theory of explanation—what a thing is matter *for* depends on its form.

I might add that this is the basis for a formal proof of the law of cause and effect. And the proof is very simple. If you combine this premise with the law of identity, you say that a thing in a given set of circumstances can (i.e., has the potentiality to) act in only one way, the way dictated by its nature. In any given set of circumstances, an entity with a certain nature has only one potentiality, and that is therefore how it will have to behave. The same entity under the same circumstanaces will, therefore, always behave that way (in other words, same cause, same effect). Anything else involves a contradiction of the nature of the entity, the ascription to it of a potentiality conflicting with its actuality. That is a perfectly unanswerable formal proof of cause and effect. I should say that this is only *implicit* in Aristotle, in the way I've just indicated, but not explicit. This is one of the places where Aristotle's Platonism, judged by the surviving documents, got the better of him, and in many places, he indicates that he does not subscribe to the universal reign of cause and effect. (I will mention some of those in the next lecture.) So apparently, Aristotle apparently had no clear idea of the universal reign of law in the universe. But in any event, he bequeathed to his followers the fundamental premises from which it does not take very much intelligence to construct an actual proof.

The importance of this discovery is that it represents the primacy of existence approach to the law of cause and effect, as against both the mystic and the skeptic approach. The typical mystic approach to cause and effect is to say the reason things are so orderly is because God wants them that way, that he derives causality, law, and order from the activities of a supernatural, designing being. That's the so-called *argument from design*, "Of course there must be a supernatural consciousness because who could make a tree behave so well if it weren't for God?" That's the primacy of consciousness approach to causality. And as against that, there's the skeptic approach, which had its adherents in the ancient world (Anecodemus is an example), and its most famous adherent in the modern world, David Hume, who denied causality altogether and said all he knows is that anything could happen at any time and if you throw a penny in the air for all he knows it could turn into Hegel. (Of course, he didn't use that example, not being imaginative enough to foresee Hegel.) Nevertheless, a truly Aristotelian point of view is to say that both of these points of views—the divine miracle point of view and the Humean skeptic view on causality—are contradictory, for they imply the possibility of an entity acting in contradiction to its nature. Either or both views imply that, and therefore both are wrong.

We've said that change is matter taking on new forms, i.e., its potentiality being actualized. But Aristotle wanted to know how this actually happens—surely potentiality cannot actualize itself. Take the examples of clay becoming a statue or bricks becoming a house. Let us look more closely into the factors involved in any process of change because we want to know what to look for in order to understand such a change. There must be something to understand because the bricks don't jump into a house just by themselves. How many factors are involved in any change? We have to understand that if we're to understand it fully. Aristotle answers in a famous doctrine called the *four causes* of a change. "Cause" here is *itea* in Greek. It is not used in the modern sense, but in a broader sense. For Aristotle, "cause" means any factor that is necessary for a change to occur, any answer to the question "why." So, in effect, this is Aristotle's definition of "why." What are you asking when you ask "why"? And he says that there are only four possible things you could mean, and only four possible answers. And the sum of those four answers is the complete answer to the question "why."

Let's take a specific example: Suppose that a man starts with some clay and molds it into a statue of Aristotle—can we isolate the four factors? One obvious factor is the clay we started with, the matter we started with, and that is the material factor, or what Aristotle calls the *material cause*. Obviously, we have the statue at the end of the stage—in other words, the new form that we have imposed on the matter—and that will be the *formal cause*. But something was required to get from the matter to the new form, some agent (in this case, a sculptor) to act upon the matter to transform it ("transform" is our way of saying "give it a new form"). This is what Aristotle calls the *efficient cause*, namely, the actual source of the motion, that which brings it about. "Efficient" does not refer to how well something works. "Efficient" comes from *facio*, the Latin root meaning "to make," so this is actually the cause that makes the transition take place. And finally, says Aristotle, there is a fourth factor—the sculptor took these actions and shaped the clay for a purpose, an end, a goal. For instance, he wanted to decorate his apartment or the agora, or he wanted to commemorate Aristotle, or whatever. He had, in other words, an end, in Latin *fines*, and thus the *final cause*, purpose. So, for Aristotle, there are really four senses of "why." If I point to this statue now and say, "Why? Why is this a statue?," you could say because there was some clay around (that's the material), or because it's shaped like a human body (that is the formal cause), or because certain actions molded the clay (that is the efficient cause), or because somebody wanted to immortalize Aristotle (that is the final cause). So, to understand a change fully, says Aristotle, you have to know four factors: the material you started with, the form it ended with, the agent that effected the transition, and the end or goal of the process. Change is a change from something, to something, by some means, for some end or goal.

This should raise many questions in your mind because we're dealing with Aristotle's metaphysics, so you should properly ask me at this stage: Does Aristotle mean that the four causes apply to *every* change? Does every change have an end, or a goal, or a purpose? Is Aristotle then a teleologist, a universal teleologist like Plato? And if he is, how does he defend such a viewpoint? And there are many other questions that we have left unanswered about Aristotle's metaphysics. What about the *Unmoved Mover*, Aristotle's so-called God, and how does he fit in? And how does Aristotle answer Zeno? What are Aristotle's views on infinity? And on other subjects—how does Aristotle defend the senses against the basic attack of the Sophists? And what problems are there in Aristotle's philosophy to which he has no answer? And what about his psychology, his theory of the human soul and its relation to the human body? And his ethics and his politics? The answers to all of these questions and still others constitute the subject of the next lecture, but you have had at least a sample of Aristotle's all-encompassing genius and integrating power.

Lecture Four, Q&A

Q: Why would a definition of "man" as "a rational mammal" or "a rational living thing" be wrong?

A: Let me put it this way: It would not be wrong according to the Objectivist view of definition, which differs from the Aristotelian view of definition. Aristotle believes that essences are intrinsic. That is to say, he believes that the characteristics making up the essence of an entity, or the class of entities, are carved out by nature entirely independently of man's state of knowledge. Therefore, whether we do or don't know certain facts, the essence is fixed once and for all by reality, and it is a fact inhering in the entity, the same way that the length, the size, and the shape are. Objectivism does not take this view. Objectivism holds that essences are objective, neither subjective nor intrinsic, and that they represent facts of reality (and, therefore, are not subjective), facts as categorized by human beings in accordance with their process of acquiring knowledge. And therefore, for Objectivism, you always have to ask in connection with definitions and essences: What is the purpose cognitively? The purpose is to enable us to distinguish our concepts, to differentiate one concept from another. The characteristics that will do this at one stage of knowledge are quite different from those that will do it in another. For instance, if you are at a very primitive stage and all you know is "thing," and you can tell that man is a rational thing and other things are not, "thing" is a perfectly reputable genus. As your knowledge expands and you begin to want to make more important distinctions than simply "thing" versus "non-thing," and you begin to tell living things from non-living and animals from plants, your genus begins to narrow to the point where it is specific enough to capture the kind of knowledge of man that is required at your present knowledge, and to differentiate man from all the other things. How specific do you get? As specific as is necessary to integrate your knowledge. If you are a biologist and you work constantly with subdivisions of animals, it is perfectly justified to say, "man is the rational mammal," as distinct from other types, in that context. But within the framework of generalized human knowledge that is not specialized, "animal" is the genus that defines "man" specifically enough without becoming too specialized. And therefore, Objectivism would say that within the framework of present knowledge, it is the best general genus for "man." Aristotle, following the Platonic influence, says that the essence is carved out by nature, and, therefore, there can be no such thing as contextual essences or contextual definitions. Although Aristotle has many valuable *rules* of definition, both he and Plato ultimately hold that the definition has to come down to an act of *nous*, that is, of an intuitive grasp. And there, unfortunately, "intuition" is used in a less rational sense, as a direct insight, and that makes the whole theory vulnerable to the charge of being implicitly mystical (which is not Aristotle's intention but is the net effect). Obviously, I couldn't hope to make the whole Objectivist view clear and wouldn't attempt to. In answer to a question on Aristotle, I refer you to Miss Rand's *Introduction to Objectivist Epistemology* where this is discussed at length.

Q: Would Aristotle favor an analytic-synthetic dichotomy?

A: If you interpret that to mean a dichotomy between the logical and the factual, then the answer is certainly no since he believes the laws of logic are facts of reality. But insofar as you interpret that to mean a dichotomy between necessary and contingent truths, then yes, he does make such a distinction, partly because he believes that essences are intrinsic. In this respect he is a Platonist. And this ties in with the point that I mentioned earlier that he does not believe in universal causal necessity. For details on this, you'll have to wait until next lecture, or read my article "The Analytic-Synthetic Dichotomy," where I discuss it.[14]

Q: When you commented that the laws of induction "had not been written out," did you mean to imply someone had discovered them but hadn't yet written them out?

A: In my judgment, Objectivism (that is to say, Ayn Rand's epistemology) has formulated the principles of the answer to the problem of induction, but those principles have not been written out as applied specifically to induction. And I trust one day, within all of our lifetimes, they will be.

Q: Could you give us an indication of what a valid defense of the principle of induction would be? Does it involve the law of causality?

---

14. This article is reprinted in *Introduction to Objectivist Epistemology.*

A: If you mean a justification of the general *procedure* of induction, Aristotle himself gives you the material for that: You are justified in generalizing because, in fact, "cause and effect" is a law of reality, and therefore, the instances that we observe are not chance coincidences, meaning that we can justifiably generalize. But if you ask me, "How do you know in a particular case that the sample you have observed is really representative of a law and not just a coincidence, or something that depends on a necessary condition that you haven't identified?," then you are asking me for the detailed theory of the actual practice of induction, and that is what I suggest you read in the book which I mentioned in the previous question, which has not yet been written.

Q: Who was the father of altruism in philosophy?

A: Would it surprise you if I said the answer is [Johann Gottlieb] Fichte? That is the answer I defend in my book *The Ominous Parallels.* Highly condensed, what it amounts to is that altruism, as the formal theory that the essence of the good is sacrifice specifically for other people, not mixing in sacrifice for God or any element of egoistic selfishness—pure self-sacrifice for others—is a post-Kantian development. It was foreshadowed by Christianity and by Platonism. There were large hunks of it, but it was mixed in with the idea that more important than sacrificing for others is sacrificing for God and mixed in with the idea that there's something in it for you, you'll get the other world, or whatever. The idea of pure, selfless total, self-sacrifice for others is a post-Kantian phenomenon. And the first famous influential, philosophically consistent altruist is the first famous influential and consistent post-Kantian, Fichte. So, you can say it was either Christianity in the sense of starting the element, or Kant in the sense of annihilating everything else, or Fichte as the man who actually did it.

Q: Did Aristotle originate the concept of "abstraction" from particulars to grasp universals?

A: There were leads in Plato, insofar as Plato said you had to have the stimuli of the senses in order to rise to abstraction. But as far as I know, as a formal theory of abstraction (as against simply recollecting stimuli), yes, he did originate it.

Q: In Aristotle's view that man is born *tabula rasa* and then develops concepts from percepts, would he include introspective knowledge as well as extrospective in this scheme?

A: Yes. You're not born with knowledge of your mental states any more than knowledge of physical facts. You have to first look in and grasp the data. And the faculty that does that, he thought, was called the "common sense" (that was his name for the faculty that is self-conscious, able to introspect and grasp the nature of the mental activities we were engaging in). And so, you need the data from the common sense, which we would call today "introspection," which you then proceed to conceptualize in the normal fashion.

Q: What was Aristotle's single most influential contribution to thought?

A: If I had to select one, I would say the laws of logic.

Q: After forming a definition, can one arbitrarily form a word for that concept, or is the word chosen based on the units of the concept?

A: If you distinguish the word from the concept, then you must mean by the "word" the particular sound or shape used, because the word *qua* standing for those particular units that it integrates is, of course, the concept. Obviously, you're free to choose any noise you want. If you get a certain group and abstract and form the class that we now call "man," there is nothing metaphysically or epistemologically sacrosanct about the sound "man," as against the sound "mensch," or "l'homme," or "homo," or "anthropos," or whatever it happens to be. And therefore, the sound is absolutely free, as you can make it whatever you want so long as you're consistent. But if you step into a developed language and propose to speak to other speakers in that language and say, "However, I intend to use words in my own special way, and hereafter, I'm going to mean by 'man' banana—now I want everyone in this rule to volunteer for a cake"—if you talk that way, that is out.

Q: Please redefine a "syllogism."

A: A deductive argument containing two premises and three terms, two of which are linked in the conclusion as a result of the linking of each of them with the third or middle term in the premises. That is a modern definition. Aristotle defines "syllogism" much more broadly to mean, any process of reasoning, or any process of deductive reasoning, but he was not familiar with the fact that there are other types of deductive reasoning (or he didn't focus on them). But a syllogism is actually a more specific type of reasoning.

Q: In what ways does Objectivism disagree with the distinction between form and matter?

A: I'd like to save Objectivism's view on Aristotle until the next lecture, but there are many different usages, they are not all the same, he is not consistent, and certain aspects are perfectly sensible, others aren't. Objectivism disagrees with the idea that universal is form, and that particular is matter, is stuff. It disagrees with that entirely, and you will see next lecture that Aristotle's formulation leads him in a terrible hole from which he couldn't escape.

Q: Was Aristotle something of an atomist?

A: He agreed that change involves rearrangement of matter, but in *his* sense of rearrangement, not merely spatial change, but change of form, where "form" means structure. For Aristotle, it is not reducible to locomotion. In that sense, Aristotle does not agree with the Atomists that all change is reducible to locomotion.

Q: Does Aristotle agree with the existence of a vacuum?

A: No, Aristotle denies the existence of a vacuum.

Q: Would you comment on the standard criticism of the correspondence theory of truth, namely, that such a theory is fruitless because we can never get outside of our minds to validate that our ideas in fact correspond to reality?

A: I would like to know what in the world is the basis for such a premise. If you hold the view of all the moderns—Descartes, Locke, Berkeley, Hume, Kant, etc.—that all we perceive is our own subjective experiences, our own intellectual mental content, which becomes a little world inside our heads, and that we are therefore cut off from reality, obviously, then, the correspondence theory would be no good. And that's just the grounds on which Kant and his followers rejected it, that reality is unknowable. But what is the justification of the premise that we do not perceive reality directly, only its effects on us? The answer is the argument that Protagoras gave, and that I gave you in this course. If you know the answer to that, then you have no problem with this argument. The answer to that is in lecture twelve.

Q: Would you suggest good translations of Aristotle?

A: There are two kinds of translations: There's the definitive translation, the Oxford edition in the twelve volumes, edited by W. D. Ross, the most famous of the Aristotelian commentators in the twentieth century, and that's the one I've been reading to you. That is the standard translation, scholarly, annotated, and as reliable as you can get. It is not very readable, but then, that is not the fault of the translator. There are occasionally translations that come out, "Aristotle for Graduate Students." There's no "Aristotle for Everyman" that I know of, but there's "Aristotle for Graduate Students" that is more readable but not very good. I remember one by Richard Hope, a translation of Aristotle's *Metaphysics* that is a little freer than the usual. As somebody once said about translations of Aristotle, that if you know Greek, you can usually understand the English translations, but the English translations are ones you really have to work at because Greek is a different language than English, and consequently, what they can express very tersely requires a whole circumlocution and paraphrase in English, because the languages are so different in their structure. And therefore, a sentence that is short and to the point in the Greek goes on and on in English, and you have to remember each part separately and build it all up again in your mind. It can be done, but it's not bedtime reading.

Q: What is begging the question?

A: Begging the question is the logical fallacy of using or assuming what you are trying to prove in advance of, or as part of, your proof. It's assuming the thing in question. One common form of it is circular reasoning. For instance, you go to a banker to borrow money, and he tells you he would loan you the money if he knew that you were reliable, but he has no verification of your reliability. And you say, "Well, I've got this friend who has known me for years, and he will vouch for my reliability." And the banker says, "Well, that would be great, but the trouble is I don't know your friend," and you say to him, "Well, I've known him for years, so don't worry. I'll vouch for him." That is going in a circle, you see. Your reasoning is, "I am reliable, and therefore, he is reliable, and therefore, I am reliable." But you're assuming your reliability in order to prove it. That's begging the question. And Aristotle maintained (obviously correctly) that any attempt to prove the laws of logic, as distinct from stating that they were self-evident, would be begging the question, because any reasoning relies on the laws of logic, and the essence of reasoning is to say, "Such and such premises, and now, since the laws of logic are true, such and such a conclusion follows." But if you tried to prove the laws of logic, if they were the conclusion of your argument, your reasoning would then be "Such and such premises, and now, since the laws of logic are true, therefore, the laws of logic are true." You'd have to use them to prove themselves. And therefore, there is no such thing as a proof of the laws of logic. You can't prove the principles of proof. All you can do is point to reality. And if the guy sees it, okay, and if he says he doesn't see it, you can try the reaffirmation through denial technique, but if he becomes like Cratylus and says, "Okay, then I won't talk at all," you can consider that you've done a good day's work.

Q: What, if any, is the difference between induction and abstraction?

A: As they're used today, it varies from writer to writer. Sometimes abstraction is said to be the process of forming concepts from percepts, whereas induction is the process of forming general principles from individual facts. But that usage is by no means standard. "Abstraction" is sometimes used for *any* mental process that consists of selective focusing in which you ignore one part of the data and focus on the rest. And in that respect, induction would involve abstraction as would concept-formation. "Induction" is commonly used to apply only to propositional truths, to arrive at full-fledged laws ("All men are mortal," etc.), whereas "abstraction" is used either for concept-formation or for the overall mental process common to concept-formation and generalization.

Q: According to Aristotle, are the primary premises of a given science arrived at by intuition (in other words, the first principles that you reach at the end)?

A: Yes. Here is another case where Objectivism would disagree with Aristotle. You see, he patterned all sciences on mathematics, which was partly the Pythagorean–Platonist influence, but partly the fact that mathematics was the one developed science where they had reached first principles, and so he just assumed that the same thing would be true in physics, in biology, etc., and that, therefore, there would be a counterpart in physics to "A straight line is the shortest distance between two points." And in fact, he thought he had found such primary principles of physics that, when grasped, are self-evident, in the same way that the mathematical axioms are, but it takes a lot of knowledge to get to them. He had no idea of the incredible complexity of science, and it's been said by a number of people that it's a good thing that he didn't, because if the Greeks knew how fantastically complicated it would be to unearth all the laws of the physical world, they would have given up. Maybe not. But in any event, it would be like asking a child who's a beginning reader to read the thirteen volumes of *The Oxford English Dictionary* overnight. It would be too much, and so you can't ask that. If you ask me a different question, "How would science come to a final explanation if it's not by intuitive self-evident principles that you reach?" I would say that answer will be dictated by your answer to the question of induction, because as part of a full theory of induction you will have to go into a theory of *theory formation.* There are, after all, other ways of arriving at general principles than simple inductive generalization. For instance, you do not arrive at the atomic theory by inductive generalization. So, Aristotle is deficient in not fully recognizing in his epistemology the crucial importance of theory-formation. For instance, you do not arrive at the atomic theory by saying, "I observe that this is made of atoms, and this is, and this is, and therefore everything is." You arrive at the atomic theory quite a different way, by saying, "Now I observe many individual facts, what would explain them?" And then you hypothesize something that is *not* directly observable in the normal case. The rules for what kind of scientific hypotheses are valid or not, is part of the issue of induction, and has to be treated along with the topic of inductive generalization. And when you have the answer there—and that will be provided ultimately by your theory of concept-formation, so it's just a matter of drawing the corollaries from the theory of concept-formation—when you have those answers, you'll know what would be the first principles and "end" a science.

Q: Would you contrast Aristotle's concept of "explanation" with the Positivists' notion that explanation is merely description?

A: Yes, certainly. The Positivists—the followers of Auguste Comte, and a whole string of them (who added in a corruption of logic in addition and called themselves Logical Positivists in the twentieth century)—declare, in essence, that there is no such thing as explanation, that all you can do is describe brute, inexplicable facts. You can give a summary of the sense data that trot by your eyes, and perhaps you can generalize and form some general rule that for some inexplicable reason, e.g., this particular sense datum is followed by this one as a normal rule. (Of course, you can never be certain according to them, and that's why the school is called "positivism.") Aristotle repudiates that entire view. Explanation is different from description, if "description" means a recitation and summary of the sense data going by you. Explanation is a conceptual identification of the causes, in terms of general principles and by reference to the nature of the acting entity. It is, therefore, *not* something accessible to a simple perceptual-level mentality. And it is something real and crucial in human knowledge and is that which enables us to rise above the animal level. In a broader sense, you can say that explanations are descriptions, e.g., the atomic theory is an explanation of many facts, but the atomic theory is a description of a fact of reality. So, in that sense, everything is a description. But then there's a big difference between description that is just a concrete-bound description of sense data and a description that is a much more fundamental account of the causes of what you observe. It's the latter sense that is Aristotle.

Q: Can you give me a line of progression of Aristotelian thinkers up until today?

A: The main Aristotelian thinkers—the *main* ones, that's all I'll give you—were Aristotle first, and passing over all the lesser followers of him in the Aristotelian school (some of whom are very good, like Theophrastus, but they don't have much to add), the next main one is Thomas Aquinas, who attempts to blend Aristotle with Christianity, but who really knows Aristotle, and who on many smaller points (smaller but vital) is better than Aristotle, i.e., he's a real philosopher, and all you have to do is learn to read him and excerpt away the religion, and he's a fascinating philosopher. There are some Aristotelians of the Renaissance, none of them very important (Pietro Pomponazzi might be the best known of the Aristotelians in the Renaissance). There is John Locke, who is, however—as are most British philosophers—a motley medley of just about everybody. He's a little bit of Augustine, and quite a bit of Descartes, and a little bit of Thomas Hobbes, and quite a bit of Francis Bacon, and some Aristotle, and it's all mashed together, as is typical of British philosophy. But if you excise him properly, you can find an Aristotelian thread running through Locke. After Locke, the next one is Ayn Rand. There is no Aristotelianism today. It died completely after Kant, whose specific effect was to annihilate the last traces of it, and so there's none in the nineteenth century at all, and in the twentieth century until Ayn Rand. Those are the main ones. The real actual main line is Aristotle, Aquinas, one quarter of Locke, and Ayn Rand.

Q: Does the acceptance of existence as an axiom say anything about its primacy? Consciousness is also an axiom, after all.

A: Yes, it does by implication. When you present the axioms of philosophy in proper order, you must begin with the axiom of existence. You could not begin with the axiom of consciousness, because the first question anyone would ask you if you said, "There is consciousness" (which, by the way, is precisely what Descartes attempts to do, as we'll see later), the first question anybody with sense will ask you is, "What is consciousness conscious *of*?" So, first you must establish existence. Only then can you establish the axiom of consciousness. In this sense, the establishing of the axiom of existence implies the primacy of existence.

LECTURE FIVE

A Revolution: The Birth of Reason (Part II)

In the last lecture, we surveyed Aristotle's epistemology and some of the essentials of his metaphysics. In regard to metaphysics, we said that reality, for Aristotle, is this world, the world in which we live, the world of concrete particular individual things as revealed to man's senses. Each particular, each primary substance, is comprised of two elements—a universalizing element that constitutes the basis for our putting it into a certain class and ascribing to it a certain nature, and an element that constitutes the basis of its uniqueness, that which makes it a "this." Recall Aristotle's specialized technical terms for these two elements: "form" and "matter." Matter is the stuff or material comprising a thing, and form represents its structure or organization. And in these terms, change is the process of matter taking on new form, so the change in no way involves a contradiction and is eminently logical, rational, and scientifically intelligible. Or using the other terminology, we could say that change is the passage from potentiality to actuality, a process we saw that occurs in orderly, predictable, lawful ways. Every change involves four essential factors, four *causes*: the material cause (that is, the material from which the change proceeds), the formal cause (which is the new structure imposed on that material), the efficient cause (which is the action of the agent that gives the new structure to the matter), and the final cause (the end, or goal or purpose, of the process, the final answer to the question "Why does it occur?").

Given that short recapitulation, let us pick up from this point and continue with Aristotle's metaphysics. The first question is: Is this four-cause analysis of change applicable to all changes of every kind? Because, as applied to human action, you might say that his analysis is obviously sensible, as against, for instance, the mechanism of the Atomists, who deny the reality of purpose. But, you might ask, what about unconscious biological change—for instance, an acorn changing into an oak? And what about non-biological, inanimate change, such as upsetting a bucket of water on the top of a hill and the water flowing down the hill? How do the four causes operate in these areas? Consider as examples the two cases I just mentioned: the acorn becoming the oak and the water flowing downhill mechanically. The first three causes (the material, formal, and efficient) still apply. In both these cases, you start from something—the acorn or the water on the top of the hill—that is the material cause of these two changes. In both these cases, you go to a new form—the oak or the water at the bottom—and that is the formal cause. And in both these cases, the change is effected by some means. Here, I don't have to specify, because there are various biological and/or mechanical processes of different kinds at work on the "matter" effecting the change, and those are the efficient causes. But the big question is: What about the final cause? Does it apply to such processes also? According to Aristotle, the answer is yes.

Why did he hold this? Whereas Plato's favorite subject was mathematics, Aristotle's was biology. He was not only a great philosopher but also a great biologist, and he tended to use biological examples and then make metaphysical generalizations from them. In biology, the doctrine of final causes has a considerable plausibility. For instance, look at the growing acorn—watch the little acorn become a sprout, and then a young plant, and so on through all the intermediate stages until it becomes a fully mature tree. Aristotle asks, can you explain this progression of stages as simply a blind reaction to outside forces that has no inherent aim, or end, to which it's striving? Observe a plant's actions—they are unconscious, but nevertheless, the plant turns toward the sunlight, and it sends its roots out reaching for water. If you put a rock in its way, within appropriate size limits, it will push against the rock to try to go around it. It seems apparent from these and countless other such facts, says Aristotle, that the plant has a goal—to live, to grow, to reach its full development, its form, its actuality. It does not seem to be simply an indifferent reactor to external stimuli. Or consider the self-repairing actions of an animal body. You break your arm, and the bones knit (beyond a certain point there's nothing the body can do). You cut your finger and the body forms a scab, and we ask why does it do that? It does it in order to keep the germs out. That's a final cause, an end, a goal. You contract a disease (to take a modern example), and the body manufactures antibodies, and we ask why—in order to fight the disease. Look at the organs of an animal body—each of them has a function, which is often described in terms of its end or goal. What are the lungs for? In order to take in air. What is the heart for? To pump blood. Etc. It seemed obvious to Aristotle that the organs and the actions of living entities have ends or goals, that their structure and functioning do not seem to be just the result of an indifferent reaction to outside factors. It seemed to him obvious that living things aim at an end, or goal, that they strive for that as far as they can, and the goal is to develop, to grow, to reach their full form or actuality. And their completed form he calls their *entelechy*, which is the final completed form of a living thing, the oak tree in relation to an acorn. This goal seems to him to be the primary factor determining the actions of a living entity.

How would you account for all this behavior except by reference to an end or goal guiding the living thing? Suppose we ask the Atomists how they would account for it. They would say it's a blind mixing and unmixing of the atoms owing to mechanical forces. Aristotle says that if we granted such a thing as a blind mechanistic mixing of atoms, that might indeed produce a few cases of acorns becoming oaks, but why does it happen regularly? What keeps the process on the track so many times? On the theory of Atomism, why isn't it the case that sometimes, by mechanistic reactions, the atoms making up an acorn are reshuffled and come out as carrots, or playing cards, or Hegel? Why do they repeatedly, regularly come out as oak trees? Aristotle granted that they do not *always* come out as oak trees, because there are stunted acorns. His expression for this is: "They happen always or for the most part." But such regularity, he says, implies an aim inherent in the process to keep it on the track. And therefore, Aristotle is a teleologist, that is to say, a universal teleologist—he believes for everything that exists, every change has a final cause. As far as the inanimate world, we won't belabor that point (his physics), but it seems that he generalized from human and biological behavior to the inanimate world as a whole. In his view, the inanimate world is ultimately reducible to four basic elements, earth, air, water, and fire—that he just took over from early Greek physics. Each of these elements, he believed, has its own natural place, its own proper location in the universe, and that location represents *its* true form or actuality, and therefore, the final cause of each mechanical change is ultimately reducible back to the aim of the elements to reach their natural place. For instance, the natural place of water is next to the earth, and therefore, if you take water way up in the air and turn it upside down, turn the pail upside down, the water is on its way back to its natural place, and that's its final cause. On the other hand, the natural place of fire is up near the heavens, and that's why when you light a match the fire goes up instead of going down, and so on.

For Aristotle, therefore, everything has an end or goal, whether it's human, biological, or inanimate. And the ultimate natural goal of a thing is to reach its form. In this sense, the formal cause and the final cause of every change become the same thing, the same form. For instance, when the acorn becomes the oak, the formal cause is the new structure, and the final cause is to acquire and develop that same new structure. And the way this is usually put is that the formal and the final causes are for Aristotle the same single fact, the same form, regarded from two different perspectives. You call it the "formal cause" when you regard the form as already attained, and you call it the "final cause" when you regard the form as being aimed at but not yet attained. This is known technically as the Aristotelian doctrine of the identity of the formal and final causes. It's a way of expressing his particular version of universal teleology.

There are many objections to this view of Aristotle's. He does not mean purposive or goal-directed behavior in a conscious sense in the case of unconscious entities, and yet it's very difficult to know what exactly it would mean to talk of an "unconscious goal-directed action." If "goal-directed action" is taken at its face value, it implies an entity with the capacity to be aware of a future state and to pursue it. What exactly it would mean to pursue a future state by an entity deprived of the capacity for awareness of anything (including of the future) remains a mystery. And Aristotle does not want to say that it's an unconscious striving, nor certainly that it's a conscious striving in these cases. Ultimately, it seems that he must leave the mechanism of such goal-directed behavior in such cases to be unintelligible (at least based on the surviving writings that we have). Many people have argued that you can give an alternative explanation of the apparent purposefulness of biological phenomena, an explanation that in fact denies that there is such a thing as purposive unconscious action. One might ask, "Couldn't living entities be built in such a way, have such a nature, that no matter what happens to them (within the appropriate limits), their necessary reaction is a pro-life course of behavior, so that it would look as though they are pursuing an end, but in fact they are expressing their nature?" And sometimes the example of a thermostat is cited in this connection—it is so structured that whatever the forces operating upon it (within certain limits), it will react in order to produce a certain temperature. Someone unfamiliar with this mechanism might say that the thermostat has an end, because it systematically acts to achieve a certain goal, but in fact it is simply expressing the laws of its nature without itself pursuing an end. In other words, you can use Aristotle's own concept that the nature, or the actuality of a thing, determines its behavior, in order to explain the biological phenomena that he refers to. You do not need reference to final causation to keep such phenomena on track. You just need an appropriate kind of efficient causation.

I want to be fair to Aristotle, so I should mention that the issue of Aristotle's teleology, and how precisely to interpret it, is a very controversial question. I've given you the standard traditional interpretation, but others are possible and have some basis in the writings that have come down to us. In particular, it's possible to interpret Aristotle's teleology as in no way implying any unconscious striving or yearning for a goal on the part of nonconscious entities. That would raise the question: "What then does teleology consist of, and how would you defend this interpretation of Aristotle?" This, however, is a technical question entirely beyond the scope of this course. For those of you who are interested, I might mention a doctoral dissertation that is being written on this exact subject by Professor Allan Gotthelf, titled "Aristotle's Conception of Final Causality," and I understand it will be available in the stacks at Columbia University sometime in the spring of 1973. And I refer those interested in this subject to that work for a thorough discussion of the complex issues involved in this point.[15]

Before we leave the subject of Aristotle's teleology, however, I do want to mention one unfortunate effect of Aristotle's teleology, namely, that it prevented him from grasping explicitly the idea of a universe run by absolute natural laws. You recall that I said last lecture that although Aristotle laid the basis for cause and effect, he himself seemed from the surviving fragments to have no clear idea of a universal reign of cause and effect, because he observed that sometimes acorns *don't* become oaks but are stunted, and sometimes little babies *don't* grow up into healthy human beings. In other words, sometimes the teleological process seems to be interfered with or break down. And consequently, for Aristotle, what happens in the physical world is not absolutely necessary. Certain things, he said, are necessary *if* the end, the form, is to be achieved, but he maintains that there is such a thing as accidental or chance factors, which can interfere occasionally and thus breech the absolute universality of natural law. Consequently, for Aristotle, laws are always expressed in the form "such and such happens always or for the most part." And the exceptions (being cases where final causality breaks down in his view) cannot be scientifically understood and are outside the province of science. These accidental facts, he says, are brute "contingent" facts (that's the later word for it), that is to say, facts that cannot be ultimately explained, brute data that we have to accept as facts. Thus, you see, even Aristotle accepts a form of the necessary versus contingent dichotomy, and that feeds very nicely into

---

15. Gotthelf's dissertation was published in the December 1976 issue of *The Review of Metaphysics* and again (with a "1986 Postscript") in Gotthelf and James G. Lennox, eds., *Philosophic Issues in Aristotle's Biology* (Cambridge University Press, 1986).

Kant's later analytic-synthetic dichotomy. If you ask Aristotle to explain such accidental, or chance, phenomena, he says that in those cases, the form was thwarted in its development by matter, by the resistance of the material element. That is an obvious Platonic carryover, a legacy of Plato's myth of the Demiurge (if you remember), who tried to shape matter to the perfection of the forms but met a certain resistance. And this kind of element does exist in Aristotle. Needless to say, this is a very bad limitation on science, because if you accept this doctrine, it prevents the world from being wholly intelligible. And that's why I stressed last lecture that although Aristotle laid the basis for causality, he did not himself have any clear idea that every event is necessitated in accordance with strict universal laws. I might mention another root of his belief in chance, or contingency, and that is that he apparently believed in free will but seems to be unclear how to reconcile free will with the universal reign of cause and effect, and that is another element feeding his view that there is contingency, chance, at work in the universe.

A last word on Aristotle's teleology: It is what is known as *immanent.* In other words, each thing is metaphysically egoistic. It is not striving to achieve an outside cosmic purpose, as for instance in the Christian version of teleology, where everything is striving to fulfill God's purpose, or for Plato, where everything is striving to satisfy an external Form of the Good. In Aristotle, the end of each thing is immanent within it, namely, each thing is striving to reach its own fulfillment, actualize its unique potentialities, reach its own form. Everything is striving to realize *itself,* and this is, therefore, very often referred to as the *metaphysics of self-realization* in the broadest sense, encompassing water going downhill and acorns becoming oaks. And as you'll see, that becomes the metaphysical basis of Aristotle's ethics. It is a universe of development in which everything is striving to develop itself, fulfill itself, ascend the ladder from matter to form, become fully and in actual reality what it has in it to become.

Let's ask the question: "What keeps it all happening?" What keeps things striving to actualize their forms? What keeps things on the go? Why are the acorns out to become oaks, and the baby busily changing into a man, and the water flowing downhill, and the sculptor shaping his statues, etc.? Why does the universe not run down, stop dead, become motionless? What is the cause of motion? And by "motion" in this question, we mean *any* change, *any* happening, *any* occurrence. Please note that for Aristotle, motion *always* existed. Motion is eternal. There was never a time when there was not motion. And his proof of this is that time itself is simply a measure of motion. A year for instance—if we take modern astronomy—is the period of the revolution of the earth around the sun, and a day is a period of the rotation of the earth on its axis. If we stopped all motion completely, then there would be no years, no days, no seconds, no time. And if so, to speak of a time when there was no motion would be to speak of a time when there was no time, since time *is* the measure of motion. And that would be a contradiction. Consequently, Aristotle concludes, time is eternal as the measurement of motion, and therefore, motion is eternal. Consequently, the cause of motion that we are looking for is not something that starts motion at a particular point in time. No, it's the eternal factor (whatever it is) that underlies all motions and explains why there *is* such a phenomenon as motion in the universe. Any particular motion can be explained by an earlier motion. Why did this thing happen? . . . because *this* one did, and why this? . . . because *this* one, and so on. But what we want to know is what explains the fact of motion as such?

So, let us engage in a chain of reasoning here with Aristotle and let us call the factor (whatever it is) that is responsible for motion "the Mover." What can we infer about it? The first thing is, it must be an eternal existent, since it is the cause of motion, and motion is eternal. Let us ask if the Mover can itself move? Answer—no. This Mover must be itself unmoved and even immovable. Why? If the Mover itself were capable of motion, as soon as it moved, the question would become "How do you explain *its* motion?" We'd have an infinite regress. If we are trying to explain the phenomenon of motion, we obviously can't do it by appealing to something that either moves or is capable of moving, because we'd be going in a circle, we'd be begging the question, we'd be assuming the thing we're trying to explain. If you want the ultimate source of motion—the *Prime Mover*, you see—then it, whatever it is, must be beyond motion. It must be immovable.

From that we can infer that it has no potentialities at all, because anything with potentialities is capable of change when its potentialities are realized or actualized. A thing that is immovable is a thing that must be devoid of potentiality. What then would it be? The only other category is *actuality*. So, this must be pure actuality, or to use the other term, it must be pure form. It will be an individual thing, not a Platonic universal. But it is not matter organized in a way that can be differently organized. Therefore, it will be an exception to the metaphysical principle of "no matter without form and no form without matter"—it will be pure form, pure actuality. And therefore, it will not be material or physical in the modern sense either, because anything physical is capable of change.

Let's observe another thing about this Mover, of which we're slowly creating a character sketch. Whatever it is—and we don't know yet fully—it must be perfect, completely perfect. Because we know that everything is striving to realize its potentiality, to achieve the higher state of actuality. And we know that it must be better to be actual than potential, and that is why everything strives to achieve the actuality. And this is inherent in teleology, at least as advocated by Aristotle. Everything is striving for the best state, the state of fulfillment. Here, in the Prime Mover, we have a being that has no unrealized potentialities, a being that is pure actuality. Therefore, it has hit the metaphysical jackpot: It must be perfect.

You might ask, how does such a Mover cause motion? Could it reach out and push the world? No, because it can't move. It can't push the world, it can't pull it, it can't even desire, because desire is a form of motion, a mental motion. It can't even say to itself in Prime Mover language, "Let there be motion," because it cannot speak, it cannot will, it's motionless, it is truly immovable. Well, what is the solution to this dilemma? How does it function to cause motion?

To understand Aristotle's answer, you have to know something of his astronomy, which was not original with him but was a standard Greek view, one that he took over from the scientists of the time, the way a modern philosopher might take over Einsteinian physics from the physicists. For Aristotle, the universe is a nest of hollow, crystalline, transparent spheres, connected along an axis. Embedded in the sides of these spheres are the various heavenly bodies—the sun, the stars, the planets, etc. The earth, he believed, is at the center, and it is stationary. These various spheres revolve around the earth, and the rotation, or the revolution, of the various spheres is responsible for the motions that we observe of the sun and the planets and the fixed stars across the sky. There is, according to Aristotle (and this also is not an original view with him), a soul, or an intelligence, connected to each of the spheres. These spheres are, in effect, semi-divine in the Greek view. They are regarded as living entities (the reason seeming to be that the heavenly motions were so perfectly ordered and so long known that it seemed to suggest to the Greeks that an intelligence of some sort had to be guiding them and keeping them on their perfect course). In any event, the various revolutions of these spheres are responsible for the motions we observe, which are communicated along the axis.

Therefore, the problem of motion reduces to the problem of getting the outermost sphere moving, the sphere in which, according to Aristotle, the fixed stars are embedded. If we could get the outer one moving or explain *its* motion (of course, it always *has* been moving, but if we could *explain* its motion), that motion would be eternally communicated along the various axes to the rest of the spheres and ultimately to the things on the earth. So, we have this nest of spheres with the outermost one guided by an intelligence, and beyond, there is the perfect Immovable Mover. If you have any power of imagination, you should be able to figure out the solution. The intelligence connected to the outermost spheres is capable of awareness as an intelligence and is particularly capable of being aware of the Prime Mover—it is *eternally* aware of the Prime Mover. And it is aware of the perfection of the Prime Mover, and it wishes with all its might to emulate this perfection, in other words, to be the most perfect that *it* can be. You ask yourself, what would you do if you were an intelligence connected to a sphere and you wanted to do the most perfect thing? You would engage in circular motion. This is the best motion because it's the only eternal motion, but if it went in a straight line, since the universe is finite, it would have to turn around at a certain point, so the motion wouldn't be unbroken. The best motion is going round and round. Consequently, the famous line that you have heard is an actual description of Aristotle's metaphysics—"It is love that makes the world go around." There is, in effect, a cosmic—if one-sided—love affair between the intelligence that moves the outermost sphere and the Prime Mover, and its motion—once it's going around—is then communicated along the axes to the rest of the spheres and the earth. So, the Prime Mover causes motion in the same sense in which a beautiful woman put at the front of the room, who was herself entirely motionless, might produce motion in her direction on the part of certain members of the class who might wish to emulate or participate in her perfection. The Prime Mover is the cause of motion in the sense of the *final* cause.

What is the nature of the Prime Mover? We must, says Aristotle, think of it as a mind, so we can now start saying "he." What do minds do? They think. But this must be a very special kind of thought process because no motion is allowed. And so, it must be a kind of motionless contemplation, not a process of sensing, or inferring, or reasoning. You can get as close to it as we as human beings can get if you look motionlessly at the tip of my finger—don't blink, and don't draw any conclusions—just, without a flicker of mental activity, look at a motionless finger. As soon as I move my finger, that wipes it out, that introduces mental motion in you, and changes your mental state, so it's disqualified. But if you can grasp a motionless contemplation, that's what the Prime Mover does.

What is the object of its contemplation? It can contemplate only something that is motionless. And the only thing that is motionless is the

Prime Mover. And consequently, Aristotle draws the conclusion that the Prime Mover thinks, or is conscious, only of himself. He describes it as pure self-consciousness, thought thinking about itself. This eternal, immutable, perfect, utterly self-absorbed mind responsible for the motion of the universe Aristotle frequently calls *theos*, "God." And this is therefore regarded as Aristotle's God.

You see that there is a strong element of Platonism here: The idea of a pure, immutable, perfect form is a Platonist idea. And it represents the primacy of consciousness in an obvious, blatant way—here's this Prime Mover, a pure consciousness detached from reality, responsible for the activities of things on earth. This is in glaring contradiction to Aristotle's distinctive approach and represents a Platonic carryover. But you see that even when he's a Platonist, he's also an Aristotelian. Even his Platonism is modified, because this is a God that would not do a religious person very much, if any, good. This God didn't create the universe. He is unmoved—the universe is eternal. You couldn't pray to this God because he couldn't hear you. This God couldn't perform miracles even if he *could* hear you. He's completely impotent. He has no plan, and he does not even know that the world exists. He has neither knowledge nor power. He is utterly ignorant and impotent. And indeed, Aristotle discusses him primarily in his physics, and it's sometimes said that the God for Aristotle is merely a footnote to physics, not a central concept. And Aristotle is frequently attacked, in spite of the Prime Mover, on the ground that he lacks any real religious feeling or interest. And that is true. The best illustration of this fact is that after he arrived at the Prime Mover theory, the astronomers came back and reported to him that one component of motion would not be enough to account for the observed motions of the heavenly bodies, and as they had calculated it, we need either forty-seven or fifty-five separate components of motion to account for the heavenly bodies, at which point Aristotle appended a chapter saying that there is not one Prime Mover, but either forty-seven or fifty-five of them. And some books seriously classify Aristotle as a polytheist on this point. That shows how seriously he took it.

The answer to Aristotle's argument is that its basic question is misguided. The question "How do you explain motion?" (in the sense Aristotle asks it) is an illegitimate question. The fact of motion, as such, must be regarded as an irreducible primary, in the same way that the fact of existence, as such, is an irreducible primary. You can explain any particular existent in terms of the actions of other existents, but the phenomenon of existence, as such, as Aristotle understands, is just there—that's where you start. And an equivalent account would have to be given of the phenomenon of motion, as such. If you attempt an explanation of motion, Aristotle's is the only one. The only explanation of motion would have to be in terms of an unmoving thing. And consequently, his is a perfectly logical answer if the question is permitted. I have to say that this argument is undoubtedly the sweetest argument for God ever offered. It is called the *cosmological argument*, the argument from the cosmos, and it takes many forms in later philosophy, deriving back ultimately from this point in Aristotle and from certain suggestions in Plato, and we will see it again in Aquinas.

We've seen so far in what ways the concepts of "form" and "matter" are central to Aristotle's metaphysics—they're the basis of his view of universals and particulars, the basis for his explanation of change, the basis for his view of causality and of an ordered universe (though he himself was not consistent on this point), and the basis for his definition of "God." Let's take about a minute to see how Aristotle used the concepts of "potentiality" and "actuality" to answer Zeno. And we'll take just one of Zeno's paradoxes because they all raise essentially the same issues. Remember the claim that you can't cross a room because first you have to cross half of it, and then half of that, and so on infinitely, and therefore there are an infinite number of distances that you have to get across, and of course that's impossible to do. The whole paradox depends, as do all of Zeno's paradoxes, on the idea that there can actually exist an infinite number of subdivisions of the distance. What is Aristotle's answer? He says this is impossible. Nothing, he says, can *actually* (now notice the word), nothing can *actually* be infinite. Here we must distinguish between the infinite and the very, very large. The infinite is not ten billion or twenty trillion zillion. The infinite is that which is greater than *any* particular quantity, which means it is no quantity in particular, which means it is a quantity with no identity, which means it is forbidden by the law of identity. Whatever actually exists, Aristotle concludes, will always be finite, limited, specific in its amount. In what sense, then, can we speak of infinity? Only, he says, as a potentiality (and there's another use of his concept). For instance, we can keep dividing a line further, and subdividing and subdividing. As a potentiality, there are no limits, so we can keep on doing it. In this sense, the line is infinitely divisible as a potentiality. But Aristotle's key point is that no matter how much we keep subdividing, we will always actually have only a finite number of parts—two parts, or four parts, or eight parts, or twenty drillion zillion parts—but always some specific number of parts. And the same is true of the number series. As a potentiality, it is infinite, and you can keep adding new numbers. But actually, whether you're going through it in your mind or writing it down on paper, you always actually have some finite specific number, even if you're counting by intervals of a zillion. There is no such thing as the *actual* infinite, and therefore Zeno's paradoxes collapse. Some of you would be curious to know how Aristotle applies this to space and time. Why doesn't he regard either of them as actually infinite? And I will be glad to answer that in the question period if anybody asks.

But now I want to see how Aristotle uses the same basic concepts—"form" and "matter," "actuality" and "potentiality"—in his discussion of psychology. And here the question is: What is the nature of the soul? Remember, *psyche* is Greek for "soul," and, therefore, psychology is the theory of the soul. Remember Plato's view that the soul is a substance, an entity, a self-contained entity that temporarily exists in the body and is capable of independent existence in another world, and remember that Plato believed in reincarnation, the whole Pythagorean wheel of birth. There was a conflict for Plato, a basic metaphysical conflict, between the soul and the body (or more exactly, between the highest part of the soul, which Plato called "reason," and the body and the bodily-influenced elements of the soul), and on that basis, Plato drew his ethics of asceticism: The body is a prison, we should flee from sensory pleasures, philosophy is the practice of dying, etc.

Consistent with his basic approach to philosophy, Aristotle wants to give a this-worldly account of the nature of the soul—a naturalistic, not a supernaturalistic, account. And he starts with the ordinary Greek meaning of the term *psyche*, or "soul." "Soul," for the ordinary Greek on the street, meant "the principle of life." It was not restricted to human beings or to conscious beings. It was the element responsible for life, whether possessed by a carrot, a dog, or a man. And, where applicable, it was the element responsible for cognition. A thing that is alive, in the Greek language, is a thing that has a soul. And we still use that language today, although if you don't know Latin you won't be familiar with it. We call a living thing an *animate* thing, "animate" being an English derivative of the Latin word *anima*, which is Latin for "soul," the translation of the Greek *psyche*. And therefore, when you say that something is inanimate, you are literally saying it lacks a soul, and that is the original Greek usage. So soul, for Aristotle, is that which makes a living thing living. And we can compare it to manness. Manness is the essence of man, that which makes a thing a man. Similarly, soul is the "living-ness" of an organism, the essence of a living thing, that which makes it a living thing.

What makes a thing the kind of thing it is? It's always its form. And so, if manness is the form of any particular man, soul is the form of a living thing. And the body, conversely, must be the matter of a living thing. And therefore, soul is to body as form is to matter. We can express the same point in the potentiality-actuality terminology. Suppose we have a handful, about ninety-eight cents worth of chemical compounds, and they are so chosen that together they have the potentiality for life, not the actuality, but the potentiality. Let us organize them, putting them together in various ways into a functioning living body. We have actualized their potentialities. Because of the new structure we have imposed, we now have actually the set of vital capacities and functions that before we only had potentially. And that, says Aristotle, is soul, which he defines as "the actuality of a natural body having life potentially in it." So, soul is to body as form is to matter and as actuality is to potentiality. At one point, he gives the example of a mark stamped on wax—the wax is the parallel to the body, and the stamp or structure imposed on it is the parallel to the soul. The soul for Aristotle, therefore, is not a thing, not an entity, but an *aspect* of a living entity. It is the name for those vital capacities that derive from organizing matter in a specific way.

The question is: What is the form of a living body? What *does* differentiate it from nonliving things? And Aristotle's answer is a specific set of biological powers or capacities, essentially, the power of nutrition, of growth, of reproduction. This is the bare minimum. When an entity has these powers, it is alive. And if soul then represents the form of a living thing, its distinctive attributes, then soul must be conceived not as a substance or a thing, but rather as a set, or a collection, of vital capacities, because these are what differentiate a living thing. And so, says Aristotle, if the eye were a complete organism, its "eye-ness," its actuality, its soul would be its power of vision. If an axe were an organism, its "axe-ness," i.e., its distinctively axe capacities, its power of cutting, would be its soul. The same thing is true with actual living things. You cannot discover the soul by dissecting the thing and hoping you'll pull out a nonmaterial ghost that belongs to another dimension. It is the name for the characteristic modes and capacities of behavior that make a living thing living. That's what soul is for Aristotle.

This doctrine has many major consequences. To begin with, Aristotle explicitly draws the conclusion that there can be no soul without a body—no form without matter, no power of cutting that floats free without the material axe, no vital capacities that float free without the entity possessing those capacities. Therefore, for Aristotle, reincarnation—the soul leaving the body and coming back to inhabit a new body—is positively bizarre, and he is nothing but scornful of that doctrine. For Aristotle—and for the same reason—there is no such thing as personal immortality. Further, with this doctrine, the metaphysical basis for any soul-body clash has been removed. Soul and body are two aspects of one integrated entity, as against Plato's view. I hasten to add that there is some Platonism in Aristotle's ethics, as we'll see, but it is not nearly as intense as in Plato, because the metaphysical and psychological foundation for it has now gone. There is no other world, there is no metaphysical soul-body opposition, and no personal immortality.

So far, I've given you just the introduction to Aristotle's theory of the soul. There are, he says, various kinds of souls—in other words, various types of vital capacities—that are to be discovered by observing the distinctive types of behavior living things engage in. There are three basic types of soul according to Aristotle. The most primitive level is the entities that just nourish themselves, grow, reproduce. All living entities have this type of soul, but one type has *only* this, and that is vegetables (or "plants," as we would call them today). And consequently, this set of powers—nutrition, growth, reproduction—is called the *vegetative* soul, or sometimes the *nutritive* soul. Next, we observe living things that have all the vegetative powers, plus the faculty of sense perception (in other words, a primitive form of consciousness). And as a result, these entities are capable of experiencing pleasure and pain when the appropriate stimuli reach their consciousnesses, and as a result they're capable of experiencing desire or aversion, and in some cases, capable of locomotion, of moving toward or from the object in question. These we call "animals," and they have what is translated unfortunately as the *sensitive* soul, which does not mean an esthete but rather a living entity with the power of sense perception. Note that this soul presupposes the previous one. The nutritive, or vegetative, soul is the precondition of keeping any entity alive, and it makes possible the higher type of soul, which will be biologically self-sustaining *and* have the capacity for sense perception. Note I said it makes *possible* the higher type. Consequently, we can say that the animal soul is the *actualization* of potentialities established by the vegetative soul. So, in that sense, the animal soul is on a higher level and represents a higher degree of actualization than plants. And finally, we reach man, who has the preceding capacities plus *nous*, the mind, the capacity to think, to grasp universals or abstract forms, to reason—he has the *rational* soul. And again, this requires the previous one—if we didn't have sense experience, we couldn't abstract, we couldn't reach reason—and therefore, again, the sensitive soul makes possible the rational soul, and the rational soul, when it emerges, is the actuality or actualization of those potentialities, and therefore, it's on a higher level than the animal soul.

The central work in which Aristotle investigated each of these souls (or sets of vital capacities) is the *De Anima*, the Latin translation for *On the Soul*. And here I want to say just a few words on two subjects—Aristotle's views on the senses and on reason.

First, on the senses: Aristotle was the first to define the five senses, to specify their organs and functions. As I mentioned in the last lecture, he was the one who suggested that error is due not to the senses but to misinterpretation by the mind. I don't have time to survey his accomplishments in this connection. However, I do want to briefly mention one element in his account of the senses: how he answered the Sophists. Remember Protagoras's argument that the qualities that things appear to have (color, sound, taste, warmth, etc.) do so only because of the sense organs of the perceiver, that these qualities are not really in the things themselves, and that, therefore, we never come in contact with reality as it really is. What is Aristotle's response? The first thing to say is that, judging by his surviving works, Aristotle is inconsistent on this subject. Sometimes he seems to agree with the Sophists—that if human senses contribute to the kind of perception we have, that would invalidate the perception. And so, part of the time, he asserts that the qualities we experience (like colors, smells, odors, etc.) exist in things themselves, entirely independently of human perception. This view is frequently called *naïve realism* ("realism" because of its stress on our perception of reality as it is, "naïve" because the people who christened this view think that it is a naïve viewpoint). The Sophists seem to have an obvious answer to naïve realism. Protagoras can say: "What do you mean those qualities are out there independent of us? They so blatantly depend upon the sense organs, and they vary with variations *in* the sense organs—how can you say that they're independent?" Therefore, part of the time, Aristotle seemed to grant that, in some way, those qualities are a function of human perception, and then he didn't seem to be able to make clear how they, nevertheless, were to be regarded as valid. His best attempt to deal with this question involved his use of potentiality and actuality. The process of sensation, Aristotle says at certain points, is a *process*, in other words, a type of change. As such, it must be a passage from potentiality to actuality. It is, in fact, a *dual* actualization, a double passage from potentiality to actuality—one that occurs *in* the sense organ (the eye, the ear, whichever), one in the *object* being sensed. Let's take them one at a time. First, the change in the sense organ.

Aristotle observed—or at least thought he did—that when you perceive, the appropriate sense organ comes to possess the particular quality being sensed. So, if you look out to see a red object and somebody looks at the eye of the seer, you can see in the appropriate light a little red image on the eyeball; it appears that the eye itself is temporarily reddened. Or if you put your hand into hot water to sense its temperature and then touch the hand itself, it seems to have acquired the quality that it's sensing, to become warm itself. You can yourself project the experience of tasting someone's tongue having eaten cherry pie, but it also presumably acquires the same quality as the taste it's experiencing. So, on the side of the perceiver, sensation for Aristotle is a process in which the quality being perceived is actually reproduced in the perceiving organ. The organ, prior to the perception, has the capacity, the potentiality, to be characterized by quality X, and sensing is the process in which that quality becomes actualized in the organ.

There is an equivalent process taking place in the object, in the thing in reality, that which you are perceiving. Before you perceive a red object, Aristotle holds, it is not actually red. To this extent, the Sophists are correct. Actual redness is somehow a function of our human form of perception and wouldn't exist if there were no human perceivers, and the same for tastes, sounds, etc. *But*—and here is his big disagreement with the Sophists—the object in reality has in fact a certain potentiality: It has the potentiality of being perceived in a certain way by a human perceiver. And that is a real fact about the object. It *is* the kind of object which *can*, given a certain perceiver, be perceived as red, or hot, or whatever, as against the kind of object which in fact *cannot*, which can only be perceived as, for instance, yellow, or cold, or whatever. In the process of sensation, says Aristotle, this potentiality of the object is actualized. The object that can be seen, for instance, as red, comes to be *actually* seen as red. The object that has the potentiality to be perceived as cold becomes an object that is *actually* perceived as cold. So, sense perception involves a dual actualization of the potentialities of the sense organ and of the object. Perception, therefore, is in contact with reality because in perception the object itself passes from potentiality to actuality, and at the end you see it as it actually is, so that redness doesn't actually exist except when we perceive, but *when* we perceive it does actually exist because our perception actualizes the potentiality of the object to be perceived as red.

Those of you who are familiar with the Objectivist theory of sense perception will be able to see that Aristotle's heart is certainly in the right place, and that if you properly developed his position, his theory on this issue *would* be the same as the Objectivist position. However, I must say that as Aristotle himself formulated this answer (and I've given you the gist of it), it is not fully satisfactory. It wouldn't and didn't stop the Sophists. You need to say more than this. Because their immediate comeback was: "We agree with you that in perception an object that has the potentiality to be seen as red actually is seen as red. In that sense," the Sophist says, "okay—there is a passage from potentiality to actuality, but the big question is, when we *see* the object as red, does that mean that in itself it actually *is* red, apart from us?" "Of course," the skeptic says, "we perceive things as we perceive them. But what we want to know is, are things in themselves *actually* the way we perceive them, or can we say only that this is the way we *see* objects but who knows what they really are in themselves apart from us?" To this objection, Aristotle offers no explicit defensible answer, at least in his surviving works. And in this sense, his views on the senses, though certainly a huge step in the right direction, are deficient. As for the Objectivist answer on this issue, I promised you that for lecture twelve.

I want to turn briefly to Aristotle's conception of the process by which *nous*, or reason, operates, i.e., the process of abstract, rational, conceptual thought that is distinctive to man. Aristotle thought of the process of thought on the model of sensation. Just as in sensation your organ actually acquires itself the quality being sensed—you actually suck in, so to speak, the sensory quality being perceived—so on the level of abstract thought. In thought, says Aristotle, you in effect suck into your mind—you imbibe, or receive—the forms of things, the abstract essences, or universals, and they become part of you, just as in sense experience the sensory qualities enter your organ and become part of you. And indeed, sometimes in terms of his own scheme, Aristotle contrasts thinking with eating, eating being one of the central functions of the vegetative soul. And he does it very sweetly as follows: In eating, in nutrition, you take in the matter of things—you incorporate that into your body—but the form is irrelevant, so you metaphorically spit out or discard the form. But in thinking, you do the reverse—you take in the forms of things, the abstractions, incorporate them into your mind, but the matter is irrelevant, so you discard or ignore it. So, in a very literal sense, thinking is a process of becoming *informed*. The abstract form actually comes into your mind. That's where we get the term "information."

Aristotle holds that the mind must be capable of receiving all forms, i.e., nothing in the universe is closed to it, and everything is knowable by human concepts. What then must be the nature of the mind in itself if it is able to receive, without any distortion, the forms of everything, all kinds of forms, throughout the whole universe? Aristotle seems to answer that the mind can have no structure or nature of its own. Because, he seems to argue, if the mind did have a specific structure or nature of its own—if it had any identity prior to the act of thinking—how could we ever know by the use of human reason things as they really are in themselves? If the human mind had a distinctive nature of its own, wouldn't we always be open to the objection, "Well, we are then just grasping the world as *we*, as *human beings*, have to grasp it, given our particular kind of thinking mechanism, so our knowledge would just be subjective, true only for human beings"? In other words, the view that Kant made his official philosophy thousands of years later. Apparently to escape this conclusion, Aristotle seems to have drawn the conclusion that the human mind—the abstract conceptual faculty—in itself has no nature or identity at all. He says that in itself, it is nothing at all before it starts to think, and therefore, there's nothing about it to distort or alter the data of reality. In itself, he says, the mind is simply *potentiality*, the capacity for receiving the forms, but nothing actually. It is, he says, the place of forms, and he seems also to have been influenced by Plato on this issue.

If you recall, Plato wanted a place, a medium, in which his supernatural Forms could be reflected, and he argued that it must be empty space, nothing, nonbeing. Plato argued for this partly on the grounds that only a thing without any form of its own would be suitable for receiving all Forms. Aristotle seems to have taken over this doctrine and translated it from cosmology to psychology and argued that the mind is like Plato's empty space—a nothing that can receive all forms. This, I interject, is a very dubious doctrine on Aristotle's part. If the mind is nothing in itself, how can it think? How can it do anything? What about the law of identity, which decrees that everything, including the mind, has an identity, that it's something, that it has a specific nature? But as soon as you say that, the skeptics rush in and say, "Aha, if the mind has a specific nature, you can never know things as they are, only things as they are thought by the human mind." In other words, they draw the Kantian conclusion. There is a tricky question here, and I think that you can understand Aristotle's problem. What is the correct answer? Put that down for lecture twelve also. It's a brief addendum to our discussion of the senses, it does not raise any new issues, and once you understand the correct view on the senses, the issue of the mind on this point falls into place without difficulty. Again, I want to say that Aristotle's views on the question of the mind's nature are obscure in the surviving works, and other interpretations are possible. I gave you the standard interpretation, which to me seems reasonable as an interpretation of Aristotle, but I wouldn't deny that you could find other elements in Aristotle that definitely ascribe a specific nature to the mind. On the basis of the existing manuscripts, Aristotle is inconsistent on this issue.

And one last word on Aristotle's theory of the mind, a point that is only of historical interest, but I mention it for accuracy. The mind, according to the account so far, is sheer potentiality, the capacity to acquire or take in the abstract forms of things. But potentiality, as we know, cannot actualize itself. Remember the four causes—the clay, the potentiality of the statue, cannot mold itself. It requires an efficient cause to act upon it, actually to transform it, to realize its potentialities. Well, says Aristotle, the same is true with mind. So, if mind is the sheer potentiality of acquiring the forms, there must be another aspect of mind, an aspect that operates on the potentiality, bringing it to actuality. Mind in its potential sense Aristotle calls the *passive reason,* and mind in its capacity of actualizer he calls the *active reason.*

In the surviving works, there are only a few broken sentences about the active reason, and it is impossible, therefore, to have any coherent theory of what he meant by it. All he really tells us (if you can even trust the translation, because one of the key sentences can be read in at least four different ways grammatically) is that the active reason is an impersonal reasoning agency, a kind of spark that operates to actualize our potential to know and bring it to fulfillment. There is, he says, nothing personal about this active reason. It's an impersonal reasoning agency. And he seems to suggest that it's independent of the body, that it existed before the body, and will survive the death of the body. In other words, it's immortal. This little fragment of Aristotle is an obvious carryover of Platonism, as far as we can judge. This view suggests that there is a nonmaterial element of the soul that antecedes and succeeds the body, and it is therefore in direct conflict with Aristotle's distinctive theory of the soul. But this view is there, and you should at least know about it, because the later Christians made a great deal of this active reason. "You see," they said, "even Aristotle, the great lover of this earth, believed in immortality." But the important point is that even granted this doctrine, Aristotle didn't believe in any *personal* immortality. There was no *you* that survived, only this abstract sparkplug, which has no psychological significance and certainly no religious significance. But in any event, that's not how most of the medievals interpreted it. And you see, between the Prime Mover and the active reason, they could really go to town to show that Aristotle is really compatible with Catholicism after all. Philosophically, that is ridiculous. But you can see that the residual Platonism in Aristotle made the medieval task of absorbing Aristotle into Catholicism at least seem possible to undertake.

Before completing our summary of his basic philosophy, I want to return briefly to the matter-form distinction as Aristotle applied it to the universal-particular question and point out a major problem that led to a big hole in Aristotle's philosophy. Remember that everything is comprised of two elements, matter and form, stuff and structure, and remember the house made of the bricks. Matter is the principle of individuation, i.e., what makes a thing this house versus all others, or it's made of these bricks—and form was the principle of universality, what made a thing a "such," what made a universal term applicable to it, why these bricks put together a certain way are called a house versus a bridge, a wall, etc., so that whenever we are applying an abstraction, a universal term, we are referring to the form of a thing. Let's follow out this analysis and see where we end up, because we end up in big trouble.

Suppose that someone says to you: "Well, you say that what makes this house this one is that it's made of these bricks versus those. But what makes these bricks these bricks? Or let's focus on a particular one—what makes this particular brick this one?" Again, we break it up into matter and form, and we say that this brick is made out of this glob of cement, and that's what makes it this one. So, this house is particular because it's made of these bricks, each of which is particular because it's made of its own particular glob of cement. But we keep going with the same question—what makes this glob of cement this one, as against any other? And again, we break it up. Let's suppose we short-circuit the process and finally hit the end. Let's suppose we say, with Aristotle's primitive physics, that the ultimate irreducible elements are earth, air, water, and fire, and suppose we say that cement is a certain form that we give to earth. And therefore, what makes this glob of cement *cement* is that it is *this* bit of earth, organized a certain way. We've hit the irreducible primitive element, and we've stripped off form after form and finally reached the basic elements. Suppose, with Aristotle, we say that it's earth that we've finally tracked down. We have the same question again—what makes this piece of earth *this* one? Again, it will have to be that it's a union of form and matter. Its earthiness comes from its form (that's what it shares with all other parcels of earth, i.e., that's the universal), but what makes it *this* bit of earth? You'll say the matter, the stuff of the earth. But now the question is: What is the nature of the matter, speaking now of earth as an irreducible element? Its matter will be the most primitive matter. What are *its* characteristics, the matter of the most primitive element? You should be able to see that you cannot ask for the characteristics of this primitive matter, because to ask for characteristics is to ask for what kind of thing it is, and that is to ask what universals it embodies. In other words, you're asking for form. All universal terms refer to form. So, when we get to the ultimate matter, it can't have any universal terms applied to it, not in itself. It must be a stuff that has in itself no characteristics. Remember, all characteristics come from form, from the way matter is organized. Matter is the source of "this," not of "such." Well then, when you get to the basic matter, in itself apart from the organization it has, it has *no* characteristics, so in itself it must be indeterminate, i.e., absolutely unique, devoid of any qualities, lacking any identity.

Aristotle calls this ultimate matter *prime matter*. It cannot exist by itself, only with form, and the most primitive form impressed on prime matter gives you the basic element—earth, air, water, and fire. You see how Aristotle got to this point—it's very logically entailed in his own analysis—but it poses the gravest, most insuperable problem to his whole theory of universals. Because if prime matter has no identity, it must then be unknowable. And Aristotle indeed says precisely that. He says that matter in itself, the ultimate individuating stuff, is unknowable. But if so, how can you know individuals? If what ultimately makes them individuals is an indeterminate unknowable stuff, then all you can know about individuals is their *non*-unique characteristics, their *non*-individual characteristics, the characteristics that they share with other things. All you can know are their *forms*. All you can know are universals. So, in this way, Aristotle seems driven in spite of himself to a Platonic conclusion, that in the last analysis and looked at from this point of view, only forms or universals are knowable because the principle of individuation is in itself unknowable.

This problem, which is just one of a number of problems posed by Aristotle's theory of universals, indicates a basic error in his whole approach to the question of universals. His basic error is to erect universals and particulars into two distinct elements within things in the world. That is the error that leads him to conclude that whenever we employ a concept (a universal term), we are focusing only on the universal element of a thing, on the form, with the result that the particularity of a thing becomes unconceptualizable, unknowable. Objectivism holds, on the contrary, that it is a basic error to attempt to divide things into two such elements, and that it is an invalid question to ask what *makes* a thing a particular. It is an invalid attempt to try to find some special element in things that are metaphysically responsible for particularity. The task is hopeless at the outset. If you look for an individuating element, you're doomed to failure, because if that element is indeterminate, i.e., nothing in particular (as Aristotle suggests), then how can it do anything, including individuate? How can a nothing in particular have the effect of making you unique and individual? On the other hand, if the element is determinate—if it is *something* in particular—then it is conceptualizable and so, in other words, it represents form, universals, that which is common to several things, and not therefore the individuating element after all. So, the situation is that an indeterminate element cannot individuate, and a determinate element cannot individuate. And the only rational conclusion is that there is no such thing as a principle of individuation, and it is a mistake to look for one. Individuality, or particularity, according to Objectivism, is an irreducible attribute of all existents: To be *is* to be particular. Every aspect of a particular is particular. And in this sense, you cannot get beneath particularity metaphysically and try to find out what is responsible for it, any more than you can get beneath motion and try to find out what is responsible for it. Particularity is inherent in the fact of existing. We don't, therefore, need a special element in things that is responsible for their particularity. Again, this is an obvious legacy of Platonism in Aristotle's part. He has the feeling that since universals are real, he has to add another element to counterbalance it and give a metaphysical basis to particularity. But that is a result of starting as a Platonist and only ending up as an Aristotelian.

A proper theory of universals will not try to construe universals as elements of particulars. Rather, it will remove universals from metaphysics and make them an issue of epistemology. In other words, it will construe universals not as elements in things, but as a human method for organizing and integrating perceptual material—a method that is based on reality, corresponds to reality, but which is the human form of grasping relationships in reality, not special elements or formal structures inhering in things out there. How this theory would be worked out in detail is extraordinarily complex, and it is *the* most complex philosophic question. Time does not permit me to say even a word about it in this course. For the Objectivist theory of universals, of concepts and concept-formation, I refer you to two sources—Ayn Rand's *Introduction to Objectivist Epistemology* or a course I propose to give, "Introduction to Objectivist Philosophy," sometime in 1974, which will have at least one lecture, possibly two, on this question (along with the rest of the material).[16] For now, I want to point out that while Objectivism agrees with Aristotle on the crucial point that universals have an objective non-supernatural basis in reality, Objectivism does not construe that basis as being that universals

---

16. This twelve-lecture course opened in New York City on September 14, 1974.

are distinct elements, or structures, in particulars. And in this sense, there are fundamental differences between the Objectivist and Aristotelian theories of universals.

To conclude Aristotle's metaphysics, let's take a final survey of the universe as a whole as seen by Aristotle, to bring out one last point. Observe that Aristotle's universe is a hierarchical structure, a series of rising levels, each level being matter for the one above and form in relation to the one below. On the lowest level is prime matter (which never exists by itself). It is pure matter without form, pure potentiality with no actual characteristics. Aristotle describes it as "the bare possibility of being something." Then come the first actual existents, the primitive, irreducible elements of things (which Aristotle believes are earth, air, water, and fire). At this stage we have the first real existent because we have form—a simple form, but form nevertheless—impressed on prime matter. And now above the elements are the various inorganic compounds. These compounds are more complex organizations of the elements, so they give new form to the matter provided by the elements. So the compounds are the actuality in relation to which the elements are the potentiality. As we know from Aristotle's psychology, these compounds, appropriately organized (in other words, given an even more complex structure), give rise to living entities. The compounds are potentially plants, the matter for plants, and when this potentiality is fulfilled, we have the new form, the new actuality, the next level—plants, the vegetative soul. And then come the animals, the sensitive soul, which as we've seen is the actualization of the potentialities established by the plant soul. And then comes man, the rational soul, which is the actualization of the potentialities established by the sensitive soul. But we still have places to go. There are a couple of things still higher on the metaphysical scale. According to Aristotle, the next highest—higher than man—are the intelligences that move the spheres. Why are they higher than man? Because they are still closer to pure actuality, pure form, and they have only one potentiality left, that is, the potentiality for circular motion, whereas man is a host of unrealized potentialities. And then finally we hit the jackpot, pure actuality, the top of the hierarchy, the exact opposite of Prime Matter—God, the Prime Mover. And so, we have a series of layers of reality—prime matter, the elements, the compounds, plants, animals, man, the intelligences, the Prime Mover—each step related to the previous as actuality to potentiality, or form to matter.

This doctrine is obviously influenced by Plato. Remember Plato's ladder of being, each level being higher than the preceding, all the way up to the pinnacle, which is the Form of the Good. Because Aristotle was a teleologist, he held that everything strives in some way for the good, for the perfect, which, in his terms, meant that everything strives for form, for actuality. In other words, actuality is better, closer to perfection, than potentiality. And therefore, unfortunately, as with Plato, so with Aristotle. He regards each level of the pyramid as higher, as evaluatively superior, to the preceding. There are metaphysical degrees of perfection, ascending from the lowest perfect level (which is prime matter) all the way up to God (the pure form, the absolutely perfect). From this aspect Aristotle adopts the view that form is the good metaphysically, matter the source of imperfection and deficiency. Here again, an obvious Platonic legacy, a highly unfortunate one, because it means that in spite of his naturalism and his this-worldliness, Aristotle's ethics and politics contain definite Platonic antimaterial influences. Because he was never able fully to free himself from his early Platonism, Aristotle's ethics and politics, as we'll see, never become fully Aristotelian, i.e., fully rational and this-worldly. And, as another consequence, all of this Platonism in Aristotle really helped the medievals in their attempt to appropriate him and claim him for Christianity. But that story we'll tell later.

Let's turn to Aristotle's ethics. In a general way, Aristotle's ethics, as you would expect, is of neither the mystic nor the skeptic variety. He does not believe that ethics is a matter of commandments or of mystical insights into another spiritual super-reality. As opposed to Plato, his ethics attempts to be naturalistic, this-worldly. It's concerned with men living on earth and attempts to guide them to successful behavior here in this life without reference to the supernatural (either as the validation of his ethics or as the goal of life). And as against the Sophists, Aristotle's is not a subjectivist ethics in which anything goes, where all feelings should be indiscriminately acted on, and might makes right. Morality, for Aristotle, does not require an appeal to the supernatural, nor a collapse into irrational whim-worshiping. In this general sense, his approach to ethics is naturalistic and objective. However, Aristotle did not know how to implement this general approach in the form of a rational, scientific, proven code of ethics. He held that ethics was not an exact science, where you could formulate precise principles and give mathematical proofs from logical premises. In ethics, he thought, you can only formulate rules true in a rough way and for the most part, and you couldn't give formal proofs. Why? You remember that science has to begin with facts, from which we then generalize, induce, arrive at the principles and turn around and deduce, systematize. And what are the facts in ethics? What are the data to start with? (I'd like to note that if Aristotle had given an analysis of the nature of life, and of the relationship between life and the concept of "value" in the form given by Ayn Rand in *Atlas Shrugged*, then he could have arrived at an objective ethics based on fact. But no such approach is anywhere hinted at in what we have.)

Aristotle said that we have to start with the way people actually behave, with what they actually value. That is the data, the facts, of ethics. You ask, do we start with just anybody? No. There are certain men whom we all recognize to be wise, good, and noble, says Aristotle, and ethics rests ultimately on our perceptions of how these men—the wise and noble Athenians—behave. We observe them, and we can then generalize, try to eliminate inconsistencies if we find any, and provide a metaphysical framework to systematize their behavior. But after all, there are many fluctuations even among wise men, many situations where our accepted general rules have exceptions, so, at best, all we'll have at the end is a more systematic account of the moral principles governing the best Athenians, not a formal science. This is all Aristotle attempts to provide. But because Athens was a good culture in many ways, Aristotle says many things that are valid in ethics. But at bottom and at the base, he has no methodology to validate his ethical conclusions. And at many points, as we'll see, his ultimate answer to an objection is: "That is how the wise man behaves. If you don't see it, it means you haven't been well brought up."

How shall we go about systematizing in ethics? Aristotle observes that values are hierarchical. Everyone pursues some things for the sake of other things—you come to these lectures for the sake of knowledge—but the knowledge of ancient and medieval and early modern philosophy is not an end in itself. You want it for a purpose, to guide your actions. Suppose that you have a career purpose. Your career is not an end in itself, but you want it as a means to support your life. And so on. Some ultimate end, some final goal (says Aristotle), must exist that we want for its own sake, and not simply as a means to something else. There must be an end in itself, and this is logically necessary because otherwise we have an infinite regress. You cannot value everything as a *means* to an end, unless something is the end, the ultimate value. Just as there must first be axioms, or *archai*, there must be an ultimate goal. And when discovered, it will serve as the standard in terms of which to evaluate all other goals and values. So, the question of ethics is: What is the end and then how best to achieve it?

We can learn certain things about the goal. It must be an end in itself, as we've said. It must be self-sufficient, something which, even if we had only it, we would have everything worth having, because everything else we want would be for its sake. And most importantly, it must be possible, i.e., it must, says Aristotle, be attainable by man on earth. This is a crucial point of Aristotle's ethics. We must remember, says Aristotle, that we are setting up an ethics *for man*—we are prescribing how this sort of entity should behave. We must, therefore, take as our given the facts of human nature, the kind of entity that we're talking about. For instance, man by nature has a body. We cannot then damn him for having a body, because that is inherent in being man, and it's a fact the moralists must begin with. Man has emotions, he has desires, he is capable of all sorts of feelings, a fact the moralists must begin with. It is ridiculous, says the Aristotelian approach, to set up as an ideal the cessation of all feeling in the way that Plato virtually does. That is inherent in man. You can't condemn him for having emotions. You can't condemn him for being capable of error. You can't condemn him for *anything* that is in his nature. It would be the equivalent—taking my own example of an ethics for dogs—if you were to say that the supreme virtue for a dog is to study the theory of relativity. You then give the dog a book of Einstein, and he sniffs at it, walks away, goes back to his bones, and you say, "You see, I always knew all dogs were rotten by nature—they are stained with sin because they prefer bones to Einstein." If that's the way a dog is by nature, then *you* are the senseless one to put forward that theory—it's not the dog's fault.

By this Aristotelian approach (with which he is not fully consistent), the doctrine of Original Sin is inherently impossible. If something is inherent, it cannot be sin. Ethics must prescribe values and virtues based on the facts of human nature, capable of attainment by man here on earth. It follows, according to Aristotle, that man at birth is neither innately bad nor innately good but is morally neutral. If he becomes good, that's his achievement. If he becomes bad, that's his fault. He cannot blame his nature or his passions—passions are facts of human nature, and, as such, they are neutral. It's what you *do* with your passions, says Aristotle, what you make of them, what form you give to them (they being now the matter)—that is what determines moral virtue.

So, what is the ultimate goal that fulfills these traits? *Happiness*—it's an end in itself, not a means to an end, and it's self-sufficient (if all you had was happiness, but you really had it, you would be lacking in nothing worth having). And it is possible if you act properly to attain it. The Greek word for "happiness" is *eudaimonia*, and Aristotle's ethics is, therefore, often called a *eudaimonistic* ethics. The word "eudaimonia" does not literally mean "happiness," although it's usually translated that way. The word "happiness," for us, suggests an emotional state of enduring enjoyment in life. *Eudaimonia*, for Aristotle, certainly included that—he emphasized that pleasure was an essential component of *eudaimonia* (the Greek word for "pleasure" being *hedone*). He emphasized that the man of *eudaimonia* thoroughly enjoyed life—but *eudaimonia* is broader than just the emotional level. It implies successful living on *all* levels, not merely emotional enjoyment but successful action, unimpeded thinking and, in general, living, functioning, acting successfully. And further, for the modern usage, "happiness" suggests primarily an inner state of the person, so theoretically you can be happy even if you're poor or persecuted by society, etc. For Aristotle, however, *eudaimonia* requires not just this inner happiness (although that is the crucial ingredient, and he is, in this respect, a true follower of Socrates), but it requires also what we might call "outer happiness." *Eudaimonia*, he tells us, requires a certain amount of money, it requires a few friends, it requires freedom, and it even requires a decent appearance and well-behaved children. You see, then, that it's an all-inclusive state, and it's perhaps best translated as a full, rich, happy, prosperous, unimpeded life of thought and action on earth. But I'll just call it "happiness."

Given this as the ultimate goal, you will see that Aristotle's ethics has no trace of the later Christian or Kantian approach to ethics, i.e., that ethics is a matter of struggling against temptation, forcing down your base impulses in order to be miserable and do your duty. Aristotle accepts Socrates's basic idea that virtue leads to happiness. Aristotle holds that the moral man has no conflict between his desires and his moral obligations. The moral man recognizes that if something is right, it will make him happy. And he gladly wants to do what is right to do it for the sake of his own happiness. The moral man thoroughly enjoys his life, and morality indeed is justified precisely because it gives him the knowledge needed to enjoy his life thoroughly. You see how opposite this is from all the ethics that came later, and even from Plato's, with its preaching of self-sacrifice for the state or the world of Forms.

The question is: How is happiness to be achieved? You can't attain it in just any old way. On this point, Aristotle agrees with Socrates against the Sophists. Happiness requires living a certain way. How? Here's where Aristotle's metaphysics enters. Everything that exists has a distinctive nature, distinctive unique potentialities. And the nature of reality, we know, is that everything acts to achieve, to realize, to actualize its distinctive potentialities, to pass from matter to form, to express in reality that which is in it potentially, to fulfill itself, to realize itself. This is inherent in each thing—the striving after its full realization. If so, what can the good life be—what can *eudaimonia* be for anything—except to act as reality and its own nature require? Suppose that you were making up an ethics for an acorn. The only thing you could tell this acorn is: "Look, cooperate wholeheartedly with the laws of reality and your own nature. Strive with all your might to actualize your distinctive potentialities and become an oak. Because if you try anything else"—suppose, for instance, this acorn conceives an ardent passion to become a willow tree—"it is doomed to frustration, to self-negation, to misery." A happy acorn, an acorn of *eudaimonia*, would be one working to actualize its distinctive potentialities.

The same is true for man. He, too, has unique potentialities, and the good life, *eudaimonia*, consists of realizing it. What is man's distinctive potentiality? Aristotle's psychology has already answered that: reason, *nous*. To be true to his own nature and the nature of reality, then, man must actualize his distinctive potentiality: reason. The life of reason is thus the life of happiness. But what in this context is reason? Aristotle distinguishes two different uses of "reason"—reason that is used to guide life, to regulate the emotions, to tell us how to act, and which he calls the *practical reason*—and reason that is used to acquire knowledge as an end in itself, just to discover and contemplate truth for its own sake, without any reference to practical consequences, and that he calls the *theoretical*, or the *contemplative*, *reason*. (I interject that this is an invalid distinction, and I will say a word later about it, but for now let's follow Aristotle.)

If there are two uses of reason, the practical and the contemplative, then the life of reason will have two departments—the exercise of the practical reason, and the exercise of the theoretical reason. And every man, for Aristotle, must exercise both, insofar as he can. In each case there will be a proper use of reason, a virtuous use (and remember, "virtue" for the Greeks means "excellence of function"). So, there will be two types of virtues. The excellent use of practical reason will give us what is called the *moral virtues*, and the excellent use of contemplative reason will give us what is called the *intellectual virtues*. Let us look at each briefly, beginning with the virtues of practical reason, the moral virtues.

Practical reason, as I said, is reason used to guide or regulate man's actions, emotions, and desires. Observe that for Aristotle, as for Plato, emotions are an independent, nonrational element of the personality that require regulation by the reason. But for Aristotle, because he believes in only one world, and because he does not believe in a metaphysical soul-body clash, he does not believe that it is as hard to control the emotions as Plato believes. He doesn't hold that there is an inherent war between reason and emotions. He believes that if you use your reason properly, you can control your emotions and live harmoniously and happily. What is the proper use, the virtuous use, of practical reason? In answering this question, Aristotle thought he detected a general principle common to all virtuous practical behavior. Whatever we do or desire, he says, we can do or desire in different amounts. We can take any human action or emotion and distinguish three amounts on a scale—the too much, the too little, and the just right. The Golden Mean. Virtuous behavior will always be the Golden Mean between the two extremes. On the one hand, the too much (the "excess," as it's called), on the other hand, the too little (the "defect," as it's called). Aristotle, in a very ingenious way, worked this out on subject after subject, ranging human traits into a three-fold column. I'll give you just four out of a great many examples.

Suppose the question is: What should your attitude be when facing threats? On the one hand, too little fear, the kind of rash person who takes senseless chances—not only walking through a cannibal colony needlessly but doing so naked—that is the vice of foolhardiness, and that's too little fear. On the other hand, there is the other extreme, i.e., too much fear, the kind we call a "coward." And virtue lies in the Golden Mean position, the just-right amount—not too little fear, not too much, but just right—courage, the courageous person. Or what should your attitude be toward food, to sex, to money? The defect would be the person who turns against these things completely, the ascetic. That is a vice. It's as much a vice as rashness or foolhardiness. Aristotle did not know what to call it, because in an extreme form it did not exist in the Greek world, and he calls it insensibility. It became the supreme virtue, or one of them, in the reign of Christianity. If Aristotle knew of the life of Saint Francis, for instance, Aristotle would be appalled at the phenomenon. But, at the other extreme are the people who are overzealous about these things, the self-indulgent profligate a la the Sophists, or Gyges when he gets his ring and runs riot. What is the proper virtue here? The Golden Mean—not too much passion for food, drink and money, clothes, etc., not too little, just the right amount—what Aristotle in the Greek tradition calls "temperance." And here it does not mean "temperance" as in the Woman's Christian Temperance Union—it means a sensible balance between the extremes. What should your attitude be in regard to social relationships? On the one hand is the person who attaches too little importance to them, what we would call a "misanthrope"—Aristotle calls that the vice of "sulkiness." On the other hand, there's the kind of person who is obsessed with people, who is obsequious and rushes around saying to everybody, "I love you, please love me"—what we would call a "social metaphysician"—Aristotle says that's the vice of "obsequiousness." And in the middle, the Golden Mean, the just-right amount—the rationally friendly person, with the virtue of friendliness. What should be your attitude toward yourself? On the one hand, the person who has too low an estimate—the person who walks around saying, "I'm no good, I'm rotten, I'm worthless"—that person has the vice of humility. On the other extreme is the person who claims for himself more than is his due, who walks around saying, "I'm the greatest thing that ever lived"—he has the vice of vanity, or conceit. And the Golden Mean refers to the person who has a high and earned self-respect, the virtue of pride.

I must leave the Golden Mean for a couple of minutes, because pride for Aristotle is the crown of the virtues—the man of pride, the man of *megalopsyche*, the man with a big soul, which is now translated as the "magnanimous man," is his ideal man in terms of the moral virtues. And his description of it in Book Four of the *Nicomachean Ethics* is the liveliest passage in his ethics, very famous, so I must read it to you even though I'll just give you a few excerpts. It will give you an idea of the type of man Aristotle admired and recommended. He's describing the virtue of pride:

> Now the man is thought to be proud who thinks himself worthy of great things, being worthy of them; for he who does so beyond his deserts is a fool, but no virtuous man is foolish. The proud man, then, is the man we have described. For he who is worthy of little and thinks himself worthy of little is temperate, but not proud; for pride implies greatness, as beauty implies a good-sized body, and little people may be neat and well proportioned but cannot be beautiful. . . .
>
> The proud man, then, is an extreme in respect of the greatness of his claims, but a mean in respect of the rightness of them, for he claims what is in accordance with his merits, while the others go to excess or fall short. . . . Now the proud man, since he deserves most, must be good in the highest degree; for the better man always deserves more, and the best man most. Therefore the truly proud man must be good in greatness and every virtue which seem to be characteristic of a proud man. And it would be most unbecoming for a proud man to fly from danger, swinging his arms by his sides, or to wrong another. . . .
>
> If we consider him point by point, we shall see the utter absurdity of a proud man who is not good. Nor, again, would he be worthy of honor if he were bad; for honor is the prize of virtue, and it is to the good that it is rendered. Pride, then, seems to be a sort of crown of the virtues; for it makes them greater, and it is not found without them. Therefore, it is hard to be truly proud; for it is impossible without nobility and goodness of character. It is chiefly with honors and dishonors, then, that the proud man is concerned; and at honors that are great and conferred by good men, he will be moderately pleased,

thinking that he is coming by his own, or even less than his own; for there can be no honor that is worthy of perfect virtue, yet he will at any rate accept it since they have nothing greater to bestow on him; but honor from casual people and on trifling grounds he will utterly despise, since it is not this that he deserves, and dishonor, too, since in his case it cannot be just. . . .

[The proud man] does not run into trifling dangers, nor is he fond of danger, because he honors few things; but he will face great dangers, and when he is in danger, he is unsparing of his life, knowing that there are conditions on which life is not worth having. [Peikoff: I interject: So much for Aristotle's view on the question of better Red than dead.] And he is the sort of man to confer benefits, but he is ashamed of receiving them; for the one is the mark of a superior, the other of an inferior. . . . It is a mark of the proud man also to ask for nothing, or scarcely anything, but to give help readily, and to be dignified towards people who enjoy high position and good fortune, but unassuming towards those of the middle class; for it is a difficult and lofty thing to be superior to the former, but easy to be so to the latter, and a lofty bearing over the former is no mark of ill breeding, but among humble people it is as vulgar as a display of strength against the weak.

Again, it is characteristic of the proud man not to aim at the things commonly held in honor, or the things in which others excel; to be sluggish and to hold back except where great honor or a great work is at stake; and to be a man of few deeds, but of great and notable ones. He must also be open in his hate and in his love (for to conceal one's feelings, i.e., to care less for truth than for what people will think, is a coward's part) and must speak and act openly; for he is free of speech because he is contemptuous, and he is given to telling the truth, except when he speaks in irony to the vulgar. He must be unable to make his life revolve round another, unless it be a friend; for this is slavish, and for this reason all flatterers are servile and people lacking in self-respect are flatterers. . . . Further, a slow step is thought proper to the proud man, a deep voice, and a level utterance. . . . Such, then, is the proud man; the man who falls short of him is unduly humble.

If you consider this in the light of what was to come philosophically —"the man who falls short of him is unduly humble"—you can't believe it. This is one of the few man-worshiping passages in all of philosophy, and it is fitting that it comes from Aristotle, who has, needless to say, been despised by centuries of Christians for this very passage and this very quality. And this, I should say, is one of the great kinships between

Aristotle and Objectivism.

Let's return to the Golden Mean. If you recall the four examples I gave you, the moral that Aristotle draws is that it's not *what* you do or desire, but the degree to which you do it, that determines virtue and vice. Virtue is an issue of moderation, of not going to extremes. You can see, I think, that there is a commonsense validity, and at certain points even a highly admirable quality, in the content of the virtues that Aristotle endorses (and I've just given you a few samples). The particular virtues that he's in favor of are generally sensible, and even noble. But as a principle of ethics, it should be apparent to you that the Golden Mean is unsatisfactory and invalid. Here are a few obvious objections.

First, notice that the trinity of attitudes that Aristotle ranges on a continuum do not in fact fall on a continuum at all. The vices in each case are differentiated from the virtues *in kind*, not just in degree (as Aristotle's doctrine requires). The obsequious social metaphysician, for instance, is not differentiated from a rationally friendly person by just having more of the latter's attitude. The obsequious person's motive and interest in people is different *in kind*, not just in degree or amount. And the same is true in all these other cases.

Second, if it *were* just a difference in degree, there would be no argument in favor of the Mean. There is no reason why a mean is valid just because it's a mean. The mere fact that some attitude is in the middle between two other attitudes doesn't at all show that it's therefore desirable. For instance, on one extreme we have never committed adultery, but on the other extreme we have committed adultery every night with a different partner. Is the Golden Mean just the right amount? Just the right amount of murder? Just the right amount of envious hatred?

Obviously, your place on a continuum is irrelevant. Aristotle tries to encompass this type of case, and he holds, in effect: "These things (like murder, adultery, and so on) are already extremes, and therefore the doctrine of the Mean doesn't apply. You can't have a mean of an extreme." But this is not a valid answer on his part. Because the question is: How does he *know* they are extremes? If you go solely by the doctrine of the Mean, we can range three attitudes on murder, or on adultery, etc., and then pick the middle. The fact is, Aristotle knew in advance that murder, for instance, is wrong, and he therefore classified it as an extreme. It's not that it's an extreme and therefore wrong, but rather, it's wrong and, therefore, he concluded, an extreme—which means that his virtues are not in fact derived from the theory of the Mean at all, rather from, as he himself says, the observations of the wise Athenians. The Mean doctrine is no proof or definition of these virtues, just a way of expounding what we know on other grounds and as such, is philosophically insignificant.

And then there is the question: How do you know what the mean *is* in a particular case? Suppose one person says never eat chocolates, and the other—a chocolate manufacturer—says eat two hundred boxes a day. What is the Golden Mean? A hundred boxes a day? Aristotle's position on this would be: "No, I don't mean the arithmetic mean. I don't mean the exact halfway point. That would be silly. I mean the just-right amount for a given person—the not-too-much and the not-too-little. And this varies from person to person. For instance, on chocolates, it depends on your health, your tastes, your money, etc. The just-right amount if you're on a diet is not the same as if you're not." The Mean, he says, is relative to a particular set of circumstances. It's not figured out by arithmetic. But then the question is: How do you *know*, given a set of circumstances, what is the mean? And you have to know if the doctrine is to be of any use to you in guiding your life. Aristotle's position is that if you take into account all of the relevant factors in a given situation, and if you're well brought up, you will just know, i.e., you will perceive what the right amount is for you by direct insight. Then the question is: What does being well-brought-up consist of? To be well-brought-up presumably is to be brought up via the Golden Mean. And the Mean is what a well-brought-up person would choose. So, it's inexorably circular. And you see again that he doesn't offer a scientific ethics, as it's based ultimately upon his observations of the wise and good Athenians. I don't want to belabor the Mean doctrine further. It's had very unfortunate consequences. Although I should say for Aristotle's own sake that he didn't originate the idea of moderation, which was an ancient Greek tradition, "Nothing in excess," that goes way back before Aristotle, and all he did was systematize it. But in any event, that particular Greek doctrine, although given Aristotle's influence, has had terrifically unfortunate consequences. It's led people to all sorts of compromising, fence sitting, contradictions and evasion on principle, even though none of this was Aristotle's intention. You need merely think of the way the terms "moderate" and "extremist" are thrown around in American presidential elections to get an idea of the devastatingly bad consequences of the doctrine of the Golden Mean (even though, as I said, Aristotle would surely never have imagined its use by modern pragmatists).

Let's look at the *intellectual virtues* very briefly, that is to say, the virtuous use of contemplative reason. In this use of reason, we pursue knowledge for its own sake—essentially science, mathematics, philosophy.

We discover and contemplate truth as an end in itself, without any concern for practical action or the existential consequences of that knowledge. Knowledge on this level is not a means to anything, but rather an end in itself. For Aristotle, this life of contemplation is the highest embodiment of the life of reason, superior to the exercise of reason in practical affairs, and the summit of rationality. This is the life that any man of adequate intelligence ought to follow, which brings us to another error in his ethics. I don't mean his emphasis on the acquisition of knowledge, but the idea that knowledge is an end in itself (as against being a means of human action and life). Why did he commit this error? There are many reasons, and here are some: In general, no Greek—Aristotle included—grasped the relationship between knowledge and life, between reason and life. This is prior to the Industrial Revolution, and I would maintain as an actual fact that it would be impossible to grasp the relationship between reason and life, philosophically, prior to the Industrial Revolution. No one did, and I would say no one could have, because at this stage of civilization, the skills needed to sustain life were manual and seemed to be obviously unintellectual. On the other hand, the knowledge that seemed pleasurable and demanding of a man's full intellectual powers (science, metaphysics, physics, mathematics) seemed to have no practical value, which it *didn't* at that early stage. And consequently, Aristotle, along with the rest of the Greeks, concluded that knowledge was not ultimately justified by its utility in life. This is an error, but certainly an understandable one at the stage of knowledge in which he was writing. In addition, there is a definite element of Platonism here, the exaltation of contemplation, retirement from action, and the hubbub of life, and so on, into private contemplation of truth. And we know that Aristotle never fully freed himself from this Platonic element in any branch of philosophy. And of course, the Prime Mover is relevant here, and that is one of the main effects of Aristotle's God on his ethics. In this life of contemplation, Aristotle says, you get as close to the divine life as you can, because all that God does is contemplate.

For these and still other reasons, Aristotle ends up advocating the contemplative life as the highest and best life. And unfortunately, he even declares that human beings are too imperfect to live this perfect life. It's not, he says, insofar as they are human that they can live thus, but only insofar as they have an element of the divine in them. In other words, he contradicts his own distinctive approach, again succumbing to a Platonic element.

This doctrine of knowledge as an end in itself has had very bad consequences. It has the effect of making Aristotle's ethics impracticable for most men, restricted in this respect, at least, to a comparative few who have the wealth and the leisure to contemplate. Most men, however, as Aristotle recognized, have to work, have to act. So, they have neither the time, the wealth, nor the ability for the contemplative life. Consequently, for them, says Aristotle, the highest form of human happiness is impossible. In this way, and in this respect, Aristotle ends up with an ethics for a comparative few, similar in this one respect to Plato.

Let's leave the moral and intellectual virtues and turn to one last point in connection with Aristotle's ethics, namely, egoism. Aristotle is a thorough egoist in ethics. He believes that each man should be primarily concerned with the attainment of his own happiness, which is to be achieved by the exercise of his own practical and theoretical reason. In contrast to Plato, there is nothing in Aristotle advocating self-sacrifice, self-abnegation, the exalting of something above your own happiness on earth. And in contrast to the Sophists, Aristotle says explicitly that the true egoist is the man of reason, not the whim-worshiping brute. The Sophist is, for Aristotle as for Socrates, merely engaged in expressing the worst element in himself, the part that isn't really him—his irrational whims and passions. As such, he is destroying his real self, his reason, and, along with it, his only chance of fulfillment and happiness. In this sense, Aristotle is a consistent champion of rational egoism, the only philosopher to be such in all of philosophy (if you are talking of the major philosophers, and not the disciples who parrot the masters). Because this is such an urgently important issue in ethics, I want to read you a few passages from Aristotle, because I think you get a feeling of the philosophy from hearing a few things in his own words that you can't get from any summary. This is also from the *Nicomachean Ethics*:[17]

> [The good man] wishes for himself what is good and what seems so, and does it . . . and does so for his own sake (for he does it for the sake of the intellectual element in him, which is thought to be the man himself); and he wishes to live and be preserved in especially the element by virtue of which he thinks. For existence is good to the virtuous man, and each man wishes himself what is good, while no one chooses to possess the whole world if he has first to become someone else. . . . He wishes for this only on condition of being whatever he is; and the element that thinks would seem to be the individual man, or to be so more than any other element in him. And such a man [Peikoff: the good man] wishes to live with himself, for he does so with pleasure, since the memories of his past acts are delightful and his hopes for the future are good and therefore pleasant.

---

17. Book Nine, from the translation by W. D. Ross.

> . . . [By contrast], wicked men seek for people with whom to spend their days, and shun themselves; for they remember many a grievous deed, and anticipate others like them, when they are by themselves; but when they are with others, they forget. And having nothing lovable in them, they have no feeling of love to themselves.

And here's another little excerpt, just a brief fragment:

> Existence is to all men a thing to be chosen and loved, and we exist by virtue of activity (i.e., by living and acting). . . . [The producer] loves his handiwork, therefore, because he loves existence.

As to self-love:

> Such a man [the rational man] would seem more than the other [the irrational man] a lover of self; at all events, he assigns to himself the things that are noblest and best, and gratifies the most authoritative element in it and in all things obeys this. . . . And therefore, the man who loves this [reason] and gratifies it is most of all a lover of self. . . . Therefore, the good man should be a lover of self.

You see how this ties in with Aristotle's advocacy of pride as the crown of the virtues. It is also a majorly important element in his ethics, one that went into eclipse and was denounced by all subsequent philosophers and not resurrected until many, many centuries later.

I can't resist adding that Aristotle had a remarkable theory of friendship—egoistic friendship—a fascinating theory, which I'd love to tell you about because it exemplifies one of the best elements in his ethics, but unfortunately, there is no time. But if you ask about friendship in the question period, I'll be glad to say a few words on it then.

To sum up our brief survey on Aristotle's ethics, you can see, I think, that Aristotle's ethics is very mixed in its merits. Much of the time he's on the right track. Many points you can agree with—his advocacy of happiness on earth as opposed to the Platonic asceticism and supernaturalism, his emphasis on reason, the acquisition of knowledge, egoism, pride—but these points, as you see, are embedded in a framework that is streaked with leftovers from Platonism, and that is avowedly not scientific or proven. As such, Aristotle's ethics was not strong enough to combat the Platonic and Sophistic rivals in the field. And therefore, to answer a question that I get all the time, this is one of the major reasons—this deficiency of Aristotle's ethics—that his philosophy did not become a major influence over all future philosophizing right away. When a philosopher's ethics is weak, no matter how many good points he has in metaphysics and epistemology, his influence on men will be significantly less because men feel the influence of any philosophy primarily through its ethics. That, after all, is the primary purpose of philosophy—to teach men how to live. As an analogy, if you offer men a magnificent internal combustion machine, but they have no idea how to use it and there is no fuel to make it run, and the alternative is a horse and buggy that actually works (to say nothing of promises of a mystic flying carpet if only they pay enough money and go to church long enough), they will choose the horse and buggy or the flying carpet over the unusable internal combustion machine. Therefore, you should not be too surprised to learn that shortly after his death, Aristotle's philosophy went into eclipse and took many, many, many centuries to exhume. But that's a story we'll start telling in the next lecture.

In conclusion, let me say a very few words about Aristotle's politics. In his political writings, Aristotle generally contented himself with describing existing states in the ancient world and making recommendations for their improvement within the framework of their basic premises. Aristotle was not a political revolutionary with fundamentally original ideas in politics—certainly not on the order of Plato who, regardless of the content of his views, was a major innovator in politics, whereas Aristotle was more the documenter, rather than the crusader. And his politics, therefore, is less interesting and important than any other part of his philosophy. To synopsize: He was not a major collectivist like Plato. He objected vigorously to Plato's communistic and totalitarian views, but Aristotle himself, in his own political writings, was certainly not a major individualist either. It's one thing to say that his metaphysics and ethics laid the basis for which his subsequent followers centuries later derived individualism—that is true—but judging by the actual politics Aristotle himself recommends (which reflects the more Platonic elements in him), you'd have to say that, unfortunately, Aristotle followed his Golden Mean in politics. He took a position that today would be pretty much described as a variant of the middle-of-the-road. For instance, he objected to Plato's view that the few ideal philosophers should have absolute power—he objected to rule by Platonic experts—but, he says, this would be ideal, but it's impractical and utopian, because there's too much risk of it degenerating into tyranny (thus conceding to Plato that this would be ideal but impractical). He also objected to rule by experts on the ground that we must have a government of *law*, not of *men*—that is a central Aristotelian idea. A constitution must be defined that spells out what the government can and cannot do. There must be laws. And we do not want a government by arbitrary decree. In this sense, he's the father of the idea of constitutional government.

On the other hand, like Plato, Aristotle has no concept that all men have individual, inalienable rights, or that the function of government is only to protect these rights. As was common in Greece at the time, he was thinking of the state as the city-state, and he thought that it had a variety of proper functions—educational, cultural, religious, economic. He says somewhere that the state should see that there are restrictions on the amount of wealth so that there's not too much or too little in any given person's hands—in general, he advocates functions of the government quite incompatible with anything that an individualist politics would advocate.

For Aristotle, as for Plato, the important issue of politics is: What group should have ruling power in the state? What group should be able to control the policies of the state? And in answer to this question, he came up with a sort of "mean" position (that is, a moderate position) as the most practical and stable type of state. He held that we don't want a state where the few wealthy upper-class aristocrats rule, because this can degenerate into tyranny or oligarchy, and we don't want one where the masses, or poorer people, rule, as in democracy, because that becomes unlimited mob rule, which is hopeless. Both Plato and Aristotle were staunch opponents of the idea of unlimited mob rule. Rather, said Aristotle, the best state is a cross between rule of the rich and of the poor, rule of the few and of the many, a state ruled neither by the mob nor by an elite of experts, but by an intermediate class—what we today call the "middle class." Aristotle called this kind of state a "polity," and he advocated it as the best, most practical constitution. In other words, a large middle class should hold the balance of power and act as a check on what today would be called the "proletariat" on the bottom and the few potentially tyrannical aristocrats at the top. So, there is a definite sense in which Aristotle differs from Plato's totalitarian philosopher-king theory, and as I mentioned, Aristotle objects to Plato's communism, but in very, very mixed and rather feeble terms. Remember, Plato objected to "mine" and "thine"? Aristotle says "mine" and "thine" are inherent in human nature, and you only create conflicts and resentments if you try to communize property and families. Better to leave people private property and encourage them to develop a community spirit voluntarily so they'll share with others voluntarily. To this audience, such an answer speaks for itself, but it is not a very powerful answer to Plato.

I should, however, point out that even though Aristotle allows the citizens of his state to have much more say than Plato does, Aristotle's state, as he describes it, also inclines in the direction of being an aristocracy run by a comparative few, even if not in nearly so pronounced a form as Plato's. For instance, Aristotle, Plato, and the Greeks, in general, advocated slavery. They had no concept of inalienable rights. Aristotle argued—and I stress again, he did not originate this view, nor was he distinctive in holding it—that there were natural slaves, men who had the capacity to understand a rational argument but not to exercise reason independently, who were, in effect, living tools, and, he said, it would be to their own benefit and to the benefit of a master if they serve and work for a natural master (in other words, those in whom theoretical reason is fully developed), because the slave gains the benefit of contact with a fully rational man to direct him, and the rational man, exempt from the need for menial work, has the leisure for contemplation. This is an obvious gross flaw in Aristotle's view, but I stress it is not a flaw in his ethics or philosophy but rather a flaw in his anthropology, i.e., in his view of mankind, and it is a flaw that he shared with the Greeks in general. The Greeks never really grasped (at least, not until the time of the Stoics, a later school) that human beings—all human beings—are metaphysically equal. The Greeks of the classical period held that men are divided into the metaphysical superiors and the metaphysical inferiors, one destined to rule the other. This is an error, but it was an error in their theory of the nature of man, not an error in their ethics. Their ethical error is a consequence of it, and they had some provocation for it—they were the only civilization. Around them was not another civilized world, but a world of crude, ignorant barbarians. And at that stage of the game, if you lived in Greece, you had a certain warrant for looking around you and saying, "We are human, and the aliens are savages."

I should also point out that Aristotle excluded women from citizenship in his state—not only slaves, but also women—on the grounds they were metaphysically inferior—again, equally invalid, but equally warranted by a study of the women in his purview. He goes so far as to build this into his metaphysics in a doctrine that has no importance at all, but he says that in conception, when men and women unite to produce a child, the woman contributes the matter (the low element), and the man contributes the form. To be accurate, on this one point, Plato was ahead of Aristotle—he recognized the metaphysical equality of women with men. Also, in his capacity as a Platonist, Aristotle generally scorned tradesmen, mechanics, that type of person, and he says that their life is "ignoble and inimical to virtue," and they too are to be deprived of citizenship or any act of participation in the state. That's the equivalent of Plato's view that the productive group is out of the state or is in a servile position. You see from these viewpoints that there's a heavy Platonic influence in Aristotle's politics. Because there's not much of great value in it, I won't pursue it further.

Let's sum up Aristotle as a whole. In looking at his overall philosophy, you can point out many errors and many bad points. To review a few: There is his inadequate account of sense perception, his inadequate account at many points on the nature of mind, his doctrines of God, of teleology, of contingency, of prime matter, of the Golden Mean, of contemplation as an end in itself, his deficient politics, and so on. All of this you must know if, as students of Objectivism, you claim any kind of affiliation with Aristotle, because these are facts that people will confront you with, and you will be amazed at what Aristotle could say.

But in the process of inventorying his bad points, I ask that you not forget what he did achieve, and in what context. Starting from a culture in which there were only Platonists and Sophists, Aristotle laid down the basic principles of a scientific epistemology: the role of the senses, the role of abstraction, the laws of logic, the types of reasoning, the basic rules of validity in deductive reasoning. He laid down the principles of a naturalistic, this-worldly metaphysics: one reality, a world of particulars, of entities acting in accordance with their natures, lawful, intelligible, graspable by man. And in ethics, the principles of a this-worldly ethics, according to which man's goal is to achieve personal happiness and personal pride by exercising his intellectual powers to the fullest. On these topics, Aristotle did not say the *last* word, but, as I have observed, he often said the *first* of any value. The pro-reason, pro-life, pro-this-world approach to philosophy, in its essence and at root, is the creation of Aristotle. And it is for that that we owe him a debt of gratitude no matter how great his other errors and Platonic carryovers.

The best summary of Aristotle's achievements—of his good points and of his errors—is given by Aristotle himself, at the end of what is now the final section of his works on logic. He is referring in this passage to his work in logic, but his remarks are applicable much more widely to his entire philosophy in all branches. This passage that I have in mind is a fairly extended one, but I think it only fitting to conclude by reading it to you and giving the last word to Aristotle himself to assess his own achievements:

> That our program, then, has been adequately completed is clear. But we must not omit to notice what has happened in regard to this inquiry, for in the case of all discoveries, the results of previous labors that have been handed down from others have been advanced bit by bit by those who have taken them on, whereas the original discoveries generally make an advance that is small at first, though much more

useful, than the development which later springs out of them. For it may be that in everything, as the saying is, "the first start is the main part," and for this reason also it is the most difficult; for in proportion as it is most potent in its influence, so it is smallest in its compass, and therefore most difficult to see: whereas when once this [foundation] is discovered, it is easier to add and develop the remainder in connection with it. This is in fact what has happened in regard to rhetorical speeches and to practically all the other arts; for those who discovered the beginnings of them advance them in all only a little way, whereas the celebrities of today are the heirs (so to speak) of a long succession of men who have advanced them bit by bit, and so have advanced them to their present form. . . . On this inquiry [Peikoff: in other words, logic], on the other hand, it was not the case that part of the work had been thoroughly done before while part had not. Nothing existed at all. For the training given by the paid professors of contentious arguments [the Sophists] was like the treatment of the matter by Gorgias. For they used to hand out speeches to be learned by heart [Peikoff: And that was their idea of teaching logic.]. . . . And therefore the teaching they gave their pupils was ready but rough. For they used to suppose that they trained people by imparting to them not the art but its products, as though anyone professing that he would impart a form of knowledge to obviate pain in the feet were then not to teach a man the art of shoe making or the sources whence he can acquire anything of the kind, but were to present him with several kinds of shoes of all sorts: for he has helped him to meet his need, but he has not imparted an art to him. On the subject of reasoning, we had nothing else of an earlier date to speak of at all but were kept at work for a long time in experimental researches. If, then, it seems to you after inspection that, such being the situation as it existed at the start, our investigation is in a satisfactory position compared with the other inquiries that have been developed by tradition, there must remain for all of you, or for our students the task of extending us your pardon for the shortcomings of the inquiry, and for the discoveries thereof, your warm thanks.[18]

18. From Aristotle's *On Sophistical Refutations*, Part 34, Richard McKeon translation.

Lecture Five, Q&A

Q: Would you please go into more detail with regard to Aristotle's view of infinity with reference to space and time?

A: To begin with, Aristotle holds that space and time are both relational in nature. Space is a relationship between entities in different places. It is not a thing, not an empty gigantic container in a way that Plato suggested. It is simply a name for the relationship that obtains between things in different places. And therefore, the universe itself is not surrounded by space, nor is there an "outside the universe," nor does the universe have a place. Aristotle defines "place" as "the innermost boundary of a container." For instance, that cup is contained by a little imaginary circle on the surface of the table, and that's its place. Since the universe is contained by no entity, it has no place—it just is. Places, and therefore spaces, are within the universe, not the other way around. And therefore, since the universe is finite, any space is necessarily finite. As to time, I've already given you his general view of time as a relation, as the measurement of motion, the now – now – now of a moving entity, and therefore, there can be no time if there is no motion. If we now ask the question, "Is the universe as a whole in time?" Aristotle would say no and for exactly the reason that it is not in space. Time is in the universe, but the universe is not in time. For the universe to be in time, there would have to be a standard of motion *external* to the universe as a whole, in relation to which you judge the universe and thus discover its duration. But there is nothing external to the universe, so that phrase "external to the universe" is meaningless. Therefore, says Aristotle, it is not true that the universe has existed for a finite amount of time (which would imply creation out of nothing), nor is it true that the universe has existed for an infinite amount of time (which would imply the actual existence of infinity, of an infinite number of seconds, which he denies, as I've said)—it is not in time *period*, finite or infinite. It is eternal, which technically means "out of time." Time considerations are applicable only to things within the universe.

Q: Does Objectivism hold that man is metaphysically the highest

form of existence?

A: No, not as the question is worded. Objectivism says you must not make value judgments as part of metaphysics, not metaphysics in the strict sense of a description of the nature of the universe. Values belong to ethics, so they belong to the evaluative branches of philosophy. And we hold it as a basic Platonic error (which Aristotle to this extent shared) to ascribe value judgments intrinsically to reality. We hold that values are objective, not intrinsic to reality, that is, they are based on facts of reality, but they presuppose a certain type of being, and are designed for the purposes of that being. If you ask a different question—"Is man the highest form of existence given a human (an objective, but a human) code of values?"—then the answer would be yes, he is the highest form of existence by human values. But then that means, given *human* values, not from God's viewpoint. And by that same principle, if an oyster was in a position to make competing claims, he would have a right to say that from an oyster's point of view, an oyster is the highest form of existence. The one respect in which you could say man is superior to all other living things is that he is the most efficacious living thing. In that sense, he is the superior one. But that is using a *human* standard, i.e., "superior in the art of survival," and is not something intrinsic in reality. It's not as though God grades everybody from the oyster on up or down.

Q: Could you briefly describe and indicate what gave rise to Aristotle's theory of intellectual intuition?

A: I can certainly do it briefly by saying that by "intellectual intuition" is meant nothing more nor less than Aristotle's view that the conceptual faculty has the power of grasping self-evident truth when it confronts it. As to his reasons for that, I gave them in the last lecture.

Q: Is it the fallacy of reaffirmation through denial to hold the primacy of consciousness premise? If not, how does one answer a proponent of this doctrine so as to point out its falsity?

A: Yes, it is that fallacy. All axioms are established ultimately—all philosophic axioms—by the technique of reaffirmation through denial. That is to say, they are established primarily by the fact that they are self-evident. You cannot prove the existence of existence to anybody, but you can simply point to reality and say, "There, look, this is existence." And if he says, "I don't see it," you can say: "Well, in other words, if nothing exists, then you don't exist, and your denial doesn't exist, and so you wipe yourself out. You have to presuppose that *something* exists in order to say that *nothing* exists." That's true. But that is not a proof that something exists, because you have to assume that something exists to utter it, too. You cannot get beneath axioms. All you can do is point to them. And then if the person has a trace of civility, he will see that the fact is self-evident, and you can proceed. If he doesn't, you can then let him define his own metaphysical status as nonexistent and proceed accordingly.

Q: What do you mean by an "invalid question"?

A: It's a question based on an unwarranted assumption. Suppose I ask you, "What movie is the universe watching?" You'd say: "Well, there's no answer and that's an invalid question. The universe can't watch a movie, because that would imply there's something outside the universe, and the universe has organs of perception——both of which are false. That assumption is, therefore, unwarranted." Suppose I ask, "Who created the universe?" That presupposes something or somebody created the universe, and the only question is who. That is an unwarranted question, unless you can establish that the universe was created, in which case it's appropriate to go on and ask, "Well, who did it then?" But only if you establish it.

Q: You said that no concept of utilitarian knowledge was possible prior to the Industrial Revolution. Do you believe that there was no equivalent, or partial approach, to the Industrial Revolution prior to the late-eighteenth or early-nineteenth century in other cultures?

A: First of all, you state my view somewhat inaccurately. I do not believe that knowledge was entirely divorced from utilitarian purposes. And Aristotle indeed has the practical reason, which is specifically the utilitarian reason. I said that they did not grasp how science, abstract philosophy, and mathematics were related to life. Primarily, the knowledge of physics, math, biology, psychology. And they could not grasp that prior to the Industrial Revolution. Do I believe there was no equivalent of the Industrial Revolution? If you mean by "equivalent" in early times that men used knowledge, they used it to make discoveries on a certain level. But if you mean they created the kind of culture that made blatant and accessible to everyone the imperative role of the mind in actually sustaining human existence, in sustaining the actual physical life of man, then, in that sense, it was only the Industrial Revolution that made it possible. Which Aristotle in turn made possible by making possible modern science, by making possible the Renaissance. And from that point of view, Aristotle created the circumstances that ultimately corrected his own doctrine.

Q: When one holds that the mind "takes in" the form of the object, doesn't that leave the object unformed, just matter?

A: No, that's just metaphorical—you don't literally suck in the form. You suck in an *equivalent* of the form, i.e., you have the same form *in kind* in your mind, but not the literal same numerical form since that actual form remains out there.

Q: Please give Aristotle's views on friendship.

A: I'll give you just a brief summary. Friendship, in the Greek view, was any mutual attraction or relation between two human beings, and it was wider than our present use. In the *Nicomachean Ethics*, Aristotle defines three types of friendship. One, the friendships of utility. These are what we would call business relationships, commercial relationships. In this case, there are certain practical advantages that you want from the other person and that he wants from you. You don't love the person for himself, but you want certain advantages from your relationship. And that's the lowest type of friendship. It's perfectly reputable, but it's not very much.

Then comes what he calls the friendships of pleasure, what we would call a social relationship, in the sense that you delight in the social pleasure that you get from this particular person. He's convivial, amusing, witty, funny, nice to go to the movies with, has a sparkling personality, etc. At this point you have a good time with your friend, but you still don't love the person for himself, but for the amusement. This essentially is the kind of relationship that children have when they have friends, or that not-fully-formed adults have. And this type of friendship, says Aristotle, is comparatively easily dissolved if and when, in effect (condensing), the person runs out of jokes. He doesn't say that, but that's the idea.

Then there is, finally, the *friendships of the good*. In this case, you love the person for himself because of his character, the values he represents. He represents all the things that you think are good, and you admire him, and you mutually help each other to live the good life. I stress that Aristotle was not a Kantian—he did not think that gaining practical advantages from such a friendship corrupts it, nor did he think that gaining pleasure from such a friendship corrupts it. He is not a Kantian, who thinks that to be a true friend you should be completely selfless and get nothing practical or pleasurable out of it: There is utility and there is pleasure in this type of friendship. But the essence of it—and it's the supremely important type of friendship—is mutual moral admiration on a profound level between two human beings who are equal morally. Aristotle draws many fascinating conclusions, fascinating (in the light of the Christianity that is to come) by virtue of their diametric opposition. It's almost as though he read the Sermon on the Mount and went out of his way to say what he thought of it. For instance, he stresses that you cannot expect to have many friends like this, i.e., you cannot say, "I love everyone, I'm friends of mankind as a whole." You must have standards, you must know the person intimately, you don't love your neighbor as such. Friendship or love is a response to values and virtues in the individual. And, he says, this implies a certain equality between the two. A superior cannot feel friendship for an inferior, and vice versa. And, he says, you owe more to your friends than you do to strangers (the exact opposite of the view that you should especially love your enemies).

There is a certain type of modern Christian called a Utilitarian, who says that the proper way to act is for the greatest happiness of the greatest number, so if you see (and this is the typical example Utilitarians give) a building on your left burning, with two strangers in it, and a building burning on your right, with your wife in it, you should save the two strangers because there are twice as many as in the other one. Aristotle would reject that emphatically. You should save your friend because you owe him more, he matters more to you rationally than the two strangers. And, he says, since you love the man *because* he's good, if and when he turns bad, you dissolve the friendship. You do not forgive in any all-embracing Christian way. It's not "Judge not that ye be judged," it's "Judge and be prepared to be judged," and if one or the other defaults, then the basis of the relationship is gone.

Aristotle goes on to ask if you can be friendly with yourself in this sense? And he says yes, if you're a good man. He says a friend is one who admires a person for his character, who wishes whatever is for the welfare of that person, for that person's sake, who lives with that person, who has the same tastes and same likes and same dislikes, who grieves and rejoices along with the person. All of this, says Aristotle, is most true of the good man's relationship to himself. He admires himself (you remember the great-souled man), he works for his own welfare, his own happiness, and he has the same likes as himself and dislikes (and there he means to contrast himself with the inconsistent villains who do something and feel guilty about it, or want something and feel frightened of it, etc.—who are inconsistent with themselves). When this kind of man, therefore, has complete friendship with himself (which is another way of saying he regards himself as the supreme value), when he does something for a friend, it is not a sacrifice. He is selfish because he is still gaining the greatest benefit for himself—he is defending his values, doing the good, being rational, and it is to his own ultimate happiness. Friendship, he concludes, is based on self-love, and you cannot admire goodness in others unless it's present in yourself, and if it's present in yourself, the first person you should admire is yourself. So that's a brief taste of what is, in essentials, a very excellent doctrine.

Q: Is there any reason, or any respect, in which Objectivism would disagree that the means to achieve happiness is to actualize one's distinctive potentialities?

A: If you mean by that, "Would Objectivism disagree that the means to achieve happiness is to live by reason?" then certainly not. Objectivism holds that reason is the means to happiness. However, Objectivism does not advocate reason simply because it is distinctive to man. Aristotle justifies the life of reason essentially on the teleological ground that reason is man's distinctive striving. And to Aristotle's defense of the life of reason, the objection is: Well, why is the fact that something is distinctive to man, per se, an argument for living that way? One very superficial philosopher whom I won't mention by name once said to me, "What if man's distinctive feature was a long nose? Would it follow, then, that you should emphasize the life of the long-nosed just because that's distinctive?" That's not even fair to Aristotle, because, he explained, given his metaphysics, why the distinctive was the thing that counts. But in any event, in a way, that kind of objection is open if you reject Aristotle's teleology. Objectivism says that you should live by reason because reason is a necessary means of sustaining life, and therefore, of achieving happiness. But the crucial middle term is the role of reason in sustaining life: Reason is through and through practical and not contemplative in that disembodied otherworldly sense. That is a basic disagreement with Aristotle.

Q: You say that Aristotle was the first influential empiricist in the Western world. Does this mean that there was one before him?

A: Yes, in a way, the Sophists are empiricists. They don't believe in innate ideas. They believe that everything begins with experience. They happen, however, to believe that everything *ends* with experience also, and that experience gives you no knowledge. So, they are skeptical empiricists, and that's just what David Hume later made all empiricists into, and that's what they all are today (with rare exceptions).

Q: Would a universal genius such as Aristotle be possible today?

A: No. There is too much known for anyone to be able to encompass it all today, and to do significant original work in every field, every special science included. A person would die prior to that time. The Renaissance was the last period in which universal geniuses were possible. But you don't have to be disheartened—content yourself with being a genius in one area. It's very hard to do.

Q: What is the Objectivist view of Aristotle's distinction between essences and properties, leaving aside the fact that Aristotle considered essences to be intrinsic rather than subjective?

A: If you leave that, and everything it implies, aside, then Objectivism subscribes to it. We do distinguish between the essence and the consequences of the essence. When, for instance, Miss Rand says that it is wrong to define "capitalism" as "the system that leads to the greatest happiness of the greatest number"—even though it does—that is based on the Aristotelian idea that the essence is the fundamental, and the properties are its consequences, and that it's a catastrophe epistemologically to confuse the two. In that sense, Objectivism subscribes to it. But essences as intrinsic (tied in with his idea that universals are formal structures inherent in things) is the heart of the metaphysical aspect of that doctrine, and with that, as I've indicated, Objectivism disagrees.

Q: When you say that no men are metaphysically superior, do you rule out the idea of inborn superior intelligence?

A: No, I do not, I'm glad you give me a chance to clarify that. I mean by "metaphysical equals," the view that all men (let's leave aside here, because it's not relevant, actually deformed men)—Objectivism holds (and this is by no means distinctive to Objectivism) that all men are metaphysically equal in the following respect: not that they are equal in intelligence (there may or may not be differences in intelligence, but that has not been established), not that they are equal in physical attributes, not that they are necessarily going to be equal in moral character (God knows, there'll be huge differences), but they'll be equal in one crucial respect, namely, they are all members of the same species, they have the same defining attributes, and all the properties that that entails. And therefore, the same moral code is applicable to all of them. Therefore, they all have an equal opportunity at birth of achieving moral perfection. And if anyone doesn't, it is his volitional default, not a congenital deficiency with which he's born. That is all that is meant by saying that men are metaphysically equal. It does not mean they have equal intelligence. Intelligence is not a prerequisite of morality (that is to say, a high intelligence is not). The full *use* of your intelligence is required to be morally perfect. But the full use of your intelligence is possible, even if the level of your intelligence is modest.

Q: Does Aristotle consider the possession of self-awareness essential to, or a defining characteristic of, consciousness?

A: No, not that I'm aware of. And it is *not* a defining characteristic of consciousness, because there are creatures on the perceptual level who are conscious but do not display any self-awareness. Self-awareness is a distinctive feature of a *conceptual* consciousness, which is capable of turning in and distinguishing itself from other things and forming the idea of itself as against other things, and, therefore, it is an attribute of the conceptual level. Aristotle certainly believed that human beings have this faculty. He ascribed it to what he called the "common sense," which was the general power of awareness, which could turn in on itself. He himself, so far as I know, ascribed it incorrectly to the perceptual level of consciousness. But I don't know that he says anywhere that that's an essential element of consciousness.

Q: Is it a vice, according to Aristotle, to believe in something so strongly as to exclude everything that might stand against it?

A: No. He did *not* make that application of the doctrine of moderation. On intellectual matters he thought you should believe strongly, firmly, and as an absolute, in what you regard as true. He had passionate convictions that he was willing to stand by. The doctrine of moderation was applied specifically to emotional matters.

Q: Would you review why it's invalid to search for a principle of individuation?

A: Look at it this way: Is the principle that you find individual or not? If the principle that you find is individual, then, are you prepared to take its individuality as a primary or not? If you do, then you've already accepted individuality as an inherent fact of existence beneath which you won't get. If you don't, then you've gone into an infinite regress of finding, of individuation of the individuator of the individuator, etc. There are certain facts that you cannot get beneath, and one of the legacies of Platonism in Aristotle is the attempt to get beneath the ungettable-beneath.

Q: Is Aristotle's concept of active reason as an impersonal spark introduced in order to avoid the charge that a personal motive controlling the intellect would make all cognition biased?

A: It might have been. There's nothing in the surviving works to warrant or contradict it. As far as we can tell, it was explicitly a view on his part deriving from the four causes.

Q: Did Aristotle distinguish for himself between epistemology and metaphysics?

A: No, those are later terms. Aristotle used "analytics" to refer to what we call today "epistemology." And he did not even have the word "logic," as I recall. *Organon* was the name given to his logical works, which was the *instrument* of knowledge. So "epistemology" is a much later term. Equally, he did not have the word "metaphysics." He called it "first philosophy." It was a later—I believe, second century AD—term. It came, if I remember, from Andronicus of Rhodes, who was compiling Aristotle's works many centuries later, and he didn't know very much about philosophy, and he found Aristotle's writing on what we call "metaphysics" shortly after he had compiled the writings on physics, and he didn't know what to call it, there being no name for it, so he called it in Greek "the stuff that I found after physics," and that came out the *meta-physics.* But if he had found it before astronomy, we'd call it "pre-astronomy."

Q: Why is mind potentiality in man, and yet the perfect self-consciousness of the Unmoved Mover (in other words, his mind) is pure actuality? Isn't this inconsistent?

A: Aristotle would say no, because these minds operate entirely differently, because their modes of thought are different. The human mind passes from potentiality to actuality—it thinks in a moving process—whereas God contemplates statically, and so his mental method is radically different from man's. And therefore, it's not a contradiction to say that the mind in one case is potentiality, and the mind in the other case is actuality. But there's an additional point—the mind also has an element of actuality—

the *human* mind, for Aristotle—and that's the so-called *active reason*, which in that respect is akin to God's mind. Aristotle describes it as pure actuality, that impersonal spark that operates our minds. And from that point of view, there is a definite parallel between the human mind and the divine mind, and many of the medievals construed (unwarrantedly) the active reason as merely God in his guise of influencer of man's thought, which is not in Aristotle. One last point on the active reason: Someone asked, "Was Aristotle's motive in any part in postulating the active reason to preserve the objectivity of human thought by means of saying that we are not guided in our thinking by secret Freudian or Marxist-type passions, but by impersonal dedication to truth?" And I did not emphasize that. In the text as it has come down to us, there is no such emphasis, but in looking up that point, I see that it is a common interpretation of Aristotle. I can't say what it's based on, but it would certainly be compatible with his view, and that may very well have been part of his motivation, although I don't think that the doctrine of the active reason as it's come down to us is the best way to defend the objectivity of the mind.

Q: Did Aristotle have any significant effect on the several centuries immediately following his death?

A: Significant effect, in the sense *I* would mean "significant," no. Several of his individual doctrines did, his school went on, and he had some very intelligent followers (Theophrastus, in particular), but no real effect of his overall distinctive approach.

Q: Could you explain why Aristotle didn't have any impact in the Greek culture, which was very rational, and how is it that he had such a tremendous impact on medieval culture that is dramatically less rational?

A: I'm not sure I have an answer. I can say only that the Greek world was already breaking up at the time that Aristotle came on the scene. The city-state, which was the center of civilization, was passing away. So, it was too late. That's the best that I can say right off the top of my head. As to the medieval period, by the time they got Aristotle, he was a treasure, which he wasn't in the Greek world. In the Greek world, they had a thousand philosophies and hundreds of years of it. And some of them appreciated Aristotle and some didn't, but he wasn't a revelation. In this barren medieval world, Aristotle struck only a few (Aquinas, Albertus Magnus, just one or two) as a fantastic treasure, which he was. And in a certain sense, he stood out in bolder relief in the medieval world than he did in the Greek world. But you'd have to give the credit to the few men. It was certainly not the mainstream of medieval philosophy that accepted him. Most hit the roof at the idea. And if you ask me, "If there had been no Aquinas, what would have happened?" I don't know. What would have happened if there had been no Aristotle? Aquinas is a vital, crucial figure in the history of the West. If there had been no Aquinas, for all I know, we'd still be in some equivalent of the Dark or early Middle Ages. Even so, it lasted for six hundred years, why shouldn't it last for twelve? And therefore, you owe your existence to Aquinas just as much as to Aristotle, although more to Aristotle because without him, Aquinas couldn't have been. But, you see, it takes only one man. That's all it takes in each era. And it was without modern means of communication. Aquinas couldn't go on television and broadcast. He couldn't even write in the newspapers. And yet within a hundred years of his death, that was the end of the medieval period. If you can do that much in that period on the basis of such ignorance in a hundred years, think what you could do in fifty—if we had them—today.

Q: You have stated that a philosophy has no hope of becoming popular if it has a weak ethics. Why then has Kant's philosophy, as opposed to Aristotle's, had the most influence on subsequent movements? Isn't Aristotle's ethics more practicable and more appealing to the man on the street?

A: A perfectly good question, but you don't interpret me entirely correctly. To begin with, Kant's ethics has certain attributes that Aristotle's doesn't: It is ruthlessly consistent, and therefore, it has the force of absolute consistency of a kind that nobody else's has, and that includes Aristotle's, with its mixture of Platonist elements and Aristotelian elements. And that's a big advantage to an ethics. Nothing is more crucial in morality than the passion that comes from absolute ruthless consistency. Kant makes no bones about it. Aristotle is not on the defensive philosophically, but he's not very enthusiastic about ethics, since that is not his forte. He is not preeminently a moralist. And therefore, his ethics lacks a kind of fire, or passion, that comes across only occasionally, as in his description of the Magnanimous Man. Secondly, Kant's ethics, however vicious it is, is universally practicable, that is to say, no one can practice it, but in another sense, it's not designed for any special class of men. Everyone can wreck his life on it equally, if he wants to try it. Aristotle's is definitely aristocratic, if you take it as a whole, because of the stress on contemplation as an end in itself, and it presupposes wealth and high intelligence, etc., and so necessarily it would seem irrelevant to the great mass of people.

Thirdly, very crucially—this is perhaps the most important, throwing the preceding two points into insignificance in a way—Kant cashed in on millennia of Christianity, eighteen hundred years of a powerfully established Christian context that was taken for granted, and he simply drove people to the wall given that context. Aristotle took the first steps in a brand-new direction without any ancestors or context at all. He had before him only Plato or the Sophists. You have to understand this point: It is much, much easier for someone today to be receptive to a philosophy that preaches reason than it would be if the same people with the same honesty and the same intelligence existed in the fourth century BC, because at that period of human knowledge, to go by reason was a complete unknown. There were no theories to say what it would consist of or what it would mean in practice. To live avowedly and self-consciously by a philosophy of reason and to know what that would mean, you would have to be a first-rate independent philosopher. It would not be possible for the decent man on the street to do it. He would have no way to figure out all the implications and applications, and how to do it, and how to solve all these endless problems. It's only after centuries and centuries where we've acquired the rudiments—and even there, mankind is still today in a moral wilderness—but now we have after Aristotle and the Industrial Revolution and modern science and the birth of the United States of America and the development of language, etc., we have some guidelines, and even those proved insufficient, for, as you know, we're in the process of losing them. And that is the crucial need of Objectivism and the Objectivist ethics. But you cannot ask, "Why did the people of Aristotle's time not endorse him, because after all, he was better than the rest?" It simply is anachronistic historically. It couldn't have happened. I don't think it could have happened even if Aristotle had had a completely consistent philosophy. It would have taken centuries and centuries to absorb such a revolution. But as it was, he had an inconsistent one, and that made it worse. But I will conclude this answer by giving one point to Aristotle, and that is: There is a sense in which Aristotle always *has* won out in human history—insofar as people act or function at all, they *do* function on an Aristotelian base, insofar as they accomplish anything of value. And in that crucial sense, the common man *does* go for Aristotle, but he doesn't know about Aristotle, and he doesn't know that you can't combine the *Nichomachean Ethics* and the Sermon on the Mount. And in that same sense, nobody can live by Kant—all they can do is destroy themselves and society in the process. That's about as much as I want to say on that question.

Q: Why didn't Aristotle catch on in the way all the others (Stoicism, Skepticism, etc.) did?

A: I'm asked that question all the time. The only thing I can say is what I said essentially so far, namely, a philosophy's effect is determined by its ethics. If its ethics is deficient, that is a mortal blow to the possibility of it guiding men at large. Aristotle's ethics is deficient, being streaked with Platonism. And you must understand something—everything I've presented to you about Aristotle is correct, i.e., I didn't distort or make him better than he is. But I'll tell you something perfectly frankly, if it's of any help to you in this connection. When I first read Aristotle, I did not appreciate his value. I could not understand why Ayn Rand was such an admirer of Aristotle. I say in my own defense that I was a teenager, and I didn't know very much of anything. But I couldn't get it. He said a few good things, but he said so many wrong things, I couldn't grasp it. In other words, prior to my being an Objectivist, I was not able to appreciate Aristotle. And I think to a large extent this is true of mankind as a whole. You can grasp the real values of Aristotle, given the nature of the manuscripts we have and the mixture as he presents it, only when you see the distinctive doctrines presented pure, as part of a whole integrated philosophy, including, above all, an integrated ethics and politics. But that's hindsight. To the people at the time, Aristotle didn't come across as an anticipation of Ayn Rand. They saw him as a philosopher for a philosophic elite, writing about a city-state that had passed into history, and the question was what to do here and now. I don't say that that's a full explanation. You can't get around the fact that however primitive and ignorant the time was, here was a genius who was ignored, and there has to be some dishonesty on the part of some people to account for this fully. But that's an area I don't care to get into as a philosopher.

LECTURE SIX

Philosophy Loses Confidence

In the last lecture, we completed our sketch of the high point of Greek philosophy—the philosophy of Aristotle. According to Aristotle, man lives in a world that is fully real and scientifically intelligible. His mind is competent to gain objective knowledge of this world, of reality, by the use of reason and logic, based on the evidence of the senses. The good life is *eudaimonia*, happiness, and it is achievable here on earth, and the crown of human virtues is pride, which is embodied in the great-souled man, expressing man's confidence in himself and his ability to deal with reality.

But if you know anything about the subsequent development of philosophy, you know that this Aristotelian approach to philosophy did not endure in the ancient world. Some five or six hundred years after Aristotle, Christianity began to become dominant, and it preached the exact opposite of all these Aristotelian tenets. It preached that man lives in an unintelligible, semi-real shadow world, as contrasted to the reality and perfection of God, that knowledge depends on faith and revelation, that life on earth is a vale of tears in preparation for a supernatural destiny after death, and that humility is man's proper self-estimate. This series of tenets together paved the way for that long night of mankind that we now refer to as the Dark and the Middle Ages.

The question is, how? By what steps did philosophy pass from the height of Aristotle to the depth of Christianity? It was during these five or six hundred years between Aristotle and the emergence of Christianity as the dominant viewpoint that man fell to his knees, to remain there for over one thousand years. Why and how? Thus, our topic: the transition from rational Greek confidence to Christian, mystical self-abasement.

This transitional period is known as *Hellenistic*, or sometimes *post-Aristotelian*, and it comprises four main non-Christian pagan schools that we want to look at: the Epicureans, the Stoics, the Skeptics, and the Neoplatonists. If you want to give a title to this lecture, call it "The Long, Drawn-Out Death of Ancient Pagan Philosophy." For the record I should say that the material we will cover is, relatively speaking, much less important than what we have covered in the course so far. Some individual points of these various philosophies have been very influential and survive to this day, so the period is worth covering. And it is absolutely necessary to know it if you are to understand the rise of Christianity. But in their essentials, the philosophies of this period are all unoriginal. They are derivatives of earlier schools, and the thinkers of these centuries are, without exception, second-rate minds. That is why, having devoted five lectures to the period from Thales to Aristotle (a period of 250 years), we can now cover in one evening four schools stretching across some 600 years. But if you think that's something, wait until the next lecture, when we'll cover more than a thousand years in one night. There's a great deal you could say, but none of it is crucial, so I'm adopting the procedure that there is such and such a point here that could be made, and if you're interested, you can use the question period to ask me.

In general, the main concern of most of the post-Aristotelian philosophers was the realm of ethics, the question of how to live. In part, there were practical political reasons for this. The Greek world during this whole period was progressively losing its autonomy and dominance. There was a series of wars and political upheavals, the old stable Greek city-state order was passing away by the second century BC, and Greece had lost its autonomy and become merely a province of Rome. In this situation, the Greeks felt that they were living in a chaotic world, where they were no longer masters of their fate, no longer in control of the world around them. It's not too much of a stretch to think of it as something on the order of the atmosphere of England today in contrast to the nineteenth century: fear, anxiety, and insecurity progressively characterized the whole period. Philosophers were addressing themselves to the question of how to achieve peace of mind in a troubled, insecure world, how to be saved from all of the evils and uncertainties of life as they saw it, and how to achieve salvation. Most of these post-Aristotelian philosophies are called "salvation philosophies," because their basic goal is to tell the individual how to achieve salvation—in other words, inner tranquility and peace amidst the chaos of a dissolving world. There is, therefore, a streak of malevolence that underlies all post-Aristotelian philosophy. The goal is not how to achieve a full life in a rational universe, but rather, how to escape being hurt too badly in a chaotic and even a hostile universe.

Epicurus

Against that background let us look at Epicurus (342–270 BC) and his most famous disciple in Rome, Lucretius, whose famous poem *De rerum natura*

(*On the Nature of Things*) is a poetic expression of Epicurus's philosophy. (Lucretius is first century BC.) Epicurus's goal, like that of most of the philosophers of this period, was to achieve happiness as he construed it for the individual. He thought that there were two main fears that stood in the way of man achieving happiness: the fear of the gods (or in general, the fears inculcated by religion) and the fear of death. According to Epicurus, the gods are presented to us by religious people as fickle creatures, with the power to interfere in human life, to inflict favors or punishment at their arbitrary decree. How could anybody have any sense of security if you believe a thing like this, if you believe that you are at the mercy of the arbitrary decrees of these allegedly divine beings? Because you never know what is coming next, you will necessarily feel anxious and helpless.

As to the second main fear, the fear of death, he said that people fear it because they're told that when you die your soul goes to an unknown reality; retribution is visited on you by some unknown standard. You're in effect delivered up to some inconceivable dimension ruled over by arbitrary powers. We have to combat these two fears. How? We need an appropriate philosophic basis to make them unwarranted. And for this basis, Epicurus looks back to past philosophic systems and selects the one he believes to be most congenial to the ethical conclusions he wants to reach. You see his procedure here: He does not originate a system of metaphysics or look at reality independently. Instead, he looks back and selects what he thinks is most convenient for his purposes out of what has already been formulated. And as such, he is a philosopher of the second rank (to be generous). And that is true of the whole post-Aristotelian period: Independent interest in major philosophic issues, in metaphysics and epistemology, is largely gone. The age of real originality has passed, and thereafter, they borrowed from their predecessors and tinkered, making minor modifications, within the framework of systems and approaches already established.

Epicurus decided that the best system for his purposes was the Atomism of Democritus. You remember the little uncuttables, the atoms, moving through the void, strictly by mechanistic laws, functioning like little billiard balls, and, on this theory, everything is just a combination of atoms constantly mixing and unmixing in different combinations. The soul is made of atoms, of soul atoms, which are perfectly physical but very round, smooth, fine atoms (you could theoretically have a handful of soul).

This metaphysics gets rid of the two fears. The gods are obviously superfluous. Epicurus still accepted the existence of gods, apparently because they appeared to people in dreams, and he didn't know how to account for this if there were no gods. But he held that the gods are made only of atoms. They have no power to interfere with human beings, for they too are just atomic collections. He thought of them as a sort of glorified race living off in seclusion somewhere, having no ability or desire to influence or affect human life. For practical reasons, therefore, Epicureanism is an atheistic approach to philosophy (as would have to be the case for any materialist), though, as I said, he did believe in the gods in the sense just mentioned.

As far as death is concerned, there is no immortality on the Atomist metaphysics. You are nothing but a certain combination of soul and body atoms. Your consciousness, your personal identity, your sense of "you" depend on a complex structure of soul atoms quivering in a complex structure of body atoms. Death is the dissolution of these structures. The atoms go floating off in new combinations. You have disintegrated, and there is no "you" anymore. And so there's no immortality, and death therefore is nothing to fear. Epicurus expressed this particular point in a famous form that is not dependent on his Atomism as such. He put it this way (this is not an exact quote, but the essence of his idea): "Where death is, you aren't, and where you are, death isn't."[19] Death, therefore, he said, concerns neither the living nor the dead. It doesn't concern the living, because they are living, and it doesn't concern the dead because they are not. Hence, the fear of death is empty. When it comes, by that fact, you are gone. Therefore, you will never know anything but life, and it is senseless to fear a state you will never know. So much for the fear of death. I observe in passing that this is a perfectly valid, unanswerable argument, and it is amply sufficient to answer today's Existentialists, who wander around moaning neurotically about death as the catastrophic metaphysical threat hanging over human life and making everything meaningless and absurd. They have not even attempted to answer Epicurus on this point.

Atomism, therefore, says Epicurus, relieves us of our two main fears. But it brings up a new problem and a new fear, namely, determinism. It takes away the fear of the gods—we are no longer pawns of the gods—but, says Epicurus, are we now to be a pawn of the laws of mechanics? Are we now passive robots without free will, reacting to the inexorable laws of physics without any control over our own destinies? Have we escaped one tyranny, the tyranny of the gods, only to embrace an equal tyranny, the tyranny of mechanics? We must, says Epicurus, find a place for

---

19. One standard translation: "When we are, death is not come, and, when death is come, we are not." From Epicurus's "Letter to Menoeceus."

free will within the framework of a materialistic, atomistic philosophy. How are we going to do this, inasmuch as there is no such thing as mind apart from atoms that is capable of making choices? How can you have free will on a materialist metaphysics?

To understand his answer, let us leave this issue for a moment and look briefly at Epicurus's physics. At one point, trying to explain the origin of the world, Epicurus hypothesized that a long, long time ago, when the atoms were in their most primitive state—before they combined into worlds—they were merely falling down in straight lines, sort of like a steady rain of atoms. He thought this because he knew nothing about the law of gravity. He thought that atoms had weight as an inherent property, that they had a certain heaviness, just the way they have a certain shape, in themselves. And, as such, left to their own devices they would just fall straight down, because things with weight, as we observe here on earth, fall straight down if unimpeded.

His problem was how to get the atoms together to make worlds from this initial rain of atoms. We need some collisions among the atoms. Since they were in a vacuum, and since they were traveling through the void, they all (he thought) fall at the same speed, so none of them would ever catch the others. The question is: How would they get together? We know they must have gotten together because they now exist in all kinds of combinations. Well, he said, there's only one way: If it were the case that every once in a while certain atoms could move sideways ever so little, just enough to collide with an adjoining line of falling atoms and start a component of motion in the sideways direction, we would thereby generate all sorts of collisions, the various atoms would smash into and away from each other and, ultimately, by strict mechanical laws, we'd bring about all the combinations that create the world of shoes and ships and sealing wax and people and planets, etc. The problem then is to get certain atoms moving sideways.

Epicurus asked himself why they would ever do this. By all the laws of physics, they should merely go down since that's what their weight dictates. Yet they must go sideways. But there's no reason for them to go sideways. Given this dilemma, Epicurus took the bull by the horns and held that every once in a while, *for no reason*—not that we don't know the reason, but that even if we were omniscient, there would *be* no reason, no cause—every once in a while, some of these little atoms lurch to the side. This is completely causeless, sheer chance metaphysically, an uncaused event. The atoms occasionally go on a metaphysical bender, so to speak. These uncaused, exceptional, sideways lurches are called "Epicurean swerves," and this represents the abandonment of the universal law of cause and effect. Most of the time, the atoms obey the laws of mechanics and are lawful, but occasional swerves are possible.

In the swerve, Epicurus thought he had the solution to the problem of free will and determinism. Because, he said, it's not true that we are pawns of inexorable laws. Our soul atoms also can swerve causelessly and can break the laws of mechanics, and they can escape their billiard ball destiny by periodically lurching causelessly. And as such, we are free to act in defiance of causal laws, and we are, therefore, in control of our behavior—we have free will.

This is the view that free will requires the denial of causality, and it is known technically as *indeterminism*, defined as the view that causality is not universal, and free will requires a breach of causality. If determinism is the view that everything is inevitable, nothing could ever happen any differently, man has no choice, indeterminism comes back with "Yes, he has, because there are no ironbound laws of reality, causeless swervings can occur."

This is, in fact, a hopeless theory. Although it's not at all uncommon—many subsequent philosophers have taken their cue from Epicurus on this issue. For instance, Kant, William James, many of the Existentialists, and many of the disciples of the physicist Werner Heisenberg have tried to defend free will by an attack on cause and effect. So it's not in any way restricted to Epicurus or atomism. I say this is a hopeless position because, among many other reasons, a human being has no more control over his actions on the theory of indeterminism than on the theory of determinism. You are no more responsible for causeless actions than for actions that are determined from all eternity by forces outside your control. For instance, suppose I were to walk casually by, minding my own business, and my arm lurches out and stabs someone in the path, and that is a causeless event. And I'm then hauled before the judge to account for my behavior—I would have a perfect right to say, "Why bring it up to me? I was minding my own business, and this Epicurean swerve took place." In other words, free will and self-responsibility cannot be salvaged by abandoning causality. I assume that the correct position on this issue you know, as it's covered extensively in the Objectivist literature. If there are any questions on how in fact you *do* reconcile free will and cause and effect, I'll be glad to discuss that in the question period. For our purposes during the lecture, I want you to know that Epicurus is one of the main originators of the attempt to equate free will with causeless action, and thus one of the main philosophers to put the concept of "free will" in disrepute. So much for his metaphysics. His epistemology is without value or particular originality or influence, so we will ignore it and turn to his ethics.

His ethics rests on what he took to be a basic observed fact of human behavior, namely, that all men want only one fundamental thing for themselves: pleasure, or the avoidance of pain. This is supposed to be a factual description of human psychology, i.e., the way people, in fact, behave and necessarily behave by their nature as human. This is a view that many, many centuries later was christened *psychological hedonism*—"hedonism," from the stress on pleasure (the Greek for "pleasure" being *hedone*), and "psychological" hedonism because it claims to be a psychological description of human behavior. As such, this doctrine is not an evaluation—it doesn't say it's good or bad to pursue pleasure—it says that is how people are. If you want a definition of psychological hedonism, it is the view that all men by their very nature as men necessarily pursue one and only one fundamental goal in all of their actions, namely, to gain as much pleasure and/or as little pain as possible for themselves. This doctrine is, therefore, a species of a broader doctrine called "psychological egoism," which maintains that all men by their nature are necessarily egoistic, but it leaves open what in particular they're after. Psychological hedonism subscribes to that and to the view that the particular thing they're after is pleasure.

On the basis of this doctrine, Epicurus formulates his ethical code. He reasons like this: If this is the way that man is by nature, then ethics must build on this fact. There is no use telling man to act for something else, if he has no alternative but to pursue his own selfish pleasure. One advocate of this view put it this way: Suppose man were so built that the only thing he could care about was lemon pies—he would be a psychological lemon-pie-ist, and if so, when you came to ethics, you'd have to say (if you're basing ethics on human nature) the supreme value is lemon pie. You would then become an ethical lemon-pie-ist, on the grounds that man has no choice. Consequently, we reach the doctrine known as *ethical hedonism*, which is now an evaluative doctrine, and it is defined as follows: Pleasure, and pleasure alone, is good in itself. Pain, and pain alone, is bad in itself. Everything else—every other candidate for value and virtue—is to be evaluated depending upon its pleasure/pain consequences. Putting it more briefly, ethical hedonism is the doctrine that pleasure is the standard of all ethical evaluation. And you see the relation between these two doctrines—psychological hedonism is a description, and ethical hedonism erects an ethics on the basis of it. Epicurus subscribed to both, and the first was really the argument for the second (although he did not always very clearly differentiate between the two). I'm not going to criticize these two during the lecture this evening. Both are false. I refer you to the Objectivist literature, again where they're covered. On ethical hedonism, there's a brief piece by me in the first issue of *The Objectivist Newsletter*, back in 1962,[20] and there's considerable discussion by Miss Rand on these topics. I'll take any further questions on these two doctrines in the question period. Also, if you're interested in the difference between hedonism and *eudaimonism*—that is to say, between an ethics that takes pleasure as the standard of value versus an ethics that takes happiness as the standard of value—and how both of those differ from Objectivism, which takes life as the standard of value, I will be glad to answer that in the question period also.

Let's now look at Epicurus's concept of the means by which the life of pleasure is to be achieved, because that is his distinctive contribution to hedonistic ethics. He did not originate Hedonism as such. It actually started with a school of followers of Socrates called the *Cyrenaics*, but the most famous early hedonist was Aristippus, who preached, in effect, the doctrine "Eat, drink, and make merry, for tomorrow you die." And his disciples were in practice indistinguishable from the Sophists. But that is certainly not Epicurus's concept of how to achieve the life of pleasure, and so he is eminently original in his idea of how to achieve the life of pleasure. He is not a Cyrenaic "gather ye rose buds while ye may"–type of hedonist.

To understand his view of the means, I'll remind you of the streak of malevolence and insecurity running throughout this era. It deeply affected Epicurus. His view was that in this kind of world, the more you care about something, the more you value it—the more passionately you desire something—the more open you are to being hurt, the more vulnerable to pain you are. If you place a premium on wealth (I'm updating the examples, but the point is his), then you watch the stock market with your heart in your throat or keep aware of the latest fiscal policies of the Federal Reserve System. Whereas, if your attitude is "Money doesn't matter to me," you are oblivious to the ups and downs of the economy. If you care passionately about another human being—you have a romantic, deep, intense involvement—a small insult or snub, to say nothing of a betrayal on the part of that person, can wound you to the depths of your soul. On the other hand, if you are indifferent to somebody (like a stranger on the

---

20. Peikoff's answer to "Why does Objectivism reject ethical hedonism?" was published in the second issue of the *Objectivist Newsletter*, February 1962.

street), and he does the equivalent, you just say, "Why tell it to me?" and it has no effect on you at all, because you don't care. This is true of any value: If you value your appearance seriously, you would look in the mirror each day and see yourself growing older. If you have a sumptuous repast and you care about it, you get a stomachache. There is nothing you can count on in this world. If you want something from the world, you only open yourself to pain. To achieve true happiness, Epicurus concludes, we must value only that which is dependent on us, ourselves. We have to be self-sufficient. Only in that way can we be in control and invulnerable to the thrusts of a cruel, uncertain world. What we need, therefore, above all, is independence, not just independence from other men, but independence from reality. Every time we care about something, we give a hostage to fate, a hostage to destiny. Every time you want something from this world, you put yourself in the power of reality, which has a chance to get at you and to hurt you.

If you want to achieve a calm inner happiness, what then must you do? How can you become independent of what goes on in the world around you? You can't, he thought, change or improve the world—that's hopeless. What you *can* do is stop it from affecting you. The ordinary man lets the world stir up in him passions, feelings, desires. The wise man, he says, should see that these are really enemies. It's your passions, your emotions, that hold you to reality. It's your emotions that suck you back into the stream of events of life and which open you to being hurt. Consequently, the wise man will conquer his emotions, stop feeling, become essentially emotionless, and in that way will become imperturbable, invulnerable. Thus, the great virtue for Epicurus is to become emotionless. You see in what way it's a variation, modification, or derivative of Plato, but with his own distinctively Epicurean flavor to it.

How should you live then once this happens? You obviously wouldn't expect to live a life of achievement, creation, action, going out in the world and fighting for your values, but just the opposite—a life of withdrawal from the world, a retirement from the cares of life, of indifference to the spectacle of daily affairs. If you want an aphorism that captures the essence of Epicurus's philosophy on this point, it's "Nothing ventured, nothing lost" or "Better safe than sorry." Wall yourself off from reality, and then it can't hurt you. And it's very appropriate, therefore, that Epicurus built a sheltered garden with good solid walls, always referred to as "the sheltered garden of Epicurus." And he proceeded to retire into the garden, live ascetically (that is to say, for a Greek), eat simple meals with a few chosen friends, hold quiet philosophic discourses, and let the world outside the garden go to hell. Hence, the greatest happiness is absence of strong emotions and, therefore, cessation of action. Notice that happiness is something negative for Epicurus—it is the state of *not* being hurt. Pleasure for him is absence of pain in the body and worry in the mind. So-called positive pleasure, the actual positive experience of pleasure, depends on positive desires, and that leaves you vulnerable and anxious.

The model of happiness should be dreamless sleep. Epicurus himself chose the example of having a good digestion. Being rather dyspeptic himself, he thought (correctly) that there were only two states with regard to digestion: Your digestion either is kicking up and causing you trouble, or it's acting well, in which case you don't notice it—neither creates a positive thrill inside. Of those two states, he identified happiness with the absence of trouble, and apparently that was one of the factors contributing to this theory. So, it is a complete mistake, historically, for modern restaurants to call themselves "Epicurean," and for the term "epicure" to mean "taking pleasure in fine food and drink." As one professor of mine put it, Epicurus's motto was not "Eat, drink, and make merry, for tomorrow you die"—this is completely false. His motto, if anything, was "Neither eat, drink, nor make merry, lest tomorrow you diet." You get the idea. Emotionlessness will make you independent of reality, self-sufficient, invulnerable, and therefore, you won't feel pain, fear, or worry, and that is happiness.

This is the essence of Epicurus's view. He mitigated it somewhat because he allowed some positive pleasures if they are not too violent, don't stir you up, or excite you and bind you to the world again. He himself emphasized intellectual pleasures and the pleasure of friendship as superior to physical pleasures, because the former, he thought, were less violent and more in your own control. He advocated a simple life of philosophic conversation in the garden with a few chosen friends, about whom you presumably do not care very passionately, so that if one of them gets sick and dies, you take it with a philosophical shrug. He said at one point that there are three kinds of desires: (1) natural and necessary, which includes food, drink, and shelter in the appropriately modest forms; (2) natural but unnecessary, which includes sex and fame; and (3) unnatural and unnecessary, which is essentially the desire for luxury. You simply live a frugal, simple life. As far as sex, here is a quote from Epicurus: "Sexual intercourse has never done a man good, and he is lucky if it has not harmed him." You see, sex is a very violent emotion, and even at best if you could tame it, it's a distraction from more tranquil pursuits. Lucretius, by the way, agrees that sexual love is to be avoided, but he says that it's all right to engage in sexual intercourse so long as it's devoid of passion. I leave this to you to project.

Notice, therefore, that we see the process of man turning away from life on earth already begun at this early stage. We have a philosophy that is materialistic, essentially atheistic, hedonistic. On the face of it, that is as nonreligious as a philosophy can be. And yet, what it boils down to in its practical recommendations is this: Withdraw, give up, retire from life, don't let yourself be hurt. Epicurus merely represents the start of this process of withdrawal, but he is not yet consistent. He still wants all kinds of things from life—pleasure, for instance (even if on the negative side), he wants his garden, he wants his few friends, he wants his good digestion, etc. By his own reasoning, if he were fully consistent, he should abandon all of these also, because any one of them could open him up to pain (as, for instance, if a friend goes bad, or his garden wall comes crumbling down or is taxed by the city administration, etc.). The possibility of pain is inherent in pursuing *any* values. In other words, the possibility is inherent in life as such. If you want to avoid it absolutely, there's only one sure way to do it, and that is death. Dead men, as the saying goes, feel no pain. Epicurus did not draw this conclusion. He is the beginning of an era, not yet the end of it. As you'll see, however, the next school is much more consistent on this point, although still not yet fully. So, let us now turn to the Stoics.

The Stoics

The Stoics, like the Epicureans, were an enduring school, one that lasted for centuries, first in Greece and then later in Rome. Their founder was Zeno (this is a different Zeno from the one who couldn't walk across a room), whose dates are 340 to 265 BC, and he had several Greek disciples, including Cleanthes, Chrysippus, Posidonius. Zeno lectured from a porch, and since the Greek for "porch" is *stoa*, he was called the porch-philosopher, and thus the word *stoic*. In Rome, when the current of civilization shifted there, Stoicism was a highly influential philosophy, much more so than Epicureanism ever was. You've undoubtedly heard of Cicero and Seneca, both of whom, although they're not pure Stoics, were deeply influenced by Stoicism. The two most famous Roman Stoics are Epictetus the Slave, who was born around the mid-first century AD, and Marcus Aurelius, the Emperor of Rome, who was second century AD. And it's often said that this indicates the universal appeal of Stoicism in Rome if a lowly slave and the mighty Emperor both were the leading lights in Rome and of the same philosophy. Because it lasted so many hundreds of years, Stoicism passed through various phases, altering its doctrines in various ways, and it's usual to divide it into early, middle, and late Stoicism, but that is unimportant for our purposes. We will concentrate on some general doctrines common as tendencies and in various forms to most of the Stoics, and we'll be particularly interested in the later Stoics as one of the main transitions to Christianity. The earlier Stoics, the Greek ones, were materialists in regard to the gods and the soul, somewhat in the manner of the Atomists. But as Stoicism developed, it became progressively more dualistic, more Platonist, more this-world versus another world, the soul versus the body, and more immortality-oriented—that was a progressive tendency in Stoicism.

The goal of the Stoics was salvation, serenity, the peace of mind of the individual in a torn world. They were influenced in this respect not only by the general temper of the times, but also by a particular school that grew out of Socrates's ethical teachings, which I haven't mentioned in this course so far—a school called the *Cynics*, the most famous of whom was Diogenes, the one with the lamp who went around looking for an honest man. Socrates had taught that external circumstances cannot harm the really good man, that what counts in life is your internal state, not your external possessions or the circumstances of society. The Cynics proceeded to develop this point beyond anything that Socrates himself had said or implied. They concluded that you should be entirely indifferent to your existential fortune, that you should scorn all social amenities—fancy clothes, material goods, even ordinary civilized manners (Diogenes, dressed very sloppily, was in a bathtub out in the street). One should, in effect, go back to nature and live like an animal, like a dog—and thus the name "Cynic" from *cynos*, which is Greek for "dog." "Cynic" literally means "the dog philosophy." And they dressed very shabbily, scorned all the amenities and were, in effect, the first hippies in the West.

In their desire for peace of mind and their scorn for external things, the Stoics are, in part, an outgrowth of this earlier Cynicism. And in this respect, they are also similar to Epicurus in the overall thrust of their viewpoint. But they did not believe that Epicurus was sufficiently independent of reality, because, as we've seen, he still wanted things from this world. The Stoic viewpoint was that we must adopt the same general line as Epicurus, but more consistently. We must stop valuing *anything* in the external world, and we must not in any way be dependent on the external world. We must stop valuing pleasure, so hedonism is out, even the negative hedonism of Epicurus. We must stop valuing friends, and we must stop valuing even life. Some of them went so far as to recommend suicide on the grounds that nothing, including life, was a value (but this, I should say, was an extreme viewpoint, and did not attract a large posterity). What we must do, they said, is achieve utter insensibility, or as it is in Greek, *a-pathy*, that is to say, the absence of feeling (which comes out in English as "apathy"), non-emotion. Emotions for them are a disease, an aberration, any emotion, emotion as such. And emotions must be obliterated across the board. The ideal Stoic is the man who hears that his wife has just been run over, and/or that he's just won a three-million-dollar lottery, and/or that he just got a new toothbrush, with exactly the same reaction—namely, "That's nice" or "That's too bad"—a perfectly calm reaction. They tell a story of Epictetus—I don't know whether it's true, but it illustrates the viewpoint—he was the slave, and his master was apparently a sadist and one day was twisting Epictetus's leg, and Epictetus is supposed to have said to him very, very calmly, "If you continue to twist my leg, the bone is going to break," and the master continued to twist, and at a certain point there was a grinding noise and a crack as the bone broke, and Epictetus is alleged to have looked at him without turning a hair and said, "I told you it was going to break." When you reach this stage, you see, nothing in the world can touch you. This is salvation.

The question is how to achieve this state. And what then should you do once you've reached it? On what basis would you then take any action at all? There could no longer be any advantage to you in seeking any particular goal, because you're in a state of apathy, having abandoned all values. The answers to all these questions require us to understand the nature of the universe and man's place in it. And if you gain this knowledge, you can attain apathy and know on what basis to act. So, we turn then to the Stoic view of the nature of the universe—in other words, the metaphysics of the Stoics.

If Epicurus is a development from Atomism, Stoicism is a development from Platonism. The best way to approach Stoic metaphysics is via the "argument from design," as it's called, a venerable argument for the existence of God on which the metaphysics of the Stoics ultimately rests. This argument was not originated by the Stoics—it goes all the way back to Anaxagoras (you remember, the man with the little seeds)—and it's implied in many, many places (all but explicitly stated in Plato himself), but the Stoics are the first school to make this argument fundamental to their metaphysics. The argument from design goes like this: Look at the universe—look how orderly, lawful, regular it is—look how complex, and yet look at the magnificent harmony of all of the various parts, all fitting into a smoothly functioning whole. Look at the purposefulness of all the parts all meshing together to achieve an overall design. Such obvious perfection and design in the universe implies a designer, a powerful cosmic soul or intelligence that runs the universe for some ultimate purpose, keeping all things orderly and lawful as a part of its purpose. Therefore, there must *be* such a cosmic intelligence, namely, God. That's the argument from design. I assume that you know the error of this argument. In essence, it assumes that existence left to its own devices, in the absence of a designing mind, would run wild and become chaos. In other words, the argument fails to recognize that order, law, regularity, means the law of cause and effect, and the law of cause and effect is a corollary of the law of identity, which is inherent in existence as such. And therefore, there's no such thing as a possibility of a disorderly existence metaphysically, and consequently, there is no need for a god to keep existence in line. A is A is quite sufficient. As to the idea that everything has a purpose, which is a different concept than "everything obeys law," you may ask what was the Stoic reasoning behind this. In general, as derivative philosophers, the Stoics accepted the overall teleological viewpoint of Plato and Aristotle. Of course, purpose *does* imply some sort of conscious agent that *has* purpose. But it's a very different concept than "law," which does *not* imply a conscious agent. And that is why the argument from design is frequently called the "teleological argument for the existence of God," from *telos*, the Greek for "purpose." This argument, I may say, appears in the *Reader's Digest* every six months or a year under the title "Twelve Reasons Why a Scientist Believes in God."

In any case, the Stoics accepted this argument as proof of God. They did not, however, believe that God is a being existing separately in another world, in another dimension, the way we're accustomed to thinking of God from the point of view of Judaism or Christianity. They took instead the analogy to the human body, the human being: Just as the soul of the human being is not outside the body controlling it from another realm but is within the body controlling it from inside and making its behavior orderly, so, they said, with the universe as a whole—God, the controlling agent of the universe, is also within the universe. You should think of him as the soul of the universe as a whole, the world soul, which forms with the matter of the universe into a single cosmic living being, a single indivisible entity. This, you see, is essentially the standard religious viewpoint, but with the attempt to give a more naturalistic account of God, trying to base the view of God's relation to the world on the model of the soul-body relation, which we can directly observe here on earth. This sort of view is called "pantheism," from the Greek *pan*, meaning "all," and *theos*, "God." The universe as a whole is matter infused with a semi-personal, omnipresent mind, or soul, guiding everything for the best. They sometimes refer to that totality as "the cosmic animal," and they give it a whole bunch of names, e.g., "God" or "Nature" or "Zeus" or "Reason" or "Providence." Two attributes of this animal (that is to say, of the universe or of God, whatever you want to call it) should be noted here. First, as already suggested, it is teleological through and through. Everything happens for the best, for a purpose of God's. This is inherent in the argument from design: The world is designed and kept orderly by God for some purpose or goal of his. And the Stoics generally took over this teleological viewpoint from Plato and Aristotle. I should say, though, that the Stoic teleology tended to be much cruder than either Plato's or Aristotle's. Plato had his comparatively sophisticated Form of the Good toward which everything aspires, and Aristotle had his metaphysical self-realizationism. The Stoics, however, generally had an anthropomorphic view of teleology. Many of them held that the purpose of everything was somehow man's welfare. So, for instance, you get a kind of crude, low-level teleology, e.g., why are there diseases?—"To combat population growth." Why are there bedbugs?—"To get us up in the morning." Why do melons have ribs?—"So we can apportion the shares equally." This is what you call a primitive teleology.

A second attribute of the divine animal: rigid determinism. The Stoics agreed with Epicurus that universal cause and effect means rigid determinism, but they took the other side of the conclusion—they said there is rigid cause and effect, and therefore, everything is determined. There is no such thing as free will anywhere in the universe, neither in man nor in God. Everything that happens is an inevitable expression of God's nature. He cannot arbitrarily will or choose anything. He's not a Christian God or a Jewish God. He's a Stoic God. Everything, therefore, is fixed for all eternity. Indeed, for the Stoics, the universe goes through rigidly fixed cycles. They were influenced here, in part, by their reading of Heraclitus, and they held that at one time the universe was a huge fire (sometimes called the "Great Bonfire"), and then, following immutable laws, it goes through various stages of development, and worlds are formed, and so on. Then, since the universe is finite, there are only so many elements. At a certain point, the original stage, the original combination must be reached again. In other words, we have another fire, the Great Bonfire—and then we go around the cycle the next time, and since the same ingredients exist following the same laws, we must go through the identical development. It's like a deck of cards shuffled according to an inexorable law: You keep going through cycles, each step repeated in the same order each time. So, on this view, you have had this lecture on the Stoics an infinite number of times already, and you came to the Hilton every Thursday an infinite number of times, and you will do it an infinite number of times in the future—I will give the identical lecture, you will ask the identical questions. I sometimes wonder why it is that we have to go through it so many times, but, you see, the idea is that everything comes back eternally. This is known as the "doctrine of eternal return," and it is a dramatic way of emphasizing the rigid, inexorable rule of destiny. I should say that this doctrine of eternal return, or eternal recurrence, was picked up by Nietzsche, among other philosophers, and subscribed to by several philosophers much later.

You might wonder at this point, how you can have an ethics at all if you hold such a doctrine. How can you say what people should do or shouldn't do if everything is inevitable, and they do what they have to do? That is indeed a problem, and it's called the "problem of freedom": If there *isn't* any freedom, how can you prescribe how men should behave? How can you hold them responsible? How can you praise them or blame them? This is a problem that the Stoics struggled with desperately but unsuccessfully. We will note the same problem under Christianity, which had it in spades and also struggled desperately with it. In general, this is a problem for any deterministic metaphysics and is, in fact, insoluble on such a metaphysics, though determinists from the time of the Stoics to the present have made endless attempts to solve this problem and to reconcile determinism with morality.

To summarize the metaphysics of the Stoics: It has three central concepts that you can put in any order you want: a teleological deterministic pantheism, a pantheistic deterministic teleology, etc.

As to the Stoic epistemology, I will mention two points of some importance for later philosophy. First, the later Roman Stoics emphasized that man was born with certain innate ideas, as a God-given cognitive endowment, to enable us to start the process of acquiring knowledge. After all, since God is everything, your mind is a part of God, and as such it contains (at birth) at least some of God's ideas, although many of the Stoics, being eclectic on this issue, also emphasized the role of the senses in a more Aristotelian manner. But insofar as they advocated innate ideas, the Stoics continued and transmitted the Platonist rationalist epistemology, and they were thus one of the main links between Plato and the rationalists of the modern era. And the second point: In answer to the question, "When can you claim absolute certainty?," the Stoics came up with the so-called doctrine of irresistibility, which, stripped of its fancy language, amounts to the following: In the process of seeking an answer to some question, you should consider and answer all possible doubts, until at a certain point you will suddenly see in an incontestable insight, an irresistible insight, that the answer in question is true. And such an irresistible insight they described as one that was "clear and distinct." I ask you to remember the terms "clear" and "distinct." You'll see what happens with this issue when we get to Descartes, who in many ways is influenced by the Stoics. I think you can see that this is a pretty feeble epistemology, and many later Stoics gave up under the onslaught of the Skeptics and said, "Well, I guess we never can be certain of any truth, merely achieve probability."

Let's now turn to the Stoic ethics. First, their view of man: What is man on this philosophy? Well, if everything is God, if God is all that exists, then a man is only a part or a piece of God. In Epictetus's phrase, man is a "fragment torn from God." His soul is part of the world soul, and his body is a part of the world body. He is not—and this is the crucial point—any longer to be viewed as an autonomous creature, as a separate individual, as an individual metaphysically on his own, owning himself without allegiance to anything but himself. That latter was the view that Aristotle had held, that Epicurus had held. It was not the view that Plato had held, and in this respect also, the Stoics reflect a definite Platonic legacy. Man is, in their terms, to be viewed strictly as a part of a larger whole, as a part of God, temporarily severed from God, but still only a part of God, owing allegiance to God—in other words, to the whole of which he's only a part. And we know that the universe, or God, has a plan, a purpose, that man is on earth in accordance with God's plan, that he has a role assigned to him in that plan. We know, therefore, that man has obligations imposed on him by the fact of not being a metaphysically autonomous entity, the fact of being only a part of a wider whole. In a word, man has *duties* that he must obey. Not for reward, gain, pleasure or for any personal advantage, but strictly because they are his duties.

Thus, for the first time we get an avowed morality of duty, in stark contrast to the approach of Aristotle or Epicurus, or even Plato much of the time. It's implicit in Plato, but to a good extent Plato held that virtues are to be practiced because they lead to happiness, fulfillment, because some advantage accrues to you. The Stoics, however, on their metaphysics of pantheism, and their view that it's hopeless to try to achieve any values in life, abandon the traditional Greek approach to morality and instead make morality an issue of doing what's right because it's right, doing your duty because it's your duty, period, regardless of any advantages or disadvantages, regardless of its effects on you. A duty-morality is essentially any morality that separates virtues from values, or actions from rewards. And it is, of course, the antithesis of the Objectivist approach to morality. If you will notice in Galt's speech, "virtue" is defined as "the action by means of which one attains value." And that very definition effaces the possibility of a duty approach to ethics. In this respect, the Stoics are one of the main sources of what Kant later took over and blew up into astronomic proportions.

I'll give you a brief quote from Marcus Aurelius on this point:

> When thou hast done well to another, and another has fared well at thy hands, why go on like the foolish to look for the third thing besides, that is, the credit of having done well or some return for it? Is not it enough that thou hast done something in accordance with thy nature? Seeketh thou a recompense for it, as though the eye should claim a reward for seeing, or the feet for walking? For just as these latter were made for their special work, and by carrying this out they come fully into their own, so also man, formed as he is by nature for benefiting others, when he has acted as benefactor for the general welfare, has done what he was constituted for, and has what is his.[21]

You don't ask, "What is in it for me to be moral?" That is a wrong approach. To be moral is to do your duty. Just as the eye doesn't say, "What is in it for me to see?," so to be an eye is to see, like it or lump it.

I think you can grasp how the road is being paved for Christianity, where ethics becomes a matter of following commandments because God commanded them, period. The Stoics were not Christians but pagans who believed that you could establish your duties rationally, not by revelation. But the basic duty-theme nevertheless appears in them. And it is their answer to the question, "On what basis should you act once you've abandoned personal values?" And the answer is, "On duty."

I should mention that, as Greeks, the Stoics were not consistent in their duty approach to morality. It was common for them part of the time to advocate duty as an end in itself, regardless of any advantages that it brought, and part of the time to declare that the justification of doing your duty is the advantages it brings to you personally—for instance, inner tranquility, peace of mind, a sense of moral virtue, happiness. In this respect, there is not too much difference between the Stoics and Plato. Insofar as their approach to morality is distinctive, both advocate placing something above your own happiness, such as sacrifice, duty, etc., but

---

21. Marcus Aurelius, *Meditations*, 7.

insofar as they're both Greek, neither ever lost the appreciation, in some form, of individual happiness as the ultimate goal of morality. So, neither Platonism nor Stoicism is consistent on this point, and you should know this for historical accuracy. I may say that the same is true of Christianity, which preaches that you should follow God's commandments *because* he commanded them, regardless of any advantage to you (which is a purely duty-approach), and yet promises otherworldly happiness for eternity if you do so (which is a legacy of the Greek idea that a reward is the justification of virtue, which was carried over by Christianity into a supernatural form). A completely consistent duty-approach to morality, which expunges every element of advantage from ethics and makes it completely a matter of selfless obedience to duty, with no value placed on happiness as a moral justification, had to wait for the time of Immanuel Kant. That was his contribution to ethics. In this respect, Kant's ethics is the sacrifice pro-duty element of Plato, the Stoics, and Christianity, stripped of every mitigating Greek feature. The Stoics, however, are not nearly as consistent or as corrupt as Kant. No Greek, however bad he became, ever dreamed of approaching the man-destroying evil later adopted and proclaimed by Kant and his followers.

What, then, *are* your duties? Their basic answer is, to live in accordance with your nature, with your reason—which is a typically Greek answer. But your nature is to be a fragment, and therefore, what your reason tells you is nothing like what the other schools said. I'll mention two characteristic Stoic duties, which in their opinion are commandments of human reason. Number one, the duty of acceptance. Accept whatever happens to you without wanting it to be different. Do not burn with passion for the things you haven't got. Do not feel anger or rebellion or protest against the state of affairs you're in, or the kind of world you're in, or the social circumstances you're in. Take the course of events as it comes. Yield unprotestingly to whatever occurs. Do not lead events, as the saying goes, but follow them. Why is this a duty? To protest would be impious—it would be rebellion against God since everything is part of his plan. And remember also the teleology—everything is for the best—so if your wife gets run over by a truck, if you could see it all from God's point of view, you would see that it's all for the best, and therefore, it's senseless to get upset over it. And anyway, everything is inevitable—your wife has been run over an infinite number of times by that same truck, so it's ridiculous. And then there is what you can call the "Grand Canyon Argument" (although that isn't the name the Stoics gave to it, but that's the idea): "Look at the vastness of the universe, the enormous number of events and the huge span of eternity

—what do your particular life and petty cares matter in the face of this?" (that's what I call the "Grand Canyon" argument because people usually recite it when they see the Grand Canyon).

For all these reasons, the wise man will tranquilly accept everything. And that's what we mean today when we call somebody "stoical." He will see that everything is inevitable, that all's for the best, that nothing external is worth having anyway, that so long as he does his duty and accepts, he has everything worth having—inner tranquility, wisdom, and virtue. To achieve this state, he must constantly suppress the enemy: his passions. He must discipline himself. He must see how his desires and aversions are nonsense in the face of God's inevitable unfolding. And if he schools himself in this, if he's really steeped himself in the right metaphysics and the right self-discipline, all of his emotions will fall away, and he will be truly insensible. Of course, it's hard to do this. It takes a process of constant willpower and self-discipline. But given enough time, they thought, it can be done. Once you do it, you are truly invulnerable. You value only what's in your power, only the state of doing your duty, i.e., virtue. That is really, in the last analysis, the only thing worth having if you're to be secure and independent of the world. Thus, the well-known idea in the expression "Virtue is an end in itself, virtue is its own reward." Everything else is inconsequential—life, wealth, health, fame, you name it. And you see the similarity to Epicurus in this withdrawal, except that the Stoic withdrawal from life is much greater than Epicurus's. Epicurus withdraws into a garden, but the Stoic withdraws into his own soul, where nothing can touch him, where he acts virtuously as an end in itself for the sake of doing his duty. That, he thinks, is just up to him alone, not dependent on a hostile world. And therefore, we have an even greater renunciation of life than we did with Epicurus.

Besides the duty of acceptance, there is a second Stoic duty, not merely the duty to wipe out your emotions, keep yourself attuned to God's plan, be apathetic. And a few advocated a kind of passive state of this sort. But most of the Stoics gave a positive content to your duty, requiring definite action and not mere passive acceptance. What kind of action did they advocate? *Altruistic* action—serving others—doing your duty to promote the welfare of mankind. What was their reasoning here? They based it on the idea that you're just a part of a whole. Just as you're a part of God and not metaphysically autonomous and therefore have duties to God and should not seek your own advantage, so in relation to mankind you're only a part. Mankind is a much larger fragment of God. And by the same reasoning that the whole is superior to the part, you owe an allegiance to humanity. And besides, it's hopeless to achieve any advantages for yourself in this world. As a Stoic, you are insensible, so no personal self-interest or private goals are possible anyway. If you're not to vegetate, all that's left is service to others. And here I'll quote from the *Discourses* of Epictetus (who always uses bodily analogies):

> A foot, for instance, I will allow it is natural, should be clean. But if you take it as a foot and as a thing which does not stand by itself, it will befit it, if need be, to walk in the mud, to tread on thorns, and sometimes even to be cut off, for the benefit of the whole body; else it is no longer a foot. In some such way we should conceive of ourselves also. What art thou? A man. Looked at standing by thyself and separate, it is natural for thee in health and wealth long to live; but looked at as a man, and only as a part of a whole, it is for that whole sake that thou shouldst at one time fall sick, at another brave the perils of the sea, again know the meaning of want, and perhaps die an early death. Why then repine? Knowest thou not that as the foot is no more a foot if detached from the body, so thou in like case are no longer a man.

Continuing from Epictetus and making the point very clear:

> What, then, does the character of a citizen imply? To hold no private interest; to deliberate of nothing as a separate individual, but rather like the hand or the foot, which, if they had reason and comprehended the constitution of nature, would never pursue or desire but with reference to the whole. Hence the philosophers rightly say that if it were possible for a wise and a good man to foresee what was to happen, he might cooperate in bringing on himself sickness and death and mutilation, being sensible that these things are appointed in the order of the universe, and that the whole is superior to the part, and the city to the citizen.

Now, that is certainly unequivocal.

The ground and essence of this viewpoint is in Plato, as we saw in his organic theory of the state. But in Plato, to some serious extent, moral virtue was justified by the happiness it would lead to. Although he was very mixed on this question, Plato's argument against the Sophists was that if you behave this way, you'll be miserable, you will have a sick soul. However, the openly religious metaphysics of the Stoics, combined with the deep sense of futility about the achievement of any personal goals on earth, has led for the first time to altruism as an official, explicit, cardinal duty, not to be justified even in the name of your own long-run self-interest. And I hasten to point out that the Stoics, as always, are inconsistent on this point and often said that altruism leads to your own happiness. But that is not their distinctive viewpoint—that's just their Greek legacy.

I should point out that the Stoics, even though they advocated altruism, are often accused, with some validity, of really being egoists. And the argument is as follows: The Stoics are primarily motivated by the desire to achieve a sense of their personal, individual moral virtue. They don't really sympathize with others in trouble, i.e., they don't burn with pity or love for suffering mankind. Since they're Stoics, they remain emotionally aloof, cold, uninvolved, apathetic. What then is their real interest in helping others? The critics answer that it is to give the Stoic a chance to exercise his moral muscle, to do his duty and thus gain the selfish sense that he has been virtuous. So, their real goal is selfish after all. This argument is valid. It shows that even the most Platonist Greeks had some tie to reality and to reason. If you contrast this Stoic approach with the later Kantian approach, you will see that, on Kant's view, if you are motivated even by the desire to achieve a sense of your own virtue, that fact alone deprives you of all moral credit for your action, because you still have a personal egoistic desire. If you get this contrast, you'll see how comparatively innocent any Greek, including even the Stoics, were on these points.

One final point on the Stoic ethics. As was typical of any duty-approach to morality, the Stoics stressed the importance of your inner motive, rather than your actual achievements in action in the world, as the measure of morality. All duty moralities, of whatever kind, hold that (1) since morality has no existential goal or reward, but consists in selfless obedience to duty, the essence of the moral man is his inner compliance with virtue, and (2) his attainments in actual reality are secondary or unimportant. Those of you who know Kant will recognize how deeply he was influenced by the centuries of Stoicism and Christianity on this point. Of course, from an Aristotelian, non-duty viewpoint, this emphasis on the primacy of motive is a fundamental error, because on a non-duty viewpoint, you will say [that] the purpose of morality is to achieve some goal in action, in the world, whether happiness or life or whatever it happens to be. And you'll say that the moral man is the one who acts in the right way to achieve this end in actual fact. His motives are important only because motives lead to action, so you'll give primacy to action. But on the duty approach, you'll reverse the order of priorities and say it's not what you actually do in life that's so important. Your inner allegiance to duty, your motive, and action are important only as expressions of the right motive.

To sum up their ethics, the Stoics preached an ascetic morality with dutiful altruistic insensibility as the essence of the good life. For the record, you are allowed three emotions: joy at the beauty of the universe (as a testament to God's goodness), hope to become virtuous, and fear of becoming vicious. As you can see, this is hardly what you could describe as an extensive emotional life.

Let us say a word in conclusion about the Stoic's distinctive approach to politics, because on this issue the Stoics did have one crucial contribution to make. They were the first major school in Western philosophy to grasp and to preach what we can call the metaphysical equality of all men. The Stoics held that *all* men—not only males or Greeks or philosophers, but all men—have some share in reason. All men are members of the same species and, therefore, each individual has a certain metaphysical dignity and value qua human and, therefore, qua potentially rational being. Every human being, they held, is to this extent entitled to respect as a human being. And politically, he is entitled to equality before the law. All men, in essence, have certain rights that others may not morally infringe. Slavery of any kind is wrong. And if, they went on, the particular country you live in has laws decreeing that some men are second-class citizens, or not citizens at all, or are slaves—in other words, that some men have no rights—this is a violation of the proper principles of laws, which should treat all men equally. Above the laws of the state, said the Stoics, there are the laws based on reality, the laws of nature, so-called natural laws. And that was their major political contribution. The only proper country is a country in which the actual laws reflect the natural laws, and those natural laws are universal, applicable to all men, rational, absolute, eternal, unvarying, moral. If the laws of your country conflict with the natural laws, then the moral man is the man who gives his allegiance to the natural law, not to the law of his country.

The importance of these doctrines to the subsequent development of the theory of individual rights, constitutional government, and the United States of America, can hardly be overemphasized. The Stoics get the credit for being the first major school to grasp this cardinal political principle. I must add, however, that in their context, it was deeply intertwined with their religious metaphysics and altruist ethics. Their basic grounds for asserting the metaphysical equality of men and the importance of what they called "natural law" were supernatural. Because all men are fragments of God, they reasoned, all men are metaphysically brothers, in a literal sense—they're all offspring of the same divine father. And it is because of this, and because God has ordained the natural laws, that all men should be treated equally. All men, as they put it, are members of one city, the cosmic city, the *cosmopolis*, and hence all men have certain rights. And, since your primary duty is to serve your brothers, you shouldn't enslave him, but live for him, so they were opposed to slavery.

You see the terribly tragic mistaken mixture here: the basis of what later became an individualist politics but tied to a supernatural metaphysics and an altruist ethics. And this mixture has subsisted to this day in the so-called conservative movement. In fact, a mystical defense of rights ultimately leads to the destruction of rights, in exactly the same way and for the same reasons that Plato's mystical defense of concepts ultimately led in modern philosophy (as we'll see) to the destruction of concepts. A mystical defense is worse than no defense, and it is self-defeating. And that's the supernaturalism.

As for the altruism, I trust that this audience understands fully how it is incompatible with the principle of rights, or of man's metaphysical equality. Here again the Stoics represent the other side of the coin from the Sophists. They have the same basic view of egoism. The Sophists say the egoist tramples over others, and the Stoics say true enough, but you should be an altruist sacrificing for others, and only in that way can you respect the rights of others. So, altruism became tied to the defense of individual rights with disastrous results. Despite these terrible errors, however, the Stoics still do get credit for advancing the first germs of what was later to be a profoundly important political development.

The Skeptics (Pyrrho of Elis)

In the light of the Epicurean and Stoic advocacy of emotionlessness and withdrawal, you might think that things are in a pretty bad state. But even though Epicurus and the Stoics have given up this world and said that you cannot achieve values here, both schools retain one firm tie to reality: Both believe in the efficacy of the human mind. Both believe that knowledge is possible by reason, whether they construe that in the Platonic or the Aristotelian fashion. Neither school, therefore, ever became religions in the sense of demanding faith or appealing to revelation or having a sacred text or a priesthood. For that to occur, one last thing had to go: man's mind, his confidence in his ability to reach the truth by reason and logic. And this confidence was the target of the next post-Aristotelian school, the Skeptics. If they succeed in their attempt, you will recognize that all is lost, that pagan philosophy is dead, and a new age is about to dawn.

If Epicurus is a derivative of the Atomists, and the Stoics of the Platonists, the Skeptics are a derivative of the Sophists. They are a school of thinkers also stretching across centuries. Again, they started in Greece and moved to Rome. The founder is Pyrrho of Elis, from which we get the adjective "Pyrrhonian skepticism." His dates are circa 360 BC to 270 BC, so he was a contemporary of Zeno and Epicurus. The Skeptics, not much better known than the Stoics, include Arcesilaus (essentially third century BC), Carneades (second century BC), Aenesidemus (first century BC), and Sextus Empiricus (flourished about 200 AD).

The Skeptics held that knowledge of anything is impossible. That's it. Even this, they stated, was not knowledge—you can be certain of nothing. Their name comes from the Greek verb *skeptesthai*, which means "to examine carefully, to investigate, to inquire," and they were always inquiring and never finding anything. And so, they came to be called "the perpetual inquirers" (as against "the finders") and finally the word "skeptic" acquired our modern meaning.

Why is no knowledge possible? The Skeptics developed a whole arsenal of arguments. For instance, on the senses, they developed at great length Protagoras's primary argument that perception depends on your sensory apparatus, and therefore, you don't perceive reality directly, only the subjective effects on your organs. The Skeptics said that perception varies with the species of entity perceiving (men and dogs don't necessarily perceive the object the same way), and it varies depending upon the specific individual within a species (for instance, the normal man versus the color-blind man), and it varies with the bodily conditions of an individual (you see spots before your eyes if you have certain sicknesses). Also, the various senses of the same individual at the same time might conflict with each other (so for instance, the classic case, if you have a cavity in your tooth, your sense of sight tells you it's tiny, and your sense of touch as mediated by the tongue tells you it's huge).

Your sense perception varies with your different relations to the object—the railroad tracks up close seem to be parallel, but at a distance they seem to converge. Your perception depends upon the medium between the object and you—for instance, the air through which the various waves travel—how do you know what the medium adds that distorts? All of these and many, many more are variations on the basic argument of Protagoras. In sum, they said, we never see things as they are, since our perceptions are influenced by all sorts of outside factors besides the nature of the object. We have no means of distinguishing true perceptions from false ones because we never get to see the object directly and therefore have no means of comparing the object with our experience. We're trapped in our own world of subjective experiences. Reality, therefore, is unknowable, and, some of them added, what makes you think there *is* a reality if you never perceive it? All you perceive is a flux of subjective impressions. How could you ever go from that to something unperceivable beyond it? Maybe it's all just a dream or a hallucination. What about reason as against the senses? Reason, they said, is based on the senses, so it's no better off than the senses. And then they used the argument from disagreement that all skeptics at all times use: Everybody claims to have the answers, everybody claims to have refuted his opponent, nobody agrees. The Stoics are teleologists, the Epicureans are mechanists, the Stoics are determinists, the Epicureans are indeterminists, and the Platonists stress universals and the Aristotelians stress particulars, etc. Who is to know? Doesn't it prove that man's reason is incapable of objective knowledge? And as far as ethics goes, all they had to do is take all the stories of the returning travelers as to how the barbarians lived, which is radically different from the way the Greeks or the Romans lived, and that goes to show there's no agreement on ethics anymore than in metaphysics and epistemology.

There were many more arguments than just these. For instance, there was an argument directed by many Skeptics against the idea of axioms, or first principles. They denied the objectivity of self-evident truths. Consequently, they said, to have knowledge, we'd have to have an infinite regress, and since we can't do that, reasoning can never lead us to knowledge, because we can't arrive at objective first principles. Some of them contested the law of cause and effect on grounds very close to that which Hume in the eighteenth century became famous for. In particular, Aenesidemus, who was a Heraclitean Skeptic, anticipated Hume's argument, so followers of Hume love to dig him up and show how venerable Hume's argument was. He argued that you can never perceive (by your senses) a causal connection, and therefore, you have no basis for believing in one. Therefore, there's no justification for induction. How can you generalize if there are no causal laws? And there's a whole standard array of Skeptic arguments. You put forth an argument and the Skeptic says to you: "How do you know you're not crazy? After all, it's possible: human beings become insane, they have delusions, maybe you've having one—prove that you're not. How do you know you didn't commit a mistake? It's possible: human beings make errors—prove that you didn't. How do you know you're not dreaming? How do you know you're not hallucinating?" And so on. In the seventeenth century, Descartes attempts once and for all to answer all of these Skeptic arguments, so we will wait until that time to discuss them, and you will see [that] Descartes makes it much worse rather than making it better. And in lecture twelve, I will finally give you the Objectivist viewpoint on all this type of skepticism.

Some Skeptics attacked the syllogism on the grounds that it was an inherently fallacious means of reasoning. If you're interested, you can ask me in the question period about their argument, which had enduring influence, and what's wrong with it. Sextus Empiricus, in particular, launched an attack on universals, as the earlier Sophists had done. Universals, whether Platonist or Aristotelian, are a myth, he said. And that subverts the whole foundation of conceptual thought and, therefore, of induction. There's no way to justify generalizations if you can't justify abstractions. And the Skeptics delighted in paradoxes. The most famous is the so-called Liar Paradox. Epimenides the Cretan comes up to you and says, "I am a liar," meaning "I am a universal liar, everything I say is a lie, everything I say is false" (including that statement). The Skeptics ask if his statement "I am a liar" is true or false. And you're trapped whichever way you turn. If you say it's true, then the Skeptic says, "Well, if it's true and it says it's a lie, then it's false. If it's true, it's false. But if it's false, then it's false that it's a lie, and it's false that it's false. In other words, it's true. So, if it's false, it's true. "So," they say, "here we have a statement that is such that if it's true it's false, and if it's false it's true. So much for human logic." A very popular paradox among later logicians, made much of by the Bertrand Russell mentality. What is wrong with this? If you're interested, ask me in the question period. On the question of God, Skeptics are agnostics.

I might mention in passing that not all the Skeptics were content to negate knowledge across the board. Carneades, in particular, was one of the first in philosophy to stress that even though certainty is unattainable, probability is possible, degrees of probability. And he is thus the father of all those modern skeptics who say: "In being a skeptic, we don't reduce ourselves to *tabula rasa* babies completely ignorant of everything. We simply deny certainty and take the middle ground between ignorance and certainty, namely, probability." What's wrong with this? Question period if you're interested.

The upshot is: No knowledge is possible. One commentator summarizes it as follows:

> Hence our attitude to things ought to be complete suspense of judgement. We can be certain of nothing, not even of the most trivial

> assertions. Therefore, we ought never to make any positive statements on any subject. And the Pyrrhonists were careful to import an element of doubt even into the most trifling assertions which they might make in the course of their daily life. They did not say, "it is so," but "it seems so," or "it appears so to me." Every observation would be prefixed with a "perhaps" or "it may be."[22]

And here's a quote from Arcesilaus: "I am certain of nothing. I am not even certain that I am certain of nothing."

Skeptics are always an easy school to deal with because, since they know nothing, you can breeze through them very rapidly. For most of the Skeptics, ethics is a completely subjective matter, but some of them worked out an ethics of a sort as follows: Socrates had said that virtue is knowledge, and knowledge is the crucial indispensable precondition of ethics. And since there was ethics, Socrates said there must be knowledge, but the Skeptics took the reverse view. True enough, they said, knowledge is the indispensable precondition of ethics, but since there is no knowledge, it follows that there is no ethics. There is never, many of them said, a rational ground for preferring one course of action to another. What should the wise man do then (the wise man being the man who knows that nothing can be known)? He should resist the seducements to which the mass of men are subject. After all, action proceeds from our ideas, right action from right ideas and wrong, harmful action from wrong ideas. The wise man, however, knows that you can assent to no ideas, knows that you can never affirm any idea, and, therefore, restrains himself from having any idea, and therefore from taking any action as much as he can. He withdraws into himself and suspends judgment and thereby is prevented from having to act. He achieves apathy, calmness, tranquility, rest within himself, and quiet indifference. So, Skeptics come to the same end as the Epicureans and the Stoics. To the extent to which a man *must* act, many of them said, he has to do what appears subjectively to him or conform to the mores of the society around him. And some of the ancient Skeptics were actual priests in various religions on the ground that you couldn't prove they were wrong to be priests—it's all a matter of opinion, and it was very convenient. So much for the Skeptics.

Now you see how all these schools—the Epicureans, the Stoics, the Skeptics—are converging on the same conclusion—the helplessness of man and the hopelessness of life. Each of these schools, in its own way, is

---

22. *Encyclopedia of Philosophy* entry on Pyrrho, author anonymous.

ripening man for the onset of a religious era. Each is sapping man's confidence in some vital area and preparing him to fall to his knees and seek divine guidance, divine knowledge, otherworldly happiness. We are now on the threshold of man's descent into the medieval abyss. We see philosophy progressively losing confidence: Man's mind is no longer capable of gaining knowledge. The senses are invalid, reason is precarious, unreliable, and life on earth is hell, inherently painful, malevolent. We have to give up the hope of happiness on earth, and we are frightened, helpless creatures. This trend became progressively more intense: We are caught in a world we cannot deal with or understand or function successfully in. We are "strangers and afraid in a world we never made."[23]

The quest was for salvation, and progressively it was felt that men couldn't achieve this on their own here on earth, as even the most pessimistic Stoics had thought. Salvation depends, it came to be held, on looking to another reality, a true, perfect reality, a reality of which this world in which we live is a mere shadow, a reflection, a semi-real insignificant byproduct. Knowledge depends upon contact with—and special help from—this superior reality. Knowledge is no longer possible on the basis of Aristotelian logic operating on sense experience. And happiness, what is it? According to this view, it is eventual escape from life on earth, from the physical, from the body, and the uniting of one's soul with true reality. So, supernaturalism in metaphysics, mysticism in epistemology, intense soul-body conflict and intense asceticism and antagonism to life on earth in ethics—these are the elements that came to dominate the whole era.

We've seen all these elements before in Plato. All the important philosophers at this time are heavily influenced by Plato. The period from the first or second century BC to about the sixth century AD (which is where we are now in our chronology) is usually classified (correctly) as a version of Platonism, but it's a version in which the worst of Plato becomes predominant, and the more pro-this-worldly sides of Plato, the more Greek pro-reason sides, are progressively ignored and suppressed.

There are two main philosophic trends from about the second century BC on through about sixth century AD. One was the continuation of ancient pagan philosophy, which we've been following since this course began, in other words, philosophy which did not become a formal religion with a sacred text, a priesthood, etc., however mystical in content it became. This pagan philosophy continued with a great deal of mysticism and very little originality until 529 AD, when the Emperor Justinian closed down the

23. From A. E. Housman's poem "The laws of God, the laws of man" (1922).

universities in Athens and ended Greek philosophy permanently. Pagan philosophy consisted of various schools, generally revivals of earlier Greek philosophers of the more mystical persuasion, especially Pythagoras (there was a whole flourishing neo-Pythagorean movement), and Plato—there was a flourishing Neoplatonist movement. The other main trend while ancient pagan philosophy was dying was the birth and rise to power of Christianity as the major philosophic source in the Western world, a process that took centuries (Christianity did not really achieve complete dominance until the fourth or fifth century AD). In the next lecture we will look at Christianity, but I want to conclude tonight on one pagan philosophy of this period in order to give you just a taste of what was happening to non-Christian philosophy in this era. You will then appreciate the caliber of competition that Christianity had or, more accurately, did not have.

Neoplatonism (Plotinus)

Now for Plotinus. He was the leading philosopher of the school called "Neoplatonism," which was the main transition between Plato and Christianity. Saint Augustine, whom we will look at next lecture, was heavily influenced by Plotinus and was vital to the shaping of Christianity. Plotinus's dates are 204 to 270 AD, so this is the first movement that we have encountered that starts AD.

Let's go straight to his metaphysics. Essentially, as the name "Neoplatonism" would suggest to you, he is a follower of Plato, with a few twists of his own. For Plotinus, there is another superior dimension beyond the world in which we live—actually, as you'll see, there are three of them. Why? Well, it's all straight Platonist in essence: This is a world of change, but reality must, as Plato and Parmenides argued, be unchanging. This is a world of imperfection, but reality must, as Plato argued, be perfect. This is a world of variety and multiplicity, of the many, but reality must be one. Remember that Parmenides even called his reality "the One," that big physical sphere. And Plato held that the universal in any category was the One in the Many. So reality for Plotinus must be an absolutely perfect, immutable, completely unified existent, which you can call "God" or "the First" or "the Absolute" or "the Infinite" or "the Good" or "the One"—"the One" for the obvious reason that it's one. It is essentially Plato's Form of the Good. What is the One like, according to Plotinus? What is its nature? What can Plotinus tell us about it? Nothing. It is, he says, ineffable. That is to say, you cannot say a word about it. If you say anything at all about it, you would be making a distinction in the One, and you would be distinguishing its existence from its nature, i.e., the fact *that* it is from *what* it is. Even if I say that the One *exists*, I make a distinction between the One and the fact that it *is*, i.e., in other words, I make the One two. And that is wrong. You cannot, therefore, say anything at all about the One, not even that it exists. You can't say that it's one or good or spiritual. It is ineffable, non-conceptualizable, non-describable, beyond anything that man's mind can grasp, incomprehensible to human reason. All we can do is say that it transcends all human concepts. We can say what it is not, but not what it is.

This gave rise in later Christianity to the school known as *negative theology*, which held that you cannot say what God is, only what he isn't, because, they said (validly) that if you give any characteristic to God, you thereby limit him. If you say that God is A, by the very fact of saying he's A, you have excluded him from being non-A. And if there's something he isn't, to that extent he is finite, limited. And therefore, the school of negative theology, which grew out of this, held that you cannot say that God is good, because what? You mean he's limited, and he can't perform evil if he wants to? You cannot say that God is all-knowing, and he couldn't attend a university class and absorb knowledge if he wanted to? You can't say he's this, because what about being not-this, also? In other words, they held the view that to have an identity is to sully God. Identity is incompatible with God—which is certainly true—and God, therefore, must lack any humanly ascribable identity, and this is Plotinus's viewpoint. You see the kinship here with Plato's ineffable Form of the Good.

If the One is reality (I'm not allowed to say that, but Plotinus wrote nine books on the ineffable), our physical world must somehow have proceeded from it or in some way be derived from it. However, not directly as there is too staggering a difference between the One, with its absolute immutable unity, and the many changing things making up this world. We need some kind of mediating levels of reality, specifically two of them, between the One and the physical world. So, we're going to have a scale going down from the One, and we'll get progressively less and less unified, less and less changeless, less and less perfect, until we finally reach the last and least real, least perfect level, this physical world. So, we'll have a characteristically Platonist hierarchical metaphysics.

The first thing to proceed from the One, the second level of reality, is a mind, which Plotinus calls "the divine mind." What does this mind have as its content? Plato's world of Forms, Plato's universals. Plato has shown that these universals must exist, but they're not in the ineffable One, so Plotinus ascribes them to the next layer of the divine mind. So, we have a mind contemplating as its content all of the Platonic Forms. And he also thought that this mind contained ideas not only of abstractions but of every particular instance of these Forms. This divine mind is less unified than the One, because now we can make some distinctions between the mind and its content, although it's still very unified compared to our minds because it doesn't think in any step-by-step fashion. It doesn't reason but rather surveys all of its content, the whole world of Forms, in one unmoving, intuitive, motionless insight. Essentially, he is drawing a perfectly valid conclusion from Plato. Aristotle had pointed out that abstractions can exist only in a mind. Plato said abstractions are real apart from the particulars in this world. Plotinus put the two together and said both are right: Abstractions must exist in a supernatural mind, which is the perfect blend of Platonism with the Aristotelian point, and it's the inevitable tendency of Platonism. And that's why in all later philosophy, Plato's world of Forms becomes thoughts in the mind of God, in a divine mind. And so the universal becomes a thought of God.

Instead of trying to study the anatomy of the divine mind (which I don't think will be of great practical significance to you), let us ask instead: How did the divine mind come to be from the One? The One, says Plotinus, is inherently creative (we can't say that, but he said it), and it, in effect, spills over or radiates out, a process which Plotinus calls *emanation*, which is his term for the process by which one level of reality gives rise to the next. What is the nature of emanation? It can't be explained literally; and all we can provide is a metaphor. Think of the One as a brilliant light, like the sun of Plato (you see how derivative all of these philosophers are), then light rays stream forth from the sun, and at a certain distance you have an area that is a little less bright than the sun itself. The rays weaken, it gets a little darker, and we have a region or dimension of reality that is less perfect, less unified than the light source. You have to think of the sun as possessing infinite energy. It never gets depleted, always shines as brightly as ever. And the emanation process, says Plotinus, takes no time to occur, so you have to imagine that light takes no time to travel from the sun to the next region if the analogy is to be exact. In other words, for Plotinus, the emanation process does not occur at some point in time. There never was a beginning of the divine mind. It had eternally emanated from the One. And this, you see, is the last vestige of the Greek view that the universe is eternal, as opposed to being created at some point in time.

The divine mind wants to imitate the One's creativeness, so it emanates the next level, the third dimension, which Plotinus calls the *world soul*, and that, you see, is the obvious Stoic element. Plato, in the *Timaeus*, also subscribed to the idea of a world soul, a soul of the whole world. It's not very important what he thought the world soul was. In effect, it also thinks, but now it thinks more like us, discursively, step by step. And therefore, its mental processes are infected with multiplicity, with change. It doesn't have the motionless contemplation of the divine mind. Since soul for the whole Greek tradition is the principle of life, and life is inherently bound up with change and motion, the world soul is much less perfect, unified, or unchanging than the higher levels. In terms of the metaphor, we're getting farther from the sun. It's getting darker.

Next stage: The world soul emanates individual souls, which emanate bodies and then inhabit them. In other words, the material world as we know it is emanated from the world soul as the last level. When we reach the material world, we have the maximum of change, multiplicity, imperfection, etc., therefore, the lowest in reality. I can't resist adding that we have here the real primacy of consciousness—minds and souls create matter, create bodies. By the time we reach Plotinus, this primacy of consciousness, which I said was implicit in Plato, has become deliberate and adopted as a matter of principle, not only by Plotinus but by all the distinctive philosophies of the period, including Christianity. They all objected to the Aristotelian idea that consciousness or, as they would put it, mind, or soul, was a metaphysically passive principle, dependent on matter and devoted only to discovering the facts of the material world. The spiritual, they all insisted, is above the material. It has metaphysical primacy, it has evaluative primacy, and it comes first in the order of being. Matter is a derivative of a spiritual principle. Consciousness is independent of matter. It is a metaphysically productive principle, whereas matter is the comparatively unreal, the derivative, simply the result of the operations of mind. Matter is a product of spirit. This is the true primacy of consciousness now become explicit. And it is the legacy of this mentality that you hear all around you when people ask where the universe came from. And you say it always existed, and they say, "But it *couldn't* have always existed!" And you ask why not, and they say, "Well, something must have created it—some mind, God, etc." And you say, well, but did God always exist, and they say "Yes." And you say, but then you're no farther ahead, and they say, "Well yes, but even so, I *am* farther ahead, because God is a mind, and I can take a mind as a primary, but I can't take a physical reality as a primary." That is the mentality throughout this late Hellenistic period exemplified by Plotinus, although he himself, as a Greek, personally believed that matter had always existed and had eternally been emanated from the world soul.

Note, therefore, that over and above the material world, we have three nonmaterial principles that ultimately give rise to this world: the One, the divine mind, the world soul. We have a *trinity* of divine nonmaterial principles over and against matter. This is very common to all of the pagan philosophies of this period. They usually held that you need two intermediaries to bridge the gap between God and the physical world. And consequently, an otherworldly trinity was very common. It was, of course, taken over intact by Christianity and became the Father, the Son, and the Holy Spirit, which was conceived by Christian theology quite on the model of Plotinus. There was nothing distinctive in the Hellenistic worship of three—the Pythagoreans had got all excited about three back in their day, and Hegel and Marx got all excited about three in the nineteenth century, so this seems to be a perennial disease of philosophy.

Plotinus had to face a problem that was long faced by religious philosophers. It was faced by Plato (even though his philosophy was not fully a religion), it was faced by the Stoics, and it was faced by the Christians. And that problem is the *problem of evil.* The problem is very simple: Evil things occur in the world (earthquakes, volcanoes that pour lava on peaceful, virtuous little Italian communities at the foot of them, diseases that run riot and attack the just as well as the unjust, slaughter, and wars, etc.). The problem of evil is that if the universe is ruled by an all-powerful good power, why does he permit evil? This has been a standard objection to religion ever since religion first appeared on the scene. Epicurus, who did not have to answer this problem (being essentially atheistic), put the problem to the Stoics as follows: He said that there are only four possibilities in theory. Either God wants to remove evil from the world, but can't, because he's not powerful enough—which would show weakness on God's part, which is contrary to God's nature as you describe him, or God is able to remove evil from the world, but he doesn't want to, which would show malignity, which is equally contrary to God's nature, or God is neither able nor willing, and so he'd be both impotent and malignant, or, finally, he's both willing and able, which is alone consonant with God as you describe him—whence then comes evil? Why doesn't God remove it? That was how Epicurus posed the problem, and religions have attempted every imaginable and many unimaginable, answers to this problem, which usually boil down to what we call evil doesn't really exist, as it's only evil from a limited human perspective. If you could only see the universe as a whole from God's point of view, you'd see that everything has a place in his scheme and his plan, and really, therefore, what we call "evil" is actually good if seen from God's viewpoint. The only thing wrong with this answer is that the advocates of it go on to say, "Of course, as human beings, we *cannot* see everything from God's viewpoint," and therefore, if you're a human being, this answer is opaque and ungraspable. If only you weren't human, it amounts to, you'd know the answer. This is an errant appeal to mysticism.

But Plotinus, with his emanation scheme, at least has a better answer to the problem of evil. And because it was a somewhat better answer than the standard ones, it was accepted by Augustine and by Christianity (although Christianity, aiming for popular success, tricked it all up with stories about Adam and Eve and so on, but that is not the essential point). So, here's Plotinus on the problem of evil.

First of all, he says, evil is associated with matter, with the physical. In view of his Platonic anti-matter tendencies and the soul-body conflict that was endemic to this whole period, that shouldn't surprise you. So, the problem of evil is really the problem of matter. But what is matter, asked Plotinus? Is it something positive? If it is, we could blame the One for emanating it, and we could hold the One responsible for evil. But, says Plotinus, the actual fact is that matter is the fourth and last level of the emanation process. If we used the metaphor of the sun, it's been getting darker and darker as we leave the One. At some point, it gets really dark, there's no more light, we get sheer darkness, and that is matter, the essential ingredient of our physical world. So, matter is not something positive. It is merely that region of reality characterized by the absence of the energy, the light, the perfection of the One. In itself, matter is unreal, an absence, nonbeing, and here again you see the enormous influence of Plato, his idea that the distinctive constituent of the physical world is empty space, the principle of nonbeing. For Plotinus, matter is where the sun's rays run out, and as such, you cannot blame the One for matter or, therefore, for evil, because that's inherent in the process of emanation. In terms of the metaphor, it can't radiate light without the light being some distance from it. And therefore, it's darker and less perfect. If the One is perfection, anything emanating from it, anything at a distant from it, must in logic be less perfect, must in logic have some metaphysical defect, so it's not the One's fault. The One is the source of light, and thus is responsible for light (in other words, for all the reality and perfection in the universe). The evil, the physical, is merely the darkness that the One didn't get to. It's not something positively existing, but rather an absence. This principle was taken over by Christianity intact and used in the following form: God is the good, evil is the deficient, the defective, whatever is not God, and therefore, evil is inherent in the world precisely because it's not

God. But since it is nothing positive, God cannot be held responsible for it, and therefore, there is evil, but God is not responsible. That's the essential Christian solution to the problem of evil, the most sophisticated one, and it's pure Plotinus and ultimately Plato.

I should mention that the Stoics had a whole variety of less profound answers to the problem of evil, quite different from this one, and a lot of theirs are still kicking around today. If you're interested, ask in the question period.

How did Plotinus know all of this? In part, he claimed to offer reasons of a Platonist sort, as I've tried to sketch in briefly. However, what about his view on the One and the emanation process? How did he know, if not by reason? And his answer was: To know the One, you must undergo a special process, which involves a long struggle, a long period of asceticism, a long period of self-discipline. You have to empty your mind at a certain point of all content, all images, all thoughts, all sense experiences, all emotions, all reason. You have to, in effect, jump outside your own narrow self and the whole physical world. And that's possible, he claims. And if you do it successfully, you will suddenly lose all sense of your own individuality and of your reason with all of its distinctions and multiplicity and logic and so on. You will suddenly merge directly with the One, and you will see what it is. Which you can't communicate to anyone who hasn't had the experience.

This state came to be called *ecstasy*, from the Greek word *ékstasis* (ἔκστασις), meaning "outside of oneself." In this technical usage, it does not mean merely strong pleasure, but rather the state of literally jumping outside of the confines of yourself and the world and merging with a deity in an incommunicable trance. And Plotinus was the great champion of ecstasy, and his biographers report that he experienced it four times in six years, which I imagine was a great strain. It's very similar to Plato's view of how you get to know the Form of the Good. Today's mystics, I may say, put forth two allegedly rational arguments in favor of ecstasy and why it reveals truths unattainable by any other means. If you're interested in those modern attempts to justify ecstasy, just ask in the question period.

I don't have much more to say on Plotinus. His ethics is just what you'd imagine it to be. By now you should be able to tell by the first three sentences of a philosopher's metaphysics what the rest of his philosophy is going to be, because we have passed the age of anything original. The ultimate goal of life is to escape this earth, says Plotinus, to go back home, to the true reality, to the spiritual world. And to be slightly flippant about it, there are two ways, the short way home and the long way home. The short way home is ecstasy, which you can hope to do for a brief period here on earth. The long way is via the "wheel of birth." Along with Plato, Plotinus accepted the whole Pythagorean reincarnation scheme with the ultimate hope of finally escaping the wheel of birth and staying at home permanently. Meanwhile, on earth, you should live ascetically, turning away from physical pleasures. Plotinus was a staunch, intense advocate of mind-body opposition and was supposedly ashamed of the fact that he even possessed a body. He took the standard Platonist approach to ethics, but much more intense than in Plato. But Plotinus is a pleasure seeker in relation to what is to come.

You see to what depths and by what main steps, Greek philosophy in every main branch has degenerated into errant mysticism. But pagan Neoplatonism was not the wave of the future, not in the form that I just presented it to you. Plotinus's philosophy, which is typical of what ancient pagan philosophers were saying at this period, is too abstract and remote to catch on with the man in the street in that form. Its essence caught on, but not in the form of a complex emanation scheme with a super divine mind and world soul. That was too abstract. During these centuries, the man in the street (or at least great, great numbers of them) wanted the same basic things: He wanted another reality. Because he felt helpless on earth, he wanted escape and salvation, having been shaped and molded for centuries by all of these philosophers. And these desires of the men on the street were ministered to by the development during these centuries by a number of low-level popular mystery cults, usually imported from the Orient, which grew steadily in the Roman Empire. These cults were primitive religions, something on the order of the Orphics that we looked at some lectures ago. They all promised salvation to their followers. There was the cult of Isis and Osiris, the cult of the Great Mother, the cult of Mythra, etc. Many of them derive from primitive, even savage, fertility rights. Most of these cults had a lot of features in common: They usually offered salvation to the believers, promised immortality, and had a complex set of rituals to be practiced and dogmas to be accepted. It was common to believe that the particular god they worshipped had died and then been resurrected. This is a carryover of the ancient fertility ritual from which many of these cults grew, i.e., the god dies in winter, and then in the spring, when things are reborn, the god comes back to life, and that's the original source of the idea of a god dying and then being resurrected, and there's a great similarity even down to tiny details. For instance, Mythraism, which was associated with sun worship, held that December 25th was a major holiday because it was the day of the sun's rebirth after the winter was over. And many centuries later, Christianity decided that, since they couldn't stamp out that pagan festival, they would make it the day of Jesus' birth. But by what we know, he was born, I think, in June.

One of these cults was a group of Jews, the cult of Jesus. Starting off as an obscure reform movement within Judaism, it was soon made into a distinct mystery cult, a new religion, primarily owing to the efforts of Saint Paul. In its essence (that is, its basic philosophic content and promises), it was not very different from all the others flourishing at the time. Nor was it immediately very popular, for there was an awful lot of competition among these mystery cults for followers. Even in the third century AD (hundreds of years after Jesus), it was considered far less significant by the educated man of the time than many other cults. It was written off as an obscure and somewhat crackpot Jewish sect. I don't have to tell you who won in this competition. The reason it won is essentially owing to tactical, strategic, propagandistic methods, rather than to its distinctive ideological content. For details, see any good history. The typical mystery cult catered only to men, following the ancient prejudice in favor of the superiority of men. Christianity emphasized equally the soul of women, and that gave them a big leg up on the other cults right off the bat. And Christianity had an immense tactical advantage in the following factor: There were a lot of people who wanted to play it safe, and so they would join three or four different mystery cults, figuring if this one doesn't have the key, the other one would. Christianity was one of the few that would not permit that. Christianity said if you join any other, you cannot join us, and if you join us, that's it. And that was enormously impressive to people who thought that they really must know what they're talking about if they're willing to stake everything on their view. It's considerations of this sort that are essentially responsible for the success of Christianity in this competition. It wasn't called "Christianity" in the early centuries, but it came to be called "Christianity" as time went on. What is the philosophy of Christianity? That is the subject of the next lecture.

Lecture Six, Q&A

Q: Please comment on the view that although certainty is impossible, probability exists.

A: That view represents a fundamental fallacy, identified by Ayn Rand as the fallacy of the stolen concept. "Probability" means an evidential state in which there is a considerable amount of evidence in favor of a conclusion, but the evidence is not conclusive. In that sense, it is contrasted on the one side with certainty, in which you have conclusive evidence, and on the other side with possibility, in which there is some but not very much evidence. Probability is an assessment of the amount of evidence, and as such, it presupposes the possibility of knowledge. All of the items of evidence that together warrant your statement of probability are themselves certainties—they are pieces of knowledge in relation to the hypothesis that what you are saying is probable. If you had no knowledge, you could never claim anything to be evidence, and consequently, you could never make any such distinction as possible versus probable versus certain. Further, if there is no such thing as certainty, there is no meaning then to the phrase "conclusive evidence," because nothing would constitute conclusive evidence, and we could never form such a concept. If so, what would be the meaning of *inconclusive* evidence? If I told you that all we have are non-gloops, and you said to me, "What's a gloop?," and I said gloops are unattainable by man—you'd say, "Well, if gloops are unattainable, non-gloops are meaningless." Probability is the negation of certainty—it is an *inconclusive* state of evidence. If we cannot attain conclusive states, then that becomes an empty concept and no negation of it has any meaning. And in that sense, it's a complete stolen concept. I'll say more about skepticism in lecture twelve.

Q: If evil is non-Godness (that's Plotinus), doesn't this still imply non-omnipotence on the part of God?

A: You mean there's something he can't do. Yes, in a certain way it does because it's still restricting God by logic. The argument is that you can't expect God to create without his creation being something other than him, because that's inherent in the very meaning of creation or emanation. Therefore, it would be a contradiction if God were to create something which was not him, and therefore, the laws of logic themselves prohibit God's doing it. Whether this is a limitation on God's all-powerfulness depends upon whether you regard adherence to the laws of logic as a limitation on God's power. Typical Christians would say that that is not a limitation on God's power. They would say God has to adhere to the laws of logic, but after all, any contradiction is not even conceivable, and consequently, when you say God can't perform contradictions, you are not saying that there is something conceivable to man that God can't do, so a contradiction is actually meaningless. And therefore, God's inability to create contradictions is not a limitation on his power, because a contradiction is outside the province of the mind to grasp. That's how the Aristotelian Christians tried to get around this point. The real religious Christians took the bull by the horns and said to hell with logic—God is so powerful he could violate the laws of logic themselves if he wanted to, and in fact does so all the time. There was one of them, Peter Damian (aka Damiani), beloved of Existentialists. He was a Christian mystic, who said that God is so powerful that once the past has taken place, God could retroactively abolish it. That's what you call all-powerful. The only other people claiming that power are Soviet officials.

Q: What is the Objectivist explanation of the Liar Paradox?

A: The Liar Paradox has as much plausibility as if I were to come to you and say, "A dog is and isn't an animal, true or false?" And then if you say to me, "Well, you said he is," and I say, "Yes, but I said he isn't, so if he is, he isn't, and if he isn't, he is"—you would say to me that is not a paradox proving anything about human logic. It merely shows that if you utter a contradiction, you are going to get contradictory results from it. Any statement that you make and put forth for someone to consider, unless you're engaged in open deception, has the implicit prefix "What I'm about to say is true." If the content of your utterance is "What I'm saying is false," then your initial statement is "What I am saying is true, and it isn't," which is a blatant contradiction. From that, you do not ask what follows, but ask the guy to go home and make up his mind. There are a thousand forms of this particular Liar Paradox. But they all come down to this: They start with a contradiction and then blame human reason for it. And then Bertrand Russell attaches an alleged paradox and bastardizes the whole of human knowledge in order allegedly to solve it. But that's something you need to know modern philosophy for: to appreciate that such an abnormal phenomenon is possible.

Q: Have there been any psychological hedonists who were not ethical hedonists?

A: Yes. I can't offhand think of the names, but in theory I've met that type. And their reasoning is this: If man is necessitated to pursue pleasure and has no choice about the running of his life, morality is out of the picture, a waste of time. There's no use telling a piece of chalk once you throw it out the window, "By the way, it's your moral obligation to fall," because if the chalk could hear you, it would answer back, "Don't bother telling me, since I'm going to do it anyway." And if man is necessitated to pursue pleasure, it's senseless to build *any* ethical theory, even a hedonistic kind, on its basis. And that is valid. But it presupposes that determinism is incompatible with morality.

Q: What is the current method used by determinists to grapple with the problem of freedom and morality?

A: The method, which goes back a few centuries, is called *soft determinism*. There are two types of determinists today, hard determinists and soft determinists. The name was given by William James, who was himself an indeterminist, and he thought that soft determinists were soft in the head, about which he is correct. And therefore, he gave the name as a pejorative term, but it stuck, and it's now used technically. A soft determinist is anybody who says determinism and morality are perfectly compatible. How do they get that? Well, as follows. Morality, they say, is one of the factors that will determine people in the future. If we have moral injunctions and we say to people you should do this and you shouldn't do that, the very advocacy of those views becomes one of the determining factors that will shape human behavior. So everything is necessitated, nothing could happen differently, but by promoting certain moral ideas and repudiating others, we thereby take onto ourselves the power to determine the future of humanity. Needless to say, the soft determinist will say, "Yes, I grant you, I myself had no choice but to advocate what I advocate. But such is determinism, and that doesn't bother me." However, they say, we must make a big distinction. For instance, take the theory of punishment. When we punish someone, which we justify on our soft determinist grounds that the punishment will have good consequences, we're not punishing him in the name of retribution for his past crimes. Retribution, they hold, would be unfair, because, after all, the person couldn't help what he did, since he had no choice. What then is the justification of punishment? Its desirable social consequences. You punish an individual in order to deter him or others from engaging in anti-social behavior (as they would put it), or you punish him in order to rehabilitate him, or you punish him to remove him from harming others. In other words, the justification of punishment is "utilitarian"—that is to say, it's concerned with the benefits on society because society is more important than the individual. So, we have two contrasting theories of punishment, the *retributive theory* and the *utilitarian theory*. The retributive theory, characteristically held by free will-ists, says that you should punish a man only if he volitionally committed a crime, in which case the justification of the punishment is justice, retribution, i.e., paying him back for what he did. The soft determinists say this is unfair, because no one had any choice about what they did, and the justification of punishment is its utilitarian social consequences. This leads them to monstrous problems, not the least of which is: What is wrong, then, with punishing an innocent man who has done nothing whatever if you can show that it leads to desirable social consequences? And soft determinists try every kind of trick to get out of that. But that is the full collectivist-altruist mentality that cannot conceive of the individual as the unit in ethics, and so it's open to all of the objections to collectivism.

Q: How do you reconcile free will with causality?

A: In essence, very easily: You do not equate causality with mechanism. Causality, as implied by Aristotle and as explicitly endorsed by Objectivism, states that everything that happens, happens as a result of the nature of the acting entity, and given an entity with a certain nature, in a certain set of circumstances, it can perform only one type of action. This, as a metaphysical proposition, does not yet state what kinds of entities exist or what kinds of actions they can perform. It leaves that question wide open as a metaphysics. If you have an independent proof that man has volition, that he does have choice (and I assume you're familiar with the Objectivist view that man's direct area of choice is whether to focus his mind or not, to think or not, and that everything else is a causal consequence of that choice)—but assuming now that there's an independent proof, that is not a violation of the law of cause and effect. A certain type of entity—namely, man—under certain circumstances—namely, he's sane, grown up, past a certain age, he's conscious and awake, and so forth, has an undamaged brain, and so on—has only one action possible to him, namely, to *choose*, and that is the type of action that he has. And he must perform it. It is causally necessitated. The proof of the inescapability of it, and the causal necessity of choice, is the complaint of the Existentialists, who go around bewailing the fact that they can't avoid choosing. But, since it's choice we're talking about, that means that the selection of alternatives by a self-generating entity is not necessitated. Choice is a subspecies of caused action and is in no way incompatible with or in violation of the principle of causality, if you understand causality in the Aristotelian and not in the mechanistic Atomistic sense of the term.

Q: Does Plotinus's theory of the world soul bear any relation to Hegel's theory of the world spirit?

A: I suppose it does in certain ways, and there is a definite influence of Plotinus on Hegel. I would just as soon, however, pass that by because to explain would take some time, and would be beyond anybody who doesn't already know Hegel, whom you cannot synopsize briefly. On the whole, however, it has been often said that certain followers of Plotinus anticipated Hegel, but actually, anything in the ancient world is very far removed from anything in modern Romanticist philosophy, certainly Hegel. But there is a similarity, even an anticipation of Hegel's dialectic threefold process, in Iamblichus, who was one of the followers of Plotinus.

Q: What was the argument of the Skeptics to show that the syllogism is invalid, and what is the answer?

A: This is an argument accepted by many British philosophers to this day, and, historically, John Stuart Mill, Francis Bacon, and several others. It claims that all syllogistic reasoning by its nature commits the fallacy of begging the question. You know the fallacy of begging the question, i.e., of using or assuming what you're trying to prove as part of the proof. And they said the syllogism necessarily commits this fallacy. Why? Well, take the syllogism: "All men are mortal; Socrates is a man; therefore, Socrates is mortal." If it is to be a valid argument, we have to be able to know the premises prior to the conclusion. But take the premise "All men are mortal"—that is a statement about all men. Consequently, they say, you would have to know independently that it's true of all men in order to be able to say it: Since Socrates was a man, you'd have to know it was true of Socrates to be able to say all men are mortal, but if you have to know it's true of Socrates to say that all men are mortal, then you're going in a circle to say, "All men are mortal; therefore, Socrates is mortal." And therefore, the conclusion of any syllogism, and indeed of any deductive argument, is in that way assumed in the premises, and therefore, you learn nothing new by syllogistic reasoning, because it's all circular. What is wrong with this argument? There's a fundamental failure to grasp the phenomenon of abstraction. What is wrong with it is this: Human beings are capable of grasping that all men are mortal without ever knowing that such an entity as Socrates existed. You grasp generalizations by induction from *certain* instances, and then, assuming you have an appropriate methodology, generalize to include the entire class on the basis of your concept of "man." Therefore, you do not have to know anything about Socrates to validate the proposition "All men are mortal." True enough, the conclusion is implied by the premise; but that is the criterion of *any* valid reasoning, and it is not *presupposed* by the premise, which is a big difference. Or as W. D. Ross puts this point, begging the question is when the conclusion is contained in the premise itself, but the conclusion of a syllogism is contained only in the combination of the *two* premises, which have to be put together—and that's precisely what reasoning consists of. And therefore, the real meaning of it is that they object to reasoning because it's reasoning. And if that were so, then you couldn't come to any conclusion. What is the status of the argument: "All syllogisms are question-begging; this is a syllogism; therefore, it's question-begging"? Did they have to know that this syllogism is question-begging to know that all syllogisms are question-begging? If so, they're begging the question. You see what I mean—these people steal concepts right and left. It's grand larceny.

Q: Who was the father of individual rights?

A: I'll give you five different answers. Aristotle—by laying the metaphysics of the reality of the individual. The Stoics—by being the first to grasp the metaphysical equality of all men. John Locke—by being the most influential definer of the concept of individual inalienable rights to life, liberty, property. George Washington and the Founding Fathers, who started the first country to grasp and be implemented on the principle of individual rights. Ayn Rand, who was the first one to give a complete philosophic system from metaphysics and, most crucially in this context, ethics, validating the concept. Those five.

Q: Please discuss the issue of life versus happiness versus pleasure as the standard of value in an ethics.

A: First, let us take the issue of hedonism versus *eudaimonism*, pleasure versus happiness. What's the difference? There are two main points. *Hedone*, or pleasure, is, as the Greek term was used exclusively, an emotional state, a state of feeling a certain kind of enjoyment or satisfaction, whereas *eudaimonia*, as we saw last time, is philosophical and a much broader concept, involving a total way of life—not only emotion, but thought, achievement, action. And secondly, *hedone*, pleasure, is a short-range, temporary feeling—you experience pleasure for a minute, or if you're lucky for an hour, but it doesn't go on in perpetuity. It's broken with intervals of indifference or pain, and so on. And so the good life for the hedonist consists of having as big a number of discreet pleasurable experiences as you can, having a sum of disconnected separate pleasures. In this sense, hedonism is a short-range mentality in ethics. Happiness represents an enduring long-range state of the total person, a character attribute, not an ephemeral feeling. For instance, we can talk about a happy person, but not about a pleased person, as a character attribute, i.e., one is enduring, the other is ephemeral. So, in these two respects, as an ethical standard, *eudaimonism* is much superior to hedonism. I should add, however, that very often today, the word "happiness" is used by hedonists as merely a long-range preponderance of pleasure over pain—that is, they interpret the concept hedonistically—and that being so, a hedonist will talk completely indifferently of pleasure or happiness, and so the distinction here collapses. This is an historical point of the relation between Aristotle and the hedonists.

As to the Objectivist view, Objectivism opposes any theory that makes an emotion, whether long-run or short-run, a standard of value. (For details, see "The Objectivist Ethics," the opening essay in *The Virtue of Selfishness*.) Objectivism holds that happiness, enjoyment of life, can properly be the ultimate *purpose* of ethics, but never the standard. By an "ethical standard," we mean that criterion, that measuring rod, by reference to which we determine the value or virtue of any other candidate. Is this action right or wrong by reference to this standard? Is this quality good or bad by reference to this standard? Is this purpose desirable or undesirable by reference to this standard? If your ethics is to be objective, your standard must be a *fact*, not a feeling, and it must be something you can prove objectively, one that determines a necessary set of derivative values. If the life of the organism is the standard, that is a fact, and it has definite objective requirements regardless of who feels what, and you have an objective ethics. But if happiness is the standard, then the first question is: What is happiness? It's an inner emotional state. And what kind of state? It's a state that comes from achieving your values. It presupposes you *have* a code of values. What was the standard of that code, and where did you get it from? If an emotion is a response to values, then to make an emotion the standard is to make your response to values the standard of values, but a response to values presupposes a code of values. So, you're going in a hopeless circle. And the result is that anybody who takes an emotion as the standard is philosophically parasitic. Regardless of his protestations, he is taking over (eclectically, usually) the values generated by philosophers who do *not* hold emotions as the standard. He's accepting and absorbing them, reacting on that basis, and then using his subjective emotion as the standard. Aristotle did not intend to be subjective—that's why he insisted that *eudaimonia* was not *simply* emotion—but it did include it, and it is a serious error. And in that one respect, Aristotle's ethics does incline toward subjectivism. I don't mean to suggest that Ayn Rand chose life as the standard because she wanted an objective ethics and that was the only way to get one, because that would be the primacy of consciousness. She proved that life *is* the standard. So, it's not that she had a desire and then distorted ethics in order to satisfy it—that would be the primacy of consciousness.

Q: Concerning the Liar Paradox, I believe the modern answer reduces to the mathematical logic of Russell and Whitehead. How would an Objectivist answer that?

A: I don't want to comment here on the mathematical logic of Russell and Whitehead. In its philosophic foundations it is thoroughly corrupt. It represents an attempt to have logic divorced from concepts altogether. It represents an attempt to have logic on the basis of a denial of universals of *any* kind, Platonist or Aristotelian or any other. The viewpoint that there are *no* universals—the typically skeptic view on that question—is called "nominalism." It's part of the lecture when we get to Hobbes, who is the first influential modern nominalist, and I will, at that point, make a big fuss about nominalism, about as big a fuss as I made about Platonic realism, and define it and explain it and give the arguments, and only on that basis will you understand *Principia Mathematica* and modern symbolic logic. But in that respect, it was the theory of universals that was started by the Sophists and the Skeptics, and it had its followers in the medieval period, and was, however, peripheral until the Renaissance. And then Hobbes picked it up, and Berkeley and Hume and Locke, to a certain extent, took it over, and the result was the complete triumph of skepticism. But I'm getting ahead of the story here.

Q: Please discuss the Stoic answers to the problem of evil.

A: Here are five points: (1) To begin with, nothing is really evil, because you should be apathetic toward everything. You should understand that the only thing that's really good is virtue, and, therefore, in that respect, there's no point in worrying about the problem. There is no real evil, except what you yourself are responsible for, namely, vice. Of course, this raised a problem for the Stoics, because their critics hastened to say, "Well, if nothing is really good or evil, why should you be in such a rush to provide these unimportant things to other people?" In other words, if, for instance, health is unimportant, why put yourself out to foster other people's health, which you should do as an altruist, according to the Stoics? If money is unimportant and it's not really good, why bother to give it to other people? The Stoic answer to that was a really petty word-chopping distinction. They said it's true that nothing is really good or evil (except virtue and vice), but certain things are advantageous, and others are not, and that you should therefore strive to give the advantages to other people even though they're not really good. Of course, the question is: Is the advantageous really good or not? And their opponents really had a lot of fun with it. (2) Another point the Stoics made, since they weren't committed to an official dogmatic view of God, is that God was limited. He's doing the best he can, but he's got a dirty job. (3) Another point was that if there were no evil, we'd have no opportunity for virtue, e.g., the essence of virtue is acceptance, and if your wife were never run over you'd never have a real chance to show how virtuous you are. (4) Another somewhat better point they made was that God works through necessary causal laws. A world of laws is much better than a world without laws, but a world which has natural laws has to function accordingly, and if the natural laws result in the lava trickling down on the Italian village, there's no way out of that situation. If God suspends the law, it would be worse still, because then we'd be living in a chaotic world. This, you see, is a much better point. The only problem with it is that it takes law outside the province of God. If you then combine that with the fact that law is inherent in the nature of existence, you destroy the whole possibility of a God with any power at all, because everything happens then by the nature of existence, so that's a good argument, but it ruins God. (5) Another Stoic argument is the so-called *author analogy*—if you wrote a novel and you put a villain in it and you were one of the characters in the story, from your point of view the villain is a very bad thing, but from the point of view of the reader of the story as a whole, the villain adds spice, drama, conflict, value. In the same way, you are actors, so to speak, in God's play: From your limited point of view, if somebody sticks a knife in your back, that's evil, but if you could see the whole play, including the final act, you would see that it's a much better story that way. Unfortunately, you cannot see the whole play, so that comes back to the point that if only you could see everything from God's point of view, you would see that it's all good. I may say that the same reasoning can be used in reverse and *was* used in the medieval period. There were people who said: "We believe everything is evil, and that everything has an evil purpose. It seems that some things are good, but that is just a snare set by the Devil to trap man and prevent him from committing suicide so the Devil can torture him longer." The logic of that argument is exactly the same as the other side and has nothing more to recommend it. Some things are good, and others are not, and you cannot escape that fact.

Q: What are the two allegedly rational arguments for ecstasy put forward by modern mystics that you mentioned last time?

A: Argument one, from "the sixth sense," and that argument goes as follows: If a blind man came up to a man with normal vision and said to him, "I don't see what you see, therefore, you must be crazy," the man would say to him, "What business do you have to criticize somebody who has a faculty you don't? If you don't have it, keep quiet." By the same reasoning, the mystics say, there's a sixth sense that gives us an insight into a true dimension of reality radically opposite to this one, a reality where everything is the One, where all distinctions are unreal. By what reasoning can you, if you only have five senses, say we don't see it? If you don't have any such sense, then just like the blind man, you should keep quiet. You're in no position to criticize. That's argument one. What is the answer? There is no identified physical basis of the sixth sense, although Duke University claims to be working on it.[24] Second, it's a funny thing that blind people have no controversies as to whether there are sighted individuals. How come? Obviously, because blind people are capable of having proved to them, objectively, in terms of their own senses, that they lack a certain faculty. Sighted people can make predictions of what will happen that they judge by their sight, and the blind person can verify that he could *not* have made those predictions, and yet he can verify them by his other senses. Consequently, there's no debate. On the question of the

---

24. At the time, Duke University parapsychologist J. B. Rhine was doing experiments on "extra-sensory" perception.

mystics, however, the exact opposite is true. It's not that the mystics are able to demonstrate a form of knowledge that we can validate or verify by our five senses, but on the contrary, they claim a form of knowledge that blatantly contradicts everything given by the five senses. The parallel would be if you told a blind person who just ate cherry pie, "There is nothing round or sweet in the universe, and I know this from my fifth sense." A blind person would have a perfect right to say, "I may be blind, but I'm not crazy."

The second argument for ecstasy is the "argument from unanimity": Mystics through the ages—east, west, north, south, ancient, medieval, modern—have had the *same* mystic experience. Doesn't that prove that it can't be just a subjective aberration, or a diseased consciousness, but that there must be something objective and real to it? And the answer to that one is yes, there's something objective to it—they all have the same sickness, schizophrenia, or whatever it happens to be—the symptoms remain constant, it's a syndrome. You prove nothing by showing that something happens repeatedly. More than that, how would you ever know that they have the same experience, since the central characteristic of the experience is that you can't say anything about it? If you judge by the hundreds of religions that exist, and which all appeal to it, and which all conflict with each other on details, they must have some differences. However, that is too stupid to discuss further.

LECTURE SEVEN

Philosophy Becomes Religious—and Recovers (Part I)

At the end of the last lecture, we reached the brink of the medieval abyss, but we did not yet take the full plunge. Now we will. We witnessed last time the protracted deterioration and final death of ancient pagan philosophy. We saw the progressive flourishing of supernaturalism, mysticism, asceticism, other-worldliness, and the quest for a supernatural salvation. We saw the rise of the mystery cults, and among them the development of the cult of Jesus—at the beginning, an obscure reform movement within Judaism, being a mystery cult of its own, and finally a full-fledged philosophy with characteristic views in every branch and department and on every subject—the philosophy that was destined to rule the West for well over a millennium. Thus, the subject for this lecture is the philosophy of Christianity after it had finally developed (by about the fourth or fifth century AD).

Jesus Christ

To begin with, I want to say something about some of the early figures and the rise of what later came to be called Christianity. And I can hardly omit at least a sentence or two on Jesus himself, whose dates are 4 BC to 29 AD. Jesus was Jewish and believed in the God of Judaism, namely Jehovah, or Yahweh, as this God is called. Jesus was a deeply religious man, preaching that God is the Father of all men and that all men are brothers, a view which in this respect is very similar to the Stoic doctrine we looked at last time. Jesus preached that the essence of morality is love, first and foremost love of God—"thou shalt love the Lord thy God with all thy heart and all thy soul and all thy mind"—and secondarily and derivatively, love of one's neighbor—thou shalt love thy neighbor as thyself. Both of these love commandments, by the way, have their source in Judaic tradition. Jesus did not originate them, but he gave them an emphasis hitherto unprecedented. As to the rest of his ethical teachings and his view of man's life on earth,

I presume that you are familiar with them, and I won't pause to recapitulate them now. The essence is in the Sermon on the Mount, to which I will refer briefly later. I'll merely say that Jesus himself seems, from the evidence we have, to have been deeply convinced that judgment day was imminent, and that in the face of this fact—in the face of the imminent end of the world—physical goods, external comforts, material affluence, worldly success, and so on, were foolish and unimportant. Give away your goods, he preached, turn the other cheek, consider the lilies of the field, for they toil not neither do they spend. Turn to God and prepare yourself to meet your maker.

In fundamentals, Jesus' teachings were obviously congenial to the overall spirit of the age in which he lived and taught. The metaphysics of supernaturalism, that's obvious, and the ethics of asceticism and otherworldliness, that's obvious. Even in epistemology the age was ripe because of its authoritarianism. And just a word on this last: As philosophy deteriorated by the time we reach the second and first centuries BC, and progressively thereafter, it became common for thinkers to defend a viewpoint not by giving arguments, but by citing authorities, by saying that some great philosopher (usually Plato or Pythagoras) had endorsed this view, so it must be true. And as the age grew more religious, the great thinkers of the past came to be viewed as inspired or illumined by God as the bearers not of rational insight, but of divine revelation. It was a period progressively ripe for a man to announce that he represented or was designated by God, was the spokesman of God. Jesus was not the only such spokesman, but the point is that in thus viewing himself, he was in harmony with the dominant epistemology of the age.

From what we can tell, Jesus' early followers, or at least many of them, conceived Jesus as a prospective founder of a Jewish state on earth, in effect as a political liberator of the Jews. They thought of him as the man designated by God to do God's work on earth, that is, specifically to liberate the Jews from tyranny. So, they called him Jesus the Anointed or Jesus the Designated (i.e., Jesus the Messiah, which is what "messiah" means). And since the Greek for "messiah" is *christos*, he was "Jesus the Christ." ("Christ" was not his last name, i.e., he was not the child of Mr. and Mrs. Christ.)

Saint Paul

It is primarily—not exclusively, but primarily—owing to Saint Paul (who was born around the beginning of the Christian era) that this Jesus movement was transformed into a distinct mystery religion. And it is thus Paul who is really responsible more than anyone else for the emergence of Christianity as a separate religion, rather than merely an obscure sect within Judaism. Where Jesus had talked about worshiping Jehovah, Paul talked of worshiping Jesus. He construed Jesus as a god, on the pattern of many of the extant mystery cults, a god who died and then was resurrected (not merely a divinely appointed political messenger or moral guide).

At the inception of what was to become Christianity, Paul laid great emphasis on several points, which I'll present in no particular order. (He was not the only one to endorse these points, but they're characteristic of him.) (1) The crucial importance of salvation, to be achieved by ultimate mystic union with Jesus, i.e., by the loss of one's own identity and the ultimate merging with God. This is a state very similar to Plato's view of the ultimate merging with the Form of the Good, or with Plotinus's ecstasy (which was not to be formulated until some centuries after Paul). (2) Paul stressed man's utter helplessness and dependence on God's grace, on God's free gift of salvation to man if man is to be saved. On his own, said Paul, man cannot earn or achieve or deserve salvation, because man is evil, corrupt, stained by sin, the original sin of Adam transmitted thereafter to all of Adam's posterity. Therefore, man needs grace—"grace" is a key term in Christian philosophy, and the best definition of it is "the unearned offering of values by God to man."

A word here about the term "sin" (in the phrase "original sin"). The term "sin" has to be sharply contrasted with the secular term "vice," or "wrongdoing," or its equivalents. When the Greeks said that something was wrong, or vicious, they meant that it was contrary to the nature of man, contrary to the dictates of reason, that it harmed the individual and violated reason. Wrongdoing for them, following the Socratic position, was essentially self-destruction. "Sin," however, is a religious term, meaning "disobedience to the will of God." It is, therefore, not so much *what* you do in actual content, as the fact that you do it on your own, by your own decision, rather than submit to the will of God. "Sin" means religious disobedience, alienation from God's will, as against the Greek view of evil as transgression against man's nature. So, Adam's sin, for instance, was not in the *content* of his act—not in the simple eating of the apple—but in doing it after God had forbidden it. But, Paul goes on, just as Adam corrupted all of his posterity by his sin, so Jesus will save and redeem them by his sacrifice on the cross, *if* you believe in him, *if* you have faith.

And thus (3), the crucial importance of faith, of acceptance in the absence of argument, of mystic acceptance in the teaching and divinity of

Jesus. And (4), the crucial importance of leading an ascetic life, of turning away from worldly pleasures, above all, de-emphasizing sex and turning instead to God as the almost exclusive focus and center of one's concern. And I might mention a fifth point under Paul before we leave him, and that is that it's primarily owing to Paul's efforts that this mystery cult became a universal religion. As we say, it became *catholic*. "Catholic" means "universal," and we still have that usage today when we say that somebody has catholic tastes. In other words, the Jesus movement after Paul was not restricted to Jews but was applicable to all men, Greek or Jew, free man or slave, male or female. Whoever unites with Jesus will be saved.

The Patristic Period

Time does not permit me to deal with the many other figures who contributed to the emerging Christianity, so, to make a long story short, let us summarize: For one thing, Jesus himself was Jewish, and there is, therefore, a large influence of Judaism on Christianity. Then, as the Jesus movement became a separate mystery cult taking Jesus as its god, it acquired further mystery cult trappings and dogmas that were not part of Judaism. And then, as its spokesmen tried to make it intellectually respectable, they tried to express Christian views in terms of concepts that they borrowed from Greek philosophy. They tried to answer the taunts of the pagans by working out a philosophy of their own. And in so doing, they borrowed profoundly from Plato and, above all, Plotinus. This amalgam of varying sources and ideas led to many sects within the early Christians, and for the sake of retaining unity, the church had to keep meeting in appropriate councils with bishops to take formal stands, declare opposing positions on a given issue heretical, and carve out the orthodoxy slowly across centuries. And once the church spoke, that was it. One thing they decided quite early was the need for a sacred text, and the reason is obvious. There was a wealth and abundance of revelations coming in at a rate you couldn't imagine. There was every conceivable kind of religious sect and sub-sect splitting off on the basis of their particular revelations, including the Cainites who worshiped Cain (the one who killed Abel), and the Ophites who worshipped the serpent that had tempted Adam. The problem was intrinsic in the nature of founding an organized religion. You could no longer use logic as the standard, but you needed *some* standard to distinguish the true from the false (in this case, the true word of God from the false). And if you're going to have an organized religion with some stability, the only solution is to decree an orthodoxy and proscribe all debate thereafter, to stamp certain texts as the definitive revelation, and, thereafter, that is the dogma, and the doors are closed to any new ones. And this is the process that gave rise to the New Testament, and also to the absorption of the Old Testament by Christianity.

This whole period of settling basic doctrinal points, declaring what would and wouldn't count as an authentic revelation, organizing the administrative setup of the church and acquiring a philosophy to unify Christian doctrine—this period lasted hundreds of years, roughly from the time of Jesus until about the sixth century AD. And this period of six centuries is called the *Patristic Period*, in other words, the period of the Fathers of the Church.

Augustine

The most famous of the Fathers was Augustine (354 to 430 AD). Early in his life, Augustine belonged to a sect known as *Manichaeism* (about which I'll comment later). Then he became a skeptic for a while. Then he discovered Plotinus and was very much taken by him, and that softened him up for a mystic experience, which he had at the age of thirty-two. He then became and remained a devout Christian. Augustine represents the first real philosopher of Christianity. He is enormously influential on its subsequent development. Indeed, I would go so far as to say that his influence cannot be overestimated. He attempts to synthesize all the dogmas and practices of Christianity into one all-embracing philosophy, which became for centuries *the* philosophy of Christianity. So, let us take a systematic look at Augustine's philosophy, with occasional excursions to earlier or later figures of this era.

First, his epistemology. In general, Augustine follows Plato. Strictly speaking, he says, we can never have knowledge of this world, which is a world of change, a world of flux. True knowledge must be of immutable truths and Platonic Forms. True knowledge is of reality, not of this semi-real reflection of reality in which we live and which we perceive through our senses. The information we acquire from the senses, he says, has practical value in daily living, but, strictly speaking, it never gives us knowledge because, as Plato pointed out, all we can get through the senses is belief. If true knowledge for Augustine, as for Plato, consists of turning away from the physical world and sensory observation, and studying immutable truths and Platonic Forms, that implies that Augustine endorsed Plato's view of a world of Forms, and so he did. As a Christian, however, he didn't believe that the world of Forms existed independent of God, because on Christian premises nothing can exist independent of God. So, Augustine followed Plotinus on this point and thought of the Forms as merely thoughts in the mind of God. God's mind becomes, in effect, a spiritual home in which reside all the Platonic Forms. True knowledge consists of turning away from this world and discovering the Forms in God's mind. Thus, for Augustine, when you study mathematics or morality, for instance, you are studying unchanging and universals laws or truths, and that means you are studying the relations of immutable universals, and that means you are studying the thoughts of God. So, in effect, mathematics, ethics, etc., are branches of divine psychology. If there were no God, there would be no such subjects, and indeed, there would be no knowledge at all. It would be like Plato without the world of Forms.

How do you gain this knowledge of the thoughts of God? Plato had said that you have a reminiscence of a preceding life, that you'd been there. On Christian grounds, Augustine is not permitted to take this view—it was orthodoxy that there was no preexistence of the soul. But then we have the question: If we can't gain the knowledge of God's thoughts through our senses, and we have no means of direct access to God's thought here on earth, how is knowledge possible? Augustine's answer is that God himself must communicate the truths to us. He must impress certain basic notions on the human mind and thereby enable man to discover the truth. Man, therefore, is ultimately dependent on God for *all* knowledge, and he's dependent on a special act of divine *illumination* as it's called. I quote Numenius of Apamea, another figure of the period: "All knowledge is the kindling of the small light from the great light that illumines the world." In this respect, man is epistemologically passive and helpless, dependent on God's act for any knowledge he has: Left to his own devices, deprived of God's aid, man could claim nothing as knowledge.

In fundamental terms, this is the Platonic approach to epistemology: Knowledge is contact with the supernatural dimension of essences, not the study of this world on the basis of sense experience. But Plato was a Greek, and as such, he held that given your preexistence in the world of Forms, you didn't need, once you were on earth, any *new* illumination from the beyond. Sense perception and reasoning to stimulate your reminiscence was all that was required on earth, culminating in a mystic vision. Augustine makes man much more helpless, much more dependent on the supernatural, than Plato ever dreamed of doing. As a Greek,

Plato had to see firsthand. He had to acquire truth by a personal excursion—before this life, of course, but nevertheless a personal excursion to the world of Forms to see for himself and acquire knowledge he could trust. Augustine, in a much more religious age, demands acceptance of God's illumination—of God's word (if, as is the case, you have no way to verify it yourself)—he demands acceptance on *faith*. Plato asked for individual mystic insight, but not faith in somebody else's revelations. Augustine demands faith, faith as such, acceptance of God's word as reported in Scripture.

I think Augustine is the more consistent of the two on their common premises because Plato and Augustine agree that man is a metaphysical dependent, simply a shadow, or an image, of another world. To be consistent, he must be an epistemological dependent also, i.e., dependent upon divine illumination for all knowledge. Plato tries to combine the Greek first-handed rational epistemological independence with a metaphysics that subverts the individual. Augustine is more consistent—in metaphysics, man is a shadow, and in epistemology, his duty is to accept the word of the true reality when it is delivered to him. His duty is to have faith. So, Augustine's epistemology is the Platonic line combined with a sense of the acute helplessness and utter dependence of man on God. The more distinctively Christian side comes out, therefore, in Augustine's discussion of faith, which means "belief or acceptance in the absence of understanding, of rational evidence or proof."

In regard to faith, Augustine's main point is that no man can set his own reason up as a judge of the truth or the falsehood of Christian teachings. To do so would be to rely on one's puny intellect and commit the sin of intellectual pride. That which God has revealed to man must be accepted on faith, it must never be doubted, it must be assented to *because* it comes from God, even if you don't understand why it's true. Once one has done this—once one starts with faith—one should then, says Augustine, go on and try to make sense of it, try to understand it. But this is the proper procedure and order of acquiring knowledge. First believe, and then try, so far as you can, to understand. In a famous line in Augustine's *Confessions*: "In order to understand the things of God, one must first believe them." The rational policy would be the exact reverse of that. And, Augustine says, if you can understand, fine, give thanks to God, but if not, recognize your limitations, recognize that God's truth is rational and he *could* illuminate you with the answers if he chose, but if he doesn't choose, you have no grounds to object. The analogy is sometimes given to Augustine and his followers and predecessors who take the line that they regard the process of acquiring knowledge like a student with a math text—the answers are written at the back of the text—you take the answer as given and try to work it out. If you can reach the answer in the back, fine, but if you can't, you start over and you say, "I must be doing something wrong because I knew the answer in advance." And, in this text, there are no misprints, because God printed the answers.

In this respect, philosophy is the handmaiden of theology, the rationalizer of theology. This is a fundamental contrast with the most mystical of even the Greeks, even with Plotinus. I note here in passing that anti-rational as this attitude is, other Christians took an even more anti-reason view. Augustine at least held that God's revelations are intelligible *in theory*, if only God gave us the necessary illumination, and that we should try to make sense of them. Other believing Christians, however, held that the basic tenets of Christianity are inherently irrational, contradictory, and preposterous. And indeed, they held, their preposterousness was the sure sign that they were true. I mention Tertullian, who is second to third century AD, one of the Fathers of the Church. He was asked about a certain Christian doctrine in which he devoutly believed, did he think it made sense, and he replied in a famous line "*Credo quia absurdum*"—"I believe it because it is absurd."[25] In other words, he was putting in as strong a way as he could the idea that he is having no truck with reason, which is a corrupt distorting element. And if this view is irrational, that's good grounds to think it's true. This is always taken as an overt anti-reason manifesto, and it is the version of early Christianity that the Existentialists most admire. They find their inspiration not in Augustine, whom they regard as too rational, but in Tertullian. This is explicit.

Let's look at Augustine's metaphysics. Here the central concept is his concept of God, which is a mixture of many elements, as you would expect. God is in part an infinite mind containing the Platonic Forms. So, to that extent, He's like Plotinus's divine mind. Augustine describes him

---

25. The meaning and source of this phrase is in some dispute. From the Wikipedia entry: "*Credo quia absurdum* is a Latin phrase that means 'I believe because it is absurd,' originally misattributed to Tertullian in his *De Carne Christi*. It is believed to be a paraphrasing of Tertullian's '*prorsus credibile est, quia ineptum est*' which means 'It is completely credible because it is unsuitable,' or '*certum est, quia impossibile*' which means 'It is certain because it is impossible.' . . . Protestant and Enlightenment rhetoric against Catholicism and religion more broadly resulted in this phrase being changed to 'I believe because it is absurd.'"

as fully real and, of course, God is the only fully real entity. He is immutable, perfect, etc.—he's just like Plato's other world, or like the Form of the Good. But that isn't *all* he is, because this is a religion now, and consequently, God can't be just a neutral Platonic set of universals; he must be given a personality. And so, Augustine describes him as a living, knowing, willing being, who is all-powerful, all-knowing, all-good, the Father of his children who loves them, who protects them, who judges them, who sends his son down to help them, etc. Most of this is straight out of the mystery cults of the time, and it's largely the primitive Judaic inheritance, not nearly as sophisticated as the Platonic inheritance.

Besides trying to combine God as a neutral Platonic world with God as a kind of infinite personality, Christianity also had the problem that many of the mystery cults of the period had: how to conceive the trinity, the trinitarian nature of God, how to relate God the Father to Jesus the Son (leaving out the third one). Christianity construes Jesus as a divine being, the Son of God, and therefore a god himself. He was, however, the Son of God, and therefore a different god from God the Father, so there are now two Gods. Although some of the other mystery cults were avowedly polytheistic, with its Judaic inheritance, Christianity is committed fervently to monotheism. This is a terrible problem. And it's worse when you add the third member of the trinity. You have three beings, each distinct from the other two. Each is God, and yet there's only one God. The ultimate position adopted formally by the Church, was that how one can be three and still be one is a mystery, one that surpasses human understanding and must be accepted on faith. There was a lot of debate about it at the time. Before the doctrine was finally settled, there were some people influenced by the Greek pro-reason view who were trying desperately to make sense of the trinity, and there were others influenced by the primitive Hebraic worship of blind faith who wanted avowedly unintelligible positions, and the latter group won out. (Most of the countless heresies on countless subjects express this tension between the Judaic and the Greek influence on Christianity, and in every case that I'm familiar with, Judaism is the source of the worst, most irrational element in Christianity, Greek philosophy the source of the better, more rational elements.)

You see now the incredible problem that Augustine had with God—he has to try to make some kind of coherence, if not sense, out of a being that has to combine emotionless Neoplatonic divine mind, the primitive Judaic loving personal Father, and the Christian trinity that is and isn't three. You can appreciate Augustine's view, stated on occasion, that God is not really knowable or understandable to the human mind. The best we can do is approximate his nature.

In any case, God, in Augustine's view, created this world *ex nihilo*, out of nothing, by an act of will at a particular point in time. Here again is a profound contrast with any Greek view. All the Greeks, Plotinus included, believed that the universe was eternal, that its constituent elements had always existed. Here was another case where the Judaic view won out over the Greek, and, as always, it created monumental problems for the Christians. The ancient pagans taunted the Christians. They asked questions like: "If God came before the stuff of the universe, why did he decide to create it at the particular point in time he did? Why not sooner? Why not later? What was he waiting around for? And why did he choose this particular place to put it in rather than some other one?" To answer such questions, and for many other reasons as well, Augustine advanced a famous and important theory of the nature of time. (Ask in the question period if you're interested.) In any event, God did create the world *ex nihilo* at a specific point in time, and he did so for a specific purpose. God has a plan. He runs every aspect of what occurs in the universe as part of his plan. Indeed, according to Augustine, God alone really has causal efficacy in the universe. Everything is determined by God. For instance, when Augustine discusses (in his *Confessions*) a journey he took, you might think that he *decided* to take it and that he is the real cause of the journey. No, Augustine says. God, behind the scenes, wanted Augustine to take it and was responsible for his journey as part of his plan for Augustine. Or Augustine relates a case where he gets a toothache and explains that God is punishing him in accordance with God's own long-range plan. God is responsible for everything that occurs, and since he's immutable, no changes in his plan are possible. It's set and fixed once and for all. Everything is predestined in accordance with this plan. And from this aspect, Augustine is a rigid, religious determinist.

This view is best expressed in the following parallel, which will give you the feel of this way of looking at the universe. The universe, on this view, is no longer a natural fact—no longer a primary, no longer intelligible in its own terms. Rather, it's like a play written by God, who becomes a cosmic playwright. The earth, the physical world, is the stage, and man is the chief actor, where his lines have been written by God, who is also the sole spectator. The play is taking place once and for all, and at a certain point, it will conclude (that's the end of the world), and the actors will retire for their critical notices.

You see the absolute contrast with the Greek view—the universe is not eternal, not natural, not a self-intelligible fact, but a specially created unnatural episode in the scheme of things. If you asked a typical Greek, for instance, Aristotle, "What is the meaning of life?"—if you asked it in a metaphysical, not an ethical context—if you just pointed to the phenomenon and said, "What is its metaphysical or cosmic meaning?," Aristotle would not understand the question. He would point to a rock and say: "What is the meaning of a rock? What do you want it to mean? It's there. Period." But, on the Christian view, life on earth is like a play by Shakespeare, and it becomes meaningful to ask what it means, what did the author have in mind? On this view, the fact of existence is not a primary but a mystery that requires some kind of unraveling. Everything is a symbol pointing beyond itself to God.

We now have the problem of evil in acute form, because the question arises: Why did God include so much evil, so much suffering, in his play? One sect of the period, *Manichaeism* (the sect that Augustine belonged to as a youth), thought that the only solution was to say that God is limited, that there is a Devil, and that he is responsible for evil, which at least makes a certain kind of sense. Christianity repudiated this as heretical. Christianity holds that God is responsible for everything, that he is all-powerful, and even the Devil, therefore, is part of his plan. Why then does God create or allow evil? Part of the time Augustine takes the view that there is no evil—if you saw God's ultimate purpose, you would see that everything is really good. But much more typically, Augustine takes the Neoplatonic solution to the problem of evil: Evil is the absence of the perfection and reality that is inherent in the creature being non-God. All things in this world are necessarily infected with deficiency—with a *metaphysical* deficiency—because they are part of the semi-real created world. If you want a pun, but which nevertheless is meant literally here, "They're made out of nothing, and therefore they're deficient." This harks back to the Platonic view of nonbeing as the constituent element of this world, and as the source of imperfection. God, from this point of view, *couldn't* have created a perfect world, a world without evil, because if you think of him as the source of light, we're now at the region where it's dark. It follows that all men, insofar as they're semi-real members of this semi-real world, are also inherently infected with evil. Men are sinners by nature. And they have no choice about it. They can do nothing about it on their own. Their evil is inherent in the metaphysical setup.

Notice here that the Church and Augustine accepted this view fully —they explicitly denied that man on his own has any choice about being good—that it is not an issue up to him, for he is helplessly evil by birth. That is the doctrine of Original Sin, which became official with the condemnation of Pelagius, an early fifth century Christian monk, who held that each human soul enters the world sinless, that it has free will, is capable on its own of shaping its destiny by its own choices, and therefore is responsible for its actions and properly to be judged by God. Pelagius denied any intrinsic wickedness in man. This view was formally condemned as a heresy (and is to this day) because it made man too independent of God. The reasoning was: If man could achieve virtue on his own, by his own will, then virtue would be *his* accomplishment, not God's. And then it wouldn't be true that everything was caused by God. And besides, the whole Christian scheme of Christ coming to earth and being crucified to redeem man would become unnecessary. If man has free will to achieve virtue on his own, he wouldn't need to be saved by divine intercession, that is, he wouldn't need any help from beyond or from the Church. And yet Christ is supposed to be the savior without whom man is lost, so this doctrine is essential to Christianity. Therefore, Pelagius was condemned, and the doctrine was taken that man on his own, without help from God, is inherently corrupt, wicked and helpless, and he cannot take a step in the direction of virtue on his own.

This viewpoint is determinism, and Christianity in this respect is fully deterministic. Free will is incompatible with man's inherent evil. It's also incompatible with God's rigid predestination, with the doctrine that only God has causal efficacy, that everything is a part of his play, and that man is merely a puppet pulled by the strings worked by God. If man has free will, what happens to the view that God determines everything, to say nothing of what happens to the view that God knows in advance everything that will occur?

If Christianity, from this point of view, is thoroughly deterministic, it is, for other reasons, incapable of accepting determinism consistently, because if it did, how would you praise or blame man? How can God hold man responsible for playing the part that God wrote him? How can God hold man responsible for an evil he couldn't have avoided? If there's no free will, isn't it hopelessly unfair for God to praise and condemn? Isn't it senseless for God to promulgate moral rules? Isn't it unfair for him to send men to Heaven or Hell? Christianity is, therefore, caught in a desperate problem: there must be absolute determinism, and there must be free will. If we had several lectures, I would indicate some of the devices by which Augustine tried to combine these two—to have his free will while eating it, too. However, we haven't the time and it is not important. The fact is, there is no possible solution on his premises, and every solution Augustine gives he contradicts elsewhere. I'll confine myself merely to giving one view of his on this question, which he took over from Paul. Namely, at certain points, Augustine limits free will to Adam. Adam, he claims, was free to choose whether to obey God or not. Adam committed the original sin, the first sin, and this was then inherited by all of his descendants, so now we have no choice, but still God validly punishes us because our first ancestor sinned volitionally. And this is the line that many, many Christians took, for instance, Milton, among many others. The whole of *Paradise Lost* is devoted to elaborating this view of the solution to the problem of freedom. It is a hopeless solution, because it takes the question back to: Was Adam free? And the same considerations as to why no man can have free will on this philosophy apply equally to Adam. Was it possible for Adam to have used his free will so as to be perfectly moral and virtuous? Well, if so, the Neoplatonist answer to evil is wrong, and that means evil is not inherent in the metaphysical setup. If the sin were really Adam's, then it's not God who is responsible, and so God is not the author of everything that occurs. And so on. And moreover, even supposing you solve this problem, where is the justice in condemning *all* men for the sin of *one*? No intelligible answer has ever been given. That is dogma, which must be accepted on faith.

On the issues of evil and freedom, therefore, the upshot is a mass of contradictions in Augustine and in Christianity. It goes like this: God is the cause of everything that's good. In fact, he is the cause of everything, since he's the omnipotent author of every event, and yet he is not responsible for evil. This world and man are inherently evil, since they're not God and are, therefore, metaphysically defective, semi-real, and yet man is responsible for his sins and properly to be condemned by God for them. Man is helpless to be virtuous on his own, yet he is to bear responsibility for vices he cannot alter. These are the foundations with which we enter ethics.

But first, one crucial metaphysical tenet of Augustine's that I have stated but not stressed, namely, that as a Neoplatonist, Augustine agrees completely with Plato and Plotinus that the world in which we live is not fully real. It is a kind of shadowy reflection of true reality, of the realm of God. This world is not a solid, substantial, real dimension. It's hard to communicate this perspective. You have to view the world as a region of comparative darkness far removed from the light and the perfection that constitutes reality. It's like a transitory drifting haze against the solid background of supernatural light. If you say you don't agree with this, but hold that matter is solid and real, Augustine answers in a famous formulation, "Of course, matter is there, it exists, but it is essentially the absence of God, so it is *prope nihil*," which is Latin for "almost nothing." That's his definition of "matter"—"almost nothing." Try to keep this view in mind and you'll have no difficulty grasping Augustine's ethics, to which we now turn.

I want to draw more widely than on just Augustine for our discussion of ethics, because in its ethics you see the essence of Christianity most clearly. To begin with, ethics for Augustine is not a matter of right living but of right loving—loving, of course, primarily God, and only secondarily and derivatively thy neighbor. In other words, the essence of the good life is not in what you accomplish or create during this life on earth, but rather in giving the proper inner emotional allegiance to the true dimension, to God. What counts above all is your inner state, not your outer actions, which are important only insofar as they reflect your inner state. This is the primacy of motive over action that we saw in discussing the Stoics. As we can also put it, it's the primacy of the inner over the outer, which is the way historians usually characterize it. And it is much more intense than in the case of the Stoics because we now have a fully religious ethics with little pretense at being worldly or rational.

This attitude, the primacy of the inner over the outer, can be expressed another way—the primacy of consciousness over existence, or, in terms of man's nature, of the soul over the body. And in this form, it's the standard soul-body dichotomy, present in Greek thought since the Pythagoreans and the Orphics, and Augustine adopts it with a vengeance. Man is a temporary union of two distinct substances, the soul and the body. Aristotle is wrong in saying that man is an integrated unity of soul and body. Augustine's definition of "man" is "a soul that uses a body." In other words, he's basically a soul with allegiance to the other dimension, and the body, since Adam's fall, has become the prison of the soul. Permit me to utter one enigmatic sentence here, which I will explain several lectures from now, and which will be intelligible only to those of you who already know Descartes. Augustine's emphasis on the primacy of the soul over the body or, more broadly, on the primacy of the inner over the outer, has had overwhelming results in every branch of philosophy, not just metaphysics or ethics. It is profoundly the primacy of consciousness approach to philosophy, and it is responsible for Descartes's distinctive approach to philosophy—his *Cogito ergo sum*—"I think, therefore I am." Descartes got it from Augustine.

Let us now turn to the content of the characteristic Christian ethics and, first, its evaluations of life on earth and of man. I have already stated their evaluations on these points, but I must let Augustine speak for himself so that you will get a real sense of his way of looking at the universe.

The conclusions in a nutshell are that life on earth is hell and human nature is depraved. But nothing makes it as clear as Augustine himself. I quote now an extended passage from *The City of God*:

> That the whole human race has been condemned in its first origin, this life itself if life it is to be called bears witness by the host of cruel ills with which it is filled. Is not this proved by the profound and dreadful ignorance which produces all the errors that enfold the children of Adam, and from which no man can be delivered without toil, pain, and fear? Is it not proved by man's love of so many vain and hurtful things, which produces gnawing cares, disquiet, griefs, fears, wild joys, quarrels, lawsuits, wars, treasons, angers, hatreds, deceit, flattery, fraud, theft, robbery, perfidy, pride, ambition, envy, murders, parricides, cruelty, ferocity, wickedness, luxury, insolence, impudence, shamelessness, fornications, adulteries, incests, and the numberless uncleannesses and unnatural acts of both sexes, which it is shameful so much as to mention; sacrileges, heresies, blasphemies, perjuries, oppression of the innocent, calumnies, plots, falsehoods, false witnessings, unrighteous judgments, violent deeds, plunderings, and whatever similar wickedness has found its way into the lives of men, though it cannot find its way into the conception of pure minds? . . . [W]ho can describe, who can conceive the number and severity of the punishments which afflict the human race, — pains which are not only the accompaniment of the wickedness of godless men, but are a part of the human condition and the common misery, — what fear and what grief are caused by bereavement and mourning, by losses and condemnations, by fraud and by falsehood, by false suspicions, and all the crimes and wicked deeds of other men? For at their hands we suffer robbery, captivity, chains, imprisonment, exile, torture, mutilation, loss of sight, the violation of chastity to satisfy the lust of the oppressor, and many other dreadful evils? What numberless causalities threaten our bodies from without, — extremes of heat and cold, storms, floods, inundations, lightening, thunder, hail, earthquakes, houses falling; or from the stumbling, or shying, or vice of horses; from countless poisons in fruits, water, air, animals; from the painful or even deadly bites of wild animals; from the madness which a mad dog communicates, so that even the animal which of all others is most gentle and friendly to its own master becomes an object of intenser fear than a lion or dragon, and the man whom it has by chance infected with this pestilential contagion becomes so rabid, that his parents, wife, children, dread him more than any wild beast! What disasters are suffered by those who travel by land or sea? What man can go out of his own house without being exposed on all hands

> to unforeseen accidents? Returning home sound in limb, he slips on his own doorstep, breaks his leg, and never recovers? . . . Is innocence a sufficient protection against the various assaults of demons? That no man might think so, even baptized infants, who are certainly unsurpassed in innocence, are sometimes so tormented that God, who permits it, teaches us hereby to bewail the calamities of this life, and to desire the felicity of the life to come. As to bodily diseases, they are so numerous that they cannot be all contained even in medical books. And in very many, or almost all of them, the cures and remedies are themselves tortures, so that men are delivered from a pain that destroys by a cure that pains. . . . From this hell upon earth there is no escape, save through the grace of the Savior Christ, our God and Lord.

And one very brief summary also from Augustine:

> Let everyone, then, who thinks with pain on all these great evils, so horrible, so ruthless, acknowledge that this is misery. And if anyone either endures or thinks of them without mental pain, this is a more miserable plight still, for he thinks himself happy because he has lost human feeling.

Addressing God and referring to all men, he wrote: "Thou did set me face to face with myself that I might behold how foul I was, and how crooked and sordid, bespotted and ulcerous."

By contrast, life for Plato was a laugh a minute and man was a superhero.

In such a state, all that counts is escape, i.e., reunion with God in Heaven. However, declares Augustine, even in theory it is not possible for all men to go to Heaven, because divine justice requires that some men be eternally damned to pay for Adam's sin. There are, therefore, two groups of men mingled on this earth—those belonging to what Augustine calls the "City of God," and those belonging to the earthly city. The former have received God's grace and are going to spend eternity in Heaven at God's side, while the latter are those who have not received God's grace and are destined to go to Hell and spend eternity attacked by worms, fire, and demons.

So, you see that it's very important to get into the right city. How do we do this? What steps can we take on our own to earn entry into the right city? None whatever. That question betrays a Pelagian bias. Remember the doctrine of Original Sin: We are utterly stained by sin, and, on our own, we cannot take a step in the direction of virtue. There is no way whatever that we can earn our way into Heaven. Otherwise, we're back in the position of Pelagius. We are helplessly dependent on God's decision.

On their own, according to Augustine, all men deserve nothing but to go straight to Hell. However, God is merciful—he decides to extend grace to certain men, to convert them from sin to virtue—and thereby permit these men into Heaven. This is a free act on God's part. Prior to grace, we are all inherently vicious, and we have no claim on God's grace—it's mercy on his part, not justice. But if all men are equally corrupt to start with, how does God decide whom to select for grace? The official answer is that this is inexplicable to man. And you see now why hope is a cardinal Christian virtue, based on the utter dependence of man on God. In epistemology, man depends on God's illumination for knowledge, above all for faith and revelation. In ethics, he depends on God's grace for virtue. And in metaphysics, man is a semi-real creature, created, run, and ruled by God. Throughout, man is utterly, totally, helplessly dependent, at the mercy of God's inexplicable decrees and decisions. This is characteristic of Christian philosophy at this period and is profoundly in contrast to *any* characteristically Greek view.

If you object that it isn't fair for God to select some sinners out of the rest and give them grace and entry into Heaven, the standard answer is that it is not that God is unfair. Here's how it's often put: imagine a millionaire who owns his money and gives some people money as a gift—well, that is not unfair to the other people to whom he doesn't give money, for they didn't have any claim on it. I might say that this is a very poor analogy. To have a more accurate analogy, you would first say that the millionaire comes in, cripples millions of victims, then leaves some of them absolutely chained and gagged and at his mercy, while handing out food and money to the rest. Then you could have a parallel, but then, you'd have a problem. However, let us pass on to the next point.

You might ask, if all this much is true, why have an ethics at all? You can't achieve happiness on earth, you can't even earn entry into Heaven—for what purpose would you take any action? What would be in it for you, the actor? And the answer is: That is a corrupt question, for God has ordained, he has commanded, that you act in certain ways, and these commandments must be obeyed because God commanded them. The highest virtue is obedience to God and doing your duty, your duty because it is your duty. Indeed, Adam's sin, as we saw, for which all mankind was condemned, was the sin of disobedience, of setting up his own code of values and not listening to God. The true Christian must abandon the attempt to work out a rational ethics, or *any* code of values, on his own. Ethics is a matter of the decrees of God, and whatever they are, you must obey. And not in the name of your own happiness—even your long-run happiness, either. You are not, in the true spirit of Christianity, to be making a practical calculation, saying to yourself, "Well, let's see, God has all this power and he wants me to do these things, so okay, I'll do it, but my inner calculation is that I'll get what's coming to me, I'll have a life of ecstasy and joy in the future, and that's why I'm doing it—it's in effect a trade with God, and he better come through when the chips are down." If you take that attitude you are anathema to Christianity. Your attitude is supposed to be "thy will be done," not "thy will be done if I get a lot of fun out of it."

I should say out of fairness that Christianity is definitely inconsistent on this point. Everybody prior to Kant is inconsistent on this point. There are several anti-duty, pro-egoist elements in Christianity. To mention them briefly: There is the emphasis on the salvation of your own individual soul, and the statement that you will be rewarded with eternal happiness if you make it, and that it's your *own* eternal happiness that you personally will experience. This quickly became the idea that otherworldly happiness is the reward for your virtue. Then the statement even of Jesus that you should "Love thy neighbor as *thyself*," which implies that you can love yourself to some extent. All of these elements of egoism are legacies of the Greek influence on Christianity, and all of them were extirpated by Kant. Until that time, however, they existed, but they were in conflict with the distinctively Christian element, which is that you obey the commandments out of reverence and love for God, and the recognition that he has created you and, therefore, has the right to make demands of his creatures. In this respect, Christianity is a typical duty ethics.

So, what is it that God commands? What does he want of us? Having created this world and placed man in it, what he wants primarily, so it appears, is that man should turn away from life on earth and turn his attention to God. Renunciation of pleasures from life on earth, concentration on one's otherworldly destiny, a brushing aside of this life as a snare, a temptation, an evil seducer of your religious purity—those are the main themes of Christian ethics. As Scripture says in a line containing the keynote to the whole ethics, "He that loveth his life shall lose it; he that hateth it shall keep it unto life eternal." Or as it's put elsewhere in Scripture, "Woe onto ye who laugh now, for ye shall mourn and weep," and "blessed are ye that weep now, for ye shall laugh."

You may think that this is a primitive view that Christianity has long since abandoned, and so I want to call your attention to a few quotes from Bishop Fulton Sheen in regard to Christianity's attitude to suffering on earth. In *Life Is Worth Living*, Bishop Sheen writes:

> Our capacity for pain is greater than our capacity for pleasure. Suffering reaches the point where we feel we can endure it no longer, and yet it increases and we endure it. But pleasures very quickly reach a peak and then begin to decline. Age decreases the capacity for pleasures, though pain never turns into a pleasure, a pleasure can turn into a pain. Tickling may be funny at first, but it can also become excruciatingly painful. Our capacity for pain is greater because the good Lord intended that all pain should be exhausted in this world. The Divine plan is to have real joys in the next life. . . . Never losing our love of God, we can then find reasons for supporting pain. If we have ruined our health by excesses, we impose upon ourselves dietary laws and avoid delicacies out of love for our health. One can do the same with the soul—one can say, "I will accept this particular suffering in order to make reparation for my own faults." Or we can also offer up our suffering for others. . . .
>
> Doctors will graft skin from one part of the body to the face if the face is burned. Those suffering from anemia receive a transfusion of blood from another member of society to cure them of that disease. If it is possible to transfuse blood, it is also possible to transfuse sacrifice; if it is possible to graft skin, it is also possible to graft prayer. We have blood banks for our own soldiers that their lives may be saved through our sacrifice of blood. Pain, agony, disappointments, injustices—all these can be poured into a Heavenly treasury, from which the anemic, sinful, confused, ignorant souls may draw under the healing of their wings. Thus through love of God, suffering becomes sacrifice. The great mystery of the world is not what people suffer, it is what they miss when they suffer. They could be minting coinage for their own salvation and the salvation of the world. The tragedy of wasted pain, the unsanctified tears, the dull aches, the nauseating pains, the infuriating double-crosses—how much of these are wasted, and thereby converted into curses, because those who suffer them have no one to love?[26]

The style on the imagery and metaphors are revealing. You can just see him hugging suffering to his breast, counting man's aches, pains, nausea, and tears like a miser counting his money, running his fingers through his treasure. And he is valid in his choice of metaphor. By the time of Christianity, suffering as such—that is, suffering on earth—has become a value. So much for Christianity as an ethics that preaches happiness on earth.

---

26. *Life Is Worth Living,* a selection of scripts from Sheen's syndicated television series that ran from 1953 to 1957.

Let's return to the early Christians, for whom there is significantly more excuse.

A study of the literature of the period, including the Bible, is required for you to gain any idea of how violently anti-life the early Church was. It preached that "Woe unto ye who laugh, for you shall mourn and weep," and it was very systematic in ensuring, if you followed its rules, that you would weep now. For instance, I wouldn't even mention the Church's attitude to business or industry if they had known about those phenomena in the modern sense, but take such simple things as food, drink, and shelter. What should your attitude be? Well, a true Christian was to pay no attention to them. "Therefore, I say unto you, Take no thought for your life, what ye shall eat, or what ye shall drink; nor yet for your body, what ye shall put on." Those are distractions and temptations because they are pleasurable. They constitute a source of enjoyment of this life. Of course, you must eat and drink; otherwise, it would amount to committing suicide, which is forbidden. The solution, declared Augustine, is to look upon food and drink as medicine—take what is required to sustain life, but stop before you start getting pleasure out of it. However, there is another peril here, which God, in his wisdom, has placed before us: Even if you eat the modest amount necessary for life, there's a certain pleasure in swallowing, in the taste, the savor of it, or in quenching your thirst, for instance, or in going to sleep when you're tired. And this seriously bothered Augustine. It's what we can call the "problem of pleasure," and the problem is how to sustain yourself in the most frugal way without enjoying it.

Many centuries later, Francis of Assisi, presented one solution to this problem. I quote from Saint Bonaventura's admiring biography: "[Saint Francis] restrained his sensual appetites with such strict discipline as that he would barely take what was necessary to support life, for he was wont to say that it was difficult to satisfy the needs of the body without yielding unto the inclinations of the senses, wherefore he would hardly and but seldom allow himself cooked food when in health, and when he did allow it, he would either sprinkle it with ashes or by pouring water thereupon, went as far as possible to destroy its savor and taste. Of his drinking of wine, what shall I say, when even of water he would scarce drink what he needed while parched with burning thirst." (I interject to say that many of the saints drank water in which laundry had been washed.) Continuing the quote: "The bare ground for the most part served as a couch unto his weary body, and he would often sleep sitting with a log or a stone placed under his head, and clad in one poor tunic, he served the Lord in cold and nakedness."

On the Christian view, this same pattern of renunciation appears in every area of life. Sex is obvious—it is to be condemned if pursued for pleasure, on the identical grounds, because sex for pleasure would be love of this world, and pleasure in this world, rather than pleasure in God. And so the Church doctrine was: Sex is permissible only for procreation, on exactly the same grounds and in the same manner as food is permissible only for medicine. One part of those doctrines (the one on food) was given up by most people in the Renaissance, but the other continued. The most consistent religious people take the same view. As to sex for Saint Francis, I won't bother to read it to you. Characteristically, he would strip himself naked and jump into a snow heap whenever he felt the onset of sexual desire, in order to rout the tempter. I refer you to *Sex in History* by G. Rattray Taylor. The book is no good philosophically—the man is a Freudian—but if you ignore his interpretation, it is filled with the most fantastic documentation of human sexual practices, including those of the Church. They're not imaginable by the wildest science fiction imagination. And today, this view of sex is the source of anti-contraception, anti-abortion—the source of the view that the truly holy people, the priests and the nuns, must abstain, etc. As to the Christian attitude to wealth, that speaks for itself, for you know the one about the rich man and the camel. What should your attitude be to yourself? Essentially, you should recognize the facts—namely, you're stained with sin, you're worthless, and you should estimate yourself accordingly. Consequently, the great virtue is humility, and the greatest vice is pride. Recognize that you are human, which means you are a miserable, helpless sinner.

Saint Benedict, in the sixth century, drew up a list of rules as to how a monk should go about acquiring true humility. He outlined a number of the steps that you should take, and here I give you a few of those steps. His scriptural text is "Matthew": "Whosoever shall exalt himself shall be abased, and he that shall humble himself shall be exalted." And now from Benedict, just a few of these steps:

> Now the first step of humility is this—to escape destruction by keeping ever before one's eyes the fear of the Lord; to remember always the commands of the Lord. The second, that a man should not delight in doing his own will and desires but should imitate the Lord. . . . Fourth, that a man endure all the hard and unpleasant things and even undeserved injuries that come in the course of his service, without wearying or withdrawing his neck from the yoke. . . . Sixth, that the monk should be contented with any lowly or hard condition in which he may be placed and should always look upon himself as an unworthy

> laborer not fitted to do what is entrusted to him. Seventh, that he should not only say, but should really believe in his heart, that he is the lowest and most worthless of all men. . . . Eleventh, that the monk, when he speaks, should do so slowly and without laughter, softly and gravely, and that he should not be loud of voice. Twelfth, that the monk should always be humble and lowly not only in his heart, but in his bearing as well. When the monk has ascended all these steps of humility, he will arrive at that perfect love of God that which casteth out all fear.

I note, by the way, a couple pages later he goes on to say that the monks "should not have personal property. The sin of owning private property should be entirely eradicated from the monastery. No one shall presume to give or receive anything except by the order of the abbot; no one shall possess anything of his own, books, papers, pens, or anything else." You see how consistent the philosophy is. Contrast Benedict's monk and Aristotle's Magnanimous Man, or Saint Francis versus the Magnanimous Man, two perfect symbols of two radically opposite philosophies.

What about what Aristotle called the "intellectual virtues"—the study of science, physics, astronomy, math, etc.—the attempt to understand by reason the laws of the universe? In book ten of *The Confessions* of Augustine, having detailed a whole host of physical temptations standing in the way of man that he has to overcome, Augustine writes a very important section, from which I quote an excerpt:

> I must now speak of a different kind of temptation, more dangerous than these [the physical], because it is more complicated. For in addition to our bodily appetites, which make us long to gratify all of our senses and our pleasures and lead to our ruin if we stay away from you [Peikoff: He's speaking to God.] by becoming their slaves, the mind in addition is also subject to a certain propensity to use the senses of the body, not for self-indulgence of a physical kind, but for the satisfaction of its own inquisitiveness. This futile curiosity masquerades under the name of science and learning, and since it derives from our thirst for knowledge, and sight is the principal sense by which knowledge is acquired, in the Scriptures it is called *gratification of the eye*.

In many translations, that comes out "the lust of the eyes." "It is to satisfy this unhealthy curiosity that freaks and prodigies are put on show in the theater, and for the same reason, men are led to investigate the secrets of nature, which are irrelevant to their lives, although such knowledge is of no value to them and they wish to gain it merely for the sake of knowing." So, science, learning, represent lusts, this-worldly loves and concerns that are futile and to be suspended. There are many more reasons why science must go. It's arrogant of puny man to pursue science on his own—what God wants man to know, God will reveal in his own good time. And if he doesn't reveal something, it is sheer snooping, it is sheer nosiness, to go prying into the mysteries of the universe. After all, it's God's world, not man's. And besides, there is no answer to any question anyway. The answer to everything is, "That's how it is because God willed it; it's a part of the plan." Everything is a miracle, and that, you see, is inherent in the idea of creation *ex nihilo*, out of nothing. There are no natural laws, all of nature is unnatural on this approach, and science is therefore impossible. Besides, your goal is not to study this world, but to get out of it, as though you were in jail, so what is the point of studying nothing or "almost nothing"? In other words, we have reached the complete reversion to the pre-Thales era, the era before philosophy and science.

You have to read *The Confessions* (the translation by Pine-Coffin in the Penguin edition) to get any real sense of the Christian approach—the acute sense of sin, the absolute power of God, the utter irrelevance of this life, including science. Augustine remarks in passing, for instance, in a line that reveals volumes—he is confessing his sins to God—and he says, "I used to study the liberal arts in those days because I was a worthless good-for-nothing," and he proceeds on as though that's self-evident. At one point in *The Confessions*, he gives himself a temptation rating, the problem of temptation being acute for Christianity. The Greeks—at least Aristotle and Socrates—never had any equivalent of this, because they held that virtue is knowledge, you can understand in reason why certain things are right, and once you understand it you will want to do it because you will want to achieve your own welfare. But the Christians have a radically different view: Virtue's content is unintelligible, and when you actually act on it, it's in direct conflict with everything that would make life enjoyable. Consequently, there's an irresistible, chronic, inescapable temptation to pursue the evil, which the Christian has to fight against constantly. Augustine summarizes the actual reason very, very aptly, but it doesn't change his mind why he's in such agony. "In this state [Peikoff: i.e., in this world] I am fit to stay, unwilling though I am. In that other state [Peikoff: i.e., Heaven], where I wish to stay, I am not fit to be. I have double cause for sorrow." And so he does.

In this temptation rating, he goes down the scale to see whether, since he has been converted to Christianity, he is still getting pleasure from things in the physical world. He checks himself on dreams, on eating and drinking, on smell. He thinks he's okay on smell but that he might be wrong. On sound, he thinks that perhaps he's overly partial to the singing of hymns from the point of view of enjoying the music—and so on and so on. But perhaps the most interesting one is that he sometimes gets pleasure out of his own humility. He takes a certain pride in his own humility, which is unspeakable. Somebody once told me about a serious and dedicated Catholic, who systematically cheated on his wife. When confronted by the question of how he reconciled this with Catholicism, he answered: "This is absolutely in keeping with my Catholicism, because the supreme virtue is humility. If I followed every commandment to the letter, I would be in terrible danger of pride. Therefore, I have to do some wicked things in order to pump up my humility." You see the inescapable problem of any ethics that preaches humility. If the top virtue is the conviction that you're no good, then as soon you achieve it, you become good, so attaining it destroys it.

I have said virtually nothing about the altruist side of Christianity, the love-thy-neighbor element, although that's the best known in the modern world. It was by no means the most important in the medieval world. It's only since Kant, since the eighteenth century, that altruism has become the big thing in Christianity. Because it's well known, however, and because you are an audience of students of Objectivism, I assume that the relation between this side of Christianity and the ones I've mentioned so far is clear. It's all part of the general process of renouncing life and forbidding independent rational judgment. Just as you are supposed to abandon independent judgment in scientific matters, so in dealing with people. Just as you want unearned grace from God, so you must extend unearned love and forgiveness to others. Judge not that ye be not judged. And just as you are to divest yourself of selfish pleasures in dealing with the physical world, so in dealing with people. You are not to love only those who give you happiness, those who meet your standards, those who are good in your eyes—that is pagan, egoistic, arrogant, this-worldly love. No, your distinctive virtue qua Christian is to love men who do *not* meet your standards, who do *not* give you pleasure, to love men who are out to harm you—"Love your enemies, bless them that curse you, pray for them that despitefully use and persecute you," etc. What they do to you doesn't matter, because it's just this life. Love of God is all that counts, and love of the enemy is proof of your selflessness and obedience. If men harm you, forgive them until seventy times seven times. If they strike one cheek, turn the other. If they steal your coat, give them your cloak also.

If they compel you to go one mile against your will, go with them two. Who are you, miserable sinner, to cast the first or even the second stone? In other words, the whole altruism love-thy-neighbor axis of Christianity, as I think you can easily see, is completely consistent with the rest of it.

I've had to omit even a brief sketch of two elements in Augustine's philosophy that I had wanted to mention but I've had no time. One is his politics, and the other is his distinctive and very influential theory of history, a theory that was particularly influential on people like Hegel and Marx, to say nothing of Mussolini and Hitler. But I'll have to save that for the question period if you ask me. For now, I want to conclude by summarizing the essence of Augustinian Christianity. And it comes to this: Man is to abnegate himself, renounce concern for his own pleasure and happiness, give up his mind, his science, his independent judgment, regard himself as worthless creature, stained by sin in the grip of an all-powerful destiny, helplessly at its mercy. His only goal is to have faith, blindly obey the commands of that power, and hope that it will take undeserved pity on him and release him from bondage one day—that glorious day when it's all finally over for him, that day when he gets his final exit permit: death.

How long can man survive on this view of man and of life? My answer in one sentence: The next centuries of human history are called "The Dark Ages."

The Dark Ages

For centuries, philosophers—particularly Christian philosophers up through the period of Augustine—had progressively been denouncing concern for life on earth, denouncing the free and independent use of reason, advocating that faith be exalted above it. They had been condemning and scorning material production, intellectual development, scientific inquiry. Well, they got their wish, and in spades. For the next four hundred years (with insignificant exceptions), reason, intellect, science, material wealth, all but vanished from the Western world. The West entered what we now call "the Dark Ages," which are usually dated from about the fifth through the nineth century AD. This was a period of barbarian rampages and chaotic violence: The Roman Empire completely disintegrated, and urban life virtually disappeared. For the most part, men lost the art of writing and reading. Life expectancy was supposedly less than twenty years. In effect, civilization was wiped out.

In particular, the West lost almost all of the philosophic and literary works of the ancient pagans. They had only a few snatches of Plato and Aristotle and a few others. I should mention here that the writings of Aristotle were preserved in the non-Christian world, where Aristotelian doctrines flourished for centuries, for instance, among the Mohammedans, while they were almost unknown in Christendom. With the exception of a few fragments, Aristotle was unknown for centuries in the Western world. It was the ideas of Plato, transmitted by the writings of the Neoplatonists and Augustine, that constituted the framework and the inspiration of such thought as existed.

What thought did exist? Apart from a few insignificant compilations by minor figures, nothing at all happened intellectually until the nineth century. So, we have four hundred years of nothing, of sheer intellectual stagnation. What happened in the nineth century? One solitary figure who has any significance at all, and even so, he has such little significance that he's only mentioned because historians are desperate to find somebody to discuss in all these hundreds of years. His name is John Scottus Eriugena, and he lived about 810 to 877. He was a mystical Christian Neoplatonist who, from the viewpoint of the Church, committed a number of heresies. For instance, in trying to avoid the doctrine of predestination and preserve human responsibility, Eriugena embraced Pelagianism, the view that man has free will and can achieve virtue on his own. And Eriugena also succumbed to pantheism, the view that all things, including men, are part of God. Christianity, on dogmatic principle, repudiates pantheism, because the religion rests on the contrast between God as the infinite perfect being and man as finite, sordid, crooked, ulcerous, bespotted, stained with original sin, and obligated to humility. If everything is God, then man is literally part of God, and then this whole scheme collapses and man's self-esteem would shoot way up, so pantheism is heretical. The upshot is that Eriugena's views were condemned officially in 855. In other words, the first thinker of any significance in four hundred years was condemned by the Church, which was becoming a political force with which all thinkers had to reckon.

What happened philosophically for two hundred years after Eriugena? Nothing. Philosophy, even on a modest scale, picks up again in the last half of the eleventh century. I won't discuss again why it started at this point. Essentially, that's a historical issue, so I refer you to an appropriate history text. In essence, however, a modest civilization painfully and gradually was reborn, starting slowly after the nineth century. Schools began to be formed to revive learning, and gradually expanded to universities at which philosophy was taught. Some fragments of the ancients still existed, and they came to be debated as to how they should properly be interpreted. And controversies began to develop among Christian thinkers connected with the schools as to how Christian doctrine should properly be interpreted. And ultimately the Crusades brought the West into contact with non-Christian civilizations, and Christians were shocked to find that the infidels laughed at them and posed unanswerable objections to Christianity, and the Christians wanted to know how to answer. And a few homegrown heretics popped up who had to be answered somehow. And for all these and other reasons, slowly, haltingly, some philosophic thought on a modest scale started again.

The Middle Ages/The Scholastics

Now a terminological note here: The period from the nineth through the fourteenth centuries, between the Dark Ages and the Renaissance, is called the *Middle Ages*, or the medieval period. And because the philosophers of this period were almost all connected in one way or another with the schools and the universities I just mentioned, these philosophers are referred to as the *Scholastics*, the philosophers of the schools. "Scholasticism" is a general name for the philosophers of the whole Middle Age period, especially those from the last half of the eleventh on through to the fourteenth. They survived thereafter, but they were no longer the dominant influence after the fourteenth. In general, the Scholastics all shared a certain approach, however different their detailed conclusions: They were all ardent Christians committed in advance of any philosophizing to the doctrines of the Church. So, they were authoritarian in their basic approach. Their concept of philosophy was (to oversimplify just a little) to spread before them the writings of the Church Fathers, of Scripture, and of whichever ancient philosophers they knew and were partial to, and then try to reconcile and make sense of this mass of authorities. In essence, they knew their main conclusions in advance, because philosophy for them was an attempt to substantiate rationally and to harmonize (so far as they could) the dogmas of the appropriate authorities. Thus, the study of the actual world around them seemed pretty irrelevant. They spent their efforts attempting to interpret and reinterpret the texts of the authorities before them, trying to get the texts in harmony with one another. And to do so, they had to make all sorts of artificial distinctions, engage in hair-splitting of all kinds, and in general turn away from any study of the actual physical world around them and immerse themselves in the study of the texts of the authorities.

What sorts of issues were the Scholastics first concerned with? Until the thirteenth century, they attempted no comprehensive philosophic systems, but they engaged in specific disputes on specific technical matters and specialized problems. To give you just a taste: One controversy that developed (I'm speaking now of the period prior to the thirteenth century) was over the problem of universals. This developed as a result of something that had survived from the ancient world, namely, somebody's translation of somebody else's introduction to Aristotle's *Categories*, and this translation of this introduction had survived. And it raised the question of universals, although it didn't answer it. The question in essence was "Are universals real or not?," to which the Scholastics in these early centuries worked out three main positions that provoked controversy. One was the position taken by the Scholastics heavily influenced by Platonism—for instance, by Eriugena, by Saint Anselm (1033–1109), an important Platonist Scholastic of this early period, and many others. These people took the general Platonist line that universals are real entities, independent of particulars, which are merely semi-real byproducts, or reflections, or emanations from universals—in other words, what has come to be called *Platonic realism*, as I defined that for you in the lecture on Plato. "Realism" is a technical term meaning that universals are real, not fictitious. This position was subjected to a great deal of criticism by various Scholastics.

What's typical of this whole era is that this position was also heavily criticized on *theo*logical grounds—it led to conflict with the Church, and it led to heresy. How? Well, you know that the higher universal always includes the lower ones—for instance, color, as a universal, embraces and includes redness, greenness, purpleness, etc. What is God on a Platonist philosophy? He is the most real entity. And if the real is equated with the universal, then God, the most real being, has to be the most *universal* universal, the widest universal, the one that embraces and includes all the others. But that means all things are included in God, and that is pantheism, and that is heresy. So Platonic realism, for this and other equivalent reasons, is unacceptable. In reaction to this, some Scholastics went to the other extreme and denied universals altogether, a view that came to be known as "nominalism." And it's attributed to a Scholastic known as Roscelin (c.1045–c.1120). Nominalism is the view that *only* particulars exist, that they have no common characteristics at all, that each is through and through unique and that so-called universals are just names that people use without any objective basis in reality. People decide to apply a certain name, a certain word, to a number of particulars as a matter of subjective convenience. But that's what it is—subjective, with no objective common denominators, no real universals uniting particulars in reality. It came to be called "nominalism" because of the theory that universals are only names, from the word *nomen*, which is Latin for "name." Roscelin is supposed to have said that universals are only *flatus vochus*, that is to say, "breathings of the voice"—in other words, they're noises we make in speaking, and that's all. They're just words. This makes all conceptual thought completely arbitrary and detached from reality. In essence, it's the position taken by the Greek Sophists and the pagan skeptics, and it is the one that was destined to dominate philosophy in the modern era, as you will see shortly. But it never became much in the medieval era and was criticized on many grounds. It, too, was susceptible to theological objections, and Roscelin had to repudiate it formally in 1093. Why? To take just one example, what happens to original sin? The idea of the Church was that in Adam's sin, we were all supposed to have become infected. In Adam's sin, human nature as such—the universal manness—was corrupted and, therefore, all the particular men. And that was the metaphysical explanation of how you could inherit somebody else's sin. But if there are no universals—if Adam is just one individual, and each of us is a separate, distinct individual with nothing in common with him—then the inheritance of original sin becomes unintelligible, so nominalism too has to go.

The third position, and the one that was finally dominant in this period, was offered as a kind of mediation between Platonic realism and nominalism, and its major author is Peter Abelard (1079–1142), the one famous for his relations with Eloise. He achieved something great for this early period, at a time when nothing about Aristotle's theory was known—he worked out a view roughly similar to Aristotle's, even if very, very primitive. And his view is often called "moderate realism," which is a foolish name, because it sounds like Aristotelianism is a compromise between Plato and the nominalists. In very brief form, Abelard's view was that the nominalists are right in one respect—only particulars exist—but human beings, using a process of abstraction, are able to discover a common nature in a number of particulars. The universal, while it existed in one sense only in the mind as an abstraction from particulars, nevertheless is not a subjective fiction as Roscelin had said, because, in fact, individual things *do* have common properties that form an objective basis for our abstractions. This position is essentially the view that Aristotle took in the ancient world, so I won't say any more about it here. As worked out by Abelard, and later much more fully by Thomas Aquinas, it has all the main virtues and problems that Aristotle's own statement of it had.

You see from this brief survey that there is nothing essentially new on this issue during this period. What *is* new is the way the whole issue becomes entangled in theological controversies and heresies. Indeed, as the philosophers of this period soon came to see, no matter what issue you discussed, you ran into the risk of heresy, of contradicting some dogma or other. And this raised for them a second main issue during this early pre-thirteenth-century period, namely, the relation of reason and faith, about which I'll now say a word just to give you the atmosphere of the times.

Some of the Scholastics, attempting merely to make sense of the authorities and the dogmas (without questioning or challenging them), started to stir up doubts despite themselves. Abelard, for instance, wrote *Sic et Non*, (*Yes and No*), a book in which he listed one hundred and fifty-eight propositions. For each of them, he quoted various Fathers of the Church in favor and simultaneously against—yes and no, you see. Abelard was a loyal Catholic. He merely wanted to make sense out of the dogmas. But it seemed to others watching the spectacle that here was the ugly voice of reason rearing itself in the midst of the paradise of Christian faith.

In general, two attitudes were taken on the issue of reason and faith. To some figures of the period, reason was a dangerous enemy of Christianity, and the whole attempt of the Scholastics to make sense of the dogmas was depraved. Let reason loose, they thought, and even if the author has the best will in the world, he's merely going to cause trouble. A true believer doesn't need to have it make sense. Philosophy—even Scholastic philosophy, they said—is the invention of the Devil. For instance, Bernard of Clairvaux, who had a mystic experience of God (so he claimed), declared, "I believe though I do not comprehend, and I hold by faith what I cannot grasp with the mind." He was a real Tertullian type, which has always been there, and reveled in the incomprehensibility. *Credo qui absurdum*—he believes it because it's absurd.

The other attitude of the time was, however, more widespread. It was represented by Anselm. It was the Augustinian attitude, in essence. Remember, you must first believe in order that you may then understand. In other words, you start with faith, which gives you your premises, and then you try to make such sense as you can out of it. Anselm and all the Augustinians of the period regarded the relation of reason to faith very similarly to the way Aristotle regarded the relation of reason to sense experience. If you take Aristotle's view, reason cannot contradict sense experience since it's *based on* sense experience. At most, reason might be unable to explain temporarily some experiences. The same for Anselm in relation to reason and faith. Faith is the *basis* of reason—it's what you start from—and therefore, maybe there'll be bits of the faith, or large hunks, that you can't explain, but that's temporary and you couldn't possibly criticize the faith. In *The Incarnation of the Word*, he put this in the following very typical formulation: "No Christian ought in any way dispute the truth of what the Catholic Church teaches. But always holding the same faith unquestioningly, loving it, and living by it, he ought himself, so far as he is able, to seek the reasons for it. If he can understand it, let him thank God. If he cannot, let him not raise his head in opposition, but bow in reverence." I think that gives you the flavor of the era better than anything else and needs no comment.

Anselm himself thought that he could make sense out of a good deal of Christianity, and in the course of his attempts, he worked out an argument for the existence of God which became very, very famous. So, I want to explain it to you very briefly—it's called the *ontological argument*, from the Greek *ontos*, meaning "being." He claims that from the very concept, or term, "God," you can prove that he must necessarily exist. Just by the definition of the term, without any need to know where the concept came from. Granting that you have an idea of God—and, he says, everybody has an *idea* of God, and even the fool who said in his heart "There is no God" has to have the idea of God to be able to utter the statement "There is no God." Grant that you have an idea of God, however you got it, from that idea alone, God's existence will be proven simply by definition. How? The definition that Anselm gave is "God is the being than which nothing greater can be conceived." Or as it's put in alternative versions of the argument, "the absolutely perfect being." Now I'm going to give you a modern statement, my own, which I think is a little clearer than his, but it's certainly his idea, for which I take no credit. Let's make a hypothetical mental chart in our minds and characterize two beings, call them "Being One" and "Being Two." And let's give each of them every Christian perfection we can imagine—they're each omnipotent, they're each omniscient, they're each all-good, they're each the creator of the world, etc. There's only one difference between these two—Being One has the attribute of actually existing in reality, and Being Two does not. Which is the Being than which nothing greater can be conceived? Which is the absolutely perfect Being? Obviously, the one that has the attribute of actually existing in reality because it has all the perfections of the other one, and on top of that, it exists, and surely it's better to exist than not to exist. For instance, I hold up two lighters, one in my right hand and one in my left. [Note: Dr. Peikoff's left hand was empty.] These two lighters are identical in every respect—they are both made of the same metal, they have the same shape, they light cigarettes the same—everything is the same. There's only one difference—the one in my right hand exists, and the one in my left does not. Which is the better lighter? It's obvious. Consequently, if you say: "I have a concept of an absolutely perfect being, but he doesn't exist," you're saying: "I have a concept of an absolutely perfect Being who lacks a perfection," which is a contradiction. Q.E.D. Logic itself demands the existence of God. How do you like that bit of reasoning?

This argument has been endlessly criticized since Anselm advanced it. Aquinas thought it was worthless. Descartes, Spinoza, and Leibniz thought it was terrific. Locke, Berkeley, Hume, and Kant thought it was terrible. Hegel thought it was terrific. And it's gone back and forth ever since that time, the Platonists all liking it, and anti-Platonists not. (Anselm was a devout Platonist.) I'll confine myself here to relating one criticism raised by a contemporary of Anselm's, the monk Gaunilo, who was a devoutly religious man and certainly believed in God, but not by this route. Gaunilo wrote a little work called "Pro Insipiente" ("On Behalf of the Fool"). And in that work he made the point that the whole argument, even if you grant all of its premises, proves nothing at all. It's all, he said, completely hypothetical. It's confined exclusively to the content of the mind and at no point makes contact with actual existence. At most, he said, it shows that if you *think* of an absolutely perfect being, you must think of it existing. But it doesn't follow that because we *think* of something as existing, therefore, it actually exists. And he gives this illustration: I think of an absolutely perfect island. (You can give it modern perfections—it has palm trees and dancing girls and the whole works.) Now imagine two such islands—they all have the same characteristics, except one exists and the other doesn't. Obviously the one that exists is more perfect because it has all the attributes of the other plus existence, so therefore, such an island actually exists. That's obviously preposterous. Why? Well, said Gaunilo, all we've proven is that *if* there is such a perfect island, *then* it must exist. But we knew that before we started—if it is, then it is. The question is supposed to be *Is there* an island, *Is there* one corresponding to our concept? And the same thing is true with God. Therefore, he said, Anselm's proof fails. That's the big contribution of Anselm.

From the brief samples so far, you see the caliber and barrenness of philosophy during the period prior to the thirteenth century. Somehow we got out of this period. But how? Many factors were at work, but the central one, the major intellectual event that altered the whole climate of opinion, was that finally, after more than six hundred years, in the century between

1150 and 1250, the West recovered all the major works of Aristotle. This occurred as a result of increasing contacts during the century with the culture of the Mohammedans, who had preserved the Aristotelian works. The Arabs themselves, so I have read, found Aristotle's manuscripts in one of the most momentous archeological discoveries in history—*the* most momentous one—they found them in a cellar in Syria sometime in the fifth or sixth century AD, and they had a flourishing civilization based on them. Once they were discovered in the West, they were translated from Arabic and other tongues into Latin, and organized and systematized, and soon became widely known. One of the main figures responsible for such translation and systematization of Aristotle's works was Albertus Magnus (Albert the Great), who was the teacher of Thomas Aquinas.

Aristotle's writings struck the thirteenth century like a bombshell. Here was a monumental, integrated, systematic, rational philosophy, encompassing a wealth of scientific information and philosophic positions on hosts of issues unheard of for centuries. And progressively, scholars wanted to know what Aristotle had to say and how it related to Christianity. At first, the Church, as you may expect, reacted properly—properly from their premises: They banned Aristotle's works outright. In 1210, it was forbidden to teach Aristotle's *Physics* in Paris, and, a few years later, the *Metaphysics* was banned. Progressively, throughout the century, the attempts to relate Aristotle to Christianity were condemned by the Church. You can see why, if you consider the violent contrast between the two philosophies of Aristotle and of Christianity. I almost don't know where to start. Take metaphysics —Aristotle says there is one reality, this one; Christianity, two realities, God versus this world. Aristotle says that the natural physical world is fully real in its own right; it is reality. Christianity says the so-called natural world is semi-real, infected with metaphysical deficiency. Aristotle says that the physical world is eternally in existence. Christianity said it was created *ex nihilo*. Aristotle says this world is fully natural, i.e., its significance and explanation is within itself, and we must understand it in terms of natural law. It is deprived of a supernatural source and significance, and it is not a theological cryptogram symbolizing an otherworldly existence. For Christianity, this world is merely the temporary backdrop of the drama of salvation, where everything has a symbolic supernatural significance, and there is nothing natural about the world, no natural law, and it's just a temporary stage for a divine play. For Aristotle, God is the Unmoved Mover, unconscious of the world, without power over it. For Christianity, God is omniscient, omnipotent. For Aristotle, there's no personal immortality. For Christianity, that is the crucial thing—the hope of Heaven, the final judgment, the final reward, etc., and the fear of the final punishment.

In epistemology, Aristotle believes in sensory experience as the foundation, and logic as the method of acquiring knowledge. Christianity believes in faith as the central concept, faith and revelation as the foundation. In ethics, Aristotle views man as potentially proud, properly proud, the great-souled man, a self-sufficient being, capable on his own of achieving everything worth having, in virtue and in value, and his goal is happiness on earth. Christianity regards man as sordid, crooked, ulcerous, bespotted, stained with sin, helpless, and his goal is escape, release to the other world, union with God.

This is a big difference, and when a force of this dimension was let loose in medieval Christendom, something had to be done. The better minds of the age could not ignore Aristotle, nor could they repudiate Christianity, which everyone took as an unquestionable axiom, as it had been literally for centuries. So, they had a real challenge to their harmonizing, reconciling proclivities. In spite of the Church, therefore, the best men set to work to try to reconcile Aristotle and Christianity. The outstanding attempt—the one that was ultimately responsible for changing the Church's attitude to Aristotle—was that of Thomas Aquinas. His philosophy, called "Thomism," was finally adopted by the Church officially as the basic theory of Roman Catholicism, although not until 1879, and it remains so to this day. I should mention in passing that Aquinas's attempt at reconciliation of Aristotle and Christianity owes a good deal to Arabian and Jewish philosophers who preceded him, and who were also struggling with the question of how to reconcile Aristotle with *their* religions, namely, Mohammedanism and Judaism. And here I might mention the very great Mohammedan Aristotelian, *Averroes* (approximately 1126–1198), who is often called "The Commentator" because of his profound knowledge of Aristotle. And I might also mention Moses Maimonides, the twelfth-century Spanish Jew, author of *Guide for the Perplexed.* And why were the perplexed perplexed? Because they didn't know what to make of Aristotle and how to reconcile it with Judaism. Moses Maimonides's answer was, in significant part, the model for Thomas Aquinas.

I presume you know already that the task Aquinas set himself is impossible. His system is nevertheless of profound historical significance, because, in constructing a Christian philosophy within an Aristotelian framework, he made Aristotelianism known and respectable and acceptable to the most advanced thinkers of the medieval world. And in so doing —although it was quite contrary to his intentions, since he was a dedicated Catholic—he unleashed the forces of pagan Aristotelian rationality into that barren world, in a way in which within a century or so of his death brought the Middle Ages to an end. More than any other single factor, it is the Aristotelianism of Thomas Aquinas that opened the door to the Renaissance.

Thomas Aquinas

And so we come to the culmination of medieval philosophy—the philosophy of Thomas Aquinas (1225–1274 or 1275). He has a monumental, ingenious philosophic system, more thorough, more systematic, than any in all of philosophy prior to his time. In its key concepts, however, it is not very original. Throughout, it is an attempted synthesis of Aristotle and Christianity, or of Aristotle and Augustine. You are already familiar with the basic ingredients of his philosophy, or at least, the most basic of the basic. What I want to do now is merely indicate some of the essentials by which he brought crucial Aristotelian views back onto the intellectual scene. I want to give you at least a rough indication of how he tried to reconcile Aristotelianism with Christianity. I'd like to stress out of fairness that my exposition of Aquinas is going to be confined *only* to the broadest of broad surveys. If you tried a full presentation—even a half full one—even a tenth full one—you would have to be here twenty or fifty lectures. In this lecture, I want to look only at Aquinas's epistemology.

In epistemology, the main problem was to reconcile reason and faith. And Aquinas did so by saying that we must distinguish two fundamentally different subjects: philosophy and theology. As he uses the term "philosophy"—and as all ancient and medieval philosophers used it—it includes not only what we call "philosophy" today, but also all the knowledge that we would put in the sciences. That's harking back to *phile* for *sophia*, love of wisdom. Philosophy is the subject that begins with the evidence of the senses and proceeds throughout strictly by reason and logic, using the Aristotelian processes of observation, abstraction, definition, induction, syllogism, the definition of *archai* (first principles), etc. It is a completely natural subject that man can pursue by the use of his natural rational faculty, without any need for divine grace or illumination, says Aquinas. And this is a radical departure from Augustinianism, for there is no need for the dogmas of faith as its basic material. Philosophy proceeds with the facts of this world as its data and primary object. At bottom, philosophy is the subject that proceeds on secular Aristotelian lines. Theology, by contrast, is the subject that begins with the dogmas of faith, with the revelations, and then tries to explore and explicate their full meaning.

Therefore, to a significant extent, these two subjects will have a different content. Philosophy is primarily concerned with the facts of this world, and what it can learn from them. Theology is primarily concerned with the mysteries of religion. There will, however, Aquinas thought, be a significant overlap between the two branches of knowledge. There will be many things that philosophy can prove rationally and that have also been revealed by God. So, you have to think of two overlapping or intersecting circles. One contains all natural knowledge, all rational knowledge, and the other contains all revealed knowledge, and in the overlap are the issues that, as part of revelation, belong to theology, and yet, as capable of independent rational proof, belong to philosophy. This overlap area Aquinas called *natural theology*, the part of theology that can be proved by reason. And he thought that it included the proof of God, of the immortality of the soul, and of several other important things.

As to the part of theology that *can't* be proved by reason, the so-called revealed theology, what is its relation to reason and philosophy? Aquinas's overwhelmingly important answer is that revelation can in no way contradict reason, i.e., it can maintain nothing that can be rationally refuted. Revealed theology *supplements*—that's the key word, "supplements"—reason, by giving us information on subjects about which reason has nothing to say one way or the other. That's Aquinas's view. For instance, he says, take the question of whether the world was created at a certain point in time or whether it's eternal. He claims, from looking at the world, that there's no way of knowing, so if you go by reason, you'd have to say, "I don't know." (That's false, but that happens to be his view.) On that issue, therefore, he says theology may properly speak, and when Scripture tells us that the world was created out of nothing, we're entitled to accept it because it does not conflict with reason but fills in a hole that reason couldn't answer one way or the other. The two subjects can't conflict, he said, because, after all, God gave man both reason *and* revelation, and God, in effect, as a good Aristotelian, advocates the law of contradiction, and he wouldn't give us contradictory faculties. So, if someone claims to give a rational proof that one of the dogmas of faith is false or contradictory, reason must, says Aquinas, proceed to prove that the objection is invalid. And it will be able to do so, he believed. If the dogma is something that belongs only to revelation, reason can't prove the dogma is true, but it should be able to refute all of the objections and, from the point of reason, leave it an open question that we then appeal to theology to decide.

I think you see the significance of this view. Going back centuries, it was the first charter of liberty and of liberation for human reason. Reason now has its own domain: the world revealed to man's senses and whatever you can learn by reasoning about it. Reason is no longer just an appendage of theology. Its domain is a fundamentally separate subject that proceeds on Aristotelian lines on the basis of sense data, not of intuition of a world of Forms. Reason is now secularized, naturalized. It is now autonomous because its data is experience, not faith. Reason's capacity to know truth, said Aquinas, is a natural power. (Here he follows Aristotle.) It requires no special divine aid, grace, illumination. In reasoning, man is on his own, and he needs no special help from God in philosophy or science. I hope you see the absolutely fundamental opposition between Aquinas's approach here and that of Augustine, to say nothing of Tertullian and his friends. For Augustine, faith is the *basis* of reason. For Tertullian, faith *contradicts* reason. For Aquinas, it is neither of these. Faith is not the basis or the antagonist of reason, merely a supplement to it—that's all.

By describing revealed theology as that about which reason has nothing to say one way or the other—by stating that faith is a supplement to reason—Aquinas implies (although that is obviously not his intention) that faith is now on the defensive, because, by his formula, a thing goes into revealed theology only if reason is silent on the issue in question. But if reason has something to say, then, according to Aquinas, it must speak out, and if its arguments are unanswerable, then the alleged dogma can't be true. In other words, Aquinas's basic epistemological principle is that the rational is an absolute that you must subscribe to. In the face of any apparent conflict between reason and faith, Aquinas himself always took the line that the basis for the lack of conflict is that the intellect had made an error. Reason didn't really conflict—so, he never personally challenged faith. But, given his formula, the way was open for others to say in the face of a conflict, "It's the faith that's wrong, not reason, so let's throw it overboard." Which is just what happened.

Aquinas didn't think a conflict would ever develop. But you know that it had to. And in fact, soon after him, it did. Pretty soon they found that reason had a great, great deal to say, and that it was mostly inimical to Christianity and to the whole medieval viewpoint.

Before leaving Aquinas's epistemology, I must say that he is a very great epistemologist if you strip off the theology that is ever-present. But if you can read it apart from that—and he himself takes great pains to keep philosophy and theology very separate—it's very easy to strip off his theology. He makes many fascinating points on questions of detail. I would have to say that on a great many questions—lesser questions, but still vital questions—he is better than Aristotle himself. That's as great a compliment as you can pay a philosopher. I think offhand of his view of the method by which the laws of logic come to be known. I think Aquinas's treatment of that question is superior to Aristotle's. If you're interested, you can ask me about that in the question period.

I want to conclude the discussion of Aquinas at this point. I've given you at least the broadest essential of his distinctive contribution to Christianity in the area of epistemology. Next lecture I'll pick up with Aquinas's metaphysics, including his view of reality, of causality, his five famous arguments for the existence of God, and perhaps I'll have a minute to work in something about his angelology, his theory of angels, and then we'll look briefly at his ethics. And then we'll trace the development from Aquinas through the Renaissance and on to the development of modern science out of the foundations laid by Aquinas. You've heard enough, however, at least to begin to appreciate Aquinas's contribution to the release and salvation of the West, and I mean salvation now in a rational sense—salvation from Plato and Augustine.

Before we move to the question period, I would like to make a statement about Tuesday's presidential election. This course is primarily concerned with ancient and medieval, early modern philosophy. But you see that the dominant figure is Plato, that Plato made possible Augustine, and if we can look ahead just a moment, Plato made possible Kant, who is simply Plato in an infinitely more clear and vicious form. And Kant's philosophy was completed by Hegel, who represents the culmination of everything that is only a seed in Plato and becomes a full-grown cancer in Hegel. Against that background, I would like to read you a quotation from something that arrived in my mail this morning. It's from an article called "Just Plain George" by Robert Sam Anson, and it appears in *Harper's Magazine*, November 1972. I don't know anything about the article except this passage:

> It is significant, for instance, that when McGovern returned home from World War II, unsettled by the experience, unsure of his values, and not at all clear what to do with himself, he fell under the influence of a pacifistic Methodist minister and philosophy professor named Donald McAnnich, and with his coaxing plunged deeply into Hegel. The German philosopher seemed to present the best of both worlds—the ethical values of the East, where society overshadowed the individual, and the more familiar rugged individualism of the West. "George was quite taken with Hegel," McAnnich once said. "He had the wholeness

> McGovern was looking for." Interestingly, liking Hegel and being infatuated with the Hegelian concept of history never led McGovern, as it did so many Hegelians, to likewise love Marx. The reason is instructive. "George could never buy something like communism. He thought it was too materialistic."

I have just one comment: Anybody who could find rugged individualism in Hegel could find Americanism in a policy of totalitarianism at home and surrender abroad. The same mentality is at work in both. Hegel at least had an epistemological basis for it—he explicitly rejected the laws of logic and said that the individual *is* the collective and vice versa, A is non-A. Whether McGovern is that deep, I don't know, but he is surely consistent on politics. The question is: Will Hegel win on Tuesday? That is up to us.[27]

27. Richard Nixon defeated McGovern in a landslide, capturing 60.7 percent of the popular vote and 520 of the 537 electoral votes. For Ayn Rand's analysis of the McGovern campaign, see her "A Nation's Unity" in the *Ayn Rand Letter* (October and November 1972). Audio of her original Ford Hall Forum talk is at www.youtube.com/watch?v=o8IT4uaTlmg.

Lecture Seven, Q&A

Q: Could you tell us about Augustine's theory of time?

A: To put it briefly: Time is made up of the past, the present, and the future. Is it real? Let's consider them separately. The past obviously doesn't exist. The future obviously does not now exist. It will exist, but it never actually exists, because when it exists, it becomes the present. So, of the three, if there's any chance for time to be real, it's only the present. But how long is the present? Suppose you say it's an hour. The whole hour doesn't exist at any one instant. So, what actually exists at any one instant? A tiny, tiny fragment of time. How tiny? It can't have any size at all, because even if it had two parts, one part would have to exist when the other didn't. In other words, the present is an infinitesimal fragment. But an infinitely small fragment can't exist, it's nothing, it has no extension. Therefore, the present is unreal also. Therefore, time is a myth; there is no time. I once heard someone present this argument and say, "I'm sorry, I have no time to answer questions, my train is leaving." However, said Augustine, we have to try to explain where the appearance of time comes from, granted that it's not a reality. And his answer is: Time is a subjective feature—it's something contributed to experience by mind—it's a product of the way the human mind operates. And the same is true of space, but those two are twins, and they always go together. Because time, for Augustine, is a feature of the human mind, and if you obliterated man, you would obliterate time. To say that something is present is to say that something is perceived, and to say that something is past is to say human beings have a memory of it, and to say that it is future is to say human beings anticipate it. It follows that since human beings came into existence only with the creation of the world, *time* came into existence only with the creation of the world. And there is therefore no meaning to the question: "What was God doing before he created the world?," because there *was* no "before"—"before" is a temporal concept and is inapplicable until the world comes into existence.

Moreover, there's no use asking such questions as "Does God know in advance what Adam is going to do?"—God is not in time. Therefore, from his point of view, there is no "in advance." God is in eternity, timeless. For him, what we call past, present, and future is one timeless span without extension. Therefore, there's no question about God knowing in advance. So, you see that this was a very convenient theory. It was the theory taken over by Kant, who says explicitly (but with more systematic arguments than Augustine's) that time and space are subjective human products, and, therefore, Kant held that true reality is unknowable. Augustine said no, true reality is knowable by faith. Kant said that, too, as he grew older.

Just a couple of last points. If you want to classify theories of time in your own mind, there are essentially three theories of time. One is that time is *objective*—that is to say, a feature of reality external to man—and *absolute*—that is to say, a reality that would exist even if all physical objects were removed. Newton, for instance, held this view, which is called the "absolute theory of time and space." Space is like a gigantic container, time is like a stream of instants, and even if you obliterated all physical things, space and time would still be there. Second is the view that time and space are *objective*—that is, they are features of reality independent of man—but they are *relational* in character, not entities. This is known as the "relative theory," time and space as relative, or relational. And, as we saw, this was the view taken by Aristotle. And third is the view that time and space are *subjective*—that they are features of the human mind—that's the idealist tradition from Augustine and even in a way implied in Plato (but not nearly so crudely as in Augustine), all the way on through Kant and his disciples. Without going further into it, what is the answer to Augustine's argument? The same as the answer—to confine myself to just one point—the same as the answer to Zeno's paradoxes. You cannot divide infinitely. You will never, therefore, reach the actual infinitesimal. Whatever you reach will always be finite. That's a lead, and I think that's all that is required. It really is a parlor game masquerading as philosophy. It's exactly on the level of Zeno's paradoxes.

Q: Does Thomas Aquinas say how we arrive at the laws of logic?

A: Yes, and this, I think, is utterly brilliant on his part. You see, Aristotle's position as he formulates it leads to a certain contradiction. Aristotle says, on the one hand, that we arrive at the laws of logic by induction—we perceive one instance of the law of contradiction, for instance, with this table, that it's not both brown and not-brown, and another and another instance, and after all, we generalize, and then we see self-evidently that the generalization is true. However, Aristotle also says that the knowledge of logic is required in order to know *anything*. And so, the question is: How can you know the law of contradiction as a result of generalizing from instances of it and, at the same time, say that you have to know the law of contradiction to know *any* proposition, including even the first instance of the law of contradiction? You see the problem. Aquinas's brilliant solution was to say that the laws of logic do *not* come to be known by induction, but rather by abstraction—abstraction not from instances of the law of contradiction, but abstraction from instances of the concept of "being" or "existing." Said Aquinas, as soon as you open your eyes and have the first sense experience, you have implicitly the concept of "being," "existing," a thing which is, and as soon as you have that concept implicitly, you have implicitly but really, actually, the awareness: "To be *is* to be; a thing is what it is, and therefore, by implication, contradictions can't exist." In other words, the process is not one instance of the law of contradiction, then another, then the generalization, but a sensation, then immediately the implicit concept of "being," and thus by implication the laws of logic. And therefore, in the first sensation, Aristotle is right, you *do* know the laws of logic. Which I think is brilliant, because Aristotle had been attacked for being in an impossible snarl.

Q: Could you tell us about Augustine's theory of history?

A: Augustine's philosophy of history was an attempt to find meaning in the progression of human history. He wrote *The City of God*, his major opus, to explain the laws governing history and therefore, to answer the question: Why did Rome fall? He wrote it right after Rome fell, and the pagans were saying that Rome fell because it turned to Christianity, instead of to the old pagan gods. Augustine's point was that Rome hadn't embraced Christianity soon enough or completely enough, and that's why it fell. But you should understand that the fall of Rome to the ancient world was the exact equivalent of what the fall of the United States to Russia would be—it was the end of the world, truly the end of the world, which immediately went into the Dark Ages and never recovered until the Renaissance. Augustine's explanation was intended to take away the onus from Christianity for this catastrophe. And his view was that history has an intelligible pattern, that it is not just a series of individual human choices and actions. It has a purpose, it is teleological—this is the theory of teleology applied now to human history. It's going somewhere—it has a direction—it's structured like a well-made play. It has a beginning, a middle, a climax, and a denouement (the climax being Jesus' appearance on earth).

This was overwhelmingly important. I don't mean merely the idea that history has a meaning, or that there are laws of history, but the idea that history has an inner motive and purpose of its own, and that as a whole it tells a story leading to an ultimate fulfillment. That is a deeply religious interpretation of history and is the absolute basis of Hegel's theory of history—that history operates through a series of stages aiming finally at the true fulfillment of the Absolute. And it is the basis of the Marxist theory of history, the view that history is the progression of economic forces moved, ultimately, by the climax it's going to reach, namely, the classless society. And it is the basis of the fascist and Nazi racist interpretation of history, that the meaning of history is the progressive realization and triumph of the Aryans. All of those are just ringing the changes on the Augustinian view. More than that, there's another crucial point. Remember the City of God versus the earthly city, the two races of men mingled on the face of the earth: the one chosen by God, given grace and promised triumph, the other not given grace by God, doomed to vice and ultimate holocaust in Hell. Augustine said that you can interpret all of history in terms of the conflict between these two cities. The members of each are predestined, and their interaction and conflict are the ingredients that make up the flow of history. This idea of a dichotomy within history—that all history can be explained in terms of the interaction of a value-superior class (a predestined collective) and a value-inferior class (a predestined inferior), and the clash and conflict between them—was taken over by Hegel, by Marx, and by Hitler, though in different forms, of course. Hegel says it is the Germans versus the non-Germans, which he substitutes for the God-oriented versus the non-God-oriented, and he is therefore a profound nationalist. Marx couches his view in economic terms: the capitalist versus the proletariat, or more broadly, the haves versus the have-nots, who have battled throughout history. And the Nazis do the same thing, but in biological terms: the Aryans versus the non-Aryans, or the Aryans versus the Jews. All of that is again ringing the changes on the basic Augustinian collectivist-determinist-teleological interpretation of history. Those are the two central points I would make, and therefore, on this point alone, Augustine has had more influence on the philosophy of history than just about any other philosopher.

Q: If to be humble in this world is a virtue, why is it a punishment in the next, and the reverse with pride?

A: I'm not sure I get that. Is the meaning of the question: "Why is it that the two worlds are in opposition to each other, such that you're supposed to be humble in this world, but you can exalt yourself in the next one, that you're supposed to be miserable down here, but you can be happy in the next one?" Is that the meaning of the question, "Why are the two worlds opposite to each other?" And if so, it's a very good question. Nobody who ever preached a super-reality ever took the following line. Nobody ever said: "Yeah, there's another world, but this one is great. Enjoy this life, live in this world, and when you're finished, then you go to another terrific world." Never was taken. The view has always been: This world is rotten, evil, defective, and so on, and therefore, get no happiness out of it, abase yourself in it, and so on, and then you'll hit the jackpot in the next dimension. There are various reasons you could give why the two dimensions have always been construed as opposed to each other. Philosophically, the answer is: because there is only one reality. No matter who says what, the human mind cannot conceive of two realities. "Reality" means "what is real, what exists, everything." And therefore, if you say there are two of them, you have to say that one of them isn't *really* real, that it's deficient, defective, and so on, and therefore, you have to sacrifice. That's the philosophic reason. If I can permit myself with the proper preface to make a psychological observation (which I normally oppose in any philosophy course), the reason is the motivation of mysticism. A people are inclined to mysticism because they're *opposed* to this world, they are *anti*-reality, and they want something that they cannot have in this reality, so they start off hating this world. So, it's not a surprise that this world comes out as poor and as the opposite in their philosophy of "true reality," as they construe it. But that's a psychological explanation, which you have to keep separate in your mind from a philosophical one, because otherwise it becomes the fallacy of *ad hominem*.

Q: According to Christianity, what is the ecstasy you will gain in the other world?

A: A spiritual happiness that will make anything that you know in this life pale by comparison. But we can't really describe it because the other world—you have to get there first. But it will really be something.

Q: What is Aristippus's view called, if not "Epicureanism"?

A: The view "Eat, drink, and be merry, for tomorrow you die"? That is called "hedonism." And it's a different type of hedonism than Epicurus's. It's sometimes called "short-range" hedonism.

Q: When the philosophers of the Hellenistic period refer to the problem of evil, do they make any distinction between the actions of men (such as murder and rape) and natural phenomena (earthquakes and disease)?

A: Oh, absolutely! There's human evil and natural evil. And the standard explanation of human evil is that human beings have free will, which is a perfection of man, and therefore, God should be thanked for giving man free will, but therefore, you can't hold God responsible for man's misuse of free will. And then on natural evil—diseases and lava and so on—that I discussed in the previous lecture.

Q: A search for an explanation of the universe has recurred in the history of philosophy. Is this a valid question from the Objectivist point of view?

A: No, not an explanation of the *universe*. "Explanation" means giving a causal antecedent, and "the universe" means the totality of everything. In terms of what would you explain everything? All that's left over is nothing. And therefore, you'd have to explain something in terms of nothing. That is the meaning of Miss Rand's point that existence exists—that is where you start—you cannot get underneath and ask *why* does it exist. You can ask why does any particular *form* of it exist, and the answer will be in terms of the actions of other elements. But you will never be able to get underneath it all and ask, "But why is there anything?," which is the question that the Existentialists or the religious people ask.

Q: What is the specific way in which Augustine influenced Hitler?

A: I really mentioned that: through the theory of history. You understand that when I say that these people influenced Hitler, Hitler was not a scholar. He did not read Augustine or Hegel, as far as I know, and certainly not Kant. He read Rosenberg[28] and Wagner and the German equivalent of James Reston.[29] So, the influence is enormously indirect, but nevertheless enormously real. The whole idea of a collectivist determinist teleological interpretation of history is Augustinian, and that is essential to Nazi philosophy.

---

28. Alfred Rosenberg was the leading theoretician of Nazism.
29. Reston was an influential *New York Times* columnist. The Ayn Rand Archives contains more than 150 of his columns clipped by Ayn Rand in the 1960s and 1970s, many containing negative marginal comments by her.

Q: Will you explain what you mean by the term "concrete-bound"?

A: Yes. Ayn Rand uses the term "concrete" in the way that Aristotle or Plato used the word "particular," meaning a specific individual existent. A concrete-bound individual, however, means essentially a nominalist, as I defined that term philosophically. It means a nominalist in practice, that is to say, a person who does not grasp that particulars have something in common, who does not therefore function in terms of abstractions, of concepts, but simply glares at separate particulars out of context and without relationship to other particulars, and is therefore incapable of learning from experience or of grasping principles. The best example I ever heard of this was a conversation related to me many years ago about a then-student of Objectivism who was trying to explain this—it was at the time that President Truman had tried to nationalize the steel industry, and this student of Objectivism was arguing against it with some non-Objectivist acquaintance, and he went into painstaking detail as to why nationalization of industry as such would be impractical, immoral, disastrous, subversive of freedom. After hearing these arguments, the person said he was absolutely convinced that the steel industry should not be nationalized. And next lecture the person had one question: "What about the coal industry?" That's what you call "concrete-bound." He sees it on steel. The real low-grade ones see it on Bessemer Steel, or they see it on this factory but not the one next door, or on this bench within the factory (but then you have to be a real modern pragmatist to get that narrow). The ordinary concrete-bounder on the street can grasp up to an industry, but industry in general and human actions as a whole, impossible. Now, that is a nominalist mentality: There are no universals, there are no concepts, and everything is a separate concrete. And you see, that is the practical result of the assault on concepts, which is the essential element of modern philosophy, not of ancient or medieval.

LECTURE EIGHT

Philosophy Becomes Religious—and Recovers (Part II)

In the previous lecture, we ended in the middle of a discussion of Thomas Aquinas's monumental attempt to synthesize Christianity with the doctrines of Aristotle, which had been rediscovered some decades before Aquinas's birth. In particular, we looked at Aquinas's epistemology—his doctrine that reason is an absolute, that man must go by reason, that whatever can be proved by man's unaided secular reason operating on sense experience is true, and that faith is only a supplement to reason, not its basis and not its antagonist. And we discussed in what way this doctrine was a charter of liberty for man's reason after centuries of the Platonizing Augustine, to say nothing of the Tertullian types.

Now let us pick up our discussion of Aquinas and proceed from Aquinas in the thirteenth century on through to the end of the sixteenth century. And first, let us look at Aquinas's metaphysics. Before I tell you its central thrust, I want to say at the outset that he was never consistently Aristotelian in metaphysics, any more than he could, as a devout Catholic, be consistently Aristotelian in any branch of philosophy. In metaphysics, for instance, he believes that a supernatural dimension—God—is the creator and source of this world. He believes that God's mind contains the Platonic Forms, just as Plotinus had said, and thus the Platonic Forms for Aquinas are logically prior to the things in this world. Aquinas often, especially in discussing the problem of evil, inclines to a Neoplatonic view of the relative unreality of this world compared to the true reality of God. He believes in all the Catholic dogmas, the trinity, the incarnation, etc. You should bear in mind that Aquinas is not a pagan. He is not a pure Aristotelian, not in metaphysics and not in any branch of philosophy. He is as close to an Aristotelian as it is possible for a devout Christian to get.

With that preface, let's turn to the distinctive Aristotelian elements in his metaphysics, the new approach in metaphysics that he brought to the Christian world. If the central problem in epistemology is how to reconcile reason and faith, the central problem confronting Aquinas in metaphysics is how to reconcile God and this world. You recall the Augustinian view that there are two radically opposite, sundered dimensions: God, who is reality, absolute reality, perfection—and nature, or the physical world, which is fundamentally unreal, which is essentially the Neoplatonic absence, the place where the rays of the One, the light of God, have run out, so it's gotten dark. And this world, if you remember, for Augustine was, therefore, a kind of gray, unreal, unsubstantial haze. God is absolutely opposite from this world. He is perfect in reality, and this world is damned, unreal, corrupt. And yet Aristotle had said there was only one reality, and that it was fully real. How did Aquinas reconcile these two views? He took over from Aristotle the view that there *is* only one reality, but that it is hierarchical in nature.

You remember Aristotle's view that there are various levels of reality, depending upon the extent to which form is actualized, i.e., ascending from prime matter, the elements, the compounds, the plants, animals, men, the intelligences that move the spheres, and then the pure form, the Prime Mover, at the very top. Aquinas adopted this whole framework. Reality, he said, is not irrevocably sundered into two opposite worlds, God versus nature. No, there are not really two kinds of reality at all, he said; there is only one. The universe forms one single real totality. But it rises in ascending levels of actuality to reach God, who is at the top pure actuality. In this sense, said Aquinas, it is right for a Christian to exalt God above the world, because God is the top of the hierarchy, the supreme form. But, he insisted, this does not imply that we must metaphysically despise or degrade the world of nature that we live in, that we must turn it into some sort of degenerate dimension infected with nonbeing. No, he says, nature, the world we live in, is part of the one reality. It is merely a lower level of the one continuous hierarchy, rising unbrokenly up the Aristotelian ladder to God. The intelligences that move the spheres give way, in Aquinas's view, to the angels. In the famous expression that captures this view, "Grace perfects nature," grace being the realm of God, nature the physical world. And whereas the Augustinian view had been that grace destroys nature—the realm of God destroys or obliterates the reality of this world—Aquinas's view is that God perfects nature.

This view is of enormous significance—it undercuts the metaphysical basis for despising this world. The earth, the natural world—with all of its creatures, including man—are now real; they exist. It's very hard to communicate to you how revolutionary this perspective is. But that's Aquinas's big contribution: This world is real. It *is*. Everything is part of one integrated universe. Following Aristotle, Aquinas equates the real with the individual, not with the universal. And therefore, there are no such things as degrees of reality. There *are* degrees of complexity of structure, and there are degrees of what Aristotle called "actuality," but there are no degrees of reality in the Platonic sense. Everything that exists, including the world of physical entities, is fully and equally there, it *is*, it's *real*. In this respect, as an Aristotelian, Aquinas agrees with Aristotle, who agrees with Parmenides—what is, is. If a thing is, then it is—the law of identity. Either it is or it isn't—the law of excluded middle. And it can't sort of be and yet sort of not be—the law of contradiction. And the result is that this world regains the solidity, the substantiality, the metaphysical stature, the reality that had been shorn from it by the Platonizing Augustinians. This world is real.

And therefore, the things in this world are fit and proper objects for human study. In pursuing science, we are again studying and in contact with reality. We are not in Plato's Cave watching the half-real shadowy reflections. We are not in Plotinus's world watching the emptiness where the rays ran out. We are not in Augustine's world watching *prope nihil*, if you remember his definition of "matter," "almost nothing." We are in reality, and science is, therefore, the study of reality. Moreover, the earth is a fit place to live in—it's man's natural home. True enough, the realm of God is man's supernatural destiny, and that's more important. But still, his natural home is a real home. It's a part of reality. It's not a place of exile from reality. As to man (and that means individual men for Aquinas, since he's an Aristotelian in this respect), man, too, gains a real metaphysical dignity on Aquinas's view. After all, man occupies a place rather high up on the metaphysical hierarchy. The angels and God, to be sure, are above man. But still, within the natural world, man is the highest being. As it came to be put, man is the highest of the natural material beings and the lowest of the spiritual ones. But notice that man is the only being who has a foot in both camps, who belongs to both worlds. As a living physical creature, he's a member of this world. But as a creature with an intellect and, as Aquinas thought, therefore, an immortal soul (and here, Aristotle's immortal active reason was of great help to him), man is destined to a life in the spiritual hereafter. Thus, man, so to speak, has a crucial metaphysical role to play for Aquinas—man is the creature who closes the gap between the physical world and the world of God and the angels. He is the link that unites the two dimensions into one reality, the highest member of the one realm, who is also by virtue of his immortal soul a potential member of the other. You can think of it as though man, for Aquinas, is the metaphysical glue that keeps the universe stuck together. And we have to always remember this in speaking of man's supernatural destiny—as we must do as good Christians. Nevertheless, says Aquinas, we must never forget that man is also a part of this world. There is not only a supernatural man with an otherworldly destiny, but a natural man with a this-worldly destiny. You should now be able to guess the ethical implications of this.

I've said that on this view held by Aquinas, science is metaphysically possible again, and it's epistemologically possible via the liberation of reason. But you might still ask me: *How* is science possible, if all events are a product of God's will? Even for Aquinas, God created the world *ex nihilo*—that's a dogma you must subscribe to it. God has a plan. Everything happens as he ordains by his will. Everything in that sense is a miracle—it proceeds from God, from God's will. How then can you have science?

Aquinas dealt with this question, too. And his answer was, true enough, everything is determined by God as part of his plan and by his will. But it so happens that God usually works through intermediate or secondary causes. An orderly, lawful, regular universe where entities act in accord with their natures is part of what God wills. A scientifically understandable universe is part of his plan. So, ultimately, it's true that only God has causal efficacy. But he expresses it by endowing his *creatures* with causal efficacy. Of course, God can intervene directly at any time and dispose with the intermediate causes. He can point in a divine way to a rock and say, "I want wine to come out," in which case, that would be a miracle. But on the whole, says Aquinas, we should try to explain events in terms of natural laws and causes, just as Aristotle said, not by reference to God's directly willing them (although he does believe in miracles). This view also was a charter, releasing man to attempt to discover order and law in the natural universe.

Now let's turn to God. I want to mention Aquinas's famous arguments for the existence of God. Since these are *arguments*, this topic comes under what we called last time "natural theology," that is, it's a theological subject matter but it's arrived at exclusively by secular reason. There are five famous arguments that Aquinas puts forth for the existence of God. None of them are original with him. I cannot go into the details of them now but will identify for you the main principle of each. (These are to this day the arguments of the Catholic Church in favor of God.)

Number one is the *argument from motion*. The argument from motion is number one, and it literally restates Aristotle's argument for the Prime Mover, arguing that motion implies a first mover, a Prime Mover, an Unmoved Mover. And therefore, there's absolutely nothing new in that.

Two, the *argument from efficient causation*. This basically restates the argument from motion in different language, speaking of causes rather than motions. You remember Aristotle's definition of "efficient cause"—the factor that brings about the existence or the motion of something, in the case of the example we used, the sculptor's actual shaping of the clay. This argument goes like this: Everything has an efficient cause that brought it into existence, which is true enough. Next premise: Nothing can be the efficient cause of itself. And that's obviously the case—nothing can produce itself or bring itself into existence. It first would have to exist before it could do anything. It follows that everything is caused by something previous, and that by something previous, and we'll have a whole series of causes stretching back, each caused by the preceding. But, Aquinas asks, what is responsible for the existence of the whole series of causes and effects? We can't have an infinite regress, or rather, to be exact, he says there may be an infinite regress of causes of causes of causes. We know from faith that there was a beginning because God created the world, but as far as reason is concerned, perhaps the series *does* go back forever. Nevertheless, he says, we must ask, what is the explanation of the whole series? Why is there anything at all? (And that, you see, is the exact parallel to Aristotle's question regarding why there is any motion at all.) And he concludes on exactly the same reasoning—there must be an uncaused cause, a first cause. This introduces nothing new but the terminology. It is, essentially, the argument from motion transferred over to causality, and the same objections are applicable to it.

The third is called the *argument from necessity and contingency.* And it goes like this: Some entities are contingent, and by "contingent," we mean that it is possible for them not to exist—as against a necessary entity that would have to exist. Some entities are contingent—they come into being, they stick around for a while, they pass away. Aquinas argues that it is not possible that *all* entities could be contingent. To simplify his argument, what it comes to is this: If every entity were contingent, that would mean that existence as a whole could pass away. And of course, it can't. Therefore, something must be necessary. And if so, either it's necessary by its own nature, incapable of going out of existence by its own inherent character, or else it owes its necessity to something else. But again, we can't have an infinite regress, so ultimately there must be something that is absolutely necessary, which has to exist by its own nature. And this, he says, is what we mean by God—the absolutely necessary being. In answer to this argument, I need merely point out to you that first of all, it's based on the dichotomy between necessary and contingent facts, which Aquinas took over from Aristotle, who took it over from Plato, and since that dichotomy is false, the whole argument, in fact, can't get off the ground. But secondly, even if you were to grant that dichotomy, it proves nothing whatever about a God. Because a Greek could answer, "Well, fine, why don't we say that the world stuff is the absolutely necessary thing, and what you call 'contingent beings' are merely different arrangements of the eternal necessary world stuff, so that we have a completely necessary thing that has no supernatural associations and no religious significance?"

Number four is the *argument from degrees.* There are degrees of various qualities that we observe. Things vary, for instance, in heat, in size, in value, and so on. Where there are degrees of a quality, there must, Aquinas argues, be an absolute maximum of that quality somewhere, which is the cause of its existence in all the lesser degrees. There are degrees of goodness, as we observe—some things are better, others are worse. There must, therefore, be a maximum of goodness that causes all the lesser degrees of goodness, an absolute goodness or an absolute perfection, and this is God. And therefore, there's a God. This argument is generally the weakest of the five. The premise—that variation in degree implies a separate entity of the maximum amount causing the lesser degrees—has no plausibility. It actually rests on the Platonic theory of Forms. Remember that, for Plato, all the qualities here in this world vary depending upon how much they reflect the perfect Form of their quality in the other World, so if there are degrees down here, that for Plato implies a maximum perfect embodiment of the quality in the other world. That's really the framework in which Aquinas is here arguing, so it's a thoroughly Platonic argument for God.

And, finally, is number five, the teleological argument, the *argument from design*, which we've already mentioned several times. That argument is very simple: There is order in the world, and everything happens either always or for the most part, says Aquinas, following Aristotle's phrase—but order, as Aristotle showed, implies final causation, implies teleology. And, says Aquinas, teleology implies a conscious being who is imposing the purpose, or end, or goal, on things. And therefore, there must be such a cosmic consciousness, namely, God the Cosmic Designer. Here, the point to challenge is the Aristotelian view that order requires a final cause. And I criticized that in discussing Aristotle's teleology. I must point out that Aquinas is superior to Aristotle in this one respect—if you *grant* final causation as a metaphysical principle of everything, then Aquinas is right, the only way to make sense of teleology is some sort of divine consciousness, and, in that respect, he draws the conclusions from Aristotle's error.

A word about the nature of God. Aquinas has, to his satisfaction, proved the existence of God, but has to face another task: He has to show that the God he has proved is the God of Christianity, not merely the Prime Mover of Aristotle. The argument from motion, for instance, establishes—if it's correct—the Unmoved Mover, and, if you recall, he's completely impotent and ignorant, unconscious of the world, without any power over it, able to do nothing but contemplate himself, his own perfection from eternity to eternity. How do you get from this God to the God of Christianity? If we had a month, I would indicate some of the ways by which Aquinas attempted this feat. Of course, it is impossible. But Aquinas takes this line: He says that Aristotle is right: God knows only his own nature, knows only himself. But we know that God is the Creator of the world, and that he contains the archetypes of everything in the world in his mind, and therefore, in knowing himself, he indirectly knows the world that he created, and therefore, God does know the world. You see that's pretty weak, because he has to resort to faith to establish that God created the world, so it's no longer natural theology. In the last analysis, Aquinas's view is that reason can prove the existence of God and can give us a few slender leads as to God's nature, but the real essence of God, insofar as man can know it on earth, depends on faith. So much for Aquinas on God.

(I have to leave out Aquinas on angels owing to the lack of time, but he had some interesting things to say about them, so if you ask me in the question period about Aquinas's angels, I will be happy to tell you a few tidbits about them.)

Let's conclude our brief survey of Thomism by looking at the main principle of his ethics. And here again he attempted to reconcile Aristotle with Christianity. Ethics has a dual nature, just as man does. Because man is in part a natural being, living on earth is his natural home, a part of ethics will prescribe for that part of man. But insofar as man is a being with a supernatural destiny, there will be a part of ethics for that side of him. So, there will be two types of virtues—the *natural virtues* for man qua natural being, and the *theological virtues* for man qua being with a supernatural destiny. And in Aquinas's opinion, these two sets of virtues do not conflict, because in fulfilling the natural virtues, in living well here on earth, he said, we develop and prepare ourselves for our supernatural destiny. Again, the idea running throughout his philosophy is that the theological elements *supplement* the natural elements, that is, they don't contradict them.

As to the natural virtues, they are Aristotelian. Following Aristotle, Aquinas emphasizes self-realization, the all-around development of one's capacities, all the various moral and intellectual virtues we saw when we looked at Aristotle's ethics: You should live by reason, you should satisfy your natural this-worldly desires (at least to a moderate extent), you should not despise the body or the physical, and you should aim at *eudaimonia*, happiness on earth. This whole side of ethics, says Aquinas, the natural ethics, is discoverable by reason alone and comes under philosophy, not theology. And he says that man by his own efforts can achieve the natural virtues—at least to some degree. We're still obeying God's will in following our reason in natural ethics, he says, because God after all is the Creator of the rationality of the universe, so in obeying reason, we're still obeying God's will. (I always thought that God would have to be very surprised to discover that what he had willed was Aristotle's ethics. But we can leave that for God to worry about.)

This naturalistic side of Aquinas's ethics released the whole system of Aristotelian this-worldly ethical values into the stream of medieval culture. For instance, even the virtues of poverty and chastity had to be modified (at least, for most men—priests and saints exempt), because after all, virtue is the Golden Mean, and you can't go to extremes—utter poverty and drinking laundry water and so on are extremes. If you want one touch illustrating the charter of liberty for human reason that Aquinas introduced following Aristotle, I refer you to his fascinating doctrine called "The Erring Reason Binds." Remember the Augustinian view that you have to accept Christian dogmas whether they make sense to you or not. If you try to set up your puny mind above God's and to judge the rationality of the dogmas, that is depravity and intellectual arrogance. Aquinas, under the influence of Aristotle, takes a diametrically opposite view here. We cannot, he says, demand more of any man than that he honestly follow his own reason. He was asked the question: "Suppose a man's reason errs, makes a mistake, and suppose the man honestly thinks that it's rational to endorse a certain belief or take a certain action, but in fact he's made an error, and the belief or action is against the Church dogma. What should the man do? Should he suspend his reason and follow the dogma, or follow his own reason even if it conflicts with the dogma?" To which Aquinas answered that a man must follow his own reason. Reason binds. You have to go by reason, even if your reason has made a mistake, as long as that is your honest conviction. And that's the doctrine, "the erring reason binds." (Needless to say, the valid reason binds just as much.) Here's a quote from Aquinas from his *Summa Theologica*: "Every will at variance with reason, whether right or erring, is always evil." That is certainly marvelous. And Aquinas himself gives the most startling example: We know that belief in Jesus, he tells us, is necessary to salvation.

Nevertheless, he says, if someone honestly believes otherwise, he would be wrong to become a Christian. Reason is the absolute. It is in this respect even more absolute than the Christian dogma. You see how utterly opposite this is to the earlier Augustinian Christian viewpoint.

While there is this whole Aristotelian side in Aquinas, the other side, especially in ethics, is always there and is often dominant. You must not get the wrong impression: Besides the natural, rational virtues, there are the theological virtues of faith, hope, charity ("charity" is a translation of *charitas*, which means "love," love of God, and it's only after the eighteenth century that it came to mean giving money to beggars). These theological virtues, says Aquinas, faith, hope, and charity, cannot be proved by reason. They depend upon God's revelation for us to know that they are virtues. They pertain to man's relation to God, not to life on earth. And they cannot be attained by us at all by our own efforts, only by God's grace. And here Aquinas accepted, as a good Christian, the whole Augustinian viewpoint, which had been proclaimed official Church dogma: Man is stained with original sin, he requires God's grace to make a step in the direction of virtue, he's predestined to Heaven or Hell by God's inscrutable decision, etc., etc. All of which, as you can project, clashes constantly with the more Aristotelian side of his thought.

If you want just one sentence on Aquinas's politics: Just as grace perfects nature, so the Church perfects the State, and just as God is supreme over nature, the Church must be supreme over the State. That is Aquinas's politics. I cannot even say it in a nutshell, but in an aphorism.

In this brief sketch of Aquinas, I've had to leave out a huge amount, including the details of the ingenious ways in which he tried to reconcile Aristotle and Christianity. And I have not emphasized the Christian elements that exist in abundance in Aquinas. I've painted primarily the better Aristotelian side because I wanted to isolate one element. For our purposes, what is crucial about him, to sum up, is this: He released reason and he affirmed that this world is real, and it's man's natural home. He gave man a significantly added metaphysical evaluative stature (and within the limits imposed by his dogmas). He advocated that man has *some* share in working out his own this-worldly destiny, that he ought to develop his human rational powers and, as far as possible, enjoy his present stay on earth. This was in the thirteenth century. The fourteenth is the end of the medieval period, and the prologue to the Renaissance.

Transition to the Renaissance

"Renaissance," as you know, means "rebirth." Rebirth of what? Of a pro-reason, pro-man, pro-this-world attitude. It is the return of man to life on earth after more than a millennium of supernaturalism. But it was not complete. The Renaissance, judged by today's standards, compared to today, is a highly religious period. Men typically did not dispute the existence of God, or the veracity of revelations, or original sin, or the incarnation, or the whole slew of dogmas. They just didn't focus on them, as they had prior to the Renaissance. Religion did not stop, but it stopped dominating people's lives. It was still there but it wasn't the controlling factor anymore. If we can borrow Nietzsche's expression, he claimed that God died in the nineteenth century (actually, he died in the eighteenth), but if we carry out that metaphor (and it's just a metaphor), you can say that the Renaissance is the time when God got seriously ill. He had his first major heart attack from which he was destined never to recover, and he slowly wasted away across subsequent centuries. As a fundamental controlling exclusive concern in human life, religious supernaturalism died in the Renaissance, never to recover.

The rest of our story, as far as we have time for it, consists of indicating what happened after Aquinas, i.e., after Aristotle and reason had been let loose. The ground had already been laid in Aquinas's separation of philosophy from theology, with the implication that philosophy had its own realm to study and was not merely a handmaiden of theology. However, in Aquinas, the full meaning of this was not yet explicit. He still had the realm of natural theology, remember, where the two circles (philosophy and theology) overlapped: theology that comes from God's revelation but which you can also prove independently by reason. And Aquinas considered natural theology to be the really important part of philosophy. So, for Aquinas, even though the philosopher does function in method independently of dogma, his most important goal in content is still to try to prove, on the basis of sense experience and reason, as much of the dogma as he can.

What had to happen for the Renaissance to occur was for Aquinas's two spheres, his two circles of philosophy and theology, to fall apart altogether so that there was no more natural theology, so that nothing in theology could be proved by philosophy. When this occurred, philosophy lost all essential connection with theology. And the whole Scholastic enterprise, therefore, collapsed. Theological issues were no longer of relevance to the philosopher but were matters of faith incapable of rational discussion.

Philosophers became men who studied this world on the basis of sense experience and reason. Their conclusions didn't bear on theology. And theologians studied God's world on the basis of faith and revelations, and their views were no longer relevant to philosophy. It was like Kipling's East and West; the twain would never meet. Once this occurred, philosophy once and for all lost its bondage to theology and set up on its own, and we had then the birth of modern science and modern philosophy.

There were many small occurrences responsible for this separation of philosophy from theology, but the two philosophers after Aquinas most responsible for this separation were both ardent Catholics: Duns Scotus (1266–1310) and William of Occam (1280–1350). Let us look briefly at each of these transition figures, from Aquinas to the Renaissance.

Duns Scotus

Duns Scotus was a true Scholastic. He excelled in subtle hairsplitting distinctions in his effort to reconcile the various authorities, make sense out of the Christian dogmas, and especially to reconcile Christianity with Aristotle. He was known as "the Subtle Doctor" because of his skill at making subtle distinctions. And our word "dunce" is the term that has come down as representing this type of mentality. It's named after Duns. But that isn't really fair, because Duns was a mixed case philosophically. In part, he was very much influenced by Aristotle, and in part, he is a typical devout religious Scholastic. Insofar as he is Aristotelian, he preached with Aquinas that all knowledge begins with experience, there are no innate ideas, and concepts are arrived at by abstraction from experience. He insisted, with Aquinas, that there are many types of knowledge that can be arrived at by man entirely on his own, by his own secular natural reason, without any need for divine illumination or divine assistance.

On the issue of natural theology, Duns is the first important voice of the future because he very much shrunk the domain of natural theology. You cannot, he argued, prove the existence of the soul in reason. You have to accept that on faith. You *can* prove the existence of a God *of sorts* in reason, he thought, but not the God of Christianity, not an all-powerful providential God, as Aquinas had thought, but that, too, is a matter for faith. And that was a big blow to natural theology. Moreover, he held—and here we come to the more mystic side of his view—it is an impious limitation on God to try to explain what he does by reference to reason. Aquinas had held that in God, the intellect (the divine intellect) was prior, or more basic, than the will. God's intellect, he held, had primacy over God's will. Aquinas had said that, first, God (his intellect) knows the rational and the good, and then as an inevitable consequence, God's will decrees that what the intellect has grasped be enacted. Duns Scotus repudiates this view of Aquinas's, and on good grounds. The Thomistic position, he says, amounts to an infringement of God's omnipotence. If God must will as his intellect declares, then God's will is restricted by his intellect. God has lost his all-powerful sovereignty and omnipotence—he *has* to go by reason, which was Aquinas's view. And, says Duns Scotus, this is intolerable. Aquinas held that reason is irresistible to man and to God. Duns reminds him that, if you're to be a true Christian, God comes above reason, and therefore, his will must be absolutely free to will whatever it jolly well chooses, without any reasons at all. God has to have a free will just like Epicurus's concept of the swerve—he decrees because he decrees—and therefore, concluded Duns, man cannot hope to make sense out of God's will or its enactments. And therefore, he thought, there's not much point in trying to apply reason to religious questions. Theology is essentially a matter of faith. You can see how that would tend to shrivel the domain of natural theology. This viewpoint by the way—that the will has primacy over the intellect—is known as *voluntarism* (from the Latin *volantas*, meaning "will"). And in Scotus, it's a divine voluntarism because it's God's will that's more basic. When you get to Freud in the nineteenth century, it becomes a human voluntarism (the id is the will), and it's a seething demoniacal force at the base of man and is more basic than his intellect, but that's many centuries of corruption later. Duns Scotus, I should say, was inconsistent since he thought God was limited by the law of identity. Even if he's omnipotent, he said, God can't will a contradiction, and that limits him to some extent.

Duns applied the same voluntarist viewpoint to ethics. Saint Thomas had said that God commands certain things to man because God sees that those are good. Scotus says, oh no, they are good because God commands them, not the other way around; otherwise, you limit God. God, says Scotus, could have willed the opposite of what he did, and then that opposite, by virtue of being willed by God, would have been the good. Here again, the net effect is to make religious ethics unintelligible to the human mind and, therefore, outside the province, or interest, of philosophy. And again, you see the systematic falling apart of Aquinas's two realms, of philosophy and theology. After Duns, these two realms essentially cease overlapping. Instead of one supplementing the other, they become separated, become virtually unrelated fields. I should point out, again on ethics, that Duns Scotus is inconsistent. The Ten Commandments, he thinks, are implicit in the law of identity, and God, therefore, had no choice about them. That is a real feat—I'd love to see somebody deduce the Ten Commandments from the law of identity.

William of Occam

Now a few words on William of Occam (1280–1350). Occam is a very interesting figure whom we have little time for. He is interesting because he blends the most radically diverse approaches to philosophy. He is an Aristotelian in many ways, but he's also a devout Catholic, a Scholastic, and he's got definite skeptic elements. So if you had to quantify him for some Pythagorean, I'd say he's about two parts Aristotle, two parts Augustine, and one part ancient skeptic, all blended. Something on the order of John Locke, but in a different form.

As to his Aristotelianism, he was a thorough empiricist: All knowledge begins with sense experience, and man is born *tabula rasa*. His theory of universals is basically Aristotelian but with a tendency to nominalism (the skeptic view that there are no universals). Starting in the next lecture, we'll see nominalism gaining ascendancy. And in fact, many people consider Occam the father of modern nominalism. I think this is incorrect. He combines elements of Aristotle's view on universals with elements of a kind of skeptic nominalism. But if you read him selectively, you could call him a very big influence on the production of modern nominalism. But that doesn't do justice to his own view. If you want another skeptic element in William of Occam, he held that since God is all-powerful, we can't be sure that there is any external world at all underlying our sense experiences. Maybe, he says, God has produced our sense experiences in our minds directly, and there really is no world out there at all. Of course, he didn't believe this, because faith told him that God had created the world. But in reason, he said, it's a possibility. And that is the standard skeptic position, and as some of you know, in a somewhat different form, it became the official viewpoint of philosophers like Bishop Berkeley and Leibniz, whom we'll get to later.

In general, however, Aristotelianism is the thrust of much of William of Occam's philosophy. He represents the completion of the tendency for theology and philosophy to separate entirely. Philosophy, says Occam, must concern itself exclusively with facts known by sense experience and reasoning therefrom. Philosophy is the science of this earth. Theology, on the other hand—now remember, he accepted theology devoutly—is completely beyond reason, and it's a mistake to try to make any sense of it at all (a viewpoint in which he's entirely correct). Reason, he says, cannot prove the existence of God, *any* kind of God, let alone the Christian one. Nor can it prove the existence of the soul, let alone its immortality. Reason, he says, cannot make any sense whatever of the Catholic dogmas. You must have faith. For all we can see in reason, God, he says (this is his own example), could have become incarnate as an ass instead of a man. You have to have faith, that's all.

Nor, he insists, should philosophers appeal to supernatural entities to explain the facts they observe. If we are in philosophy, he says, then we have to throw out the occult—throw out the demons and the ghosts and the devils and the angels, all of which we believe on faith, but that's theology, not philosophy. In philosophy, we go by facts. And he uttered in this connection a truly famous principle: *Entia non sunt multiplicanda sum praeter necessitate*, i.e., "Entities are not to be multiplied beyond necessity," a principle known as Occam's Razor. The meaning is: Do not make up arbitrary entities and then appeal to them as explanations for facts. If you can explain a fact strictly by appealing to natural entities, the things you observe, do not multiply entities uselessly and start appealing to a whole galaxy of disreputable supernatural entities. And it's called Occam's Razor because it cuts out that whole occult dimension. Occam's Razor has been very influential since his time, and, in the form in which I presented it to you, it's valid and very important. It depends, however, entirely for its interpretation on what you mean by "necessity"—it says entities are not to be multiplied *beyond necessity*. But if you start getting rid of entities right and left, whether they're necessary or not, on the grounds of Occam's Razor, then you cut your throat with Occam's Razor. And that is what all the moderns do with it, use it in ways that Occam wouldn't have dreamed of doing. But as Occam intended, it's a valid and important principle.

I might note finally on Occam that he carried the voluntarism of Duns Scotus to its consistent extreme. God, he said, is not limited even by the law of identity, and therefore, it's senseless to try to make sense of theology. God could have commanded even the opposite of the Ten Commandments. He could have made murder a virtue. He could have made lusting after your neighbor's wife a virtue. He could have made hating God a virtue. And if he had, then it would be our religious duty to practice those activities. The commandments that we have as of now are just a function of God's arbitrary will and have to be accepted on faith. Again, there's no use trying to make sense of God by reason.

Reason and Faith

By this point, there's an unbridgeable gulf between faith and reason. The final seal on this gulf was placed by the rampant mystics of the period, of which there were many. You may have heard of Meister Eckhart, a rampant, frenetic, bizarre medieval mystic beloved of the Nazis many centuries later. And you may have heard of Nicholas of Cusa. These men agreed that sensation is the basis of human knowledge, and that reason is based on sense experience. Therefore, they said, reason can know only this world. If we want to know God, we need a super-Neoplatonic, mystic, ecstatic union with the transcendent unspeakable dimension. That position reinforced the view that if you're going to go by reason, you'd better say goodbye to God. If you want a taste of what these mystics offered, here is Windelband's summary of one of the typical mystic doctrines of this period:

> The goal of all life is the knowledge of God, but knowing is being; it is the community of life and of being with that which is known. If the soul would know God, it must *be* God; it must cease to be itself. It must renounce not only sin in the world, but itself also. It must strip off all its acquired knowledge, as the Deity is nothing, so it is apprehended only in this knowledge that is a not knowing. And as nothing, that nothing, is the original ground of all reality, so this not-knowing is the highest, the most blessed contemplation.[30]

So you see how stuff like this would drive people to reason and away from theology.

I'll mention one more step in the collapse of the medievals' precarious attempt to reconcile faith and reason, and that was the doctrine of the "twofold truth," as it was called. It was accepted by many people, including the followers of Averroes (the twelfth-century Mohammedan Aristotelian commentator I referred to). The doctrine of twofold truth held that faith and reason were inherently in conflict, in contradiction, and that there are two orders of truth, the truth in theology and the truth in philosophy, and that the very same idea can be true in philosophy but false in theology, and vice versa. This was a charter of liberty to all the thinkers who used it. They could pursue the boldest course intellectually, come up with doctrines in blatant

30. Wilhelm Windelband, *A History of Philosophy*, Volume I (New York: Harper, 1958), p. 337.

defiance of the Church teachings, and when the authorities raced in to challenge them, they would say, "I'm not challenging the Church. My doctrines are true in philosophy, but they're not true in theology. There are two truths." You see how this helped further to secularize philosophy, to make it the subject of reason.

In the doctrine of twofold truth, you see the ultimate result of Aquinas's forlorn attempt to reconcile reason and faith. The two have come to confront each other as naked opponents. But there's a deeper epistemological reason why such a clash *had* to develop, why it's hopeless to attempt to reconcile faith and reason, even on the lines attempted by Aquinas, and his was the noblest and best attempt. Remember that Aquinas had said there'll never be a conflict, because faith can speak only where reason is silent, where the evidence for or against something is nonexistent, and therefore we fill in the gaps by faith. Now, what is wrong with this? The answer is: Reason is *never* silent—it always has something to say. When there is no evidence *for* a viewpoint, then the principle of reason is the onus of proof principle, which is that the onus of proof is on the man who asserts that something exists, the man who asserts the positive. If there's no evidence for the positive, your rational obligation is to accept the negative and say, in that context of knowledge, the thing doesn't exist. That's the rational position.

To tell a man that he can have faith in the positive because there's no evidence either way, is therefore to tell him he must violate the method of reason at its root. In other words, he must violate the commitment to going by evidence. And such a contradiction of reason at its root will necessarily express itself sooner or later throughout the content of your conclusions, so that faith will come out as in systematic conflict with reason. In essence, you cannot combine faith with reason, any more than you can combine God with this world, or Aristotle's ethics with the Sermon on the Mount. It is one or the other across the board. As soon as this discovery developed firmly enough in enough people, we reach that attitude of mind that led to the Renaissance. The attempt to apply reason to God had failed in spite of centuries of effort, and men's alternatives were increasingly either to revert to Tertullian (and some of them did, as we'll see shortly) or else to turn their reason away from God and back to this earth. Aristotle's treatises had shown them how much you could learn about the physical world just by observing and studying it, which was a revolutionary discovery in that era and irresistible to the better minds after the centuries of barren Scholasticism. There was an awakening of Aristotle's scientific mood and interests. Men began to expend their energies in behalf of life on earth, to observe, to reason, to invent, to explore, progressively to seek their own self-development, their own welfare, and to discover how much was possible to them on earth. Here's an eloquent summary:

> In the Middle Ages, it is fair to say man had submitted to nature as he found her. It had not occurred to him that he could control her and by harnessing her to his uses, improve his natural lot. Or when the possibility of such control *did* enter his mind, it appeared as magic, and all attempts to actualize it were promptly condemned by the Church as an invocation of Satan's aid against God's purposes, and as the practice of a black art. But now the discovery that nature could be manipulated at will by experiment, and thus made subservient to human ends, was sure to be followed by the discovery that her forces could be mastered and her ways altered by man to suit his preferences.
>
> This awakened sense of power over nature went hand in hand with the sense of the self-sufficiency and dignity of the natural man, which was one of the great characteristics of the Renaissance. . . . The 14th century is as much a prologue to the Renaissance as it is an epilogue to medieval thought. It was astir with the naturalism, scientific, moral and philosophical, that was to color and direct the thinking of the next two centuries. It was groping towards the great discoveries in astronomy and physics which were so soon to be made, and which were so profoundly to influence the new speculation. It had prepared their advent and their acceptance by breaking in large measure the shackles of the past. It had sown the seeds of doubt, respecting the necessity of reckoning with anything supernatural in the conduct and the salvation of human life. It had asserted the power of the unaided human reason to work out satisfactory solutions of the manifold problems with which humanity was confronted.[31]

When this attitude sunk in deeply enough in enough minds, the Middle Ages were over, and the rebirth began. And so, we have reached the Renaissance.

The Renaissance

The Renaissance is essentially the era of the fifteenth and sixteenth centuries. By the time you reach the late sixteenth century, early seventeenth, you're out of the Renaissance and into the modern world, into specifically

31. Fuller, *History of Philosophy*, pp. 428 and 431.

the beginning of modern philosophy as a distinctive development. Some people date the Renaissance from 1453, but that is preposterous. You may as well say it started at high noon on a Tuesday. It's a fundamental philosophic attitude, and it stretches across centuries, the fifteenth and sixteenth centuries.

In *Atlas Shrugged*, Ayn Rand writes, "The road of human history was a string of blank-outs over sterile stretches eroded by faith and force with only a few brief bursts of sunlight when the released energy of the men of the mind performed the wonders you gaped at, admired and promptly extinguished again." In our survey of the Dark and Middle Ages, we have just come through a long sterile stretch eroded by faith and force. Now it is our pleasure to examine the achievements of one of the few bursts of sunlight in human history. Our pleasure is going to be diluted, because we'll see the seeds of the next era of faith and force being planted again right from the beginning. We'll see the forces at work to extinguish the wonders released during this period. But let's at least look briefly at the wonders.

Philosophically, the Renaissance is an age dominated by three fundamental tenets: In metaphysics, this world is fully real and intelligible to man. In epistemology, man's means of knowledge is sense experience and reason based on the senses. In ethics, the goal of life is happiness on earth to be achieved by developing one's capacities and one's intellect to the fullest. All of these are Aristotelian, passed on by Aquinas. In this sense, the Renaissance is at root an Aristotelian period. I said it, and I say again—it was not complete, it was not consistent. You would be shocked at how religious they were in the Renaissance in comparison to the atheism that is the essential undercurrent of twentieth-century Western civilization. They believed in God and the Bible, the Church, the afterlife, faith, revelation—the whole bit—but it was no longer the dominant cultural force. The attitude was, "Yes, this is all true, but now let's get down to business." As a *cultural* force, mysticism died in the Renaissance. There's a danger in thus accepting but putting to one side all of this religion. For one thing, it prevents people from forming a rational new ethics. And the Renaissance in that respect was a chaotic, licentious, brutal, deceitful age. People didn't put forth a new ethics; instead, they blindly rebelled against the old one, and they became Sophists in reaction to Plato (that's what it amounts to). And that then gives ample room for people to say: "You see what happens when you leave religion. We need to reassert the old code." So, I don't mean to suggest that this is a safe view. In fact, it's this view that ultimately led to the downfall of the Renaissance.

Nevertheless, let us look at some of the achievements of the Renaissance.

Perhaps its greatest achievement was its view of the ideal man. The ideal man was no longer Saint Francis. The emphasis was on all-around development of man's faculties—on human dignity, self-respect, pride, culture, achievement. Man was regarded as a self-sufficient, responsible, independent entity, and he should fulfill his potentialities for reason.

Leonardo da Vinci

I can't resist paying a brief tribute in passing to the man who is to the Renaissance what Saint Francis is to the medieval period: *Leonardo da Vinci* (1452–1519). He is not a philosopher, only a universal genius. But needless to say, it is not the case that everyone in the Renaissance was like him, any more than that everyone in the medieval period was like Saint Francis. But they are two perfect symbols to contrast two different views of life. While one was doing all the things I'm about to read, the other was busy drinking laundry water and plunging into snow heaps. Here is B.A.G. Fuller's description of Leonardo, under the heading "Universal Genius":

> Strong, handsome, skilled in all athletic exercises, an accomplished musician, completely a man of the world, the friend of kings and princes and endowed with an extraordinary personal charm and magnetism—Leonardo would by these qualities alone have satisfied the standards set for the perfect Renaissance gentleman. Clad, however, in this outward magnificence walked probably the most universal genius of all time. [Peikoff: I enter the brief demur of Aristotle there.][32]

And then he discusses Leonardo's painting, his work in architecture, military innovations, his system of canals, his efforts to invent flying machines, submarine boats, devices for enabling man to walk on water. And then he continues: "Leonardo was not simply a supreme artist and inventive genius; his inventions, like his art, were incidental to a consuming curiosity regarding the structure and operations of nature."

And then he goes on to detail Leonardo's discoveries in the field of pure science—his investigations of the laws of perspective and chiaroscuro. He

---

32. Fuller, *History of Philosophy*, p. 11.

was led to the verge of the laws of inertia and acceleration, the molecular theory of liquids, the undulatory theory of light and of sound, etc., etc. There isn't even time to itemize the table of contents. And what was his attitude to the Church?

> Although he lived and died at peace with the Church, Leonardo, like many another man of the Renaissance, took his Catholicism with a grain of salt. By temperament a spectator, he was amused or disgusted, rather than outraged, by the abuses that were so soon to precipitate the Protestant and the Counter-Reformation. But he openly expresses his contempt of the monks, of the cultus of the Virgin and the Saints, and of the sale of indulgences, discredits the story of the flood, and apparently denies the Divinity of Christ. His whole attitude is summed up in his remark that if we are doubtful of the evidence of our senses, we may well be still more doubtful of things of which there is no sensible evidence, like the being of God and the soul and other such things about which people are always disputing and contradicting one another.[33]

And jumping to his conclusions:

> Such was Leonardo da Vinci, courtier, athlete, musician, painter, sculptor, architect, hydraulic-civil-mechanical engineer, military and naval engineer; inventor, mathematician, physicist, astronomer, geologist, biologist, botanist, physiologist, philosopher—a mind forever voyaging through strange seas of thought alone.[34]

When you reach a period where such a man is possible and universally admired, you are not in the medieval period anymore.

I won't say anything about the artistic accomplishments of the Renaissance. Look at a series of medieval paintings, and then look at something by Michelangelo, and that will speak much more eloquently than any lecture I can give you. I do want to say a word about the inventions of this period. It was during this period that the compound microscope was invented, the telescope, thermometer, the barometer, and the air pump. Clocks were greatly improved, and all of this precise instrumentation made possible the development of modern science. The crucial invention was Gutenberg's printing press, which made the communication of ideas open to virtually

---

33. Fuller, *History of Philosophy*, p. 15.
34. Fuller, *History of Philosophy*, p. 16.

everybody, as against the medieval period, where you had costly monk-copied, hand-copied manuscripts. The printing press was the catalyst that made thought result in action in a speed and in a manner unprecedented hitherto. It took Christianity four centuries from Jesus until the time of its dominance because it couldn't use the printing press. It took Marx much less time. (It wasn't *only* the printing press; he had all the centuries of Christianity to rely on.) But still, the whole intellectual process has been enormously speeded up since the printing press, and television is a continuation of that phenomenon. What the printing press did was open up the possibility of education and the world of thought to everybody, rather than just the rich.

As to exploration, this is also the period when the surface of the earth was opened up. In 1492, as you know, Columbus discovered the new continent, America. During this period, Vasco da Gama rounded the Cape of Good Hope, and Magellan founded an expedition that resulted in the circumnavigation of the globe. You can't underestimate the importance of that either, the impact of it. When Columbus took off, everybody told him that he'd fall off the end of the world, because the world was flat: If you went too far, you'd go off the end. Man was regarded as having an absolutely circumscribed position beyond which he must not venture. According to something I read, Columbus had a mapmaker, and for all the parts whose location wasn't known, they put the word "Terror" on the map. His principle was, "Where unknown, there place 'Terror.'" And you can get an idea of what the world was like. It was in the Renaissance that for the first time we had the idea of a wide-open intelligible world in the narrowest physical sense. The map came to be known, it was safe to take voyages, and the world was open to man's conquest and enjoyment. Even picnics are a Renaissance phenomenon, where you go out and commune with nature and enjoy the grass as an end in itself, not because you want to give testimony to God's horticultural powers.

On the social-political level, with the loss of the authority of the Church (a loss abetted by the Protestants), you find the rise of the nation-state. So, it becomes meaningful to talk of France, Germany, England, as against Christendom. National languages progressively became fashionable, and that was helped by the printing press. Gradually, the monastic Latin fell into decay. The feudal order broke up. Money began to be used for investment, economic profit became a goal, trade became freer and on a comparatively worldwide basis. It is not, as some alleged historians say, a period of capitalism. It is a period of absolute monarchy, politically. There were still social classes, aristocracy by law, and so on. All that you can say is that the guild feudal system was definitely breaking up, and *with* America and the Industrial Revolution, capitalism did come into existence. But that is still several centuries away. Nevertheless, the Renaissance was a comparatively freer period politically. It was less status-conscious than the medieval, more individualistic. It was not the freedom of the stability of a rational constitution, but the freedom of chaos. But at least it had it to that extent. The groundwork began slowly to be laid for what would centuries later become capitalism and the United States.

The Protestant Reformation (Martin Luther and John Calvin)

Now let us look at the big religious development in the Renaissance, and that is the Protestant Reformation. The famous names associated with this are Martin Luther (1483–1546) and John Calvin (1509–1564). You must have heard of the abuses of the Catholic Church, the tyranny of the clergy, their amassing of wealth by exactions from the populace, the sale of indulgences, promising Heavenly forgiveness if only you paid enough money, and that goes for your dear departed ones in the other world also—if you paid enough, you could promote them in Heaven. I'll give you an idea of what went on in the medieval period under the Catholics (note the hierarchy of values): "In 1517, the following scale of fees was charged. For an indulgence in the case of sodomy, 12 ducats; for sacrilege, 9 ducats; for murder, 7; for witchcraft, 6, and so on down the line." Here is a sentence or two from one of Johann Tetzel's sermons (he was a dispenser of these indulgences): "Do you not hear your dead parents crying out, 'Have mercy upon us—we are in sore pain and you can set us free for a mere pittance. We have born you, we have trained you and educated you, we have left you all our property, and you are so hard-hearted and cruel that you leave us to roast in the flames when you could so easily release us.'" That's what you call a religious abuse. And there was all the hypocrisy, the reliance on pomp and sacraments and rituals so that God fell into the background. There was the blatant corruption of the Papacy. Leo IX in the sixteenth century is supposed to have said to his brother, "God has given us the Papacy. Let us enjoy it."

That is what the Reformation was rebelling against, and it caught on. Monks deserted their monasteries, priests got married, churches were invaded, the images were broken, the rituals were parodied, and Christianity was irrevocably split in two between its Catholic wing and its Protestant wing.

What was the philosophy of Protestantism? It really had no organized, systematized philosophy. Its basic principle was the right of each man to read the Bible and commune with God directly and personally, to understand God's message on his own and in his own way, without benefit of clergy or formalized systems of dogma, particularly without benefit of Thomism or Scholasticism, which Luther was violently opposed to. I may say that, initially, the persecutions by the Protestants of dissenters were as strong, if not stronger, than those of the Catholics. But eventually, their very lack of formalized dogma proved a liberating influence as well as a significant factor contributing to freedom of thought. There were sects continually splitting off or forming new interpretations, and without a formalized dogma, you couldn't accuse these sects of heresy and sin. And if you look at Protestantism, you see the endless proliferation of sects, as against Catholicism, which has rigid control over what you can and can't believe.

You may be surprised to learn that the actual philosophy of the founders of Protestantism, people like Luther and Calvin, was a reversion to the very, very worst of the medieval views—to Augustine and beyond. Luther linked the corruption of the Church to its Aristotelianism, with its this-worldly attitude. He thought that Aristotle was monstrous, and he referred to him at one point as "that damnable, proud, cunning heathen Aristotle." He wanted a real uncompromising religion, and he sure got it. He all but outdid Augustine in preaching that man was thoroughly depraved and sinful, absolutely dependent on God's mercy for entering Heaven—there was nothing man could do on his own to earn entry into Heaven—everything was rigidly predestined, completely determined. He wrote, "I wish the word 'free will' had never been invented." Everything is completely a function of God's plan, and man is entirely at God's mercy. His doctrine was that works are unimportant (in other words, what you do and how you live are not essential, but that what is important is that you have faith and believe in God and in the gospels). Faith over works is Luther's big principle: Faith unadulterated by reason, ritual, or action was the cardinal tenet. And, under the influence of Luther, Protestant theologians to this day (like Reinhold Niebuhr, for instance) are infinitely worse than Catholic theologians, who are still to some extent controlled by Thomas Aquinas.

The best thing to see what Luther advocated is to let him speak for himself, because he writes clearly, and whatever you say about him, he's not mealy-mouthed. In epistemology: "Aristotle is to theology as dark is to light." What about reason? "Reason is the Devil's harlot, and can do nothing but slander and harm all that God does and says. If, outside of

Christ, you wish by your own thoughts to know your relation to God, you will break your neck. Thunder strikes him who examines. It is Satan who tells us what God is, and by doing so, he will draw you into the abyss. Therefore, keep to revelation and do not try to understand." Pretty clear. He says in his *Lectures on the First Psalm*: "Whoever wants to be a Christian must tear the eyes out of his Reason." And that's true. What about his metaphysics? Well, "We are not masters of our actions; from the beginning to the end, we are slaves." In other words, complete determinism. "Free will after the Fall is nothing but a word." In other words, Adam had free will, but it's gone now. "Man must completely despair of himself in order to become fit to obtain the grace of Christ. This false idea of free will is a real threat to salvation, and a delusion fraught with the most perilous consequences." He's a full-fledged voluntarist, as you would expect—"God is inscrutable and unknowable will. Of God's will there is no cause nor reason. There is nothing equal or superior to it. It in itself is the rule of all things. If there were for it any rule or measure or cause or reason, it wouldn't be the will of God. Not because he *ought* to will thus is that right which he wills; on the contrary, because he wills thus is that right which he wills." That's the straight voluntarist position.

What about man? "By nature, all of us are liars born of original sin in blindness." If you're that rotten, what should you do? "Cursed and condemned is every kind of life lived and sought for selfish profit and good. Cursed are all works not done in love, but they are done in love when they are directed wholeheartedly not toward selfish pleasure, profit, honor and welfare, but toward the profit, honor and welfare of others." What happens to your body is unimportant. "Of what benefit is it to the soul that the body is free, is hale and hearty, that it eats, drinks, and lives as it pleases? On the other hand, what harm comes to the soul from the fact that the body is in bondage, is sick and weary, hungers, thirsts, suffers? The influence of none of these things extends to the soul." And therefore, don't worry about the body. Politically, as you would expect, Luther is a rabid authoritarian. Just a brief quote: "Fear and trust God. God has commanded that you should honor the government. Even if you despise the government for other reasons, you dare not do so any longer because of the word of God." Governments are ordained by God and your duty is absolute blind obedience to the secular power. Beyond that, Luther was a fervent German nationalist, a fervent anti-Semite. From his *On the Jews and Their Lies*: "Fie on you, fie on you, wherever you be, you damned Jews, who dare to clasp this earnest glorious consoling word of God to your maggoty mortal miserly belly, and are not ashamed to display your greed so openly."

Paradoxically, the ultimate result of all this was positive because the lack of a formalized dogma—the emphasis on the liberty of the individual conscience—was enormously anti-authoritarian. It broke up the monopoly of the Catholic Church, and Protestantism could never establish an equivalent monopoly. Moreover, the philosophy of Protestantism, and particularly its morality, is so extreme, so anti-reason, so anti-life, that it can't be lived by. And the emphasis on faith over works suggests you don't *have* to live by it. It's not *how* you live, it's what your faith is that counts, so that the effect of Protestantism was to separate religion and life. Aquinas had tried to reconcile reason and religion so that you could actually practice religion here on earth. Protestantism separated the two so far that you had to live your life without much reference to religion, and then go to church on Sundays. And the result is that, although Protestantism philosophically is much worse that Catholicism (given Aquinas), Protestant countries are generally more this-earth, more independent, more rational, and more productive than Catholic countries. And so you have England, the United States, and Germany for instance, as against Italy, Spain, and South America. (France, I may say, is untypical in this respect.) So much for Luther. Hitler knew perfectly well what he was doing when he made Luther's birthday an official Nazi holiday.

Continuing with the Renaissance, our theme now is the rediscovery of antiquity. Just as the spatial boundaries on earth were opened up, so were the frontiers of time opened up. In the Dark Ages, as you know, men in the West were ignorant of the ancient world and its achievements. By the time of the Renaissance, antiquity was rediscovered in all of its glory. They unearthed the manuscripts of the pagans, they translated them, and virtually everything we have today came to be known during the Renaissance. And almost all the schools of the ancient world flourished again. There were the standard controversies between the Aristotelians, the Platonists, the Neoplatonists, the Pythagoreans, the Atomists, the Epicureans, the Stoics, the Sophists, the Skeptics. For the two hundred years of the modern world, until the seventeenth century, there was nothing new philosophically. That period consists of the revival of Greek philosophies and the supplanting of the medieval tradition. Sometimes put, it's the period when the West went to school for two centuries, to the schools of ancient Greece, relearning what was known in the ancient world. There were still theologians and Scholastics in abundance, but their time was progressively up.

Such philosophy as there was during the Renaissance, you may be surprised to learn, was Platonism in one form or another. There was every kind of view that the world is the body of God, pantheism, Neoplatonism, excessive mysticism, a lot of alchemy, magic. It was an eclectic, chaotic period intellectually, with a pronounced bent toward Platonism. Why? The answer is a tragic, tragic irony: Aristotle was identified as the philosopher of the Scholastics, the philosopher of the Catholic Church, owing to the Scholastics' appropriation of him. And consequently, the rebellion against the Church and against Catholicism took the form of a rebellion against Aristotle, whom almost everybody package-dealt with the Church. And this is one of the most tragic ironies in history, from which we are suffering to this day. And it will explain why superficial commentators refer to the Renaissance as the period in which Platonism rules and Aristotle is supplanted. Poets had the effrontery to write poems on the hero who slayed the tyrant Aristotle. This package-deal was deliberately fostered by the Church. They would sometimes take specific theories from Aristotle's physics—not his philosophy, but his physics—theories which Aristotle would have been the first to abandon if he'd seen the evidence against them, and then the Scholastics would refuse to consider the evidence, blindly adhere to Aristotle's specific scientific theories in the face of overwhelming evidence to the contrary, and proceed to persecute, torture, and even kill the scientists of the period "in the name of Aristotle."

Many of the deaths of the Inquisition were perpetrated in the name of Aristotelianism. For instance, Pietro Pomponazzi, a good Aristotelian of the period, had a disciple, Vanini, who was burned at the stake. Giordano Bruno, who preached that the earth is not at the center of the Heavens, was burned at the stake. Tommaso Campanella, a strongly religious mystical Platonist, was sentenced to twenty-seven years in jail. Galileo was forced to recant his views. It was not just the specific incorrect scientific or astronomical theories of Aristotle, moreover, that the Church did this with. The *philosophic* ideas of Aristotle were thoroughly distorted to mean something quite different from what Aristotle had meant, and then used allegedly in the name of Aristotle to fight the scientists and the independent thinkers. For instance, you remember that Aristotle had said that there are self-evident axioms, but he had gone on to say that these must be carefully defined, based on sensory evidence, limited to those that you can prove objectively to be self-evident. But in the hands of many Church Aristotelians (not the Thomists), it turned into the idea that we can start from any premises which appeal to us and erect floating systems regardless of observational evidence, and if one of these systems is opposed by factual evidence, so much the worse for the evidence. You have no idea the mentalities at work here. For instance, Galileo discovered the four moons of Jupiter—prior to that there had only been five planets, the sun, and the moon. In other words, seven heavenly bodies (not counting the stars). But seven is a sacred number—the Sabbath is the seventh day, candlesticks have seven branches, there are seven major churches in Asia, and so on. Some people refused to look through the telescope. Here's a quote from a professor of philosophy at Padua, who refused to look through Galileo's telescope to see the satellites of Jupiter: "There are seven windows given to animals in the domicile of the head [Peikoff: two eyes, two nostrils, the mouth, two ears—seven]. From this and many other similarities in nature, such as the seven metals, etc., which it would be tedious to enumerate, we gather that the number of planets is necessarily seven. Moreover, these alleged satellites of Jupiter are invisible to the naked eye [Peikoff: Get the progression here.] and therefore can exercise no influence on the earth, and therefore would be useless, and therefore do not exist. Besides, from the earliest times, men have adopted the division of the week into seven days and have named them after the seven planets. If we increase the number of planets, this whole and beautiful system falls to the ground."[35]

When this sort of thing passes for Aristotelianism, it is no wonder that there is a rebellion. But then it's not a rebellion against Aristotle, regardless of what it's called.

During the Renaissance, this rebellion took two predominant forms. One trend, as I already mentioned, was the Platonist trend—nothing original at all, just eclectic mystical Platonism. The second was the rebellion of the scientists, the men who were on the premise of opposition to books, systems, theories, whether Aristotelian, Platonist, or any other. Let us go to the facts, as they put it—let us study the book of nature, not the books of men. Let us sweep aside all the traditional views and go to the things themselves for an unprejudiced examination of their character by observation and unaided reason. Let's start from scratch, scrap everything, and found philosophy and science once and for all on firm foundations. Of course, the men of science, in spite of themselves, were influenced by philosophy—they couldn't escape it—in part, insofar as they were truly scientists, they were influenced by Aristotle but also in part, unfortunately, by Plato

---

35. Although this "reasoning" has been attributed to "some Paduan philosophers," the generally accepted source is Francesco Sizzi, a seventeenth-century Italian astronomer.

and Platonism, which was everywhere in the atmosphere.

These two trends interacted. The Platonists had to make terms with science, and their great attempt was Descartes. As for the scientists, I'm sorry that I can't call them Aristotelians, because they were mixed from the beginning, and they slowly, gradually merged into the Sophist school centuries later (that is to say, the philosophers of science—the working scientists, not so badly). We're going to look at science now and continue with it after some lectures on Descartes and his followers. But now I want to turn to the development of modern science, and I'd like you to look at both the good and the bad developments in the philosophy of modern science as it developed. It was, of course, science, the great achievement of this period, and the most influential philosophically. Let's look at a few of the key figures and spokesmen for the new science.

Copernicus

Copernicus (1474–1543). We've talked about opening up the world, and this is the key to the times. If the Kennedy administration hadn't taken it over, I would say the slogan of the Renaissance is "New Frontiers." Invention unlocks the secrets of nature, exploration unlocks the surface of the earth, research unlocks antiquity—and Copernicus unlocked the astronomical universe. You know the old geocentric view of the earth at the center and the hollow spheres inside each other with the heavenly bodies implanted in them, revolving around them—that was Aristotle's view. Copernicus did not invent the heliocentric view, the view that the sun is at the center—that was known in antiquity—but he made popular the view that the sun is at the center of the solar system and the earth revolves around it. This thought led others (Giordano Bruno, for example) to the view that there was nothing especially privileged about man's solar system, that there was an endless number of such systems, and that the universe was an infinite collection of bodies—that space was infinite, and the earth counted for very little in the cosmic scheme of things. The significance of this was that man no longer had a metaphysically privileged place in the universe. The earth was no longer the center of the universe. The protective crystalline spheres were shattered, and an open endless physical universe awaited discovery. There are commentators who say that this showed man's unimportance. Not true. Man had *discovered* it. It was a triumph of the intellect. But what this heliocentric view *did* have an effect on was religion—the Bible story of creation, the view that this earth was a stage setting for the enactment of God's drama and that God spent his time watching the proceedings. This view never recovered from the Copernican Revolution. If it's an endless universe with endless worlds, God, people began to think, just hasn't got the time to sit around watching some species on a remote planet lost in infinite space. The Copernican Revolution, in that sense, was an astronomical knife in the back to religion. The only other comparable knife was Darwin in the nineteenth century.

I hasten to add that you cannot refute religion on scientific grounds. Religion is a philosophic issue, and Copernicus does not refute the existence of God. The way was open immediately for religious people to incorporate Copernicus and say, "God is infinite, so he can watch Adam and Eve on an infinite number of planets, and therefore, the fact that earth is just one tiny speck in the universe doesn't mean he isn't interested." All that Copernicus really affected were fundamentalists, who interpreted the Scriptures literally, and that is inessential to philosophy. But it was a serious setback for religion and for the reasons I've mentioned.

I should also mention Tycho Brahe (1546–1601), who made a host of observations and measurements of an astronomical nature and William Gilbert (1544–1603), who inaugurated the scientific study of magnetism.

Johannes Kepler

Let's now take a look at Johannes Kepler (1571–1630). Kepler discovered the laws of planetary motion, building on Tycho Brahe's data. He discovered that the planets move around the sun in *ellipses*, which was an enormous shock, because the Greeks had always said the circle is the perfect figure. And when they found that the planets don't go in circles, everybody was staggered. And that was an enormous impetus to observation and scientific study of the world because the message was: Think what you can learn by actually studying the facts. Moreover, Kepler discovered that the speed with which the planets move can be calculated mathematically according to certain simple laws that govern all the planets. Wherever he looked, he saw mathematical relationships of the most surprising kind—*mathematical* relationships. For instance, the planets were known to speed up and slow down in their courses around the sun, and the issue was how to find any regularity in their changes of velocity. If the medieval world had known about it, they would have looked for an answer on this order: "Well, when it's hot, they go faster, and when it's cold, they go slower; or when it's dark, they go faster, and when it's light, they go slower" (assuming that they had even tried to explain it, and not just say God willed it). Kepler found a mathematical law dealing with numbers and geometrical figures. He found that if you draw a line from the focus of the ellipse—the point where the sun is—to the orbit of the planet, and another line to another point on the orbit, you will have a triangle. Do the same with another two points and you get another triangle. And he found that if the two triangles are equal in area, then the times required for the planet to go from the first point to the second are the same, in other words, equal areas are swept out in equal times. This was absolutely unsuspected. Imagine, the planets function according to geometrical figures, their speed a function of the area that they sweep out. He also discovered that every planet takes a certain amount of time to circle the sun—call it T in appropriate units—and it has an average distance from the sun—call it D. For each planet, you'll get two different numbers. He worked it out and he found out that it invariably is the case that T-squared equals D-cubed. If you multiply the time by itself, and the distance by itself, you get the equality. You must not underestimate the utter shock of this discovery, that simple numerical geometrical relationships govern the laws of nature. This was absolutely unexpected, and yet it took place. And you'll see what happens to it in a moment. In that sense, Kepler is enormously important to the development of science and philosophy, because of discovering the first crucial mathematical laws.

Francis Bacon

Let's look at Francis Bacon (1561–1626) (the one who did *not* write Shakespeare's works). He is not so much a scientist as a philosopher of science, one of the first spokesmen for the new science. And as such, he is not an originator, but a very eloquent formulator of many of the ideas that were germinating in the scientific world. Here are some of his key ideas. One famous line of his, "Knowledge is power." This is an attitude that he did not originate, but the attitude that it expresses is a new phenomenon in the Western world. It is in contrast to the medieval world, and in contrast to the ancient world, even Aristotle. Remember, Aristotle had held that scientific knowledge is an end in itself—you contemplate simply for the satisfaction of your curiosity. Bacon expresses the attitude of the Renaissance: Knowledge is not an end in itself, it is *power*. If you have enough knowledge of the laws of nature, you can remake the world to serve human purposes. Nature is not something to be gazed at passively, but something to be used and exploited to satisfy human goals. Man becomes an *active* creature, rather than a passive, tranquil observer. This is an indispensable contribution of the Renaissance to human thought. Without it, the Industrial Revolution would have been impossible. By itself, it's not enough—you also needed political freedom for the Industrial Revolution—but this attitude that knowledge is power is a mark of the modern mind, not of the ancient or medieval mind. And as a consequence, Bacon held (as did the people of this period) that if we study nature, we can make limitless progress. There are endless new vistas to discover and new things to invent and new improvements to make in human life. Again, this contrasts radically not only with the medieval view, but with the Greek view. Both Plato and Aristotle had the idea, being at the very beginning of knowledge, that everything essentially was known, that perfection so far as man could achieve it was reached, and that there was no more progress, simply a static situation, remaining at the level already attained. The idea of permanent progress in human development is a Renaissance contribution.

Another crucial idea of Bacon's: "Nature, to be commanded, must be obeyed." If you want to achieve your goals and get what you want from nature, you must understand its laws and obey them. There's no use praying or trying to get around nature. If you want to *produce* a certain effect, you have to know the cause, and if you want to *remove* a certain effect, you have to know what cause to eliminate. A very, very pregnant crucial aphorism—"Nature, to be commanded, must be obeyed"—one of the best aphorisms in the entire history of thought.

We must, says Bacon, have the right methodology, the right means of acquiring knowledge. We must know how to learn. This is again a typically modern attitude. Ancient and medieval philosophy, although they have a great deal to say on epistemology, are dominantly centered on metaphysics as the crucial branch of philosophy. Modern philosophy centers on epistemology as the dominant branch of philosophy. Modern philosophers, with a few exceptions, are highly conscious of the theory of knowledge. They are highly conscious that before you go into "What is the universe like?," you have to first validate your method of knowing it. And therefore, progressively, epistemology comes to dominate the scene—to the point of insanity in the form it takes in twentieth-century movements, where metaphysics is thrown out altogether and philosophy is exclusively epistemology. But this emphasis on epistemology goes all the way back to the Renaissance. Again, I stress that the Greeks were interested in epistemology, but they were not *centered* on epistemology the way most philosophers were from the time of the Renaissance.

As to Bacon's epistemology, he says that we have to break clean from all the errors of the past. And he could quote the Bible here—"Except as ye become as little children, ye shall not enter the Kingdom of Heaven." We have to become like little children, epistemologically. Almost everything that we believe is wrong. We are seduced right and left by prejudices, superstitions, faulty methods of thinking, which plunge us into fallacies of all kinds. So, he proceeded to define four categories of errors that we have to get rid of, which he called the "Four Idols." This is presented in every elementary text on the history of philosophy, so I'll zip through it quickly.

There are the Idols of the Tribe. Those are the ones, the fallacies, that he believed are inherent in human nature as such, i.e., they derive from belonging to the tribe of mankind. For instance, the tendency to treat abstractions as things, e.g., (using modern examples) to talk about "the state" or "society" or "Washington" as though it were an entity. Or the tendency to reject evidence that doesn't conform to your particular pet viewpoint and to look only for supporting evidence, and thus to engage in hasty generalizations. Or Bacon himself lists as one fallacy, one idol of the tribe, the deceptiveness of the senses, the tendency of human beings to rely on the senses, which he believes deceive us via illusions. He believes that if we correct them by instruments and experiments, they're okay. But you see this is already a crack in the door at the outset—here's the philosopher of science ambivalent about the validity of the senses.

Then there are the Idols of the Cave. Those are the fallacies deriving from the peculiar mental or physical constitution of each individual. Each person lives in a cave of his own, you see, with his own personal distortions over and above the ones that come from being a member of the human race. For instance, the tendency to interpret everything from the viewpoint of your own particular specialty. So a physicist, for instance, will characteristically say, "There is no such thing as mind; all that exists are the laws of mechanics," or a mathematician will say, "Ethics isn't a science, because you can't quantify it." Or the tendency of some people to be conservative (in the very broad sense here), "Everything new is bad," as opposed to other people to be "progressive," "Everything old is bad." That would be an idol of the cave.

Then there are the Idols of the Marketplace. Those are the fallacies that derive from the association of men with one another, and that means primarily from language, which is the medium of association. So that, for instance, because words exist, says Bacon, we think that things corresponding to those words must exist. People talk about fate, destiny, chance, fortune, and because they use those words, they think there are such things. That's an idol of the marketplace. And there are ambiguous and vague words that get people into trouble.

And finally, there are the Idols of the Theater, and these are the false ideas that have resulted from unsound systems of philosophy that have been widely accepted. He calls them "idols of the theater" because he regards previous philosophies as "stage plays representing worlds of their author's creation." He's being sarcastic about all previous philosophy and launches an all-out attack against previous philosophy, theology, intellectual tradition of all kinds. He is particularly virulent in his attack on Aristotle. In part, it is the very package-deal that we already observed—Aristotle is allegedly the Scholastic. In part, Bacon is opposed to the syllogism—it doesn't give you new knowledge. All it does is apply what we already know—"All men are mortal; therefore, Socrates is mortal." We need, says Bacon, a new method of arriving at knowledge, not a worthless method like the syllogism, which does nothing but tell us in our conclusion what we already knew in the premises anyway. Aristotle's logic had come to be called the *Organon*, which means "the instrument." Bacon wrote one called the *Novum Organum*, "the new instrument." And the new method that we have to use, he says, is not syllogism, but *induction*—we have to observe and generalize to arrive at laws. *This* is the way to acquire knowledge, not deduction or the syllogism. And I interject here: Aristotle, of course, recognized induction way before Bacon, and he was the one who defined it for the first time. Moreover, Bacon uses a syllogism to refute the syllogism. His argument is "Everything that doesn't teach you something new is worthless; the syllogism doesn't teach you something new; and, therefore, it's worthless." That's a syllogism. Has he learned something new from it or not? He's using the syllogism to attack it, as do all the opponents of the syllogism.

What I *will* say, however, is that Bacon made great improvements in the method and type of induction that had been used prior to his time. I don't believe that he originated this, but he is the formidable spokesman for a new theory of induction, in what came to be called *experimental induction*. The Greek method was called *induction by simple enumeration*, which means induction simply by enumerating examples—you see this man die, this man die, this man die, this man die, and after a while, you generalize and say, "All men are mortal," and so on. Simple enumeration was really the only method of induction known to Aristotle and the ancient world. And it has great problems. You might strike coincidences—this Chinese man is a laundryman, and this one is, and this one is; therefore, all Chinese men are laundrymen. And there may be exceptions to your rule, qualifying conditions that make it less than universal—this crow's black, and this one is, and this one is, but there may be an albino crow. And above all, simple enumeration leaves man passive—he has to sit around and wait for the instances to trot before his eyes. But the modern method of induction, of which Bacon is one of the early formulators, is not by simple enumeration, but by experimentation. Suppose you want to establish the value of a certain drug. If you go by enumeration, you never can get very far, because there are too many factors operating, and you don't know what is really responsible. Suppose you observe a thousand people take the drug and they get better. Was that due to the drug, or did they have some dietary factor in common, or did they belong to a certain race, or was it a normal process where the disease would heal itself no matter what? But the modern method is to control the variables—divide your subjects up into two groups, match them factor for factor (everything that might conceivably be relevant to the effect you're investigating), and then give the drug to one group and not the others (presumably you'd do it with rats and not with people in this case). And then, perhaps on the basis of maybe just twenty-five or fifty examples (if you've chosen your subjects appropriately), you can establish a causal connection and generalize a universal principle with a degree of certainty that you cannot approach if you follow ten thousand crows around and observe, "Yes, this is black, and this is black, and this is black, but what about the next one?" The method of controlled experiments—of subjecting all relevant factors to human control—and then systematically altering the one factor you're interested in to see what effects that will have—that was the method of experimentation. And it really is indispensable to any sound inductive method. It's not the whole story, but it's an important ingredient, and Bacon was one of the first formulators of this method. And you see again the emphasis on human activity. Just as knowledge is power, and, therefore, the goal of science is to go out and act and do something, so in method, man should go out and do something with the factors—control them, alter them, experiment—not wait passively for the instances to confront him. So again, that common denominator that man is an active being in goal and in method—that is a Renaissance contribution.

Notice that Bacon is still an empiricist—all knowledge rests on sensory observation and induction therefrom. There are, he agrees with Aristotle, no innate ideas. The world is lawful, reason can know the world, the world is worth knowing—all that is Aristotle, and in that sense Bacon is fundamentally Aristotelian. But his antagonism to deduction and his ambivalence on the senses is already a crack in the wall.

Galileo

Galileo (1564–1642) was the real founder of modern science. Isaac Newton was born the year that Galileo died, and between them, modern science reached its maturity.

Galileo discovered certain basic laws of motion governing all material bodies in the universe. One of them was the *law of falling bodies*: All bodies, no matter of what size or weight, fall with the same acceleration. Whether you drop a feather or a rock, they fall with the same acceleration (in a vacuum, of course). And this is mathematically measurable—it's thirty-two feet per second per second.

What became clear to Galileo before it became fully clear to anybody else was the crucial value of mathematics to science. That was prepared for in part by Kepler and others, but Galileo was the one who really gets the credit for it. He, more than anyone else, is the one who grasped that physics requires mathematics if it is to develop. Prior to this time, physics and mathematics were regarded essentially as two separate subjects, approximately the way today you regard esthetics and chemistry—you take one course from one professor, and one from another on different days, and they have the most tenuous, if any, connection. But you wouldn't get an esthetic chemistry, or a chemical esthetics. That was the position of mathematics in relation to physics until Galileo. Galileo was the man who created the concept of mathematical physics, and in that sense he is the father of modern science.

What was the value of mathematics? They observed that mathematics gave you an exactness that you couldn't get otherwise. If you say that something is long or hot or fast, you can't do very much with that knowledge. But if you say it's 10.2 feet, or 93.7 degrees, or it's moving at a rate of 32 feet per second—if you transfer a quality into a quantity—you have a precision in your knowledge of nature that is otherwise unattainable. And as a result, you can discover relationships in reality that you could never hope to discover on a qualitative basis. You could see things getting faster, but only if you measured exactly could you discover that acceleration under gravity is uniform. You can discover a law unexpected on the basis of observation, a precise mathematical law, and it turned out that these laws existed and were being discovered by scientists in all sorts of areas. As some of them put it (they all believed in God), it was if God was a mathematician and had built the universe on mathematical lines. And because precise laws had been discovered, combinations of them suggested still wider laws that would explain the earlier ones. And on the basis of a handful of mathematically formulated laws, Newton explained almost all phenomena in physics and astronomy then known (the discoveries of Kepler, Galileo, etc.). It appeared to them that if you tried to unravel the universe strictly in qualitative terms, you were limited to a few vague generalizations, like Aristotle with his earth, air, water, and fire, but if you approached it quantitatively, the whole universe opened up to human understanding. And as a result of this precision, exact predictions could be made, and therefore, knowledge became power—control over the world could be exerted in a way that would be unapproachable without mathematics. So that on the basis of Newton's discoveries, for instance, you could predict to the last fraction of a second when the apple would fall, how fast, where it would be each second, when the tides would rise and fall, how high, how fast, how the planets revolve, the path of the comets, the behavior of gasses—everything then known. Galileo, in sum, established that the true task of physics is to discover the mathematical relationships governing bodies in motion. And this was as fruitful an approach as could be dreamed of.

Here we have to give credit to Pythagoras, with his mystical world of numbers. Many of these scientists were Pythagoreans, and they looked for mathematical law even in the face of the belief of everybody else that it's hopeless and you'll never find it. They looked on the grounds that Pythagoras had said that all things are numbers, and if we look long enough, we'll have to find the numbers. For instance, Kepler was a Pythagorean, a really weird Pythagorean. Remember that the Pythagoreans in the ancient world believed that music was mathematical, and since everything was mathematical, they believed the heavenly bodies gave out music, the music of the spheres. They associated music and the heavens, because both were mathematical. Kepler goes so far as to identify the vocal range of each planet. For instance, Jupiter is a basso; Mars, a tenor; Venus, a soprano; Mercury, a falsetto; and the Earth sings "Mi fa mi," for "Misery, famine, misery." Now you see the fantastic combination of errant mysticism and modern science, and it's not a clean break by any means with mysticism. But we must say for the record that Pythagoras, in spite of all his mysticism, finally bore serious fruit.

Let us now take a look at the universe established by the scientists and contrast it with the medieval viewpoint. To begin with, modern science de-spiritualized nature. Science declared that physical nature was nothing but the movement of small bodies, of atoms, of which one movement is the cause of the other, operating according to simple, inexorable mathematical laws. There was no room left for spiritual powers of any kind—for supernatural powers, for occult powers—to operate. And here they used Occam's Razor. Entities are not to be multiplied beyond necessity. One can, the scientists said, explain the whole world strictly on the basis of matter in motion, so let's wipe out all spiritual entities in physical nature. Away with angels, devils, gods, world souls, essences. As a result, teleology was rejected. Mechanism was adopted. Teleology, remember, is the view that everything is purposive, everything aims or strives for some goal, which implies some of some kind of consciousness controlling things. And when they de-spiritualized the physical world, they abandoned teleology in favor of mechanism. The rallying cry was: There are no final causes in nature, only efficient causes. And again, in contrast to the Greeks and the medievals, they held the view that the whole universe is homogeneous. The Greeks and the medievals had tended to exalt the astronomical universe (the heavens) and to say that the part on earth was of lesser value, or different in kind. Even Aristotle held that view. Modern science said no, the universe is homogeneous throughout. The laws that apply to the heavens and the material that exists in the heavens are the same as the material and the laws of earth (which is our modern perspective). So you see here that it is the mechanistic, atomistic, materialism of Democritus that won out and became the philosophy of modern science. And these people were all influenced by the ancient Atomists.

I must point out that some of them (particularly the philosophers, not the scientists) tended to generalize, and they asked, why should the animals, why should man, be an exception to the principles that govern the entire physical universe? Man, too, must be simply matter in motion, and that's all. There's no distinction in principle between the animate and the inanimate. Mind can be explained materialistically and mechanistically as a kind of motion of material bodies according to mathematical law. That's the position that we'll see Thomas Hobbes takes.

If you want an overview, you can say that modern science has four main roots, three of them traceable back to the ancient world: (1) Its basic philosophy in epistemology, metaphysics, and ethics is Aristotelian—the senses, reason, denial of innate ideas. This world is fully real, intelligible to man, and worth studying. The proper processes are induction and deduction, and human life on earth is a value. All of those premises, which are indispensable to modern science, are Aristotelian. In that sense, modern science is Aristotelian at its philosophic base. (2) In specific content, the next main contributor was Democritus, because modern science adopted mechanistic materialism for its theory of nature. And they needed this to fully implement Aristotle's metaphysics. Aristotle had implied that the whole world is lawful, but his teleology, remember, had led him to the idea of chance and the belief that some things violate law. Mechanistic materialism (as applied now strictly to the physical world) was needed in order fully to implement the idea that the universe is lawful. (3) Pythagoras, because Pythagoras combined with Democritus was the key factor in being able to grasp the laws that mechanistic materialism told us existed. Pythagoras supplied the idea that the key to law is mathematics. (4) Man is an active being. That supplied both the inductive methodology of experimentation, and the goal, knowledge is power. So, to summarize, you can say that, on an Aristotelian base, the idea of combining Democritus and Pythagoras, on the premise that man must act—that combination gave rise to modern science.

I have referred to the good and the bad in modern science, and I've given you some warning signs of the bad in Bacon, and, by the way, Galileo did not share Bacon's contempt for deduction. But I now want to look at one crucial premise of Galileo's that was instrumental in undercutting modern science and effecting the subsequent transition back to Platonism, skepticism, and, ultimately, Kant. Galileo declares that a crucial distinction can be made between two kinds of sensory qualities. On the one hand, colors, tastes, smells, sounds, hot and cold, textures, etc., and on the other hand, size, shape, number, motion, rest. Whom does this remind you of? Democritus and his distinction between the qualities that the atoms have in themselves and the subjective qualities they appear to have because of their effect on us. Galileo took this distinction over from Democritus and embedded it into the heart of modern science, so that it became scientific orthodoxy thereafter. Therefore, this distinction was accepted by Descartes, by Hobbes, by Spinoza, and by Locke. It was Locke who gave the distinction its modern name: "primary qualities versus secondary qualities," primary being the shape, size, number, motion or rest, and secondary being all the rest.

What is the difference between them? Well, they said, (1) the primary qualities are mathematically measurable, i.e., they are quantifiable. You can give us a precise mathematical description of the shape of something, or the size, or its rate of motion. But can you tell us how beige something is, or how cherry it tastes, or how rosy it smells, etc.? No. If reality is, as Pythagoras said, the place that is par excellence mathematizable, then the qualities that can't be quantified are not real. That was one argument. And then (2) they argued that the so-called secondary qualities vary from person to person, from perceiver to perceiver. The color-blind man sees gray and the normal man sees red. The man with a cold in his nose tastes cherry pie as bitter versus the man without a cold, etc. On the other hand, the primary qualities remain the same for everybody, and you can measure them. If it's six inches, it's six inches, whether you've got a cold in your nose, are color blind, or are standing on your head. And therefore, they argued, on that ground also, it looks like the secondary qualities are dependent on the perceiver, and therefore subjective, whereas the primary qualities are not. And thirdly, they argued, it's quite easy to conceive of matter without these secondary qualities. Think of air, for instance—it doesn't bother you at all that it has no color, it has no sound, in most cases no detectable temperature, and in fact, for a long time, men didn't even know it existed. On the other hand, if you try to take away one of your primary qualities, the whole thing obliterates in your mind and there's nothing left. Try to imagine a piece of matter of any kind that has no size at all, no shape, no number, is neither moving nor at rest, and it obliterates. And so, they said, this is further confirmation of the fact that the primary qualities are intrinsic in reality. The secondary qualities are just our subjective human way of perceiving what's out there in reality. Colors, sounds, tastes, smells, textures, warm, cold—none of these, they said, exist in reality but are merely subjective effects in us of what's really out there. And a common example later given was that it's like the tickle of a feather—when you tickle somebody with a feather, where is the tickle? Is the tickle out there in the feather, or is the tickle just the effect on you? Obviously, the tickle is just the effect on you. If there were no you, there would be no tickle. Well, they said, the same holds true for *all* of the secondary qualities. And for the same reasons—how do you know the tickle isn't there? It's not mathematically measurable, it varies from person to person (some people giggle and others don't), and you could easily imagine matter that is not ticklish. But you can't do that with the primary qualities.

Consequently, concluded Galileo and his followers, the senses are deceptive. The world is not what it looks like at all. The world of science is a strange, remote world of mute, colorless, textureless, odorless particles, having only size, shape, and motion. All the rest is a subjective illusion. As I said, just about everybody picked this up. It is a dichotomy going back to Democritus that has had catastrophic effects. And it leads to people like Bertrand Russell saying there are two tables in this room, the table of common sense—which is green and solid and peaceful and so on—and the table of science, which is a berserk mass of charges whirling back and forth and shooting off cosmic rays and so on, and Bertrand Russell spent a good part of his life trying to get the two tables back together into one table, and finally confessed that it couldn't be done (at least in certain moods he thought it couldn't be done). This is a vital issue, and you will soon see the catastrophes that derive from this primary-secondary quality distinction.

Niccolò Machiavelli

Let us go back in time and see what is happening in the value realms of philosophy, in ethics and politics. I said that there were the Platonists and the scientists. What effect did the new science have on value theory? Let's look first at the new science and the Platonists. Let's take as our example of an early political theorist learning to speak as a scientist, Machiavelli (1469–1527). He was one of the earliest to develop what is called the modern scientific attitude to values, and that came about as follows: Science consists of observing the facts and then explaining them. In science, you don't say what you would like the facts to be—you record the way they are. The purpose of science is *description*, not *prescription*. How do you apply that to ethics and politics? Well, said the so-called moralists of science, *we* are not going to tell men what they *ought* to do; ethics consists solely of describing what people actually *do*, and the "good" means what men want, not what they ought to want, just as "gravity" is how bodies act, not how they ought to act. This came to be known as the *naturalistic*, or *realistic*, view of ethics (as opposed to the *idealistic* view that ethics has something to do with values). Their argument again was: Any science—including ethics—has to be concerned with facts, not with values.

Values do not come under the domain of facts. There are no values out there in the world intrinsically, as an inherent feature of things. Nothing is good in itself. It is good only to someone, which means it is good only if somebody arbitrarily decides it's good, which means it is good only subjectively and, therefore, is outside the bounds of science. Here you see the dichotomy: Values are either out there in the world as independent entities (that is to say, they're intrinsic), or they are arbitrary human constructs (that is to say, they are subjective). Those influenced by science on this question decided to take the view that values are subjective and that their sole function is to describe without comment the values people actually hold. Those influenced by Plato took the view that values are intrinsic and part of the furniture of the universe. So, you reduce back to Plato versus the Sophists—intrinsic mystical values versus subjective values. And modern science firmly aligned itself with the subjective viewpoint. And today it's a bromide—science has nothing to say about values; science gives us means, it doesn't give us ends, etc. The idea of a third possibility, that values are *objective*—neither intrinsic in reality, nor subjective, arbitrary constructions of human beings—was never dreamed of prior to Objectivism. I cannot elaborate on that topic in this course, but I recommend "What Is Capitalism?," the first chapter in Ayn Rand's *Capitalism: The Unknown Ideal*, for the Objectivist viewpoint.

In any event, Machiavelli combined this so-called realist approach with a strong dose of secularized original sin. Men, in his viewpoint, are essentially stupid, irrational creatures, incapable of self-government or rational control of themselves. They are moved by passion, not reason. Therefore, the only feasible government is a strong monarchy—the same type of argument that Plato gave, that Augustine gave (and that Hobbes is going to give in the next lecture). If we don't have a powerful government, we'll have universal slaughter, says Machiavelli. The king will probably turn out to be a tyrant, since he also is a man, but what can you do when you deal with people? If you'd said, "Why don't you tell people how they *ought* to behave? Why don't you set standards of good and evil to which the rulers should adhere?" Machiavelli would answer, "I don't set standards—I'm a scientist. Whatever men aim at is the good by definition, and whatever acts produce this end is virtue by definition. If men want power, then the acts that produce power are virtue. And they *do* want power, everybody wants power, that's the way people are, there's no 'ought' about it. Politics is therefore the art of developing those qualities that will enable you to achieve power." And the qualities that will do it best, says Machiavelli, are force and fraud. Therefore, if you employ them ruthlessly enough and cunningly enough, you will achieve your ends. In his manual *The Prince*, he gives many tips as to how to do it. This is the so-called realistic approach, but actually it's completely subjectivist. What was the alternative that was offered? Once they abandoned teleology—the idea that reality sets certain purposes for man—they could think of no objective way to prescribe a code of values. And so they drew the conclusion that you take men as they factually come, observe their desires without comment, and merely describe for them the best way of achieving their ends, whatever those ends happen to be.

Thomas More

Against this trend were the Platonists, who believed that values are intrinsic, that there's a Form of the Good or some equivalent out there in reality, and that all you have to do is commune with it and you'll know what's really good. They preach ideals based on intrinsic goodness. And then by a funny little coincidence, every single one of them preaches that the ideal is a socialist or communist state. And here the arch example is Thomas More (1480–1535), one of the fathers of socialism. In *Utopia*, he advocates a complete communist state.

You see the alternative you're offered. Notice that both sides recommend force. More says: We must have rule by the learned because most men can't grasp the intrinsic good by themselves, so they have to be compelled. That's pure Platonism—the philosopher-king, in effect. Machiavelli says there *is* no intrinsic good. He concludes, therefore, that there's no rational way of dealing with men, and therefore we must use force. So we're back again to Plato versus the Sophists. As it came to be put during this period, the crucial need is to find room for objective values in a world of fact. And the consensus of philosophy progressively was that it cannot be done—either you have a mystic experience (or a religious ethics), or you become a Machiavellian skeptic.

So you see the problems beginning to emerge as we reach the end of the sixteenth century. In metaphysics, God is not yet dead, and the religionists have yet to make their final attempts to save him, to reconcile God and science—while the materialists are busy denying mind and purpose and saying man is just a complicated machine. In epistemology, you see the attack on the senses and on deduction, and that bodes very badly for the future. And in ethics, we are back to Plato versus the Sophists. So far, however, these are all tendencies, suggestions, not yet full systems. The future course of modern philosophy awaits the seventeenth century, when two philosophers laid down the first full modern systems of philosophy and became between them the founders of modern philosophy. One of them was the materialist Thomas Hobbes, and the other tried with all his might to reconcile science and Catholicism, and he became the real father of modern philosophy, René Descartes. Those two, Hobbes and Descartes, are the subject of the next lecture.

Lecture Eight, Q&A

Q: Could you tell us about Aquinas's angels?

A: I'll say two things about Aquinas's angels. He believed in angels—everybody believed in angels at that time, so it wasn't even debatable. And he had them all arranged hierarchically. If I remember, there were nine orders of them, ranging from the lowest to the highest, and they had all sorts of different powers—and he pursued angelology systematically. He knew more about angels than any of us in this room know about living creatures. Of course, he had many problems with the angels. Here's one: The angels are purely spiritual beings, with no bodies and no matter, but matter is the principle of individuation on Aristotle's and Aquinas's philosophy. So the question is, what makes any particular angel *this* angel rather than any other, since they lack matter? How do you distinguish one angel from another, if an angel is pure form? Aquinas's answer was: No two angels have the same form. Think about that—it means that each actually belongs to a different species and is the only representative of its species that is possible. But that begs a big question—why call them all "angels" then? Do they have anything in common? If not, you shouldn't call them all "angels." If yes, there has to be something that individuates and distinguishes one from the other. He had a terrible difficulty with angels in this respect. And there, again, is the problem of trying to reconcile Aristotle with Christianity.

The more interesting thing about angels, though, is the way they acquire knowledge. And this is very instructive. I was first taught this by Miss Rand as an epistemological lesson. She knows[36] a great deal about Aquinas's angels, and she uses that expression all the time as a very helpful way of capturing something. The angels, not having physical senses, do not arrive at concepts by abstraction. They directly contact the forms in God's mind. Therefore, they grasp the abstraction in one act of contemplating the form. And, says Aquinas, in the act of grasping the abstraction, they thereby know every particular instance that will ever come under it. The importance of this is not that there is such a species, but it's very helpful to keep

36. Note: "knows" was correct. Ayn Rand died ten years later, on March 6, 1982.

in mind because that is precisely what human beings are not. The essence of *human* epistemology is to grasp abstractions by seeing a number of instances and abstracting. But the fact that you grasp the abstraction, even though you grasp it fully clearly, does not mean that you are automatically conversant with every instance that will ever come under it. You have to make a separate act of thought to say, "I know this abstraction, and here is a new fact, and therefore, I put the two together and I come to this particular conclusion." And there are a great many cases of people who hear an abstraction, understand it, and then fail to apply it to some case and reproach themselves when they hear the answer on the grounds of "Oh, I should have known that." All that kind of guilt (assuming you're not just stagnating intellectually, but you're doing your best) comes from the implicit assumption that you should be able to operate like Aquinas's angels, and that if you know, for instance, that mind and body are integrated, you should know every blessed subdivision and sub-instance of that—theory in relation to practice, and idealism in relation to practicality, and all the rest of it—and if you miss one, that goes to show you're no good. That's a real source of guilt that should be abandoned, and the best way to abandon it is to follow Miss Rand here and say to yourself: "I'm not Aquinas's angel. As a human being I have to grasp particulars by applying my abstraction by a new act of thought in each particular case, and the things I grasp, fine, and things I don't, as long as I'm open and working, is not held against me." I found that enormously helpful when Miss Rand first taught me that.

Q: Why did the forces of reason and science not wipe out Christianity entirely?

A: They did, but it takes time. You cannot have a thousand years in which something is regarded as a self-evident axiom and everything is integrated around it, every human circuit and concern and premise, and expect that because you challenge the base, the rest is all going to quickly be obliterated. This is where the fact that human beings are not Aquinas's angels comes into the picture. They have to grasp with each new concrete, "Oh yes, that's Christianity and I've rejected that, and oh yes, this is, and I've rejected that"—it doesn't take as long to undo as it did to build, but it's very similar to the process by which you recover from a neurosis. If it takes you twenty years to build up a good-size neurosis, it might take you, let us say, several years to overcome it but not as long as to build it up. But on the other hand, you might hear the most brilliant lecture and be intellectually convinced of what's wrong with your neurosis, but you have to uproot it one application at a time until you begin to automatize the new viewpoint. Mankind as a whole functions the same way. It's very rapid—five centuries only, essentially, since the Renaissance—and already the latest wing in Christianity is proclaiming atheism, you know, "God is dead," as a new school of Protestant theology. Religion is gone now. There are a lot of other bad things, and a lot of bad legacies of religion, but religion is not only not a dominant force—it is not even a *non*-dominant force today. In the West, for practical purposes, atheism rules. It's not even controversial anymore. You have to go out of your way in the Bible Belt to find somebody who will even argue for it. And in that sense, Christianity has gone. I mean, the buildings are around, but that's about it. You can't have an a-historical view as though all of mankind sits down and reads Aquinas and says, "All right, let's start over." It just doesn't work that way.

Q: Please describe More's Utopia.

A: Bertrand Russell, of all people, has a good description of it.[37] I'll give you just a few excerpts, but this will surely be enough to give you the clue to *Utopia* (1516). This is Bertrand Russell's description of it, but on this point, he actually is accurate.

> There are in Utopia fifty-four towns all on the same plan, except that one is the capital. All the streets are twenty feet broad and all the private houses are exactly alike, with one door onto the street and one onto the garden. There are no locks on the doors and anyone may enter any house. The roofs are flat. Every tenth year, people change houses, apparently to prevent any feeling of ownership. All are dressed alike, except that there is a difference between the dress of men and women and of married and unmarried. The fashions never change, and no difference is made between summer and winter clothing.
>
> Everybody, men and women alike, work six hours a day, three before dinner and three after. All go to bed at eight and sleep eight hours. In the early morning there are lectures to which multitudes go, although they are not compulsory. After supper, an hour is devoted to play. Six hours work is enough, because there are no idlers and there is no useless work.
>
> Some men are elected to become men of learning and are exempted from other work while they are found satisfactory. All who are concerned with government are chosen from the learned. . . .

---

37. See Russell's *History of Western Philosophy*, Book Three, Chapter IV.

> [Peikoff: That's pure Platonism.]
>
> Family life is patriarchal. Married sons live in their father's house and are governed by him unless he is in his dotage. If any family grows too large, the surplus children are moved into another family. [Peikoff: You see the complete collectivism here.] If a town grows too large, some of the inhabitants are moved into another town. If all the towns are too large, a new town is built on wasteland. Eating at home is permitted, but most people eat in common halls. Cooking is done by women, and the waiting by the older children. Men sit at one bench, women at another. Nursing mothers with children under five are in a separate parlor. [Peikoff: You see the mentality—it's all planned out down to the last semicolon of how the rest of mankind will live its life forever.] All women nurse their own children. Children over five, if too young to be waiters, stand by and marvel in silence as their elders eat. They have no separate dinner but must be content with such scraps as are given them from the table.
>
> As for marriage, both men and women are sharply punished if not virgin when they marry, and the householder of any house in which misconduct has occurred is liable to incur infamy for carelessness. Before marriage, bride and groom see each other naked; no one would buy a horse without first taking off the saddle and bridle. And similar consideration should apply in marriage. There is divorce for adultery or "intolerable waywardness" of either party, but the guilty party cannot remarry. . . .
>
> People have no money, and they teach contempt for gold by using it for chamber pots and the chains for slaves. Pearls and diamonds are used as ornaments for infants, but never for adults. . . .
>
> [One man in the book] preached Christianity to the Utopians, and many were converted when they learned that Christ was opposed to private property. The importance of communism is constantly stressed. Almost at the end we are told that in all other nations "I can perceive nothing but a certain conspiracy of rich men procuring their own commodities under the name and title of the common wealth."

That sounds like George McGovern, but it's More. It goes on like that, you get the idea—a full-fledged Platonic little dictatorship. Bertrand Russell's comment on this, by the way, is that it is "astonishingly liberal." But he doesn't like it because, "It must be admitted, however, that life in More's Utopia would be intolerably dull. Diversity is essential to happiness, and, in Utopia, there is hardly any. This is a defect of all planned social systems, actual as well as imaginary." That is the totality of his comment, and then he goes on to the next chapter—there is not enough diversity for him. The fact that it is a complete dictatorship and would stifle any and all human creativity, he doesn't consider worth mentioning.

Q: For developing the philosophy of Objectivism, is there a beginning, a genesis? Is there a word, phrase, sentence, or single idea that is a logical place to start? If so, what?

A: Yes, there is. There are two words, that is, one word that is the logical place to start, and that is "existence," or if you want it in the form of a sentence, "Existence exists." What is, is. That is the primary of Objectivism from which we then go on to the existence of consciousness, the faculty of being aware of existence, and the basic law of existence—it is what it is, the law of identity—and then from there develop the system. But the foundation is existence.

Q: I thought that there was no proof that Jesus actually existed? Is there such proof? If so, what is it? And could you tell us your source for his dates?

A: It's a special academic game that people play, "Was there really such and such a person?" They do that with Socrates, and you periodically will see somebody come out with the claim that there was no such person as Socrates—Xenophon and Plato made him up. Or there was no such person as Jesus, and so forth. I regard these as absurd, because we have got the evidence of the Scriptures, and those are historical documents. If Scripture reports that somebody tapped a rock and wine came out, you don't accept it, but if Scripture reports that there was a man who preached certain ideas, and if you see everybody and his brother jumping to embrace those ideas, and you see a whole religion develop out of them, it is ludicrous to say there was no person there. If there wasn't, there was somebody else who did the same thing, so what difference does it make? So what have you accomplished? There was no Jesus, there was somebody named Bill Smith, who preached at the time of the first decades that we now call AD and that you should love the Lord thy God with all thy heart. This is just senseless. I certainly believe in Jesus on the same grounds that I believe in Socrates: historical evidence. Where did I get his dates? From the encyclopedia.

Q: Would you please briefly review the dichotomy of necessary versus contingent facts, and the error therein?

A: I didn't cover it at all, because I referred you to my article titled "The Analytic-Synthetic Dichotomy" for that. But basically, the people who believe in necessary versus contingent facts believe there are two kinds of facts. Certain facts must be the case by the very nature of reality. For instance, that fire is hot, that water is wet, etc. And those facts they call "necessary." Other facts, they say, *happen* to be the case, but we could imagine a world in which they were not the case. For instance, that water freezes at zero degrees Centigrade. Couldn't you imagine a world where everything was the same, they say, but water froze at five degrees (assuming you hadn't defined "zero" as the freezing point of water)? That man has reason is a "necessary" fact, because that's part of the definition, but that man has two eyes, well, you could imagine a man with an eye on the top of his head, or coming out the back of his neck, or on the tip of his little finger, and, therefore, man could have five eyes, so it's just contingent. That's the nature of the dichotomy. It was subscribed to in various ways by Plato, by Aristotle, by Aquinas, and as you'll see, by Leibniz and Locke and Hume, and it has many disastrous consequences culminating in Kant. There are a great many errors in this, but just to take one or two central ones: There can be no such thing as a contingent fact in the sense here used. *Every* fact is necessary. If you believe in the law of identity, then you believe in the law of causality. i.e., you believe that everything that happens does so as an inexorable result of the nature of the entities involved, and that given the entities and the circumstances, *if* anything else had happened, that would be a contradiction, which is prohibited in logic. Therefore, in that sense, metaphysically, everything is necessary, and it is dictated by the nature of the entities involved.

A contingent fact—a fact that metaphysically could have been otherwise—would mean an entity that could have acted in defiance of its nature, which would mean a contradiction. Therefore, the whole idea of contingent facts is out. Don't confuse free will with contingency. There is such a thing as volition, but I've already commented in an earlier question period that volition is a subcategory of causality, not a violation of it. What are the roots of this confusion? There are many, but I'll confine myself to one since that's not the central subject here. If I borrow from my formulation in that article, you must make a clear distinction between metaphysics and Walt Disney. The fact that you can imagine something proves only that you have the capacity to fantasize, and it has no philosophic significance. Those who take the wrong position say, "If Walt Disney could draw it, it's possible, and therefore, it's just contingent that man has two eyes because Walt Disney could draw him with five. But even Walt Disney couldn't draw water that wasn't wet, or fire that wasn't orange, or whichever, and therefore, that puts a limit on reality." But what Walt Disney or your imagination can or can't project is of no objective significance whatever. You can imagine what you can imagine only because you're ignorant. I don't mean that insultingly, but I mean this: If you knew the facts involved in man having two eyes, and every biological neurophysiological antecedent of that fact, and you saw *why* man had two eyes and why that was in the nature of him, you could no more imagine man having five eyes than you could imagine the contrary to any fact the reason for which you see. You can imagine the opposite only insofar as you are ignorant of, or evade, the knowledge of why things are as they are. No argument based on ignorance proves anything about reality. In reality, everything is necessary, and there is no such thing as a fact that happens to be but doesn't have to be.

Q: Did Aristotle's principles of definition anticipate Bacon's principles of scientific induction?

A: I do not see the connection you imply. For Aristotle, definitions are not simply linguistic. You are correct in saying that, for Aristotle, definitions are a mode of objective knowledge of reality, of facts of reality, and that classification is an objective fact, not a declaration of how you're going to use certain vocabulary. It doesn't follow, though, that because definitions give you objective knowledge of reality, they therefore give you the methodology of induction. Aristotle himself has very little to say about the correct methodology of induction. All he really tells us is that there are three kinds of induction—the induction by which we arrive at the axioms (like the laws of logic) which consists of seeing a few instances and then grasping self-evidently the universal proof, but that's applicable only to axioms. That's so-called intuitive induction, using "intuitive" to mean the capacity to grasp the self-evident. Then there's ordinary induction—when you see three puppy dogs wag their tails and they're happy, and you generalize that all puppy dogs wag their tails when they're happy. That type, Aristotle said, is suspect. That's simple enumeration. All it does is give you the material for a generalization, but you have to validate it by deductive means. He did not know any methodology by which to validate it inductively, experimentally. And finally, for Aristotle, there is what is called *induction by complete enumeration.* That is, if, in some case, you could actually study *every* particular first under a universal, then you could state the generalization with complete confidence. But you wouldn't need the generalization, because you'd already know every particular. And that's all Aristotle recognizes, those three types, and therefore, his theory of induction is definitely defective. If you want to hypothesize that if you took Aristotle's theory of definition, combined it with a proper theory of universals, reinterpreted it, and then applied it to the question of induction, would you come up with a valid theory of induction? Yes, you would. But Aristotle didn't do that, at least not judging by what we have.

Q: How is it possible to overemphasize epistemology?

A: It's possible to overemphasize anything. I do not mean, however, that epistemology is not crucial. Objectivism agrees that epistemology is the most crucial subject of philosophy, and that philosophy is *essentially* epistemology because (a), ethics and politics depend absolutely on epistemology, and therefore, epistemology is much more fundamental, and (b), Objectivism holds that metaphysics is a very, very delimited subject. A great deal of what traditionally went into metaphysics, Objectivism holds, is the function of science to discover, and therefore, Objectivism does not have theories on the nature of the mind-body relationship or on the nature of matter (is it atomic, etc.), and all those questions that went into metaphysics really belong in science. Objectivism holds that the essence of metaphysics is the law of identity and its corollary the law of causality, and a few of the more obvious implications of that, and the primacy of existence, but beyond the fundamentals, Objectivism holds that the essence of philosophy is epistemology, and in that sense, we certainly agree with modern philosophers.

So what did I mean when I said that modern philosophy overemphasizes it? Perhaps "overemphasizes" is a misleading word. Modern philosophy followed this progression. With Kant, it came to the conclusion that metaphysics is impossible. With the Logical Positivists in the twentieth century, it came to the conclusion that not only metaphysics, but also ethics and politics are impossible, which left us with the view that philosophy is *only* epistemology, which is to say a study of the means of knowledge divorced from any awareness of reality, or any practical consequences of it. Which, of course, was impossible and useless. Which led, therefore, to the Analysts—the latest wave of modern philosophy in the twentieth century—that even epistemology is useless and impossible, and that therefore, philosophy does not exist as a subject. And that is the current view. You cannot have epistemology unless you have a metaphysical foundation for it, and there's no point in having it unless you're going to draw the practical cash-value conclusions from it. And consequently, if you make philosophy *exclusively* epistemology, you end up having no philosophy at all. And that's just what the moderns do—they say there's no such subject as philosophy, no distinctively philosophic questions.

Philosophers are, in effect, hecklers, who walk around listening to the man on the street speak, and they tease out little puzzles for the hell of it. Now, that is abysmal trivia, garbage, and junk, to put it technically. I don't say that that's implicit in Bacon or any of the others' emphasis on epistemology. I think the switch to epistemology is very valuable, if it doesn't result in a complete obliteration of metaphysics and the other branches of philosophy. Unfortunately, the epistemology that caught on was skepticism. And the result was that it swamped everything else. It's the same pattern in which the Sophists abandoned metaphysics and ethics because of their skeptical epistemology. So I was wrong, or misleading, if I said that you can overemphasize epistemology. What I should have said is that a skeptical epistemology is a corruption that will destroy all of philosophy.

Q: Would you please describe the modern view of the meaning of Occam's Razor?

A: I had referred to the corrupt uses of it. Yes. For instance, Occam's Razor is often used to support materialism, and the argument is: Occam said, "Don't multiply entities beyond necessity." Well, why have mind *and* matter, if we can explain everything with just matter? Why multiply entities and have two starting points, when we can start with just one? Of course, that's a complete corruption of Occam's Razor, because Occam says, "Don't multiply entities *beyond necessity*." But the question is: Is consciousness necessary? Obviously, it is. Or I've heard modern Pragmatists say: "Why base logic on reality? Who needs reality? Let's say logic is okay just because it works, so to hell with reality. Why have logic *and* reality, two things, when we could have just logic, one thing?" That's Occam's Razor used to slash your throat.

Q: Were there no philosophers in history, before Ayn Rand, who made any significant attempt to provide an objective base for values?

A: Here you must distinguish between an attempt to provide an objective *base* for values versus grasping the category "objective" as distinct from the intrinsic and the subjective. On the former, there were several philosophers who tried an objective, as opposed to a supernatural or avowedly subjective, base. Aristotle tried that. Many of the Greeks in part tried that. Spinoza tried that. Several modern philosophers tried that. In other words, if you take that in the sense that "didn't appeal to the supernatural and didn't say anything you feel is correct," even John Dewey claims to be in that position—he denounces subjectivism and supernaturalism. But, if you ask me, "Were any of these attempts successful?," then I say no, they were not, and they collapsed either into supernaturalism or subjectivism or both. Why? Because, in order to defend it correctly, you have to know what the objective *is*, as a category distinct from the intrinsic and the subjective. You have to know what it means to say value is *objective*, so that it's not simply a feature out there in the world that requires an intuition (and makes it intrinsic), or an arbitrary invention in the mind (and, therefore, subjective). You have to grasp the metaphysical category of the *objective*, as against the intrinsic and the subjective. If you can do that—and the whole philosophic approach that that implies—then you'll be able to found an objective ethics. To my knowledge, no one has grasped the objective as distinct from the intrinsic and the subjective prior to Ayn Rand. The objective has always been equated with the intrinsic. And that was one of the major problems of all philosophy. And here I'll have to refer you to *Introduction to Objectivist Epistemology*, which is a thoroughly objective—as distinct from intrinsic or subjectivist—approach to concept formation, and on that particular point, even more to the essay "What Is Capitalism?" in *Capitalism: The Unknown Ideal*, which has an extensive discussion of this trichotomy, and of what's wrong with the intrinsic and the subjective as categories.

Q: If Aristotle's philosophy had been completely consistent, with no traces of the primacy of consciousness, so it could not have been integrated with Christianity at any point, would it have had more or less impact on the medieval period?

A: That's a fascinating question, and any answer could only be speculative. I would say, ultimately, it would have had *more* power because this monolithic, consistent system diametrically opposed to Catholicism and Christianity would in the long run, as soon as men were free, have triumphed completely and stamped out medievalism and all of its modern heirs more fully than they were stamped out, given the attempt to take over Aristotle. But on the other hand, I say it would have been a much more bitter struggle, and people like Aquinas and so on would have been literally taking their lives in their hands to come near Aristotle. He might have been so completely suppressed that it became centuries—or his works might have been burned completely, and everyone who came near them burned also—

in which case, they could have been lost altogether. On top of which, you mustn't overlook the fact that Aquinas was not a pagan, nor was Albertus Magnus or any of those others. It's hard to predict which would have won if they felt it as an absolutely naked choice, God or Aristotle, and you cannot have both—I wouldn't swear as to which. I've read, for instance—I do not know whether this is true—that Aquinas, at the end of his life, in his last year, claimed to have had a mystic experience and said that all of his writings were unimportant, and he now sees the truth mystically. I don't know if that's old age talking—he was only forty-nine or fifty when he died—or because he was fundamentally a Catholic, or what. But no one could know that. So, my own guess would be, if the writings were allowed to survive, they would ultimately have triumphed more fully. But there would have been a bitter, bitter, bitter struggle, and how long it would have taken to allow them into the stream of thought, I don't know.

LECTURE NINE

The New Breach Between the Mind and Reality

We are now at the real beginning of the modern era, the start of systematic, distinctively modern philosophy in the seventeenth century, after the intellectual transition from the medieval era has been completed. The systems propounded at this point in time will be decisive in shaping the course of subsequent philosophy. If there's any hope for the future of modern philosophy, you will have to get it tonight.

The two philosophers whom we will look at tonight—the ones who, between them, founded modern philosophy—are Thomas Hobbes and René Descartes. To alleviate the suspense, I'll give you a preview and tell you in a sentence what to expect. Hobbes is a derivative of the ancient materialists and ends up as a total Sophistic skeptic. Descartes is a derivative of Plato and Augustine and implants the essence of the Platonic approach deeply into the very fabric of modern philosophy. Hobbes denies consciousness, and Descartes casts doubt on physical reality. Between them, modern philosophy begins in a disastrous fashion, and things have gotten worse ever since.

If you asked me if there were any major modern philosophers influenced essentially by Aristotle, I would answer: If there were any such (and really there weren't), it would be John Locke, whom we will consider next lecture. And you will see what a weak and, at best, one-third Aristotelian he is.

Thomas Hobbes

With this advance word of warning, let us turn first to Thomas Hobbes (1588–1679). Hobbes is the first British philosopher to construct a complete philosophic system on the basis of the discoveries of the new science. In the previous lecture, we discussed the scientific discoveries and the scientific worldview that was formed on the basis of these discoveries. Hobbes takes as his starting point the view of the world propounded by the new science and proposes to take all branches of philosophy for the first time under the new science. He is one of the first really influential and systematic modern philosophers. He is contemporary with Descartes but not as important or influential as Descartes. Therefore, he has not won from historians the title of "Father of Modern Philosophy". But that should not detract from his importance. In a way he was ahead of his time—his impact and influence were delayed. His metaphysics became enormously influential, really, only in the nineteenth century; his epistemology, ethics, and politics only in the twentieth. In the seventeenth century, he primarily has the function of a horrible example to the other philosophers of the time, who regarded his conclusions as horrendous, and who believed that they must avoid Hobbesianism at all costs.

I said that he claims to be the arch proponent of modern science. What then is his attitude to God, revelations, theology, etc.—are they thrown out? And the answer is yes. You should understand for accuracy that Hobbes himself is not an atheist. He frequently refers to God. He even gives the first cause argument in favor of God. He calls God an incorporeal spirit and suggests at certain points, indirectly, that God is the source of ethics. But none of this in Hobbes has any philosophic significance, because it contradicts every element and principle of his distinctive philosophy. Some commentators hypothesize that Hobbes retained these references to God out of prudence. After all, it was still not one hundred percent safe politically to be an atheist, for there were still religious authorities and persecutions at this time. The seventeenth century is still too early for avowed atheism, which did not become a cultural phenomenon until the later eighteenth and particularly the nineteenth century. So we can ignore the religious vestige in Hobbes. By the logic of his philosophy, in consistency, he has to be an atheist, and virtually everybody takes him as that, in spite of these few references. There are often very bitter anti-religious remarks in Hobbes. For instance, when he defines "religion," he explains that there are two kinds of fear—justified and unjustified. For instance, a justified fear would be the fear you feel if a wild animal is suddenly let loose at you. An unjustified fear would be the fear that people feel in walking under a stepladder. Within the category of unjustified or irrational fear, he goes on, there are two kinds: irrational fears that are not publicly endorsed—that we call "superstition"—and irrational fears that are publicly endorsed, and that is religion. This is hardly a pro-religious viewpoint.

Hobbes prides himself on being scientific, naturalistic, rational. He is, like all philosophers of this period, enormously conscious of epistemology, of method. You must have the right method to philosophize, he insists, and like so many of the philosophers that we've seen and that we'll continue to see, he believes philosophy must follow mathematics in its method, and specifically geometry, which was the best developed and clearest example of mathematics known at this time. The essence of the proper method of philosophy is: Start with certain axioms, or basic principles, and then proceed rigorously to deduce their implications. According to Hobbes's biographers, one day when he was not yet cognizant of geometry, he stumbled on the forty-seventh theorem of Euclid, and he read it and said that it's impossible and can't be true. And he slowly worked his way back through the preceding theorems until he reached the axioms, and he is supposed to have said words to the effect of, "By God, it really is true," and he promptly fell in love with geometry if it could give a demonstration like this. And this must be what philosophy is—it must be completely deductive, starting with the basic premises of science (which Hobbes takes as his starting point) and deducing their consequences for mankind in all realms.

Let us look first very briefly at his metaphysics. He is a complete, thoroughgoing materialist. Matter in motion is all that exists. It is governed by the laws of mechanics. Everything happens exclusively by what Aristotle calls "efficient causation." There is no purpose, no end, no goal-directed behavior, nothing of what Aristotle calls "final causation" anywhere in the universe. So, this is a standard mechanistic materialism, in effect, the billiard ball metaphysics.

What about man? Man is no exception, he says, to the universal truths discovered by science. Man, too, is only a mechanistic materialistic entity. And therefore, man is completely determined, free will is a myth, everything is determined by the laws of motion operating upon matter. This is the metaphysics of the ancient materialists. What about mind, consciousness, spirit, soul? There are no such things, says Hobbes. Anybody who believes in these things shows that he is a holdover, or a carryover, from the old-fashioned medieval religious period. These things have no place in a scientific philosophy. Science, he insists, demands materialism. Mind, or consciousness, is a supernatural legacy. We have dispensed with ghosts, he says, we have dispensed with demons, now let us be consistent and dispense with mind also, on the same grounds. The mind is supposed to be a spiritual entity. What is a spiritual entity? If it means anything, it means a body-less body, and a body-less body is a contradiction in terms. So much for mind.

Here's the false alternative: For centuries, the Platonists and Augustinians had been saying that mind (or consciousness or soul) is a supernatural element, the part of man akin to the world of supernatural Forms or God. And Hobbes agrees, saying that if there were a mind, that's what it would be—supernatural. But he rejects the supernatural, and therefore ends up as a materialist. In other words, he doesn't challenge the point and the basic premise that mind is supernatural; he merely takes the other side of the same coin. And you'll see this same procedure again in his epistemology. If the mark of a great philosopher is his ability to challenge entrenched fundamentals, to think as an innovator in terms of basic principles rather than merely accept the principles and alternatives already popular, then you'd have to say that Hobbes is not a great philosopher, not in any branch of philosophy.

His attitude to mind, I must say, is very popular today, particularly among people who pride themselves as being "scientific." And you can find it defended by sundry physicists, vast numbers of psychologists, particularly behaviorists. I've already mentioned this under our discussion of Democritus, and I've discussed what's wrong with materialism, so I won't repeat that now. You will see that a materialist *always* has to smuggle in consciousness, in spite of himself, whenever he deals with man, with cognition, with ethics, with politics. And you'll see that, as we now turn to the most important part of Hobbes's philosophy, his epistemology.

Hobbes's epistemology was destined to be enormously influential, though not for a few centuries. In many respects, for those of you who know twentieth-century philosophy, you will see that Hobbes is a real twentieth-century soul. He is the blood brother and the ancestor of the Logical Positivists and the Pragmatists and that whole school that derives from Anglo-American skepticism.

All knowledge, he says, is based on the evidence of the senses. There are no innate ideas. In this respect, he is a thorough empiricist. There is nothing in the mind that was not ultimately based on sense experience. This is the attitude taken by modern science, by Bacon, by Galileo, and, ultimately, it is an Aristotelian element. How does Hobbes, as a materialist, account for such a thing as sensory perception? He says that, according to the laws of mechanics, matter external to our bodies strikes our bodies in certain places, those places that we call the senses, and that starts certain parts of our bodies quivering, oscillating, shaking, moving back and forth. This motion is communicated by various nerves and so on to the heart or brain (he didn't necessarily commit himself to the brain, but I'll leave out the heart hereafter), the appropriate part of which (the brain) starts moving, and so we have a motion in the brain produced by the impact of external matter in our bodies. And that's a sensation—a motion in the brain. That's all it is. Now, you say, the sensation *is* the motion? Is it that, or is it that the motion *appears* to us, or is *experienced* by us, as a sensation? And Hobbes often says yes, a sensation is really the way we experience the motions in our brain. You might ask why motion in the brain yields a sensation, an experience, and not just motion, the way motion does when you strike any complex machine. Who or what, you might ask, is *doing* the experiencing if there is no conscious entity? And you might ask why motion in the brain yields a world of green, red, hot, cold external objects, rather than at least the experience of motion in the brain? To all of these questions, Hobbes has no answer. On his premises, there *is* no answer. He has to assume and smuggle in consciousness. By his premises, there should be motion in the brain, and that's all. That somebody should know about it, or experience it, is inexplicable without consciousness. But we can pass by this problem because many others are pressing.

We said that somehow this motion in the brain produces the experience of an external world. But is our perception of the world valid? Can we trust the senses? Do they tell us what the world is really like? Answers Hobbes firmly, no, they do not. Why not? Because he accepted the distinction of Democritus and Galileo that there are two kinds of qualities. We've already discussed this distinction, the kind that Locke subsequently called the "primary versus the secondary qualities." The secondary qualities—colors, tastes, odors, etc.—are, says Hobbes, merely the effects on us of what's *really* out there. The real world is therefore not remotely what it appears to be. It's colorless, odorless, soundless, invisible, temperature-less—all it consists of is quantities in motion, with size, with shape, with number.

The senses, therefore, are great deceivers. He says this quite explicitly: "Whatsoever qualities our senses make us think there be in the world, they be not there, but are seeming and apparitions only. The things that really are in the world, apart from us, are those motions by which these seemings are caused. And this is the great deception of sense." You see the contradiction he's in at the outset—all knowledge rests on the senses, and we don't get off the ground before he's denouncing the senses. So, you can figure out where we're going from there.

Now, you might ask: How can we know that the senses are deceiving us? And Hobbes answers: by thought. For instance, by the various arguments used by philosophers to establish that secondary qualities aren't real, the arguments that I gave you last time—that we can't conceive of matter without the primary but can without the secondary, or that the primary don't vary from perceiver to perceiver and the secondary do. In other words, by a process of thought, says Hobbes, we can correct our senses. But he also says that thought is based on the evidence of the senses. How can thought correct the evidence on which it's based? If you're an empiricist, and you say that all knowledge rests on the senses, and then you say the senses deceive you, clearly you are lost. There's no means of correcting the senses if they're your sole foundation of knowledge. If you criticize the senses and take Plato's way out via innate ideas, that's a different story. But if you are an empiricist and denounce the senses, that is the equivalent of committing epistemological suicide, and it will lead to the view that reality is unknowable. You will shortly see Hobbes come to that conclusion.

I'd now like to introduce you to some technical philosophic terminology. Hobbes's view is that we do not perceive reality directly. We perceive only the appearances of reality to us, the effects of reality on us, the way it affects our brains and senses. We don't perceive reality directly, as it really is. In effect, we're all locked up inside our own minds—or, let me correct that: inside our own *brains*, inasmuch as there is no mind. We know our own experiences directly, and that's all. Perception, therefore, is really a species of introspection, looking out doesn't really exist. All looking out is a form of looking in.

This viewpoint is called the "causal theory of perception" and is defined technically as the view that reality is the cause, but not the object, of our perception. Aristotle, being an advocate of the validity of the senses—being a naïve realist—says that reality is the cause of our experience, and it is the *object* that we experience. We directly experience reality. We open our eyes, or whatever sense modality that we use, and there is reality given to us. The advocate of the causal theory, however, says that we do *not* directly experience reality, only the inner content of our mind as the result of the influence of reality on us. Reality, he says, exists as the *cause* of our experience, but we don't directly encounter it.

Some advocates of the causal theory stop there and say reality is unknowable since we never encounter it. Some, like Hobbes, go on to say that some of our experiences are *similar* to reality, and some are not. Some, in the technical phrase, *represent* reality, or stand for reality, and some do not. Of course, in Hobbes's case, the primary-quality experiences represent reality, the others do not. If you add this point, you are said to believe in the representative theory of perception, which is the view that you do not directly perceive reality, only its effects on you, but that some of your experiences nevertheless are similar to or represent reality. Hobbes subscribes to the causal theory *and* the representative theory of perception. Of course, if you were to ask him: Since you never perceive reality, how do you know that some of your experiences represent it?—that's what later thinkers asked him, but we'll wait and see for that. For now, I just hope you get clear the terminology—the primary-secondary quality distinction, the causal theory of perception, the representative theory of perception—because the results of this trinity of ideas are disastrous.

How do you know there's a reality at all if you're locked up experiencing your own subjective experiences? Of course, the advocates of this viewpoint say that there must be a reality that caused our experiences—that's the causal theory of perception. And, the representative ones go on, I can infer something about reality in order for it to have caused the particular kind of experiences I had—that's the representative theory of perception. But their central point is that reality is known by inference, not by perception, not directly, not self-evidently. Later philosophy proceeded to challenge this inference, to ask *why* does there have to be an external world causing my experiences? Why couldn't God, for instance, directly cause my experiences in me? That is the position taken by Bishop Berkeley. Why does there have to be a cause at all? Let's go by the observed facts—all we observe is our own experiences, therefore, that's all we have a right to believe in. That is the position taken by David Hume, who threw out the law of cause and effect along with reality. Now, you see that by this route, the whole external world will shortly vanish.

However, that's looking ahead. Hobbes still believes in reality—there is an external reality—and he thinks that our senses are trustworthy at least in regard to the primary qualities. But the process of destruction of reality has started.

There is more to mental processes than sensing. Hobbes holds that every so-called mental process can be explained strictly materialistically and mechanistically in a rigidly deterministic fashion. All "mental" activity is really motion in the brain. For instance, you have a particular sensation, then that sensation starts to be interfered with by other motions as new stimuli strike your senses and start up new motions. And so, Hobbes says, the original motion begins to "decay" (that is his word), and you therefore experience it as somewhat fainter and more blurred than you did the original sharp experience, and that's due to the new motions that are entering your brain and obscuring the old motion. This decaying sense is called "imagination," or "memory." And by "imagination" here we mean the faculty of forming mental images. For instance, right now, form before your eyes a visual image—you can have images in any sense modality, but the commonest are visual, so we will restrict ourselves to that—right now, form before your eyes a mental image of your mother, of her face. What is the explanation of that, according to Hobbes? It's that at one point, you actually perceived your mother, and started certain motions going in your brain, and those motions, by the law of inertia, are still there, but other motions have come in to obscure them. So, when you go to look at your mother, you're seeing a faded, decayed sensory experience, and that is an image. If this happens while you're sleeping, you're said to be dreaming, and this is why images are fainter and paler and more blurred.

We now reach a crucial point: What about thought? Abstract thought, concepts, man's cognitive distinction and glory—how does it fare in this philosophy? To tell you the brutal truth in a sentence: Hobbes equates thought with image. "Image," "idea," "thought," "concept"—all those are synonyms for Hobbes. And an image, we know, is merely a decaying sense experience. And a thought, therefore, or an idea, or a concept, is really only a sense experience, or an image thereof. This viewpoint has a technical name: *sensualism*. Sensualism is the doctrine that all cognitive elements really are sense perceptions. Or to put it another way, it is the view that man has only one cognitive faculty, the faculty of sense perception. The power of thought is not a distinct cognitive faculty, but a form of the faculty of sense perception.

Do not confuse sensualism with empiricism, for there is a vital distinction. Empiricism is the broader of the two terms. It is the view that all knowledge begins with experience, that there are no innate ideas. But that leaves open two possibilities. A philosopher, given an empiricist base, can then go on à la Aristotle and say: "Granted that all knowledge begins with experience, man nevertheless has the power of abstraction, and therefore the power of forming concepts, which are not simply names for sense experience. Therefore, he has the power to gain knowledge of reality by reason and thought, which he couldn't have gained exclusively from sense perception, even though it's ultimately based on it." That would be an Aristotelian empiricist. A sensualist is a radically anti-Aristotelian empiricist. He believes with empiricism that all knowledge begins with the senses, but he is a pessimistic empiricist. He believes that knowledge not only begins with the senses but ends with the senses. His view is that the senses constitute the *only* cognitive faculty man has (the senses plus their decayed remnants, images), and therefore, what cannot be learned by sense perception cannot be known. There is no such thing as acquiring knowledge by reason other than what you could acquire by perception. That is the sensualist view. It is particularly attractive to modern empiricists. You will be hard put to find any empiricist in the modern world who is not a sensualist, for a reason that I'll explain shortly.

Why do I stress sensualism? Why is it a vital issue in philosophy? Because consider what happens to abstract conceptual thought if you are a sensualist. In fact, images, like sense perceptions, are thoroughly individual, particular, concrete. Suppose I tell you to form the image of banana—you cannot form an image of banana in general. If you inspect your image (even if it's blurred), focus on any part of it and you'll see that your banana is either yellow or green or brown, big or small, on its end or not, striped or not, peeled or not. And if you have the capacity to form tactile images, you either taste an acrid image or whatever it happens to be. That banana image, and all images across all modalities, is thoroughly particular, even if blurred. Animals have the capacity for images. If thought is only decaying sense, if it's only particular images, how do men differ from animals? It used to be said that man can abstract, can grasp universals, not just gaze at concretes, and that he grasps universals by a process of thought. But if "thought" is just another name for decaying sense perception, then how does man grasp universals? How does he grasp common denominators? How is he able to abstract? Or does he? And if not, how does man achieve his uniquely human attainments?

This brings us to Hobbes's theory of universals. We'll tie in sensualism in a minute. Hobbes's theory of universals is the heart of his epistemology. I've referred several times to the theory of universals, which was destined to be dominant in the modern era: nominalism, which was the theory of universals endorsed in essence by the ancient Sophists and Skeptics, and by certain medievals and to a certain extent William of Occam, among others. But nominalism didn't become a dominant influence on philosophy until the modern era. And of all the modern nominalists, Hobbes is the first important influential one. After him you will see that Locke follows him about one-third of the time, and Locke is about one-third to one-half nominalist. Berkeley is a thorough nominalist, and Hume outdoes Berkeley, if that's possible. And the Logical Positivists in the twentieth century, the Pragmatists, the Existentialists, the Analysts are nominalists with a devotion and a devoutness equal to that of the medievals' belief in Catholic dogma. So now is a good time to understand modern nominalism, at least in essentials.

I should say, for accuracy, that Hobbes is not a complete or consistent nominalist. He's the seventeenth century, remember, and there's a limit to how corrupt you can be in the seventeenth century. Therefore, elements of Aristotle's approach survive in Hobbes's writings. But they are not what is distinctive. The dominant thrust of his philosophy is nominalism. So, I want to look now at nominalism and go beyond Hobbes here, and survey some of the main arguments offered by modern philosophy (some by Hobbes, some by others) to defend this viewpoint.

If we put it negatively at the outset, nominalism is the denial that there are universals. Nominalism is the view that every particular is unique, that there are no real, identical common denominators that objectively unite particulars into classes. Universals are a myth, a subjective human creation. What Plato and Aristotle called "form" doesn't really exist. What kinds of arguments are put forth for this? Let me give you three. There are many more, but those three will suffice to give you an idea.

I made up my own name for the first one—I call it the "I can't find it" argument. It has two parts, the first briefly against Plato and the second more extendedly against Aristotle. It starts off with the premise of empiricism—all nominalists are empiricists and go only by the basis of the sensory evidence. As applied to Plato, it's clear how they would reject his viewpoint. For Plato, universals are supernatural elements, and the nominalist says, "I am naturalistic, scientific, empirical, I believe only in what can be justified on the basis of experience. And, he says, we certainly do not sensorially experience universals, only particulars. There is no basis in experience for Plato's Forms." And that's valid. You might object (and I hope you do) and say: "Well, that's fine as against Plato, but what about Aristotle? Aristotle said you *could* grasp universals on the basis of experience by a process of abstraction." Remember the process of focusing only on what's in common among particulars and ignoring their individual differences. To this the nominalists answer: "There is no such process as abstraction in Aristotle's sense of the term. Aristotelian abstraction is a myth." They say, "Whenever we try to follow Aristotle's advice—whenever we take any group of particulars and concentrate only on the alleged common identical common denominators after we strip off the particular aspects, we find nothing left."

And here's where we get the "I can't find it" argument. They say, "When I ignore the differences that individuate every particular, there's absolutely nothing left to be aware of." Take "man" for instance. To form the concept of "man," the nominalist says, let me try Aristotle's way—I'm supposed to contemplate a whole bunch of men and ignore everything that isn't identical. I have to ignore their height, because they vary in height, and I have to ignore their weight, because they vary in weight, and I have to ignore skin color, because they vary in skin color, and I have to ignore their intelligence, because they vary in intelligence, and I have to ignore their legs, because there are amputated men and men with one leg, and so on, and so on. Let me set aside everything that varies from particular to particular, and what's left? Well, what I have before me is some kind of mystic entity that has no height, no weight, no color, no etc., no etc.—it's nothing, it's a myth. All that exists are particulars. If you take away the particular characteristics of a particular, there's nothing left to contemplate. Every particular is particular. It's particular in every respect. Ignore its particularity and you've ignored the thing. Do that with the whole group and you end up with a big fat zero. Conclusion—universals are a myth. Or take, for instance, "red" (a favorite nominalist example)—"red," the color. Look at a deep red and a light red and a pink red and a rose red, and the whole business of reds. Ignore the particular shade of each and then focus on what's left. Well, the nominalist says, what's left isn't dark, it isn't light, it isn't pink, it isn't un-pink—it isn't red, it isn't anything. It's a myth. In reality, he concludes, there is nothing the same among particulars—or if there is, we can't find it. That's argument one.

If you're an ingenious enough nominalist—and they are ingenious—you can do it with any concept, truly any. Consequently, there is no use in trying to stump them by finding some esoteric concept with which you can't do this. I've had nominalists as professors in school for over a decade. And there is no concept for which they can't do this. The essence of the argument is: "Only the perceivable can exist, universals are not perceivable entities, therefore, they don't exist." Or to put it another way: "Only the particular can exist, universals are not particular, therefore, they don't exist." Plato held the same premise, "Universals are not particular," but then drew the opposite conclusion, holding that they must exist in a supernatural world. Nominalists draw the opposite conclusion. I'm sorry that I can't deal with this argument in this course, because it would require a whole theory of concept formation, but it is dealt with in detail in Ayn Rand's *Introduction to Objectivist Epistemology.* As a clue, I ask you to note the idea underlying this argument: If universals have any foundation in reality, they must be specific elements or objects in reality that you can directly contemplate. And then, since the nominalists can't find those elements in reality, they proceed to deny that they exist. In other words, their premise is "If universals exist, they must be intrinsic ingredients in things," as both Plato and Aristotle in their own ways had said. Then they find that they can't find these intrinsic ingredients, and so they conclude that universals are subjective. So you see the same dichotomy on universals as we saw last time on values—either it's intrinsic or it is subjective. What is left out? The category of the objective, as against the intrinsic and the subjective.

Let's look at argument two, the "borderline case" argument. And this one goes as follows: If, like Plato or Aristotle, you believe that there really are universals, how do you account for borderline cases? A "borderline case" means a particular, a concrete, that overlaps two or more of our present conceptual categories, and therefore seems to pose a dilemma in terms of how to classify it. The nominalists argue that on Aristotle's view (we can ignore Plato), there should be no such thing as borderline cases, because, after all, classification is dictated by nature. Either a concrete exemplifies a given universal or it doesn't. And therefore, there should be no indecisiveness, no option, no debate as to how to classify. If the thing exemplifies the universal, then it objectively belongs to a certain class, and if not, not. But, the nominalist goes on, the fact is that we are overrun with borderline cases. Their favorite example is the color spectrum. Where do you draw the line between red and orange? You can study and study and scrutinize it under a microscope, but you can't find any point at which redness sharply stops and orange starts. There's a borderline area which some people say is red with lots of orange, and other people say no, it's orange with lots of red, and other people say oh no, it's a new color, it's orangey-red or reddish orange, etc. What, says the nominalist, is the answer? The fact is, he says, *every* shade, from the most extreme red on through, merges into the next. We have a continuum, with nature giving us no place to draw the line. Yet if redness were a real universal, it should be the case that you have redness up until this point and then the universal leaves and you don't have it anymore. It's true, says the nominalist, all the shades resemble each other, they are similar, but there is no one element common among all the reds, cutting them off from the oranges. In the borderline area, we draw the line by arbitrary human decree. And there are options—no one is right or wrong as to where he draws the line. It is arbitrary. In other words, reality gives us no objective grounds on which to form classes.

Let me give you one more example of this argument. You define "man" as a "rational living being," following Aristotle. The nominalist says "fine," then he asks: What would you do in the following situation: A spaceship lands in your backyard, a hatch opens, and out of it slithers a thing that looks exactly like a spider—it's got a hairy body and the legs of a spider and so on—and it slithers over to you, points its face directly toward your eyes, opens its mouth and says, "I think, therefore I am," and you engage this spider in conversation and you find he is majoring in Descartes on some other planet—he is a rational living being. Now, says the nominalist, is this a man? It's a living being that has the power to reason. Is it a man or not? That depends. Are you going to include having a certain type of body in your concept and definition of "man"? If you do, then no, this is not a man. If you decide *not* to include a certain type of body and say that all that really counts, all that's essential, is rationality, then yes, it is a man. How will nature, he asks, tell you? It doesn't say. You can catalogue the facts of this spider and of what we ordinarily call "man" until you're blue in the face, and nature won't decide what counts, what the standard for entry into the class "man" is. Again, the spider is a borderline case, and there's no place to draw the line. Conclusion: There is no manness, no redness, nor *any* universal out there in reality. In reality, there is a series of rough similarities, or resemblances, that fade off imperceptibly into new phenomena.

Human beings draw the line arbitrarily on the basis of *convenience*, their subjective, arbitrary convenience. For instance, suppose you happen to be interested in philosophic discussion, and that is what's really important to you. Then you will say: "Well, I don't care whether this spider has a human body. It has what counts to me, and that's essential. Therefore, this spider is a man." That's the essence *you* will define. On the other hand, suppose you're primarily interested in sex, and it would be very awkward, not to say impossible, to have sex with this spider—then you will say that having a certain kind of body is essential to being a man, and therefore, this spider is not a man. But that's your subjective decision. And the nominalist will go on, if you include a body, where do you draw the line? What about pygmies? What about the missing link? What about crippled men? What about dead men? And so on and so on. You get the idea. As they put it, "Men create classes; they don't discover them." They create them by deciding how to use names. Universals, therefore, are really only names, collective names, and thus the word "nominalism" (from "name"). Now I will dictate to you a formal definition of "nominalism" (my own, but it captures the essence of the theory): "Universals are merely collective names arbitrarily imposed by men on roughly resembling particulars by the standard of subjective human convenience." I will answer this in lecture twelve.

Now a final, brief indication of a third argument, one that derives from the problem of individuation. You remember Aristotle's troubles with finding an individuator. It couldn't be determinate, otherwise, it's conceptualizable and comes under form, and it couldn't be indeterminate, otherwise, it's nothing in particular, and how would nothing in particular individuate? The nominalist just loves this spectacle because, he says, that is the kind of problem you get into when you say that universals are real, that they're really out there in reality, because once they're real, you then have to add an individuating element, and it becomes hopeless. We must, he says, take the other approach—things are individual by nature, and we don't have to individuate them because there *are* no universals, universals are a myth, and so we have no problem of individuation. Here again, you see the idea that universals are subjective because they're not intrinsic.

I note that nominalists do not dispense with abstract terms. Obviously, "nominalism" itself is an abstract term, and they couldn't speak at all if they dispensed with abstract terms (except for uttering proper nouns like "Tom," "Dick," and "Harry"). Their standard line is that "collective names," as they call it, are convenient—they enable us to communicate our thoughts to other people, among other things. It's very nice to have one term to refer to a number of particulars, they say, instead of having to refer to every particular by a separate word. It's a big time-saver. Suppose you wanted to say, for instance, that Socrates, Plato, Plotinus, Tom, Dick, Harry, etc., are all mortal. Think of the time and trouble you save—think of the convenience—in being able to condense all of these statements into the shorthand statement "Men are mortal," instead of having to say it for the endless collection separately. But the nominalist's main point is that this is *all* that universal terms are—they're nothing but collective names, shorthand, convenient ways of referring at the same time to a group of particulars. They're nothing but a convenient human linguistic device, a kind of shorthand linguistic code, with about the status that shorthand in writing has, which is nothing but a convenient human writing device. It doesn't give you any special insight into reality.

If you ask a nominalist: "But why are certain classifications convenient and others aren't? Why do certain collective names work, and others don't? Why can't I, for instance, make up the term 'gloop' to stand for the people on my right, Greek philosophers, the linoleum in the north half of Manhattan, and all the ships in the British Navy that weigh more than four tons? That won't be convenient. Why, if everything is unique, if there are no real common denominators?" To which the nominalist answers that it's true that there are no real common denominators, but there *are* similarities, or resemblances. That's real. Rough similarities, rough resemblances, but still, they're there. For instance, Tom, Dick, and Harry are more like each other than any one of them is to a carrot. There's nothing identically in common among Tom, Dick, and Harry—each is unique in his own way—but still there is a rough resemblance among them. Of course, there are resemblances also between them and a carrot, but the resemblances are closer between the three of them than between any one of them and the carrot. Therefore, the nominalist says, usually it's more convenient to have one term for those three, and for the other things that resemble them closely, than to have a term for Tom and Dick and the carrot, because the resemblances are much more pronounced. In a word, they say, reality *suggests* which classifications are more convenient because it does present us with groups of more or less resembling particulars. But they insist we stick to our view that reality does not dictate or necessitate any one classification over any other. It wouldn't be wrong to stick Tom, Dick, and the carrot together, because after all, there are some similarities—vague, but there. And it is not right to do it the way we do it now, because in fact, there is nothing identically in common. Classification, they insist, is not a matter of truth or falsehood, merely of convenience or inconvenience, and classification that adheres to the more pronounced similarities is usually the more convenient. But it's up to us to decide where to draw the lines, how close the resemblance has to be in order to qualify for the same term. Our subjective interests, therefore, decide what classifications to erect upon the rough similarities that nature presents us with. Reality gives you hints, but that's all. It's never coercive.

I might point out that since a nominalist denies thought (that is, abstract thought, which he equates with decaying sense, with images), he does not say that the power of thought is man's distinctive cognitive capacity, because animals have the power of images also. He says that what differentiates man from the animals is his ability to impose names on particulars. In other words, his ability for language, his ability to speak. Man, says the nominalist, is the talking animal. If you ever heard that, that's a nominalist speaking. Somehow these convenient arbitrary noises, words that man uses, have the power to make possible all of man's distinctive cognitive achievements. How does this naming power make possible man's achievements? I have never heard a remotely sensible explanation from a nominalist on this point, so I won't take any time on this question. In actual fact, talking is a consequence of thinking, unless you are just babbling like a parrot. An animal that could associate arbitrary names—in other words, noises—with its sensations, and assume that's all it could do, is a nominalist animal that would be no better off cognitively than a mute animal. It would not acquire the cognitive powers of man. Aristotle is correct that man is the *rational* animal, and as a result, he has the power of articulate speech. But it is man's reason, not his talking, that is the root of his distinctiveness. But a good working test of a nominalist is this definition of "man" in terms of language, "the language using animal." That's a sure sign of nominalism.

Now let's bring in sensualism. What I want you to see is that nominalism and sensualism imply each other, i.e., if you accept either, you must accept the other. Nominalism, as posed by traditional philosophy, is a metaphysical viewpoint: Universals are unreal, i.e., they don't exist in reality. Sensualism is an epistemological issue, dealing with what kind of cognitive capacities man has. But if you start with either, you're led to the other. For instance, if you start as a sensualist and you say man has only the faculty of sense perception, then you will never discover universals, because those can be discovered only by abstraction, by thought, not by sense. If you are a sensualist, all you'll find is sense experience, and consequently, you will deny that there are any universals—that is, you will end up as a nominalist. In reverse, if you start as a nominalist—in other words, there are no universals, only unique particulars—then you will reason, but then there's nothing for human beings to do but perceive these unique particulars, and the name of perceiving a particular is "sense experience." Abstraction, conceptual awareness as a distinct cognitive state, becomes impossible, because there are no real common denominators to be aware of. There is no possible object for *con*ceptual, as distinct from *per*ceptual, awareness. The real reason that philosophers are sensualists is that they are nominalists. They defend nominalism as scientific, as empirical, and then they're brought immediately to sensualism. This is what happened to Hobbes, and to almost every other modern empiricist. And so, nominalism-sensualism has been grafted onto empiricism from the time of Hobbes in the name of science and the rejection of mysticism. That's why today most philosophers would deny that Aristotle is an empiricist—because he is not a sensualist or a nominalist, and they have forgotten that there is a type of empiricist that doesn't subscribe to these things.

Nominalism has many disastrous epistemological consequences. Let us look at the ones endorsed by Hobbes. To begin with, what happens to definitions on this philosophy? Definitions are supposed to be statements of the essence of some class, of those fundamental characteristics that make it what it is and differentiate it from all other classes. But if classification is a subjective and arbitrary human product, then so are definitions. After all, the nominalist says, *you* (or society, if he's a social nominalist) subjectively created the class, you drew the lines, you subjectively decided to pick out these particulars and impose one name on them, you decided what would qualify. Therefore, it's up to you to specify the so-called essential characteristics of your arbitrary classification. "Essential" means whatever you've decided is necessary to belong to the grouping you've subjectively made. Just as classes are dictated by names, so essences are dictated by names. As it's put technically, there are no real essences, only nominal essences ("nominal essence" meaning an essence dictated by arbitrary naming procedures). Says the nominalist: Take anything you want, and you can make it the defining characteristic of a class if you choose. Suppose you say, "I want to make featherless biped-ness—two legs without feathers." Fine, then you can make that essential to being a man. And of course, a plucked chicken will be a man, and that's okay, it's your definition, it's a free country. It's not false, because any definition is arbitrary. You just decided on an unusual grouping, that's all, which may not be as convenient as the norm, but then for some purposes, maybe it will be. Definitions merely express the way you are naming things. They merely say how you intend to speak. They are verbal, linguistic, *conventional* as it's put ("conventional" meaning a product of arbitrary human choice). Definitions, as the nominalists insist, are neither true nor false. But if there *is* an objective basis for classification—that is to say, for conceptual thought, the nominalist viewpoint is completely untenable.

So what happens to general principles? "Man is mortal," "Socialism is slavery," "Altruism is evil." The truth of general principles, on anybody's theory, depends upon one's definitions. By certain definitions of the key terms in the principles I just gave you, those three are true, but by other definitions, they're crude falsehoods. For instance, a communist retorts: "I have my own definition of 'slavery.' 'Slavery,' by my definition, is the state of being wrapped up in bondage to your own selfish interests, whereas true freedom, I define as the state of being released from confining personal concerns and being compelled to serve and love your brothers." If slavery is being egoistic, and freedom is being compelled to be self-sacrificial (and this is the Platonic and Hegelian definition of freedom and slavery), then socialism is freedom, and capitalism does rest on slavery. The communist in the example I gave you at least comes forth with a definition and says his is correct and yours is wrong, and assuming he used logic (which he didn't), you could argue with him. The nominalist, however, hears your dispute, and he enters and says: "Look, what's the use of arguing? There's nothing to choose between your two sides. Definitions are arbitrary, and therefore all the general principles that rest upon them are equally arbitrary. General principles are a matter of semantics." That's the nominalist tip off—you just start disputing over the use of words. The communist wants to use "slavery" one way, and you define it differently. But there's no objective definition, and therefore, there are no objective general truths. General principles are all subjective, i.e., they follow from the usage of words. Your principles merely express your particular word usage. They don't express facts of reality. They merely say that the way you use names, socialism and slavery go together. Well, that's okay. But it's no better than the way the communist uses names, according to which capitalism and slavery go together. If you say, "Well, after all, what really *is* slavery?," they say, "What really is slavery? Slavery is whatever you make it—definitions are arbitrary." As it's put, there are no real definitions, only nominal definitions. Hobbes says explicitly that general statements are merely "a conjunction of names." He gives the example: I (Hobbes) say, "Man is a living creature," you might think that's a fact of reality, but no; I've merely said that I'm going to use words in such a way that anytime I call something "man," I'll also call it "living creature." I'll have made a subjective arbitrary decision, and I've conjoined two names. That's just a subjective predilection.

What then can *reasoning* hope to accomplish on this viewpoint? Reasoning requires premises, general principles from which we reason. When you reason, you say, "Granted such and such truths, then such and such follows." But suppose that your premises are merely linguistic—they just express your arbitrary word choices. What status will your conclusion have? Obviously, no better than the premises. Your conclusion will merely state, "Given that you use words in certain arbitrary combinations in the premises, then to be consistent you must use those words in a certain other arbitrary way in the conclusion." If your premise had stated facts of reality, then so would your conclusion, and reasoning in such a case could give you knowledge of fact. But if your premises are just linguistic conventions, then reasoning is just playing with words. If I give the typical syllogism, "All men are living beings; all living beings are mortal; therefore, all men are mortal," the nominalist would say that all you're doing in this alleged reasoning is saying that if you used the word "man" in such a way that you arbitrarily won't call anything a man unless he's a living creature, and if you use the word "living being" in such a way that you arbitrarily won't call anything a living being unless it's mortal, then to be consistent, you must use the word "man" in such a way that you won't call anything a man unless you *call* it mortal. In other words, reasoning gives you only the consequences of your arbitrarily chosen definitions. The whole reasoning process is severed from reality. I said "playing with words," but Hobbes has his own definition—reasoning is "reckoning with names." To put the same point another way, all reasoning is conditional or hypothetical—it tells you only that *if* you use words in certain ways, then you must use them in other ways. It tells you only what Hobbes calls (and please take note of this) *rela-*

tions of names, as against *matters of fact*. We'll return to that in a moment. Reasoning never tells you absolutely that such and such is a fact, but that it's always conditional and linguistic. Reasoning, by a nominalist metaphysics, never can give you knowledge of facts. And here you see the obvious tie-in to sensualism—only the senses, not reason, can teach you about reality.

It wouldn't take much work to anticipate the consequences of severing reason from reality in this fashion. Anything that you believe as a result of reasoning from general principles based on definitions becomes linguistic. I leave it to your imagination, and, in fact, I'll show you some consequences shortly.

Can we ever know, according to Hobbes, that facts exist? Since we don't know them by reasoning, can we ever know facts at all? Is everything a linguistic convention? No, says Hobbes; he's not that modern. Certain statements do express matters of fact. They do tell us facts about the actual world. It's not true that everything is a linguistic convention. Well, what statements are those? The only statements that a sensualist can grasp are those that come from direct sense perception, or images, and memory of sense perception. For instance, if you open your eyes and you see a little furry creature with a tail meowing on a rug, you can say, "A cat is on the mat," and that statement is factual, guaranteed by direct experience. If you listen to a piece of music and you have your eyes on your wristwatch and you see that it lasts for twenty minutes, you can say, "This piece of music lasts twenty minutes"—that's a fact, one that doesn't depend upon your arbitrary conceptualization. But any truths that go beyond what's given to you in sense experience—any truths that depend on human definitions, concepts, general principles, reasoning, as against simply passive, sensory staring—any such truths are merely verbal, conventional, non-factual. So "A cat is on the mat" is a matter of fact. "Cats are necessarily mortal" is conceptual, rational, and therefore, linguistic—that's a relation of names. "There are four mountains north of a certain point in Colorado"—that's a matter of fact because you just look and see. "Two and two equals four" is a general principle that depends on your definitions; that's just a relation of names. "Many Russians are hungry today"—that's a matter of fact because you can go there and see them and look at the hunger pains. "Communism, by its nature, is anti-life" is semantic, i.e., a matter of the way you use words. In all cases, the general principle is what you cannot substantiate simply by opening your eyes, and therefore, it is linguistic, conventional, non-factual.

For Hobbes, there is a basic dichotomy, two fundamentally different types of statements: matters of fact given in direct sense experience, as against relations of names, which are linguistic, conventional, non-factual truths, based on definitions and reasoning. I cannot overemphasize this distinction, which you'll hear over and over again in many variants. And if you combine it with the necessary-contingent dichotomy that goes back to Plato and Aristotle, the result is the following dichotomy: on the one hand, brute contingent sensory facts, and on the other hand, logical, necessary, conventional, conceptual truths. The factual contingent knowledge coming from *per*ception; the necessary but verbal knowledge coming from *con*ception, from linguistic manipulation. And that, when it develops fully, is the analytic-synthetic dichotomy, named by Kant and endorsed to its hilt by both Hume and Kant. We will see it growing further.

Even though Hobbes talks about matters of fact, he also says a few pages away that the senses don't give us knowledge of reality. Then what? The senses don't give us knowledge of reality, nor does reason. What then *does* give us knowledge of reality? Says Hobbes, in the last analysis: "Nothing"—he's a complete skeptic. And you might ask: What happens to Hobbes's own philosophy then? It's no better than anybody else's. All skepticism is self-refuting in that way. You might be surprised to know that Hobbes agrees with you. He says the truth is unknowable by man, because there's no objective standard to appeal to when men dispute. You ask, if men disagree, how then are they to decide? Hobbes had a very direct answer: The best way of ensuring that there will be a resolution of human disputes is the king, who is to have a very efficient police apparatus. There must be *some* way for men to deal with one another. But there's no way for men to be reasonable, even if they sat down with the best will in the world—there would be no objective principles to appeal to. There's no reason behind one set of definitions versus another. If we are to have order out of chaos, we must have a king or a dictator, and the only ultimate reason for accepting any theory or philosophy or idea in any field would be: The man with political power commands you to obey it. This is the philosophy of "might makes right" in the deepest sense—might makes *truth*, any truth, not just ethical truth—and for this reason, Hobbes is one of the early totalitarians in the modern world. He's one of the founders of the theory of modern dictatorship. And was beloved by the Nazis.

Before we leave Hobbes's epistemology, I want you to observe what has happened to this arch materialist, epistemologically. As far as the senses are concerned, we are left locked up in our own minds contemplating our own experiences, divorced from reality. As far as reason is concerned, all we can do is manipulate words, which we put together arbitrarily, divorced from reality. In other words, reasoning tells us how we use words in our own minds. Both of man's cognitive faculties are separated from reality. So, here we have the arch materialist withdrawing totally into . . . consciousness. Consciousness has become divorced from existence. It has its own world of experiences and verbal manipulations, all of it sundered from reality. This withdrawal into consciousness, in a different form, forms the fundamental premise of Descartes, and between Hobbes and Descartes, the primacy of consciousness becomes launched as the foundation stone of modern philosophy.

Let's finish Hobbes very briefly—his psychology, ethics, and politics, which are obvious consequences of what we've said and just rattle themselves off if you've come this far with them. Man is essentially the same as a machine, merely a more complicated one, because his actions are determined by the laws of motion, including his desires and aversions. His whole so-called emotional life is just various jigglings of various parts of his brain and his body. According to the laws of mechanics, there is no free will. Hobbes holds that it happens to be the case that when a material stimulus strikes the body, one of two reactions will take place mechanistically: Either you will start moving in the direction of the stimulus, and then you are said to desire it, or you will start moving away from it, and then you are said to have an aversion to it. For instance, if I hold a snake up before your eyes and dangle it, by the laws of motion you move back. If I hold up a million dollars, you move forward.

Now, says Hobbes, men give the name "good" to their desires, and the name "evil" to their aversions. Therefore, "good" and "evil" are merely names, signifying "I like" or "I do not like." Therefore, Hobbes is an avowed subjectivist in ethics, in *all* value theory. His subjectivism has three main roots: Metaphysically, it comes from his materialism. It's pointless to advise a determined machine what it *ought* to do since it has no choice. You cannot talk a machine out of obedience to the laws of mechanics, and therefore, if man acts a certain way, he acts as he must, and there's no objective basis for saying that this behavior is good or this is bad, this is better or this is worse. He reacts as he must. Secondly, epistemologically, nominalism is at the root of his subjectivism. If reason, in general, is impotent to yield objective knowledge, obviously it's impotent in ethics. And thirdly, Hobbes is trying to be "scientific." He is very much influenced by these people who said that to be scientific in ethics you must confine yourself to *de*scription, not *pre*scription. That's another root of modern ethical subjectivism. So "good" means "I want it," arbitrarily.

What do people want? What are their characteristic human desires, according to Hobbes? In spite of his materialism, he's a good Christian, with a typically Christian view of human nature as black, depraved, stained with sin (although he doesn't call it sin), but he has essentially the Augustinian view of man (he doesn't call it that). He is touted as being realistic because he's a thorough cynic. His view is that everybody wants to satisfy his desires, and the basic desires of all men are (1) to grab as much material wealth as they can, no matter how; (2) to protect themselves against the rest of their fellows, who are equal predators trying to grab their wealth; and (3) to gain fame and glory in the eyes of their fellows. In effect, he views men as brutal, grasping, whim-worshiping social metaphysicians by nature. And that he defends by saying, "Look around you." And in the Christian world, everybody was willing to say, sure, that's the way people are. Needless to say, Hobbes is taken as representative of the view that all men are egoists. And this concept of man is carried on as the egoist view of man. And it is the Sophist concept of egoism that Hobbes subscribes to.

How should you treat others then if they disagree with you? Force, physical force, is the only way—both to hit them before they hit you and to grab material goods before they get to them. Because you can't reason with men (for all the reasons we've mentioned), men must live by force.

Which brings us to Hobbes's famous politics. If we didn't have a government—let's call it what he calls it, a "state of nature" (which is a state without a government)—life in such a state, he says, would be, in a famous phrase from *Leviathan*, "Solitary, poor, nasty, brutish, and short." Because a state of nature with all these savage killers (namely, men) running loose would be a state of war, the war of all against all, where everybody is like Gyges in the myth out to cut everybody else's throat. Now, says Hobbes, life could be fine, it could be peaceful, if men would obey certain principles—for instance, the Golden Rule—but they won't, left to their own devices. They won't because they are too rotten (although he doesn't use that word). And even if one of them had some good will and decided to, he'd be crazy to in a state of nature, because if he weren't out to kill off everybody else, or get to them before they got to him, they would get to him first. And therefore, says Hobbes, in a state of nature there is no morality, there is nothing of objective values, anything is permitted, anything goes.

This is intolerable, says Hobbes. There must be a way out. Well, he says, suppose men were to contract with each other, to make a solemn vow to each other—each one to say to the other, "Look, let's pick one of us and say, 'I will turn over all my power to him if you do the same, and you do the same, and you do the same, etc.' We'll give absolute power to a single sovereign, a despot. We then will be deprived of the means of creating civil strife. The sovereign will keep us all quiet and peaceful by force and threat. We will have to behave out of fear of what he will do to us." Therefore, says Hobbes, we should have an absolute dictatorship. The sovereign can do *anything*, because there is no objective morality and therefore, no objective rights. Can you say, "But didn't the sovereign promise to keep peace?" No, the sovereign doesn't make any promises. As Hobbes says in a famous line, "Covenants without the sword are but words." In other words, a promise not backed up by a gun is meaningless. You make a promise with all the other subjects, but the king is the one with the gun to enforce it. Therefore, the king himself is not bound by any promises, because there's nobody to enforce his obedience. The king is still in the state of nature. And consequently, he is unlimited and can do whatever he chooses. And your goal, your obligation, is unqualified obedience to him. You are forced to do whatever he says, and, by the way, that will be the right thing because the king's precepts are the standard of morality and the standard of truth. The king creates morality by his precepts. Good is what the king decrees. Therefore, rulers must be scrupulously obeyed. You cannot criticize the state. For Hobbes, the concept of an unjust action on the part of the state is a self-contradiction. The state *defines* "justice." Hobbes adds that you can do anything that the sovereign hasn't forbidden you to do.

This Hobbesian view is all over the place today among advocates of "democracy," not quite in this clear cut of a form. But when they say that we can't have laissez-faire capitalism, because people would run amuck, or if we didn't have building ordinances and left it to private capitalists, obviously their greed and power lust would have them put no foundation in, or they'd try to save money by leaving the third story out and going right to the fourth, so we need regulatory agencies. And we can't leave the draft to volunteers, because only bureaucrats can tell when a country is threatened. All of that is the Hobbesian line: People are savages, irrational brutes, and only a small handful who have physical power know what to do.

To conclude our discussion of Hobbes, I want to observe that whereas on the surface there is a profound opposition in every main field of philosophy between Plato and Hobbes, when you come down to essentials, observe how the alleged opposition leads to the same ultimate practical consequences. In metaphysics, Hobbes is a materialist, Plato an idealist (true reality is nonmaterial). But Hobbes's materialism says there is no mind, and therefore, a few steps later, we have to use force in politics.

Plato's idealism says there is so a mind—there's a whole supernatural world—and therefore, for the cave dwellers, we have to use force. Or turning to epistemology, Hobbes's nominalism says we can't know anything objectively, therefore, dictatorship. Plato is the rationalist, the Platonic realist, not the nominalist, and therefore, a mystic who says knowledge is reserved for a special elite, and we must have dictatorship by the philosopher-king. In ethics, Hobbes is a thorough egoist (so-called)—men are selfish cutthroats, and therefore, they must be ruled by force. Plato—oh no, men should sacrifice for others, they should love their brothers, and therefore, their brothers have every right to tell them where their services are needed, and therefore, force. In other words, from all of these alleged alternatives, you end up with the same politics—in essence, you are back to Plato versus the Sophists. Which is the state of modern philosophy at its outset.

René Descartes

Let us turn to René Descartes (1596–1650). Descartes is more influential than Hobbes, significantly so, so please don't be deceived by the fact that I give him less time, which I do because in many ways his philosophy is less complex to present. Descartes is justifiably acknowledged as the father of modern philosophy. He was brought up by the Jesuits, received a thorough Scholastic training, and was a devout Catholic. Nevertheless, Descartes says, he is going to make a fundamental new beginning in philosophy. He says that he is going to be much more fundamental in his approach than any other modern philosopher. Hobbes, for instance, takes over modern science uncritically. Descartes accepts the conclusions of modern science—that is, the scientific conclusions, not materialism. But, he says, in effect: I want to question it, I want to question everything, right to the root. I want to erect a philosophic system from scratch, without taking over anything from other people uncritically. And therefore, this is going to be the beginning of a new era in philosophy.

I may interject to say that, as you'll see, Descartes's ideas are not new. His distinctive contribution is actually to institutionalize the primacy of consciousness, that is to say, the Platonic-Augustinian viewpoint, to plant it into the very heart of modern philosophy. He is the father of the modern primacy of consciousness. Ever since him, that viewpoint has been more explicit and virulent than ever before. How did he do it?

Like everyone else of this period, Descartes is very conscious of method. One of his early works is *Rules for the Direction of the Mind* and another famous one is the *Discourse on Method.* He tells us that we must accept nothing blindly, nothing arbitrarily, not because we feel it, not because others believe it, not because our temperament points to it. We must be guided exclusively by objective reason. This sounds fine, but it all depends on what he means by "reason." All men, he says, are by nature equipped with reason. Reason *is* capable of knowing reality. Hobbes is wrong. Reality is rational, it's intelligible, it can be known by the human mind. Why, then, are men so confused, so uncertain, in such chronic disagreement? Descartes noticed that when he went to school, what he was taught in one class was contradicted by what he was taught in another class. He said the trouble is that people just plunge in haphazardly, without a firm foundation, without any systematic method, and that's why they end up in such chronic disagreement.

So what method should we use? You shouldn't be surprised to learn that Descartes says we must model philosophy on . . . mathematics. Mathematics, he says, is the one science that enables us to achieve clear-cut, indubitable certainty. What enables mathematics to do this? It starts from basic self-evident axioms (which are indubitable, perfectly certain), and proceeds logically to deduce their consequences. And that, he says, is what we must do in philosophy. That way, we will achieve a philosophic system that is absolutely certain, not a matter of opinion. It will be a definitive statement of the truth to end all disagreement, a philosophy to end all philosophy.

The crucial question is: How are we going to get our fundamental axioms? They must be absolutely certain because everything else rests on them. If there is one chance in a hundred, in a thousand, in a trillion, that a proposition is not true, it is unacceptable to Descartes as an axiom, because then it would infect all the rest of our knowledge with that same uncertainty. Well, says Descartes, there is only one way to proceed in our search for fundamental axioms: We must examine every idea we can think of. We must search through the whole range of human thoughts. And of every thought we must ask: "Can this rationally be doubted? Are there any rational grounds on which to doubt this idea?" Notice that it has to be *rational* grounds—you can't just arbitrarily say, "This might be wrong," you have to give a reason. And if there are any grounds, one chance in a thousand, that the idea is wrong, we have to abandon it and look further. We may come back and reinstate some of the ideas that we threw out in the beginning, but we throw them out in the beginning because they are no good as the foundation of knowledge. We want the indubitable, the absolutely certain. If we find nothing at all that fulfills this test, then we should close up shop, that's the end of philosophy, period. But, if we find even one idea that can't be doubted, then our base is established.

This process is known as "Cartesian doubt." A Cartesian doubter is supposed to be very different from a skeptical doubter. A skeptical doubter doubts because he delights in showing you can't be sure of anything. A Cartesian doubter doubts because he's supposed to be desperate to find something that escapes the possibility of doubt. Cartesian doubt, if you want a formal definition: the method of establishing a fundamental certainty by doubting everything that one can conceive of any grounds for doubting. Let me say that this method is wrong. It is disastrous. If you approach philosophy this way, only catastrophe can result, as you will see in a moment. What is wrong with this apparently innocuous method of finding certainty, by means of doubting everything that could be doubted, until you find a final inescapable one?

Let us follow Descartes in the famous process of Cartesian doubt. What can we doubt? I'm going to read from Descartes. He writes very clearly. (French and British philosophers write clearly, as against German philosophers.) And I'm going to constantly interject comments, so try to keep clear when it's me and when it's Descartes. He's going to start from the most obvious point. "Surely, I cannot reasonably doubt that I am here, seated by the fire, attired in a dressing gown, having this paper in my hands, and other similar matters. And how could I deny that these hands and this body are mine? Were it not perhaps that I compare myself to certain persons devoid of sense whose cerebella are so troubled and clouded by the violent vapors of black vile [Peikoff: In other words, they're crazy.] that they constantly assure us that they think they are kings when they are really quite poor, or that they are clothed in purple when they are really without covering?"

In other words, there is such a thing as insanity, which is characterized by vivid hallucinations and very often by firm delusions. In both cases, the person has no insight. That is supposed to be one of the distinguishing characteristics between a psychotic and a neurotic—a neurotic knows he's sick and a psychotic doesn't. This phenomenon exists, holds Descartes. Is it not possible that my belief that I am seated here in a dressing gown, and so on, is a psychotic delusion or hallucination? It happens to people. How do I know it didn't happen to me? Is it possible—not probable—but possible? There is one chance in a million that I'm a raving lunatic, and that all of this is a delusion. If so, I can't accept it because I want the indubitable. That is, so to speak, the insanity division of Cartesian doubt.

Now we go on. "At the same time, I must remember that I'm in the habit of sleeping, and in my dreams, representing to myself the same things, or sometimes even less probable things, than do those who are insane in their waking moments. How often has it happened to me that in the night, I dreamt that I found myself in this particular place, that I was dressed and seated near the fire, whilst in reality I was lying undressed in bed. On reflection I see manifestly that there are no certain indications by which we may clearly distinguish wakefulness from sleep."

People dream. One of the characteristics of a dream is that you very rarely know that you're dreaming—you take it as real, you feel fear, passion, etc. This to you is reality. And then you wake up with a start and you say, "Ah, it was just a dream." Well, is it possible that you're dreaming right now, that you are actually home in bed and are having a vivid dream of a lecture on Descartes, and any moment you'll wake up? Well, says Descartes, it's possible, isn't it? There's one chance in a thousand, in a million. Can't be certain . . . out. That is the dream division. There's no use in saying that the way to tell the difference between a dream and awake is to pinch yourself, because, Descartes will say, how do you know that you're really pinching yourself and not just dreaming that you're pinching yourself? So he's going to assume the worst because he wants certainty.

Continuing: "Now let us assume that we are asleep and that all these particulars—for instance, that we open our eyes, shake our head, extend our hands and so on—are but false delusions. And let us reflect that possibly neither our hands nor our whole body are as such as they appear to us to be." In other words, maybe the whole thing is a dream. Maybe the whole physical world is a dream or a huge hallucination. After all, can you trust the senses? Even if you don't take the view that the senses are *always* wrong, everybody, says Descartes, grants that the senses are *sometimes* wrong, and if the senses are sometimes deceptive, how do you know in any particular case for certain that they're not deceptive in this particular case? Since you can't be certain of any conclusion about the material world, it might be a hallucination, a delusion, a dream, a deception.

We go on. "Surely arithmetic, geometry, and other sciences of that kind, which only treat of things that are very simple and very general [Peikoff: which don't depend on the senses] contain some measure of certainty and an element of the indubitable. For whether I am awake or asleep, two and three together always form five, and the square can never have more than four sides. And it does not seem possible that truths so clear and apparent can be suspected of any falsity." You can imagine, it seems self-evident, that a square has four sides. But people have been wrong about the self-evident. They thought that it was self-evident that the earth was flat. How do you know they're not wrong in this case? Is it possible? There's one chance in a thousand. You can't be certain. Suppose you say, "But I'll give a proof, I'll give an airtight argument with premises leading to a conclusion." The answer comes back: People commit fallacies in their reasoning, i.e., they reason invalidly and think honestly that they have arrived at the truth. How do you know you didn't commit a fallacy? Is it possible? One chance in a thousand?

Descartes finds still another basis for doubt, even of mathematics—"I have long had fixed in my mind the belief that an all-powerful God existed, by whom I have been created such as I am. How do I know that he has not brought it to pass that I am deceived every time I add two and three? But possibly God does not desire that I should be thus deceived, for he is said to be supremely good? Well, we cannot be certain that God is supremely good. He may be an evil genius, no less powerful than deceitful, who has employed his whole energies in deceiving me. I shall consider therefore that the heavens, the earth, colors, figures, sound, and all other external things, may be nothing but the illusions and dreams of which this demon has availed himself in order to lay traps for my credulity." That's called "Descartes's demon." How do you know it doesn't exist? Is it possible? I don't see why it's impossible, he says, that there could be an all-powerful wicked being, who would delight in deceiving me, and every time I add two and three and get five, he rubs his hands in glee that he took me in. And his way of taking me in is to make "two and three equals five" seem so clear that we never think of questioning. Descartes is not going to be trapped by the demon. "At the end, I feel constrained to confess that there is nothing in all that I formerly believed to be true of which I cannot in some measure doubt, and doubt not merely through want of thought or through levity, but for reasons which are very powerful and maturely considered." You get the idea. There are all these possible sources of error—dreams, hallucination, delusion, insanity, sensory deception, fallacies, misidentification of the self-evident, etc.—all of it, so to speak, symbolized by the demon. The demon really represents the possibility of error.

The issue, therefore, is really this—and Descartes doesn't say it, but this is the actual meaning of Cartesian doubt: How can man ever achieve certainty? Because to say you're certain about something is to say you cannot possibly be wrong. That's what it means to say you're certain. On the other hand, man is a fallible being, and a fallible being is a being who *can* be wrong, who is capable of error. And therefore, the problem posed by Cartesian doubt is the problem of how a fallible being can ever attain certainty. On the face of it, it seems like an obvious impossibility. How can a being capable by nature of error ever reach a state of saying, "I'm incapable of error"? That's the problem posed by Descartes's philosophy that the demon symbolizes. That's the problem, by the way, that I will answer in lecture twelve. But now let's follow Descartes.

It seems that we're in a pretty hopeless state. But wait. I said that I might be dreaming, says Descartes. Well, *I* must exist in order to dream. I said I might be thinking insanely. Even so, *I* must exist in order to think insanely. I said I might be deceived by an evil demon. But *I* have to exist in order for him to deceive me. I said I'm conscious of my inadequacies, my ignorance, my doubts. *I* have to be, to be conscious of them. You say I think incorrectly, but the very fact that I think at all immediately establishes one thing: Even if all my thinking is wrong, even if I reach total despair and I'm left with nothing but thoughts that I doubt, in order to doubt, I must exist, i.e., in order to think, even if incorrectly, I must exist. "I think, therefore, I am." In Latin, *Cogito ergo sum.* That's the axiom, called "Descartes's Cogito."

The basic, unquestionable premise, the undoubtable, is the existence of yourself, your (consciousness). The very act of doubting your consciousness establishes your consciousness, because to doubt is to display a certain kind of consciousness. Notice that all that Descartes has established is that his *consciousness* exists. The argument works only for that. One of his opponents tried to establish the existence of the body in the same way, and he said, "I walk, therefore, I am"—*Ambulo ergo sum.* Descartes dismissed that as ridiculous because, he said, you might just be imagining that you're walking, you might just be dreaming that you're walking, you might just be thinking that you're walking—the whole material world, including your body, might be an illusion,. But you can't just be dreaming or imagining that you're conscious, because to dream or imagine *means* to be conscious. If somebody says to you, "You just think you're thinking," you say to him, "Fine, if I think I'm thinking, I'm thinking," because by "think" he really means, "I'm conscious, conscious in any form." That's what he means by "I think." Therefore, the fundamental indubitable truth is "My consciousness exists," as uttered by Descartes or by anyone of you who is conscious. The fundamental axiom, the basic premise, the starting point of philosophy, of all knowledge, is the existence of consciousness.

I cannot emphasize enough that at this point in Descartes's philosophy, that we do not yet have any grounds to believe that there is a physical world, other people, that you even have a body or that Descartes even has a body—legs, arms, heart, etc. He knows only that he, Descartes, as a consciousness, exists. In other words, what he maintained is: You can be certain of the existence of consciousness *before* you can know there is a physical external world. Consciousness has logical priority. And, therefore, if we are to find out that there's an external world (and Descartes thought there was one), we must infer its existence somehow from the content of consciousness. We are not given existence directly. We are given directly only consciousness. This viewpoint is known as the *prior certainty of consciousness*, for obvious reasons. The place to start philosophically, the easiest thing to know, is your own consciousness. It is a self-contained entity that you directly and immediately can discover, and that we contradict ourselves in the process of trying to deny. It's logically unassailable. But the external world—existence, reality—is still doubtful. For all we know at this stage, there may be no external world at all, only our consciousness, and everything else might be a figment of our imagination, a gigantic deception perpetrated by the demon.

Now consider this: Consciousness could, for all we know, exist by itself without there being a reality. It's a self-contained independent entity that does not require a reality metaphysically. Therefore, consciousness is not the faculty for *perceiving* reality, because if it were, in the act of being conscious, it would be aware of reality. Since we know consciousness first and *don't* know existence directly, we are *not* in immediate contact with reality. We have to try to *prove* that there's a reality, we have to try to deduce it from our own consciousness, from our axiom. We are, as I think you can see, in an impossible position. On the one hand, consciousness metaphysically does not require reality, and yet, if we are to find out that there is a reality, we have to deduce it from consciousness. But how can you deduce reality from consciousness if consciousness doesn't require or imply a reality? Obviously, you cannot. We'll see Descartes's feeble attempt in a moment, but it's so feeble that nobody of any significance followed Descartes in it, because it's embarrassing.

The upshot was that almost all philosophers accepted Descartes's prior certainty of consciousness, and then there was a hopeless struggle to scrounge up a reality. But they couldn't do it. And so, one by one, and more and more, reality dropped out of the picture. All that existed was consciousness and its experiences. That has come to be called "the problem of the external world," bequeathed by Descartes: What makes you think there is one? Which many philosophers proclaim is insoluble. Now you know why I said that Descartes was the founder of the primacy of consciousness. He himself believed in reality, but his method of defending that belief rested on the prior certainty of consciousness—in other words, upon the independence of consciousness from reality, upon the view that reality must be a derivative of consciousness, which means upon the primacy of consciousness. That was the fatal blow at the base of Descartes's system, from which mankind never recovered philosophically.

What is wrong with the conclusion of the prior certainty of consciousness? I don't think I have to tell you. It is a logical impossibility for there to be a consciousness without existence. Otherwise, what is it conscious *of*? It is a logical impossibility for anyone to know that he is conscious without *knowing* that there is an existence—otherwise, what does he know he is conscious *of*? Here I refer you to Galt's crucial statement, "Existence exists and consciousness is the faculty for perceiving that which exists." Existence and consciousness are both axioms. They start off together, in any proper philosophy, with existence first. That's the disaster implicit in Cartesian doubt as a method. It leads inevitably to the prior certainty of consciousness, and therefore, to the primacy of consciousness. As to the error of Cartesian doubt itself as a method, what led us to this conclusion, that, as I said, I will discuss in lecture twelve.

I want to clarify the enigmatic remark I made some lectures ago that I promised I'd clarify. Descartes did not originate the *Cogito* argument. In slightly different form it was actually originated by Augustine, as you should expect. Recall that I emphasized Augustine's changing of the focus of philosophy from the outer to the inner, the soul, or consciousness. As part of his philosophy, Augustine had explicitly advocated the prior certainty of consciousness. And Descartes here is giving a somewhat different form and enormous prominence and emphasis to this Augustinian viewpoint. And since Augustine is Plato made Catholic, you can see that Descartes is fundamentally a Platonist.

Let's continue. We want to try to establish the existence of the external world, in which Descartes himself believed. How are we going to do it? Descartes says that if only we can establish that there is no demon, no perpetual deception being practiced on us, then we'll be entitled to trust our minds. So, the problem of the external world becomes the problem of getting rid of the demon. How will we prove that there is no demon? Descartes says, only if we can prove there's an all-powerful and *good* God watching over us. A perfect God wouldn't permit demons to go around deceiving us, nor would he stoop to deception himself. Therefore, our scenario goes from *our* consciousness to *God*'s consciousness—from the mortal consciousness to the immortal, infinite consciousness—before we can finally get to the external world . . . hopefully.

At this point, Descartes launches into a whole series of arguments for the existence of God. They are standard. Of course, he can't use the argument from design—the argument that the whole world is so orderly, therefore, God must have created it—because he doesn't know there's a world yet. But he picks up the ones that he can from ancient and medieval philosophy. He can say, "Here I am, somebody must have created me, I didn't, so it must be God." He uses Saint Anselm's ontological argument, which he thinks is terrific. He has another argument that I'll give you a brief taste of, called the *argument from the cause of the idea of God.* And that argument goes like this: I have an idea of God. (Descartes's definition of "God," by the way, is "a substance who is infinite, eternal, immutable, independent, all-knowing, all-powerful, and which created everything which exists." In other words, a perfect Christian God.) Now, he says, this is the idea of a perfect being. Where did I get this idea? What caused it in me? Did I make it up myself? No. Why not? Because the cause of anything must be at least as perfect as the effect. The less perfect can't cause the more perfect. How do you know that the less perfect can't cause the more perfect? Says Descartes, in a pregnant utterance, that is "clear and distinct." You remember that phrase from the Stoics? Here it is again. The less perfect, the less real, can't cause the more perfect, the more real. That is "clear and distinct," obvious, self-evident. I, however, am imperfect and finite—that's obvious. Consequently, I couldn't cause this idea, because this is an idea of an absolutely perfect being, and therefore, itself shares in absolute perfection. Therefore, only an absolutely perfect being could have caused it in me. And therefore, it did. And therefore, there must be such a being. Therefore, God exists. Q.E.D.

The idea of God, he says, is "the mark of the workman impressed on his work." It's as though God turns out each soul, stamps his trademark on it, and the trademark is the idea of God, and then when the soul becomes adult and introspects, it finds the trademark, and that's the idea of God, and from the perfection of the trademark it infers the perfection of God as the cause. I won't bother to criticize this argument, but I do want to point out how Platonic the argument is. The more perfect can't be caused by the less perfect. How does that follow? Only if you accept Plato's view of degrees of reality and degrees of perfection—there's a higher really real, really perfect world, and our world, which is a dependent derivative, not as real or perfect. And since the higher world is true reality, it is the source of the imperfect reflections down here. Things down here get such goodness as they have by sharing in the rays emanating from beyond. This is the essence of this argument—our idea of God is a ray of perfection shining in our imperfect persons, so it must come from beyond. In other words, he takes the Platonic metaphysics as self-evident, and his other arguments are typical. (Modern commentators delight in demolishing his arguments for God, so we don't have to waste time on that.)

Now we almost have a physical world. First the soul, then God, now we're on the threshold of establishing that there is a reality. After all, says Descartes, God gave me all my powers, including my cognitive powers. He would never have given me the power to judge truth or falsehood unless I could trust myself. God wouldn't purposely deceive me—he wouldn't deliberately make me wrong—because God is not a deceiver. How do we know? Because God is perfect. And anybody who engages in deceit is obviously not perfect. I note here, in passing, the fantastic introduction of value judgments, as though they are self-evident, at a point where we don't yet even know that there is a physical world—we are nevertheless in a position to pass value judgments on lying. Notice also that Descartes believes that the validity of human consciousness depends upon God. If there weren't a good God, we couldn't trust our minds. This is a blatantly Augustinian element, as against Aquinas—man's mind is not self-validating but must be validated from beyond by God. And that is another reflection of the true Augustinianism of Descartes.

We're now ready for the physical world. Now we can trust ourselves. Descartes says: "Nothing more is left for me to do except to examine whether corporeal things exist." That's the last question, and then we're finished. So how do we get the physical world into the picture? Descartes says, you have to grant that we perceive things that *appear* to be physical objects. We don't cause these experiences in ourselves, because we can't alter them at will. You can't, for instance, will the sight of me away. And therefore, the cause of our experiences must be somehow outside of us. You might ask: Couldn't God directly cause our experiences in us without the intervention of any physical world? No, says Descartes. Why not, you ask? Is it because we perceive directly the material world? No, obviously, we don't. If we directly perceived the material world, we wouldn't have the primacy and prior certainty of consciousness. No, says Descartes, we know that God doesn't cause our experiences directly in us and that they must come from the material world because we conceive matter as clearly and distinctly different from God. *Why* do we, on this philosophy? No answer. We just do. Therefore, a material world exists, because otherwise, God would be deceiving us in something that is "clear and distinct" to us.

You don't have to be surprised that nobody followed this particular root to an external world. It is much better, it's healthier, to get rid of reality right off the bat, than to drag it in in this feeble, arbitrary way.

I would like you to observe how hopeless this whole approach of Descartes's is: He's gone through all of this argumentation (and a good part of it I left out) as to why we can trust our minds. All the arguments for God, and if there's God he wouldn't deceive us, and therefore, we can trust our minds—and the whole business. He's satisfied, yes, we can trust our minds. Suppose you grant that all of his argumentation, every step of it, from the *Cogito* on, is impeccable to the human mind. You can't find a thing wrong with it. Has he, therefore, validated the human mind? Obviously not. If there were a demon, which is his hypothesis at the beginning, then at the end of this whole incredible chain of reasoning, as Descartes says, "Now I've validated the human mind," the demon would sit back and chuckle to himself, "I really took him in that time."

The wider point here is that there can be no such thing as an argument to prove that the mind is reliable. If you call in question the reliability of the mind, the validity of the mind, what do you propose to use to answer the question? If you say, "You cannot trust human arguments, but here's an argument to show that you can trust them after all"—well, if you can't trust them, you can't trust them, period, and that cuts out your own argument. Either the validity of the human mind is an axiom, or all is lost. It cannot be established by reasoning, because reasoning is an act of that very mind. And when I say all is lost, I mean *all*, because, as later philosophers were quick to point out, even the *Cogito* itself does not stand on Descartes's premises. How do you *know* that just because I think, therefore, I am? Descartes's answer is "'I think, therefore, I am' *must* be true; it is so clear and distinct." But the answer is, it's no clearer and distincter than "Two plus three equals five" or "A square has four sides." In all these cases, the opposite is a contradiction. But if we can't trust our minds—if something could be blatantly contradictory to us and nevertheless be correct—then we cannot trust *anything*, including even the statement that we have minds or engage in doubts. We are wiped out entirely. In this way, Descartes is really the source of all modern skepticism. Although he claims to be putting an end to skepticism, he, more than anybody, entrenched ancient skepticism deeply into all modern philosophy. His typical follower accepted the method of Cartesian doubt, threw out the *Cogito* as arbitrary, and ended as a complete ancient skeptic. So if in one respect, Descartes is the father of Idealism—in other words, of the primacy of consciousness and of the mentality that dispenses with or degrades the external world—in another sense, he's the true father of modern skepticism. So in one stroke, you see, he reinstituted the Sophists and Plato (Plato via the primacy of consciousness) and closed the door to Aristotle.

Let's look at Descartes's epistemology, and then come back for a few final words on one more aspect of his metaphysics. Are the senses valid? No. Descartes accepts the primary-secondary quality distinction. The senses deceive us. They do not give us any knowledge of the real nature of the material world. All that is actually real, in his terms, is *extension*, which means "three-dimensionality"—spread-outness in space with the appropriate associated characteristics (size, shape, quantity, motion). The senses, says Descartes, are useful for practical purposes of living. But they do not give us objective knowledge about reality.

To gain true knowledge, what do we do? As we said at the outset, we must model ourselves on mathematics. We need self-evident axioms. Where do we get our basic premises? In theory, there are only three choices: (1) You look outward to get your basic axioms, à la Aristotle; (2) you look upward, à la Augustine; or (3) you look inward, à la Plato. Descartes has rejected the senses as a source of axioms. He is being very modern and secular, and therefore, he rejects God as a source of axioms. And the only remaining choice is: Look inward. You have to introspect to get your basic premises. Does this mean then that there are ideas in the mind apart from sensory data, ideas acquired by some means other than the senses? Yes, says Descartes. How did we get them? We are born with them. They are innate. And here Descartes follows Plato, although he does not believe that *all* knowledge is innate, merely certain crucial fundamentals (e.g., the idea of God and certain mathematical ideas). Descartes does not believe in the preexistence of the soul—that's prohibited by Catholic dogma—and he, therefore, follows the Augustinian view that innate ideas are our heritage from God. So what do we do to acquire knowledge? We look inward and try to discover our innate ideas. Notice that an idea is no longer a form of awareness of reality but rather a self-contained thing inside our minds that we rummage around to find. And the primacy of consciousness that Descartes subscribes to *forbids* the idea that an idea is a form of awareness of reality. If an idea were an awareness of reality, then whenever we thought or had an idea, we'd be aware of reality and there could be no prior certainty of consciousness. On the other hand, if an idea isn't an awareness of reality, we'd have to be aware of reality to get it, so it couldn't be innate. In other words, the real epistemological expression of the primacy of consciousness is innate ideas. And that's why Plato believed in them, and that's why Descartes believes in them. Consciousness has to have its own domain, its own independent content to focus on, detached altogether from reality. That's what innate ideas serve epistemologically.

How do we distinguish innate ideas from these falsehoods and confusions that we have acquired through the senses and through commerce with other people? Because by the time we come to philosophize, we're grown up, and our minds are grab bags of conventional notions and popular prejudices and true innate ideas. How do we distinguish the authentic article, coming from God, from the arbitrary prejudices, beliefs, and so on? Can you do it by observing reality and checking? Oh no. The answer is that it must be something in the nature of the idea itself that certifies that it's the true article, the real innate idea. What is it? It's *clear and distinct*. "The things which we conceive very clearly and distinctly are all true." (He has the grace to add that there is some difficulty in ascertaining what those are.)

What does this mean? Descartes did not advocate subjectivism but thought that his clear and distinct innate ideas were objectively self-evident. But in fact, this has led to the idea that axioms are subjective, because there is now no way of validating axioms by reference to sense experience, by reference to reality. Whenever Descartes gets stuck, he has a clear and distinct intuition and then he goes on from there. He wants to prove God and he gets stuck, but the perfect can't be caused by the imperfect—that's clear and distinct, and on he goes. He wants to prove the external world. It must be clear and distinct but different from God. The conclusion the moderns draw is that there *are* no axioms. And so the fight is poised between the Cartesians who say, "Yes, there *are* clear and distinct innate axioms," and the other side who says, "Oh, it's all ridiculous subjectivism. There are no self-evident axioms." Descartes is right that knowledge requires self-evident axioms. But the crucial fact is that axioms must be objectively based on reality, which means based on the direct testimony of the senses. Everything else has to be logically proved. In this sense, Aristotle points the right direction. An axiom for Aristotle must be reducible to the directly perceivable. But that's the primacy of existence approach, which Descartes rejects out of hand. And the result of Descartes's approach is that pretty soon, more and more of his more careless followers begin to take more and more of the most grotesquely arbitrary ideas and say, "It's clear and distinct to me; therefore, this is my axiom." Pretty soon altruism becomes self-evident. Or there must be a God—after all, I clearly and distinctly conceive that somebody must have created the world. Etc. And then the reaction sets in. Hobbes's view takes over: "It's all linguistic, it's all arbitrary, there is no objective self-evidency." So you see the choice you're given: Descartes, posing as a champion of objectivity, comes up with axioms as being clear and distinct and innate, which means not based on reality. Hobbes says, "Ach, they're all arbitrary and linguistic," which means not based on reality. On the crucial point, they agree.

What then is the total method of knowledge for Descartes? You look inward, you find your clear and distinct ideas (you do this by a process that he calls "intuition"—intuition for him is the process of grasping clear and distinct ideas), and then you deduce their consequences. If you get stopped at some point, you have a new intuition of a clear and distinct idea, crank up the machine and go on again. Basic knowledge is innate in the mind and is grasped by direct introspection, or "intuition," as he calls it, and deduction therefrom.

This is the model of *rationalism*: the idea that reason alone—"reason" here meaning the faculty that intuits and deduces—leads to all knowledge. For Descartes, the senses, observation, inductive generalization—they are basically unimportant. They may be useful for practical purposes, they may even be fruitful in suggesting ideas to us to refer to our intuition to certify, they may remind us of our innate ideas (à la Plato). But the senses and induction do not tell us what reality is like. We find that out from innate ideas. How do we know our innate ideas are true since they're not based on observation? Descartes answers, God gave them to us, and God wouldn't deceive us. Those who followed quickly pointed out the hopeless circularity of this answer: He has to use his innate ideas to prove that there's a God, and then use the God to prove that he can rely on his innate ideas, which is a hopeless circle from which he never extricated himself.

Notice how consistent Descartes is epistemologically and metaphysically within the framework of the primacy of consciousness. If consciousness is the faculty of thinking, as he says it is, and thinking is the awareness of reality, then consciousness is not independent of reality, and there can be no prior certainty. But if there *is* a prior certainty of consciousness, then thinking must have some object other than reality, some aspect of consciousness as its content. Otherwise, consciousness is not self-sufficient. It must have some content of its own apart from reality. And Descartes says yes, and that content is innate ideas. So, in other words, the primacy of consciousness metaphysically and necessarily implies the breach of consciousness from existence epistemologically. And that breach, in turn, reinforces the primacy of consciousness, because the person says: "I never perceive reality; how do I know it's there? All I know is consciousness." So, you have a vicious circle, from which there is no escape, except by saying that the starting point is "Existence exists."

Now for a few points on Descartes's metaphysics, specifically on the mind-body question, for which he is famous. There are, for Descartes, two things that exist: consciousness and matter. And therefore, he is regarded as a *dualist* in metaphysics, because there are two kinds of things, consciousness and matter—two essential components to reality—as against Hobbes, who says that only matter exists, or as against Plato, who tends to deny that the physical world is actually real. Descartes thinks that both are real, the physical world and consciousness. He calls them each "substances," and his definition of "substance" is "a thing which exists in such a way as to stand in need of nothing beyond itself in order to exist." You can see the trouble in this definition if consciousness is therefore a substance.

So, the two substances are the mind substance and the body substance, what Descartes calls the *res cogitans*, "the thinking thing," and the *res extensio*, "the spread-out thing," or "the extended thing." And he adds that really God is the only substance because everything else depends on God, but we can omit that complexity.

So, we have two completely self-contained substances, or worlds, independent of each other, unconnected, a kind of metaphysical laissez-faire in which each leaves the other alone, and neither one requires the other. Thus, I have achieved a terrific thing, Descartes holds, by splintering the universe in two divisions, because I have found a way of retaining thought, purpose, free will, in a world in which matter is necessarily mechanistically determined by physical laws. Matter, I agree, the *res extensio*, is a completely material mechanical system, just as Hobbes and the scientists claim it is. He believes in God and in final causes. There is a purpose to everything that happens, even in the physical world. But final causes are inscrutable to human beings, and therefore, as scientists, we shouldn't look for them. We should content ourselves with ordinary natural scientific laws. In that sense, the scientists are absolutely right. But he says that God introduced a certain quantity of motion into the world when he created it, and then he withdrew, and from then on the world obeys the laws of modern science. Therefore, scientists can study it with impunity. Not only have I preserved the domain of modern science, I have escaped the catastrophe of Hobbes. I have found a place for mind in the world of matter, and therefore a place for all the things that are crucial to our Catholic religion. Mind is purposeful, so even though matter operates only by mechanism, mind is teleological. Mind thinks—that's the essence of consciousness, it's the thinking thing, the *res cogitans*, so we're not simply, as Hobbes said, creatures whose brains oscillate according to stimuli. We can think and come to objective conclusions.

Descartes is a strong believer in volition because he has a clear and distinct idea of it. As to the question of how you reconcile free will with God's causation of everything, he says that this is incomprehensible to man, so we shouldn't consider the question. Mind is immortal. Because it's entirely independent of matter, it can exist without matter. And this is the best proof of immortality ever offered. We make everybody happy—both the scientists and the religionists. We carve the universe in two. We render unto God the things that are God's: the mind; and unto Galileo the things that are Galileo's: the material world. Thus, Descartes's famous reconciliation of science and religion. Notice, by the way, that free will, purpose, and the power of thought get in under the power of religion and have been associated with it ever since. So, to this day, if you say you believe in free will, the power of thought, or the reality of purpose in human psychology, most philosophers and almost all psychologists routinely say, "Oh, that's some religious crackpot." That's the legacy of Descartes.

We come finally to man. How do we make sense of man? He is the creature who is a union of the two substances, of mind and body. And the shocking thing is that, in the case of man, these two utterly disparate independent substances can actually influence each other. They can interact. For instance, in sense perception, something physical strikes my mechanical body, and after the appropriate jigglings and mechanical oscillations, suddenly an event leaps the gap and in the *res cogitans*, there is a mental experience. That's body influencing mind. And the other way around. Watch, I'm now going to describe to you a mental event, namely, an intense desire to raise my right arm straight in the air. Now watch—there goes the *res extensio* following straight up in the air. So, obviously, there's two-way interaction.

The question is: How can there be interaction between these two absolutely separate, absolutely different, completely independent substances? This is known as "the problem of interaction." And the problem is that the body is part of a mechanical system that moves only on physical contact, but the mind is not *in* space, not physical, and therefore, it can't contact the body physically. So, how can the mind move the body? And, moreover, if it does, think of the trouble we're in—if the mind moves the body, the body is not exclusively in the realm of mechanics, and then all the materialists and the physical scientists scream that we've introduced supernatural influences. But if the mind *doesn't* influence the body, that means the soul is impotent and that there is really no free action. Our mind is just a little helpless nothing with thoughts that have no influence on our actions, and of course, all the theologians have a fit. So, we're in bad trouble. That's the so-called problem of interaction. (I have to say, parenthetically, that this is not a legitimate philosophic problem, unless you set up, as Descartes did, two absolutely separate, absolutely independent substances, and then wonder how you are going to get them back together gain. There is no justification for his assumption that there's nothing in common between mind and body if you reject Descartes's arbitrary split, which is generated by the primacy of consciousness.)

Descartes's answer is that interaction is possible because God has united these two substances marvelously—which means, it is metaphysically incomprehensible. But, he says, at least the problem goes no further than man. Animals don't have to have souls for religious purposes, and therefore, animals are strictly mechanical systems devoid of consciousness. Your cat and dog—all animals—are devoid of consciousness. They are little automata, little mechanistic systems, aware of nothing—they feel no pain, they feel nothing. Of course, a whole school of materialists immediately rose and said, "If we can get rid of consciousness in animals and explain all of their actions exclusively by materialistic factors and dispense with consciousness, why not with man, too?" And so, Descartes is the father of modern materialism as well.

In *The Concept of Mind*, philosopher Gilbert Ryle (1900–1976) satirized Descartes's view, but with a very clever satirical description, calling Descartes's view of man "the ghost in the machine." And that is correct. There is this spiritual entity—it is a ghost devoid of matter—rattling around inside this mechanical system, and never the twain shall meet—except by miracle. Ryle, as an arch materialist, draws the conclusion: "Down with consciousness." But his characterization is correct. Descartes's theory becomes even more fantastic in the details. He thought he had found a point in the body where the *res cogitans* meets the *res extension*: the pineal gland. Needless to say, that left him open to fantastic ridicule, and his followers were eager to find some way out of this impossible theory of interaction. Since they accepted all of his premises, interaction was incomprehensible to them also. And therefore, all but one of them drew the conclusion that we must explain the appearance of interaction while denying the existence of interaction, so let's explain why it looks like there is interaction. The Occasionalists, for instance, a very minor school that included Arnold Geulincx and Nicolas Malebranche, argued like this: There is no interaction, and when it appears to us that a physical event in the body is causing a mental experience in the mind, what actually happens is, on the *occasion* of the physical stimulus, God intervenes and directly arouses the experience in our mind, and on the *occasion* of an act of will in the mind, God intervenes and causes the body to move. Therefore, to the naïve observer, it looks as though the mind influences the body and vice versa, but actually God is the cause of the apparent interaction. This, of course, is bizarre, and Spinoza and Leibniz set themselves as one of their tasks to explain the appearance of interaction more sensibly, while also denying the fact.

I think you can see the disasters implicit in Descartes's philosophy. From different aspects he is at once the father of modern Idealism, modern materialism, modern skepticism. In other words, of every destructive trend of all the subsequent centuries. You see why he's considered the father of modern philosophy. As to ethics, Descartes did nothing original in that field. He was not particularly interested in ethics or politics. If you could classify him at all, he's a combination Catholic and Stoic. But he has no special influence in these areas.

I think you get a better idea why Objectivism stresses that the two fundamental axioms of philosophy are existence and consciousness, with existence coming first. If you start with consciousness, you get Descartes. If you deny consciousness, you get Hobbes. In either case, you get catastrophe. What is the result of the disaster? If there's no consciousness, à la Hobbes, then man is cut off from reality, incapable of knowing it. If reality is in doubt, as in Descartes, the same result. In both cases, you have a fundamental breach between man's mind and reality, either by denying the mind or by casting doubt on reality. And this breach between man's mind and reality is the fundamental theme uniting Hobbes and Descartes. This is the theme we will see intensified and developed when we look at three followers of Descartes—Spinoza, Leibniz, and Locke.

Lecture Nine, Q&A

Q: Isn't it clear that the concept of "time" or of a "mat," for that matter, is a reasoned abstraction, and its difference from the concept of "mortal" is only of degree, not of kind?

A: In other words, why does Hobbes distinguish between two types of truths since *all* truths depend upon concepts and definitions? Hobbes is not very clear on that. His modern followers say that the so-called factual truths are really the truths that are independent entirely of conceptualization. And they (that is, the consistent modern followers) say that the so-called factual truths are raw sense data descriptions that actually can't be put into words. The closest you can come to them are things like "Here now green." And actually, even that uses concepts. So, the most you can do to be completely consistent is to say that "matters of fact" are the things you point to, without using concepts or definition—"there, there, there"—and you can't say even *that*; you can just point. And that is the view taken by Logical Positivism, by many Pragmatists, by a whole school of Hobbesians who are much more consistent. And I grant you that it is true that *all* propositions depend upon conceptualization, and if conceptualization is arbitrary, then *all* propositions are arbitrary. And in that one respect, Hobbes's modern followers are more consistent.

Q: Do you agree that there are some things man cannot conceive of, even in the Walt Disney sense? For example, matter without primary qualities?

A: No, not in the sense meant by this question. Do not confuse conceiving with having an image. Objectivism is not nominalism. It does not equate thought or conception with imagery. You can't have an image of an electron, but you can conceive it. On the other hand, you *can* have an image of a little triangle on a blackboard leaping off and trotting through the park, but that does not mean that you have got a concept. Rather, your image represents a complete contradiction. Image and concept are completely different phenomena. And if you ask, "Can I conceive the opposite of an established truth?" the answer is, if by conception you are going to allow evasion in and say, "By suppressing enough knowledge that you have, can you conceive of such and such?" I answer that by evasion and ignorance, anybody can conceive of anything. I can conceive of matter without primary qualities as easily as I can conceive of matter without secondary qualities. Why? Because I don't think of the facts. But on the other hand, if by "conception" you mean a state of mind based on the full context of the evidence available, then I say the opposite of *any* proposition would be a contradiction—any demonstrated proposition—and consequently, the opposite of *no* true proposition is conceivable. And therefore, Objectivism rejects out of hand the idea that some propositions are contingent, and you can conceive the opposite, and some you can't. For further details, see in my article on the analytic-synthetic dichotomy.

Q: In the light of Hobbes's position that reason is conditioned, is he then the major forebearer of the German polylogist systems?

A: Well, indirectly. One type of polylogism is the view that logic itself is conventional, linguistic. More generally, polylogism holds that logic is not universal and for all men, but different men have their own logics—different races, for instance, or different economic classes, or different linguistic groups. In the removing of conceptual truths from reality, in that broad sense, you can say that Hobbes, as the influential nominalist, is the ultimate modern source. But he just picks up the nominalism of earlier philosophers. He himself did not think of applying it to logic. Even Hume didn't think of applying this to the laws of logic themselves. The laws of logic had to await Kant's attack to explicitly remove logic from reality. And even there, Kant thought that Aristotelian logic was implanted in our minds and inescapable, even though subjective. And it waited until the twentieth-century Logical Positivists to draw the conclusion that what Hobbes said about relations of names is applicable to logic also. So, it's essentially a twentieth-century development. And in that sense, Hobbes is only indirectly and partially responsible for it.

Q: Why does Hobbes place such a value on the absence of social strife?

A: I guess it would be for commonsense reasons. Life under the conditions he describes would be solitary, poor, nasty, brutish and short, and he happens to want companionship, civility, and long life, which is not too confusing.

Q: But is that just a whim on Hobbes's part?

A: *Everything* is a whim, according to Hobbes.

Q: But why should that be applied to other people?

A: Why should his whim be binding on anybody else? If the sovereign that gets in agrees with it and puts you in jail if you disagree, his whim is correct, and if not, not.

Q: Hobbes starts his philosophy by appealing to the method of mathematics and ends up denouncing mathematics as being detached from reality. How does he reconcile those two?

A: He doesn't. Hobbes is the seventeenth century, and remember, the things that became explicit in the eighteenth and nineteenth and, above all, the twentieth are simply in germ in the seventeenth. Hobbes is one-part empiricist, one-part rationalist, you see, starting from axioms and deducing all truth, and one-part skeptic. I emphasized the skeptic part in him because that was the most influential. But there's a lot of rationalism in Hobbes and a lot of skepticism in Hobbes. British philosophy throughout this period is about one-part skepticism, one-part Aristotelianism, and one-part Platonism, all mixed up. That's what's called "British common sense." You'll see that same mixture in Locke exactly. Berkeley is more consistent as a Platonist, and Hume is pretty consistent as a skeptic.

Q: Would Objectivism agree with the primacy of the will over the intellect, since man's free will consists in focusing his mind, and therefore the will comes first?

A: An ingenious question, but "no" is the answer. The primacy of the will specifically means that the intellect is a derivative, incapable of objectivity, a consequence of irrational—nonrational, to be exact—willing factors that are more basic, and which color and distort all the conclusions of reason. In this sense, Objectivism denies the whole dichotomy between will and intellect, and refuses to say which is more basic. And that is vital to the whole Objectivist theory of free will. The will, according to Objectivism, *is* the intellect; it is not a separate faculty outside the intellect that turns it off or turns it on or points it in this direction or points it in that direction. Free will is the intellect's power to focus itself, that's all, and therefore, there is no question of whether the will is more basic than the intellect. That whole dichotomy presupposes a soul-body split—that the intellect is one thing, and the will belongs to the body (in a normal interpretation, although sometimes they reverse it—the intellect pertains to the senses and this world, and the will pertains to the spirit)—but in any case, there's a clash between the two, and which is more important? Objectivism denies the mind-body opposition, and therefore, the whole will-intellect dichotomy.

Q: What if someone defined "man" as "a featherless *tri*ped," meaning a three-legged creature without feathers—wouldn't Hobbes be able to call this definition false on the basis of sense perception?

A: No, not on his premises. He would say that you have defined a thing that we have no instances of, but you're free to do that if you want. We've got lots of classes where there are no instances—"fairy," "demon," "gods," etc. Throw in another one if you want. All I can say is that there are no instances of it, but that doesn't stop you from having it. It's not false. All definitions, you see, are hypothetical—"*If* there is anything with these characteristics, then the name will apply to it." You're saying, "*If* there were a three-legged thing without feathers, I'd call it 'man.'" "Okay, good luck," he would say.

Q: Would you give some examples of Descartes's applications of mathematics to philosophy?

A: I already have given you the major one, namely, the concept of deduction from self-evident axioms as the essence of the method in philosophy, which is essentially a mathematical method, as against the observational inductive approach to knowledge. Another is Descartes's emphasis on quantity as the true feature of reality, metaphysically; the primary qualities being the quantitative ones, you see. And there are many more. Descartes himself was an accomplished mathematician, but we're not here to discuss his achievements in mathematics.

Q: Since the metaphysical and epistemological fundamentals of modern science are heavily Aristotelian, why did modern science adopt a skeptic-subjectivist ethics?

A: Well, here you have to distinguish between science qua scientists and science qua the philosophers of science. Scientists, the actual working scientists, insofar as they accomplished anything (and they did accomplish marvels in the modern world) functioned as Aristotelians, regardless of what they preached. They studied the world by observation, they believed you could acquire knowledge by reason, they weren't sensualists, they weren't skeptics, they didn't try to remember their recollections of a preceding life, they weren't Platonists—they didn't search for their innate ideas—they functioned as Aristotelians. But the philosophers who were busy interpreting their works drew all kinds of Platonist and skeptic conclusions out of it.

You ask why. Well, philosophy precedes science. Science does not lead to philosophy, but the other way around. No scientific discovery will change a philosopher's mind, nor should it, because science itself rests on a metaphysical-epistemological foundation. What happened is that the results of science, which rested on an *implicit* Aristotelian base, were systematically distorted by philosophers to justify subjectivist/skeptical/nominalist conclusions. The proof of the power of philosophy is that the scientists themselves, not being philosophers, began to spout officially the very corrupt ideas that they were taught by philosophers. Because you cannot permanently insulate science—the actual practice of science—from philosophy, the result is that in the nineteenth century, but particularly in the twentieth, scientists in their actual working lives began to be irrationalists, began to be skeptics, began to be subjectivists and nominalists. And what you see today is the actual collapse—I don't mean just of psychology, which never got started before it collapsed—I mean of biology, I mean of physics, I mean of mathematics, the actual hardcore sciences. The signs of that process are in the theories of modern mathematicians, ninety-nine of a hundred of whom are followers of nominalism (even if they've never heard the name), of every kind of subjectivism, and Bertrand Russell and that whole crew dominate the field of mathematics entirely. Physics is being overrun with irrationalism—there's the Copenhagen interpretation of quantum mechanics. There's quantum mechanics itself, with its fantastic ideas, denying the law of cause and effect, some of them claiming that subatomic particles are and are not corpuscular at the same time and respect, and that this refutes the law of contradiction. There are the fantastic interpretations placed on Einstein's theory of relativity. There's the theory in biology that molecules have memory. I mean, you can't keep science separate indefinitely. At the beginning, riding on an Aristotelian remnant, it was able to accomplish marvelous things. But that's only for so long.

Q: Did Hobbes believe that men should voluntarily give up their power to the king?

A: Yes. He believed that men should voluntarily contract. All are equal in the state of nature. And therefore, they should voluntarily contract to give up their power to a dictator. It may surprise you to know that many, many commentators declare that Hobbes is really the father of modern democracy, because he said that men should reach dictatorship by the consent and agreement of all individuals, and therefore, it's government by the consent of the governed. And you know what democracy is, so I guess it's true. Democracy is unlimited majority rule, and the majority can determine anything, including to have a dictator. So why not? It's very revealing as to what democracy is if they will say that Hobbes is one of its fathers.

Q: Can you explain the relation, if any, between nominalism and the modern empiricist view that all knowledge by induction is probable, never certain?

A: Oh yes, the relation there is very direct. Knowledge by induction is knowledge that tries to arrive at generalizations. Universal propositions such as "All men are mortal" or "All hot stoves burn," etc.—no amount of sensory observations is going to establish universals, because they have a limitless number of instances. Either, therefore, you validate those by some *conceptual* means, or you pile up instances and say who knows what's going to happen tomorrow? If conceptual means are detached from reality, you are left in the position where you *can't* know what's going to happen tomorrow. These people have no right even to say it's probable. They should say with Hume, who was a consistent nominalist in this respect: "I haven't the faintest clue what's going to happen tomorrow. I don't even know if there's going to *be* a tomorrow." This problem of induction is inherently connected with the problem of universals and concept formation.

Q: What is the role that man's awareness of his own mortality has played in philosophy?

A: The short answer: It depends on what period of philosophy you're looking at. In periods where men are comparatively happy with life on earth, mortality is not an issue. Aristotle, Epicurus represent the Greek attitude (not Plato, who is untypical and unhappy with this life), but Aristotle and Epicurus represent the Greek attitude—life is great, let's enjoy it, we're going to die, but so what, because when we die, we won't be there, and it doesn't mean anything. On the other hand, in proportion as men are opposed to life on earth and/or feel insecure or unhappy, then they regard death either as a glorious escape (which is the typical Platonic supernatural medieval approach to it), or they regard death as a horrifying threat because it puts an end to their life before they've had a chance to make any meaning or sense out of it (and that's the Existentialist modern plaint). But the concern with mortality as such is an aberration. It comes either from hatred of life or terror of one's own inadequacies. It is, therefore, a peripheral issue in philosophy, a pathological phenomenon.

LECTURE TEN

The Breach Deepens . . .

Our subject in this lecture is three followers of Descartes who formed the bridge between the rationalism of Descartes in the seventeenth century and the subjectivism and skepticism of Berkeley and Hume, respectively, in the eighteenth century. The three that we are going to cover are two Continental rationalists, Spinoza and Leibniz, and one British empiricist, John Locke. In terms of his actual influence on later philosophers and on later cultural developments, Locke is definitely the most important of the three. I am, however, giving him comparatively less time than the other two tonight, only because his ideas are largely unoriginal in metaphysics, epistemology, and ethics. In politics, where he shines, his views are very easy to understand, and therefore, the presentation of Locke takes less time than Spinoza and Leibniz.

Let's begin with Spinoza and Leibniz. Your understanding of the history of philosophy requires that you have some knowledge of perspective, of who is and who isn't crucially important. So, I want to say at the outset that Spinoza and Leibniz are *not* major turning points or profoundly influential philosophers. They exerted some, but comparatively little, influence on subsequent philosophers, and virtually no direct influence on the man on the street. Virtually nobody is a Spinozist or a Leibnizian, the way people are Hobbesian or Cartesian or Platonic or Aristotelian. In a way, these two are the least influential of the major world-famous first-ranked philosophers. I include them in this course partly because they're world famous, partly because they do have one major function in the history of philosophy: They perpetuate and transmit Cartesian rationalism. They develop the philosophy of Descartes to its ultimate consistent consequences. And in so doing, they produce such bizarre philosophic systems that it occurred to philosophers watching the spectacle that something major was wrong with Descartes—in other words, with the general rationalist approach to philosophy. And the ground was thereby prepared for a school emphasizing that knowledge begins with sense perception—in other words, for the empiricist school. You will see that the systems of Spinoza and Leibniz are ingenious, complicated, deductive systems that are dream worlds of thought, intellectual castles in the air, unrelated to the world, to life as we actually experience it day by day. And their very remoteness from this world produced the empiricist reaction to them.

I should add that certain individual points of these philosophers definitely did influence later philosophers. Spinoza, for instance, had a vogue in Germany in the late-eighteenth and early-nineteenth centuries and is one of the formative influences on Hegel. And Leibniz formulated certain concepts that were utilized by Freud, and, in other ways, he definitely helped to influence Hume and Kant. So you mustn't think that these people are *only* curiosity pieces. But they are certainly not the equivalent in influence of the major ones we've been stressing. Therefore, I will synopsize only the key points and conclusions necessary for our purposes, and not attempt anything like a detailed exposition or presentation, even of their basic arguments. In this lecture, you will get a kind of hit-and-run of Spinoza and Leibniz.

Baruch Spinoza

Baruch Spinoza (1632–1677) was about eighteen when Descartes died. Spinoza's sources are, in part, medieval Jewish philosophy—he was himself a Jewish philosopher. He was taught a great deal of Scholasticism and was thoroughly familiar with the Scholastic tradition, and he was familiar with the developments of modern science. One of the primary goals of his philosophy was to reconcile his religious heritage with the developments of modern science. You will see in him a peculiar blend of religious mysticism and logical modern science. Remember that Descartes also had attempted to escape the materialist conclusions of Hobbes by finding a place for what he regarded as the religious conclusions in the world of science, and Descartes had done it by dividing the world up into two substances: Mind belongs to religion and matter belongs to science. Spinoza is also interested in finding a place for religious worship in a universe properly studied by the physicist. He wants to save both. But his solution is rather different than Descartes's.

Epistemologically, Spinoza was a rationalist—he is the second famous Continental rationalist. Accordingly, he believes that the proper method of acquiring knowledge is the mathematical method, in particular, the geometric method. That is to say, we must model philosophy on geometry. It must start with basic axioms, self-evident axioms, which are clear and distinct (you remember that expression of Descartes's), which are grasped intuitively in Descartes's sense (i.e., self-evident), which do not require proof, and they are then the foundation for everything else. All subsequent knowledge will be acquired by deduction from these clear and distinct starting points. This was Descartes's program, but Descartes, if you recall, had not been very rigorous about it. He had proceeded along the path of his deductions, and every time he was stuck, he had a new intuition of a "clear and distinct idea" to help him along the path and smooth the transition on to the next series. Spinoza, however, is much more rigorous about applying Descartes's method. He wants to apply the method literally and make philosophy exactly like geometry. You're not allowed to have subsidiary intuitions along the way. You must, he says, specify every one of your axioms and definitions at the very outset, and once these are laid down, every step must be deductively proved, rigorously. We must really emulate geometry. And the title of Spinoza's famous work is *Ethica ordine geometrico demonstrata—Ethics Demonstrated in Geometric Fashion.* And it is exactly in structure like a geometry text. It starts with numbered axioms and definitions, and it deduces the theorems, each one numbered—there are about 260 altogether—and it's common in discussing Spinoza to say "Proposition 78, book I," etc.

Since Spinoza is a Continental rationalist, you can guess what his attitude to sense perception is—he takes the Cartesian view. Sense perception is inadequate, confused, basically an invalid form of knowledge. He subscribes, with Descartes, Hobbes, and Galileo, to the distinction that Locke christened the "primary-secondary quality" distinction, the view that matter is really only extension, three-dimensionality, spread-out-ness in space, and therefore, the way matter looks to us with sound and color and taste, and so on, is really deception. By the senses, says Spinoza, we cannot distinguish what really pertains to things in reality and what are just the subjective secondary effects on us. Sensory knowledge is, therefore, confused and inadequate, and it won't tell us what really exists. The senses are helpful for practical purposes. They may even be helpful as a suggestive stimulus to make us think of ideas that we subsequently validate by deductive means, but we can know nothing about reality *only* on the evidence of the senses. The true method of knowledge is to focus on our clear and distinct ideas and then deduce the consequences. This is typical Cartesian rationalism. And as we'll see, Spinoza assumes as self-evident, as clear and distinct, a great many Scholastic Platonic ideas, just as Descartes did.

Let us turn to Spinoza's metaphysics. What is the nature of the universe? Where does Spinoza start? You remember that Descartes had begun with the *Cogito*, with the self, and had then gone on to prove the existence of God and finally the physical world. Spinoza has a different starting point. His philosophy starts with the proof of the existence of God, and his basic proof is a version of Saint Anselm's ontological argument. Spinoza's argument amounts to this: I have, he says, the concept, the idea, of an absolutely independent, self-contained infinite being. Let us just reason from this idea. If such a being exists, it can't be because some outside entity brought it into existence, because if so, the being would be a product of outside factors, and it wouldn't be completely independent, completely self-contained. In other words, it must be such, if it exists at all, that its very nature requires it to exist. Its essence, as Anselm puts it, implies its existence. But if a thing is such that its essence implies its existence, which means from the very concept of such a thing, you can conclude that it must exist. Therefore, it does. You got that? This is, in effect, Anselm's argument. But instead of talking about the concept of the most perfect being and concluding from its definition that it must exist, Spinoza somewhat changes the initial definition. And his argument is open to all the objections that Anselm's is—that it's all hypothetical and proves only that if there is a being answering to your definition, then there is one. But we knew that in advance. The question is, *Is* there one? In any event, we pass on.

This absolutely independent entity is infinite. And Spinoza takes this seriously. What does it mean to be infinite? It means not to be limited. If you contrast this entity with a human being, the human being is limited, or finite, in two ways. It has only two attributes—mind and matter (or body)—and each of those attributes is finite in amount—it has a finite mind and a finite body. In contrast, the infinite, independent, self-contained being (called "God") has infinite attributes, since God is infinite, he has infinite attributes, i.e., an infinite number of different attributes, and each of them is infinite in extent, in quantity. So, he is not limited in either of the ways that we are. The idea that God is infinite is a perfectly typical position. The point is that Spinoza takes it seriously, which few philosophers prior to him did. He argues as follows: If God is infinite, if he possesses infinite attributes, each of which is infinite in extent, how can there be room for anything else to exist besides or in addition to God. God is the being who has every imaginable and unimaginable attribute, an infinite number, and an infinite quantity of each. He must then be *everything*. There is no attribute left for anything else to have. So, we can only conclude that God is the only thing that exists—a perfectly logical deduction from the premise.

You might ask, what about the world, what about physical nature, what about reality? The answer: God *is* the world. "God" or "Nature" or

"Reality" are just different names for the same one independent infinite entity. This view is called *pantheism*, the view that God is identical with the totality of the world. God is everything, and everything is God. We have seen this view in the Stoics in ancient Greece.

When Spinoza says that God and the universe, or nature, are only two different names for the one same totality, isn't this merely semantics? And the answer is yes and no. But mostly no, it's not semantics, because he conceives the universe in such a way that it has very, very religious attributes. There is a legitimate usage of the term "God" as applied to the universe as Spinoza conceives it. However, in one sense, Spinoza is an atheist—if you conceive God in the traditional Judeo-Christian fashion as a supernatural being beyond the world of nature, with a personality, a will, a plan, etc., looking down at the spectacle from his own dimension and having his own purposes, interfering with the course of nature, and performing miracles—if *that's* your idea of God, then Spinoza is an avowed atheist. He says that God *is* nature, not a ghostly Father controlling nature from beyond. And by the way, this position subjected Spinoza to the fiercest, vilest form of attacks from his contemporaries. He is the only really world-famous Jewish philosopher in all of thought, and the Jews formally excommunicated him for being a horrendous atheist. He denies that God created the world out of nothing—he believes the universe is eternal. He denies that God has a personality, that he's a loving or providential Father—you cannot pray to Spinoza's God anymore than you can pray to the totality of reality. He has no plan, and Spinoza is a real polemicist against miracles, against the argument from design, "Only God can make a tree," that *Reader's Digest*–type argument.

I have no time to quote Spinoza here, but I do want to at least mention that he makes many very, very good remarks criticizing the traditional religious view. There is a definite rational, scientific side to Spinoza, which is very admirable as far as it goes, and very uncharacteristic of the seventeenth century. So, bearing that in mind, let us proceed with Spinoza's system.

The first thing to recognize is that if everything that exists is in God, or is a part of God, then it can obviously be understood only by seeing its relation *to* God. This is a typically religious attitude in a *non*-pantheistic philosophy: Everything depends on God and can be understood only as caused or produced by God in some way. The question is: What does this mean if you're a pantheist? It can't be that God has a plan and by an act of will produces everything, because God *is* everything, not an outsider imposing his will. At this point, Spinoza takes a turn, determined by his rationalism. The universe, he believed with Descartes, is a logical universe, and after all, that's why we can study it geometrically, with axioms leading to theorems. Reality is a logically related integrated totality, where everything happens as it does as an inevitable, logical consequence of previous events and the nature of the whole.

So, religion said that everything comes from God, and rationalism said that everything happens geometrically (in other words, by logical necessity, from basic principles). Spinoza puts the two together and says that everything comes from God geometrically, or logically. In other words, he puts together religion and geometry in a pantheistic form. And the upshot is his view that reality, or God (and Spinoza use those two as synonyms), has a certain basic nature, and from that basic nature, every single aspect of reality follows inexorably, with the same logic as theorems in geometry follow from axioms. For instance, if I use the definition of a triangle and the appropriate axioms, I can deduce the absolute necessity of the angle sum of that triangle being 180 degrees (and we're here talking of a Euclidean triangle). Any alternative would be logically impossible, a contradiction, and therefore it would be forbidden by the laws of logic. That's the model to keep in mind to understand Spinoza's view of the universe. *Everything* that exists, *everything* that happens, for him, is related to the basic nature of reality in the way that the angle sum of a triangle is related to the nature of a triangle. And if, therefore, you clearly grasp what is the nature of reality, you will see that everything—the smallest aspect and the broadest principle—is logically inevitable, and any alternative would be a logical self-contradiction, forbidden by the very laws of logic themselves. When we say that God is the cause of the world, we really mean that God, or reality, has a certain basic nature, and everything follows logically from this nature. God causes the world in the same exact sense that geometric axioms cause their theorems; in other words, He logically implies the world. And anything else would be a self-contradiction.

If you drop the religious references, what Spinoza is saying is that we live in a rational, logical world, one that is governed by an ironclad law of cause and effect, and that law of cause and effect itself is guaranteed by the laws of logic. And he is correct in this view. He has been attacked endlessly by people following David Hume for believing that the universe is logical, when Hume allegedly proved that it wasn't. So, I want to emphasize that, stripped of its religious aspects, the core of Spinoza's view on this one point is certainly correct. However, Spinoza draws from it a conclusion that Objectivism certainly would not. Namely, he holds that if you believe in an ironclad logical universe where everything happens according to the law of causality in accordance with the laws of logic, you must then be a determinist. And he is, accordingly, a determinist: Since man is also part of reality, he is also a logically inevitable consequence of the total nature of reality, and every aspect of him—his thoughts, his emotions, his actions—are as absolutely logically necessitated as the angle sum of a triangle. If man did *anything* differently, even the tiniest thing differently from the way he actually did, that would violate the very laws of logic themselves and would involve a contradiction. Therefore, Spinoza is sometimes referred to as a *logical determinist*, meaning by that: determinism via the laws of logic themselves. We cannot, says Spinoza, even imagine in fantasy an alternative to any human action, thought, or emotion that has ever occurred, any more than you could imagine a round square, because the alternative to anything that happens would be a contradiction. We do, says Spinoza, have a sense of freedom, but this is an illusion, caused by the fact that we do not understand the causes operating. If a stone, he says somewhere, were rolling downhill in complete blind obedience to the law of gravity, and if it were conscious, it would probably think to itself, "How free I am going down the hill." But the stone is completely moved by factors outside of its control, and its illusion of freedom is an illusion caused by ignorance. It looks to the future and doesn't realize the past factors that are necessitating its behavior. And so for man. In this respect, Spinoza is perhaps the most rigid determinist in the whole history of philosophy. And, you see, he derives it from the law of cause and effect, from the idea that the universe is rigidly logical. And therefore, the problem he poses is: How do you reconcile free will with the laws of causality and logic?

We've said that God is the world. Let's now ask: What kind of world is it? Or put the same question another way: What kind of being is God? For Spinoza, there's only one independent entity, which is the universe, which, following the terminology of Descartes, he calls a "substance." Remember Descartes's definition of "substance" as "a thing which is independent of everything else." There's only one such substance according to Spinoza, namely, the universe as a whole, or God. What then is the status of mind and matter? Descartes thought they were each substances, so he is classified as a dualist. But, for Spinoza, mind and matter cannot be substances, since only the totality is the substance. And therefore, mind and matter must be properties, or *attributes,* of something. Well, of what? Obviously of the only thing that exists, namely, God. Therefore, mind and matter must be two attributes, or properties, belonging to and expressing God's nature. They must be two attributes of the one reality, namely, God.

Now we have a problem. An attribute, in this terminology, is supposed to express the basic nature of a substance. It's supposed to tell you what essentially a substance is. And on the face of it, mind and matter are radically different things. Consider, for instance, an actual physical earthquake and a mental phenomenon that corresponds to it, i.e., your thought of that earthquake. With these, we could list radically different characteristics. For instance, your thought of the earthquake doesn't make any noise, but the earthquake does. Your thought of the earthquake doesn't destroy human lives, but the earthquake does. And your thought of the earthquake is at no particular point in space and doesn't register on the Richter scale, but the earthquake does, and so on. Mind and matter, in other words, seem to be radically different. How can one single entity, namely, God, be at the same time essentially mind and essentially matter? How can two such different properties both express what God essentially is? How will we understand this? If you're not a rationalist, you will say, "I had better start over again and check my basic premises by observation and see how I got into this now." But if you are a rationalist, you will proceed headlong with your chain of deductions because you've got your clear and distinct axioms, and so you just take the bull by the horns and go on from there.

In principle, you've got two choices: You can say, "One of those two isn't really real. Mind and matter aren't both real, so one of them is really an illusion, an appearance," and that would solve the problem, because then you'd say that God, for instance, is really only mind, and so we don't have to explain how he can also be really matter because matter is an illusion—if you regard that as a solution, that's one possibility. The other possibility is to take a bold leap, and the bold leap is the leap that Spinoza took. Namely, these two properties are not really different but are ultimately the same. Mind and matter are just two different ways of expressing the same thing. In other words, either you get rid of one of them and say it's just an illusion, or you say there's no problem because the two aren't really different. Leibniz took the first alternative, and you can guess which one he got rid of as unreal, namely, matter, under the influence of Descartes's prior certainty of consciousness. Spinoza took the other side.

What does it mean to say mind and matter are the same, ultimately? They are two different expressions of God. Here I must resort to an analogy. Consider two different languages, French and English. And suppose the stand-in for God in this analogy is a discussion that can be in French or English. Suppose that the exact same discussion were taking place in two different rooms. There's a point-for-point correspondence, i.e., every time a question was asked in French, the same question was asked in English, and when the answer was given in French, the answer was also given in

English in the next room. These are two self-contained little discussions. It would be the same discussion manifesting itself in two different forms. Notice that French and English in this analogy don't divide the discussion between themselves—it's not as though half the discussion is French, and half is English—*all* of it is in French, and in the next room, simultaneously, all of it's in English. That's the pattern on which you have to understand Spinoza's theory of the relation of mind and matter. They are two different expressions of the one same reality, two different forms in which God's nature manifests itself. Each expresses completely what God essentially is, just as each of those two languages expresses the discussion completely in the analogy. And each expresses the *same* underlying reality, just as it's only the one discussion. It's just that God happens to express or manifest himself in two different forms. So, it's not that reality is *partly* matter and *partly* mind, as Descartes said. No, mind and matter don't divide reality. The whole of reality, or the whole of God, is completely expressed by mind—the mind-series of events, the mind-language if you want to look at it that way—and the whole of reality is completely expressed by matter, the body- or matter-language if you want to look at it this way. And therefore, mind and matter are ultimately the same. They are, in effect, two different expressions of one identical reality.

It follows that there must be a point-for-point correspondence between the mental and the physical. Since each expresses the same reality, and does so in a rigidly logical inevitable fashion, the two must parallel each other. Just as in the analogy of the two languages, we can translate back and forth—for every sentence in the one discussion, there'll be an exact counterpart in the other—because each expresses the same discussion in the same order. And so there's a point-for-point correspondence. For every French word, there's an English equivalent.

So with mind and body. We can translate back and forth. There are two series of events: the mental series and the physical series. This viewpoint is known as "the metaphysics of psycho-physical parallelism," which means mind-body parallelism. It's the view that there's an exact point-for-point parallelism between mental and physical events, and that the reason there is such a parallelism is that, ultimately, the two sets of events are really the same phenomenon, or the same one entity.

Before we go any further, I should remind you that there are an *infinite* number of attributes, not just mind and matter, because God is infinite. You might ask me about the other infinite things minus two. Spinoza says these happen to be unknowable to the human mind. So, in the analogy, you have to think that the same discussion is going on in an infinite number of languages, from eternity to eternity, but we're only tuned into two of these languages, so to speak. We all live in countless other worlds beyond the mental and the physical ones, and they happen to be unknowable to us. We can leave the unknowable ones and come back to just the two we know, the mental and the physical.

You might wonder what would possess anybody to take a view like this. And there are several reasons, of which I'll mention just one: It avoids the problem of interaction. Remember the problem that Descartes bequeathed: Mind and matter are radically different. One is in space and moves only on physical contact by mechanical law, whereas the other is exclusively a conscious thinking entity and does not occupy space. How could the two of them possibly influence each other? It's a miracle, said Descartes. God is great, God is marvelous, and somehow, incomprehensibly, he allows them to influence each other. Spinoza is much more rigorous and consistent, as he won't permit that kind of miracle. He says that the solution is that there *is* no interaction—mind cannot act on matter, matter cannot act on mind. There is no mutual influence at all. Each of these two attributes is a completely self-contained, closed system. Events in the mental world are caused only by preceding mental events. Events in the material world are caused only by preceding physical events. Just as in the analogy, French doesn't cause English, and English doesn't cause French. They are two self-contained little dimensions that run parallel to each other. Where would anybody get the idea that there's interaction? He mixes up his series. Suppose, for instance, you hear a question in English, and then you rush to the French room, and you hear the answer in French—you might think that the French questions interacted with the English and produced the answer. But that's obviously your confusion. So, said Spinoza, I can account for the *appearance* of interaction while denying the actual existence of it: Whenever you have an act of will (for instance, to move your arm), the arm will move. And that's the apparent example of mind influencing matter. Whenever I stick a pin in you, which is a physical event, you'll experience a little pain, which is a mental event. But that doesn't mean there's any causal interaction in either direction. Each series goes its own way. The reason that the act of will in the bodily movement or the sticking of the pin and the experience of pain seem to be causally related is that they are actually the same one event manifesting itself in two different languages, expressing the same one reality. We just get our languages confused, you see. And therefore, there will be parallelism between the two.

From Spinoza's point of view, there are great advantages in this scheme.

We have saved a mechanistic material physical world of science entirely untouched by mind, and so mind can't influence matter and the scientists are presumably happy—they now have their preserve of a strict mechanical world to study, and no mind is going to interfere with the laws of mechanics. On the other hand, we haven't done it at the price of falling into Hobbes's trap of denying mind and thought and purpose, and we have saved a world of thought and purpose independent of matter. And we did it—although this is basically a Cartesian division—we have done it in a way without being unintelligible like Descartes was, because we can account for the appearance of interaction while denying the fact.

You can see that while this is a fantastic viewpoint, it is *not* because Spinoza is inconsistent. On the contrary, it is because he is *so* consistent. Spinoza is a much superior philosopher to Descartes. Granted the basic premises, Spinoza carries them out to the bitter end. Descartes gets scared and has a new intuition and turns himself on to the next direction. And Descartes was not the man to come in conflict with the Church.

You might wonder how psycho-physical parallelism applies to rocks and rivers and inanimate things. This is a debated point in Spinozistic interpretation. Spinoza *seems* to say that *everything* is, to some degree, animate, alive, or even conscious in a way, and that the correlate of every physical fact is some kind of mental state, but this is a highly debated point, and we don't have to pursue it here.

But we have another problem. If mind and matter are two expressions of the same one reality, what is this reality in itself apart from its expressions? It can't be mind, because mind is just an expression of it, and it can't be matter, because matter is just an expression of it. This is where my analogy to the discussion breaks down, because the discussion is there and is a reality apart from the French or English that is being spoken, namely, people having thoughts, and so it's possible to talk about two manifestations. But here, what are the manifestations manifestations *of*? There's apparently nothing for reality in itself to be, because, remember, *all* attributes are expressions of it, an infinite number. Apparently—and again this is a debated point—Spinoza believed that God (or reality) in itself apart from its manifestations, was actually nothing, and all the manifestations were, therefore, really manifestations of a cosmic metaphysical zero. To try to make this intelligible, you must remember the school of negative theology that we discussed: the idea that God can't be limited. You can't give him any attributes or qualities, because if you give him any identity, then he's A versus non-A, and that's impious and irreligious. And it was common, in the negative theology tradition, to deny any characteristics to him, i.e., you have to say he is really nothing. Spinoza, I think, really belongs to the school of negative theology (although this is debatable). And you see the mysticism involved here. At the core of the Spinozistic universe is this mystical indeterminate uncharacterizable entity, lacking identity, which manifests itself in all these attributes. As one commentator puts it in a pregnantly bizarre statement, "God is everything, and therefore nothing."[38] There are people who say that's not fair to Spinoza, because for Spinoza, "God" is just a name for the various series—for the mind series and the body series—and he's not anything underneath them, that's all. But it seems unlikely that this is his view, because the attributes are supposed to parallel each other, because they are two expressions of the same one reality. Which raises the question, expressions of *what*? Some people say that they are expressions of each other. But since "each other" is an expression, you have expressions of expressions. Of what? So, it seems that you're driven back to nothing.

The situation is actually still worse than this, because we've talked up until now of mind and matter in general as being identical attributes. What about particular, specific individual minds, and particular, specific, individual material things? How do tables and chairs, or your individual mind and my individual mind, fare on Spinoza's metaphysics? Here you should be able to foresee. He is a pantheist. God is the whole, the single integrated substance. What is going to happen then to reality or individuality of what we call particular things? Spinoza's answer is going to be that particular things are just separated aspects of the whole. Individuality is not really real, neither mentally nor physically. There are no autonomous independent entities at all. There is only the one cosmic substance.

Consider, for instance, matter—we know that its essence is extension, three-dimensionality, spread-outness. Strip off all secondary qualities from matter. No color, so it's invisible, and there's no texture, so you can't touch it, and there is no sound, so it makes no noise, etc. Now ask yourself: How does this pure extension differ from space, ordinary empty space? And, says Spinoza, there *is* no difference between matter as it really is and space. And this is plausible when you strip off all the secondary qualities, and when you have only extension left, well, space is supposed to be extended. He did not, by the way, originate this conclusion. Descartes also equated matter, *true* matter, with space.

So, you can't break space up into separate hunks. Any divisions you make in space are only a fragmented human way of looking at it. All that really exists is the indivisible infinite slab of space. If I tell you to focus on

38. Source unknown.

this little piece of space over here, that's obviously an abstraction, and it's not a separate real entity. Since Spinoza equates space and matter, that's his view of physical entities. So, when he talks of matter, he doesn't mean bodies that you can weigh and measure and dissect and sit on and kick around. That is the world of appearances. In the material world, individual entities are mere appearance.

What about individual minds? Are they real? No. Individuality is unreal in mind just as it is in matter. Of course, if you introspect, you feel that there is a *you* that is distinct, definitely you, and absolutely different from everybody else's mind. But that is the crude, confused level of sense perception. If you reach the level of abstract thought, says Spinoza, you will come to realize that that isn't true. Remember that for Spinoza, mind and matter are ultimately identical. Which means that your *thought* of an object is really ultimately identical with the object. When we think of an earthquake, or we talk about the actual physical earthquake, the thought and the object (the earthquake) are really two different expressions of the same thing; they're really identical. Your mind is all of *your* ideas (in other words, everything you think about), and *my* mind is all of my ideas (everything I think about)—but we both think about the same thing, namely, the universe. And therefore, my mind is the same as your mind. You get that? This is a triumph of geometric deduction over reality (although Spinoza wouldn't put it that way). In other words, says Spinoza, we can conclude that in the deepest sense, each of us—intellectually, psychologically, mentally—is all of the others. In a word, there is parallelism between the two spheres, and there must always be an exact correspondence. If individuality is unreal in matter, it must also be unreal in mind. There is only an infinite slab of space and an infinite divine mind, or system of ideas. Our own sense of personal identity, therefore, our own personality, our own sense of uniqueness, is a confusion. It's the way things appear to us. But in actual reality, all so-called separate bodies are merely modes or aspects of one slab of space, and all so-called minds are merely modes or aspects of one cosmic, infinite mind, or system of ideas. And if you add that mind and matter are ultimately identical, so that space and the infinite mind are really the same thing, you will come to the final conclusion that everything is ultimately one, and ultimately identical to everything else. In other words, distinctions are unreal.

You see the very Platonic (even Neoplatonic) character of this viewpoint. And here is the real influence of Plato again. On the one hand there's a true reality that consists of a cosmic system of ideas and a slab of space—that's pure Plato—as against a world of appearances, which is not true reality. There is reason, the faculty that knows true reality, versus the senses, the faculty that knows the world of appearances. And there's even the Platonic idea that individuality and distinctions are not ultimately real. Remember Plotinus's view that everything is ultimately the One. All of this Platonic mysticism comes out again in Spinoza. And that shouldn't surprise you, because this world is *always* metaphysically degraded by rationalists.

After they get finished with their deductions, this world always ends up as an appearance, a reflection, something of a lesser status. True reality is always some superior realm. And this is the essential illustration of the connection between rationalism (as that term is used philosophically) and religion. And it's inherent in the very rationalist approach, because if the senses are no good, then the world must be basically different from the way it appears. If a rationalist came out at the end of his chain of deductions with a world that was identical to the world given us by the senses, he would be in a ridiculous position. Why be a rationalist to begin with then? And therefore, you always end up with a superior reality, and nine times out of ten you end up with Plato's.

There's a final problem—an epistemological one—that I want to mention in dealing with Spinoza. (I'm skipping dozens of points.) Let us grant him the best, i.e., let us grant him that his axioms really are clear and distinct and unanswerable, and that he has deduced all of their consequences unanswerably. He has a perfectly consistent unobjectionable system. We must observe, however, that all of his axioms and theorems are *general* propositions, universal propositions. Imagine that there is a blackboard before you with a whole bunch of particular triangles inscribed on them. You do not have a clear and distinct insight innately that some particular triangle is three feet away from another one and has to be by the definition of "triangle." Nothing in the definition of "triangle" will tell you that. You don't have a clear and distinct insight that there are ten triangles on that board drawn in white chalk, and that that must be so by the nature of reality. The most you could have would be some general proposition of the order, "Triangularity has certain properties." And no one, I may say, in philosophy has ever claimed innate knowledge of particular things, because a knowledge of particular things too obviously depends upon experience. From Plato on, the knowledge that comes above experience is always explained as universal knowledge. You know, for instance, A is A perhaps, but you don't know that A is a puppy dog. You know that two and two is four, but you don't know those two students are to the left of those two students. You know man is rational, but you don't know that man is marvelous at geometry. Well, where are we then? At the end of all of our deductive reasoning, we have knowledge only of general, universal truths.

So, how do we ever get knowledge of particular, individual, specific, concrete, actually existing entities and events? How do we get to see the necessity of particular events? And Spinoza has told us that everything is logically necessary and that as a rationalist he will explain everything.

To jump ahead, let me relate an anecdote in regard to Hegel, who took the same view as Spinoza that everything is logically deducible by rationalistic fashion. One day, Hegel was confronted by an obscure gentleman known as Herr Krug, who held up his prosaic pen and said to Hegel: "All right, you claim to be able to deduce the entire universe, including everything that is in it, by rationalistic deduction. Here's my pen—my particular, real, concrete pen—go ahead and deduce it from your categories or your principles or whatever it is you start with. I'm waiting for you to show how my pen follows." According to the story that has come down to us, Hegel answered, in effect, "I'm a philosopher and I can't be bothered with pens." In other words, he used his fame and prestige to crush poor Herr Krug. And you see why. At best, he could maybe deduce the theorem "Pen-ness implies inkiness," some general principle. But why there must be this particular pen here and now, he couldn't do it. And you see why. He couldn't derive existence—concrete, real, actual existence—from concepts in consciousness. And that was the problem that Descartes bequeathed, and here it's breaking out again—how do you get from concepts in consciousness to the actual facts of existence? Which means for Spinoza, how can we ever know the necessity of particular things in the world if we are locked in consciousness studying universal principles and concepts?

Spinoza answered this question in his own way. He said that there is actually a third kind of knowledge, which is the highest kind of knowledge. The lowest kind is sensation or sense perception, which is confused knowledge. It tells you *that* particular things exist, but doesn't tell you *why.* The next level is rational knowledge, and that involves the grasping of clear and distinct general principles and the deduction from them—in other words, Descartes's approach. And that's fine, says Spinoza, that gives you true knowledge, but only general knowledge. And then finally we get to something that he called *scientia intuitiva,* which is essentially intuitive knowledge, but that's a different use of "intuition" from Descartes's.

To make a long story short, intuitive knowledge is a mystical vision, in which we grasp in an ineffable insight how every actual concrete particular thing necessarily comes from God. When you have this vision, you see how Herr Krug's pen had to be by the nature of the whole totality. But it is an ineffable, mystic, trance. Spinoza's pantheism is not a matter of semantics. And you see that the most consistent rationalists usually end in a mystic vision of some kind. Plato ended with his vision of the Form of the Good, and Plotinus ended with his ecstasy. The explanation of it is very simple—since they don't derive their concepts from percepts, they can't derive percepts from their concepts, and consequently, they are left with only a mystic recourse.

We can now make a prediction. The rationalists, in the person of Spinoza, declare that reality is logical, and then they construe reality as a super-realm from which they cannot deduce the actual facts of this world. If you are familiar with the extent to which false alternatives exist in philosophy, you shouldn't be surprised to find that their arch enemies, the empiricists, will say, watching the failure of the rationalists to deduce the actual concretes of this world, "Aha, this proves that reality is illogical, or at least non-logical, that things don't happen for logical reasons, they just happen, they are brute, unintelligible, contingent facts." And that viewpoint is all over the place today. If today you should ever say to a professional philosopher that you believe that reality is logical—if you should ever say, so help you, that the real is rational (that being a phrase immortalized by Hegel), you are done for. Because I know a professor (and not just one), who to this very day, in spite of all my arguments with him, insists that I am a follower of Hegel, or, in some moods he thinks of Spinoza, because I hold that reality is rational. And if you hold that reality is rational, you must be a rationalist who believes that everything is deducible rationalistically. The answer is that reality *is* governed by logic,[39] but only a proper epistemology, not a rationalistic one, will enable you to discover its laws. But you can't communicate that to certain mentalities.

We must now leave Spinoza. He has a very famous ethical theory, but it hasn't been particularly influential compared to other theories. So, I would have liked to have said a few words about it, and if you ask me in the question period about Spinoza's ethics, I will give you the highlights. In any event, we can say for Spinoza that his system is certainly ingenious, it's thoroughly worked out in deductive fashion, and if you consider it as an integration of the most diverse elements, it's certainly original, even if often baldly contradictory.

39. In his answer to the first question in this lecture's Q&A, Dr. Peikoff makes it clear that reality is "logical" or "rational" only in the sense that it's governed by the law of identity and the law of cause and effect (not that reality thinks).

Gottfried Wilhelm Leibniz

Let us go on now to Gottfried Wilhelm Leibniz (1646–1716). Given that he died in 1716, we are creeping into the eighteenth century. I will be even briefer on Leibniz. He, too, has an ingenious, complicated overall system, more fantastic than Spinoza's, with profuse argumentation at every step—essentially all fallacious—I am omitting almost all his arguments and just giving you a quick sketch to give you an idea.

He, too, is a rationalist, at least three-quarters of the time. He made some fun of rationalism, and there are even some anti-rationalist features in his philosophy (as we'll see), and scholars distinguish two Leibnizes, the pure rationalist Leibniz and the mixed Leibniz. But we're going to look only at the mixed Leibniz, because that's the one that was most influential.

As a rationalist, he believes that reasoning alone can discover the nature of the universe. There's the usual opposition to the senses. The crucial knowledge, the foundational knowledge, is innate, we introspect to grasp it, and then we deduce its consequences.

In his metaphysics, he disagrees with Spinoza's pantheism. He believes that finite substances, or entities, are real. It's not true that we're all parts of God. And this was the orthodox Christian position, and Leibniz certainly is eager to be orthodox. He does believe in God, and he believes that God is infinite, and he has no answer to Spinoza's argument as to why if God is infinite there is no room for anything else. He just goes about his business. He is not the one to take risks like Spinoza.

Let's look at one of these finite substances, like a table or a chair or a rock or a mountain—what is it really? It is compound. The world is filled with things that are compound, i.e., substances consisting of parts. That's what "compound" means, "consisting of parts." If there are compounds, there must ultimately be simple substances. After we break the compounds down to their ultimate constituents, we must reach the ultimate indivisible substances. And the technical name for indivisible is "simple." And these simple substances will themselves have no parts; otherwise, they too would be compound. Such a simple substance Leibniz calls a *monad*, from the Greek word *monas*, meaning "one, that which is one." These monads, or simple substances, are the atoms of nature. The whole universe is made up of these monads.

This will sound to you like the atomic theory, and Leibniz in his youth was attracted to Democritus. But this is a different period of time with different influences, and he goes Democritus one step better. He says that monads, the ultimate atoms of things, cannot be material or extended in space at all. Why not? Because if they're extended, he argues, they would be divisible, at least in thought. We could, for instance, even if the little, tiny thing was a quarter of an inch or a zillionth of an inch, we could separate the left half of it from the right half in our minds, so it would still be divisible and not simple. But we've proved that there must be simple entities comprising the universe. And therefore, extension can't be an ultimate attribute of these monads. So, they're not material, they're not extended, they're absolutely indivisible even in thought. And therefore, they're not in space, because you have to be material to be in space. (The main fallacy here is the fact that dividing something in thought in no way entitles you to say that it's divisible in reality. You see the typical Cartesian jump from consciousness to existence—"I can conceive of dividing it, therefore, it can be divided"—and that's the typical adherence to the prior certainty of consciousness.)

In any event, Leibniz proceeds from this foundation to a long chain of reasoning, again consistent to the bitter end like a good Continental rationalist. Monads, we said, are not extended, they're not spread out, they're not material, they don't occupy space. But they must have some nature. What could it be? For various reasons, but essentially the influence of Descartes, who established that everything that isn't matter must be mind, Leibniz concluded that the monads are ultimately minds, souls, consciousnesses, perceiving beings, using "perceiving being" in the widest sense for a nonmaterial focus of awareness.

What do the monads perceive? Obviously, they can perceive only other monads because that's all there is. Each monad, says Leibniz, perceives every other monad in the universe, and each monad is a living mirror of the entire universe of monads. And "perceive" here means "is aware of." It's not restricted to sensory perception, and, as you'll see, there are various grades of monads.

What distinguishes one monad from the other? How do you tell where one monad stops and the next one starts? They're all minds perceiving the universe. What makes this particular monad *this* one rather than *that* one? In other words, what's the source of individuality of the monad? It is in *how* they perceive, answers Leibniz. Some monads perceive clearly and distinctly, some obscurely and confusedly. The universe, therefore, is an infinite number of monads perceiving each other, each with its own precise degree of clarity and distinctness. No two have exactly the same degree of clarity—otherwise, it would be the same monad. That's the only thing that individuates, that differentiates one monad from another. So, we have an infinite continuum. On the bottom is the lowest, most confused, most unclear monad—in effect, a sub-freshman monad—and it goes on up to the monad that perceives with absolute, total, perfect clarity, and that is God, and every possible shade of clarity is represented.

This viewpoint, that reality is essentially nonmaterial (though not necessarily in the monad form) is, as you know, called "idealism." And Leibniz is a staunch proponent of idealism, which represents the ultimate triumph of the primacy of consciousness. When you reach idealism, consciousness swamps existence completely, and existence is just a collection of consciousnesses. And so this is the final upshot, you see, of Descartes.

We've seen the major objections to this view, but I can't resist pointing out that the whole case is eloquently clear in Leibniz. The monads, he tells us, are perceiving beings. What do they perceive? Other monads. But other monads are only perceiving beings, too. What is there to perceive? Nothing. This whole universe is absolutely empty. It consists of a whole infinite number of consciousnesses, each perceiving (with an infinite number of degrees of clarity) nothing at all. This is the triumph of consciousness without existence. And it's as good as an example of the flaws of idealism, or the primacy of consciousness, as you'll ever find. But we can leave this problem because others are pressing in.

The monads are minds, and Descartes had said that minds are independent substances. And you remember that a substance is that which exists in such a way as to stand in need of nothing beyond itself in order to exist. A mental substance for Descartes is a completely self-contained, locked-in, independent entity. Leibniz insists with Descartes that this is true. Each monad is absolutely impervious. It's a self-contained independent little world. No monad, he says, can in any way whatever influence or affect any other monad. And that follows Descartes. Descartes had tried to sneak in interaction among his constituents, but he couldn't make it intelligible. Leibniz here follows Spinoza—there is no interaction, no influence at all. Each substance is completely independent in its own little world. As he put it in a famous metaphor (but only a metaphor), "The monads have no windows from which anything can enter or go forth." (That's just a metaphor because they're not physical, so obviously they have no windows. But it's a way of saying that they can't influence any other monad nor be influenced by any other.) And ever since this formulation they have been called the *windowless monads*. From conclusions of this sort, you can sympathize to some extent with the empiricists, who hear all this, and they say, "Oh, to hell with deduction."

To continue with Leibniz—we have real problems now. Even supposing there was something to perceive, how can the monads perceive each other without being affected by one another? How does the monad that is my mind perceive, for instance, the monads that are your body, since those monads can't act on my monad? Well, the solution to all problems is always God. God, says Leibniz, endowed each monad with all its perceptions in potential form when he created it. In effect, you can think of it as an analogy: God stuck a certain motion picture film in advance inside each monad. And your conscious experience, life, is locked up in your own little world watching the film roll on, and you're locked in your own projection booth. So it *seems* as though you're being affected by other monads, but you really aren't. Every experience is set in advance by God when you're created, and your conscious life just rolls inevitably inside your own projection booth.

We can leave this for a moment and ask: What, for Leibniz, is matter? It also must be a collection of monads because everything is. You say to me: Isn't matter composed of perceiving entities? Surely matter isn't conscious. Well, says Leibniz, no, it isn't conscious, and it perceives unconsciously, without being aware that it's perceiving. And so he introduced the concept of "unconscious awareness," or "unconscious perception." And I should just mention in passing that this is one of the earliest mentions in history of the concept of "unconscious awareness," although it was hinted at by others. Of course, it was taken over by Freud, and although misused mystically by Freud, it is a valuable psychological concept. It's not startling today to talk blithely of unconscious motivation, unconscious premises, etc. But it was startling in the seventeenth century, and therefore, Leibniz does get credit for developing this concept to some extent, even if you don't want to give him credit for the metaphysical motives that led him to endorse it. Only conscious beings, in fact, can be unconscious at times and over specific issues. How a completely non-conscious entity, like a chair, can be unconsciously aware without ever being *consciously* aware of anything, Leibniz does not explain. But that's the least of our problems.

In any case, we have an infinite range of monads. Four general groups. The lowest, most confused, most unclear monads, which have only unconscious perceptions, constitute matter. They are what Leibniz refers to as the *naked monads*. And you can think of them as monads in a deep coma, or monads that are fast asleep. A material thing is actually a cluster of naked monads. It looks to you as though it's extended, physical, three-dimensional, but that is confused sensory appearance and not what it really is. If a collection of naked monads clusters around one dominant monad that is considerably clearer than they are and is now conscious and has memory and sense perception, we call that totality an *animal*. And if a group of naked monads clusters around one dominant monad that is still clearer, which has risen to the level of rational knowledge, we have a *human being*. So, each of you is, in effect, a high-class monad and a group of fellow-traveling naked monads. And finally, if you get the absolutely clear infinite monad, that is *God*. So, everything is really a colony of souls, of windowless monads.

I might add that, for Leibniz, even though matter is only the appearance of monads, he does say the naked monads do, after all, *appear* to us as matter. And we can describe the naked monads by mechanistic scientific laws. Of course, the world of physics is an illusion, but it is an illusion that we live in and one that happens to obey the laws of physics. And therefore, says Leibniz, it's perfectly all right to go ahead and study it scientifically. We must, however, remember that the universe is really a set of living minds created and determined by God. This is known as Leibniz's compromise between religion and science.

Let's go back to the problem of mutual influence. We can call it the *mind-mind problem* since there's no mind-body anymore. If nothing can influence anything, why do things *seem* to influence each other? This is wider now than merely the problem of how does one perceive the other, although that's part of it. We must ask not merely how do we account for *perception*, but how do we account for *any* form of apparent influence of one monad on another? It seems that I experience an act of will—and that takes place in my dominant monad—this collection of naked monads that I call my body moves as a result, so it seems. A pin comes into my body, and I then experience a pain—isn't that influence from one monad to another? It seems as though if we just have one billiard ball hitting another, first the one rolls as one collection of naked monads does something, and then the other one rolls—isn't that influence? Or when we all look at this water pitcher, we all have presumably the same experiences, and isn't that an example of influence, the same real set of monads out there acting on all of us at the same time and causing the same experience in us? Leibniz denies that there is any such influence in any of these cases. The monads are windowless. There seems to be influence only because God has worked it all out in advance. We are really looking at nothing but the motion picture in our heads, but God has synchronized and organized all of our experiences so that influence appears to exist, even though it doesn't. God has arranged, for instance, that whenever I have an experience of will, that will be followed by an experience of bodily action. Whenever I have an experience of a pin entering my body, I will have an experience of pain. Whenever I have an experience of a billiard ball hitting another, I'll have an experience of a second one moving. And whenever we all have the same experience, that's because God has arranged for us all to see the same picture at the same instant. In other words, God has organized all of our perceptions in advance, so that they all mesh, all synchronize. He has pre-established a harmony between them. And that is Leibniz's theory of *pre-established harmony.* It's his solution to the problem of interaction, among other problems. There is no interaction—God has pre-established a harmony so that there appears to be interaction.

Let's ask a final question: Why did God organize our perceptions the way he did? He could have fed us a totally different stream of experiences, and still synchronized them all. Why does God show all of us this movie and not some other movie? Or if we put the same question in more familiar terminology: Why did God create the world as he did? Why does the world contain the kinds of things in it that it does? Why does it follow the kinds of scientific laws that it does? After all, says Leibniz, other universes are logically possible. Why, therefore, this one?

Notice that in asking this question, Leibniz has abandoned rationalism. He has given up the attempt to see this world as logically necessary given the nature of reality. He's decided, in effect, that Spinoza's failure means that it can't be done. Remember that Spinoza couldn't deduce the concretes of this world from general principles, and I warned you then that a reaction would set in. Well, Leibniz represents the first indication of that reaction in a major way. If you asked Spinoza, "Are other worlds possible?," he would say "ridiculous," any more than if you asked him, "Why did God pick these geometrical theorems rather than some other?"—he would say no other theorems are possible. Objectivism would here agree with Spinoza—there is no other possible universe, and therefore, there's no sense to asking the question, "Why this one?" But Leibniz has given up on that question, which sounds the death knell of rationalism, at least for a century, until Hegel, under the influence of Kant, revivified it. He has concluded that reality is *not* completely logical.

Leibniz still retains a vestige of rationalism. God, he says, cannot produce literally any world, i.e., he is limited to a self-consistent world, a world without contradictions. You can't have a world where the angle sum of a triangle equals 179 degrees—impossible, because that contradicts the definition of a triangle. So a possible world for Leibniz is a logically non-contradictory world. Spinoza and Objectivism would say that that limits the possibilities to one, namely, the actual world. But not Leibniz. He says that before the world is created, God spreads out in his mind all the possible worlds (and there are a great many), and he asks himself, "Which one should I actually create?" Being good, he wants to create the best of these worlds. You ask, can God create an absolutely perfect world? Says Leibniz, no, he cannot, because anything God creates must be finite, must be limited, since it's not God. And that which is finite and limited, we know from thousands of years of Christianity and Platonism, is necessarily imperfect. And therefore, there must be some evil in the world. That's logically required. You see here the obvious acceptance of the Augustinian, Neoplatonic solution to the problem of evil. But, says Leibniz, God does the best he can, given the limitations forced upon him. He chooses the best of all the possible worlds. He chooses the world that has as much order, variety, and goodness as is consistent with the laws of logic. And thus, Leibniz's famous line from the *Theodicy*, "All is for the best in this best of all possible worlds." That is his solution to the problem of evil—if there's evil, that's because God is operating under certain constraints. This viewpoint, by the way, I cringe to state, is sometimes referred to as "metaphysical optimism."

It was very unfortunate for Leibniz's timing that his book came out just around the time of the Lisbon earthquake that destroyed three-quarters of the city, and which was immediately followed by a gigantic tidal wave killing fifteen hundred people. This was too much for Voltaire, and so he wrote his satire *Candide*—Dr. Pangloss there represents Leibniz. And if I may say so, in my opinion, *Candide* is actually a stupid book. However, it has one clever line of satire—not very profound, but clever—he has his hero Candide and Dr. Pangloss go through a whole series of detailedly described catastrophes, holocausts, and so on, and then he has poor Candide in a bewildered way look up at one point and ask, "If this is the best of all possible worlds, I wonder what can the others be like?" That's about the substance of Voltaire's contribution to human thought.

Let's conclude Leibniz with one last epistemological point. Notice that truths fall into two classes for him: (1) those that even God can't violate, those whose opposites would involve a contradiction—in other words, those that are logically necessary in *any* universe, in all possible worlds, their opposites being literally inconceivable. "Two and two make four," for instance, or "A is A," or "The angle sum of a triangle is 180 degrees." These are the truths certified by logic, the truths of reason. And (2) there are the truths that result from God's decision, from his goodness, from his purpose, from his having created this particular world rather than all the others he could have created. In the case of these truths, they *could* have been different had God so decided. These truths are not logically necessary; they are *contingent*. They happen to be the case in our world, but they don't *have* to be the case. They are true as a matter of brute fact. For instance, "Bodies fall when you drop them," "The planets travel in elliptical orbits,"

"There are nine planets," etc. So, on the one hand, we have the "truths of reason," logically necessary truths that we can learn apart from experience. I may have introduced you to the philosophic term *a priori*, which means "prior to experience." The logically necessary truths are *a priori* for Leibniz. They are the purely conceptual truths, true of all possible worlds, but they don't pertain only to this actual world. On the other hand, there are the factual, contingent "truths of fact," the ones that we learn only from experience, and they are not *a priori* but *a posteriori* (*a posteriori* means only "dependent on experience"). Think for a moment—who does this dichotomy remind you of? It should remind you of Hobbes. Even though he was different in certain ways—remember, he contrasted relations of names with matters of fact. For Hobbes, relations of names were linguistic. That isn't true for Leibniz. The truths of reason are eternal laws of reality for him—even God can't violate them. And for Hobbes, matters of fact didn't come from God's will. But if we leave aside those differences, we have two philosophers agreeing on the following distinction (among others): the truths that are learned by reason and are necessary versus the truths that are learned by experience and are brute, contingent facts. Two radically different philosophers, so it seems—an ardent theist (Leibniz) and a virtual atheist (Hobbes), an ardent idealist and a passionate materialist, a Continental rationalist and a more-or-less empiricist. And yet we have that same basic cleavage and dichotomy. You see how the ground is being laid for Kant. By the time he comes on the scene, this dichotomy is regarded as self-evident, and he proceeds to build on it.

If you observe the progression from Descartes through Spinoza and Leibniz, you will see what happens given the rationalist approach to philosophy. We start with allegedly self-evident, clear, and distinct principles, underived from sense experience, which means, in actual fact, with *arbitrary* first principles, even though they are allegedly innate and inherited from God. And we proceed to deduce the consequences from these starting points. Whenever our conclusions conflict with the testimony of the senses, we write off the senses as confused, inadequate, deceptive, invalid, and proceed to deduce doggedly. The result is the construction of a number of opposed, imposing philosophic systems, all contradicting the others, all more or less completely removed from the everyday commonsense world given us by the senses. We have a series of intellectual castles in the air, as I mentioned at the outset, free-floating castles unrelated to and often in direct conflict with sensory data. That is the consequence of an approach whose essence is the manipulating of concepts cut off from sense experience. And it is an obviously unsatisfactory and invalid approach to philosophy.

We turn now to a school that reacted strongly against the rationalist approach, a school that claims to be radically opposed to the rationalists. And this school asserts that there are no innate ideas, that all knowledge is based on the evidence of the senses, and that the way to arrive at knowledge of reality is *not* to engage in conceptual manipulations within our minds, but to open our eyes and look at the actual world. This viewpoint, as you know, is called *empiricism*, the view that there are no innate ideas and that all knowledge begins with experience. The eighteenth century in philosophy is the century dominated by empiricists, who pride themselves as being men of common sense, concerned with practical life. They say that this world, here and now, that we perceive is real (although, as you'll see, they don't say that for very long, but at least they start off saying that). To solve philosophic problems, they say, we must appeal to concrete facts, not get lost in a chain of floating abstract deductions. Our ultimate description of empiricism is going to be much less flattering than this. When we get to the end of this development, you're going to be hard put to choose between Leibniz and the empiricist approach. But we'll watch and see it happen.

John Locke

Let's begin with the man often called the "father of British empiricism," John Locke (1632–1704). He is not really the first—Bacon and Hobbes, among others, preceded him in the modern world. Locke was eighteen when Descartes died, and Spinoza was his contemporary, so we're backtracking slightly to take up this school.

Locke was a strong advocate of reason. All men have it, he held. All men have the capacity to learn the facts, the capacity to agree. And they must always follow reason. We must be objective. We must not let our passions or our prejudices sway us. We must go by the evidence scrupulously, factually, impartially. I should say that Locke does make appropriate overtures to the religious camp. He is himself a deeply religious Christian and wrote a great deal in defense of Christianity. But he does draw a clear line between faith and revelation on the one hand and reason on the other. And in philosophy, only reason counts. We can therefore ignore the faith side of Locke, but it's there.

Locke is very similar to the rationalists in his general pro-reason attitude, a general attitude that lasted among philosophers until the time of Hume and Kant. And it was at that point that the consequences of all the different definitions of "reason" caught up to philosophers. Usually it takes fifty, seventy-five, a hundred years, for the practical results of a philosophy to manifest itself. Kant died in 1804, and by the mid-nineteenth century, reason, culturally, was on its way out. You can look around today to see what happened by the mid- and late-twentieth century. Nevertheless, at this point in time, we're still in the seventeenth century, a very pro-rational period. And you must understand this; otherwise, you'll never grasp why the seventeenth century is called "the Age of Reason," or the eighteenth century is called "the Enlightenment." *We* now see the disasters implied in their philosophies, but obviously, *they* didn't. So, all of the major thinkers were still confident about the power of reason. The rationalists and the empiricists differed in their theories regarding what reason was and how it operated, but they did not differ about the fact that reason is an absolute and that we must accept it, as against dogma, emotion, prejudice, etc. That was in itself a very important attitude shaping cultural developments.

Locke holds that we must use the right method in philosophy. We must first inquire into the nature and powers of the human mind, find out what it is and isn't fitted to deal with, what rules it must follow. And the first thing we have to establish is that the mind at birth has no innate ideas, no knowledge. It is a white paper and dark chamber, an empty cabinet, a *tabula rasa*. What writes on the paper, or fills the cabinet, or illuminates the chamber? Only experience. Locke devotes the first book of his famous *Essay Concerning Human Understanding* to an all-out polemic against innate ideas. Here are some of the many arguments he offers.

It had been argued by some philosophers that there are certain ideas universally accepted by all men, and this must prove they were innate. Locke answers that that doesn't prove anything of the kind. If there are universally accepted ideas, that could be because the issue in question is so obvious that nobody could escape it. It doesn't have to show that it was born in us. Moreover, he says, there is really no universal agreement. Even on such a thing as the law of contradiction, he says, it isn't true that everyone agrees—savages, imbeciles, babies have never even heard of it, and they're not even conscious of the law of contradiction. The innate-ideas advocates came back with: "Well, they aren't conscious yet. You have to come to the stage of reason in order to grasp that you have those ideas." Locke answers that such is the case for *all* ideas. Are they all innate, then? Why do we have to discover them if they're innate? As for moral ideas, he says, there is no universal agreement even among civilized adults. Locke is not a relativist in ethics—there are such things as correct ideas in ethics—but they require proof, and if they need to be proved, he says, they are not innate. Even the idea of God is absent from some people, and it differs from tribe to tribe and group to group. So much for the idea that there are universally accepted ideas that must, therefore, be innate.

Moreover, he argues, to call an idea innate is usually a way of trying to protect it from criticism. These rationalists come in and say that their innate ideas come from God, and therefore, if you challenge their innate ideas, they contend that this is an attack on God. That is wrong, says Locke. It amounts to entrenching your prejudices under the protection of the Almighty. You take your arbitrary subjective views and masquerade them as a word from on high. We have to reject that. We have to establish our principles by an appeal to the facts as we experience them.

Another argument that he gives is of a quite different type. Even suppose that we were born with certain innate ideas, the ones that the rationalists make such a big fuss about would be useless to us, even if we had them. For instance, suppose we were born with such an innocuous idea as "What is, is" (which is another formulation of "Existence exists"). What have you got when you've got that? asks Locke. You can't deduce any concrete facts from it anyway. (We'll see whether Locke needs this, but he's already a typical modern empiricist, scorning broad abstractions as essentially irrelevant or useless.)

His arguments are very uneven, and the rationalists could and did answer them all. Leibniz wrote a whole work called *The New Essays on Human Understanding* specifically to refute Locke. Locke left out the single crucial argument against innate ideas, namely, that an innate idea is a contradiction in terms. An idea is a form of awareness of reality. An innate idea would be an awareness of reality prior to any contact with reality, which is obviously an impossibility. But you'll see soon why Locke didn't and couldn't use this argument.

In any case, he establishes to his satisfaction that man is born *tabula rasa*. And now, he says, I will prove to you positively that we get all ideas from experience. How? I will undertake to show for any idea you name how it has its ultimate sources in experience. And if I can do this, that will cut the ground out from under the advocates of innate ideas.

For Locke, there are only two basic sources of experience: outer and inner. By "outer," he means the five senses—"sensation" is his name for the faculty of sense perception. By "inner," he means what we would today call "introspection," the faculty of looking into the content of your own consciousness. His term for that is "reflection." So the two sources of experience, sensation and reflection, are the only ultimate source of all our ideas and concepts. From "virtue" to "God" to "art" to "the theory of relativity" (had he known about it), there's no other possible source. Some people objected: "Surely we don't get every concept from experience. What about 'centaur,' for instance, or 'golden mountain'—we couldn't get these concepts from experience." Locke says, well, of course. What we get from experience are the basic, irreducible building blocks, out of which all our other concepts are later constructed or compounded. We may never, for instance, have seen a white circle, but we have seen circles, and we have seen white, so we can put the two together in our mind and get the idea of a white circle. But in that sense, the idea of a white circle still comes ultimately from experience. What we get from experience are the irreducible components of all our later ideas. We get the atoms of knowledge from experience, and we then build up the compounds.

Locke's name for these atomic ideas, using the traditional terminology, are "simple ideas." And "simple," in philosophy, means "indivisible, irreducible." A simple idea is an idea that can't be reduced to constituents, an irreducible unit that you have to experience directly in order to understand. From sensation, for instance, all of the following (and there are many more) are simple ideas—"red," "green," "hot," "cold," "bitter," "sweet," "rough," "smooth," "moving," "rest," "space," "extension," "unity," "existence," etc. No mind, says Locke, can invent or construct one such simple idea. They come straight from experience, and without the necessary experience, you cannot understand the idea. If you were congenitally deaf, the word "loud" would remain a mystery to you, i.e., you have to be able to hear, and then you'd say, "Loud, oh yes, I know what that is." From reflection or introspection, we grasp all the states and activities of our own minds—"willing," "feeling," "reasoning," "pleasure," "pain," "judging," "perceiving," "remembering," etc. In other words, the mind acts on its simple ideas, and, by introspection, can observe those actions. And again, we must experience these ideas, these internal ideas, these ideas of our own inner actions, if we're to understand them. If you have never in your life felt a pain or anything approaching it, the word "pain" will be a mystery to you—you don't know what it stands for. No one can invent a simple idea. Imagine that I told you, "Invent the taste of roast buffalo"—you just can't do it. If I told you that it's one part pineapple and three parts banana split, you could maybe do it. But if it's a simple idea, you have to taste it to know.

In addition to simple ideas, there are "complex ideas," built out of simple ideas. In other words, the mind for Locke is not passive. From a comparatively small stock of simple ideas, by various operations we can produce an endless quantity of ideas. This shouldn't surprise you. The piano has eighty-eight keys, and the whole wealth of piano music comes from those eighty-eight simple units combined in different ways. Similarly, the whole fabric of our knowledge comes from a handful of simple ideas put together in various ways.

According to Locke, there are four mental operations we use to make complex ideas out of simple ones. One is *repetition*—we can repeat a given idea over and over. For instance, "One, one, one, one," and if you do it twelve times, you'd get the idea "dozen." Or two, we can *compare* two or more simple ideas, view them side by side and grasp their relationship. And that's how we get the idea of "bigger," or "to the left of," and so on. Or three, we can *combine* simple ideas. For instance, we can observe in a cigarette one simple idea of its whiteness, and one would be its hotness, and one would be its smoothness, and we put them all together to form "cigarette," and that is a combination used to form the complex idea "cigarette." And finally, says Locke, we can *abstract.* "Abstraction" he defines as "the separating of one idea from all those which accompany it in reality." And that's the source of general ideas. So, for instance, we look at a number of men and we pull out or separate the idea of "rationality" and "animality," and we thereby form the general idea "rational animal," or "man" in general.

I won't go into Locke's theory of abstraction, because it's complicated and unnecessary for this course. Obviously, his theory of abstraction is going to be crucial for his theory of universals. And without going into details, I'll just say that Locke's theory of universals is a very confused mixture of different elements. There is a certain Aristotelian element in his writings in regard to universals, but there's also a very strong nominalist element. If you have to classify him, I would say on the whole, and with appropriate exceptions, that Locke is a nominalist on the theory of universals. He does not really believe in the Aristotelian concept of abstraction. He *does* believe that existents possess real natures, real essences that makes things what they are, and that explains the properties of things—to that extent, he follows Aristotle. But, he adds, the real essence of a thing is unknowable in most cases. All we can know are the essences that we arbitrarily create by our linguistic practices, the Hobbesian essences. You'll soon see the results of this mixture in Locke. But in sum, there is grave trouble in Locke on the theory of universals, and since there's a large element of nominalism, you will expect a definite skeptical element in Locke. And if you expect it, you won't be surprised when you hear about it.

I want to look more closely at the process I referred to a moment ago, the process of forming compound ideas of entities, material entities, what Locke calls "material substances." Locke assumes that experience gives us directly only isolated simple ideas—separate sensory qualities, in effect. And so we ask the question: How do we arrive at the concept of integrated entities? And he answers: We observe that certain qualities, certain simple ideas, go together constantly in our experience. And we, therefore, come to associate these qualities together in our minds as one unit, one entity. So, we build up entities, or ideas of entities, by an active mental process of synthesizing, or uniting, or combining in our minds, a set of coexisting simple ideas. So, for instance, I observe this cigarette, and one simple idea would be cylindricality, and *that*, I notice, when I touch it, goes along with smoothness. And *that* I notice, when I put my finger at the tip, goes along with hotness, and *that*, when I look at it, goes along with whiteness, and so on. There's a whole cluster of such ideas, and I observe them going together repeatedly, and at a certain point I say, "I'm going to give a name to this cluster of coexisting qualities—that's a 'cigarette.'" And thus, I get the idea of an entity, a material substance, a thing, a cigarette.

This account led Locke immediately into an obvious question: What keeps the qualities of a thing together? What makes this one unified entity? Why don't the qualities float off? Why, for instance, don't we have a little cylindrical white patch over on the left which has no texture at all, so that when you go to touch it, there's nothing there, and no temperature, no burning point, and over on the right, meanwhile, when I put my finger there, I get a burn, but all that's there is the hot without the little white cylinder. And in front of me, I feel the smoothness and there's nothing else there? This doesn't happen, says Locke. But why? Is there any necessity in these coexisting qualities staying together? Well, he says, there must be something that holds them together. An entity, a material entity, must consist of something over and above its qualities. There must be some kind of support or bearer. And this phenomenon he calls the *substratum*, which means "the spread-under." It is like a metaphysical pincushion, or like a metaphysical glue in which all the various qualities are stuck, and which keeps them altogether.

Now, says Locke, we can draw support for such a thing as a substratum over and above the qualities from our ordinary language. If I say to you, for instance, "What qualities does this cigarette *have*?"—notice I say the cigarette *has* the quality of whiteness, cylindricality, heat, smoothness, etc. If it has them, it must then be something over and above the qualities. It must be the thing that possesses all of these qualities. And therefore, there must *be* something over and above the qualities, the substratum in which they inhere, which binds them together, which possesses them, which makes them altogether one thing.

What are the characteristics of the substratum? You should see immediately that it cannot have any characteristics of itself, because if it had any qualities, the immediate question would be, "What keeps *those* qualities together?," and we'd have to have a sub-substratum to keep the substratum stuck together, and so on. The substratum (and every material entity), says Locke, is "Something I know not what." As much as I appreciate Descartes's view that we must have clear and distinct ideas, this happens to be a confused and indistinct one, Locke says. But nevertheless, it's a necessary idea, because we can't make sense of material substances without a substratum. For those of you who remember Aristotle's Prime Matter—that little uncharacterizable nothing-in-particular on which all forms are imposed—this is it showing up again in Locke in the form of the substratum.

Just to make it worse, Locke is a dualist like Descartes. He's not an idealist or a materialist. He believes in two kinds of substances, material and spiritual (minds, souls, selves), and he applies exactly the same analysis to *spiritual* substances. What, he asks, unites all the activities of a mind into *one* entity? What is the "you"? We say *you* think, *you* dream, *you* imagine, *you* will—what is the "you" that performs all these activities, that binds them all together, that makes it one entity rather than just a disparate stream of activities? There must be, he says, a something that has all those mental attributes, that performs all those—the "I," the "you"—and that is the substratum. And again, it is "something I know not what" that sticks your mental properties together. Locke, believing in God, says that God is a big cosmic infinite substance, and so, in this respect, he's like Descartes. I want you to remember Locke on substance. I'm not going to criticize it now, and Berkeley and Hume did quite well in criticizing this doctrine. You should see that, in this respect, Locke is no empiricist, because if you're going to go on the basis of experience, you cannot possibly justify the idea of "something I know not what." But if you reject it, as Berkeley did partially and Hume did completely, you're back to Locke's question, "What keeps all the qualities together? Why doesn't the universe disintegrate?" To which Hume said, "It does all the time," but we'll wait until we get there.

Now let us sketch in Locke's metaphysics. What is the first thing we can know to exist, going in order? You might say that since Locke is an empiricist, he must believe that the first thing you know to exist is the physical world. If you think that, you'll be disappointed. According to Locke, the first thing we can know to exist—the self-evident primary with which philosophy begins—is your own mind, your own self. Of that we have a direct intuition, he says (using that in Descartes's sense—a direct self-evident knowledge of the self). He simply repeats Descartes's *Cogito*, that the mental self, the mind, is the most certain thing of all. And thus, Locke is a firm advocate of the prior certainty of consciousness, and in this respect, a thorough follower of Descartes and Augustine.

What comes next? Can we at least go from the self to the material world? No. You have to remember that Descartes is not called the father of modern philosophy for nothing. Remember where Descartes went after the self? He went to God. And so does Locke. The next thing is God, he says. If we get the self by direct intuition, direct self-evidency, we get God by demonstration, by deduction. And he proceeds to offer a standard proof of God that isn't worth discussing. It amounts to "I exist. I must have had a cause, since I'm a thinking being, and the cause must have been very powerful, and it must itself have been a conscious being." And in effect, he finally reaches the idea that there is a being who is the source of all existence, all thought, and that is God. That's a quick run-through of that argument, but it has no value. So God is the next certainty, after the self. And according to Locke, we can be more certain that there is a God than of anything else outside of us (except for ourselves). Here again, he's a straight follower of Descartes.

What about the material world? Locke certainly believed in it—after all, he's an empiricist and believes in material substances. Well, I've been saving the truth for you. We don't, according to Locke, perceive the material world, i.e., we do not *directly* perceive the material world. What we directly perceive is only ideas in our own minds, experiences, sensations in our own minds. Again, a pure Cartesian position, and it was taken for granted by all of Descartes's followers. Consciousness is a self-contained, locked-in entity that contemplates only its own experiences, its own ideas. If you ask Locke, as we asked Descartes: "How do you know then that there *is* an external material world?," Locke would say with Descartes, "Well, it's obvious that we don't create our own experiences, because they are not subject to our will, and we can't get rid of them by an act of will." Suppose we say: "How do you know they're not all a dream? A dream is involuntary. When you're in the middle of a dream, you can't get rid of it by an act of will." Locke says no, material reality must exist as the cause of our experiences. We don't perceive it, so we have to infer its existence, but it must exist as the cause of our experiences. How do you know, Berkeley asked, that God doesn't cause our experiences in us directly, and there is no material world at all? Locke's answer, after a fair amount of equivocation, amounts to this: "Oh, nobody can really be that skeptical." *Why* they can't, given his philosophy, is a big unanswered question. He's in a worse position than Descartes here. At least Descartes had an innate guarantee that God is good, and therefore, if he had a clear and distinct insight that there was a material world, okay, if you accept his epistemology. But Locke is an empiricist. How can an empiricist verify an unperceivable reality? Obviously, he can't, and therefore, it's not going to be very long before there is no reality for the empiricists.

In other words, Locke had all the problems that we have seen with the causal theory of perception. Remember what the causal theory is: Reality is the cause, but not the object, of our experience, i.e., we don't directly perceive reality, only its effects on us. Reality is something we have to reach by inference. And Locke accepts this for the same reason that Descartes and Hobbes and Spinoza and all the rest do. Can we know the nature of reality, you ask? Yes, says Locke. Our experiences resemble, or copy, or represent the things out there in the world, so that although we are caught up in our own little world of consciousness, it happens that our little world of consciousness corresponds to, or represents, what's out there. And therefore, Locke subscribes not only to the causal theory of perception, but to the representative theory of perception.

Of course, he does not believe that *all* of our experiences represent reality, only one part of them. Locke is the one who christened the "primary-secondary quality" distinction, the one who introduced those terms. In the primary qualities, he includes all the standard ones plus solidity (because he wanted to distinguish it from empty space). The primary qualities, he says, resemble reality as it actually is. The secondary qualities are merely like the pain we experience when we put our hand in the fire—they are the effects on us of what's out there, but they do not represent real qualities in the object. They are subjective. And his arguments are the standard ones: You can conceive matter without the secondary qualities, not without the primary; the secondary vary from person to person, the primary are invariant, etc.

Locke's views on the senses and the physical world—in essence, the three strands, the primary-secondary quality distinction, the causal theory of perception, the representative theory of perception—all of these repeat the conclusions we've already seen in Hobbes, Descartes, and others. You can be prepared, therefore, to expect the worst possible result in future philosophy. Here is an empiricist, an advocate of common sense, accepting all the doctrines that lead to the unknowability of physical reality. If the empiricists, along with the rationalists, accept this, you can expect that it won't be very long before reality exits altogether from the philosophic scene. And that is what Berkeley and Hume between them achieved (if you call it an achievement), and that's what we will see in the next lecture.

I want to turn to a final aspect of Locke's epistemology and metaphysics. He also believes in the necessary-contingent dichotomy among truths. He does not characteristically express it in these terms. For those of you who've read the essay, you'll know that he distinguishes four different types of propositions, but I won't go into that kind of detail. The necessary-contingent dichotomy is what it comes down to. On the one hand, we have those propositions that we can establish by Descartes's methods—by direct self-evidence, or deduction from the directly self-evident. These propositions, says Locke, are eternal necessary truths, absolutely certain, and we can see why they must be true. On the other hand, there are the propositions that we establish by observation, sense experience. And in these cases, says Locke, we do not get any necessity. We observe brute facts: Such and such qualities happen to exist, as our senses report, and such and such qualities happen to coexist together, as our senses report. So, there are, in effect, the necessary truths established by reason versus the contingent truths established by the senses—a dichotomy that by now you should be used to.

Let us turn to the necessary truths, the truths established by reason. What is Locke's view of their status? To make a long story short, Locke wavers with regard to the interpretation of these. Part of the time he suggests the typical rationalist view that the necessary truths represent eternal laws of reality, necessary principles that even God can't violate. Part of the time, however—more of the time, insofar as he's a nominalist—he takes the typical Hobbesian view that necessary truths are merely the results of our linguistic decisions, our semantics, our nominal definitions. And therefore, they don't tell us anything about reality but merely express the way that we use words, so that they're conventional, arbitrary, semantic. On this question, Locke is a thoroughly inconsistent mixture of Hobbes and Leibniz. And you see what an eclectic Locke is: He picks pieces from the most opposed philosophies and sticks them together, even though they're diametrically opposed to each other. This approach, by the way, is called "British common sense."

Turning to the truths that are established by sense experience—the contingent truths—can we ever, asks Locke, reach complete certainty in their case? And in essence his answer is no. At best we can achieve only probability in regard to the truths learned by the senses. That's his dominant view. Why? Consider a typical example—suppose you consider gold and the properties of gold. You observe that gold—I mean the ordinary element—combines a series of qualities that go together repeatedly in our experience. It's metallic, it's yellow, it has very great weight, it behaves in various ways when combined with other substances. There's a whole list of separate properties you can rattle off. We observe that these qualities coexist repeatedly in our experience. Can we understand *why* these qualities go together? His answer is, no, we can never understand why these qualities go together. We can see that in fact they *do* go together; but we have no means to know that they *must* go together, nor that they will go together in the future. If we could grasp the real essence of gold, as Aristotle had thought we could, then we could see how all of the properties follow from the essence. We could see why gold *must* have the properties it does, and our knowledge would be certain and necessary. But, says Locke (and in this part he's a real nominalist), we can't grasp real essences. All we can grasp are *nominal essences*. In other words, we decide arbitrarily to call a certain cluster of coexisting qualities by the same term. And we thereby *create* the phenomenon gold, but gold doesn't express a real necessary union of properties out there in the world. It is merely our human subjective classification. And since we see no necessary connection among the properties that we have jointly labeled "gold" we see only that they *happen* to go together, but we're unable to grasp any real essence that would explain why. For all we can tell, maybe tomorrow they'll stop going together, or we'll encounter something with *all* the properties of gold except that instead of being yellow, it's green with pink polka dots, or instead of being heavy, it's lighter than water, but in every other respect it's the same. Who knows? How *can* you know, asks Locke? As a nominalist, you can't. You're confined to observing what's before you. The upshot for Locke is that all observational knowledge, all empirical knowledge, is at best probable.

You might ask: Why is it even probable if we can't grasp any necessity? Why is there even some likelihood that the combination of qualities that we encountered so far will continue tomorrow? That's exactly the question Hume asked, and in the answer, he wiped out cause and effect, holding that there isn't even any probability. So, you see how, on issue after issue, Locke's formulations lay the basis for the worst skepticism, which is going to break out shortly after him.

I should make clear that Locke himself was not a skeptic. He is teeming with the *seeds* of skepticism, but the seeds did not grow into a full David Hume in Locke. In fact, based on our very brief summary of Locke's metaphysics and epistemology, the best thing to say is that he is not anything consistently. There are three separate philosophic strands in Locke, all in conflict with the others, all popping up repeatedly and clashing in his discussion of various philosophic questions. And the three strands as *I* would identify them are (1) a large hunk of Cartesian rationalism—for instance, Locke's emphasis on intuitive and deductive, clear and distinct truths; the fact that he begins with the *Cogito*, or the prior certainty of consciousness, the idea that we perceive only our own ideas. Then (2) a definite element of Aristotelianism. He did have a real respect for this world. Even though he was a devout Christian, there is no supernaturalism or overt mysticism in his philosophy. As part of his Aristotelianism, he insists on the senses as the base of knowledge, even granted his views on the nature of the senses. He insists that the unit of reality is the individual, the particular, the concrete, and he emphasizes reason, which he views as the faculty that operates on sense perception. All of these very important ideas are Aristotelian. And then finally there is (3) the Hobbesian nominalism, and all of the skeptic elements that it led to in Locke. So, in effect, to put in a crude mathematical formula something which can't be quantified, I would say Locke is one part Descartes, one part Aristotle, one part Hobbes, which means if you put it more deeply, one part Plato, one part Aristotle, one part Sophists, all blended and glossed over by British common sense.

This combination obviously cannot survive, and the first thing to go was the Aristotelianism, because it couldn't survive within the framework of a mixture of Descartes and Hobbes. And with only Descartes and Hobbes left, and the rationalist approach discredited via the constructions of Spinoza and Leibniz, the end result had to be what it was (assuming nobody else came on the scene), namely, the final triumph of complete skepticism in David Hume. So much for Locke's metaphysics and epistemology.

Let me say just a little about Locke's ethics. In ethics, as in metaphysics and epistemology, Locke is an eclectic mixture. And again, you can distinguish three main strands in his viewpoint, all helter-skelter tossed off. In part, he's a hedonist—a psychological hedonist and an ethical hedonist. Remember that psychological hedonism is the view that all men live for pleasure—that that's a law of human nature, and it was a standard Greek view, even though it's erroneous as a universal observation. An ethical hedonist is someone who says that a person *should* live for pleasure; pleasure is the good, and the test of right and wrong is maximizing pleasure. Whatever acts lead to the greatest amount of pleasure are right. There is this definite hedonist element in Locke. But then, over and above that, you have to remember that Locke is a devout Christian, and he often says that God is the author and creator of morality, that God has commanded his creatures to live a certain way, and therefore, "virtue" means "obedience to the divine commandments." You see this incredible mixture of ancient hedonism and medieval Christianity. And there's still a third element, which is his heritage from the rationalists. To a certain extent, he accepts the typical rationalist view that ethics can be demonstrated geometrically, i.e., that from the very nature of certain concepts you can establish good and evil deductively without reference to God or pleasure, simply by reference to the laws of logic.

How does Locke combine all these elements? He doesn't really, but if you had to, his view would be something like this: Ethics means obeying the commands of God, and God commands us to behave as long-range hedonists, and since God is rational, so are his commandments, and they're therefore geometrically demonstrable. That's the closest I can make a synthesis out of Locke's ethics. And I won't comment further on such an incredible mixture. You see that Locke's ethics, like his metaphysics and epistemology, is an incongruous mixture of the most diverse elements.

In conclusion, let us turn to Locke's politics, by far the most famous branch of his philosophy and a direct, extremely important influence on the Founding Fathers of this country. Before I utter any reservations about Locke's politics (and I have many), I want to say something about the good things. And it does have many profoundly good things. The constituent elements of Locke's politics are not always original with Locke, but he was the first man in Western philosophy to bring them all together and give the theory of inalienable individual rights its first comprehensive influential statement. His famous work on politics is *The Second Treatise of Government*, which was published in 1690. And in it—it's a rather brief book—he argues forcefully against any form of absolute political control, and in favor of individual rights, and strictly limited government. And the man he has in mind, although he doesn't mention it, is Hobbes, whom he's out to refute.

Let me synopsize Locke's political views. There is, Locke argues, a natural law, a law of nature, an objective rule, defining men's proper social and political relations to each other. This rule is a commandment from God, but it is graspable and provable strictly by human reason. This part of his politics is obviously the ancient Stoic view that we looked at many lectures ago. The law of nature, according to Locke, is that even before governments exist, in a state that he calls the *state of nature* (which simply means a condition without government), all men should exist as free, independent, equal beings. And when he says "equal," he doesn't mean economically equal or intellectually equal, but equal in one respect only:

All possess certain inalienable, individual rights granted (in his opinion) by their creator. And those rights are *not* the right to Medicare, guaranteed employment, and three months in Florida for your lumbago, but the rights to life, liberty, and property. These rights, says Locke, cannot be interfered with by the government. They do not come from the government. They logically precede the government. And indeed, it is to *secure* these rights, to enable us to be safe and secure in their exercise, that we should establish governments. That, he says, is why men should make a *social compact*, or contract, with one another and leave the function of protecting rights to the government. They will not themselves attempt to punish criminals, men who infringe their rights, but will delegate that task to the government. The government, therefore, is not the ruler of the people, but its agent. Government has the task of protecting men's rights, and above all, their right to the property that they have created by their own labor, and to which they are, therefore, entitled. Government, therefore, he concludes, must be by consent of the governed and must be strictly limited in its functions.

So why have a government at all? Locke answers that a government gives you three great advantages that a state of nature without government would not have. It enables us to live by a code of objective laws that we can appeal to in case of disputes; it provides objective, impartial judges (if you have a decent government) to apply the laws in particular cases; and it has the power to back up the sentences of the judges, to enforce the laws, thereby ensuring that each man will be free and secure within the sphere of his individual rights. So, each man, according to Locke, will be able to live by the guidance of his own reason. None will be able to force his views on others. Men, thought Locke, are by and large good. They are rational beings. And here he was in profound opposition to Hobbes. Men do not need an omnipotent ruler to tell them what to do. Left to their own devices, by themselves, they can achieve the good life, and achieve peace and harmony and happiness on earth. And, he adds, if and when a government begins seriously to abuse its powers, to violate men's rights, to enslave them instead of protecting them, then the people have every right to declare a revolution, to overthrow such a tyrannical government, and reestablish the proper rights-respecting kind of government.

That is a brief sketch of Locke's politics, and I think you can see its enormous virtues. In essence, Locke's politics derives from the Aristotelian element in his basic philosophy—from his emphasis on this world, man's reason, the rationality of men, their ability to run their own lives by their own minds, the reality and importance of the individual. The two other elements in Locke—the mystical (i.e., the Cartesian-Christian side) and the skeptical (the Hobbesian-nominalist side) are largely *implicit*. He was stopped from making them the dominant or explicit themes of his philosophy. And consequently, they do not break out in substantial ways in his politics. That is the explanation of why Locke, with his incredibly mixed philosophy, could have such a comparatively good politics.

But these other elements are present in his philosophy. And the subsequent course of philosophy consisted of suppressing the Aristotelian element in Locke altogether, and of transmitting to later centuries only Platonism and skepticism in progressively more intense forms. And the result was that Locke's politics could not last. Politics cannot stand by itself. It depends directly on ethics, and still more basically on metaphysics and epistemology. As the metaphysics and epistemology, and therefore the ethics, of later philosophers turned violently Platonist, skeptic, and Kantian, the result was that approval of Locke's ideas dropped off sharply among philosophers and intellectuals and cultural trend-setters, so that by the time you reach the nineteenth century, intellectually speaking, Locke's politics were swamped, overcome altogether by every variety of a proliferating collectivism, largely generated by the derivatives of Hume and Kant—Hegel, Marx, and the whole unholy crew thereafter. This is why Locke's politics, with all its virtues, could not endure. What would make it endure? Only a complete, systematic, rational philosophy, across the board, in every key branch and issue of philosophy. That, unfortunately, is what Locke did not provide.

I don't want to imply by my praise of Locke's politics that, as he formulated it, it is completely free from objections. You cannot escape your metaphysics and epistemology, and if something is only a partial element, it will show up in your conclusions. And Locke's confused metaphysics, epistemology, and ethics *did* have some influence even on his politics. You see, for instance, his references to God as the source of natural law, the source of man's rights—that's a Christian influence on his politics. And if we had time, I could give you many other examples of errors in Locke's politics, cases where his formulations are inexact or dubious or outrightly dangerous—cases where his doctrines on matters of detail or implementation leave the door wide open for the modern socialist to plunge in with both feet and wreak havoc, cases where his mixed-up philosophy leads him to glaring contradictions. But these details are not really central to this course.

I think we have to come to a twofold conclusion. In part, we have to regret deeply that Locke presented his politics in the philosophic framework that he did, because it means that he never really had a long-range chance to become a permanent influence on the life of mankind. But nevertheless, we have to express our appreciation to Locke for the excellent elements that *are* in his politics. True, it's Aristotle who deserves the deepest credit for these elements, and true, Locke made many errors. But it is *also* true that, whatever his errors, Locke is one of the pillars on mankind's road to the discovery of a rational social order. And it's owing to his direct influence that the Founding Fathers were able to hold the views they did and to create the United States of America. This, I submit, is an achievement for which Locke will, and properly should, always be remembered.

Lecture Ten, Q&A

Q: What is the fallacy in distinguishing, as Leibniz does, between the logically possible and the real?

A: I've really covered that, but I'll review it briefly. The "logically possible" means the noncontradictory. *Any* alternative to the reality we have would, in fact, be contradictory. And therefore, any alternative would be impossible. Why would any alternative be contradictory? Because the law of cause and effect is an expression of the law of identity. Every entity acts as it does because of its nature and could not act differently without contradicting its nature. Consequently, given an entity of a certain nature, it must act as it does. Consequently, nothing could occur differently from the way it actually does. The attempt to distinguish the logically possible from the real is to make the real non-logical, which means not dictated by the law of cause and effect or the laws of logic, which means, not in harmony with the laws of logic, which is a violation of the basic principles of logic. And therefore, the whole attempt is wrong. For further details, I suggest that you refer to my article on the analytic-synthetic dichotomy, which discusses that question at greater length. The idea, however, of a possible universe different from ours—speaking here not now of a planetary system or a galaxy, but meaning the total of metaphysical reality—the idea of another possibility is wrong. There is no other possibility. That's involved in "Existence exists"—no other existence exists, no other existence is possible. Even the concept of "possible" has to be defined by reference to this existence—"possible" is what is compatible with this existence—there's no other reality to have a base of any other possibility.

Q: If observation is invalid, how does Spinoza show that his basic axioms are true? He can't deduce them from anything more primary.

A: He would say, "Sure, that's why you have to start with clear and distinct self-evident ideas, which are neither sensory nor deductive; they're simply clear and distinct." But in a deeper way, Spinoza would say—a point that I left out of the lecture, and a point which was very influential on Hegel—*all* ideas are true. Even the ideas that you consider to be totally false are really substantially true. And here, he defends this viewpoint by reference to his psycho-physical parallelism. To every mental phenomenon there is a physical correlate. To every thought, there must therefore be a corresponding object. And if "truth" means "the correspondence of a thought to an object," every thought must have its truth. What do we call "error"? Error is a thought that gets attached to the wrong object, that's all. It's like a misplaced truth. So, for instance, if you have a hallucination of a pink rat, we say you're wrong, but that doesn't mean there is no physical object associated with the pink rat. It's just that you got mixed up as to what the physical correlate is—the actual physical object is not a pink rat, but a pint of alcohol in your blood, let us say. So, in this sense, there are no false ideas. All ideas are guaranteed to be true by virtue of the fact that all ideas express inevitably the development of God. That doesn't mean that on a lower level there aren't superficially false ideas. And Spinoza would say, for instance, that Descartes is wrong on certain points. But that's on a lower level, so to speak. On the deeper level, all ideas are true, and therefore Spinoza is correct. This particular theory was developed by Hegel into what was called the "coherence theory of truth"—that all ideas have a degree of truth, and that there's no such thing as a completely false idea. But it's hinted at in Spinoza, and that's one of the reasons that Spinoza is said to have an influence on Hegel.

Q: Wasn't Spinoza an advocate or champion of individual freedom, even though he didn't believe individuality was real?

A: Yes, he was. Spinoza was a definite individualist politically. Let me take this opportunity to say something about Spinoza's ethics, because that will help to clarify how an individualist could believe that individuality is unreal. The whole seventeenth century is a germinal individualist era. That's what laid the ground for all the individualist revolutions of the eighteenth century and for America. And therefore, to a certain extent, Spinoza is reflecting in his individualism the cultural climate of the emphasis on reason, this world, science, the individual, which seeped into everybody's thought. In this sense, the cultural climate of the Age of Reason was infinitely superior to anything in the twentieth century in this cesspool of irrationalism. So, to some extent, no matter what a philosopher's foundation was, he absorbed an individualist politics. Even Kant has large elements of individualism in his politics. They're in grotesque conflict with the rest of his philosophy, but he didn't see fully the political conclusions. His immediate followers did, but he didn't.

Spinoza's ethics, like his philosophy in general, is a blend of two elements. Just as his metaphysics and epistemology are part religious mysticism and part logical pro-science view, so his ethics is partly a kind of Stoic-Platonic otherworldliness and contempt for the world of appearances, and yet partly it's a this-worldly, naturalistic egoism. Spinoza is classified as an egoist in ethics. And there are many points that, out of context, students of Objectivism would very much approve of and agree with in Spinoza's ethics. I'll give you just a sample of the egoistic, this-worldly side of Spinoza. To begin with, he is a psychological egoist, i.e., he believes that all men are necessarily egoistic in their actions. He believes that the basic motivation of all men is self-assertion, self-fulfillment, self-preservation. This is incorrect, but it is a reflection in Spinoza of the common Greek advocacy of psychological egoism. And Spinoza goes on with the Greek view: This is good. Men *should* be selfish. He is an ethical egoist, but how can he be an egoist if he holds that the individual self is only appearance? And his answer would be: That is how it appears. We do appear to be separate individuals, and we must act accordingly. What do you think of that? It's not a very substantial foundation.

Virtue, he says, therefore—and he insists on this—is not self-sacrifice. Virtue is self-fulfillment, self-perfecting, perfecting the power of the mind to think and of the body to act. And the result of virtue, says Spinoza, will be personal individual happiness, pleasure, which is the proof of the truly moral man. All of this, you see, is in a general way within the Greek tradition in ethics. And you can find many points to agree with in Spinoza's views. For instance, his insistence that pleasure is not bad but good, that life is to be lived and enjoyed. Quoting from Spinoza: "Assuredly nothing forbids a man to enjoy himself save grim and gloomy superstition." The wise man, he says, enjoys the things of this life. And Spinoza has many pungent things to say about those who are obsessed with the afterlife, and who tremble in the face of death. The wise man, says Spinoza, pays no attention to death whatever. He doesn't waste his time brooding about it. "His wisdom is a meditation not of death, but of life." Spinoza doesn't believe in any personal immortality: When you're dead, that's the end. And then all the Christians chimed in, "Well, if there was no personal immortality, if we didn't fear an afterlife, no one would be moral." To which Spinoza answers—a very clever answer: "To say that the man who does not believe in personal immortality has no incentive to right living, is not less absurd than to suppose that because he does not believe that he can by wholesome food sustain his body forever, he should wish to cram himself with poisons and deadly fare; or, that because he sees that the mind is not eternal and immortal, he should prefer to be out of his mind altogether and to live without the use of reason. These ideas are so absurd as to be scarce worth refuting." You can find a lot of that in Spinoza, and he's very interesting from that point of view.

But, mixed in with this-worldly egoism is a profound strain of Platonism and Stoicism, deriving from the Platonist elements in his metaphysics and epistemology. Most men, he says, are slaves to their emotions, to emotions that are thrust on them by external causes, causes that they do not really clearly and distinctly understand. And the result is that most men spend their lives buffeted and ravaged by blind emotions—hatred, fear, envy, guilt, rivalry, etc. In a famous section of his work on ethics, a section entitled "Of Human Bondage," Spinoza tells you how to escape from bondage to such emotions. And how do you do it? You must understand the universe fully. You must see how everything follows inevitably from the nature of reality—in other words, from the nature of God. You must see that nothing could possibly have been different. And then you will experience serenity, tranquility, acceptance, peace of mind. You won't feel fear, you won't feel hate, you won't feel any emotional rebellion. Who can rebel against the inevitable when he sees it clearly as inevitable? You can see the obvious Stoicism of all of this. We must, he says in a famous phrase, "perceive the world *sub spatie aeternitatus*," which means "under the aspect of eternity." Which amounts to: We have to lose the narrow, petty perspective of our own confining cares and concerns, and see the universe from the aspect of the grand totality. And then we will see that all is really one, all is inevitable, we really are the same as each other, and we will find peace. So, there's not much left of his egoism when you combine it with the rest of his philosophy, because if I am you and you are him and we're all ultimately identical, then living for myself becomes living for the whole totality of the universe, and the whole distinctively egoist character of the ethics is gone. In any event, the crowning virtue for Spinoza is what he calls "the intellectual love of God," and since "God" means "reality," it's the intellectual love of reality. In other words, the full understanding of the universe by man's intellect, and the dedication to grasp and explain everything about the universe by human reason, until finally the totality has been mastered. In this respect, Spinoza is an arch champion of the full, free, unfettered, scientific use of the human mind (that's his scientific rational side), but he uses it to prove the deterministic rigidity of the universe and the importance of turning away from the petty cares of this world and immersing one's self in the contemplation of eternity. So again, you have that major mixture of Platonist mysticism and naturalistic, scientific, rational egoism. But if you consider just the egoist element, you can find a lot in Spinoza that's very interesting. I've often, in conversation, been accused of being a Spinozist—it doesn't last for very long when they hear what the rest of my views are—but there is to that extent a certain similarity, out of context, on certain points.

Q: I've always heard determinism expounded in relation to a divinity, or man's genes as the causal factor. Considering Spinoza's pantheism and lack of individuation, I don't understand how determinism applies.

A: Well, you're quite wrong. Determinism is the view that everything that happens is inevitable. It doesn't have to be God and it doesn't have to be genes. It can be atoms following mechanistic laws, à la Democritus and the materialists. It can be your id and your toilet training, à la the Freudians. It can be your economic environment, à la the Marxists. It can be the logic of reality, à la Spinoza. "Determinism" is a very broad abstraction. God and genes are only two popular versions of it. There are many others.

Q: Was the mysticism of the Continental rationalists resisted by the scientists of the time?

A: Mostly, no. Scientists do not set philosophic trends. They are human beings like everybody else, and they accept the dominant philosophic trends. Now, qua scientist in this period that we're talking about (seventeenth and eighteenth centuries), they were much more rational than today's scientists. I don't mean that their theories were superior, because there are obviously great virtues in some modern scientific theories, but I mean as men, they were more rational on the whole, because the intellectual climate was more rational. But, in their extra-scientific activities, there were weird mystics among the scientists, not the least of whom was Isaac Newton, who believed that space and time were the sense organs of God. So much for the idea of scientists being impervious to mysticism. If you go to Southern California, you'll see what scientists are like philosophically.

Q: [Follow-up question]: Was this a factor checking the immediate popularity of Continental rationalism?

A: No. Continental rationalism was checked, if it was, by the British empiricists, who were to some extent influenced by science and admirers of it, but primarily they derived from Aristotle, and from Descartes himself as you see in the case of Locke. So scientists, as scientists, are not factors in the history of intellectual development. They are products along with every other field.

Q: An altruist does not respect the rights of others. There is no reason, therefore, for others to respect the rights of the altruists. This means there is nothing wrong with killing the altruists. Do you agree?

A: How's that for a short argument in favor of murder? Now, what is wrong with this argument, just as an intellectual exercise? It starts, "An altruist does not respect the rights of others." How do you know? Are you talking about the *actions* of every altruist, or the *theory* of altruism? Are you saying that every advocate of altruism goes around robbing, raping, and murdering? That is bizarre. Most of them are very law-abiding, and they spend most of their time writing books. Or are you saying that their *theories*, if consistently applied, politically would lead to the abolition of rights and dictatorship? If you say that, then yes, that's true. But the fact that somebody advocates a theory is not justification for killing him, even if it's a theory, which, if consistently applied, would lead to murder. You do not kill somebody for an idea. Here you have to remember that *you* are an advocate of individual rights, even if your opponent is not, and his individual rights include the right to propagate utterly false, vicious, destructive ideas. When can you step in? Only when he begins to *act* on those ideas in the form of initiating physical force against an innocent victim or victims. At that point, you step in, and you do so not because of his theories, but because of his actions. If you don't keep that idea in mind, you obliterate the idea of individual rights, you obliterate the distinction between thought and action, and you are, therefore, in the position where someone can just as well come up to you and say: "Most egoists in history have preached dictatorship and brutality, and since you're an egoist, even if you don't advocate it, this is likely to arouse in the masses the lust to brutality, and therefore we'd better kill you before you cause trouble." You would object to that if done to you, and the same thing goes the other way. I don't mean that the deductions are the same in quality. I mean that you do not initiate force because of disagreement of ideas. You distinguish between the theory and the action.

Q: If the dichotomy of necessary and contingent facts is false, how does one apply this to human actions? Is it wrong to imagine that a man could have acted differently than he has?

A: I covered exactly that question in my article on the analytic-synthetic dichotomy. No, certainly a man has free will and thus could have acted differently than he did. But I would not apply the term "contingent" to that. That is why we have the term "volition." Volition is not in conflict with the law of cause and effect. Volition is one subspecies of cause and effect. But it is the kind of action that allows alternatives. I would never call that "contingent," though, because "contingent" implies causeless, divorced from cause and effect, divorced from logic, brute, unintelligible. There is no such phenomenon in the human or the non-human parts of reality. What there is, is a universe governed by iron cause and effect, everything must act in accordance with its nature, and man has a specific nature compatible with that law, but the nature of man is such that he has the faculty of choice. Therefore, you could imagine different actions. But I wouldn't call that "contingent."

Q: Is Leibniz's reasoning correct that there must be ultimate, indivisible substances composing reality?

A: That is just the kind of question I refuse to answer. In my opinion, that is physics, not metaphysics. I would never engage in any deductive attempt from abstract philosophic principles to determine whether the ultimate constituents of reality are atomic or continuous. That is pure armchair rationalism if you attempt that. There is no way philosophically of answering those questions. And consequently, I do not want to end up with my own theory of monads or the equivalent. That is not the province of philosophy.

Q: Did Leibniz's pre-established harmony imply determinism?

A: Yes. All your perceptions are determined in advance, and Leibniz is in that respect a thorough determinist. There are attempts on his part to reconcile determinism and free will and modify it, but substantially he is a full-fledged determinist. Any of those cases where everything is synchronized in advance . . . well, since the whole physical series is determined, the whole mental one is also.

Q: Would Plato's Form of the Good or Plotinus's the One, necessitate a best-of-all-possible-worlds, since perfection (which was also perfectly good) must radiate or emanate in the best or most perfect of all possible ways?

A: Yes. If you say that the world is run, directly or indirectly, by a fundamental feature that is the apex of reality, is perfect, and is responsible for everything else, then you believe that there is an ultimate good purpose running everything, which makes you a teleologist. And all teleologists in that respect believe that this world is as good as it can be. Does it mean, therefore, that Plato and Plotinus believed that other worlds were possible? No. They weren't Christian, remember. They were Greek. And the Greeks believed that the whole universe, including even the debased physical world (even if it were debased) was eternal and emanated eternally. So the idea of other possible worlds is a distinctively Judeo-Christian view. That was not in any of the Greeks, except by the implication of the necessary-contingent dichotomy. They thought that individual *facts* within this world could have been different, which is a mistake on their part. But nevertheless, as a general rule, the Greeks did not believe in the idea of another possible world. Would this imply determinism in their ethics? First of all, determinism comes under metaphysics, not ethics. But would this imply determinism, that everything happens for the best? Not necessarily, because they could take the view that everything happens for the best, but one of the best things is that man has free will, and that adds to the perfection of the world. That's the typical Christian answer. And therefore, even though everything happens for the best, man has free will, and therefore that view is not deterministic. That answer is ultimately incompatible with an all-powerful God, but it's been a very common answer.

Q: Do you recognize any validity in Locke's view of simple ideas? Could you explain where he went wrong with this approach?

A: I explained that I do not believe we are given simple ideas as discrete, separate qualities, but that they are acts of later analysis. As I will explain in the final lecture, I do not believe we spend our time contemplating our ideas or our experiences; we are directly aware of reality. Objectivism rejects the causal theory of perception in its entirety. So, in all of those respects, it's wrong. So, if you ask me: Do I recognize *any* validity in the idea of simple ideas? Only this much: Not *all* ideas can be reduced to other ideas; there can't be an infinite regress of definitions; and therefore, there must be some such things as simple ideas, that is to say, ideas of direct sensations that you get directly from experience and which can be defined only ostensively, by pointing to instances of them. I don't always agree with Locke that what he regards as an example of a simple idea *is* such an example. But the basic idea of simple, unanalyzable ideas is valid, if you don't misuse it in the countless ways Locke does.

LECTURE ELEVEN

. . . and the Attempt Collapses

The final two philosophers to be covered in this course are Bishop George Berkeley and David Hume. Both are eighteenth-century philosophers, both are British empiricists, both are derivatives of the trend developed by John Locke, and both are typical of the final epistemology offered by the period known as the *Enlightenment*. The seventeenth century is called the *Age of Reason*, and the eighteenth, as a result, the *Enlightenment*, but the philosophers of the Age of Reason put forth deeply Platonic and/or skeptic notions of what reason consists of. And the result was that the dominance of reason, of the explicit advocacy of reason, had to come to an end. And the two philosophers of the Enlightenment period with whom it *does* come to an end are Berkeley and Hume. Both of these philosophers, I hasten to add, are, in their own view, staunch advocates of reason. But when you see what their systems are, you will see why other contemporary and later philosophers said that reason has had its chance and has failed. And the result was the ushering in of an era of avowed mysticism and irrationalism, starting in the late-eighteenth century and intensifying, without exception, to the present day.

Bishop Berkeley

Let us start with Bishop George Berkeley (1685–1753, and he was about nineteen when Locke died). As a bishop, Berkeley, needless to say, is a deeply religious man. One of the main goals of his philosophy was to combat what he regarded as a major obstacle to religion, namely, *matter*. That is to say, the concept of an external, independent physical reality. This, he believed, was always a thorn in the side of religion. Religion preaches that God created matter *ex nihilo* (out of nothing), and there were always skeptics (and others) around to ask how you could get something out of nothing. The belief in matter always gave way periodically to people like Hobbes, who said we could explain everything in terms of matter and thereby deny the soul, deny God, deny immorality. The belief in matter gave rise to mechanism, the idea that the laws of mechanics, the laws of physics, explain everything that happens, so we can dispense with God's purpose, with God's plans, with God's miracles. But, thinks Berkeley, if we can get rid of the material world—if we can show that there *is* no external physical world—we will once and for all have cut the base out of the materialists, the skeptics, and the atheists and in the most profound way. And he is correct: The material world *is* the philosophic enemy of God, so he knows what to attack.

Berkeley, as I said, is an empiricist. He agrees with Locke that all knowledge comes from experience. There are no innate ideas. We can acquire knowledge only on the basis of experience. But he is much more consistent than Locke was. He accepts all of Locke's basic premises and uses them to demonstrate the nonexistence of the physical world. He is, therefore, classified as an *idealist* (in the technical philosophic sense). With Berkeley we end up with a world of individual minds, presided over by God, each contemplating its own experiences. And thus, we have a universe very similar to Leibniz's, but now we reach this kind of idealism not via the rationalist route of Leibniz, but via the empiricist route of Berkeley. And because empiricism was much more influential in the Anglo-American world than rationalism ever was, Berkeley is the first really influential modern empiricist.

I first want to look at Berkeley's arguments against the existence of an independent material world. You must understand that when we talk about an external material world, we mean anything external to the mind, and that includes your brain and your body, your arms and legs and liver. All of that goes when the physical world goes.

Let's first of all get clear what Berkeley is driving at before we hear his arguments.

Consider the example of a toothache, and ask yourself the question: Can you have a toothache without experiencing it? Can a toothache—not a tooth now, but a toothache—exist or be real if you in no way perceive it, experience it, or are aware of it? Suppose I point at someone say, "I'm sorry that you have such a raging, searing, painful toothache this evening." And you say to me: "What do you mean? I don't feel any toothache at all. I'm not aware of any such thing." What if I came back with: "Well, what's the difference whether you're aware of it or not? After all, facts are real whether or not people are aware of them. A is A. Don't facts exist independent of consciousness?" You'd say to me: "Well, look, this is a very special kind of existent you're talking about. A toothache is an *experience.* It's something that exists only in the mind. It is not an external fact." You would say that the very reality or being of a toothache exists in its being perceived. If nobody experiences the toothache, the toothache is unreal. The Latin for the viewpoint is an expression made famous by Berkeley: *Esse est percipi. Esse* is Latin for "to be." *Est,* Latin for "is," and *percipi* is Latin for "to be perceived." In the case of a toothache, you would say, *Esse est percipi*—its being consists of its being perceived; if it weren't perceived, it would not exist. It would be nothing.

Berkeley proposes to argue that matter—every kind of matter and every quality of matter—is in the identical metaphysical position as the toothache. Not only color, sound, taste, temperature, but extension, three-dimensionality, solidity, size, shape, motion, *everything* pertaining to matter is just a set of experiences, a set of ideas in the mind. In the case of matter, he is going to argue *esse est percipi.* And there is, therefore, no independent external material world at all. This will be the proof of what Objectivism would call "the primacy of consciousness." Physical existence is going to become a series of subjective mental experiences. And thus, Berkeley's philosophy is referred to as *subjective idealism*—"idealism" because it believes that true reality is something more basic than the material world, "subjective" to contrast it to Platonism (which holds that true reality is the nonmaterial, unconscious world of Forms), and to contrast it to the later view of Hegel, who holds that there is one cosmic consciousness, the Absolute, which constitutes true reality. Berkeley believes that separate individual minds are real—each individual subject is real—and reality consists of these individual minds and their content.

How does Berkeley defend a viewpoint like this? He gives a great many arguments in his work *A Treatise Concerning the Principles of Human Knowledge,* and also in a famous series of dialogues between two characters, *Hylas* and *Philonous.* ("Hylas" derives from the Greek word *hyle* for matter, so Hylas is the man who believes in matter, and "Philonous" is the mind-lover, the idealist in the technical sense. And, of course, Philonous wins all the arguments). I'm going to give you two of the major sets of arguments that Berkeley gives. There are many more, but these two will be ample for our purposes. One set derives from the causal and representative theories of perception, which I have stressed many times in this course. The second set derives from the primary-secondary quality distinction.

Let's look first at the argument from the causal theory of perception. This is the viewpoint accepted by Hobbes, Descartes, Spinoza, Leibniz, and Locke, the viewpoint that what we directly perceive is not reality but rather the experiences in our own minds. Remember their basis: Our senses obviously process the data we get, and there we are at the end of the chain perceiving only the resulting effects on us. Therefore, we don't directly perceive reality, only its effects on us. But, they all claimed, reality must exist to be the cause of our experiences, and thus, the name: the *causal* theory of perception. And, they went on, although we don't directly perceive reality, we can know something about it, because some, at least, of our experiences represent or copy or resemble reality. Locke had taken that view. Here is where Berkeley takes off and begins to slaughter both the causal and the representative theories of perception, and in the process annihilates the material world.

Let's start with the representative theory of perception. Berkeley asks Locke: How can a sensation or an idea or an experience—which is what you say we directly perceive—how can any one of those things resemble or copy or be *like* something that is *not* a sensation, an idea, or an experience? Consider the sensation or experience, for instance, of a shape, like a triangle. Locke says that sensation of a shape is just like the real shape out there in reality. What does it mean, asks Berkeley, to say that my experience of a shape is just like the real shape in reality? My experience is certainly not triangular, doesn't occupy space at all. My experience has no size, but the real triangular entity has size. The real triangle might be moving at the rate of thirty miles an hour, but my experience is certainly not moving at the rate of thirty miles an hour. It is therefore entirely gratuitous to talk about a similarity between a mental experience and a physical object. A sensation or an idea, he says, can resemble only another sensation or idea. What does it mean to say that mental contents resemble or copy reality? It doesn't mean anything legitimate. So much for the representative theory of perception.

Continuing with the same overall argument. Assume for a moment that there is some meaning to saying that our ideas resemble or represent reality—how can Locke say that any of his sensations or experiences resemble reality, even assuming it were meaningful to say so? To know whether his experiences resemble reality, he would have to do what? He'd have to have some access to reality, and then compare his experience on the one hand with reality on the other and see whether they were similar. But according to Locke, this is impossible to do because he never comes into any contact with reality. Suppose that I open one hand to you and show you a quarter, and my other hand is closed behind my back, and you have no access whatever to what (if anything) is in my other hand. And now I say to you, "Does the thing that I have in my open hand (the quarter) resemble, or not, the thing in my other hand?" Your answer would be, "I have to know what's in your other hand." But suppose I say that you can never perceive what's in my other hand. Then your conclusion would have to be that you haven't the faintest idea whether what I have in my hand does or doesn't resemble the other, because you have no access to it. Indeed, if you never could come in contact with the content of my other hand, you would have to say it was unknowable to you. And that, says Berkeley, is precisely the position that Locke is in with regard to the material world. If we perceive only our own experiences, we have then got no way to go outside of our experiences and compare them to reality. And therefore, if the causal theory of perception is correct, the material world must be unknowable.

But, says Berkeley, accept this much: If there were a material world, it would be unknowable because we never perceive it. We perceive only our own experiences. Berkeley just adds another premise, which is perfectly logical. He says that the idea of an unperceivable material world is a contradiction in terms. The idea of an unperceivable or unknowable material world is a contradiction in terms. What do we *mean* by a material object? If you go by common sense, you mean by a material object something that can be seen, touched, tasted, smelled, heard, etc. Suppose that I hold up an empty hand and tell you, "Take a look at this apple." And you say to me, "What apple?" I say: "Well, this is a special kind of apple. It happens to be unperceivable and unknowable. You can't see it, you can't taste it, and you can't touch it." "Well," you'd say to me, "how do you distinguish that kind of apple from nothing whatever? If it's a physical apple, it *must* be perceivable. A material thing is a thing capable of being perceived, or experienced." Which is obviously true.

Now we combine these two premises. Looking at the argument, you find a simple syllogism with two premises leading to a conclusion. Premise one, "A material thing is a thing capable of being perceived." Premise two, "The only things we're capable of perceiving are experiences in our own minds." That's the premise of Locke—all we perceive are the experiences of our own minds. What follows from those two premises? "A material thing is a thing we can perceive, and the only things we can perceive are experiences in our own minds." The conclusion must be: "A material thing is a collection of experiences in our own minds." Therefore, it's true that we can perceive material things directly, but that's because material things are simply experiences in our own minds. In other words, says Berkeley, I'm merely combining two premises that no one can object to. On the one hand, a premise of the common man on the street, with his good common sense, and on the other, the premise that all philosophers grant. The common man says a material thing is a thing capable of being experienced, and I agree. Philosophers contribute the second premise: The things we experience are the ideas in our own minds.

I put the two together, and my conclusion is, therefore, "A material thing is a set of ideas in our own minds."

Now we move in for the kill: An idea, a sensation, an experience in the mind, is in the same category as the toothache—it can exist only when it is being experienced. An un-sensed sensation, an un-thought idea, an un-perceived perception, an un-experienced experience, is a contradiction in terms. Unless the mind experienced its own experiences, those experiences wouldn't exist. The very being of an experience consists in its being perceived. But matter, as I've demonstrated (he claims), is a set of experiences. Final conclusion: Matter exists only insofar as it is being experienced. Therefore, in the case of matter, *esse est percipi*—to be is to be perceived. So much for the external world. Q.E.D.

I quote from Berkeley from his treatise on human knowledge:

> It is indeed an opinion strangely prevailing amongst men, that houses, mountains, rivers, and, in a word, all sensible objects have an existence, natural or real, distinct from their being perceived by the understanding. But with how great an assurance and acquiescence soever this principle may be entertained in the world; yet whoever shall find in his heart to call it in question may, if I may mistake not, perceive it to involve a manifest contradiction. For what are the aforementioned objects but the things we perceive by sense, and what do we perceive besides our own ideas and sensations; and is it not plainly repugnant that any one of these or any combination of them, should exist unperceived?

Notice, Berkeley says, that he is a champion of the senses—he is an empiricist. He believes the senses are perfectly reliable. They give you reality. Except that reality is the experiences in your own mind. In fact, says Berkeley, I am the one real assured champion of the validity of the senses. You can be sure that your senses aren't deceiving you and that your experiences are correct because they *are* only what you experience them to be. As long as you believe in an external material world, he says, there's always the question, How do you know that your experiences are giving you that world as it really is? If all that exists is your mind and its experiences, then you can be sure your experiences are correct, because your experiences have no nature other than what you experience them to be. Your toothache is only however you feel it to be. And since matter is all in that category, you can rest assured with your experiences of matter because it's whatever you experience it as.

You see that on the premises of Locke, this argument is unanswerable.

You see the disasters implicit in the causal and representative theory of perception. Therefore, the question for anyone who wants to retain the physical world is: How can one answer the Cartesian-Lockean argument? And remember their argument is that we must perceive reality by its effects on us, and that seems unanswerable. And those effects seem to be in some way a function of our particular sensory constitution. If we had a different constitution, it would produce different effects. Aren't we then inevitably pushed back into our own consciousness, each of us experiencing his own private experiences, cut off from access to reality? To which Berkeley comes along and says that if you're cut off, there *is* no such thing as reality. And here we're back all the way to Protagoras's original argument against the senses, which has now blossomed in full. That is the point that I'm going to discuss at length in the next lecture. There are many people who disagree with Berkeley vigorously and haven't the faintest idea how to answer him. For instance, there was a school of materialists in France, who declared that Berkeley's viewpoint was an insane delusion, but unfortunately irrefutable.[40]

All right, let us look now at the second argument that I will give, the argument from the primary-secondary quality distinction. This no longer depends on the causal theory of perception, so let's not assume that viewpoint, and let's start afresh. Nevertheless, says Berkeley, I will still show you that matter is a set of ideas in the mind. This time, his taking-off point is the traditional standard distinction between primary and secondary qualities that goes all the way back to Democritus (although the terminology is Locke's). Remember that philosophers have traditionally distinguished between these two qualities on the basis of two main arguments—the conceivability argument, and the variability argument. The conceivability argument says, "I can't conceive matter without primary qualities, but I can easily conceive it without secondary qualities, and therefore, that goes to show that one set of qualities is intrinsic in matter, the other is dispensable." And the variability argument is: "Certain qualities, the secondary ones, vary from perceiver to perceiver, and that proves they are subjective, a function of the sensory constitution of the perceiver. Whereas others, the primary, are invariant, constant, the same for all perceivers, and that goes to show they are contributed by the real physical object."

Berkeley says that he intends to wipe out both of these arguments and get rid of the material world thereby. So let's first consider the conceivability argument. Well, he holds, maybe Locke can conceive of matter

---

40. Windelband, *History of Philosophy*, Volume 2, p. 472.

that has primary qualities and no secondary qualities, but I, Bishop Berkeley, cannot. Can you, he asks, ever imagine a shape (to take that example of a primary quality)? Go ahead right now, try—visualize a shape (for instance, a big triangle) without a color. As soon as you obliterate the color in your mind, what happens to your image of the shape? It disappears. Of course, you might do it with some other secondary quality—if you were blind, you might imagine running your hands over this triangular shape and getting some sensation of warm, smooth surface. But if you obliterate that also, what is left of the shape? A shape that can't be seen, a shape that can't be touched, a shape devoid of color, texture, and every secondary quality. Well, says Berkeley, I can't tell the difference between that and nothing at all. Shape is inseparable from *some* secondary quality—let us say color—and if the color exists only in the mind, then the shape that we see must exist only in the mind also. Take another example, the supposed primary quality of motion. Suppose I say, "Over to the left of me here is something moving. Go and visualize it but strip it of all secondary qualities." Can you conceive it? Can you imagine it? Can you visualize it? Obviously, you cannot. If you strip it of all secondary qualities, it evaporates. You can do this with *all* primary qualities. The general point, says Berkeley, is that you perceive the so-called primary qualities only by means of the secondary qualities, so if the secondary are unreal and subjective, existing only in the mind, so must the primary be. In any event, they must be in the same boat metaphysically. If one is in the mind, both are in the mind; if one [is] in reality, both are in reality. So much for the conceivability argument.

I'll interject here to call your attention to the fact that I have deliberately been equivocating on one point—Berkeley asks if you can *conceive* shape without color, and proceeds to answer the question "Can you *visualize*, or *form an image* of, shape without color?" Switching the question from "Can you conceive?" to "Can you visualize?" will suggest to you that Berkeley equates an abstract concept with an image. And that should suggest to you right away that Berkeley is a nominalist, which he is, an avid, full-fledged nominalist. And this particular part of his argument depends upon his nominalism. Nevertheless, that is not his whole argument, and the rest continues even without it. So, let us pick up the rest of it.

Suppose you say: "All right, Berkeley, you have shown to me that primary and secondary qualities are in the same boat, and that I can't say one half is in the mind and one half is in reality. Well, I'm going to then go completely in the other direction—I will say *all* of them are intrinsic in physical objects; *none* of them exist in the mind." Very well, says Berkeley, now

I will prove to you that the very same argument, showing secondary qualities to be only mental and subjective, applies equally to primary qualities. Namely, the variability argument. Remember the reasoning—since facts are facts, they don't depend upon the perceiver, and therefore, if something varies from perceiver to perceiver, it must be mental. Well, says Berkeley, I propose to show you an obvious fact: All primary qualities vary from perceiver to perceiver just exactly as the so-called secondary qualities do. They are just as dependent upon the conditions of our perception, and if such variability proves subjectivity, it proves that the primary qualities are just as subjective as the secondary ones, and thus the whole distinction collapses.

For instance, consider the question of size, which is supposed to be a real orthodox, kosher primary quality. Is size independent of the conditions of perception? A standard example given by followers of Berkeley is: "What is the size of the sun? Is it the size that you see if you take an Apollo spaceship and head right straight for the sun? Obviously, you're going to get a much different experience than if you look at the sun from the earth, which makes it look about the size of a fifty-cent piece. Is the size of it the size with your ordinary eyes, or the size under a magnifying glass? What if there were a race with magnification built into their eyes? They would see everything bigger than we do. So, size obviously depends upon the structure of your organs and your distance from the object. It's variable. If variability proves subjectivity, size is subjective." Now, what about shape? Now, here, the standard thing for a professor of philosophy to do is to take a quarter or a penny and walk into the middle of a class and say, "So you believe that this has a real shape?"; and the students, not yet having been completely corrupted, say yes. Then he proceeds to have each of them describe the shape, and, of course, he is so located that they all perceive it from different perspectives. Some people say they see a perfect circle, and other people say no, they see an ellipse slanted in one direction, and other people say no, they see an ellipse slanted in another direction, and certain people see only a tiny little rim, etc., and they all come up with different descriptions of the shape. To which the professor says: "Well, you see, the shape varies with the perception. There is no such thing as *the* shape, any more than there is *the* color or *the* temperature or *the* size—it all varies with the perceiver. If variability proves subjectivity, shape is just as subjective as color and size." As far as motion is concerned, we can bring in Einstein and the so-called relativity of motion, which is supposed to prove that something can be moving or at rest depending upon the frame of reference of the observer, so that even motion is variable and therefore subjective. And even such a hardcore primary quality as number—whether there's one quarter or two—is supposed to be a function of our experience, and variable. For instance, press in your eyeball and you will suddenly see this single quarter multiply into two. For a Berkeleyan, the kind of eyes we have determines what quantity we observe. And therefore, number, shape, size, motion, are all variable, and therefore, they are all in the category of the so-called secondary qualities. The whole distinction breaks down, all qualities are subjective, and in all cases, therefore, *esse est percipi*.

You see the problem that we are in. On the one hand, we *have* to make a distinction between primary and secondary qualities because, after all, our senses contribute *something* to our experience, so doesn't it seem sensible on the face of it to say that there are qualities that derive from the kind of senses we have, and qualities that derive from the object, and therefore, there are two kinds of qualities? And that was exactly the reasoning by which the primary-secondary quality distinction was arrived at. But on the other hand, as soon as you make the distinction between two kinds of quality, whatever test you use to justify that distinction, Berkeley and his followers come along and prove that whatever argument shows that the so-called secondary are subjective applies just as well to the primary, and you end up with no reality at all. So what is the answer to this particular problem? That's part of the same issue of the senses, on which we will spend a good amount of time in the next lecture. The conclusion for Berkeley is that the whole physical world with everything in it—all the furniture in the earth—is nothing but a series of experiences in the mind and would not exist if there were no beings perceiving it.

There are people who try to refute this by direct experience. I point out to you that that is a hopeless proposition to attempt to do. You cannot, by direct experience, refute Berkeley, because he will demand that you prove by experience that something exists when you are not experiencing it. And of course, you can't do that: Whenever you experience it, you're experiencing it. It's like the story of the drunk who was told after he reached a sufficient stage of intoxication that the streetlight went out whenever he closed his eyes and came back on whenever he opened his eyes. And he closed his eyes and opened them as rapidly as he could, and looked up, and he said, "Oh, it isn't true, the light is on," and the man told him, "Of course it's on, your eyes are open. It only goes out when your eyes are closed." Obviously, you cannot refute that by experience, because you'd have to see it when you're not seeing it. And therefore, the question is: How do you refute Berkeley, since, according to many people, the only way to refute him would be to perceive something existing when you're not perceiving it, and you can't do that? The way to refute him is to refute the premises that led him to this conclusion. By the way, a camera will not refute him. There are people who say the way to answer Berkeley is to set up a camera in a vacant room and then come back and expose the film, and then show the picture, and that'll show the room was still there when nobody was experiencing it. But Berkeley would come back in such a case and say: "That doesn't prove anything. As soon as you left the room, the camera disappeared, the whole room disappeared, nothing existed when you didn't perceive it, and as soon as you came back, the camera came back in and the film came back in with its particular alteration." If you want to know why it was altered, I'll tell you shortly. In other words, he has to be answered on philosophic grounds.

That's the thrust of Berkeley's philosophy. We can cover a few last points before we leave him. Some philosophers ask: "Isn't matter more than just the sum of the qualities? What about the substratum that *has* those qualities?" You recall Locke's substratum, the thing underneath the qualities that sticks them all together, the thing with the qualities that Locke described as "something I know not what"? Berkeley has no difficulty whatever disposing of the substratum. And in this respect, he is perfectly correct. The idea of a substratum is the idea of something without any identity—which is a completely invalid idea. Locke was contradicting his own philosophy completely in endorsing it, and Berkeley's quite right to throw it out.

I might mention that Berkeley, being a bishop, was not a hundred percent consistent with regard to the issue of the substratum. He wanted to keep the *spiritual* substance, the soul, the self, because religion required that. And so he said that in the case of the soul, there were not only the mental processes we engaged in, but also the substratum that bound and united them. How could he possibly keep the substratum in the mental realm, having denounced it in the physical? It's true, he said, that we don't have any clear idea of the substratum, but we have a *notion* of it. Obviously, an extraordinarily lame viewpoint, and Hume had no difficulty getting rid of it in the spiritual world. It's hopeless to try to keep it in either realm.

You may ask this question: If Berkeley truly believes that *esse est percipi*, does that mean that stars, for instance, don't exist when you're not perceiving them? Or, taking the gentleman in the very back row, if no one is perceiving the back of his head, can we conclude that it does not exist? Or what about your apartment if there's no one there now? The famous example was: What about the tree out in the park, the tree in the quad, the quadrangle? Does it not exist if no one is perceiving it? To which Berkeley's answer is: "I don't mind you using the terminology that it exists when you don't perceive it, so long as you understand that its existence depends upon *somebody's* perception. To exist is to be perceived—*esse est percipi.* So, to say a thing exists when you are not perceiving it is either to say *if* you looked, you'd see it (in other words, a statement about a material object is really a prediction about some mind's future experiences), or else to say a thing exists when you're not perceiving it is to say that some *other* mind, or spirit, is perceiving it." But you don't have to worry, says Berkeley, because even if no human mind is perceiving your apartment or the back of your head or the tree in the quad, there is always some mind perceiving everything, and thereby keeping everything in existence. And guess who that is? *God.*

There is a famous limerick that expresses Berkeley's philosophy on this point. The first stanza explains the problem, and the second is the solution, and it goes like this:

> There was a young man who said, "God
> Must find it exceedingly odd
> That this tree which I see
> Still continues to be
> When there's no one about in the quad."

And the answer is,

> "Dear Sir, your astonishment's odd,
> *I* am always about in the quad.
> And that's why this tree
> Still continues to be
> Since perceived by, yours faithfully, God."[41]

That's Berkeley's viewpoint.

His followers, in later decades, abandoned God, and we were left with the viewpoint that existence goes out of existence when it is not perceived. And in this sense, *esse est percipi,* although they may not know it, is the perfect metaphysics for any evader, because their premise is, "If you don't

---

41. "God in the Quad" (1913) by Monsignor Ronald Knox, a noted Biblical scholar. Leonard Peikoff's memory of the limerick was almost perfect, the main difference being that "perceived" in the last line should be "observed."

look at it, it's not there." And here is a full-fledged metaphysical demonstration, allegedly, of this viewpoint.

A last point on Berkeley—Dr. Samuel Johnson is famous for allegedly having given a refutation of Berkeley. And his refutation consisted of taking a stone and kicking it. By which he wanted to express his exasperation at what he took to be Berkeley's denial of the reality of the physical world. He said, in effect, that you are denying reality to our experiences. When I kick this stone, it's a real solid stone. It's not a mental image, or a dream, or a hallucination, or an experience. It's *reality*. How can you have such a concept as "reality" if everything is mental? If you deal with followers of Berkeley (and there are quite a number of them today, and I believe Einstein at one point claimed to be a follower of Berkeley), you should know that they are vehement in saying that they're all in favor of reality. But, they say, reality is not an issue of something existing *external* to the mind or *independent* of the mind. Reality is an issue of the kind of experience that takes place *in* the mind. There are three kinds of experiences, and we can separate them on many counts. (1) Some experiences are involuntary—we can't get rid of them by an act of will—whereas others we can. You can banish obvious fantasies and mental images by an act of will, and by that very fact they are disqualified for being part of reality. (2) Some experiences are vivid, sharp, clear, while others are faint, pale, indistinct, blurred, vague. In this case, we normally take the faint, blurred ones and say, "Oh, that isn't reality, that's a dream," whereas the sharp, clear ones, we say, "That's reality."[42]

(3) And most important, some experiences are well-behaved. They are connected in a regular manner with previous and subsequent experiences. They are orderly. They obey what we call scientific laws. On the other hand, other experiences are wild and bizarre. They do not fit nicely into the scheme of the rest of our experiences. So, for instance, what is the difference for Berkeley between a pink rat that you see after you drink a lot, and a pink rat that is an actual rat, on which somebody poured pink paint? What's the difference? A normal non-follower of Berkeley says that the hallucinatory rat exists in the mind and the real rat exists outside of the mind. Berkeley says nonsense—both rats exist in the mind—but the difference is [that] the hallucinatory rat is not well-behaved. If you take the real rat and you take the experience of a knife, and with that experience

---

42. American poet laureate Richard Wilbur's 1950 take on Johnson's rebuttal: "Kick at the rock, Sam Johnson. Break your bones. But cloudy, cloudy is the stuff of stones."

you cut into the experience of a rat, you will find another experience—blood. Whereas if you take the experience of the hallucinatory rat and try and cut into it with the experience of the knife, you won't get any experience of blood—it doesn't bleed. And therefore, it is a badly behaved rat. And consequently, we regard it as a hallucination, not as real. And therefore, the only difference between reality and unreality (or fantasy) is that reality is that set of involuntary, vivid, lawful mental experiences, whereas unreality is either voluntary, blurred, or, at minimum, wild. And therefore, he says to Dr. Johnson: "I don't deny that you kicked the stone. But the point is, all you had was an experience of a stone, followed by an experience of a toe, followed by an experience of a pain, all following one another in a lawful way, and therefore the whole thing took place in the mind."

If you say: "But mustn't there be a cause of our experiences? Maybe we make up the voluntary pale ones, but what about the lawful, vivid, involuntary ones—we don't make them up, since they're involuntary. *We* don't impose law on them, but they follow laws. If it's not an external physical world that causes our experiences, where do they come from?" You're right, says Berkeley, they must have a cause, and they must be produced in us by something external to us. And given the variety and order and lawfulness of these experiences, we can only infer that they must be caused in us by a being that is "wise, powerful, and good beyond comprehension." In other words, by God. God feeds us our experiences directly and imposes law and order upon them. Reality, therefore, is a series of finite minds contemplating their own experiences, fed to them all by the infinite mind, God. You see, therefore, a reality very similar to Leibniz's view. So much for Berkeley's contribution to philosophy—the end of the material world. Berkeley, however, is not as extreme as you can get. He's still a bishop. He believed in God, he believed in the soul, he believes in cause and effect, even if of a divine sort. He has taken Locke's premises part way to their ultimate conclusion, but not the full way. That honor goes to David Hume.

David Hume

Let us now turn to David Hume (1711–1776), the last, the most influential, and the most consistent of the three famous British empiricists. In fact, he is so consistent, so rigorous about deducing the final consequences from the premises of Locke and Berkeley, that he represents a complete dead end philosophically. If you think Berkeley's (or Leibniz's or Spinoza's) universe is strange, you haven't heard anything yet. I'll quote you an anticipatory summary of Hume from Bertrand Russell in his *A History of Western Philosophy*: "It is therefore important to discover whether there is any answer to Hume. . . . If not, there is no intellectual difference between sanity and insanity. The lunatic who believes that he is a poached egg is to be condemned solely on the ground that he is in a minority, or rather—since we must not assume democracy—on the ground that the government does not agree with him." And Russell concludes this paragraph: "This is a desperate point of view, and it must be hoped that there is some way of escaping from it." Which he never found.

Hume is the arch skeptic in philosophy. I should add that one could become even more skeptical than Hume by applying his conclusions even more rigorously. You might wonder how you can become more skeptical than to reach the stage where you can't tell whether or not you're a poached egg. The answer lies in twentieth-century philosophy with the modern Pragmatists and Logical Positivists—Hume is their top favorite among historical philosophers—but they are *really* consistent, and they regard Hume as old-fashioned in certain ways (which he was, since there's a limit as to how much is possible even in the eighteenth century), but you have to wait until you study contemporary philosophy for that. Hume is quite consistent enough for us now.

Hume's place in the history of philosophy is the final invalidation of reason. At least, that's what people took it to mean. He comes to the conclusion that reason is impotent to give us any knowledge at all, and he claims to prove this position in reason. All of the preceding philosophers, with a few exceptions, fall into two types: They were either philosophers like Descartes, Spinoza, Leibniz, Locke, Berkeley—all of whom claim to be very pro-reason, regardless of their conclusions or interpretation—or they were the outright mystics like Tertullian, and we didn't mention Pascal, and people like that who appealed blatantly to faith, the heart, mystic revelation, etc. Hume is the first modern philosopher to attack reason in a major way, and to do it in the *name* of reason. You may think Hobbes anticipated him, and he did, but Hobbes is really old-fashioned by comparison to Hume. Hume is the first influential *neo*-mystic, meaning by that term, "the man who uses reason to invalidate reason." He dealt reason the philosophic knife-blow, and then Kant came on the scene and finished it off permanently.

Hume is an empiricist. He does not believe in any innate ideas. He believes in a *tabula rasa*, experience being the source of all subsequent cognition, and in this respect he follows Locke: From experience we get simple, unanalyzable, self-contained ideas ("blue," "rough," "straight," "loud," "pain," "will," etc.), and then we form complex ideas, which we build up by putting together or compounding the simple ideas. Hume's name for the simple ideas is "impressions." These are the direct, immediate, unanalyzable experiences, the units out of which all other cognitive elements are constructed. To this extent, he is a direct follower of Locke. But Hume takes a direction that we saw in Hobbes, Locke, and Berkeley, and which I'm now going to emphasize in Hume. Hume declares that as an empiricist, one must be a nominalist. And Hume is an arch nominalist, nominalism being the rebellion against universals, either of the Platonic or the Aristotelian kind. A rebellion allegedly in the name of sense experience, empiricism, science. We don't, say the nominalists, perceive any such entities as manness, banana-ness, subway-hood, etc. There are no sharp lines in nature. Remember the borderline case—everything blurs into everything else. Consequently, if universals are supposed to be sharp, fixed, abstract entities that have some being in reality, that is a myth—there are no such things. There are no universals, just human-naming procedures. On the basis of our observation of certain rough resemblances, we decide what name to call a group of particulars. But the only universal is the word, or the name. Classification is an issue of our subjective convenience. And, you recall, this position is always associated with sensualism. Nominalism holds that there are no universals, and sensualism holds then that there is no such thing as the awareness of universals, i.e., there are no such things as abstract ideas or concepts. All we have are percepts. This is a straight Hobbesian viewpoint. What we call an idea (or a thought, or a concept) is only a fading or decaying image of a sensory percept. The sensualist is the man who says that concepts are really ultimately only percepts, and he's the man who takes sensory perception as the key to consciousness in every form and refuses to grant that conceptual consciousness is a distinct form of awareness. And this is done in the name of being empirical, scientific, anti-mystical.

We've seen some consequences of nominalism and sensualism. We saw in Hobbes the view that classification is arbitrary, definition is arbitrary, general principles are arbitrary, and we finally ended up in Hobbes with the need for an absolute dictator to solve disputes because reason is helpless. But Hobbes, you might recall, wasn't a consistent nominalist. You might wonder how much more consistent you can be as a nominalist. You will soon see.

The first thing, then, to recognize is that Hume is an extreme nominalist and sensualist. The only types of cognitive element that he recognizes are direct experiential impressions. He grants that you can use the term "idea" (as distinct from "impression"), but then you have to follow Hobbes's view that an idea is merely a faint copy (an "image") of an impression. It's equally concrete and specific. The only difference, says Hume, between a so-called abstract concept and a direct percept is the vividness, the intensity, the vibrancy of the percept, as against the relative paleness and diffuseness and blurriness of the image. So if you want to have the thought of "man," just form a little blurred, un-vibrant, un-vivid image of a man, and that is the totality of the abstract idea, or concept, "man." And thus for all so-called ideas.

On the basis of this nominalism, Hume formulates a principle implied by nominalism but never before made as explicit. And since he is explicit, he can be much more consistent about it than prior nominalists. This principle is a certain theory of meaning, so let me just say a word about the meaning of "meaning." The meaning of a term (as that is used in philosophy) is what it stands for, what it communicates, what it refers to. A term or a word or a phrase is said to be meaningful if it stands for something if it has a referent. If I say, for instance, "glass of water," I could point and say, "There is the referent, that's what it stands for," and consequently the phrase "glass of water" is meaningful. On the other hand, if I say "gloop," and you say to me, "What does it stand for?," and I say, "It has no referent, it stands for nothing," then obviously it is meaning*less*.

If you are a sensualist, what referents can a term have? There are only two possibilities: either a direct sense percept or the fading image of one. Those are the only kinds of cognitive elements we're in contact with. So we have a simple test to determine if any word or phrase is meaningful: Every meaningful word or phrase must be such that one can either directly perceive its referents or at least form an image of its referent. This is sometimes called "the empiricist theory of meaning," but more properly called the "sensualist theory of meaning." (It's called the "empiricist theory" because almost all empiricists after Hume are sensualists.) And therefore, there's a very simple test: When somebody puts forward a word, you ask, "Can you perceive the referent?" If the answer is no, "Can you form an image of the referent?" and if the answer is no, the word is noise; the word is like "gloop"—just empty sound. Can't a word stand for a concept as distinct from a percept or an image? And the answer is that on a sensualist philosophy there is no such thing as a concept distinct from a percept or an image. Percepts and images are all we can ever know. And therefore, since our words must have referents, they can be meaningful only if they refer to percepts or images.

Let me give you an example: Take "spatial extension," as apart from color or tactile quality. Think of it in the old sense of a primary quality, simply three-dimensionality. Can you have a percept of such spatial extension, apart from color and so on? No, you can't. Can you form an image of it? Well, that's just the test we tried under Berkeley, and you can't. Then what conclusion can we come to? The phrase "spatial extension" is meaningless, just noise, like the word "gloop"—it stands for nothing perceivable or imageable. I have heard this applied by modern followers of Hume to such a concept as "electron"—you can't perceive it, you can't form an image of it, and I have heard an ample number of modern physicists declare that the concept "electron"—if used to designate some alleged real particle that's out there but that can't be perceived or imaged—is meaningless noise. It's more common for philosophers of science than physicists to say this, but I've heard it from both. This is an application of Hume's theory of meaning. Please understand this: Hume is not saying that all meaningful terms must be *based* on observation—Aristotle would say that. But on Aristotle's view, you could get the concept of "electron" from observation by a process of abstraction and reasoning. Hume is saying that any meaningful term must stand directly for a percept or an image. There are no concepts apart from percepts or images.

This sensualist theory of meaning, one of the most influential tenets in all of twentieth-century philosophy, was started in a major way by Hume. It represents the final outcome of nominalism and sensualism. And it's the key to the whole procedure of Hume's skepticism: He picks some central philosophic term and then asks, "Can you perceive its referent directly?" And you say no. And then he says, "Can you form an image of it?" For instance, you *can* form an image of a golden mountain, so that's meaningful. But in the key terms that he produces for analysis, you can't. They are just noise. And thus, you get the philosophy of a creature devoid of the capacity to form concepts. Because of Hume's influence, it became much more popular among mid-twentieth-century philosophers to denounce your opponent's ideas as meaningless instead of calling them false. You see, to say that an idea is meaningless is to dismiss it as even beneath falsehood—it's just noise. If I come in the room and say, "Ish da triddle de gloo-gloo, true or false?," you'd say it's neither; it's just noise. In this respect, to say that your opponent's view is false is already thought by these people to be a compliment, because you're at least saying his ideas are meaningful and say *something*, even if false. The modern Humeans dismissed every viewpoint as meaningless. Some of them went so far as to say, "What do you mean by the word 'meaning,' or 'meaningful'? Can you perceive a meaning? What color is it? Can you form an image of it? Then it must be meaningless. The word 'meaningful' must be meaningless." That, you see, is as consistent as you can get.

A twentieth-century gentleman named Ludwig Wittgenstein wrote a whole book (*Tractatus Logico-Philosophicus*), at the end of which he discovered that he had proved that he could not meaningfully say most of what he had said in the book—by the very definition of "meaning" that he had given in the book. So, he stopped. And he ended his book on the sentence, "Whereof one cannot speak, thereof one must be silent." He had a kind of mystic experience that certain things are meaningful and other things are not, and he could not proceed any further to put it into words. This has embarrassed many of his followers, who evade all over the place, but that's beyond our scope—now that's the twentieth century, so let's go back to Hume.

Let's take some key terms and see if they can withstand the application of this Humean theory of meaning. Take the expression "external world," or "external reality," and see if it has any meaning. Most philosophers prior to Hume believed that we do not directly perceive an external world but perceive only our own experiences and have no access to an external world. But they believed it must exist as the cause of our experiences. That's the causal theory of perception. And Hume agrees that we directly experience only our experiences. In this respect he, like Berkeley and Locke, is in the tradition of Descartes. But now, he says, let us apply the theory of meaning to the phrase "external world." What do people mean by the expression "external world"? Well, he says, they mean two things together. One, the external world is supposed to be something apart from our experiences, something distinct from our experiences. And two, it's supposed to be something that continues in existence even when no one experiences it. So, those are the two criteria of an external world, something distinct from our experience and something that is continuous, which goes on existing, whether we experience it or not. That's what's meant in saying reality, or the world, is external to us.

Let's take each of these in turn. Can you perceive something distinct from your experiences? Perceive? Not if you accept Descartes's view that all you perceive is your experiences. Obviously, you can perceive only your own experiences. You can't perceive something distinct from your experiences if you accept Descartes's and Locke's view. What then happens to the words "distinct from experience"? Since you don't perceive anything distinct from experience, the phrase "distinct from experience" has no referent, nothing that you can perceive. It must become . . . meaningless. What about the idea of continuity, of something existing when you are not perceiving it? Can you perceive something existing when you're not perceiving it? Obviously not. If you're perceiving something, you're *perceiving* it, so you're not perceiving it existing when you don't perceive it, so both of these terms end up as meaningless. We have no percept of something distinct from our experiences. We perceive only our experiences and have no percept of something existing when we don't perceive it. Since we perceive only when we perceive, we therefore have no referent for either ingredient of the phrase "external world." But if we have no perceptual referent, by the theory of meaning, the phrase is meaningless. And therefore, the phrase "external world" is just noise.

If you try to answer Hume and say, "But look, after all, inherent in the very concept of 'existence' and 'consciousness' is the distinctness and continuity of existence." And if you then proceed, "Existence exists, consciousness is the faculty for perceiving it, A is A (the law of identity), now just grasp these concepts and you will see." You won't get any further than that and Hume will say to you: "Concepts? What are you talking about? All we have are percepts and images. I don't perceive existence apart from consciousness." And that's true that you don't perceive when you're not perceiving. Consequently, on nominalist grounds, Hume would refuse even to hear any such argument.

Hume asks himself, "Since 'external world' is a meaningless, fantastic idea, why do people think there *is* an external world?" From his point of view, it's a fantastic belief. There's more evidence for a Santa Claus on Hume's philosophy than there is for an external world. At least we see people dressed up as Santa Claus, but we never come into any contact with something distinct from our experience. His answer as to why people entertain this "fantastic" hypothesis is that our experiences seem to show a certain constancy. For instance, look at this lectern. Now look away for an instance, perhaps at your fingertip, and then look back. If you don't pay strict attention or blink your eyes, you get a sudden shot of blackness, and then you open your eyes again and see the lectern. If you don't pay strict attention to the procession of your experiences—to the fact that they're constantly interrupted—if you don't focus on those interruptions, you will tend to glide from one frame to the next without grasping the cuts, the holes, the breaks from second to second. The result is that since we're all intellectually lazy, according to Hume, we tend to fill in the interval between these experiences. It isn't real to us that there are all these cuts, because we're too lazy. We imagine that the thing, the lectern, is still there between our experiences, and therefore that it is distinct from our experiences. But that's a product of what Hume calls our "imaginations." Our imaginations are lazy. They have a tendency to fill in the gaps. They invent fictions. But, says Hume, my point is that it *is* a fiction. If we go by direct experience, we have a series of discrete experiences and no evidence for continuing entities. The idea of an external world is a meaningless myth.

Having gotten rid of the material world, clearly there can be no external material entities in the universe, no material substances (in the traditional terminology). But Hume is not content with the attack I've given so far on material entities. He launches an independent one, to which I now want to turn.

Do we, he asks, have any evidence of material entities or substances? He proceeds to answer no, on the basis of Locke's premise. The scenario is always the same—you start with Locke and then show the disaster that follows. Locke had said a material entity is a collection, or bundle, of qualities or simple ideas, inhering in a substratum, and the substratum was supposed to be what ties the qualities together, what makes it one unified entity. Otherwise, Locke reasoned, these self-contained qualities could exist by themselves and separate and disintegrate. But we build up entities by recognizing that these independent qualities are kept together in the substratum that is of such a nature that I know not what it is. Berkeley, if you recall, blasted this substratum as lacking any identity. Hume agrees—the substratum is gone. And on this point, they're obviously correct: the destruction of the substratum idea of being a nominalist or a sensualist. We don't even have any concept, let alone percept or image, of the substratum. It has no identity at all, and it's nothing in particular, so it's perfectly valid to reject it.

What then would Hume say in answer to Locke's question: What *does* keep these bundles of qualities together, what *is* the thing that integrates qualities into entities, where *are* there recurring combinations of identical qualities? Berkeley's answer was that God arranges it that way. He feeds us our experiences in that order. In Hume, as you'll see, God is out. So, he has a simple answer: If you are in a position where something is inexplicable on your premises, simply deny it. Hume says there *are* no recurring bundles of the same qualities. In fact, the qualities constantly change partners, so we have no problem. There is, says Hume, no reason why the qualities that happen now to go together to make up what we call a material entity should not suddenly split apart, disintegrate, so that instead of an entity, we have merely a succession of disjointed separate qualities. You remember the example I gave you in the last lecture: A

Humean would say that there's nothing to prevent the qualities that make up a cigarette from suddenly splitting apart from each other and showing up in different parts of this room, so that the white color might travel to the rear without tactile qualities, without temperature. And over here, where the tape recorders are, would be a nice smooth texture, but you'd see nothing, and over on my left, a hot burning point, devoid of texture, color, etc. According to Hume, this state of affairs is perfectly possible. What we call an "entity" is simply a cluster of independent qualities that happen to go together for a while—they just happen to, that's all. We have a bundle of qualities, a loose collection that can at any instant disintegrate and leave us in a universe of floating qualities without things or entities.

This, says Hume, is not just a theoretical projection; it actually happens all the time, but people do not pay careful attention. We *never* perceive enduring entities, he says, only constantly shifting sets, or bundles, of qualities constantly changing their partners. Suppose I'm walking down the street looking at a building. Most people believe that this represents a certain enduring combination of qualities—that they can look at it, look away, look back, see the same set, the same size, the same shape, the same color, etc. Hume says that if you go by actual experience, you *don't* see the same set of qualities each time, you see a new bundle each time you look. As you get closer, for instance, you see something bigger. The sun comes out and you see a different color. You get a different perspective. You see a somewhat different shape. You pass by under the building and look up and see a radically different shape. Your eye goes up to the very top to the spire, and you get a completely different experience than when you were looking down at the base. Etc. What we really experience, says Hume, is a succession of different bundles of qualities constantly changing. What we call the entity is really a loose collection of shifting qualities.

You might object: "Isn't Hume confusing two entirely different things: the entity, which endures, and our changing forms of perceiving it, our changing perspectives on it. The entity is one thing—it is what it is, and it's not affected by our varying perceptual conditions. All you have to do to answer Hume and discover a stable entity in reality is abstract away from our changing experiences and form a concept of the entity as it is independent of our varying forms of perceiving it." But if you said that to Hume, you know that his sensualism would forbid it. Abstract away, he would say, form a concept? There are no such things. All we have, all we can know, is the stream of sense data that goes by right before your nose. And even our nose is a temporary union of sense data. If this stream constantly changes, if we don't sense an enduring entity, then there's no basis for an enduring entity. If we go by sense data alone, we must conclude there are no such entities. There's a Heraclitean flux of sense qualities, constantly changing, shifting, appearing, disappearing. What we really experience is a succession of different bundles, each closely related to the previous but nevertheless different. Therefore, we don't *need* a substratum to tie them together. What we call an "entity" is just a name for a loose collection of qualities constantly changing partners. Why do you have the illusion that you see the identical entity enduring across time? Because the various bundles, moment by moment, have a rough resemblance to each other, and again your imagination is lazy, it fills in the gaps, it doesn't pay any attention to the actual difference, it imagines that it sees the same enduring entity, but this is just a reflection of the laziness of your imagination.

I've indicated to you where Hume is wrong on this point, and that if you're able to rise to the conceptual level, you *can* defend the view of enduring entities apart from our changing perceptions. He is here drawing the final conclusions from Locke's viewpoint. But we still have Locke's original question to answer, so let's leave Hume for a moment. And Locke's question, if he heard this much, would be, "Well, why? What keeps the qualities of a thing together?" After all, Locke would say, we directly perceive only these little atomic simple qualities. *Something* must keep them together. And if it's not the "I know not what," what is it?

If you grant Locke's premise that what we directly perceive are these little atomic, self-contained qualities, you are in bad trouble. Then you do need a metaphysical glue to integrate them. So, you must contest Locke's premise. The truth is that we do not observe any such thing as atomic, self-contained, simple qualities. We do not observe loose collections of independent qualities at all. If we're going to be empiricists, we should be honest empiricists—that is to say, true to the actual observed facts—and if we go by the actual observed facts, we will see that we directly observe *entities*, integrated entities. The separation from an entity of its various qualities is a work of analysis that human beings perform *after* they have first experienced the integrated entity. Consider an experience of an apple. Do you as an adult separately observe a simple redness and a roundness and a smoothness and a shininess, etc., and then put them all together? No, you do not. You directly observe an *apple*, the integrated totality of these qualities. And only later, by an act of selective attention, can you focus on *this* quality or *that* one apart from the rest. The world of direct experience is a world of directly given entities. Individual qualities are not the *starting* points of experience but are much later stages of abstraction *from* what we experience. And you must remember that an abstraction, a mental separation, cannot exist in reality apart from the thing that it's abstracted from. You can *think* of a certain quality apart from the others that it goes with in reality *only* by mentally ignoring its accompaniments. But you must remember that in reality, it's inextricably connected to its accompaniments. Locke's procedure is, in actual fact, that first he perceives the entity, then he abstracts the qualities, then he makes his individual qualities (that in fact are separable only in thought) separable in reality, and then he has the impossible problem of trying to put them back together again. The fact is that no glue, and no unknowable substratum, is necessary to preserve an integrated material entity. The qualities, to put it simply, do not have to be put back together because in reality, they never were apart.

What caused Locke's confusion on this point? The answer is that Locke confused two different levels of consciousness, ones that I haven't yet mentioned in this course, but because it's an important issue, I want to comment at least briefly. There are actually three different levels of human consciousness. We've been talking throughout this course of *perception* and *conception*. But it's time now to mention the third—namely, *sensation*. And I want to distinguish, therefore, *perception* from *sensation*, the perceptual level of consciousness from the sensory level of consciousness. It's true that as babies, we start at the lowest level of consciousness, the sensory level, which is the first, chronologically. We don't perceive entities or objects immediately as babies; we're merely bombarded with disconnected sensations. We reach the next stage of knowledge, the perceptual level, when our brain has learned to integrate this disconnected, unintelligible bombardment of sensations into solid, integrated entities—"apple," "Mother," "bed," etc. That stage is the perceptual stage. And then we are ready, after a certain accumulation of knowledge, to move on—by a process of abstraction and concept-formation—to the conceptual stage.

So, Locke is right in one respect: At one point in the past, we *did* get from reality a disconnected bombardment of sensations. But the crucial thing is that we do not now get such a bombardment, and we *cannot*. If we are now conscious, thinking men, to say nothing of philosophers, we start at the perceptual stage, at the stage of perceiving entities; we no longer experience the sensory stage. So, how do we even know that it once existed? And the answer is—only by inference, by a process of complex reasoning. When we get to the conceptual stage, we discover that we have means of perception—we discover that certain information comes from our eyes, and some from our fingertips, and some from our ears, and so on—and then we realize that at one time, as babies, we must have gotten a disconnected set of data that our brain had to learn to integrate. But we can't now experience that baby's disintegrated state. We can only infer that something like it must have existed. And the crucial point is that our inference depends on and starts from our present perception of entities. So, there are the three levels: the sensory, the perceptual, the conceptual. In the order of time, you have the sensory, then the perceptual, then the conceptual. But in terms of conscious experience, where we have to start as thinkers and philosophers, the first stage is the perceptual stage. Then we simultaneously go forward to the conceptual stage, and then, having developed a conceptual apparatus, we infer back to the existence of the sensory stage. We can infer back only by abstracting from our perceptions of entities. In this sense, the existence and the direct perception of entities is a prerequisite of discovering the sensation stage. You have to keep clearly in mind the difference between these three levels of consciousness. If you equate the perceptual with the sensory, then you're in Locke's position—you have a whole set of disjointed sensations and you need some unintelligible glue to stick them together. If you equate the conceptual with the perceptual, then you are in the nominalist-sensualist position (and you know the catastrophe implicit in that). And if you do *both* of those things, so that the conceptual equals the perceptual equals the sensational, then you are in Hume's position. You are left literally in the state of a newborn babe or a low insect (I say "low" because the higher animals at least have the perceptual level). You are left in the stage where you are bombarded with disconnected sensations, unable to integrate them into entities, unable to form concepts, lost in a hopeless, chaotic, unintelligible, disconnected jumble—namely, the universe of Hume. In this respect, Hume represents the absolute disintegration of human consciousness into atomic, disconnected sensations. Well, so much for what is wrong with Hume on this point.

We've been talking so far about material entities. What is Hume's view of *spiritual* entities—of the soul, the mind, the self? Berkeley, as you know, had also gotten rid of material entities, but he had clung to the self, the thing that *does* the thinking, *has* the experiences, and so on. And he had claimed to have a notion of that, even if not an idea. Hume does not have Berkeley's religious axe to grind. So, he proceeds to demolish the self as easily as he demolished material entities, given Locke's premises. Hume asks: "What is this 'self' that everyone is talking about? Let me introspect and see if I can find it. What is it supposed to be? It's supposed to be something distinct from my experiences—from my wishes, my thoughts, my beliefs—it's supposed to be that which *has* the experiences, that which *does* the thinking, *does* the wishing, *does* the believing. And it's supposed to be something unchanging, something that remains the same and constitutes our personal identity. After all, our thoughts, our experiences, our emotions, our mental content constantly changes, but the basic 'I' or 'ego' or 'self' is supposed to be unchanging. Well, let me see if I can catch it perceptually," says Hume. And now I quote from his *A Treatise of Human Nature* regarding his introspective hunt for the self:

> For my part, when I enter most intimately into what I call *myself*, I always stumble on some particular perception or other, of heat or cold, light or shade, love or hatred, pain or pleasure. I never can catch myself at any time without a perception, and never can observe any thing but the perception. . . . If anyone, upon serious and unprejudiced reflection thinks he has a different notion of himself, I must confess I can reason no longer with him. All I can allow him is [Peikoff: And this of course is sarcasm on Hume's part.] that he may be in the right, as well as I, and that we are essentially different in this respect. He may perhaps perceive something simple and continued which he calls *himself*, though I am certain there is no such principle in me.
>
> But setting aside some metaphysicians of this kind, I may venture to affirm of the rest of mankind that they are nothing but a bundle or collection of different perceptions, which succeed each other with an inconceivable rapidity, and are in a perpetual flux and movement.

That is the famous passage in which Hume proposes to demolish the self. The word "self" is a meaningless term because it stands for nothing we can experience. When we perceive introspectively, all we perceive is a collection of individual experiences, thoughts, feelings, etc. We have no contact, says Hume, with an unchanging "I" underneath all of these experiences which has them, and therefore, there is no meaning in referring to such an "I" or "self"—no perceptual referent, no image, meaningless. Personal identity is therefore a myth. I am a flux of ever-changing experiences, and so are you. We are each a bundle of experiences. This is sometimes called the *bundle theory of the self.*

What is the explanation for the belief in this myth? It's our imaginations that delude us. Because one state of consciousness merges smoothly into the next, there are always great resemblances between the content of your consciousness at any one instant and its content at the next instant. And therefore, we don't pay attention to the differences. Our imaginations smooth things over by inventing the fiction of enduring self-same entity, or self. But this is a fiction. If you attend closely, introspectively, you see only a succession of different psychological states, that's all. You're just a loose bundle, psychologically.

So, what's wrong with this view? The objections to it are legion. I can't resist pointing out the stolen concept—did you hear his formulation? "When *I* enter most intimately into what *I* call 'myself,' *I* always stumble"—"I" do all these things, and there is no "I." He's using the self to deny the self. But what is the basic error? Again, it is his sensualism and nominalism. What, after all, is the self? (I am here now speaking from the point of view of Objectivism.) The self is your consciousness, your faculty of awareness, the entity that perceives reality. Why can't Hume find it? What does he want? Since he's a sensualist, he's upset that he never finds a percept of pure consciousness. He always finds consciousness of this or that content. He never perceives consciousness except with some content. And since the content is always changing, he bewails the fact that he never perceives an unchanging pure consciousness. What does he want? He wants to perceive consciousness without any content, but you're never going to do that. By the very nature of consciousness, consciousness is the faculty for perceiving *something*, for perceiving *some content, some object.* A consciousness without a content, a consciousness conscious of nothing, is literally a contradiction in terms.

How in fact do we arrive at the awareness of our consciousness, or self, as distinct from its changing contents? Again, only conceptually, by a process of abstraction—we abstract away the various contents and focus on the fact of conceptual awareness, the entity that is consciousness. In other words, we ignore the contents and arrive at an awareness of our faculty of consciousness as such—that which does the thinking, makes the connections, feels the emotions, etc. But consciousness can't exist in *fact* except as consciousness *of something*, and so you cannot perceive consciousness except perceiving it as consciousness of something. If, like Hume, you deny the conceptual level, you will never find an enduring selfsame consciousness, or self. You will find only a string of conscious experiences, and you'll always catch consciousness occupied with some content or other. And since the content is always changing, you will moan, "Where is the unchanging 'I'? Where is my personal identity amidst all this flux?" When the fact is that it is really very simple; it's easy—you *do* directly experience your "I," your consciousness. But in order to identify it and defend its existence, you must reach the conceptual level to which Hume, on principle, never ascended.

Where are we now? What do we have in Hume's universe? We have a bundle of impressions, or experiences, images, and so on. Impressions of what? Nothing. The external world is a myth. Experiences experienced by whom? Nobody. The self is a myth. You might think this is as far as we can go in skepticism: impressions of nothing by nobody. But there is still more. There is one very famous and incredibly influential point of Hume's that is almost universally accepted today by philosophers. There is still one more link tying the world or tying experiences together, which must be shattered if we're to end up with a real poached-egg mentality. And that is the law of cause and effect. Remember, Berkeley had believed in cause and effect coming from God. Hobbes had believed in cause and effect—*every* major philosopher prior to Hume believed in cause and effect. Hume now sets his nominalism and sensualism to work to demolish cause and effect, too. So now we'll look at Hume's greatest "achievement," his destruction of the law of cause and effect.

Again, we follow the standard procedure: Let's take the term "cause." What does it mean? We say "A causes B." To take a classic simple example, we take a rock and throw it at a window, the window shatters. We say, "The rock caused the window to break." What does it mean to say one thing caused another? Well, says Hume, people think there are three points involved. Two of them, as we'll see, are okay, and one—the vital one—proves to be meaningless.

One thing involved in the causal relationship is *spatial contiguity*, togetherness in space. The rock actually touches the window, for instance, in the process of its breaking. That's very simple—we can see the two of them together in direct physical contact, so we have a direct perceptual referent for the phrase "spatial contiguity," or "spatial togetherness," and therefore, that's perfectly meaningful.

But that is not enough. The causal relationship also involves *temporal* contiguity—the window breaks immediately after the rock strikes it. And again, says Hume, that's a perfectly respectable phrase, "temporal contiguity," because we can observe one thing happening immediately after another in time, and therefore, that is perfectly meaningful.

But spatial and temporal contiguity, after all, do not yet give us the essence of the causal relationship. A coincidence can have these two characteristics. For instance, suppose I causally touch this lectern and while I'm in direct contact with it spatially, at the next instant a bomb explodes, and the whole building comes down. You would say maybe the two events were spatially and temporally connected, but that is just a coincidence since there's no causal connection, and maybe someone in the next room let off a bomb at the same instant. What is the crucial factor, the vital ingredient, in the concept of "causal connection"? Hume says it is *necessary connection*. Not only spatial and temporal contiguity, but necessary connection. When we say, "A causes B," we mean more than that the two go together in space and the two go together in time. We mean that the first *necessitates* the second, that the two have a compulsory connection to each other, that granted the first, the second must happen, that the first *produces* the second, that the first *makes* the second happen, etc., all of those being synonyms for "necessary connection."

Let us now put this strand of "necessary connection" to the test of the theory of meaning. Do we ever perceive or form an image of necessary connection between events? Watch it very closely. I don't have a window here to demonstrate, so just project that I take a rock and I throw it at the window. You see the rock sailing slowly across the room. You could stand there right next to the wall with a magnifying glass to watch—you see the rock moving, touch the window—so far there's no necessity, just a rock, right?—next thing you see is that the fragments shatter, right? No little flag came out and said, "The next event is unavoidable." There was no booming voice from the sky that said, "What comes now has to be." There was no Doris Day singing "Que sera, sera." We perceive that the two events go together in space and time, that's all. We never come in contact with any such phenomenon as necessity. What is necessity like? Is it red? Is it loud? Is it hot? Can you form an image of it? What does it look like? What would it taste like? Obviously, we cannot form a percept of necessity; we cannot form an image of necessity. It must, therefore, be an utterly meaningless term. The phrase "necessary connection" must be just noise, like "gloop," and so must any of its synonyms—the synonyms of nonsense are nonsense. And therefore, when you say that one thing produces another, or makes it happen, or given the first the second must happen, all of those are equally meaningless. Now let's have Hume speak for himself on this. First, he states, in *Enquiry Concerning Human Understanding*, his nominalism and sensualism:

> It seems a proposition which will not admit of much dispute that all our ideas are nothing but copies of our impressions [Peikoff: That's his sensualism—an idea is a faded copy of your sense experience.] . . . . To be fully acquainted, therefore, with the idea of power or necessary connection, let us examine its impression; and in order to find the impression with greater certainty, let us search for it in all the sources. from which it may possibly be derived.

He conducts a scrupulous search, all over the place, looking for necessary connection, if only he could find it.

> When we look about us towards external objects, and consider the operation of causes, we are never able in a single instance to discover any power or necessary connection, any quality which binds the effect to the cause and renders the one an infallible consequence of the other. We only find that the one does actually, in fact, follow the other. . . . There is not in any single particular instance of cause and effect anything which can suggest the idea of power or necessary connection.

If an idea is a name for a fading experience, a copy of an experience, and there is no *experience* of necessary connection, then there is no *idea* of necessary connection, so the phrase must be meaningless. Therefore, when you take a knife and put it in somebody's heart and twist it, one event is observing the knife go in, and the next event is you see the man turn pale and lie down on the ground. Those are two events that are spatially and temporally contiguous, and that's it. You cannot say that the one made the other happen. All you have a right to assert—in fact, the only thing that is *meaningful* to assert—is that the two events go together in space and time. You observe that one is right next to the other, that one is right after the other, but you can't observe that one is *because* of the other. And that's right: You can't *observe* the causality.

Why do you think there is a necessary relationship, if, in fact, this is a myth? Again, because you have an overactive imagination. In this case, you have a hyperactive associative mechanism. Two events that, in fact, have no necessary connection (or it would be meaningless to say so), two events happen by chance to go together so many times in your experience that after a while you form the habit by custom, by conditioning, to expect the second when you encounter the first. That is the source of the irrational idea of "necessary connection." You observe, says Hume, repeated conjunctions—two events that happen to go together repeatedly—and you begin to associate the two and expect the second after the first. For instance (and this is not his example), suppose you were brought up by an irrational mother, and for no reason at all, every morning when you sat down at breakfast to drink a glass of orange juice, just as you picked up the glass of orange juice, she had a huge strap, and she smashed the kitchen table with it. Now, this happened day after day, and there's no causal connection, but that's just the kind of mother you have. After a while, as you pick up the orange juice, you flinch in the expectation of the strap, and you come to associate the two by quantity of repetition. Well, Hume says, this is exactly the relationship in *every* case where we assert cause and effect. Causality is merely a subjective expectation on our part, completely irrational without any justification. You can use the word "cause" if you want, but then all it means is that two events are repeatedly conjoined up until now in our experience, and we, therefore, have the accompanying irrational, baseless expectation that there's some connection between them, but in fact there is no connection. Here is Hume's famous conclusion:

> All events seem entirely loose and separate. One event follows another, but we never can observe any tie between them. They seem conjoined, but never connected. And as we have no idea of any thing which never appeared to our outward sense or inward sentiment, the necessary conclusion seems to be that we have no idea of connection or power at all, and that these words are absolutely without any meaning when employed either in philosophical reasoning or common life.

That's an uncompromising Humean statement.

Suppose you contest this and say: "Oh, that's ridiculous. Causality is not just a matter of habit. Causal sequences are necessary. Their opposites are literally inconceivable. We couldn't even imagine their opposites happening." Hume comes back with a famous example. He says that you can perfectly well imagine the opposite happening. He gives the example of Adam as the first man. Across the garden Adam sees a flame. Is Adam able to know before he experiences the behavior of the flame that the flame is going to consume him if he puts his hand into it? No, Adam hasn't the faintest idea how this orange tongue that's flickering is going to behave when he puts his hand into it. Prior to experience, if we had asked Adam, "Is it going to make you six feet taller, burn your hand off, or turn you into a pumpkin?," Adam would have said, "I haven't a clue." Well, says Hume, what does he get *after* experience? After experience, he's got a burned hand. But he doesn't have any more understanding of *why* this took place. As far as he can see, the fire could just as well have turned him into ice or into a pumpkin. In other words, it is a matter of brute fact—it happens to be the case—that fire up until now burns or warms. But it's unintelligible why this is so, and we can easily conceive the opposite. If someone were to say that we could explain by reference to scientific law why fire does what it does, Hume would say: "Scientific law? Scientific law is based on cause and effect. Cause and effect depends on necessary connection, and that's meaningless. So much for scientific laws." All we do is let our familiarity with certain arbitrary sequences delude us into thinking that the connection is intelligible, when actually it's completely unintelligible.

Suppose you tried to give Hume a proof in logic that every event must have a cause that necessitates it. Hume says, go ahead and try, and I'll show you that you can't give me any such proof. Is your proof going to rely on reason, he says? You answer, "Certainly, I'm going to give a rational proof." Well, says Hume, by reason we can prove only truths whose opposites would be contradictory, logical contradictions. Reason teaches us that we have to believe something because the opposite would be a contradiction. So, we could prove that two and two is four because if somebody denied it, we could show him he was contradicting himself. Anything that is a contradiction is inconceivable—you can't conceive a round square, for instance, because the two sides annihilate each other. Is there any difficulty in conceiving that the law of cause and effect is false? Would any contradiction be involved, he asks, in conceiving it? No. The opposite of the law of cause and effect, he says, is perfectly conceivable. It's easy to understand. It's not like a round square, which obliterates itself. It's perfectly conceivable. Take the idea, "There are events that don't have any causes." If this were a contradiction, we shouldn't even be able to grasp it; it should be like "married bachelor." But, says Hume, there's no difficulty in grasping this. Just imagine (I'm making up the example, but this is his idea), imagine you're walking down the street and suddenly an apple pops into existence out of thin air. Nothing preceded it, it's not a hallucination, it just is there without any cause. Walt Disney could draw it. Hume says that this is perfectly conceivable: There's no contradiction in it—if there were a contradiction, you couldn't conceive it, but you understood my story, so you must be able to conceive it, whereas if I said, "A round square popped out," you'd say, "I don't know what that is." If it's conceivable, there's no contradiction. If there's no contradiction, reason can't prove it. Reason proves something only if its opposite is a contradiction. Therefore, the law of cause and effect cannot be proved. Since it can't be proved in reason, and we know there's no basis for it in reference to experience, we conclude that the law of cause and effect is bereft of any foundation of any kind, in reason or in experience. It is, therefore, a myth.

The objections to this Humean viewpoint are legion, which I'll just indicate briefly. Notice that Hume assumes that if he can visualize an event that takes place allegedly without a cause, that that's the same as saying he conceives it without contradiction. If Aristotle heard this argument, he would say: "You are visualizing an event that implies a contradiction, and therefore, you are actually conceiving nothing but an irrational figment of your own imagination. You have an image, but not a logical concept." What would Hume's answer be if he heard that? "What's the difference? An image *is* a concept. If I can form an image of something, I've formed a concept of it." That is his nominalism—a concept is an image. So, if you can form an image, you can form a concept, and if you can form a concept, then it's obviously logically possible. Therefore, if you can form an image—any arbitrary, fantastic image—the thing it stands for is logically possible. That is the end result of reducing concepts to images, the way the nominalists do.

You might think you would satisfy Hume if you gave him the proof of cause and effect that we developed from Aristotle's philosophy. You remember the argument that had essentially two premises—"Actions are actions of entities" and "Entities have identity," in other words, they are what they are, the law of identity, and therefore, to make a long story short, they can act only in accordance with their nature. If you were to reincarnate David Hume and give him this argument, he wouldn't bat an eye. Because, observe each premise—"Entities?," he would say, "What is that? All we have are loose floating bundles of qualities." And that's all that he, as a nominalist-sensualist, can encounter. And therefore, the premise about entities existing is already out and so is the base of any proof of cause and effect, given his nominalism. And as for the law of identity, is that supposed to be a necessary general truth? Then, as a nominalist, that must be linguistic, semantic, just the way you use words—it doesn't say anything. In other words, causality has already come fairly far down in philosophy. First of all, you have to have the conceptual level to validate your knowledge of anything, including of causality. So, there's actually nothing new to answer in Hume's attack on cause and effect. If you can answer his nominalism and sensualism, if you can defend a valid theory of concepts, then his whole attack on cause and effect crashes to the ground along with the whole rest of his philosophy. On the other hand, if you *cannot* answer his nominalism and sensualism, then you are lost, and everything is lost. And you see again the crucial importance of a valid theory of concepts.

In any event, for Hume, the collapse of cause and effect leads to overwhelming, insoluble problems. It leads him to complete and total skepticism because, if there is no cause and effect, how can we predict the future? How can we generalize? How can we say that because things have happened a certain way in the past, therefore, they will happen that way in the future? How can we ever formulate scientific laws? How can we even *have* science? To all of which Hume's answer is, "You can't." We have, he says, no reason on earth to assume that nature follows law. We have no reason to assume that nature is uniform. We have no reason to assume that the future will be like the past. This is known as the *problem of induction*: What makes you think that because something has happened a certain way repeatedly in the past it will, therefore, happen that way in the future? If there are necessary connections in reality—if there are actual laws that nature must obey—then you can validly generalize from experience under the appropriate circumstances. But if you destroy causality and reduce nature to the unintelligible, to a brute conjunction of events without any necessity, then *anything* is possible at the next instant, and the fact that something has happened a thousand times proves *nothing* about the future; it's been a run of coincidence.

People often misunderstand Hume, and they think that he is saying, "Well, you can never be certain about the future, you can only have a degree of probability." He goes much beyond that. He says you can't even have the faintest trace of probability with regard to the future. Every occurrence is a brand-new event, all events are loose and separate, there is no necessity about any conjunction of events, and therefore, you haven't the slightest reason to assume that the future will resemble the past in any respect. If I throw a penny up in the air, up to now, the penny has come down, and you might be inclined to say, "Well, there's a good chance it will come down again." But in Hume's philosophy, there's only one chance in infinity it will come down. It might just stand still. It might go straight up. It might turn into Hegel. It might become a quarter. It could do *anything*. You say, "But it's come down so many times in the past." Well, I've heard Humeans say that just goes to show that we've had such a run of good luck that we shouldn't expect it to continue.

So, we've reached a total dead end, an absolutely shattered universe. We have loosely floating qualities, no entities, no reality, no self, no causality, everything a brute, contingent fact. Let's mop up some final points.

Is there *any* necessary knowledge, according to Hume? Anything we can know as necessary? Yes, he says, but not matters of fact. Anything that talks about the way things actually are, any factual statement, is contingent. We derive it from experience—it is empirical, *a posteriori* (using the term I introduced last time, which means "dependent on experience"). Where, then, do we get necessary knowledge? Only in what Hume calls "relations of ideas." If I utter the statement, "Bachelors are male," I can know that that has to be true because, says Hume, it is a matter of definition—I *define* "bachelor" as "an entity, one of whose characteristics is being male." This is a necessary truth; one I can count on. But it doesn't tell me anything about facts. It would be true even if there were no bachelors. It's necessary because we make it so by our arbitrary nominalistic definitions. If it stated an actual fact of reality, he would say, how would you ever know it is necessary? Therefore, this kind of truth, the so-called relations of ideas, we arrive at by reason or thought or analysis. In their case, the opposite would be a contradiction. They are learned by definition, not by experience, so they are so-called *a priori*. Thus, we have the standard dichotomy that we have seen in so many different forms: As it exists in Hume, the linguistic truths versus the existential or factual truths, the logical truths versus the factual truths, the truths of reason (which are necessary but detached from reality), and the truths of experience (which pertain to facts but are contingent). You see that this is a variant of the standard dichotomy, and this dichotomy is what Kant then picked up and called *analytic truths versus synthetic* truths, the analytic being the ones you arrive at by analysis, the logical truths so-called, and the synthetic being the ones that tell you actual empirical information.

Given this (which is not original with Hume), what happens to metaphysics if you accept this dichotomy of necessary relations of ideas that are linguistic versus the contingent factual empirical truths? Is metaphysics supposed to be factual? The advocates of metaphysics say certainly: Metaphysics tells you facts about reality. If it's factual, it has to be empirical. Is metaphysics supposed to tell you contingent, empirical hypotheses? No, the advocates of metaphysical principles, like cause and effect, for instance, say they are necessary. Well, there's no such alternative possibility as a factual necessary truth. If it's necessary, it's linguistic; if it's factual, it is not necessary. Is metaphysics supposed to be linguistic? No, say its advocates. Is metaphysics supposed to be contingent then? No, say its advocates. Well then, says Hume, metaphysics as such is out. There is no room for any such subject. If you say to Hume: "But what about 'Existence exists,' 'A is A,' 'Consciousness is the faculty for perceiving reality,' 'Every event has a cause,'" he would say, "Did you mean those propositions as expressions of your arbitrary linguistic usage?" You would say, "Certainly not, I mean those to be facts of reality." He would say, "Did you arrive at them by sensory perception, and do you regard them as simply contingent truths?" You would say, "Certainly not, those are laws and principles of reality." He would say, "No such category. It's either a subjective relation of ideas, or it is a brute contingent sensualist-type fact." Therefore, as far as metaphysics is concerned, throw it into the fire—a viewpoint echoed in the twentieth century by many schools that are neo-Humean. The upshot in Hume's viewpoint is this: If you are certain about a proposition, if you understand why it must be true, if it's really reliable, it's detached from reality; and on the other hand, if it has something to say about the real world, you can't be certain about it and you can't make any sense of it. If you know it must be true, then it's not about the world—it says nothing about facts, but just expresses linguistic conventions. If it says something about facts, then it is contingent, uncertain, unreliable. And if you prove it by experience, it's contingent and unreliable, and if you prove it by logic, it is an arbitrary convention. So, you're trapped either way, you cannot win, and you end up in a complete skepticism.

Let us look briefly at some final topics, which we can race through briefly because you now know the essence of Hume's philosophy. On God: God cannot survive on a Humean philosophy. God is supposed to be a spiritual substance who is the cause of the world. But every item in that statement is eliminated—there is no "world," no "spiritual substance," and no "causality." And consequently, God is out. And Hume takes great delight in demolishing God. He's particularly interested in the argument from design, and he loves to take on religious people and make mincemeat of their viewpoint. There are passages in Hume which indicate that religion is still a sensitive subject and that he is loath to come out as a complete atheist, but obviously any belief in God would be completely incompatible with his philosophy. In essence, his view would be that "God," as a term, is radically different from anything a sensualist can come in contact with, and therefore, it's a meaningless noise. And therefore, Hume is essentially anti-religious. If you read his detailed arguments, I may say, you would find them a mixture of astute objections—he's a fairly good polemicist—but he's always a Humean, and to untangle his good objections from his crazy Humeanism, which are all mashed together, it's easier to refute God on your own without help from Hume.

Hume's assault on God contributed heavily to the fact that after this period, no influential philosopher again attempted to prove the existence of God in reason. Kant was very religious, though he did not think you could prove God in reason. Hegel—well, Hegel is Hegel, and his God is hardly the same as anybody else's God. Nietzsche said, correctly, in the nineteenth century, "God is dead," meaning religion was a dead issue, and in the twentieth century, one whole school derivative from Hume and Kant says that God is a noise like "gloop," standing for nothing at all, and another school says that if you *do* believe in God, you have to go by absurd feelings because God is not graspable by reason. So, God didn't survive the eighteenth century philosophically and never again had the importance that he did in Descartes, Spinoza, Leibniz, Locke, and Berkeley. There are people who think that this is good, and that Hume has done a great service (combined with a few other philosophers) in getting rid of God. I would not agree with that. Because, as an Objectivist, I would say the concept of "God" is bad because it is anti-reason and anti-reality, but in Hume, God is thrown out *along with* reason and reality, on the same grounds. And this is a very, very bad mixture. I remember once asking a brash sophomore if he believed in God, and he said, "Of course not, God doesn't exist; *nothing* does." That is the Humean mentality. And it helps to explain to you why it is a mistake to call Objectivism "atheism." Objectivists are atheists; we deny the existence of God. But *all* sorts of people deny the existence of God, including Hume and the communists, but for different reasons. And therefore, to know that somebody is an atheist is to tell you nothing about the essence of his philosophy. It tells you only that there is one aberration that he did not commit. But that leaves open a very large field.

To say a word about Hume's view on ethics: It should be obvious that his ethics is compatible with the rest of his philosophy. It is a thoroughly skeptical-subjectivist ethics. The question he raises is: How can you ever defend an ethical or evaluative proposition? If we have to base everything on experience, experience only tells us what *is* the case. How do we ever get a knowledge of what *ought* to be the case? Did you ever touch a desirability? Did you ever smell a goodness? Obviously, you cannot grasp or imbibe value terms through the senses or images. And if that is our only means of cognition, there is obviously no way to validate value premises. So, here we have the old problem of deriving values from facts, and of course, Hume declares it can't be done. In fact, there's a parallel here—just as he claims you can't get a "must" out of an "is," i.e., you can't get a necessary connection out of a fact, so, he says, you can't get an evaluation out of an "is," you can't get an "ought" out of an "is," you can't get a value out of a fact. And therefore, value judgments are gratuitously arbitrary in their foundation. No rational ethics is possible. Ethics must begin with subjective desires and feelings, and when we say something is right, or some equivalent value term, we ultimately must mean that is what we desire. Ethics is a matter of feeling. Reason, therefore, says Hume, is and must be a slave of the passions. In other words, we have again, essentially, the Sophist viewpoint in ethics. So, there is nothing new in his ethics; it's the same skepticism as in the rest of his philosophy. The answer to his specific charge that you cannot get values out of facts is contained in Galt's speech, and it's also in "The Objectivist Ethics," the essay by Miss Rand, so I won't comment on that further.

To summarize Hume's philosophy, I think the best thing is to let him summarize it himself. This is from *A Treatise of Human Nature*, in which he expresses his arch skepticism. I read you these passages because they're famous and explicit, and, because he's British, they're intelligible:

> 'Tis not solely in poetry and music we must follow our taste and sentiment, but likewise in philosophy. When I am convinced of any principle, 'tis only an idea which strikes more strongly upon me. When I give the preference to one set of arguments above another, I do nothing but decide from my feeling concerning the superiority of their influence. Objects have no discoverable connection together, nor is it from any other principle but custom operating upon the imagination that we can draw any inference from the appearance of one to the existence of another.

In other words, nobody can know anything. This is arch, complete skepticism, absolute bankruptcy: Philosophy, idea, science, and theory are all a matter of taste and feeling.

You say you can't live by this philosophy, and you think that that is an objection to Hume. You may or may not be surprised to know that Hume agrees with you. He says quite explicitly, "No, you cannot live by this philosophy." He says in a famous passage (which I won't take the time to read, but it amounts to this)—he writes that "external world" is meaningless, and "self" is meaningless, and "causality" is meaningless, and so on, but then he says he leaves his writing, and he goes and dines with friends, plays a game of backgammon (he uses that example), and lives in the normal world with everybody else. And then he says he comes back, and he reads what he wrote, and it seems to him so strange and ridiculous that he wants to throw it all out, but he can't find anything wrong with it. What is his solution to this dilemma? The solution, he says, is that skepticism is a disease that comes from living by reason, and the only way out is to pay no attention to the conclusions of reason.

> This skeptical doubt, both with respect to reason and the senses, is a malady which can never be radically cured, but must return upon us every moment, however we may chase it away, . . . Carelessness and inattention alone can afford us any remedy. For this reason, I rely entirely upon them, and take it for granted, whatever may be the reader's opinion at this present moment, that an hour hence he will be persuaded that there is both an external and an internal world.

You get the idea. In other words, you cannot live by philosophy. You have to be careless and inattentive to it because you can't live by reason. And you do not have to, because we are not only rational creatures, but we are also *natural* creatures, which means we have instincts, we have imaginations, we have feelings, and our feelings and imaginations and instincts will invent the fictions we need and will take us through life prosperously as long as we pay no attention to reason and philosophy. If you think you've got a reason for believing what you do, you haven't. The actual cau—I can't even say "cause," because there are no causes—but the actual something-or-other of your beliefs is simply instinct. A famous line of Hume: "'tis only because it costs us too much pains to think otherwise." There's just a pragmatic matter of instinct. In other words, in the last analysis, irrational, unphilosophical, unthinking blind instinct is superior to reason, thought, and philosophy. That's the final upshot of Hume's philosophy. Reason is impotent, nobody can know anything, reason can't give you a knowledge of reality, external reality is a myth, entities are a myth, the self is a myth, cause and effect is a myth, logic is a subjective construction, nobody has any reason to believe anything, you can live only if you ignore reason and function by irrational instinct, only if you throw reason and philosophy into the fire and follow your irrational passions.

This is the end result of trying to philosophize after having invalidated the conceptual faculty. And one of two things had to happen at this point: Either a champion of reason in a valid sense had to appear, somebody who finally validated man's conceptual faculty, or the arch destroyer of all time would appear and put the final seal on man's philosophic demise. And the second is what happened. The man who came on the scene right after Hume, the man who set himself the task of answering Hume, the man who said he was going to avoid the floating constructs of the rationalists and the skepticism of the empiricists—that man was Kant. And, in the process of giving his answers to these schools, he once and for all removed reason from the philosophic scene altogether. That, however, is the story for another course, not this one.

We have now traced the story from Greece, beginning with Thales and his friends eagerly trying for the first time to probe into the nature of reality, and we have gone now all the way through David Hume, where the attempt finally collapses with a sickening whimper. And on this melancholy and even disastrous note, we have to conclude our presentation of the Founders of Western Philosophy: From Thales to Hume. In the next and final lecture, I offer you a final ray of sunshine, so as not to leave you in the depressed state that you are probably now in. Namely, the Objectivist answer to some of the key problems that we have postponed discussing so far.

Lecture Eleven, Q&A

Q: You said that Kant removed reason from the scene altogether. It's hard to see how he could have removed it further than Hume. Could you sketch how he did it?

A: That's a good question, but I don't know how to answer it briefly. Hume still has operating in his mind the idea that reason would be, or consciousness would be, the faculty for grasping existence, only it happens to be that he doesn't believe in existence or think we can grasp it. But at least he represents the last ray of the idea that *if* there were reason, it would consist of grasping existence. Kant denies that completely. He turns reason into a faculty that *creates* existence, at least the existence that we actually live in, and therefore corrodes and corrupts human epistemology much more deeply than Hume does. A skeptic says, "I don't know." Kant goes much further and says, "I *do* know, and what knowing consists of is creating, by means of a collective, human-wide delusion, a made-up mythical world that we live in." That's much worse than Hume. But if that isn't clear to you, you have to study Kant. And even then . . .

Q: How can Hume ask if we can conceive the opposite of the law of cause and effect, since it is a conception and it would be meaningless to begin with?

A: No, the answer is, by "concept," he would mean "form an image of"—can you form an image of the opposite of cause and effect? And he and his followers would say yes you can, you can form an image of an event without a cause, namely, for instance, the apple I mentioned during the lecture. And as long as you can image it, for them, that's forming a concept of it.

Q: According to Berkeley, how can God exist independent of his being perceived?

A: I left out one point from Berkeley. There are two ways to exist. If it's a soul or a mind, its existence doesn't consist of its *being* perceived, but of its actually being capable of *perceiving*. So, in its case, *esse est perciperi*, "to be is to perceive." And since God perceives, since he has experiences and ideas and so on, he exists in the way that a mind or a soul exists—as a perceiving entity.

Q: How would Hume deal with 100 percent predictability? For instance, a certain mass of rock thrown with a certain force will *always* break a window a certain way.

A: Hume would say you have no way whatever of knowing this. All you would know is that up to now, that kind of rock has behaved this way. But you haven't got one reason in a million to believe that it's going to behave that way in the future. So, he would say, "I don't account for 100 percent predictability; there is not even 1 percent predictability." He's wrong, but that is what he would say.

Q: Is the issue of meaningful versus meaningless terms, as used by philosophers, valid? I.e., is the standard of the existence of a referent for meaningfulness valid?

A: You need to untangle many things. But to be brief, yes, certainly, a meaningful term has to stand for something. In that respect, it must have a referent. That's correct. Otherwise, it would stand for nothing and would be meaning*less*. But the crucial point is that the referent does not have to be *perceivable*, as long as it is *conceivable*. In other words, in a valid philosophy, a term is meaningful if it stands for something to which the human mind can have cognitive contact or relationship. But that contact does not have to be restricted to sense perception or images. There are many things that we *cannot* know by direct perception that we *can* know by conceptual means (concepts, being themselves ultimately derived from percepts, but not being the same as percepts). And in this respect, I would say that a term is meaningful if it has a referent that is either perceivable or conceptually definable.

As to the broader issue, no, I do not believe that the criterion of meaning (if you want it more specific than I've just given you) is a valid philosophic question. It's a question that arose only under the influx of a wave of nominalism and sensualism, which led philosophers to the conclusion that three-quarters, if not more, of the issues that had been traditionally discussed were meaningless. And so they got off on this wild kick of asking what meaningfulness consists of, and they forgot about the questions. As an Objectivist, I take the view that the definition of "meaningfulness," beyond the brief account I gave you here, is *not* a legitimate philosophic question. If a statement does not consist of undefined terms or does not violate the laws of grammar, it is meaningful. If you say "The cow and up," that's meaningless. If you say, "The gloop hit the triddle," that's meaningless. But if you say, "The cow hit the frying pan," that's meaningful, because the terms are defined, and the grammar is English (or whatever language you're speaking). It is not the province of philosophers to become lexicographers, contrary to modern trends.

Q: By Hume's premises, how can our past experiences cause us to form a habit and hence arrive at our false idea of cause?

A: A good question. No answer to it. Hume throughout gives causal explanations (alleged causal explanations) of our false beliefs—our belief in entities and the self and the external world and so on. Having denied causality, he has no business giving such explanations, a point that is commonly made in polemics against him. And therefore, he has to say that our belief in causality (if he's consistent) like causality itself, or like *any* phenomenon of the world, is an inexplicable, brute, unintelligible, contingent fact, which he can't make head or tail of. And in falling into the tendency to give a causal explanation of our mistaken belief in causality, he is using causality while denying it, and thereby contradicting his own philosophy.

Q: Will you give Objectivism's differentiation between a concrete and a concretization?

A: A "concrete" is a metaphysical term—it stands for any particular, any specific individual thing—a concrete man, a concrete wristwatch. "Concrete" here does not mean "made out of cement." It is contrasted with an *abstraction.* And the more common philosophic term in the history of philosophy is what is called a "particular." That's what Objectivism means by a "concrete." A concretization is an epistemological process in which, to clarify some theory, you provide a concrete example, that is, you name or identify some concrete that would illustrate or clarify a theory. So, for instance, I just *concretized* for you the concept of "concrete" by giving you a particular example—"a concrete river," "a concrete man." In offering those examples, I am concretizing for you the concept "concrete." That's all there is to it. Concretization is the offering of a concrete, intellectually, to clarify a point.

Q: If Hume says that the meaning of a concept or a word is its refer-

ent, how can he accept the analytic-synthetic distinction, which depends on distinguishing meaning and referent?

A: Let me bypass what Hume says on that and tell you what his modern followers say, which is that you must distinguish two different kinds of meaning. If a term is supposed to be "factual"—that is, refer to actual experience—then it must have a referent in actual experience. But on the other hand, if a term is being used as part of what Hume calls "a relation of ideas," then its meaning is entirely different—it is meaningful if you equate it with *other* words. So, for instance, if I say a bachelor is an unmarried male, the meaning of the word "bachelor" is "unmarried male," all of it, a little world of definitions cut off entirely from reality. That's what's called *semantic meaning* by many philosophers and is contrasted with *factual meaning.* Of course, there is no such phenomenon as semantic meaning in this sense (speaking rationally). But then, if you were to speak rationally, you wouldn't accept the analytic-synthetic distinction. But in other words, they say there are two kinds of meaning: Some terms are meaningful because they relate directly to experience, and some terms are meaningful because we build them into a web of constructs, arbitrary definitions, and their meaning is the arbitrary definition we give.

Q: How can Hume claim that his is a philosophy of reason when he claims to be an arch empiricist and is against reason on principle?

A: I'm not sure that the intention of this question is clear. An empiricist, if that term is used very broadly, is not somebody who denies reason, but somebody who declares that reason must take its point of departure from experience, rather than build upon innate ideas. In that sense, the fact of saying you're an empiricist doesn't mean you're against reason. Hume's philosophy derives from empiricism, sensualism, nominalism, and skepticism, and in that sense ends up being against reason. It's not from being an empiricist, but from the particular interpretation he puts forth. And he would say, "I'm not against reason. My whole philosophy is perfectly rational. I've given the rational proof that reason is hopeless."

Q: If Hume has to fall back on the concept of natural creatures with instincts, emotions, and so on, doesn't he necessarily refute his original empiricist premise of no innate ideas? If so, didn't he see this and offer any explanation?

A: You must understand that for Hume, instincts, emotions, etc., are part of the impressions we are directly given. Just as we are directly given the simple ideas, including certain emotions, passions, and feelings, which for Hume do not derive from our ideas or from our intellect at all. They are irreducible primaries. They are part of our given empirical equipment. And therefore, he feels no compulsion to offer any explanation of emotions. Emotions are just there. Whatever emotions we have, we have, and that's it. They are raw elements like sensations, with no further explanation offered. Since he offers no explanation of anything, it shouldn't surprise you that he offers no explanation of emotions either.

Q: If you asked Hume to put his hand in a fire a few times and see if this would be the time his hand wouldn't be burned, would he do it? Assuming not, what would be his reason?

A: Undoubtedly he wouldn't do it, and he would say because he's a creature of instinct. Being a creature of instinct, he is conditioned to expect irrationally that the flame would burn him, and he prefers to live by his irrational instinct.

Q: Why did certain philosophers develop a preference for certain psychological processes (namely, sensations and perceptions), which they held to be valid and meaningful, and reject as meaningless or nonexistent other psychological processes, such as conceptualization and understanding, whose existence are equally identifiable introspectively?

A: I tried to explain that in the process of giving the course. They believed that concepts were not based on reality. And therefore, they reconstrued what is, in fact, available introspectively. (If it will make you feel better, think of that noise coming from the next room as a secondary quality, and therefore, it's not really real.) In other words, concepts do pose a certain problem that percepts don't. I'm not saying that the conclusions of philosophers are valid, but concepts are not directly perceivable in reality the way percepts are. Percepts represent a direct contact with reality, but concepts are indirect. And therefore, if a philosopher says, "Yes, I can grasp perception, but I don't know what conception is," it represents, to be sure, a profound default on his philosophic task, since the essence of philosophy is the theory of concepts. But on the face of it, it is more intelligible than if he were to say, "I grasp concepts but I deny percepts," because percepts are much simpler and easier to grasp. And in this sense, I would offer that as a partial explanation. But the full story is the whole nominalist argumentation.

Q: On Berkeley's premises, is it enough for an object to be perceived by *any* mind in order for it to exist, or must it be by *your* mind?

A: No, it can be by any mind, he says. And since God is always perceiving, everything always exists and is sustained by God. His followers got rid of God, and in the process, they were left with each contemplating only his own experiences, which had no source. (That didn't bother them, because they followed Hume, so they dispensed with cause and effect.) But then the question was: How did they know that any other human beings existed? Even any other human minds? Because their only contact with other human minds was by the experience of their bodies, and their bodies were only experiences in their own mind. And so they ended up with the idea that all that exists is one's own mind and its content, and that everybody else was simply a figment of their imagination. And that is the viewpoint known as *solipsism*, "I-myself-alone-ism," which is the upshot of Berkeley's idealism. But Berkeley himself, a bishop, would not take this viewpoint.

Q: Are metaphysics or epistemology, as two branches of philosophy, an effect of the adherence to the mind-body dichotomy in philosophy?

A: No. You do not have to subscribe to the mind-body dichotomy—*dichotomy*, mind you, I'm using the word of the questioner, meaning "two opposites"—in order to advocate a distinction between metaphysics and epistemology. All you have to subscribe to is a distinction between knowledge and the object of knowledge, between consciousness and existence, quite independently now of the makeup of consciousness, or whether existence is physical or nonphysical. If there is something to know—a reality—and something to *know* it—a consciousness—that already raises two questions: What is the nature of reality? What are the means of knowledge? And consequently, metaphysics and epistemology derive from the distinction between existence and consciousness, no matter *how* construed. From that point of view, the subjects themselves do not presuppose any dichotomy between mind and body.

LECTURE TWELVE

Objectivist Answers to Selected Philosophic Problems

Our subject is the Objectivist answers to certain selected problems that arose in the history of philosophy in the period from Greece through David Hume. And I must at the outset delimit our assignment. Objectivism denies that any philosophic question can be answered in a vacuum. It holds that all philosophic problems and issues are interconnected, and, therefore, that a full answer to any one philosophic question would require the presentation of a full system of philosophy. Such a presentation of the Objectivist philosophy is obviously impossible in one lecture, so throughout this presentation, I am counting on a considerable knowledge on your part of the philosophy of Objectivism. I am assuming that you're generally familiar with the Objectivist literature, particularly with Ayn Rand's *Introduction to Objectivist Epistemology*, with its presentation of the Objectivist theory of concept formation, and that you're familiar with Galt's speech, with its overview and summary of Objectivism. And I'm assuming that you understand in particular the Objectivist views that we have already covered or mentioned in this course—above all, the three fundamental axioms of Objectivism: (1) "Existence exists," what we have been calling the "primacy of existence"; (2) the axiom that one exists possessing consciousness, consciousness being the faculty of perceiving that which exists; and (3) "A is A," the law of identity (along with its reformulations), the law of contradiction and the law of excluded middle. I'm counting also on your knowledge of the fallacy of the stolen concept—the fallacy of using a concept while denying or ignoring a more basic concept on which it depends.

I'm assuming an overall knowledge of Objectivism in order to concentrate on three basic issues. First, *the senses* and all the tangled questions we have postponed now until this lecture. Then, a discussion of the *borderline-case problem* that arises in the theory of universals. And finally, a brief discussion of the *problem of certainty* and of what is wrong with the method of Cartesian doubt.

The Validity of the Senses

Why is the issue of sense perception so crucial to epistemology? Because man is born *tabula rasa*—he has no innate ideas. The senses are man's first and primary means of coming into contact with reality, of perceiving that which exists. The senses provide man with the basic evidence that is the foundation of our entire cognitive structure. Everything that we know derives ultimately from the evidence provided by our senses. In particular, all concepts are formed on the basis of sensory evidence. Concepts are forms of organizing, relating, integrating, unifying sense experience. As such, the validity of human concepts—the issue of their relation to reality—depends on the validity of man's sense perceptions. If the senses are invalid, then at one stroke the whole edifice of human knowledge collapses, and all concepts—*all* concepts—are immediately invalidated.

For a moment, forget all the objections raised against the senses across the centuries. Imagine, if you can, that you were in a rational class on philosophy, and the professor was discussing the issue of the validity of the senses. What would he have to say positively, apart from answering the countless objections accumulated through the ages? In essence, he would have very little to say. He would say that the proposition that "Man's senses are valid" is an expression of the axiom that man is conscious.

Why? Well, what is meant by the term "valid perception"? The answer is: It means a perception of existence, of reality, a perception whose object is an existent, something that is. Notice that I do not say a valid perception is a perception of reality "as it really is." The phrase "as it really is," in this context, is a redundancy. There is no such thing as reality as it really isn't. There is no unreal reality, no nonexistent existence. To perceive reality "as it really is" is simply to perceive reality, the one and only reality there is.

What would be the status of an alleged sense perception that was not valid, a perception that was not a perception of existence? It would have to be a perception of nonexistence, i.e., of nothing, i.e., it would not be a perception at all, not a form of consciousness or awareness. If "invalid perception" means (as it does) "a perception of something other than existence," it means a state of awareness of nothing. And as such, it is a contradiction in terms. This is true for any perceiving species, whatever its organs and means of perception. If it perceives, it perceives something that is. In other words, its perceptions are valid. To say that man's perceptions are *invalid* is to say that man has no means of awareness of reality, i.e., that he is unconscious. For this reason, the issue of the validity of the senses is contained in the fundamental axiom of consciousness. In stating that man is conscious, one implies that man's means of awareness *are* means of awareness. In other words, his senses are valid.

Don't be confused here by the phenomenon of dreams or hallucinations. Dreams, hallucinations and equivalent phenomena are not sense perceptions. They are not examples of man sensorially perceiving something other than existence. Once a man acquires a certain content of experiences from his perception of reality, it is possible for him, under certain circumstances, temporarily, to detach his consciousness from the perception of reality and contemplate instead the stored and remembered sensory images in his mind, the content he originally acquired from the perception of reality. In such a case, he is not engaging in sense perception at all. He is turning his consciousness in on itself and contemplating his own stored content of experiences, images, etc. Such a phenomenon is possible only because he has initially acquired this content—acquired it or, at least, its ultimate constituents—by direct perception of reality. The phenomena of dreams, hallucinations, etc., presuppose a prior contact with reality. Such phenomena do not prove that consciousness can sensorially perceive something other than reality. They prove the opposite: Only because man *does* perceive reality when he senses, is he able, under certain circumstances, to acquire the kind of mental contents that then makes it possible for his consciousness temporarily to turn in on itself and contemplate the data thus initially acquired from a direct awareness of reality. For the rest of this lecture, therefore, please forget about dreams, hallucinations, and phenomena of that nature. I am talking about sense perception, and sense perception is always perception of existence, of reality, of things that are.

Against this background, let us turn to the central argument against the senses—the one raised by Protagoras in ancient Greece, and accepted in various forms by the overwhelming majority of philosophers ever since. You recall the argument: "How can you ever claim to perceive reality by means of your senses? After all, you perceive reality only by means of your particular sensory organs, your sensory apparatus. If your sensory organs were different, your perception would be different. All you can say is, 'This is how reality appears to me, granted my particular sensory apparatus.' You can never know how things really are in themselves."

So I would like you to consider this argument, which we have encountered repeatedly in the course, and consider it carefully from the point of view of Objectivism. The argument objects to the fact that man can perceive reality only by specific means, the sense organs. Since this is so, the argument claims, you can never perceive reality "directly," or never perceive reality "in itself," only reality as processed by your sensory apparatus, merely how *your* consciousness gets reality. Ask yourself: What is the ideal of this viewpoint? What would its exponents regard as an actual perception of reality? What would they call "perceiving reality directly"? Only one thing: if man could jump outside of his own senses, i.e., outside of his means of awareness, outside of his consciousness, and somehow go out to contact things without benefit of sense organs, without having any specific means of perception at all. This, according to the argument, would be a true perception. The perception that this argument yearns for, and in the name of which it condemns human perception, is perception by no means and, therefore, in no specific form. Perception no-how. So long as you perceive by any specific means, they write that off as invalid. That, they say, is just *your* type of sensory mechanism, *your* specific type of consciousness. That's merely the form in which a consciousness of *your* kind perceives. Since man's consciousness is something specific, since it operates by specific organs and agencies, by specific means and in specific forms, it is invalid. That is the meaning of the argument.

Observe that this argument is wider than an attack on *human* consciousness. It is in fact an attack on *all* consciousness, of any kind whatever—animal, human, Martian (if such a thing exists), divine (assuming for purposes of pedagogy that it exists). Are an animal's percepts valid by this argument—any animal now, regardless of the nature or keenness of its sense organs? The thunderous answer is *No*. After all, the animal still has specific sense organs. It, too, perceives reality only as it perceives it, reality as it affects *its* consciousness. What about the Martian? Suppose he has radically different sensory apparatuses—he has no eyes, no ears—imagine that he has a bulbous receptacle on his (or its) forehead, which twitches, and an appendage on the equivalent of its nose which buzzes, so that the Martian perceives reality in terms not of color or of sound, but of some kind of twitches or buzzes. Obviously, these are of a kind we do not gain from *our* senses, so I cannot describe them further to you. But the question is: According to Protagoras's argument, would this Martian perceive reality? No: The Martian would perceive reality only as it affects a Martian-type of consciousness, only as processed by Martian organs. Even God's consciousness, assuming he exists and assuming he perceives somehow, is invalidated by this argument. In whatever way God perceives, Protagoras could come back to him and say, "You, God, perceive reality only as it appears to God. You perceive only the effects of reality on the divine means of perception. You perceive reality only in a divine form. So again, you don't perceive reality directly, truly, validly."

What sort of consciousness then could perceive reality validly, even in theory? And the answer would have to be: a consciousness that is not limited to *any* specific means of perception, a consciousness without any means of consciousness, a consciousness that perceives in no specific form at all, a consciousness that isn't this type of consciousness as distinct from that type, a consciousness that is nothing in particular—in other words, that has no identity. This is the ideal of the Protagorean argument, and this is its standard for epistemology. The only consciousness that could perceive reality is a consciousness without identity, a consciousness that is nothing—in other words, that doesn't exist. The Protagorean argument attacks human consciousness not in the name of an allegedly *superior* consciousness, but in the name of a zero, a nothing, an entity without a nature or identity. And as such, the argument invalidates *all* consciousness, *any* consciousness, consciousness *as such*, human or any other kind.

It is by this means that philosophers have come to accept the following disastrous idea: If a consciousness has identity, it cannot perceive reality. Or, putting it another way, if consciousness is something, it cannot perceive anything. And then, as usual, given this false premise, philosophers proceed to divide into two opposed camps, both accepting the same basic premise. One side is the skeptics, who later became the Kantians (later, that is to say, after Hume and the termination of our course), and they declared that consciousness *does* have an identity, it *is* something, and therefore, it doesn't perceive reality. The other side, desperate to defend the validity of consciousness—and most of the so-called naïve realists are in this side—says, "Oh yes, consciousness can perceive reality, because it has no nature, it is nothing in itself." What is common to both of these theories? The following absurdity: If consciousness is a something—if it has a nature, if it has specific means of perception—perception is impossible. Paraphrasing Ayn Rand, it is having eyes that stand in the way of seeing, having ears that stand in the way of hearing, having specific organs of perception that make perception impossible.

By contrast, what is the Objectivist position? A is A. Everything that exists is what it is, with a specific, delimited, definite, finite nature. Everything is rigidly bound by the laws of identity and causality. And all of this applies not only to facts of the physical world, but also to consciousness. Consciousness—*any* consciousness—is something. It has a specific nature. Each conscious species perceives by specific means and in a specific form, a form that is determined by its particular means of perception. This is the base from which all epistemology must proceed, and by reference to which all epistemological concepts and standards must be defined. Because consciousness has identity, we must always understand "perception" to mean "perceiving reality by some means and in some form." There is no such thing as perceiving reality no-how, by no means, in no form. For instance, speaking of human perception, we perceive an object, say, by means of light waves reflected from its surface to our eyes. That is the means, and the resultant form is color. We perceive a different aspect of existence by means of certain vibrations striking our ears. That is the means, and the resultant form is sound. We perceive still another aspect of existence by means of bringing certain sensory receptors into contact with the energy states of various molecular combinations. That is the means, and so the form is heat or cold. In all cases, the object of our perception, i.e., what we are perceiving, is a fact out there, a fact in reality. But in all cases, we are perceiving it by a certain means, and so in a certain form. The contrast between the Objectivist view and what I'll call the "traditionalist" view, is this: The traditionalist view holds that if you perceive reality by a certain means, then you are not perceiving reality, only its effects on you; a means of perception is incompatible with perceiving existence. Objectivism says the exact opposite. It says that only the existence of a means of perception makes consciousness possible. The fact that consciousness must perceive in a certain form does not invalidate consciousness—that's what makes it possible. The traditionalists say identity is the obstacle to the perception of reality. Objectivism says only because consciousness has identity can it perceive reality. And since this is true in any process of knowledge, we must always distinguish the object (what you know) and the *how* (the means by which you know it). The object is reality. The "how" determines only the form of your perception of reality. But all forms of perception are *forms of perception*, i.e., forms of awareness of reality. As such, all forms of perception are valid.

You can see the fundamental error of the causal theory of perception as we have discussed it. It is true that reality is the cause of our perceptions, but it is also true that our perceptions are perceptions of reality. Distinguish here between two statements that may sound similar, but there is a life and death difference between them. The Objectivist view is: Man perceives reality *by means of* its effects on his consciousness. The causal theory of perception says man does *not* perceive reality, but only its effects on his consciousness. Objectivism says that the object is reality. The causal theory of perception makes the *means* of perception into the *object* of perception, thus invalidating man's consciousness, cutting it off from reality. The truth is that we do not perceive effects while being locked up in consciousness. We perceive reality directly, and we do so by means of the operations of our sense organs. So much also, by the way, for the representative theory of perception. Our experience does not "represent" or "copy" or "stand for" reality. It is directly *of* reality. It is not that a separate world is reproduced in consciousness and that we are confined to that world of consciousness, and we then have to engage in arguments about whether it does or doesn't correspond to an external reality that we never perceive. This entire viewpoint is false. Our experience is directly of reality.

If you think about it, you will see that the advocates of the causal theory of perception and the representative theory of perception use stolen concepts all over the place. What is an "experience" or a "perception" or a "sensation" or any equivalent term? These terms designate *states* of consciousness, not *objects* of consciousness. A sense perception is a state of awareness, an unanalyzable awareness of reality mediated directly by a sense organ. And equivalent definitions are applicable to a perception, a sensation, etc. *Nobody perceives experiences.* Let me repeat: Nobody perceives experiences. We perceive *things*, things in reality, and then we give the name "perception" to our awareness of these things. To speak of perceiving perceptions or experiencing experiences is to speak of being aware of your awareness. Which immediately raises the question: your awareness *of what*? Consciousness requires an object. We do not sit locked up in our consciousnesses, perceiving its perceptions of its perceptions of its perceptions, and so on to infinity, with nothing being perceived. We perceive reality. And we can be self-conscious, i.e., we can be aware that we are aware, aware that we are perceiving. But for this to be possible, we must first be aware of something, of an object, of an existent.

Let us now turn to a series of questions and objections raised by philosophers regarding the fact that not all consciousnesses perceive reality in the same sensory forms. This much is true: Animals have different capacities of sense perception from humans. There are variations in the structure of human sense organs. And if you want to, for pedagogical purposes, go ahead and project a race of Martians who perceive reality in the form of the twitches and buzzes I mentioned earlier. In other words, let us grant the fact that there are many different forms of sense perception possible, depending upon the different types of consciousnesses that exist. Many philosophers think that this poses a grave objection to the senses. What objection? The most common one is this: If two different consciousnesses perceive the same object in different forms, owing to their different means of perception, doesn't this lead to a contradiction? To take the standard example, a man with normal vision looks at a given object and says, "It's red." The color-blind man looks and says, "It's gray." And then the question goes: Isn't this a contradiction? It can't be both red and non-red, can it? So somebody's sense experience must be wrong.

The answer to this objection is: No contradictions between any form of perception and any other are logically possible. When a person says, "This object is red," what is he validly entitled to mean by the statement, bearing in mind everything I've said up until now? He must recognize that he is perceiving the object in a certain form, determined by his specific means of perception. He cannot evade the issue of means and pretend he has some kind of mystic revelation of the object, and that the nature of his specific means of perception is irrelevant. What then can he validly mean by the statement, "It is red"? And the answer is the following: "It is an entity in reality of a specific nature such that when it acts upon *my* senses, I perceive it in the form of red color." And this is true—that is what it is. Now the color-blind man says, "It is gray." What can he validly mean by the statement? "It is an entity in reality of a specific nature such that when it acts upon *my* senses, I perceive it in the form of gray color." And that is true, that is what it is. Both are true statements. Neither is in conflict with nor contradicts the other. And if the Martian comes in and says, "It is twitchy," the same applies to him—it is an entity in reality of a specific nature such that when it acts on *his* senses, he perceives it in the form of twitchiness. In sum, each man and Martian must recognize that his perceptions are perceptions of reality. They are not whims. They are not subjective inventions or distortions. A man has no choice regarding the nature of his perceptions. Each of his perceptions is an inexorably determined effect caused by an object in reality acting on his particular organs of perception. If each perceiver properly defines what he is entitled to claim about the object, there is no contradiction at all. Where is the appearance of a contradiction? Only if one of them thinks, "I have a mystical contact with reality; I perceive without benefit of sense organs; I just (so to speak) wrap my consciousness around the object and see it 'really,' while everyone else is seeing it invalidly." But this attitude represents a crucial error and is what causes the trouble.

Here's another question deriving from the fact of differences of sensory forms: If consciousnesses can perceive in different forms, and they derive all of their conceptual conclusions about reality from their sense experiences, doesn't this mean that the various consciousnesses will come to different conceptual conclusions about the nature of reality? The answer is no. Differences of sensory form do not matter and have no epistemological importance at all. The conceptual conclusions—the *conceptual* conclusions—you will come to about reality will be identical, whether you are human or Martian, possessed of normal vision or color blind, or you name it. Take the normal human being. We perceive reality in terms of color, tactile sensations, and so on. We have these sense data. Now what do we do with them cognitively? They are the *material* of knowledge, but they are not yet conceptual knowledge. What do we do with our sensory data to build the structure of human knowledge?

As you know from *Introduction to Objectivist Epistemology*, we observe similarities and differences in our perceptual materials, and we proceed then to abstract, omit measurements, integrate, form concepts—in other words, rise to the conceptual level, and then proceed conceptually to discover the laws of reality, formulate our scientific theories, and so on. What is the function of the senses in this process? Twofold. One, to give us the basic evidence of existence, of what is. And two, more specifically, to give us the evidence of similarities and differences among existents, which evidence is then the basis permitting us to rise to the conceptual level. Now ask yourself: What difference does it make in what *form* you perceive the initial data from reality, the initial similarities and differences, and thus are enabled to develop to the next cognitive stage? So long as your perceptual form permits you to develop a knowledge of similarities and differences—and every perceptual form does this—the rest is the work of the mind, of the conceptual faculty, not of the senses. And differences of sensory form are irrelevant.

The simplest case in which to see this is the case of the so-called red-green inversion. This is a question that's sometimes asked: How do you know that whenever you perceive what you call "red," the man next to you perceiving the same object *doesn't* have the experience that you have, but has the experience of green of what you would call "red," and vice versa? So, your red and green perceptions are inverted or reversed. Apart from the fact that this is a baseless fantasy, assume for the moment it were true. So what? He still classifies objects precisely as you do. He puts all objects of a certain group together as similar in color, the very ones that you put together. He contrasts this group with the other, and so do you. You both classify and conceptualize in exactly the same way. So what difference does it make that you grasp these two groups initially in different sensory forms? It makes *no* difference. In fact, it wouldn't even come up, since you'd never even learn about such a difference if it existed, because all of your conceptual activities would be the same as his in regard to these objects. You'd call them by the same word (since words are ultimately defined ostensively, by just pointing), and the whole construct in sum means nothing at all. The same principle is true of the Martian with his twitches and buzzes. Whatever similarities he perceives in his twitchy-buzzy form are there, they are real, and his concepts, therefore, reflect objective facts of reality, just as yours do, except that what *you* hold in the form of color, the Martian holds in the form of twitches. What wider significance does this have? None. In this respect, and as an analogy only, you can compare the sense perceptions to a language.

A language is a unified system of signs by which you hold all your concepts. And every language is capable, in principle, of saying whatever there is to be said. There is no contradiction between French and English, for instance. Both languages refer to the same reality, the same facts, both are equally valid. The difference is only in the form of the signs. Well, in an analogous way (and this is just an analogy), you can think of sensory form as a language. You can think of your perceptions of reality as written in—held by you—in a specific sensory form, a specific code by which you hold and have your perceptions of existence. In contrast to language, this is not a manmade code. It is completely determined by the facts of reality and the nature of your consciousness, its means of perception. There is no choice in this case, as there is in the case of which language you will speak. But the relevant point that there can be many such sensory codes possessed by different species is as irrelevant as in the case of language, where there *are* many, because all of them are just so many sensory codes to enable the perceiver to grasp the same ultimate facts of reality. For this reason, all perceivers will agree about the nature of reality, and none will contradict the others.

In actual fact, there are only two differences between the various sensory forms that do—or theoretically might—exist. One, how much information is given directly by the senses of a particular species, and two, what *particular* information is given directly. In other words, some sensory forms are superior, not in terms of validity—all are equally valid—but in terms of the *quantity* of evidence they give the perceiver directly. And some can vary in terms of what *type* of information they give.

Let us consider each of these cases briefly. First is the case of senses that give different amounts of information. Take the case of a totally color-blind man, who will not be able directly to discriminate differences that others can by simple perception. Suppose he perceives everything as the same shade of gray. He therefore gets less direct information about the differences in reality than we do. Does it follow that he then has his own physics? No. He must then learn, by inference from what he *does* perceive directly, that there are facts here outside of his range of direct perception. The study of the phenomenon of light will give him ample evidence of such facts. At the *end* of his cognitive quest, he will end up with the same physics as the normally sighted person. Just as, for instance, we have come to learn of infrared and ultraviolet ranges of the spectrum by inference from what we *do* perceive, even though this information is not given to us directly. Or just as we are able to discover frequencies of sound outside of the human range of hearing, frequencies that dogs, for instance, can hear.

Consider the second point of difference. If you want an example of a completely different kind of information given by a sensory apparatus, let's be bizarre for a moment: Imagine a species of atoms with consciousness. Given the scale in size of an atom, let us say that they perceive the atomic structure of things directly. So, for them, the fact that matter is atomic is not a theory to be reached by inference, as in our case, but that they actually perceive only whirling clouds of particles. You might be tempted to say, "Oh, well then, their form of perception is more valid than ours—they see things *really*." But that would be wholly false. By the very fact that their consciousness (as we are hypothesizing) operates on a submicroscopic range of perception, by that very fact they do not gain from the senses the kind of information *we* get directly. We get information directly—real information about reality—that they don't. We have to infer submicroscopic objects, but they have to infer macroscopic objects like this table or the Empire State Building. Given the scale of their senses, they can't directly take in large-scale physical objects. So, it takes a genius among *their* species to reason to the conclusion that there must be special forces in reality binding these whirling particles together into objects too large to be grasped directly. In effect, the genius in their species is required to reach the conclusions available to the morons in ours, and vice versa. No form of perception can perceive everything directly. Why? Because A is A. Any sensory apparatus is finite, i.e., limited. By virtue of being able to perceive one aspect of reality with one type of sensory apparatus, you cannot then expect to perceive directly some other aspect if it would depend upon a different scope or kind of sensory apparatus.

Therefore, I conclude that all forms of sense perception—*all*—are valid. That no contradictions are possible among them. That all perceivers, regardless of differences in form, regardless of what particular information they get directly from perception and what they must reach by inference, will, if they're rational, end with the same conceptual account of the nature and laws of reality.

Have we finished with the issue of the validity of the senses? Not yet. There is a final crucial question. And that question can best be put: What is the metaphysical status of the sensory qualities we perceive? To make the issue clear in its crudest terms, if you discuss the senses with anybody, you will often be asked, "*Where* are the qualities you perceive or experience?" Where, for instance, is color, warmth, solidity, heat, size, shape, etc.? Are they only in here, in the mind, only subjective? Or are they out there, in reality, intrinsic in things, part of things in themselves? The subjective idealists, like Bishop Berkeley, say that all sensory qualities are subjective; they're all in the mind. The typical naïve realist says that all sensory qualities are intrinsic in the objects in reality. And then the Descartes–Locke axis, which is usually called *critical realism*—they are kind of the Republicans, or compromisers, of sense theory, who say that there are two kinds of sensory qualities—the primaries (extension, including size, shape, etc.), which are intrinsic in things in reality, and the secondaries (color, sounds, smells, tastes, etc.), which are subjective, existing only in the mind.

The point I want to make is that Objectivism disagrees with all three of these theories. Before criticizing them, I want first to explain the Objectivist viewpoint on this issue as defined by Ayn Rand, and which she has communicated to me in a lengthy series of discussions. Then after presenting the Objectivist view, we can turn briefly to criticizing these theories.

The first point to note is that sensation is the product of an *interaction*, a physical, physiological interaction between two entities—the physical object and the relevant sense organs of the perceiver. Each of these entities is essential to the end product, which is the sensation. Without the physical object, there is nothing to perceive, i.e., no sensation. Without the sense organs, there is no means of perception, i.e., no sensation. The process of sensation is a process of physical interaction between two entities in reality.

If you think about this viewpoint, you will see that it immediately invalidates any question that asks, "*Where* is the sensation or the sensory quality?" There is no answer because the question is invalid. You cannot ask such a question about anything that is the product of a physical interaction. Take a simple example having nothing to do with the senses: an Oldsmobile and a Cadillac collide. A collision is a type of interaction between the two cars. Does it make sense for me to ask where is the collision? Is it in the Oldsmobile? Is it in the Cadillac? In the ashtrays? Under the seat covers? All of these answers are senseless because the question is senseless. The collision designates a relationship between the two entities and cannot be declared to be in one as against in the other. In one sense, it is in neither; it is a process in which both partake, but which is not a thing located in either one by itself. In another sense, the collision is in both, because it is a process in which both partake. Or take another example, this time involving the senses. I play a phonograph record of a Viennese operetta and ask you, "Where is the operetta? Is it in the record? Is it in my ears? Is it in my brain? Is it in my mind?" These are clearly foolish questions, because the answer to all of them is yes and no, depending upon the aspect in question. The operetta *is* in the record, in the sense that the record is so structured that when a certain needle moves over its surface in a certain way, a human perceiver will hear the music. But the operetta is not in the record all by itself, as though some kind of submicroscopic soprano were nestling between the grooves, belting out tiny notes to herself. The same is true for the ears—is the operetta in your ears? If so, where—the outer ear, the middle ear, or the inner ear? Is it in your brain? Is it in your mind? Well, in one sense, obviously, no. When you listen to the operetta, you are not humming subvocally to yourself. You are not just imagining or hallucinating but are hearing an event in reality. It is not just "in your mind." In another sense, obviously, the operetta *is* in your mind, in the sense that if no one were conscious, the record could spin forever, and no one would hear any sound. So where is the operetta? In the record? In the air vibrations? In the ear twitches? In the nerve cells? In the brain's gray matter? In the consciousness? The answer is: all of these and/or none. The question is invalid.

The same principle applies in regard to all sense experiences. Since they are the products of a physical interaction between entities and reality, it is a fundamental error to ask, "Where are the sense qualities—in the object out there or in the mind in here?" The answer, as in the previous case, is both or neither. In other words, the question is invalid. What you *can* say is only two incontestable facts: One, without consciousness, no sensation—in other words, no conscious states would exist. States of consciousness are *states* of consciousness and would not exist without consciousness. In this sense, if there were no perceiving beings, there would be no perceptions, no sensations. And the second, just as obvious and just as important, consciousness is consciousness of *something*, of an object in reality, and without the "something," without the object, there would be no sensations or perceptions either. The sensation or perception is not an invention of consciousness but rather a form of awareness of the object.

This brings me to the next point: As a form of awareness, sensation is a cognitive process. By means of this physical interaction of object and sense organ, man gains information, real information, an enormous amount of information, about the facts of reality. A sensation is *not* a subjective effect divorced from the object. It is not a creation of consciousness that has nothing to do with the object. On the contrary, the precise nature of your sensation is a result of the total properties of the object in question and will lead to the ultimate conceptual discoveries of these properties. You can, in this respect, think of man's senses as entities that operate to sum up—that is the key term here—to sum up an enormous range of facts about the object in reality being sensed, to give you a whole body of information, condensed in the form of a single sensation. All of science, in fact, is nothing more than the unraveling of the conceptual identifying of the information summed up implicitly in our sensations. For instance, you open your eyes and see that an ashtray is red. Here, in the form of a single sensation of redness, you receive a vast amount of information about the object, although you must rise to the conceptual scientific level to be able to identify this information. What is it about the object that is indicated by the perception of it as red? That it is an object that absorbs certain kinds of light waves and fails to absorb others, and that to do so, it has to have a certain kind of surface structure, and that this involves a certain kind of physical-chemical constitution on its part, etc. If it's an apple that's red, the red indicates, in addition, that the apple is ripe, i.e., that it's undergone a certain biological development, has reached a certain stage of maturity, with everything this implies. So, far from it being true that redness is merely a subjective state of consciousness, divorced from reality, redness is actually a summary in the form of a single sensation of a whole host of properties possessed by the objects in reality.

It is not necessary that every perceiver in the universe gain this information in the form of a red sensation. There could be, as we have seen, different forms of perception, different kinds of sensation, as a result of the interaction of the object with different kinds of senses. But the cognitive point here remains unaffected by this. Whatever the form of the sensation, our sensations summarize a host of facts about the entity in reality. They are the product of the total entity in reality. And all of science is the unraveling of the information they implicitly contain.

This cognitive role is true of *every* sensation. Consider the case of the tickle. Advocates of the primary-secondary quality distinction love to compare the so-called secondary qualities to the tickle you get from a feather. The tickle, they say, is subjective, and it tells you nothing about the feather; it's merely the subjective effect in you. In fact, this is completely false. The tickle gives you definite information about the feather. It summarizes, in the form of a single sensation, a whole body of information about the properties, the structure, texture, etc., of the feather. If you doubt this, a simple experiment will show it to you—try drawing a variety of different objects across your body, and you will get a different summary from your sensations, revealing to you the nature of radically different objects. Draw a rose thorn across your arm, and you will not get a tickle, but a scratch. Does this indicate something about the nature of the rose thorn in reality, as against the feather? Does it give you information about a real fact of reality? Try drawing the edge of a razor blade across your skin, and you will not get a tickle or a scratch, but a sharp cut. Try drawing a pipette dripping sulfuric acid across your skin, and you will get neither a tickle nor a scratch nor a cut, but a searing agony. In all these cases, you are gaining information about the entity. You are perceiving a whole range of facts about the entity, summed up in the different cases in the form of different sensations. Are the sensations, then, just inventions or products of consciousness, divorced from facts of existence, not indicative of facts of existence? No. They are cognitive elements. And if this is true of a tickle, which is the bastion of the secondary-quality people, it is obviously equally true of all the so-called secondary qualities. They are not independent of the objects that produce them. They are not noncognitive subjective effects on us "in here" but are objective indicators, in a certain form, of what is out there.

From having one sensation, you cannot acquire all of the knowledge implicitly summed up by that sensation. If I touch a baby with the tip of a knife and he feels the pain, he has only a single—and to him inexplicable—sensation, and so far has not learned any facts about the knife. He merely feels the subjective effect of the knife on him. So long as we are on the most primitive level of consciousness—the level of being bombarded with single sensations—so long as we do nothing cognitively *with* them, then to that extent the sensation is simply a feeling in consciousness that generates no information about the entities in reality. What must the baby do to begin unraveling, actually acquiring, the information implicit in his sensation of pain? He must utilize *all* of his senses in relation to the knife—he must look at it and observe its shape, finger it, and observe its sharp edge, pick it up and feel its solidity, drop it and hear the thud it makes on falling, etc., etc. After such a sensory survey appropriately performed, the brain of the baby learns to integrate all these separate sensations into an entity, and the baby rises to the *per*ceptual level, where he is aware not merely of separate sensations, but of integrated percepts—in other words, of entities. At this stage, he is in a position to grasp at least part of the information initially implicit in the sensation of pain. The knife causes him pain, and he can grasp it because it is solid and sharp, as against the feather that is very different in texture and structure.

At this point, on a primitive level, by means of having integrated his sensations into an entity, the baby can begin to unravel the information given by his separate sensations and grasp what about the entity caused those sensations. A separate sensation by itself does not directly give him information about the object. By itself, it is a feeling in consciousness. But when he has integrated it with all the rest of the sensory data from the object, the individual rises to the level where he can grasp entities, and thus be in a position to begin extracting from his sensations the information they contain implicitly. Those who declare as a formal theory in epistemology that sensations are nothing but subjective feelings, subjective effects that are devoid of information about reality, are thus ascribing to mankind as a whole the cognitive primitiveness of a newborn baby. Their epistemological model of man is: "He possesses only the knowledge available to a newborn infant who has not yet risen to the perceptual level." The infant, they declare, gets only subjective effects from his sensations, no information about reality. Therefore, neither does the adult, who has integrated his sensations and reached the perceptual level.

Beyond the perceptual level is the conceptual, the distinctively *human* level, the level on which scientific explanation becomes possible. Once *that* level is reached, man can begin to define explicitly the information about the knife implicit in his sensations, and only partly accessible even on the perceptual level. Now he can enter into an analysis of the knife's structure and density and the nature of the body's receptors and nerves, and so on and so on—in other words, the kind of analysis required fully to grasp the causes of the sensation of pain, the facts about the knife, which make it a source of pain as against a feather. But the conceptual level, as you know, is a development from the perceptual, which is in turn an integration of the sensational stage. The point is that the information reached explicitly on the conceptual level was there in the sensational stage, implicitly contained and summed up in our sensations. If it were *not* there, we could never have risen to the conceptual level. So much for the idea that the so-called secondary qualities are nothing but subjective sensory effects in the mind, devoid of cognitive significance in relation to objects.

Having said all this, have we now satisfied the advocates of the so-called secondary qualities? Have we now satisfied them that color, sound, etc., are real and not subjective? You might think so, but the answer is still no. At this point they will argue as follows: Let us take red as the example of all such so-called secondary sense qualities. Red, they will say, is not an intrinsic quality of things in themselves. You yourself admit that red is an effect, an effect on human consciousness, of what exists out there in reality. So redness, they conclude, is not a quality of things in themselves but merely an effect produced by more basic factors in reality (light waves and so on) operating on your sense organs. That's the argument we want to turn to.

Let's follow the implications of this argument as Ayn Rand pointed them out to me. Red is declared to be not an attribute of things in themselves, because it is not a causal primary, in other words, an irreducible fact without any deeper cause underlying it. Because our perception of red has a cause, a cause involving both the object in reality and our sense organs, for that reason redness is disbarred from the status of a real attribute of things in themselves. So, by this standard, the only facts that qualify as attributes of things in themselves are causal primaries, in other words, attributes which cannot be explained by reference to anything more fundamental, attributes that are irreducible, ultimate facts of reality, which are not in any way the product of deeper causes. If being a causal primary in this sense is the standard of being "really real," how are we to tell what is a causal primary and what is not? At one point in human knowledge, people *did* think redness was a causal primary. They thought that redness was an intrinsic property of things without any underlying cause. And then it was discovered that light waves underlie red, and that red is an effect of light waves on our sense organ. Are light waves causal primaries? Are they irreducible facts of reality without deeper explanation? Obviously not. According to the latest theory, light waves themselves are effects, expressions, of various energy and/or particle combinations. Is energy, subatomic particles, a causal primary? The point is, how would you know? Only one way: You would have to know every attribute of matter, every constituent of physical reality, in order to be able to say, "I have surveyed the totality; I know everything there is to know about the physical world, and thus, I see that X (whatever it is) is the ultimate ingredient, the basic cause of everything else, the real constituent out of which everything else is made and which everything else reflects." You would have to be omniscient, literally omniscient, to grasp that this X is the ultimate unit and cause of every other phenomenon in reality. To declare that only causal primaries qualify as real attributes of reality is to declare that man can never claim any of his knowledge as knowledge of reality—in other words, as knowledge—until he is omniscient. Which means, he can know nothing until he knows everything. If so, how is he supposed to get to the stage of knowing everything? To deny redness the status of reality on the grounds that it is an effect of deeper causes, to denounce man's senses because they only provide us with effects, is to declare, "I won't accept the validity of the senses unless what they give us are the causal primaries of reality, the ultimate elements or attributes which underlie everything else, the irreducible building blocks of the universe. I demand that the senses give me ultimate causes, not effects. And since they give me effects, they are invalid." That's the meaning of the claim.

This is a classic example of what Ayn Rand calls the *fallacy of rewriting reality*. The fact is, reality does not give us by perception the ultimate causal primaries of existence. It gives us effects, qualities that are real, but which are the products of complex underlying causes acting on our senses, causes which modern science is nowhere yet near unraveling completely. By what logical right does an individual stamp his foot in a petulant state and declare, "If *I* had created reality, we would have been given the ultimate causes by direct perception; since we're not given them and only effects, our senses are no good and knowledge is impossible and I'm leaving"? This is obviously a grotesque departure from reality and a grotesque standard by which to judge the senses. But let us follow this construct up for a few minutes because it will be clarifying in regard to several points.

To begin with, if redness is an effect and, therefore, not intrinsic in things in themselves, this obviously applies to *anything* that can be causally explained in like manner. It applies to sound, temperature, texture, etc. What about extension itself, that bastion of the Cartesians and the Lockeans? Is extension a causal primary? Is three-dimensional extension in space—with its correlates of size, shape, solidity, etc.—a causal primary in the sense I earlier defined? At our present state of knowledge, we cannot say. There may very well be deeper causes in reality, ultimate factors making up reality, which take on the form of extended objects when perceived by man, just as they take on the form of red, green, hot, cold, etc., objects. As Bishop Berkeley pointed out—and in this one respect he is correct—there is no presently known standard by which to distinguish metaphysically between the status of the extension qualities and the colors, smells, etc. They are all in the same metaphysical boat. I want to be clear here—I do not mean to imply that I know that extension is *not* a causal primary. The point is that you would have to be omniscient to know one way or the other. At the present stage of human knowledge, it is entirely arbitrary to draw a line and declare that red is an effect, but extension is irreducible and intrinsic in reality.

So, I want to take a bold leap for pedagogical purposes. Let us assume that extension—and that means, therefore, that size and shape and so on—is an effect, in the same manner as red, green, hot, cold, etc. Let us assume that the entire world of matter as we perceive it is an effect, an effect produced by the operation on our sensory apparatus of the ultimate causal primaries which make up reality in itself.

Let us assume that we have discovered the actual causal primaries in reality, the ultimate elements of things in themselves, the basic irreducible building blocks of reality in itself, which underlie and give rise to everything that we perceive, giving rise to the entire physical world as we know it. What these ultimate primaries are, I do not pretend to know. For purposes of this construct, let us call them "puffs of meta-energy." I deliberately choose something esoteric and undefined without pretending to know what it means. Let us assume, in sum, that we have reached omniscience, penetrated to the core of reality in itself, and discovered that things in themselves are puffs of meta-energy, and that what we perceive as a material world of three-dimensional objects—with color, shape, size, etc.—is all an effect on us of various combinations of energy puffs acting on our means of perception. So, things in themselves are really combinations of various energy puffs. Suppose now this whole construct were true. The crucial question is: What would it prove about the validity of the senses or the status of the sensory qualities we perceive? And the answer is: nothing of any epistemological significance whatever. The point here is this: If everything is made of energy puffs in various combinations, so are human beings. And it is still an iron, inescapable fact of reality that when the energy puffs that comprise external reality interact with the energy puffs that comprise human beings, when all of these puffs enter into all of the combinations that they enter into, the inexorable result is the material world as we perceive it with all of the kinds of entities and qualities it possesses. This is a fact, a fact of reality, not a creation of consciousness. It is a fact that when such and such energy puffs unite in such and such a combination with other ones, the result is a man with all of his properties, or an orange, or a buffalo, or a planet, or a feather, etc. So, whenever we perceive one of these material objects, we are perceiving reality. In other words, energy puffs in a certain combination. And every sense perception gives us real information about that particular combination of energy puffs. Does it mean that extension, size, shape, color, etc., are unreal just because they are effects of the energy puffs in certain combinations? Certainly not. The exact opposite is true—if they are effects of the energy puffs, by that very fact they are real, real products of the real puffs that make up reality. We did not invent the puffs. We did not invent their capacity to unite into forms that bring about a material extended world. We did not create the physical world by any subjective act of our consciousness. It is a metaphysical fact of reality that certain puffs, in certain combinations, produce, when perceived by a human being, an extended physical world, and that every sense perception we have gives us information about the puff combinations that exist. It is an intrinsic fact of things in themselves that X puffs combined with Y puffs combined with Z puffs—man's senses—yield solid, three-dimensional, extended objects.

On this account, if we pursue it, the whole material world would be an effect, an effect of things in themselves acting on the puffs that make us up and constitute our sensory apparatus. But the material world would be an effect—a *real* effect—and therefore, a real fact. You do not deny the reality of something by explaining it. You do not make something subjective by giving a causal explanation of it. You do not detach it from reality by showing that something in reality produced it. The exact opposite is true. If you have shown that the cause of something exists *in reality*—if you have shown that reality itself produced certain facts—then you have given the most solid metaphysical foundation there is to those facts. You have shown that they are inherent in metaphysical reality itself. If the whole construct I have given you were true, it would change nothing about the validity of the senses, or the reality status of the sensory qualities we perceive. In this manner, *all* of the sensory qualities we perceive are inherent in reality, in things in themselves. They are real. They are not human inventions or subjective products of consciousness.

Now you can see why Objectivism rejects the primary-secondary quality distinction. It is not true that extension is really out there intrinsically, and color and the rest are really just subjective effects on us. *All* of the qualities we perceive are facts of independent reality as perceived by human consciousness. There is no basis whatever to divide the properties we perceive into the extension-connected one, and the colors, sounds, textures, etc. There is no warrant for claiming two kinds of sensory properties, those that belong to the object and those that are created by consciousness. The actual facts are: There are objects in independent reality that have various attributes in themselves. Human beings have the faculty of consciousness and perceive those objects by certain means, and thus, in certain forms, forms inexorably dictated and determined by the nature of the objects in themselves, part of which includes the nature of man's sensory apparatus.

The only *valid* distinction you can make in this context is between the primary causes in reality—the energy puffs in my construct—and the derivative manifestations of those puffs (all of their expressions, effects, results). You can distinguish between cause and effect in this way. But that is not the distinction between primary and secondary qualities as the traditional philosophers make it. Here you have to be precise about the meaning of terms. If the phrase "primary quality" means "quality intrinsic in reality"—in other words, quality that is a real fact, as against a subjective product of consciousness—then, as we have seen, *all* the qualities we perceive are facts, *all* are real, *all* are primary, red and green as much as size and shape. On the other hand, if by "primary quality" you mean "exists in the objects that are irreducible primaries in reality, the objects in themselves apart from their effects, combinations and interactions," then *none* of the qualities we perceive are primary in that sense. In either event, the traditional primary-secondary quality distinction collapses. There is no basis to assume that the causal primaries in reality possess in themselves the exact same form as our sense data, since we know that our sense data are effects and that we perceive by certain means. But by the same token, you cannot pronounce our sense data as invalid on this ground. It is only by *starting* from our sense data that we can ultimately, conceptually, unravel the information they contain, and finally end up with a conceptual account of the energy puffs or whatever it is we reach at the summit of the cognitive quest.

You can see also why Objectivism denies not only Bishop Berkeley's subjective idealism—or the whole primary-secondary quality viewpoint—but also naïve realism. What the naïve realist does is to treat all the qualities we perceive as causal primaries, intrinsic in objects, independent of man's form of perception. He doesn't explain the facts of man's perception. He takes no account of the fact that men perceive in a certain form, that consciousness requires *means* of consciousness, that the properties we perceive are the product of an interaction between the objects in reality and our sensory apparatus. And as a result, as soon as the naïve realist confronts the fact of two perceivers perceiving the same object in different forms—for instance, the color-blind versus the normal-sighted person—the naïve realist is lost and falls back to the claim that one of their senses must be deceptive. And as soon as science offers the causal explanation of some quality that we perceive, the naïve realist is also lost, and feels that it threatens the reality of the quality he perceives. In short, naïve realism is properly named—it is naïve. Its basic intention—to preserve the validity of human consciousness—is correct. If you want to put it this way, its heart is in the right place. But it has no means to implement or defend this intention or to support or justify its claim that man's senses reveal reality. Objectivism is not naïve realism. It is not so-called critical realism. It is not subjective idealism. It is Objectivism.

I hope that after this lengthy discussion, the issues involved in this problem are now clear to you. I want to note in conclusion that several of my formulations on this issue are new in this lecture, and I believe they are clearer than formulations I have given on the issue of the senses in the past, where I believe that my statements in several cases may have been misleading. So, I would like to state for the record that the points I have made hereby supersede any other formulations of mine that you may hear if you hear older tapes of mine dealing with the subject of the senses, and that specifically includes my lecture on Objectivism in the Modern Philosophy course, which is the companion to this one.

The Problem of the Borderline Case

Let us now turn to the problem of the borderline case, which is one of the chief arguments put forth by modern philosophers to defend their nominalist theory of universals. A full answer to this question would require that I offer you a presentation of the Objectivist theory of concepts, and contrast it to the Platonist, Aristotelian, and nominalist theories. I will not attempt such a presentation now. I'm assuming that you have already read and understood *Introduction to Objectivist Epistemology*, that you understand the Objectivist view of the nature and formation of concepts (because there is a limit to what can be done in three hours), and above all, of why concepts are neither intrinsic (in the Platonist or Aristotelian manner) or subjective (in the nominalist manner) but, rather, objective. If you understand this much, you will not have any difficulty with the borderline-case question, and indeed, that issue is referred to in Miss Rand's book.

The borderline-case argument is one of the basic arguments used by nominalists to justify their claim that there is no objective method to determine where to draw the lines when one is grouping concretes together in the process of concept formation. A typical example of the argument, for instance, as we discussed in the course, is: Where do you draw the line between red and orange? Are the intermediate shades red or orange, or neither? Isn't any decision arbitrary and subjective? What has reality to say on this question? Or to give you a new example: Someone invents an object that is just like a table in all respects—it's a manufactured object, it has a flat, level surface for holding other objects—but it attaches to the ceiling and hangs from it by chains. And then the nominalist asks you, "Well, is it a table or not?" How would you decide? In some respects, it's very much like tables as we originally defined them—"manufactured objects, flat, level surface with supports to hold other objects," and so on, but in certain obvious ways, it's different. How different can it be from our original conception of tables and still qualify? Where do you draw the line? Isn't it, ask the nominalists, all arbitrary and subjective? There are endless examples of this sort. Let us first pose and answer the question in general terms, and then apply the answer to these examples.

The problem in its most general form may be posed as follows: We classify concretes on the basis of similarities and differences, but the concretes in a given class will differ in various ways from each other and will be similar in various ways to concretes in other classes. By what standard, then, do we draw the line? Or, as it's more usually put, we have formed some class, some concept, on the basis of similarities that we have detected among a given set of concretes, and we have defined the concept accordingly. Then we discover a new concrete that is in some respects like the members of the original class, and in some respects different. How do we decide what to do with this new concrete? Should we put it in the original class, which may involve broadening and redefining the original class, or should we form a new concept for the new concrete to distinguish it from the concretes already conceptualized, or is there another alternative still, and if so, what is it?

The general answer is determined by the function of concept formation in human knowledge. Concepts, according to Objectivism, are integrations of percepts. They enable us to isolate a set of concretes, which we can then treat as a unit for specialized study. Whether or not to form a new concept, therefore, to encompass some newly encountered concrete, depends upon the degree, or extent, of the differences separating the new concretes from the others we know, i.e., it depends upon whether the differences in question are fundamental. When the differences are significant or fundamental enough so that it is no longer practicable to study the new concretes in terms of one's concepts to date, and when the phenomenon is widespread enough so that one has to deal with it, then one coins a new concept.

Observe that there is no way of specifying in numerical terms how great a difference qualifies as significant or fundamental. In this respect, there is an optional element in the formation of new concepts. In some cases, the formation of a new concept to cover a newly discovered concrete is mandatory. In other cases, it is invalid and impermissible to form a new concept. And in other cases, it is optional. Now I want to illustrate for you these three types of situations.

First of all, the mandatory. I ask you to recall Miss Rand's point that definitions are contextual. The function of a definition is to distinguish, in terms of fundamentals, the existents in a certain class from all others known at a given stage of knowledge. Definitions depend upon the context of knowledge, because the characteristics that serve to differentiate one group of concretes from the rest depend in part on the nature of the concretes and in part on the context of one's knowledge. Recall Miss Rand's example of the child's initial implicit definition of "man" as "a thing that moves and makes sounds," the child not yet having discovered and discriminated various animals, automobiles, etc. At this point the child grasps, let us say, only the distinction between inert and silent objects (like chairs and tables) and the people around him. He may select "moving and making sounds" as the characteristic differentiating men from all the other objects he knows. Within the context of his knowledge, he has successfully isolated men from the rest of what is known to him. To that extent, his definition is correct—it is contextually valid.

Now let's foreshorten a complex process to get back to the borderline case from this takeoff point. Let's assume that the child discovers locomotives and landslides. At this point it is mandatory for him to form a new concept (actually, concepts) to cover the new phenomena, and mandatory to redefine "man" so as to keep that concept separated from his new discoveries. If he tried not to form a new concept—to include locomotives, landslides, and men under one concept with one name, to treat them as a unit in his further dealings with and study of them—he would find himself defeated in his attempts to expand his knowledge, defeated by virtue of the fact of there being just too many profound differences in reality among the things he is attempting to deal with as a single class. He would find that some "men" talk, while others hiss and rumble, that some "men" walk on legs, while others role on wheels. In sum, their characteristics, structure, components, behavior, are radically different, and thus virtually nothing learned about some "men" would be applicable to others. To keep track of his knowledge it would be necessary, in spite of himself, to distinguish the talking men from the rolling men, and so on. Which means that he would be forced, if he is rational, to form separate concepts for the entities he had lumped together. In this kind of case, the differences are too fundamental and far-reaching. And this is the type of case in which it is mandatory to form new concepts to cover a newly encountered concrete.

Now look at the impermissible case. Start again with the child in the above example, with the same initial definition of "man" as "a thing that moves and makes sounds," and assume that he has so far seen only white men, and now encounters Blacks for the first time, and decides to erect a new class so that there are now "men" and "Blacks" as two separate concepts.

Here is the opposite error: taking an insignificant difference as the basis for forming a distinct concept. And again, the child would find that the facts of reality would force him to alter his concepts here, because the color in this case affects virtually nothing about the entities involved. It is a nonsignificant, nonfundamental characteristic. Whether a given shade of color is present or absent, hosts of characteristics will remain similar in the two allegedly different classes he has formed. If he sets out to study men and then Blacks, he will find that virtually *everything* that he learns about the one—in anatomy, psychology, physiology, etc., etc.—is true also of the other, so that the distinction he has erected is, in fact, useless in enabling him to organize his field of knowledge. This does not mean that one cannot subdivide the concept "man" according to various special characteristics, by means of specific concepts, such as "Black," "Caucasian," etc. It *does* mean, however, that such concepts must be recognized as *subdivisions* of one broader class, and that as such, they all share crucial characteristics that require being conceptualized together into one unit, namely, the concept "man."

Turn now to the optional case. Imagine finally that having formed a given concept, you encounter a concrete that is neither crucially different (the way locomotives and landslides are from men) nor crucially similar (the way black and white men are), but somewhere in between. And here we can use the hanging table as an example. In this type of case, precisely because the nature of the concrete neither *demands* a concept, nor *forbids* one, one's procedure is optional. You have three choices in this specific type of case: (1) Since its purpose and general structure are the same as for tables, except for its being attached to the ceiling rather than the floor, you might decide to include it under the class of "tables," which will then require an appropriate alteration in your initial definition of "table," on the usual pattern of contextual redefinition. And if necessary, you may then decide to subdivide "tables" into two species—"floor tables" and "ceiling tables"—and even give separate names to the two types. That's one possibility. (2) Since its construction will involve a number of *differences* from tables—for instance, you can't normally use this hanging table outdoors, it requires some specific means of being attached to the ceiling, and it's not easily movable—you may decide to form a new concept to designate this type of entity, treating it thus as a concept on a level with tables, rather than as a type of table. That's a second possibility. (3) You need do neither of these things. You need not have any one concept to designate such an entity. You need not either subsume it under the old concept nor make up a new one, but merely identify its status as intermediate by means of a *descriptive phrase*—"entity like tables in such and such a way, and unlike them in such and such a way."

Please note this fact: It is not the case that every phenomenon must ultimately be subsumable under one concept. There are phenomena that can be handled cognitively, fully adequately, by a description formulated in terms of a number of other concepts, phenomena that do not require the formation of a single concept to cover them, not now or ever. For shorthand, I will refer to this as the *descriptive handling* of certain concretes, as distinct from the *conceptual handling* of them. That description will be in terms of concepts already formed. The point of the distinction is only that no *single* concept need be formed to handle such phenomena. In other words, we do not form a single concept, a single word, for everything in the universe. All sorts of phenomena are handled descriptively in terms of a number of other concepts. Indeed, all conversation and writing are descriptive in this present sense. For instance, if I say, "It is a beautiful winter evening; the air is crisp and the sun is setting with a golden glow," I have used a whole series of concepts—"beautiful," "winter," "evening," "sun," "glow," etc.—to identify and communicate a certain phenomenon. There is no *single* concept to stand for "beautiful winter evenings with crisp air and golden sunsets," nor is there any *need* for such a single concept. The descriptive handling serves all cognitive purposes perfectly satisfactorily. When you have a case such as the "hanging table," therefore, there is nothing to say that you must have one concept to identify it, either an old one or a new one specifically formed for it. It is optional in such a case whether to handle it conceptually or descriptively.

In cases like the hanging table, Objectivism recognizes a number of optional alternatives—including the possibility of descriptive handling. This approach clearly differentiates Objectivism from the traditional realists like Plato and like Aristotle. On the traditional realist view of universals, whether Platonist or Aristotelian, essences are intrinsic in things: Each entity has an essence intrinsic to it, and as we've seen in this course—an essence apart from any relation to man's knowledge or man's mode of cognition. So on the traditional view, "tablehood," or "tableness," is a phenomenon that inhabits all tables intrinsically—it's present in all tables, absent in everything else, and given any concrete it either has the essence in itself or it doesn't have the essence in itself. And consequently, there can be no options—no option, for instance, in the case of the hanging table; either it has the intrinsic essence of tableness in it, in which case it *must* be subsumed under the concept "table," or it *doesn't* have it but has instead a *different* intrinsic essence, in which case it must be subsumed under some single *new* concept naming that essence. In either case, there can be no option and no possibility of descriptive handling. Consequently, Platonists and Aristotelians alike find the borderline case examples a serious embarrassment, because they have no means of deciding, in such cases, which entities have which intrinsic essences. And ultimately, if you press them far enough, they have to rely on "intuition." Which means that their theory ends up being subjective in spite of themselves. It is the defenders of intrinsic essences who find the borderline-case problem difficult, if not impossible, to answer.

But the Objectivist theory is that essences are *objective*, not intrinsic, and therefore, there is no such problem. Concepts, according to Objectivism, are human forms of cognition, forms of organizing our perceptual material for the sake of enabling us to expand our knowledge beyond the perceptual level. Essences, according to Objectivism, are characteristics that are contextually determined and serve to differentiate our concepts. There is nothing in this position to say that *every* concrete must at some point be separately conceptualized. There may be a great many concretes for which there is no cognitive point in handling with a single concept. There may be concretes that are not so fundamentally similar to some earlier-conceptualized group that it's mandatory to subsume them under an old concept. And these concretes may not be sufficiently widespread, and/or of sufficient cognitive importance, for us to have to conceptualize them separately at all. If you then ask me, "But what class do such concretes fall into, what is their essence?," the answer is: We have not *formed* a class for them—in the sense of a single concept with its own definition and essential characteristics—and there's no need to. They can be handled descriptively by identifying their relations to the nearest relevant classes. Again, granted that essences are not intrinsic, it is not the case that there must be a single concept to cover every concrete we encounter. There are certain cases where the procedure is optional—where you can either subsume a phenomenon under an old concept, or form a new one, or merely handle the phenomenon descriptively.

The question comes up, "Doesn't the existence of optional cases mean that concept formation in these cases is subjective and arbitrary?" To which the answer is, no, it does not. Note the following facts here. To begin with, the cases where it's optional are dictated by the facts. It is the actual nature of the concretes in question that determines that it is optional how to treat them in the particular case. If you are to have an option whether or not to include it under an earlier-formed concept, a new concrete must be neither crucially different nor crucially similar to the concretes already encountered. And if it is crucially different, one *cannot* include it under the old concept, and if it is crucially similar, one *must* so include it. Note also this: Precisely because these borderline optional concretes are not in fact crucially similar to or different from those already known, the alternative modes of handling the new concretes are *all* correct, and it makes no difference which policy is adopted in a particular case. For instance, if you put the hanging tables into the old class of "tables," this would imply that there are some significant similarities between the hangers and the tables. And that's true; there are. Or if you form a new concept for the hangers, this would imply that there are some significant differences from the tables. And this is true; there are. Or if you do neither and form no single concept for them, handling them merely in a descriptive phrase, this would imply that neither the similarities nor the differences are overriding. And this is also true. Consequently, all three choices are in accordance with fact, none contradicts the others, and in sum, there is no foothold for subjectivism to enter on this point.

You can note in this connection that different languages often manifest the fact that there is an optional area in concept formation, and yet this in no way implies subjectivism or contradiction from one language to another. Most key words are translatable in a single word from one language to another. But most languages have certain words that are *not* translatable by one word in other tongues. These words are still translatable, but, in another language, the translation may take a phrase or even more to communicate the phenomenon identified in the first language by one concept, in one word. This is a case where one language handles *con*ceptually what another handles descriptively. And you see that neither language is wrong—neither contradicts the other—each is translatable into the other. The principle is the same when applied to borderline-case examples. No one option in those cases contradicts the others, each is legitimate and valid, and there is nothing in this to warrant a subjectivist conclusion.

Let me give you an analogy: Suppose you have a stack of books to classify on library shelves. The intrinsicist would say: "The correct order of these books on the shelf is dictated exclusively by the intrinsic character of the books. For instance, I intuit that they must be alphabetized by author." And if you say to him, "Well, couldn't it be by subject or title?," his answer is only, "No, I've had the intuition, the intrinsic factor here is X, that's what must dictate the organization." Then the nominalist (the subjectivist) comes in, and his viewpoint is that *any* method of arranging them is as good as any other. Decide by your arbitrary whim or take a poll of society. Put the red books on one shelf and stick in some tomatoes if you want to. Put the smooth books in front with Kleenex and so on. The

Objectivist *ob*jective approach, in contrast—saying that essences are neither intrinsic nor subjective—holds that you would have to keep in mind two things: the purpose of the classification, and the nature of the material to be classified. In other words, the conscious purpose and the facts. And given these, certain arrangements will be nonsensical and invalid. But in certain circumstances there may be an option—perhaps in a given case the purpose is served equally if it's alphabetized by author or by title. You see the analogy. The cognitive purpose of conceptualization *and* the factual nature of the concretes in question jointly determine when to conceptualize and when there is an area of optionality.

Let's apply this discussion to the example of orange and red. Here we are dealing with a literal continuum, so no exact cut-off point is dictated by reality as the line of demarcation. Consequently, a certain range is left optional. If you decide for some purpose to draw a line, then within certain limits, it would make no cognitive difference where the line was drawn. It is a fact of reality that the exact point makes no difference and that there is a limited range where it's optional. Notice, however, that no specific line *needs* to be drawn. You can very well handle the intermediate shades descriptively, without trying to apportion them either to red or to orange. You can merely describe "those transitional stages intermediate between red and orange, progressing from a very reddish orange to a very orangey red." Or you could, as is done by painters, give every discriminable shade a separate, distinct name, i.e., form a separate concept for every distinguishable shade. All such options exist, and, on the grounds we've already discussed, all would be valid, none would contradict the others, none implies subjectivism in concept formation.

So to sum up the borderline-case issue: The borderline case puzzles and confuses people because they implicitly believe that essences are intrinsic, and consequently, they feel there should not be any optional area in concept formation. Then when they find that in certain specific cases there *is* an option, they swing over to the nominalist axis and are ripe for the subjectivist plucking. The truth is that essences are objective. This accounts for the fact of optional cases without implying any form of subjectivism. On this issue, as on so many others, the false dichotomy of intrinsic versus subjective has wreaked its usual havoc and confusion. So much for borderline cases and for nominalism, at least for this lecture.

The Error of the Method of Cartesian Doubt

In conclusion, let us turn briefly to Descartes and the error of the method of Cartesian doubt. In an alleged quest for certainty, Descartes reasoned, "To establish certainty, I must first refute the possibility that I am in error." He observes that people commit errors—they go insane, they mistake their dreams for reality, they misinterpret sensory evidence, they commit fallacies, etc.—so, he thinks: "How can I be sure of anything, even of 'Two plus three equals five'? How do I know I am not committing an error in a given case, no matter how clear and distinct it seems to me? How do I know that a demon is not deceiving me, so that truth is forever beyond my grasp?"

In essence, what is his procedure? He takes the fact of human errors—in other words, of human fallibility—and uses it to conclude that it is therefore impossible for man to be certain of any of his knowledge. The essence of the argument implicit in Cartesian doubt is this: To be certain means you *can't* be wrong, to be fallible means you *can* be wrong, and therefore a fallible being can never attain certainty.

Descartes himself, as we have seen, thought that he escaped this problem through the *Cogito*, and that "I think, therefore, I am" was completely certain. But as we have also seen, the *Cogito* does not escape the demon if the demon exists. If Descartes's argument invalidating human cognition is correct, it invalidates the *Cogito* along with everything else. It invalidates human consciousness across the board. Nothing whatever escapes this.

So, what is wrong with Descartes's approach? Out of all the countless fallacies one could mention, I'm going to confine myself to a few brief points. To begin with, I can't resist pointing out to you the stolen concepts used by Descartes. He argues, "People have been in error; therefore, man can never know if or when he is right on some question." The obvious question is: If man can never know what is right, how could he ever know that he was or ever had been in error, that he had ever been deceived or made a mistake? How could he ever form such a concept as "error" if deprived of any knowledge of what is correct? "Error" means "departure from truth." If truth is unknowable, you could never form the concept of a departure from it. Inherent in calling an idea mistaken is some knowledge of what is true, by reference to which one condemns a given idea as false. So, for instance, a man says to you, "Two plus three equals seven"—you can say that it isn't true. Why not? Because you know in this case that two plus three is five, and by reference to this, you condemn as false, the claim that it's seven. But if truth were not knowable to us—if we couldn't know what two and three *is*—how would we ever be in a position to say about any answer, "It's not correct"? Now, you might say, "Well, couldn't you know that a given answer was false because it's inherently self-contradictory, even if you didn't know the truth?" You're not escaping the point, because you're still referring to your knowledge of the truth—in this case, of your knowledge of the truth of the laws of logic. If you literally couldn't know truth at all, as Descartes's argument implies, you couldn't even say that a contradiction is an error. The very process of classifying something as an error presupposes that you have discovered the truth in some respect on that question, the truth by reference to which you see that the old belief was mistaken. Deprive man of knowledge of the truth, and you deprive him of the concept of non-truth and the ability to recognize it. So, Descartes's position here is the exact reverse of the correct one. He uses errors to undercut the possibility of knowledge of the truth, whereas, in fact, it is only one's knowledge of truth that enables one to form the concept of "error" and to recognize specific errors when they are committed. He holds that man is fallible and can err, and therefore truth is unattainable. The fact is, to be able to identify the existence of errors logically presupposes that man is able to know the truth.

What went wrong, then, with Descartes's argument? It takes off from the premise that man is fallible. So, let us ask, what is the actual meaning of saying man is fallible? It means only one thing—man is not *automatically* right (underscore that word). He is not built in such a way that error is impossible to him by his nature no matter how he uses his consciousness. He is not built in such a way that the mere presence of an idea in his consciousness requires that that idea be true. That man is fallible doesn't in the least imply that his ideas can't be right, or that he can't know for certain they *are* right under the appropriate circumstances. That man is fallible means merely that you can't rely on the *mere* presence of an idea in your mind as the guarantee of truth. You must *do* something with an idea before you can know it's right.

What must you do? Well, man must form his conclusions by a specific method, a method that will distinguish true ideas from false ones. He must subject his ideas to a test designed to distinguish which ideas are correct and which incorrect. He must, in a word, *validate* his conclusions. This and this alone is what is involved in man being a fallible being. If he were infallible—if error was a metaphysical impossibility to human consciousness—we would not need any test to distinguish true ideas from false ones. There couldn't *be* any false ones. We would not need to go through any process of validating our ideas. You could form them in any old way that you wanted because erroneous ideas couldn't enter your consciousness. But since man is *not* constitutionally infallible, his responsibility before endorsing any conclusion is to ensure that he has performed a process of validating it. "Fallibility" does not mean that man can never know what is true. It means he cannot know what is true just because an idea is in his head. Again, to know it is true, he must validate it by a certain method.

What is the method of validating human ideas? That is the subject matter of an entire science, namely epistemology. *The* question of epistemology is: "By what method does man validate his ideas and therefore claim them as knowledge?" Here I'm going to remind you of what you already know on this question. In essence, the process of validation is: Man must ground his knowledge on the direct evidence of the senses (that's the foundation), and he must then scrupulously derive all of his conceptual conclusions from the initial sensory evidence, guided step by step by a process of logic, of logical inference, going back ultimately to the facts directly accessible to sense perception. Logical inference, in conceptual form, based on sense perception—this is man's method of validating conclusions. Of course, this is just a summary sentence, and you must not oversimplify here. For the present, however, I'm assuming that you understand that the process of validation in particular cases can be extraordinarily complex. When I speak of validating an idea by using logic or reason, I assume you understand that the application of this process can involve a complexity of factors, and you don't assume that some one simple argument will prove any conclusion on anything out of context.

What then is the answer to the problem of how man, a fallible being, can achieve knowledge? The answer is: He can achieve knowledge by validating his conclusions by a process of reason and logic. When he has used reason and logic on some idea, he is no longer relying on the mere fact that the idea occurred to him. Hence, the fact that his consciousness is not automatically infallible is now irrelevant, irrelevant to his ability to achieve certainty. He has now demonstrated that his idea is true, and hence he can be certain of it.

I'll give you a simple example: A child is adding up the same figures, 2 and 3. Before he is able to reason and see the proof, you merely ask him, "How much is two and three?"; any old number could have occurred to him, and he could very well be wrong. That's what's meant by saying man is fallible—he's capable of error. But now assume he's studied arithmetic, and he's defined the terms and understood the proof, understands logic, and sees how if two and three were anything other than five, that would be a contradiction. At this point when he says two and three are five, he has obliterated the earlier possibility of his being wrong on this question, because he has now taken rational steps to validate his answer and now he, on this question, can no longer be in error.

So, what the Cartesian approach amounts to is the following gross *non sequitur*: Because man can't be certain *apart* from using a validating process on his ideas, he can't be certain even when he *has* used a validating process. We can put the Cartesian approach another way. It amounts to saying: It is possible for man metaphysically to be in error; therefore, it is possible for each and every man—including the men who have scrupulously used reason and logic on some questions—to be in error on every question. This is clearly a gross *non sequitur*. When you say that error is possible to man, you mean it is possible *under certain conditions*, namely, assuming a man hasn't employed the appropriate validating process. It does not follow that error is possible under *all* conditions, including the conditions that enable a man to know that he is right. Under those conditions, he can know he is right.

I want to give you a different example to illustrate the general point about claiming that something is possible, because the error hinges on the idea, "But it's *possible* you're wrong, isn't it?" So, consider this example: We know that it's possible for a human being to run the mile in under four minutes. It's possible because it's been done repeatedly. And we know that it is possible for a human being to be pregnant—it happens all the time. Suppose now I go over to an elderly crippled gentleman, rocking in his wheelchair and I say: "Maybe you'll give birth to a child next week after you finish running the mile to the hospital in 3.7 minutes. After all, you're a human being, and these things are possible to human beings." If I said that, the elderly gentleman would have every right to assume I had lost my mind. If he deigned to answer me at all, he would reply, "What is possible to human beings in general, as a species, and in some circumstances, is not necessarily possible to each individual human being in every specific set of circumstances." The same principle is applicable on the issue of error and is no less fantastic when committed on that issue. If you want to use Descartes's argument, you might just as well reverse it and argue as follows: I maintain that this room is filled right now with Campbell's Creamed Mushroom soup. You can't be sure this is an error; after all, human beings are capable of reaching the truth, aren't they? And I'm a human being. So, maybe this is the truth. It's possible, isn't it? That is exactly the same fallacy as in Descartes. You cannot derive from a generalized statement of what is possible to a species under some set of circumstances, the conclusion that that event is necessarily possible to every member of the species under every set of circumstances. In this case the individual, the Campbell's soup individual, is not and cannot be right, just as in countless cases we know, because we have proved our answers that we are not and cannot be wrong.

A conclusion is certain, according to Objectivism, when *all* of the available evidence in a given context of knowledge leads to that one conclusion, and no evidence suggests even a possibility of an alternative conclusion. There are innumerable cases where this is so, and there are, therefore, innumerable cases of valid human certainty.

In order to complete even the bare essentials of the answer to Descartes, I have to make a final point. Precisely because man is fallible and needs to validate his ideas by a process of logic, the assertion of arbitrary ideas is cognitively worthless. By an "arbitrary idea," we mean "one put forth without any evidence or proof," i.e., epistemologically speaking, without any standing at all. Since logic is man's standard of arriving at knowledge, no idea put forth in the absence of logical backing is deserving of any consideration or attention at all. A man has no epistemological right to espouse an idea without showing its credentials, i.e., without giving you at least some evidence in favor of its possible truth. If he gives you evidence, then you can consider the idea, discuss it, weigh the evidence, and decide whether he's right or not. But if he gives you no evidence, it is not your responsibility to refute his arbitrary assertion. Your proper response is to recognize that, bereft of evidence, his claim is rationally to be dismissed, and I mean dismissed—given no consideration—until and unless evidence on its behalf is forthcoming.

This is the point that is summarized in the very crucial logical principle that *the onus of proof is on him who asserts the positive*. It is not your responsibility to prove a negative, to disprove a man's arbitrary assertion that such and such is the case. It is not your responsibility, and it is not possible for you to prove that it is not so if he asserts it arbitrarily. It is his responsibility to prove that it *is* so. I will be very happy in the question period to elaborate on the onus of proof principle, which I would like to do, to define it more fully and to explain its deeper justification. For now, I want to show you how it arises in a discussion of Cartesian doubt. And the best way to see it is for me to give you a sample dialogue with one of these Cartesian doubters.

Let's say you put forward a proof of some point—you've specified your premises, defined the concepts, checked all the relevant facts, etc., you've laid out a logical rational case for your conclusion which integrates all known evidence. And the skeptic then says, "Well, that's all very fine, but you cannot be certain." And you ask him why not. And he says: "Well, how do you know you haven't made a mistake in applying logic? How do you know you haven't committed a fallacy somewhere? How do you know you haven't erred in applying the validating process?" You then say, well, where is your evidence that I've committed a fallacy? Go ahead, point out a flaw in my reasoning, give me a counter argument, mention a fact I've overlooked. The skeptic says: "I can't do that. I don't quarrel with your particular conclusion. I have no evidence at all against your specific conclusion. What I want to know is, how do you know you *didn't* commit an error? It's possible, isn't it? Prove that you didn't commit an error." If your patience holds out, you might ask him at this point, "Did you have any particular error in mind that I am supposed to prove I didn't commit?" And here the skeptic has to say: "No, I can't specify the error; I don't know what it is. My viewpoint is that maybe it's there. I want you to prove you haven't committed an unspecifiable, undetectable error. I can't tell the difference between your argument and a perfectly valid one. But still, I'm not sure. I want you to prove that this non-perceivable error does not exist." This is the point at which the assertion of the arbitrary and the demand to prove a negative comes out in full force. Here is a case of a man, the skeptic, indulging in a completely gratuitous, wanton, arbitrary assertion, namely, "Maybe there's an error," without a jot of evidence to support it, and demanding that you refute his baseless claim. This is the point in the discussion, if you've lasted this long, in which you waive the onus of proof principle in the face of the skeptic, indicate succinctly the epistemological status of arbitrary assertions, refrain if you can from the moral comment, and depart.

To summarize: Descartes first grants anyone the right to raise any arbitrary assertion he wants, to the effect that maybe he, Descartes, is in error, and then he decides he can be certain only if he can refute these arbitrary doubts. And then, of course, he can't, and ends up retreating into doubt as his only absolute. The valid procedure would recognize that to *doubt* without a basis is the epistemological equivalent of—and is, in fact, a form of—*asserting* without a basis. Both are arbitrary, both are epistemologically disqualified by the very nature of human cognition. The truth is that to establish certainty, all you have to do is prove positively on the basis of the full context of evidence available that your conclusion is true. In other words, you have to prove that you *are* right; it is not incumbent upon you to prove that you are not wrong when no evidence of error has been produced. Therefore, I advise you to reject out of hand all questions beginning "How do you know you are not . . .?" As in "How do you know you are not . . . wrong, crazy, insane, deceived, dreaming, hallucinating, etc.?" The answer to all such questions should be, "What makes you think I am?" In epistemology, as in law, you are innocent until and unless proved guilty. Reject out of hand all claims beginning, "But it's possible, isn't it?" "It's possible you're wrong, crazy, insane, dreaming, hallucinating, etc." The answer is that nothing can be claimed even as a possibility in the absence of specific, defined evidence.

All of the attacks on certainty are done by evading a point I mentioned briefly earlier, namely, that certainty is *contextual*. A proposition is certain when, in the full context of the evidence available, all of the evidence without exception points to that conclusion. So, I want to conclude this discussion of Descartes by giving you an example of a certainty. This is an example I've used before, but I find that it's helpful because it makes something concrete.

Given the evidence that you have available to you now, you can be certain, objectively certain, that it is I, Peikoff (not an imposter), who is lecturing. I use this example because I had an instructor in college who was a fanatic on the view that there could be no certainty. And he walked in one day and said, "You think I'm me," he said to the class, "me" being Professor X (I won't use his name), "but how do you know I'm not an imposter, a consummate actor taking Professor X's place?" Well, let's apply that to the present case for a moment. How can you be sure I'm me and not a consummate actor? And the answer is that all the evidence, all that is available to you, leads consistently and without exception to the conclusion that it's me—the occasion, tone of voice, content, my appearance, etc., etc. Now a skeptic walks in and says, "But it's possible it's an actor, isn't it?" The question you should ask is: "On what basis do you assert that it is possible? Can you give even some evidence for it, even a slender foothold of a fragile thread of a beginning of an intimation?" And the answer is—none whatever. Contrast this (just to engage in science fiction for a moment) with a situation where you could validly in that context be uncertain. You see me lecturing, but my voice occasionally breaks, sounds funny. At certain angles I seem to look different from the past. Occasionally, I utter some quite dubious remarks. And so on. On this basis, you might begin to entertain some hypotheses. You still have no conclusive evidence yet. But you have at least *some* evidence that would be consonant with a number of different hypotheses. So, you could now assert validly in this context, "Well, maybe he's sick, or maybe he's very upset," or whatever. These statements that such and such is a possibility are now warranted by some evidential basis. But so far you couldn't validly hypothesize I was an imposter.

But now let's carry out the example—suppose I suddenly came out for Immanuel Kant as the greatest philosopher in history, and you notice that one ear begins to sag a little, and I didn't recognize people I've known for years, and so on and so on. Now you have evidence to raise a whole bunch of possibilities—"Maybe he's gone crazy," "Maybe he's an imposter." And then, to end this epistemological story, the mask suddenly falls off and Boris Karloff stands revealed. You can say, "Now I'm certain it was an imposter."

The point is that certainty is contextual, and you cannot challenge any claim to certainty with the arbitrary declaration that something else is possible. So, if you ask me, "Is certainty attainable?," I would answer appropriately, "Certainly certainty is attainable." So much for Cartesian doubt and the problems it raises.

Well, ladies and gentlemen, we have now completed this course on the founders of Western philosophy. We have traced the development of philosophy from its beginnings in ancient Greece through its collapse with David Hume. And I have tried within the limits of the time available to indicate to you the essentials of the Objectivist answers to some of the central problems posed by traditional philosophy. I believe I have now at least touched on every point that I promised throughout the course that I would discuss. So. I want to take this final opportunity to thank you all for your attendance at this course, and for your interest. I hope you have enjoyed it; I have enjoyed having you as a class. Thank you.

Lecture Twelve, Q&A

Q: Given your brief statement of meaning, would you regard the concept of "God" as meaningful or meaningless?

A: In the sense that I think is meant by this question, I regard the concept as meaningful but invalid in the sense that it designates no entity in reality. You can distinguish between metaphysically meaningful and epistemologically meaningful. A concept is metaphysically meaningful if it designates something actual or possible in reality. On the other hand, if it is devoid of connection to reality, it is to that extent metaphysically without referent, metaphysically meaningless. This does not however mean that the term "God" is in the category of the word "gloop," which I just made up and which stands for nothing whatever. When a person talks about the issue of God, I can understand what it is he thinks he is saying about reality, and I can point out the contradictions, the problems, the flaws in his reasoning. I could not do that if he uttered, "Ish da triddle de tweedle, true or false?" And therefore, I think you must grant that the term is meaningful in the epistemological sense—that is, that you can grasp what the intention is, but in fact it has no referent in reality.

Q: What is the answer to Berkeley's argument that it is meaningless to say your experience of something resembles, or is just like, the real thing?

A: Well, there is no answer to that because, if you *were* trapped in a world of consciousness studying only your own sensations, it *would* be meaningless to say that your sensations resemble real things. Sensations are not entities that can be compared to or contrasted with things. You can't say your sensation is three inches long, and the thing you're perceiving is six inches long, therefore, your sensation is half the size. The point of the Objectivist view of the senses is that in sensation we are *not* contemplating the contents of consciousness, but we are contemplating directly the thing, so there are not two things to compare to each other, the entity and the awareness of the entity. The awareness of the entity is only the *awareness* of the entity and does not have intrinsic characteristics that you can then put side by side and say it's like or unlike the entity. That was the point of my rejection of the representative theory of perception.

Q: Could you explain the relation of the concept "causal primary" to the Objectivist theory of cause and effect? What are causal primaries causes *of*?

A: A "causal primary" in this sense means "the ultimate irreducible elements of reality, that out of which everything else is comprised, and the operation of which produces all derivative effects." So, for instance, we can break up matter, macroscopic solid matter, analyze it in terms of molecules, their laws and behavior, molecules in terms of atoms, atoms in terms of electrons, and so on. In the sense that I meant it, the energy puff (and remember, that was just a construct) is what you reach at the very end of the line. And from that aspect, by calling it a "causal primary," I mean in the analysis of the ingredients of reality, this is the final irreducible you reach that cannot itself be analyzed in terms of anything more primitive. What is its relation to cause and effect? It's a cause, and the rest of the phenomena in reality would be its effects. I don't know what other meaning there would be to that particular question.

Q: How is the law of noncontradiction grasped, and what is its relation to the axiomatic concept of "identity"?

A: That is somewhat off of our main points tonight, but I guess it's more or less a free-for-all tonight. Once you grasp the law of identity (A is A), the law of noncontradiction is a self-evident corollary of the law of identity. The law of noncontradiction is simply a restatement of the law of identity and has exactly the same status of self-evident truth. You say to me, "Why must it be the case that nothing can be A *and* non-A at the same time and in the same respect?" And the obvious answer is, because if it were A and non-A, the two parts would obliterate each other and it would be nothing, it would have no identity. The example that I use for classes, for instance, is to tell a student who wants to see this point, "You got a grade of 74 in the exam." And he says, "Fine, at least I got a C." And I say, "But I left out the fact that you also *didn't* get 74." And he says, "What, you mean you graded it at two different times?" And I say, "No, at the same time, you got 74 and you didn't." And he says, "Well, you mean you were using two different standards, and by one standard one and one the other?" And I say, "No, same time, same respect, same standard, you did and didn't get 74." And then he throws up his hands and says, "But then I didn't get any grade at all!" And that's the point—he didn't. The 74 annihilates the non-74 and vice versa. The grade has no identity. In other words, a contradiction is a violation of identity. A thing that is A and non-A is a thing that is nothing, and therefore, the law of noncontradiction is a restatement for epistemological purposes—to guide human thinking—of the basic metaphysical law of identity.

Q: What is the Objectivist view of the nature of mind? Is it a faculty, an entity, or a process?

A: Would you accept the following one sentence answer (because that's all I'll give you): It is a faculty possessed by an entity (the human being) whose essence is to perform a process (namely, the process of consciousness, which is a state of action—of sensing, integrating, conceptualizing, etc.). So from different aspects, it is all of these.

Q: Do clairvoyance and mind reading exist?

A: If you want a one-word answer, no. Here is a perfect case of the onus of proof principle. There are ten thousand disreputable nonexistent phenomena that have their champions in today's world. If you grasp the onus of proof principle, you will have an epistemological burden removed from your shoulders of a kind that is almost unequaled by grasping any other point. If you don't grasp the onus of proof principle, you will think, when someone claims clairvoyance or mind reading, stigmata, Indian rope climbing, and the whole crew of things, ESP, etc., "Well, now I have to go and prove that they don't exist." The fact is, the onus of proof is on the people who claim that such entities or processes do exist.

I have had several questions asking me if I would elaborate on the onus of proof principle. To give you briefly a deeper indication of why that principle is true: It is because man is not infallible and omniscient that he cannot ever validly assert arbitrary declarations. It is because he's not infallible that he must adhere to the correct epistemological rules to claim that anything is true. Here you must understand what is wrong with an arbitrary assertion. By "arbitrary" we mean, "an idea put forth in the absence of evidence of any sort"—no perceptual evidence, no conceptual evidence, a sheer assertion devoid of any attempt at validation. In effect, a blind cognitive whim, adhering to no logical rules or standards, merely uttered by fiat.

I said during the lecture that any such statement deserves no epistemological consideration or attention at all. Your proper attitude toward it should be as though the statement had not been made (cognitively speaking), which means that it is not your responsibility to refute arbitrary assertions—in other words, to rack your brains to try to find or imagine arguments showing that what is being said is false. It is a fundamental error on your part if you even *try* to do this. The rational procedure in the face of an arbitrary assertion is to dismiss it at once without further discussion or argumentation, merely identifying that it's arbitrary, and as such inadmissible. This is where the onus of proof principle comes in. What does it mean to say that "the onus of proof is on him who asserts the positive"? The first thing to grasp is what is meant by "positive." It's not necessarily the grammatically or linguistically positive, because you can express a negative content with an affirmative term. For instance, I can say, "The man is innocent," "The man is guilty"—both statements are grammatically affirmative, but the positive one there is the statement, "The man is guilty," he *has* committed a certain crime, a certain phenomenon did exist; the negative statement is "The man is innocent," he did *not* commit the crime, a certain phenomenon did *not* exist. In other words, the positive is an existence-affirming statement, a statement saying that something or other exists. The corresponding negative would be a statement denying that the thing exists. If you understand this, then the onus of proof principle tells you that if a person asserts a positive statement that X exists, he is required to adduce evidence supporting his statement. If he does, then you must either refute his evidence or accept his statement. But if he offers *no* evidence for the existence of X, his claim must be rejected without argumentation. In such a case, the corresponding negative that X is *not* true, or does *not* exist, must rationally be endorsed, and no evidence or proof of the negative in such a case need or can be given. Why?

The basic reason is metaphysical—it's the fact that existence exists, and *only* existence exists. In other words, there is no nothing. (That harks back all the way to Parmenides.) The distinction between something and nothing is the cardinal one in this context. A thing that exists is something, it is, it's out there in the world, and as such, it has effects, consequences, results, by which at an appropriate stage of knowledge, it's at least possible, in principle, for one to grasp and prove, either directly by simple perception or indirectly by its secondary consequences (as, for instance, the way we discover and prove the existence of atoms). But a nonexistent is nothing. It is not a type of existent. It is not a special constituent of reality that gives off special effects or consequences that one could hope to detect. For instance, somebody asserts that there's a convention of green gremlins over in the corner of the room. Now, gremlins don't exist, they are nothing, they are not a constituent of reality. What would be a possible answer to someone who says: "Prove to me now that those gremlins don't exist. Give me an argument. Point out to me the effects or consequences of the non-gremlins in reality"? Obviously, there can be no special effects, consequences, traces, signs, or manifestations of non-gremlins. It is preposterous to say, "Point out to me the facts in reality that follow from the nonexistence of gremlins," because the gremlins are nothing, and therefore, nothing follows from nothing. The rational view of negative propositions is: Nothing is nothing. A negative proposition is to be established by showing that there is no evidence for the corresponding positive proposition. That's all that validating a negative can consist of. How would you establish, for instance, that there is no mouse in this room now? The only way you would do it is to show that there is no evidence *for* the existence of a mouse, no evidence for the positive, and thus the negative is validated, not directly but indirectly by the absence of evidence for the positive. It is not as though you have special perceptual evidence of a non-mouse, like some kind of special dark vision revealing non-mousehood. There is no special positive perceptual evidence against the mouse. There's no anti-mouse vision that you can have. There is merely no evidence *for* the mouse, and nothing else is required. That is the principle to keep in mind as applied to *all* issues, whether on the perceptual or conceptual level. If there is no argument, no evidence, for declaring that a murder took place or that a disease or clairvoyance or God exists, then the absence of evidence for the positive is all that is required to validate the corresponding negative. And that's why you cannot prove a negative. All you can do is show that there is no evidence for its corresponding positive. You can refute a positive if it's false, assuming the person gives evidence for it that he has misinterpreted—you can then show him his misinterpretation. Refuting a positive consists of showing that there's no evidence for it, of showing that some alleged evidence is not actually evidence. And in that way, you can refute a positive. But you cannot directly prove or establish a negative. All you can do is show that the corresponding positive is based on no evidence. And that's why a person who utters an arbitrary positive, by that very fact, has refuted himself and invalidated his position.

Q: Is it philosophically necessary for causal primaries to exist?

A: I would say yes, on the grounds that there is no infinity, and therefore, ultimately, reality must consist of something. But please don't ask me what it consists of, because I'm not a physicist.

Q: What is the Objectivist view on symbolic logic?

A: The same as the Objectivist view on numerology. In other words, if you mean by "symbolic logic" that concoction that owes its source to Bertrand Russell and his several ancestors, derivatives, contemporaries, and successors, Objectivism rejects the entire field as invalid. It rejects it as invalid on many grounds, the only one of which I'll mention is that Objectivism denies that logic is arbitrary, that you can start with any logical construct or system you wish, make up any logical rules you want, and then proceed to derive any conclusions you want. Objectivism holds that if that's the procedure you want to engage in, give it any name you want except "logic" or anything to do with philosophy. Say that you have a predilection for playing a particularly foolish, pointless game. And then, all right, if you want to do that in your spare time and you don't tell other people about it, there's nothing wrong with that. But to make an alleged subject out of that—to define "implication" and so on in the crudely arbitrary ways that these people do, and then to declare, "This is just another alternative to Aristotle, and in fact is superior to Aristotelian logic"—nothing could be more incompatible with the Objectivist viewpoint.

Q: When a person says, "It is possible this plane will crash," can I validly use the onus of proof principle, since it is metaphysically possible that planes crash? How do I answer?

A: Well, that happens to be an example I used in another lecture, so I don't know if that's just a coincidence. Here you have to distinguish two different statements—it is possible metaphysically *for* something to happen, which does not warrant you in saying it is possible epistemologically *that* it will happen. Those are not the same statements. When you say that something is metaphysically possible, you are ascribing a certain capacity to an entity under certain circumstances. For instance, "Man has the possibility of walking. It is possible for him to walk." And that is not an epistemological use of the term "possibility," but a metaphysical one. You are describing a faculty or capacity or potentiality of man, and it is a certainty that he has that potentiality. When you say it is possible *that* so and so will happen (and the normal usage in English is that it is possible *for* something to happen, indicates the metaphysical possibility, the capacity), but when you say it is possible *that* such and such *will* happen, you are giving now an assessment of evidence; you are saying there is some evidence, even if the evidence is not conclusive, that the phenomenon in question will take place. And here you contrast "possible" to two others—"probable" and "certain." There is a scale of evidential assessment. On the lowest level, when you have *some* evidence, you say, "It is possible that such and such will happen." As the evidence mounts, at a certain point you say, "It is more than possible; it is probable that such and such will happen." And as and when the evidence becomes conclusive so that everything points to this one conclusion and nothing points in any other direction, at that point you say that it is certain.

The relevant point is that you cannot pass from a generalized statement that something is metaphysically possible to a given kind of entity, to the epistemological conclusion that, therefore, you have some evidence that that possibility is being actualized. Now contrast these two types of situations using the airplane example. You're in an airplane. Granted that an airplane metaphysically has the capacity to crash. In that sense, it is possible for it to crash. After all, it's not a feather, it has weight, it's large, it's up in the air, there is a law of gravity, and so on and so on. Airplanes have the metaphysical capacity of crashing. They also have the metaphysical capacity of *not* crashing, of landing safely and without any difficulty at the airport. Both of those are metaphysical possibilities. You're on a particular plane. By what right do you attach yourself to "It's possible *for* it to crash," and say, "Therefore, it's possible *that* it will crash." You go by the actual evidence. And here, the actual evidence is much more complex. Assuming you got on the airplane at some place that has a decent screening system, and it's a reputable airline, and it's a sunny day, etc., then you say in the normal case, "It's possible for this plane to crash; it's also possible for it not to crash, and all the evidence I have points to the fact that it will land safely, and none against." In which case, it is invalid to say suddenly out of the blue, with no basis, "Maybe it will crash." On the other hand, suppose the engine starts to knock and the pilot announces, "We're running out of fuel," and the clouds are closing in, and so on and so on, at a certain point, you can say, "You know, it's actually possible that this plane will crash." At that point, when you have some evidence, you are entitled to say, "It's possible *that* it will crash." But you must have some evidence. The abstract possibility that airplanes in general can crash under some circumstances does not entitle you to say about any particular plane, in the absence of any specific evidence, that it's possible this one will crash on this flight.

Q: Can you be certain of a conclusion if you know that knowledge relevant to it exists that you have not examined?

A: No. The question I'd like to understand is: How did you know that knowledge relevant to it exists? Did you find that out because you made a partial study of the subject and you yourself know that the facts you have are very fragmentary and don't suggest any particular conclusion and that there's much more material already known? That's one thing. Or did you find it out because you made an exhaustive study of a subject, you have a full case, and somebody arbitrarily tells you, "If you studied another fifty years you'd find out you're wrong, only don't ask me how or where." But assuming it's actually that you have reason to believe that relevant knowledge exists that you haven't examined, then no, you can't be certain. Certainty is contextual, but that means you must have the full evidence of the knowledge available to you. What you *can* say in such a case is: "On the basis of the knowledge I have so far investigated, everything I see points to this conclusion, and I know nothing that points elsewhere. But, if I also know for specific reasons that there may be evidence elsewhere, then I keep that in mind, and I don't declare I have certainty until I investigate the relevant knowledge."

Q: Is the ultimate standard for new concept formation (versus just inclusion in a group) "usefulness to further conceptualization"?

A: No, I would certainly not say "usefulness," if you mean that in any pragmatist use of the term. The ultimate standard that I've tried to indicate is: the facts of reality as interpreted according to the method of a conceptual consciousness. And the purpose of conceptualization is not to feed on itself; the purpose of conceptualization is not further conceptualization. The purpose of *all* conceptualization is the grasping of facts of reality. And therefore, you form a new concept or not according to whether that will, given the facts of reality, objectively promote a knowledge of reality.

Q: Is there any difference between the statement "This is X's apparent shape" and "This is X's shape as it appears to me"?

A: Yes, I can grasp a difference between those two—suppose you are looking at something from a great distance and your viewpoint is obscured, and you say: "It appears to me that the man in the distance has a very large stomach, but I can't see that clearly at this distance and I'm not sure. So, his apparent shape is an obese rotundity, but I can't be sure." On the other hand, you come right up to him, and you see him, and you're standing right there, and you investigate, and you say, "Mr. X's shape as I perceive it, as it appears to me, is, let us say, definitely circular." If that's the case, then there's no doubt. In other words, the word "apparent" there could be used to express doubt about the actual nature of what you're perceiving.

Q: If differences in forms of perception are attributed to different quantities of information available to the perceiver, doesn't that contradict your assertion that all perceptions are equally valid?

A: I said that there can be differences in forms of perception, and that one form can be different in the amount of information. How does that contradict my statement that all perceptions are equally valid? The fact that you are not given everything does not mean that what you *are* given is invalid. There's no relationship between quantity and validity. If your senses give you—let us just pick an arbitrary figure out of the air—5,000 facts, and somebody else's senses give him 10,000 facts, on what grounds would you say your 5,000 facts are no good because you have fewer facts than he does? A fact is a fact. Validity is a question of the relation of your cognitive mechanism to reality. The most you can say is that the normally sighted person, as against the one who perceives no color gradations or color changes, gets more information, just as the person who has 20/20 vision gets more information than the one whose eyes let in much less information without the correction of eyeglasses. In that sense, one form of sense perception can be superior to another, but that is a matter of how much is given to you directly, and how much you have to reach by inference. It is not a matter of the validity.

Q: On the question of certainty, in the hypothetical case where an actor successfully pulls off an impersonation, can it be said that the deceived had knowledge and was contextually certain?

A: Yes. Suppose you all believed it was me, but I was an imposter, and then after you were completely convinced and you wrote it out in blood and you were willing to sign your life on it, it turned out that you had made a mistake. Doesn't that prove that you really were wrong? It proves that you made a mistake. But remember, you cannot from that draw the conclusion that maybe you will be wrong the next time. The fact that you are wrong once tells you there is a certain area where you should be a little more careful, go over where you were wrong and define to yourself what was it you left out the time before that enabled you to make a mistake. And when you identify that factor and correct it, whatever it may be or however complex it may be to name, when you grasp it then, you know, you have put to rest that source of error. You will be aware of that from here on in, and you will proceed with greater confidence as a result of the error. I don't mean to impugn the motives of the questioner, but this type of question is very typically used to allegedly prove that you can't be certain, because you said you were certain, and it turned out you were wrong. Inherent in the question is the giveaway—by saying it turned out you were wrong, it means the questioner knew what the truth really was. And if he is able to know it, you are able to know it. So, even if it turns out that you are completely wrong on some question, there is no logical warrant for that to impair your epistemological self-confidence in the future if you proceed according to a logical method in the future.

Q: In what context and with reference to what actions or attributes of specifically human entities can the term "subjective" be validly used?

A: Well, not to give you a whole detailed analysis, the term "subjective" can be validly used to designate a type of error, a type of departure from reality on the part of a conceptual consciousness. To begin with, the term "subjective" cannot, for all the reasons I mentioned in the lecture, be applied on the perceptual level. Nothing on the perceptual level can be subjective. Everything on the perceptual level is the product of an inexorable physical interaction between the object and the sense organ. The concept "subjective" is applicable only on the conceptual level and only because man has free will, because consciousness is not automatically infallible. It is therefore possible for him to use his consciousness on the conceptual level in a way that departs from the facts of reality. I don't mean here an error. If a person is rational and bases his conclusions on the evidence but makes an honest error, that person is not subjective; he is simply mistaken. In exactly the same way that a person can be completely honest in a moral issue and yet mistaken, so he is wrong but not immoral. "Subjective" as an epistemological term is not synonymous with "mistaken." It means "a mistaken content coming from a method that represents a departure from reality at its root." For instance, a man says to you, "I believe the earth is flat"—you know, the Flat Earth Society that I think there are still remnants of somewhere in Britain—and you ask him why, and he says, "I feel it, I feel it very strongly, and that's it." You can say that this belief is subjective, and this man is being subjective, meaning he is placing the subject above the object. And meaning by that, he is treating his consciousness as an entity that dictates to reality, so his arbitrary feelings create the corresponding facts. That is true subjectivism. The subjective is the view of the primacy of consciousness applied to human beings, that human feelings can shape or mold facts. And in that sense, the term "subjective" can validly be used to designate a type of departure from reality. It cannot, however, validly be used to designate any *fact* of reality. Notice that even the *phenomenon* of consciousness itself is not subjective. Man's faculty of consciousness exists. That is a fact. It exists not because we want it to exist or don't want it to exist. It exists in fact. And in that sense, it is an objective fact in the same way that any fact is objective.

INDEX

P

R

Printed in Great Britain
by Amazon

47537619R00341